Psychiatric Terror

PSYCHIATRIC TERROR

*How Soviet Psychiatry Is Used
to Suppress Dissent*

SIDNEY BLOCH
PETER REDDAWAY

Basic Books, Inc., Publishers

NEW YORK

Published in Great Britain by Victor Gollancz, Ltd., under the title, *Russia's Political Hospitals: The Abuse of Psychiatry in the Soviet Union.*

Library of Congress number: 77-75238
ISBN: 0-465-06488-4

10 9 8 7 6 5 4 3 2 1

To Vladimir Bukovsky, Semyon Gluzman and all defenders of humane psychiatry in the Soviet Union

ACKNOWLEDGEMENTS

PERMISSION TO reprint three of the appendices in this book, in amended translation, is gratefully acknowledged. Appendices VIII and IX appeared first in *A Chronicle of Human Rights in the U.S.S.R.*, Nos. 10, 1974, and 13, 1975 (Khronika Press, 505 Eighth Avenue, New York, N.Y. 10018). Appendix VI appeared first in *Survey*, Nos. 94–95, 1975 (135 Oxford Street, London W.1).

The authors are also grateful to the following copyright holders for permission to reproduce material: to the *Guardian* for the open letter signed by 21 Soviet psychiatrists that was included as a "Letter to the Editor" on 29 September 1973; to *New Psychiatry*/IPC Magazines for Dr Voikhanskaya's article (appendix X); to Macmillan, London and Basingstoke, and Alfred A. Knopf, Inc., for extracts from *A Question of Madness* © Zhores A. and Roy A. Medvedev, 1971, translated by Ellen de Kadt, translation © Macmillan London Ltd, 1971.

All quotations and articles from the Soviet press have, except where otherwise indicated, been translated by the authors, who take no responsibility for accuracy of content. As is usually made clear by the context, the content is often far from the truth, and is quoted to demonstrate that this is the case.

CONTENTS

disturbed patients on the dissenter (p. 217);
Conclusion (p. 219).

second false start in the USA (p. 324); The overall situation in mid-1974 (p. 326); Events in Britain 1974–1976 (p. 327); The Plyushch campaign and developments in France and Switzerland (p. 330); A Soviet counter-blast (p. 334); The WPA and the 6th World congress in Honolulu, August 1977 (p. 335); The release and emigration of Bukovsky (p. 339).

LIST OF ILLUSTRATIONS

following page 160

FOREWORD

by Vladimir Bukovsky

THE PROBLEMS WHICH the authors analyse in this book are exceptionally complex.

The peculiar features of the Soviet political system, the Communist ideology, the uncertainties and difficulties of the science of psychiatry, the labyrinths of the human conscience—all these have weirdly woven themselves together to create a monstrous phenomenon, the use of medicine against man.

Paradoxical though this phenomenon seems, it is, apparently, symptomatic of our times, times in which the highest achievements of human thought, science, and technology have suddenly boomeranged against man, putting his very existence in doubt. The rapid development of technology threatens to break down our ecology, and the discovery and exploration of atomic energy have made possible the complete destruction of life.

When Pinel first removed the chains from the mentally ill and thereby freed them from punishment as criminals, who would have guessed that two centuries later prisoners would look with fear at Pinel's successors, preferring chains to their "care"?

These pernicious phenomena have unexpectedly brought to the fore such apparently old-fashioned concepts as human conscience and man's moral and ethical principles. Evidently a profound and lengthy reconsideration of habitual values will be needed, a re-thinking of accepted ideas, if we are to find a way out of the situation which has come about. Serious, fundamental research is essential, which will make it possible to examine every facet of these complex and dangerous phenomena.

One such piece of research is this book. For many years I have studied the question of psychiatric abuse in the Soviet Union, and can therefore judge accurately the enormous amount of work performed by the authors. Without doubt, Bloch's and Reddaway's book will be a kind of encyclopaedia, an indispensable source for all those interested in the problem of psychiatric abuse. Among its merits are the impeccable documentation, the detachment of the analysis, and the combination of a scientific method and a fluent, readable style. I believe that all this will ensure for the book a wide readership and will also assist, ultimately, in the cleansing and resurrection of Soviet psychiatry.

For most Western people it is psychologically difficult to grasp the atmosphere of a country in which phenomena like those described in this book have become routine. I often see looks of incomprehension when I describe life in the Soviet Union. Sometimes I deduce from the questions put to me that no understanding exists at all. Occasionally I am overwhelmed by despair and lose faith in the power of the human word. It is virtually impossible to explain the degree to which life in the USSR is unreal. It is not, there, theories and conclusions which develop out of the raw material of life, but, on the contrary, the raw material of everyday life is created to fit in with the ruling theory. Life does not develop normally and naturally in accordance with its inner laws, but is created artificially in ways calculated not to undermine the basic principles of the ideology.

The ruling doctrine asserts that being determines consciousness. As Socialism has been built in the USSR, and Communism is being built, the consciousness of people must be exclusively Communist. Where, then, can belief in God appear from, if for 60 years atheism has been propagated and the preaching of religion outlawed? And from where does an opponent of Communism come—in a Communist society?

Within the confines of Communist doctrine there are only two possible explanations: the cause must lie either in subversive activity directed from abroad—i.e., every dissenter has been bought or recruited by the imperialists; or in mental illness: dissent is just a manifestation of pathological processes in the psyche.

As life in the USSR does not develop freely, but is "interpreted" by the party, these two principles mean that every dissenter whom it is difficult or inconvenient to pursue under the first heading is automatically assigned to the second.

The Soviet psychiatrist is a part of the Soviet system. He cannot say, "I find no symptoms of illness in this person". He cannot reach his conclusions inductively, he must follow the prescribed deductive method. He cannot regard dissent as a normal phenomenon generated by the realities of Soviet existence: if he did, he would become a dissenter himself. And not everyone is capable of that: family, children, professional career and the quiet life are automatically put at risk. Ahead lies nothing but harassment, persecution, condemnation, quarrels and lack of understanding in his family—relatives accusing him of selfishness, and of indifference to his children. Also the incomprehension of those around him, his colleagues— what's the point of it all? Do you really think you can change anything like that? You can't shift a mountain with a shovel! And in truth, one has to be decidedly "different" to become a dissenter in the USSR.

Now, when I hear from all sides so many high-sounding words and assurances of sympathy and support, when I hear condemnation of dishonest Soviet psychiatrists, when I see amazement in people's eyes—"How could doctors be so venal?"—I involuntarily find myself wondering: who among you, if you suddenly lived in the Soviet Union, would choose the freedom to be different? Would many of you be so eccentric as to want to be persecuted for the sake of an abstract honesty before your conscience?

I fear that not many would prove capable of acting out in such conditions the righteous incomprehension which they voice now. Evidence for this view is the outcome of the world psychiatric congress in Mexico in 1971, when the question of Soviet abuse was simply swept under the carpet. A sad episode, which, I trust, will not be repeated this year in Honolulu.

Bonn, 22 January 1977

PREFACE

THE AUTHORS MET each other for the first time in early 1972 in London some weeks after the World Psychiatric Association's international congress had conferred in Mexico. The congress was highlighted by an intense controversy over the alleged misuse of psychiatry in the Soviet Union for political purposes, an issue we both felt to be of great importance.

One of us, Peter Reddaway, has taught politics since 1965 and developed a special interest in Soviet dissent. Study of the régime's methods to combat dissent followed naturally and before long he had collected substantial evidence that psychiatry was one of the instruments used for this purpose. He soon became convinced that Soviet psychiatry warranted special attention in its own right. As a result he helped to found in February 1971 a small *ad hoc* research group, composed mainly of psychiatrists, human rights experts and specialists in Soviet affairs—the Working Group on the Internment of Dissenters in Mental Hospitals.

The other author, Sidney Bloch, while living in Australia, had heard vaguely about allegations of psychiatric abuse early in 1971 but only after coming to Britain the following year did he learn more about them. Perhaps like most psychiatrists at the time of the Mexico congress, he found it difficult to believe that Soviet colleagues were involved in unethical practices. On joining the working group and collaborating in its research, he soon agreed that something was seriously amiss in Soviet psychiatry. He was sensitive on such issues, having become steadily more concerned in recent years about the vulnerability of psychiatry to misuse. He had confronted matters such as his power to intern and treat people compulsorily; the undefined boundaries of his professional rôle; and the lack of sufficiently objective criteria in the diagnosis of mental illness.

In 1972 we agreed on the desirability of a book to record and analyse Soviet abuses but personal circumstances prevented our commencing work on one. In any case, the range of sources was still limited and there seemed little chance that a visit to the Soviet Union would yield much fruit: we would certainly not be allowed to visit prison psychiatric hospitals, and the sort of free discussion needed to fill gaps in our knowledge would be difficult with dissenters and impossible with official psychiatrists. Such gaps were numerous, as prior to 1972 no formerly hospitalized dissenters had yet emigrated except for Valery Tarsis, and his experience had been limited.

But we continued our research and in 1973–74 Reddaway could press ahead more quickly during seven months of sabbatical leave at Columbia University. He is grateful to the university's Russian Institute and Research Institute on Communist Affairs for jointly giving him a senior research fellowship to enable him to do this. During his leave he succeeded, among other things, in interviewing four psychiatrists who had recently emigrated from the Soviet Union.

Bloch also had the opportunity to pursue research while holding a Harkness fellowship in the Stanford University Department of Psychiatry and Behavioural Sciences in 1973–74. He would like to thank the Commonwealth Fund of New York for giving him the fellowship and Stanford University for its hospitality.

In the spring of 1974 we met in New York and soon after decided firmly to collaborate on a book. Next January Bloch visited Israel and took the opportunity to question in depth five Soviet immigrants—two psychiatrists, and three dissenters who had been hospitalized for non-medical reasons. Over the next eighteen months we continued to interview such people whenever the chance arose, travelling for the purpose to Toronto, Boston, New York, Paris, Moscow, and Leningrad. In the Soviet Union Bloch interviewed—his wife Felicity interpreting—Vladimir Borisov, Gennady Shimanov and Yury Shikhanovich, all previously hospitalized for their dissent; close friends of General Grigorenko; and the leader of the Soviet-based campaign to free Leonid Plyushch from a special psychiatric hospital, Tatyana Khodorovich.

The first drafts of various chapters were written separately, then revised jointly on several occasions; we each take responsibility therefore for the whole text. At certain places in the book the pronoun "we" is used for convenience, to avoid the pedantry of always indicating which co-author is meant. To reduce the number of references, we have sometimes omitted those concerning a dissenter who figures in appendix I, as they can be found there.

We would like to thank all those people we interviewed in the Soviet Union as well as the following émigrés: Viktor Fainberg and Zhores Medvedev, both now in Britain; Alexander Volpin, now in the United States; Ilya Rips, Grisha Feigin and Yaakov Khantsis, all now living in Israel; Vladimir Bukovsky; and Leonid Plyushch and Natalya Gorbanevskaya, both now in France. We are also indebted to several ex-Soviet psychiatrists: Boris Segal, Boris Zoubok and Edgar Goldstein, all living in the United States; Marina Voikhanskaya, now in Britain; Felix Yaroshevsky, now in Canada; and three other psychiatrists who have emigrated from the Soviet Union and requested anonymity for fear of retribution to their families still there.

We are very grateful to Mrs Elizabeth Sumorok for a magnificent job in typing the manuscript. We also thank members of the secretarial staff of the Departments of Psychiatry at both Stanford and Oxford universities.

Kathy Reddaway, Tamara Kolakowska, Peter Dornan, Martin Dewhirst, Naum Korzhavin, Alexander Lunts, Raymond Sturgeon and the Working Group on the Internment of Dissenters in Mental Hospitals helped us in various ways in the preparation of this book—to them our appreciation.

S. B.
P. R.

Psychiatric Terror

Chapter 1

THE VULNERABILITY OF PSYCHIATRY

THE NATURE OF psychiatry is such that the potential for its improper use is greater than in any other field of medicine. Why should this be so? Several factors suggest themselves: psychiatry's boundaries are exceedingly blurred and ill-defined; little agreement exists on the criteria for defining mental illness; the mentally ill are often used as scapegoats for society's fears; and the psychiatrist commonly faces a dual loyalty, both to the patient he is treating and to the institutions to which he is responsible.

Arising from these general factors are more specific issues: there is no consensus on how to define the degree of dangerousness of the patient to himself or to others and thus the need for involuntary hospitalization; there are no satisfactory criteria for determining whether or not a defendant in court is fit to plead on psychiatric grounds, nor for deciding whether he was mentally responsible for the commission of the offence.

It is useful to distinguish from the start between psychiatry's improper use and something which is only a peripheral concern of the book—its poor practice. Psychiatrists, nurses and other mental-health professionals may act incompetently or inconsiderately or negligently towards their patients. Not uncommonly, inadequately-trained staff, working in poor conditions and under extreme pressure, may act cruelly towards "difficult" patients. Over-tranquillization is one example of poor practice which may result from the needs of the staff to contend with patients who are irritating, impulsive or aggressive. Even the most well-intentioned staff may conduct themselves in ways which they subsequently regret.

Psychiatry's Ill-defined Boundaries
What is an appropriate rôle for the psychiatrist and where does his work start and end? Intense and continuing debate

surrounds the question both within and outside the psychiatric profession.

Dr Ewald Busse, a former president of the American Psychiatric Association, has argued that the psychiatrist should limit his field strictly to the suffering patient and his needs: ". . . Psychiatric services should not be the tool for restructuring society or solving economic problems or for determining new human values. Psychiatric services should be continued as patient-oriented activities designed to reduce pain and discomfort and to increase the capacity of the individual to adjust satisfactorily."[1]

By contrast, another former president of the association, Dr Raymond Waggoner, has called on his colleagues to adopt the rôle of social visionaries:

> In sum, I plead for a psychiatry that is involved with fundamental social goals. I plead for a psychiatry that would eschew isolation altogether and assume its proper leadership rôle in advancing the total health of our nation. I plead for a psychiatry that is at once concerned with individual liberty and communal responsibility. And I ask of psychiatrists that they be not only pragmatists but also dreamers with a vision of the future.[2]

No matter the outcome of this debate, developments in psychiatry of recent years show that psychiatrists have travelled far beyond the walls of the asylum that was traditionally their place of work. Today their functions extend to the military, schools, universities, child-guidance clinics, the courts, prisons, and a variety of other social institutions.

What is Mental Illness?

Despite the development of psychiatry as a scientific discipline over the last 100 years, the fundamental question of what mental illness is still haunts the profession. As regards most of the conditions the psychiatrist treats, there are no satisfactory criteria available for their accurate definition. Unlike in other branches of medicine, many of the conventionally-labelled psychiatric disorders are based only on clinical observation rather than on recognizable pathological changes in the nervous system. No tests have yet been developed to determine objectively the presence or absence of most mental diseases. Thus Dr Ronald Liefer, a leader of the American "radical psychiatry movement",[3] can argue that:

> The criteria for medical disease are physico-chemical while the criteria for psychiatric disease are social and ethical. To diagnose and treat physical disorders we use methods of physics and chemistry. To identify and eliminate mental disorders we use methods of social communication, evaluation and influence. . . . Every medical speciality except psychiatry has in common an ultimate interest in the structure and function of the human body as a physico-chemical machine. Psychiatrists, on the other hand, are interested in, and intervene in, human conduct and social processes. . . .[4]

Liefer's position is less extreme than that of Thomas Szasz, a psychiatrist well known for his contentious view that mental illness is in fact a myth and that psychiatrists essentially deal with people who experience problems in living; labelling them with a mental disease is completely unjustifiable and inappropriate.[5] Although we regard the views of Liefer and Szasz as much too extreme, the psychiatrist does indeed face considerable problems in conceptualizing mental illness. Strict medical criteria for the determination of mental illness are often lacking; this forces the psychiatrist to rely, more than other doctors, on social factors. As a result, a variety of ethical problems can readily arise, and all this tends to compromise the objective, scientific stance that most psychiatrists crave. A good illustration is the dilemma many psychiatrists encounter in their approach to homosexuality.

Homosexuality appears in the 1968 edition of the diagnostic manual of the American Psychiatric Association[6] as "sexual orientation disturbance (homosexuality)". The diagnosis is applied to individuals whose sexual interests are "directed primarily towards people of the same sex and who are either disturbed by, in conflict with, or wish to change, their sexual orientation. This diagnostic category is distinguished from homosexuality, which by itself does not constitute a psychiatric disorder." This definition constituted a major change, as, previously, homosexuality had been defined as abnormal. It still is when one checks the comparable British diagnostic manual. There, we find a reference to it as a sexual deviation, defined as "sexual attraction with or without physical relationship between members of the same sex".[7]

Controversy has raged in the last decade over the status of homosexuality as a psychiatric disorder, and whether it should be viewed as a normal variant of sexuality or as a pathological deviation from normal sexual development. On the one hand, an American task force of psychiatrists unanimously agrees that "homosexuality arises experientially from a faulty family constellation . . . and represents a disorder of sexual development".[8] On the other hand, a member of the New York Gay Activists Alliance bitterly asserts that: "The illness theory of homosexuality is a pack of lies, concocted out of the myths of a patriarchal society for a political purpose. Psychiatry— dedicated to making sick people well—has been the corner stone of a system of oppression that makes gay people sick."[9]

The change in the approach of official American psychiatry accompanied the profound shift in society's attitude to homosexuality during the 1960s. Earlier, society, and psychiatry along with it, saw homosexuality as a deviation from conventional sexual behaviour and branded it accordingly as a disease. The natural questions that follow are how psychiatry decides when a particular behavioural pattern deviates sufficiently from the norm to warrant its designation as illness, and who determines which behavioural norms are acceptable as reflections of health. The psychiatrist is called upon to establish, or at least legitimize, a scheme of normality which suits society's attitudes and values.

The Psychiatrist as Oppressor

The new notion that psychiatry is a component of an oppressive system has received considerable attention in recent years, particularly with the emergence of various forms of "radical psychiatry". Both psychiatrists (e.g. Laing, Liefer and Szasz) and active groups of lay people contend that psychiatry is a cog in the wheels of the establishment, and, as its agent, has the function of maintaining the *status quo*, of preserving the socio-political order. Labels like social engineer and behavioural controller are commonly used to depict the psychiatrist's rôle.

Thus Liefer states, in a sweeping way that is typical of radical psychiatry:

> The state has assumed most of the traditional social functions of regulating and controlling human conduct. Because all moral codes are not codified in law, and because the power of the state is limited by rule of law, the state is unable satisfactorily to control and influence individuals. This requires a new social institution that, under the auspices of an acceptable modern authority, can control and guide conduct without conspicuously violating publicly avowed ideals of freedom and respect for the individual. Psychiatry, in medical disguise, has assumed this historical function.[10]

For Szasz, the tools and methods of psychiatry are perfectly suited to this social function. Labelling and classification are two essential ingredients. "To classify another person's behaviour is usually a means of constraining him. This is particularly true of psychiatric classification, whose traditional aim has been to legitimize the social controls placed on so-called mental patients."[11]

Adjustment to Society as a Criterion of Mental Health
The concept of "adjustment to society" has been used commonly in psychiatry as a criterion of mental health. But for the critics discussed above, it confirms the political stance, either covert or overt, taken by the psychiatrist when he makes those who behave in ways unacceptable to society modify their behaviour so that they can re-find their place in the community, adjusted to its norms and mores. The critics resent this socio-political function and call upon the psychiatrist to urge the powers that be, especially governments, to modify the social and political system and pay more attention to people's rights and needs. Mental-health workers are summoned to participate in direct political activity, to strive for an improved society. Since, it is argued, psychiatric illness has its roots primarily in economic, political and cultural inequities, it is here that psychiatrists must operate most actively.

The Predicament of Dual Loyalty

Beyond the private relationship that exists between a psychiatrist and a patient who pays for a personalized service, the thorny issue of dual loyalty faces the psychiatrist. Once he works within an institutional setting—e.g. army, prison, health service—the possibility exists that the interests and goals of the institution to which he is responsible may conflict with those of the patients whom he treats. The aware psychiatrist is then faced with the dilemma of which party has priority.

The psychiatrist employed by the army, for example, has the responsibility of contributing to the efficiency of the organization by sorting out those soldiers who disrupt that efficiency. It is not fanciful to see how "disciplinary problems" may become construed as psychiatric disorders and the soldier labelled accordingly. Often, because the psychiatrist is employed by a complex institution with its requirement for regular procedures, and depends on it for his livelihood, the organization's interests are placed above those of the individual. One of the authors (S.B.) grappled with the problem of dual loyalty early in his career. A young university student was referred to the psychiatric clinic by the police with an injunction either to have himself treated for homosexuality or be liable to prosecution. S.B. felt trapped as he strove both to satisfy his own professional integrity *vis-à-vis* his patient and to fulfil the requirements of the law. (At that time, homosexuality was regarded as an offence.) The needs of each were irreconcilable.

Hospitalization without Consent

The rôle of the psychiatrist as a professional with responsibilities to society, confers on him exceptional authority, notably the legal power to place a person in a mental hospital without his consent. Involuntary commitment is similar in several respects to imprisonment: the patient is deprived of his liberty, often loses most of his rights, and is subjected, without choice, to an array of institutional rules and regulations.

The customary reason for forcible hospitalization is dangerousness—a person is a danger either to himself or to others and the commitment is made to protect the community or the individual. Since the process by which he commits a person involuntarily involves a great measure of uncertainty, the psychiatrist often finds himself in a predicament. No reliable objective criteria exist to determine whether or not someone will behave dangerously; approaches to the concept of dangerousness vary considerably among psychiatrists. One psychiatrist concedes that "the record has not been good with respect to the accurate prediction of dangerousness in the mentally ill".[12]

Efforts have been made to establish strict criteria for the "likelihood of serious harm". The 1970 Massachusetts Mental Health Reform Act, for instance, stipulates them in a detailed and specific fashion. As a result, during the first year under the new act as compared to the last year under the old, involuntary commitments diminished from 77 per cent of all admissions to 28 per cent.[13] But this dramatic drop has not eliminated the possibility of widely differing interpretations, within the new guidelines, of what constitutes dangerousness.

Commitment statutes in many countries remain exceptionally vague and ambiguous, and in some they go well beyond the relatively narrow criterion of dangerousness to embrace such ill-defined concepts as the need for treatment, poor judgement, and lack of self control.[14] An illustration of wholly inappropriate criteria for involuntary commitment came to light in 1972 when it was discovered that two women had been confined in an English mental hospital for 50 years. Originally, each had been declared "morally defective" after bearing an illegitimate child, and had been hospitalized for this reason alone.[15]

The lack of guidelines for compulsory commitment was clearly shown in an analysis of compulsory admissions to mental hospitals in England and Wales from 1964 to 1970. There was considerable variation both between different geographical regions, and within the same region over time. Since there were no major administrative or other changes during the period to explain the variations, the investigators concluded that they stemmed mainly from the attitudes of individual doctors.[16] The authors felt that "compulsion is used much more frequently than is necessary and that it is arbitrarily employed". The findings confirm a commonly held assumption that psychiatrists play safe and opt for compulsory hospitalization when doubt exists about the level of dangerousness of a patient.[17]

The Right to Treatment
Critics who have attacked the procedure of compulsory commitment have also raised the banner of "the right to treatment". They argue that if a person is to be hospitalized involuntarily, he should be treated actively; the psychiatrist should be more than a mere custodian. A landmark case in this regard was the unanimous decision by the US Supreme Court in 1975 that a state does not have the right to confine in a mental hospital a mentally-ill person who is "dangerous to no one and can live safely in freedom".[18] Thus Kenneth Donaldson gained his freedom after 15 years of compulsory confinement and a long series of legal battles.

The court established that the plaintiff had not received treatment during his commitment, but did not consider the broader concept of the "right to treatment". Over the past decade, certain experts in mental-health law have struggled to establish this right. They argue that a patient has a fundamental right to adequate treatment in exchange for being deprived of his liberty. Simple custodial supervision of a patient does not constitute treatment in their view. The legal issues involved in the "right to treatment" will almost certainly come to the Supreme Court before long.[19]

Psychiatry and the Court
Some of the problems discussed above also contribute to the complex relationship which exists between psychiatry and the courts. The borderland that straddles them is full of snares. Since objective criteria for diagnosing most mental illness are unavailable, it follows that the criteria to establish whether a defendant was mentally ill at the time he committed the crime are also wanting. Paradoxically, the court calls upon a psychiatrist for an expert opinion, even though usually aware that his expertise is limited and patchy. Although the court must ultimately make decisions about the defendant's fitness to plead and his criminal responsibility, it transfers many of the tricky questions to a professional group which is not sure to provide an objective, accurate evaluation. Legal decisions like that in the Durham case of 1954 in the USA (that an accused person is not criminally responsible if his unlawful act was the product of a mental disease or defect) provide only general,

ill-defined guidelines for the examining psychiatrist. They leave unanswered the questions of what constitutes mental disease or defect and the criteria for establishing that the disorder was sufficient to justify labelling the accused as not responsible.

Even when it is concluded that a defendant is either unfit to plead or not criminally responsible on the grounds of mental illness, his subsequent fate is often uncertain. The customary recommendation by the court is for treatment in a psychiatric institution but its duration and nature are frequently not clearly specified, primarily because the course of the patient's illness and his response to treatment (assuming that this will be provided) are often unpredictable.

The Use of Psychiatry in the Soviet Union as a Form of Repression

Our goal thus far has not simply been to catalogue all the immense ethical and social difficulties that the psychiatrist encounters, but rather to provide a *mise en scène* for the specific issue we focus on in this book.

From now on, we look at one particular pattern of the misuse of psychiatry, prevalent in the Soviet Union, namely the labelling of sane dissenters as mentally ill and in need of compulsory hospitalization and treatment. Why do we select the Soviet Union alone? Although this form of misuse has sometimes occurred elsewhere as well, in no other country, to our knowledge, has it become widespread and systematic, the expression of a deliberate government policy. Those cases we have studied have been only occasional or localized in character. While our information on most of them is insufficient for us to make firm judgements, some appear to have involved at least a degree of psychiatric abuse.[20]

More than likely, with assiduous research, more cases akin to those described in reference 20 could be brought to light in other countries; but this task is beyond our capacities. Instead, we have focused on the Soviet Union, which strikes us as a special case, and on which voluminous documentation is available.

The use of psychiatry as a political weapon in the Soviet Union is in many ways unique. With the development of various modes of dissent by Soviet citizens in the 1960s, reports began to emerge that substantial numbers of human-rights activists, nationalists, religious believers, and would-be emigrants, almost all mentally healthy in the eyes of their families and friends, were being declared insane by psychiatrists and thereupon confined compulsorily for indeterminate periods to psychiatric hospitals. Rather than receiving appropriate care there, the dissenters were encountering brutal and punitive "treatment", apparently in an effort to stamp out their nonconformist behaviour.

Allegations were subsequently made both in the Soviet Union and in the west, that psychiatrists were being employed in the battle against dissent as part of a systematic, state-directed policy, whose objectives appeared to be: the avoidance of a full-scale criminal trial with all its attendant publicity, the indefinite compulsory internment of dissenters in mental hospitals, and the discrediting of their convictions as those of mentally-sick people.

Our aim is to examine these allegations and to assess their validity. Initially, we take a brief look at the history of Russian psychiatry with special emphasis on its relationship to the state. Then follow a history of the politicization of psychiatry since the first well-documented case in the early nineteenth century, and an account of how its more recent occurrence has become known.

To illustrate the nature of the abuse, we discuss in detail four cases of dissenters labelled as mentally ill and forcibly hospitalized. The first two typify the process of criminal commitment in which the dissenter is charged with an "anti-Soviet" offence, declared not responsible on the basis of his insanity, and ordered by the court to receive compulsory treatment in a psychiatric hospital for an indefinite period. The other two cases exemplify the process of civil commitment in which the dissenter is involuntarily confined to a hospital under the provisions of a directive concerning disturbed persons who are "a social danger".

The next three chapters are both descriptive and analytic; they deal more generally with the main features of psychiatry's misuse—conditions in the psychiatric hospitals and the "treatment" given to dissenters there; the rôle of the psychiatrist, his motives and the nature of his diagnostic methods *vis-à-vis* the dissenter; and finally the dissenters themselves, the types of people usually selected for psychiatric repression and the factors underlying the selection. Appendix I presents data in summary form on those dissenters whose internments are well documented.

In the final chapter, we discuss the international reaction to the abuse, particularly that of the psychiatric community, and the efforts to curb it. We also examine the counter-response of certain Soviet psychiatrists to Western criticism. In Appendix 2 we suggest some steps through which the misuse of Soviet psychiatry might be combated and its occurrence elsewhere inhibited. Other appendices provide the texts of specially vivid and illuminating documents.

Chapter 2

SOVIET PSYCHIATRY:
EVOLUTION AND CHARACTER

THROUGHOUT HISTORY THE theories and practice of psychiatry have tended to be linked inextricably to the norms, values and ideologies of the society within which they functioned. This relationship is particularly well demonstrated in the case of Soviet psychiatry. To draw a brief sketch of the development of Soviet psychiatry, within the broader fabric of medical and social history, will increase our understanding of how its current misuse to stifle political dissent has evolved.

The discipline of psychiatry was non-existent in medieval times in Russia, as elsewhere in Europe.[1] The roots of mental disturbance were regarded by all levels of Russian society as supernatural; the insane were possessed by demons and evil spirits. Care of the afflicted was assigned to the monk, who occupied the *de facto* rôle of "psychiatrist"; the monastery served as an asylum, and exorcism of the harmful spirits was the therapy of choice. The monk's rôle in this system was partially legitimized as early as the tenth century by Prince Vladimir's statute that it would be mandatory for the Church to provide shelters for widows, orphans and the mentally ill. Monastic responsibility for the latter was further institutionalized in 1551 by Ivan the Terrible, who ordered the higher Church Synod to accept a therapeutic responsibility by "hospitalizing" the insane in monasteries, there to "receive enlightenment and understanding of truth" through religious and moral correction.[2]

The rule of Peter the Great saw a major innovation in attitudes to the insane. In 1723 he decreed the creation of special hospitals for the mentally ill. Although there were minimal practical effects from this directive, the tsar laid the ground for the subsequent transfer of psychiatric practice from the realm of religion to that of medicine by explicitly forbidding the placing of mental patients in monasteries. The shortcomings in his programme were the complete absence of any psychiatric institutions to replace the monasteries and the primitive state of Russian medicine. Tsar Peter had recognized the latter deficiency earlier in the century when he established Russia's first medical school. Also foreign doctors were encouraged to come to Russia during this time: they worked either exclusively with the nobility or in the state's military service. Later the medical faculty of Moscow University was established and its first medical degree was awarded in 1768. Efforts were now made to train Russian doctors both at home and abroad.

Peter the Great's psychiatric hospitals continued to remain more an idea than a fact. Peter III issued a similar decree in 1762, calling for the creation of special houses for the insane, but again with poor result. Only in the following decade, through the endeavour of Catherine the Great were the first mental hospitals actually built and utilized. In 1776 a psychiatric shelter with 25 beds was attached to a Moscow hospital, and in 1809 a psychiatric hospital opened on the outskirts of the city. By that year more than a dozen psychiatric facilities had come into existence.

Although additional institutions were established in the first half of the nineteenth century, their staffing and facilities, and the funds allocated to them, were quite inadequate to satisfy the need. The treatment and care provided were also of poor quality. However, some attempts were made at reform. A notable figure in Russian psychiatric history, Professor Sabler, on attaining the directorship of the Moscow Psychiatric Hospital, introduced a series of improvements: the name "madhouse" was altered to "hospital", the use of chains as a method of restraint was abolished, patients' case records were kept and annual reports made, and occupational and recreational activity was encouraged.

The most radical change in the organization of Russia's health service followed the freeing of the serfs in 1861 by Alexander II. The development of the *zemstvos* or local government councils was the most important administrative reform. These bodies were granted selected powers of self-government including the responsibility for developing and administering health services. During the next few years the *zemstvos* assumed authority for hundreds of medical facilities including mental institutions. By 1892 34 mental hospitals containing 9,000 beds and staffed by a total of 90 psychiatrists were financed and administered under this system of local government.[3]

As the mental hospital system expanded and progressed, so the quality of Russia's psychiatrists began to improve. Academic psychiatry was introduced with the appointment of Ivan Balinsky to the first chair of psychiatry, in the Military Academy of St Petersburg. Balinsky also organized the first psychiatric society in 1862. The creation of other chairs soon followed, held by academics who contributed significantly to psychiatric knowledge, particularly through their comprehensive descriptions of a variety of abnormal psychological states. Sergei Korsakov was the most celebrated of these figures. In addition to his academic pursuits, Korsakov, in his Moscow clinic, also continued Sabler's innovations by eliminating the physical restraint of patients, removing bars from windows and opening the doors of isolation rooms.

The ferment pervading Russian society around the turn of the century paved the way for a greater stress on the humane treatment of psychiatric patients; the social consciousness of Russian psychiatry was increasingly aroused. In 1911 Korsakov's successor, Professor Vladimir Serbsky (the Serbsky Institute for Forensic Psychiatry in Moscow, founded in 1921, of which we shall hear more in later chapters, was named after him), severely criticized the régime for its neglect of social welfare. Serbsky's leadership was a cogent factor in the founding of a national association of psychiatrists who believed that the roots of mental illness were to be found in the unjust social and economic conditions of Russian society. The volume of criticism from the medical profession as a whole, on the inadequate state of health services, reached a crescendo in the final years of tsarist rule.

Not surprisingly, the October 1917 revolution ushered in a new era for medicine and psychiatry in the Bolshevik state. The contemporary Soviet medical system originated in the many changes that occurred in subsequent months. The *zemstvo* model of medical care was entirely revamped through the establishment of a centralized People's Commissariat (later renamed Ministry) for Public Health. The formidable task before it was the total reorganization and co-ordination of the health services of the fledgling state. With the proclamation of a federally structured USSR in 1922, health commissariats were ratified in each of the constituent republics, all under the direction of the federal people's commissariat. Soviet psychiatry, like all other branches of the health service, has since remained under central control, with the ministries of health in each of the Soviet republics subordinate to the federal ministry.

The exposition of the organization and principles of Soviet psychiatry which follows describes mainly how the system is supposed to work, how it works ideally. The reader can then grasp the formal structure. At the end of the chapter we present a critical view of how the health services operate in practice. This should help to illuminate the characteristics of Soviet psychiatry described later in the book.

The federal minister of health* is today a figure of considerable power, appointed by, and in theory answerable to, the Supreme Soviet of the Soviet Union. He is advised by a variety of specialists including a psychiatrist, currently Dr Z. Serebryakova. She plays a significant rôle since all policies in the practice of psychiatry, no matter their source, must ultimately meet with her approval. Changes may be suggested by psychiatrists occupying positions lower down in the hierarchy, but their implementation requires the sanction of the top tier of the Ministry of Health. There is little chance of independent psychiatric policy, even at local level, since all psychiatrists (except those who work in the prison psychiatric hospitals which are administered by the Ministry of the Interior, and military psychiatrists) are employees of the Ministry of Health and are thus subordinate to superiors in all administrative matters. With such a hierarchical system, change is slow. There is a deliberately planned uniformity of psychiatric practice throughout the country.

In addition to the ministry's chief psychiatrist, the Institute of Psychiatry of the Academy of Medical Sciences also performs an important advisory rôle for the Ministry of Health. As a result, the institute and its director wield great power in the determination of psychiatric policy. The institute is

* He sits on the Council of Ministers or government, which has about 100 members, but he is neither on the council's presidium of a dozen senior ministers nor on the party's politbureau which in practice lays down the broad policies to be executed by the council.

particularly instrumental in shaping the training and research patterns in psychiatry. The present director of the institute, Professor A. V. Snezhnevsky, is one of the very few psychiatrists to hold individual membership of the academy. We shall come across this man frequently in later chapters.

The Post-revolution Development of Psychiatric Services

With the reorganization of the health system following the Bolshevik revolution, a policy of psychiatric service was adopted based above all on the prevention of mental illness.* The core of the new system was the psychiatric out-patient clinic situated in each administrative district. It remains so today.

An initial medical consultation usually takes place in the local all-purpose health clinic. A patient with a psychiatric condition who warrants more specialized attention is referred to the nearest psychiatric clinic. Such clinics serve a population of about half a million people. Here, ideally, the staff aim to maintain the patient within the community and admission to hospital is avoided if possible. Some clinics do contain a small in-patient unit for patients who require a short period of hospitalization. The clinic may also offer the facility of day care with the patient attending daily throughout the week and returning to his home each evening.

An important feature of the clinic is the industrial workshop. Work plays a pervasive rôle in the treatment and rehabilitation of psychiatric patients. The goal is to keep patients productive, either with a view to a return to their former jobs, or to retraining them for other more suitable posts. This aspect of psychiatric treatment reflects the Soviet attitude to work: the official ethos calls for every citizen to be socially productive and a contributor to the welfare of society.

Most day patients therefore participate in work therapy. Contracts are established between the clinic workshop (workshops also exist in the mental hospitals) and industry for the manufacture and assembly of a variety of goods. Patients occupied in the workshop receive small payments for their work, in addition to an invalid pension. As there is, at least in

* The importance of prevention was seen in the setting up in 1925 of the Scientific Research Institute for Neuropsychiatric Prophylaxis in Moscow.

theory, guaranteed employment in the Soviet Union to every citizen, patients probably have less fears than in the West about securing a regular job on discharge from the clinic.

More severely ill patients who are unable to maintain themselves in the community and need more comprehensive care are admitted to the regional mental hospital. There, most of them are treated over a period of several weeks or months and subsequently referred back to the clinic for follow-up supervision. The liaison between the mental hospital and its related clinic is apparently limited, with only minimal contact between the two staffs beyond the formal referral.[4] In addition to regional mental hospitals, some general hospitals contain small psychiatric units but this is a relatively minor aspect of the Soviet psychiatric system. Prison psychiatric hospitals exist for the treatment of the mentally-ill offender, and we discuss these in chapter 7. The psychiatric colony, usually situated in a rural area and agriculturally-based, is designed to meet the needs of patients requiring long-term care, sometimes for life.

The Therapeutic Approach

Conventional psychiatric treatment has in recent decades been based on the ideas of Pavlov, one of the most celebrated figures in the history of Soviet medical science, who died in 1936. Pavlovian ideas and research findings have remained of fundamental significance to Soviet medicine in general. A joint session of the Academy of Sciences and the Academy of Medical Sciences met in 1950, and, under pressure from party ideologists, cemented the Pavlovian foundations of medicine and of several other fields as well. The academies resolved to take the necessary steps for the further development of Pavlov's theories and for their application to medical practice, pedagogy, physical education and animal husbandry.[5]

This period saw extensive purges in scientific circles and is a sorry chapter in the history of Soviet science as a whole. In biology for instance, the Lysenkoists were given all the powerful positions by the party. They promulgated a particular body of theory which denied the right of biologists to entertain different views, and went as far as purging opponents. Lysenko's views were later shown to be those of a charlatan and he himself was

officially repudiated. Zhores Medvedev, a biologist who is a
focus of our attention in chapter 6, has written a vivid account
of this tumultuous phase in Soviet science.[6]

With the "Pavlov session" of the two academies, psychiatry
entered a similar period of turmoil. Pavlov's physiological
theories of higher nervous activity and its regulatory mechan-
isms, were incorporated into psychiatric thought and became
entrenched as the sole viewpoint, attaining the status of dogma.
The whole field of psychiatry was remoulded to conform to
Pavlovian doctrine. "Anti-Pavlovian" psychiatrists were removed from important positions and either forcibly retired or
transferred to posts in remote parts of the country. Many of
them were Jews, and indeed the process took place within an
anti-Semitic context, whose culmination was the execution of
the twenty leading figures in Yiddish culture in 1952 and the
infamous Doctors' Plot of 1953.

Pavlov's theories were artificially synthesized with the
Marxist view that man's behaviour is a consequence of social
and economic conditions prevailing in his society, to form a
basis for psychiatric treatment. This stance was intensely
critical of the theories of Freud, which had been effectively
taboo in the Soviet Union since the 1930s. At that time Freud's
works became generally inaccessible and translation of them
into Russian ceased. The Soviet rejection of Freud centres on
two main issues: the significant rôle given by him to man's
instincts in determining behaviour, and the highly individualistic quality of psychoanalysis, in which the patient is
encouraged to become independent, autonomous and responsible for himself. The party ideologues have resolutely opposed
the theory that man's behaviour is mainly determined by
irrational and unconscious factors and egoistical drives. There
has been a similar rejection of Jung, Adler, and the neo-
Freudians such as Horney and Sullivan, even though the ideas
of this group are barely known to Soviet psychiatrists.

The Soviet model of treatment involves biological, psychological and social dimensions. The stress on the biological basis
of mental illness is reflected in the widespread use of tranquillizing and anti-depressant drugs. These are the same drugs
that are used commonly in Western medical practice. Underlying the Soviet reliance on drugs is the Pavlovian theory that
normal functioning of the nervous system results from a balance

of excitation and inhibition. An imbalance of these opposing functions occurs in mental illness but is reversible by the action of certain drugs on the brain.

Other physical treatments are also used, although less commonly. Insulin coma treatment, rarely applied today by Western psychiatrists, still retains a place in the Soviet Union. It consists of the administration of insulin sufficient to induce a comatose state, which is subsequently reversed; this is repeated several times over a period of weeks. Electro-shock treatment and narcotherapy or sleep treatment are also used. Psychosurgery—surgical interference with brain function, particularly the destruction of parts of the fore brain, as practised in the West to a limited extent—has been banned in the Soviet Union.

Psychological treatment* is characterized by its directive and educative qualities. Ziferstein, an American psychiatrist who observed the use of psychotherapy over a thirteen-month period whilst visiting the Bekhterev Psychoneurological Research Institute in Leningrad, has provided a clear description of it.[7] The psychiatrist promotes a supportive emotional climate by conveying his interest, concern and appreciation of the patient's positive qualities; he offers direct guidance to the patient on how problems of living should be tackled in a realistic and mature fashion; and he interprets the patient's neurotic pattern of behaviour and his resistance to change. Generating negative feelings in the patient is studiously avoided since this would disturb the positive emotional climate and prove anti-therapeutic. The aim of psychotherapy is the gradual promotion of an attitude of optimism in the patient.

Ziferstein's impressions were confirmed by members of the United States Mission on Mental Health which visited the Soviet Union in 1967 to study the country's psychiatric facilities.[8] The visitors saw their Soviet counterparts as extremely active in psychotherapy, using techniques of guidance, education, advice and exhortation, as well as providing a warm and supportive relationship.

* Dr Boris Segal, formerly head of the Department of Clinical Psychology and Psychotherapy of the Moscow Institute of Psychiatry, and now living in Boston, has written a comprehensive review of "The Theoretical Bases of Soviet Psychotherapy". See *American Journal of Psychotherapy*, 1975, Vol. 29, pp. 503–523.

The social dimension of treatment is closely related to the psychological. We have already noted the importance attached to work therapy in the workshops of the clinics and mental hospitals. Work is a major tool in the therapeutic arsenal and reflects the Soviet view of it as basic to the life of every citizen. The psychiatrist wields considerable power in shaping the economic and social world of his patient; he has the authority to intervene in a number of ways: by modifying the work schedule of the patient, recommending further training or education, classifying the degree of invalidism and thus the amount of welfare benefits received, changing his place of work, requesting new housing. An employer or other relevant authority is normally obliged to comply with a psychiatrist's recommendations. The powers granted to the psychiatrist are based on a reciprocal relationship between him and the state. The latter employs the psychiatrist for his therapeutic and socializing skills, and he in turn makes use of the state's resources.

The psychiatrist's social therapy is intimately bound up with a view of society in which, while the welfare of the latter is paramount, that of the individuals who make it up is also important. Thus guaranteed employment, job security, a pension and free health care and education are viewed as necessary ingredients of society. Ultimate therapeutic success can only be achieved when the community provides institutions and a system of regulations which safeguard the citizen's welfare. The social measures cited are, to the psychiatrist, prophylactic in their effect. The maintenance and improvement of mental health is a social endeavour in which the psychiatrist plays a central rôle. A good illustration of the system is the participation of the clinic psychiatrist in activities within the community; education in mental health for example, is offered in factories and schools.

The concept of the collective dominates social therapy. An emphasis on the group, or the community, is a cardinal feature of Soviet society; the need and objectives of the collective take priority over those of the individual. The latter operates within a variety of collectives such as the family, the trade union, the party organization, the factory, the collective farm, and in each case he must consider the needs of the collective before those of his own. One of the psychiatrist's tasks is to hasten the patient's reintegration into the collective and a position of social responsibility. Promotion of individualism in the patient has no place in Soviet psychiatric treatment. A reflection of the psychiatrist's attentiveness to the collective rather than to the individual is seen in a clause of the Soviet physician's oath which states that he must "work conscientiously wherever the interests of society demand".[9]

The strong official ethos of collectivism generates in Soviet psychiatrists—and also in the more conformist sections of the public—an intolerance of deviance from conventionally accepted norms and values. Social behaviour involving particular styles in clothing, hair and manners, certain attitudes to religion, an interest in some forms of art, literature and music, sexual practices such as homosexuality (a criminal offence)—all behaviour recognizably different from that of the broad collective—is prone to be viewed by psychiatrists with suspicion and distrust, and as evidence of possible mental illness. The psychiatrist's active re-education of the patient entails "presenting to him values and standards of behaviour that are considered correct, realistic and *socially desirable*".[10] [Our italics]

The ready labelling of unconventional behaviour as socially deviant provides fertile soil for its redefinition as psychiatrically abnormal, a natural foundation on which the use of psychiatry for social repression can take place.

Psychiatry and Political Ideology

As part of his oath, the Soviet physician swears: "in all my actions to be *guided by the principles of communist morality*, ever to bear in mind the high calling of the Soviet physician and my responsibility to the people and the Soviet state".[11] [Our italics] This clause extends further the priority granted to the collective over the individual, by calling on the doctor explicitly to pursue Communist values in his practice. Yet these values are accepted by probably only a minority of the population. Only one in ten of all adults belong to the Communist Party, and many of those do so only for careerist reasons. Many non-Communists are, of course, influenced by Communist ideology, but many others reject it, some in part, some completely.

Communist morality is inculcated in the physician from the

start of his medical career, when, as a student, he is obliged to attend a course of studies related to Marxism-Leninism. According to Field's research, during the period following the second world war, no less than 250 hours were set aside for this subject. This compares with 297 hours then devoted to anatomy and 213 hours to surgery. The same emphasis obtains today.*[12]

Stalin highlighted the need for political enlightenment in the professional work of scientists in his declaration that:

> ... there is one branch of science which Bolsheviks in all branches of science are duty-bound to know, and that is the Marxist-Leninist science of society ... a Leninist cannot be just a specialist in his favourite science; he must also be a political and social worker, keenly interested in the destinies of his country, acquainted with the laws of social development, capable of applying these laws, and striving to be an active participant in the political guidance of the country.[13]

A typical quotation of 1952 from *Medical Worker*, the organ of the Ministry of Health, relates political consciousness more specifically to the physician: "In order to be a worthy representative of the physician's noble profession, it is necessary not only to have an excellent professional education, but also to be well acquainted with the principles of Marxism-Leninism."[14]

Of more pragmatic significance for the psychiatrist (and for all professionals for that matter) was Stalin's pronouncement that political qualifications took priority over professional ability and experience. Good political qualifications involved a person's loyalty to the party and its ideology, and his preparedness to comply with party directives. The political criteria and their pertinence in the life of the professional remain almost as solidly entrenched today. This is well illustrated by the high proportion of positions of authority in the health service which are occupied by party members.

Thus the party, through its pervasive presence amidst the echelons of power, plays a dominant rôle in controlling all

---

* According to Dr M. Voikhanskaya, until 1975 a Leningrad psychiatrist, and other competent sources, 25 per cent of the medical curriculum is devoted to political studies. The subjects covered are Bases of Marxism-Leninism, Political Economy, Dialectical Materialism, Historical Materialism, History of the Communist Party and Scientific Atheism.

aspects of the country's health service, including the professional activity of its doctors. We shall come to see how crucial this pattern of authority is in the use of psychiatry to stifle dissent.

Field captures the essence of Soviet medicine's submissive relationship to the party and the régime:

> Ideology . . . occupies a place of central importance in the Soviet scheme, both as doctrine and as a practical instrument of control. Yet the régime does not so much want conformity with doctrine or even belief (in the sense of a religious conviction or faith) as a "positive identification with the party as a trustworthy custodian of all fundamental doctrinal questions". It is natural, then, that the regime should be particularly concerned with the Soviet intelligentsia and this intelligentsia's receptiveness to party ideology and, more important, with its "correct" interpretation of party policies and its readiness to execute orders and directives in the spirit of these policies.[15]

The Health Services in Practice

As noted earlier, this chapter has looked mainly at formal structure and principles—rather than the practice—of the Soviet health system, with special reference to psychiatry. Beyond doubt the practice is often very different. As yet, however, no probing and comprehensive account of medical practice "on the ground" has been written. The reason is simple: no foreigner would be allowed to do the necessary field-work, and no independent-minded Soviet citizen who somehow circumvented all the obstacles would be allowed to publish his findings.

In these circumstances the assessment of a judicious and independent critic like Dr Andrei Sakharov is of value, even if it cannot be based on systematic data. In 1975 he wrote in a book as follows:

> . . . Medical care for the majority of the population is of a low quality. It takes half a day to get to see a doctor at a clinic. . . . The outpatient has virtually no choice as to what doctor he will get. . . . At the hospitals, the patients lie in the corridors, where the air is stuffy or else there is a draught. . . .

For an ordinary hospital, the budget allocates less than one ruble per day per patient for everything. . . . But for privileged hospitals the budget allocates up to fifteen rubles per day per patient. . . . In the provinces there is almost no modern medication and even Moscow lags far behind the Western countries in the range of medication available. . . . The system of medical education has been seriously undermined. . . . The general ethical and professional decline has spread to the doctors, who held out longer than others. Those unquestionable gains made by medicine in the first decades of the Soviet régime (in paediatrics, in combating infectious diseases, etc.) are now threatened.[16]

Sakharov's assessment is the more significant because it coincides with that of numerous recent émigrés from the Soviet Union to whom we have talked, including a number of psychiatrists and doctors. It also coincides with the personal experiences of the health service of one of the authors (P.R.), when he lived in Moscow as a research student in 1963–64.

Even the official Soviet press, in rare moments of candour, partially agrees with Sakharov. In 1976, for example, an article in the *Literary Gazette* pointed to the problems facing the Soviet health service. According to the author the hospitals were seriously under-financed. He strongly recommended the setting up of a medical fund, to tap the population's charitable instincts. The fund would permit the purchase of expensive apparatus and the enlargement of crowded hospitals. Ministry of Health officials favoured his scheme.

At present patients

are sometimes lying in the corridors; and at holiday times it is painful to see that all hospital patients have to go unattended and unfed. In fact many have to remain untreated at such times, except in the most drastic cases, and are usually ignored by their neighbours in other beds who may be lucky enough to have visitors or relatives to care for them, and even to give them their necessary medicine.[17]

Also in 1976, an article in *Izvestia* described the chronic bribery which prevails in many hospitals. The author detailed the long string of bribes which a patient had to give to orderlies, nurses and doctors at different stages of a hospital stay so that his operation could eventually take place.[18]

The sum total of our reading and interviewing leads us to believe that, as in Western countries, the general quality of the psychiatric services in the Soviet Union is lower than that in most other branches of medicine. Evidence for this view appears in chapters 7 and 8 and in appendix X where Dr Voikhanskaya describes the ordinary city mental hospital in which she worked before emigrating.

Finally, we should also note a trend in Soviet psychiatry which differs from the strong tendency in Western countries to treat as many patients as possible as out-patients rather than in-patients. By contrast, the Soviet authorities have been building mental hospitals at a rapid rate, the number of beds for patients with mental and nervous diseases having gone up between 1962 and 1974 from 222,600 to 390,000. The latter figure represents 13 per cent of the beds available in 1974 in hospitals of all types. Moreover, it evidently does not include a substantial number of psychiatric patients kept in geriatric facilities. Also, the expansion in the quantity of psychiatric beds is due to continue in the years up to 1980.[19]

After this brief outline of the development of Russian psychiatry and its relationship to the state, we can now consider how the relationship has been exploited by the régime to suppress dissent.

Chapter 3

PSYCHIATRIC ABUSE: ITS HISTORY AND HOW IT BECAME AN ISSUE IN THE SOVIET UNION

AFTER SERVING IN the tsar's army in western Europe, the Russian philosopher Pyotr Chaadayev (1793–1856) returned home. Disturbed by the condition of Russian society and impressed by features of western European tradition and culture he wrote a "philosophical letter" critical of the tsarist régime that was published in the Moscow journal *Telescope*. The result was a prompt denunciation initiated by the chief of the secret police of Nicholas I. Nicholas himself retaliated by officially declaring Chaadayev insane and by exiling the *Telescope*'s publisher. Disguising his repressive motives under a mask of benevolent paternalism, Nicholas proclaimed:

> I consider this to be a farrago of insolent nonsense worthy of a lunatic. . . . The essay of P. Y. Chaadayev which appeared in the *Telescope*, and the thoughts expressed in it have aroused feelings of anger and repugnance in all Russians without exception. But the horror quickly turned to sympathy when they learned that their unhappy compatriot, the author of the article, suffers from derangement and insanity. Taking into consideration the unwell state of this unfortunate person, the government in its solicitude and fatherly concern for its subject, forbids him to leave the house and will provide free medical care with a special doctor to be appointed by the local authorities from among those under their jurisdiction.[1]

Thus by tsarist decree Chaadayev was detained in his home over the next year. On attaining his freedom, he continued his literary and political activities. Two further "philosophical letters" were published during his lifetime in France, but not in Russia. The complete series of his eight "letters" was published only after his death.

The Chaadayev incident occurred in 1836 and in all likelihood was the first instance in Russia of dissent curbed by resort to psychiatry. Why such a procedure was used is not fully clear but it did serve to undermine Chaadayev's reformist ideas by discrediting them as those of a madman. The concept of "reformism" will reappear several times in the story of the "madness" of dissenters. However, the practice of repressing dissent by psychiatric means was only occasional and localized during tsarist times; it was neither systematic nor a state-directed policy.

The Early Soviet Period

During the early days of the revolution the labelling of dissenters as mentally ill continued to be a rare event. When it did occur, the goal was to defuse the political rôle of individuals viewed as a threat by the then shaky Bolshevik government. Two well-known cases demonstrate the régime's unsuccessful efforts to accomplish this result. In November 1918 Maria Spiridonova, a leader of the Socialist Revolutionary Party, was brought to trial and sentenced to one year in prison. An alliance between her party and the Bolsheviks had collapsed and friction between them had increased to such an extent that in mid-1918 the Socialist Revolutionaries were vigorously suppressed.

Granted an amnesty and prematurely released, Spiridonova rallied her followers and attempted to rebuild the party's structure. She began an incessant attack on the government for the wrongs she believed it had committed against the people. All Bolshevik efforts to undermine her growing public success failed. Spiridonova had become a major political force and had to be checked; her inevitable arrest ensued. The Bolsheviks were now in a predicament. Spiridonova was regarded as a hero by masses of people, she had not committed any crime, another trial and sentence would only provoke increased opposition, and yet her power constituted a real danger. The Moscow Revolutionary Tribunal contrived a scheme to resolve the predicament—confinement to a sanatorium, a move obviously anticipated by Spiridonova. In a letter smuggled out of prison she wrote:

> I have a feeling the Bolsheviks are preparing some especially dirty trick for me. It would be difficult for them to kill me,

and to send me to prison for a long term would not do either . . . they will declare me insane and put me in a psychiatric clinic or something like that . . . they want to strike a moral blow at me. To save their position they resort to every possible means . . .[2]

Later she heard the Tribunal's verdict:

As the tribunal in fixing its sentences is not influenced by any feelings of revenge for enemies of the revolution, and as it intends to cause Maria Spiridonova no unnecessary suffering . . . the Moscow Revolutionary Tribunal declares as follows: Spiridonova is to be banished for one year from political and social life and isolated in a sanatorium where she is to be given the opportunity of healthy physical and mental work.[3]

Was this a strategy inspired by the memory of Nicholas's 1836 proclamation, an attempt in other words to reduce her prestige? Spiridonova is no doubt correct in her own forecast of the tribunal's decision: confinement in a sanatorium could serve the purpose of discrediting her. She would be removed from political power and influence on the grounds that she was physically and mentally unwell. Her ideas were those of a disturbed mind. Spiridonova in fact never entered a sanatorium. She remained confined in a Kremlin guardroom in distressing physical and psychological conditions until her escape in April 1919.

The second case where confinement to a sanatorium was attempted but failed was that of Angelica Balabanoff. Her "mental illness" was only hinted at. An influential figure in the Bolshevik Party and international labour movement, she knew, and collaborated closely with, many of the leaders of the revolution including Lenin and Trotsky. In 1920 Balabanoff protested about several mistakes she felt had been made by the revolutionary leadership. She expressed her anger directly to Lenin. This was a period of great danger for the Bolsheviks: the White Army was advancing on Petrograd, even Moscow was threatened. It was within this situation that Balabanoff was ordered by the Central Committee to enter a sanatorium.

. . . I was amazed to receive an official order . . . to leave Moscow for a sanatorium. I thought at first that the order must be the result of an error . . . no special concern had been shown about the state of my health before this. When I made further inquiries I discovered that there was no error —the Central Committee wished me to "take a rest in a sanatorium" . . . "I am neither sick nor old enough to retire," I told the general secretary of the party, Krestinsky. "I am strong enough to work and I want to keep on working."[4]

When Krestinsky realized that Balabanoff would not comply with the order, he resorted to another tactic to remove her from the central political arena by instructing her to take charge of a propaganda train to remote Turkestan. The committee's strategy had been foiled by Balabanoff's resistance and the sanatorium manœuvre was abandoned.

The Stalin Period

Information is scanty on the practice of interning or attempting to intern dissenters in mental hospitals during the Stalin period. It is not until the late 1930s that the régime appears to have initiated a systematic policy of internment. An illuminating account of this period is provided by a psychiatrist who left the Soviet Union for the United States soon after the second world war. He described his experiences in a series of four letters to the *American Journal of Psychiatry*. The first appeared in 1970 when allegations of the political use of psychiatry were beginning to be voiced in the West. The identity of the psychiatrist has never been disclosed and, at the time of publication, was withheld at his request. The journal's editor commented, however, that he was satisfied with the credentials of the writer, who had been a member of the American Psychiatric Association for many years.[5]

The psychiatrist, a native of eastern Poland, automatically became a Soviet citizen in 1939 when the Red Army occupied that region. After Hitler's attack on the Soviet Union he fled eastwards and joined the staff of a mental hospital in Kazan. This, he recounts, was a 400-bed institution used exclusively for the treatment of politicals and serving the entire country.*

* The Kazan institution has housed a number of well-known present-day dissenters including Victor Kuznetsov and Natalya Gorbanevskaya; the latter is discussed in chapter 5.

The hospital was in the grounds of an ordinary mental hospital but was run independently, under the direction of the NKVD (the name of the secret police at that time). Corroboration of this information appears in the *Chronicle of Current Events*, the main journal of the human-rights movement in the Soviet Union, to which we turn later in this chapter. In a report on prison psychiatric hospitals, the *Chronicle* wrote that the first hospital of this type was "already in existence before the war, in Kazan. There is still a special section for politicals dating from that time."[6]

The psychiatrist differentiates two types of political inmate at Kazan. The first was sane people confined for political reasons. One such "patient" he learned about on his arrival in 1941 was Jan Pilsudski. Pilsudski was discharged from the hospital some weeks after an agreement had been reached between the Soviet Union and Sikorski's Polish government-in-exile, on the treatment of Polish political prisoners. As he was mentally normal, both his admission and his release from the institution were clearly determined by political factors.

Another case vividly described is that of a Moscow factory worker who declined to contribute a month's salary for the war effort, a "voluntary" state requirement for all workers and farmers. He claimed that his salary was too meagre both to keep himself alive and make the contribution. Steadfast in his refusal, he was arrested, detained in Moscow's Lubyanka prison and there diagnosed as schizophrenic. He was then transferred to the Kazan hospital and again diagnosed as a schizophrenic. The psychiatrist believed the "patient" to be sane, but presumably felt under pressure from fellow staff to concur with their diagnosis. The added fact that the "patient" had been charged with counter-revolutionary propaganda made it all the more personally hazardous for the psychiatrist to dispute the diagnosis and question the need for hospitalization. Furthermore, by arguing for the man's sanity, he might well have rendered the "patient" vulnerable to what would probably have been a harsher form of punishment—imprisonment or detention in a labour camp, and the possibility of his death there.

The second type of political inmate was indeed mentally ill. People of this category had been sent to Kazan because their delusions and other abnormalities had a political content. One schizophrenic patient, for instance, had the delusion that he was Trotsky. Another patient believed that Judaism had the power to destroy the world (political anti-Semitism was punishable by law). In fact, the psychiatrist emphasized in his correspondence that *most* patients at Kazan were mentally ill and that only a minority were sane and held there solely because of their political convictions.

Our earliest detailed information on the route by which most politicals reached Kazan comes from Naum Korzhavin. A poet born in 1925, he informed us about his experiences of early 1948 in the Serbsky Institute for Forensic Psychiatry.* Although then a convinced Stalinist, he had been arrested a few days earlier for writing "anti-Soviet" poems. He recalls that the Serbsky was then a relatively humane institution, with a benevolent staff, including the head of the section for politicals, Professor Khaletsky.

Korzhavin's stay was reasonably pleasant compared to prison: he read, wrote poetry, participated in occupational therapy, and at no time received any treatment. Two commissions examined him. As a result of the first examination conducted by about a dozen doctors, in the presence of his criminal investigator, he was transferred to the institute's section for politicals. Here, he gained the impression that the staff were hoping to rule him mentally ill, and not responsible, thus to spare him the ordeal of a concentration camp. The second commission, however, found him responsible, whereupon he went into Siberian exile for several years.

Korzhavin concluded that, from what he could ascertain, in 1948 at least, the practice of placing healthy people in mental hospitals was not malicious in intent but benevolent.

Paradoxically, at about the time of Korzhavin's detention, these humanitarian attitudes attracted the attention of the authorities. A commission headed by R. S. Zemlyachka, a veteran party functionary, inspected the institute; its report expressed indignation that "here they have created a sanatorium" and ordered the director "to tighten things up": the

* The Serbsky Institute for Forensic Psychiatry was founded in 1920 and has served as the main centre in the Soviet Union for the teaching and research of forensic psychiatry. It also operates as an assessment unit for forensic cases from all over the country. We shall discuss it in detail later in the chapter and in chapter 5.

régime had to be made more severe and fewer defendants were to be ruled not responsible. Korzhavin reports that—apparently to help implement this new policy—a forensic psychiatrist called Daniil Lunts was brought into the political section. We shall come across Lunts frequently in subsequent chapters.

One of the most illuminating cases of a political ruled insane in the early 1950s* is that of Ilya Yarkov, the author of an autobiography published in *samizdat*,† and smuggled out to the West.[7] Although Yarkov does not feature in other *samizdat* documents, we have no doubt that his vivid and carefully-written autobiography is authentic. It was sent to the West by Vladimir Bukovsky, together with a photograph of the author, who had died in 1970. Chapter seven of Yarkov's story, written in about 1963, deals with the period 1951–54 during which he was interned in three different prison mental institutions in Gorky, Kazan and then Chistopol, all situated a few hundred miles east of Moscow.

In 1928, Yarkov, a native of Kuibyshev and then about 35 years old, was apprehended by the police, tried and sentenced for "counter-revolutionary activity". Twenty years later, he reports, the authorities decided to create a large new category of political prisoner by simply re-arresting those people who had served sentences as politicals in the 1920s and 1930s and were still alive. Yarkov fell into this category and was arrested in 1951. The secret police thought he was a dangerous leader of some sectarian group. Soon they discovered that he had simply been writing a biography of the leader of an early twentieth-century Tolstoyan sect.

Under interrogation Yarkov did not hide his dislike of the secret police as an institution. He explains to the reader that he had always been an intellectual oppositionist or "heretic", but he was not against the Soviet system as a whole.

* Other early cases include ex-President Paets of Estonia, held in Kazan from 1941 to 1956 (*Kaznimye sumasshestviem*, Frankfurt, Possev, 1971, p. 479); the Leningrad mathematician Revolt Pimenov, interned under civil commitment in 1949 (*Chronicle* 15); the cultural and political figures listed by S. Pisarev (*Survey*, 1970, No. 77); and those listed by Yarkov (see below).

† An acronym, *samizdat* literally means "own publishing house". A manuscript usually gets into *samizdat* when an author types out copies of his work and distributes them to friends and associates. The manuscript is typed and retyped repeatedly until a substantial circulation has been achieved.

The police had no evidence of him having committed any actual crime—such as propagandizing his "anti-Soviet views". So, unable to concede that they had arrested him in error, they switched tack, discovered that he had suffered a mild mental illness many years earlier, and sent him for psychiatric examination. This took place in the psychiatry department of the Kuibyshev medical institute, in the presence of his police investigator. Here he sensed the police influence, which "somehow required that I be turned into a madman". One of the psychiatrists put a leading question to him: "Whom do you love more, Lenin or Stalin?" With his investigator present, Yarkov found it impossible to see where medicine ended and police work began. He was duly ruled not responsible.

On the basis of the three years he then spent in psychiatric hospitals he reflects that they were used for people "arrested under article 58 of the criminal code* (and this one alone!), against whom charges clearly would not stick. . . . Either there had been a false denunciation which ultimately had no foundation, or there was not enough material to support the charge." Here Yarkov anticipates the reader criticizing him for naïveté, and points out: "It should not be forgotten that it was, after all, 1951 and not 1937 [the highpoint of Stalin's "great terror"]. In 1937 various extra-judicial forms of oppression against 'dissenters' were permitted on a large scale; but in 1951 some minimal legal checks, however relative and conditional, were nevertheless required."

Hence the resort to psychiatry. And, as Yarkov stresses, what a promising resort for the police it was: "How many people can one find in our country nowadays with totally undamaged nerves, without neurosis or psychosis, without one or another 'oddity' or 'eccentricity'? The past decades have laid their imprint on all of us. . . . A specially important cause has been the war of 1941–45."

As a result of the police use of psychiatry, in three years Yarkov met

> a great mass of people who were definitely intelligent and developed personalities, often well educated, sometimes profoundly cultured, people whom not one self-respecting

* Article 58 of the Stalinist, pre-1960 code, covered an enormous range of "anti-Soviet" acts.

doctor in a "civilian" hospital would dream of detaining for years on the pretext that they were "nut-cases". Plenty of such "nut-cases" surround us in everyday life, occupying senior posts, showing an unusual capacity for work, active in science and literature. No one thinks of placing them in a hospital, behind prison bars. Not until they fall by chance into the orbit of the secret police. Then everything is turned upside down and back to front.

Elsewhere Yarkov describes his sane fellow inmates in terms which would also apply to the well-known dissenters with whose internment twenty years later this book is largely concerned. They were "very interesting, definitely outstanding and original people, whose whole 'guilt' lay essentially in the fact that, as regards their psyches, they were more sensitive, more intolerant to social injustice, dishonesty and cruelty than the man in the street, and they reacted to such things with greater concern".

Yarkov regarded a substantial minority of his fellow internees as being as mentally healthy as the rest of society. The majority, however, were suffering from psychiatric illnesses, while one good friend of his went out of his mind under the strain of separation from his family and deep resentment at his unjust fate.

The three hospitals contained large groups of Muscovites, who had mostly been assessed in the Serbsky Institute, militant Latvian nationalists from Riga, and devout Orthodox Christians, interned for their religious activity. Yarkov paints vivid pen portraits of many friends and acquaintances. There are, for example: the artist, Mitrofanov, who had spent no less than twenty years in prison hospitals for having fought for the Poles during the Soviet invasion of Poland in 1920; the biologist Kozhevnikov, interned as an opponent of Lysenko's ruthless dictatorship in biology; the well-known writer Mark Krinitsky, aged 78 when Yarkov first met him; the Jewish tailor Khanan Lyakhovitsky, one of the few Trotskyists to survive imprisonment in Kolyma; the chauffeur Fedotov, whose only crime had been to drive for Trotsky and other early Soviet leaders; and the doctor Fyodor Strizhenov, who had treated an Englishman later pronounced a spy, and who, on his release, resumed work and eventually retired in a blaze of glory.

Yarkov also befriended a man called Dzhumabayev from the Kazakh Republic. He had been an official in the republic's finance ministry until accused in the early 1930s of "oppositional" activity, belonging to a seditious group and participating in an anti-Soviet conspiracy. An ardent and convinced Communist, Dzhumabayev had spent nineteen years in prison hospitals by the time Yarkov met him, and he had accepted his lot. Since the party had decreed that Dzhumabayev was insane and in need of treatment, and the party was always correct in its judgement, he had acquiesced. Although he had not agreed with the original criminal charges laid against him, he believed that it was his duty to the party to comply.

Among the patients who were definitely mentally disturbed, Yarkov was friendly with Mikhail Burshtein, who exhibited delusions of persecution. This was confirmed in 1960, six years after both men had been discharged, when Yarkov received an odd letter from Burshtein in which he described himself as a German and called himself by a German name. Burshtein, a research psychiatrist prior to his hospitalization, had demanded greater freedom to conduct his research programme and, if this were not forthcoming, the right to emigrate. He had immediately been arrested, accused of treason, declared insane and hospitalized.

The psychiatrists Yarkov met in the three hospitals varied considerably. The head of the psychiatric section of the prison hospital in Gorky, for instance, Dr Evsei Maidansky, is described as a perfect example of a person uniting the rôles of doctor and police officer, yet a very pleasant man. Another Gorky psychiatrist, Dr Nadezhda Velikanova, was decent and cordial. The opposite could be said of Dr Elizaveta Lavritskaya, an elderly psychiatrist on the Kazan staff. She was a cruel woman who often humiliated and punished her patients. Her favourite form of punishment was the "roll-up" treatment, strikingly described by Yarkov.* Sheets of wet canvas were rolled around the patient's body. As the canvas dried, it became tighter and tighter, making breathing progressively more difficult. The degree of tightness and the duration of the roll-up varied according to the reasons it was prescribed for.

Although the orderlies were ordinary criminals serving their terms in prison psychiatric hospitals instead of forced-labour

* The "roll-up" has been described by several dissenters—see chapter 7.

camps, Yarkov found the majority of hospital personnel generally pleasant. Nurses and female orderlies were often kind, and the administrators "tried to show politeness and consideration, or at least restraint". Yarkov never underwent treatment of any kind, and in summer he and his fellows could spend the whole day walking in the grounds, conversing with each other. There was complete freedom of speech and some inmates "cursed Stalin the whole day long, from morning to night".

The commissions which visited the hospitals about twice a year from Moscow were usually chaired by a secret-police doctor who often had the rank of general.* The decision when to recommend an inmate's release depended, Yarkov and his friends believed, on the highly secret term of imprisonment which the authorities had prescribed for each one of them: "all the rest was *pro forma*". This view sounds plausible enough, as nowhere does Yarkov mention the subject of recantation: i.e. the "admission" that your anti-Soviet acts were the result of your mental illness, and a statement of gratitude to the doctors for curing you. Neither the hospital staff nor the visiting commissions, it appears, had any duty to persuade inmates into such a course of action. As we shall see, this task was soon given to them.

Post-Stalin Attempts at Reform

During the period of Yarkov's compulsory hospitalization the infamous "Doctors' Plot" episode occurred. In January 1953 Sergei Pisarev,[8] a party member since 1920 and for many years a party official, submitted a report to Stalin criticizing the secret police for its fabrication of the non-existent "plot" to poison leading political figures. Before long he was arrested. Pisarev spent the initial seven weeks of his detention in the Serbsky Institute for Forensic Psychiatry and then, having been declared insane, he was confined for four months in the psychiatric section of the hospital in Moscow's Butyrka prison,

* This frank approach was changed, probably in the mid-1950s, since when the psychiatrists have formally been civilians, employed by the Serbsky Institute. The latter, in turn, is outwardly subordinate to the Ministry of Health, while in fact it is controlled by the Ministry of Internal Affairs, or MVD.

and for nearly a year and a half in the Leningrad Prison Psychiatric Hospital. The diagnosis reached by the Serbsky psychiatrists was schizophrenia, yet later on three occasions during his Leningrad hospitalization Pisarev learned that his psychiatrist there, Dr L. A. Kalinin, had reported that he was "healthy and fully capable of accepting responsibility for his actions". Pisarev continues:

... on all occasions, the commission* ... which, unlike Kalinin, had no idea whatever of my condition, was obedient to the administrative organs and "disagreed" with him. On all three occasions, the head of my department (Dr Kalinin) recorded his personal opinion in the files. My case remained "undecided" and they continued to hold me in detention. In order not to compromise the Serbsky Institute, I should mention that on all three occasions the commission suggested that the diagnosis "schizophrenia" be replaced by the diagnosis "paranoid psychopathy". In order to disprove both these diagnoses, I was obliged, at my own insistence, instead of being given my freedom, to spend in the hospital of the Gannushkin Psychiatric Research Institute a further two and a quarter months (December 1954–February 1955). It was only after this that it was finally proven that I was neither schizophrenic nor even any kind of paranoid psychopath (on this point, you may, if need be, obtain confirmation directly from the Gannushkin Institute).

After his release in 1955 Pisarev mounted a campaign to combat psychiatric misuse, concentrating particularly on the Serbsky, which he saw as the root of the evil. He presented evidence to the party's Central Committee of numerous cases in which the Serbsky had diagnosed mentally-healthy people as insane and in need of compulsory treatment. He cited the names of many scholars, writers, artists and party workers who had been labelled insane and hospitalized along with genuine patients for periods of several years. The Central Committee responded by appointing a commission under the chairmanship of a senior party official, A. I. Kuznetsov, and comprising eminent professors of psychiatry and directors of important

* i.e. the panel of psychiatrists assembled to assess whether further treatment was required or not.

psychiatric institutions. The commission conducted a thorough investigation of the Serbsky Institute and visited the prison psychiatric hospitals at Kazan and Leningrad.

The commission's carefully prepared report, however, was never considered by those who had ordered it. For two years it was carefully concealed from the Central Committee by the responsible official* who then consigned it discreetly to the archives. Despite this development, Pisarev was able to report that some changes did in fact take place in both the Leningrad and Kazan hospitals. Conditions for patients, both political and genuinely ill, improved and the psychiatric staff, which included many new, freshly-trained specialists, more frequently repudiated the unjustified diagnoses made by the Serbsky Institute.

In 1970 Pisarev revived his campaign when he wrote a letter to the Academy of Medical Sciences, to which he appended details of his own psychiatric experience of seventeen years earlier. The letter was mainly an indictment of the Serbsky Institute, at whose hands he had suffered:

> . . . the unending and frequent mistakes and diagnoses made by the Serbsky Institute . . . compel me to ask for your attention. The causes of the mistakes lie in the fact that this purely medical institution is, *de facto*, *not subject to constant supervision and control by the public health authorities*. The special hospitals for its "clients", which are used in the first instance (and in recent times predominantly) for political prisoners, are not even formally subject to their control. . . . All the facts I presented [i.e. in 1955] were completely corroborated by the evidence. . . . Among the . . . "mentally ill" people sentenced to indefinite isolation the commission discovered hundreds of absolutely healthy persons. It listed systematically the perversions of the truth in the diagnoses given by the institute, in particular by D. R. Lunts (at that time a senior lecturer) and a number of other people. It was documentarily proved that through the fault of the diagnostic institute under investigation, Soviet psychiatric hospitals, and above all the two notorious special prison hospitals for political prisoners in Kazan and Leningrad had, year after year, been filled up mainly by persons responsible for their actions. By

* Almost certainly, V. M. Churayev.

that time, it had already been recognized that three-quarters of these people had been innocent sufferers and the victims of illegal repressive measures.

Pisarev also provided some historical data regarding prison psychiatric hospitals. Their use for politicals had been initiated by Andrei Vyshinsky, a subordinate of Nikolai Ezhov, the head of the secret police in the years 1936–38. At that time and since, the prison psychiatric hospitals (later renamed special psychiatric hospitals) had remained under the control of the Ministry of Internal Affairs—the ministry which also directs the operations of the police, the prisons and the labour camps. The commission had concluded that as part of reforming the Kazan and Leningrad hospitals they should be transferred "*in toto* to the supervision of the Soviet Ministry of Health" and thus away from the influence of police and prison authorities. Pisarev complained, however, that:

> . . . it is an indubitable aggravation of the abnormal situation described by the Central Committee's commission, and a frightening proof of the increase in the illegal political repressions facilitated by the Serbsky Institute, to find that, instead of the complete abolition of the two special hospitals which are outside the system of the Ministry of Health, additional new hospitals of a similar type have, in recent years, appeared in other cities.

(We discuss the special psychiatric hospitals in chapter 7.)

As for the Serbsky Institute, ostensibly functioning under the aegis of the Ministry of Health, Pisarev regretted that no real changes had occurred since the commission produced its findings. The psychiatrists most implicated were still there, none had ever been prosecuted under the law: "The Institute . . . complacently utilizes pseudo-scientific phraseology in order to cover up the dishonest actions of officials in the investigation and Procuracy organs." Pisarev thus believed that the Serbsky medical staff remained under the domination of officials of the Ministry of Internal Affairs. He concluded:

> There can be a radical elimination of these harmful abnormalities only if the supervision of all special psychiatric

hospitals is transferred in its entirety to the public health departments so as to ensure that both they, and more especially the diagnostic institute (Serbsky), are placed under the direct, continuous and exceptionally vigilant control and management of the Ministry of Health, with the participation in such control of the whole of our medical community.

Despite Pisarev's initiative and the work of the investigating commission in 1955–56, there was no halt to the practice of interning sane dissenters in mental hospitals. An important reason was probably the implicit support for it which came from Mr Khrushchev. The party leader was keen to convince both domestic and foreign opinion that his régime had put the Stalin era behind it and no longer held any political prisoners. Against this background, *Pravda* reported him on 24 May 1959 as, in effect, equating social deviance with insanity:

A crime is a deviation from the generally recognized standards of behaviour, frequently caused by mental disorder. Can there be diseases, nervous disorders among certain people in the Communist society [of the future]? Evidently there can be. If that is so, then there will also be offences which are characteristic of people with abnormal minds. . . . To those who might start calling for opposition to Communism on this "basis", we can say that now, too, there are people who fight against Communism . . . but clearly the mental state of such people is not normal.

A flagrant example of abuse occurred just as the investigating commission's report was being shelved, when Nikolai Samsonov was shunted into the Leningrad Special Psychiatric Hospital. Detailed information about Samsonov appeared in the form of an obituary published in the *Chronicle of Current Events* shortly after his death in 1971.[9] He was born in Leningrad in 1906. On his graduation from Leningrad University in 1929, he began an auspicious career as a geophysicist. He occupied important research positions and published many professional papers over the next 25 years. His contribution to Soviet geophysics was recognized with his receipt of several decorations including the esteemed Stalin Prize.

In 1956 Samsonov submitted a treatise entitled "Thinking

Aloud" to the party's Central Committee. This dealt with the creation of a bureaucratic élite and the erosion of Leninist principles: he called for a return to these principles. Soon after the dispatch of the document Samsonov was arrested and charged with counter-revolutionary crimes. During the criminal investigation that followed he underwent a psychiatric examination. The examining commission, headed by Professor Torubarov of the Serbsky Institute, concluded that Samsonov was mentally ill and not responsible. The court accepted the commission's conclusions and ordered his transfer to the Leningrad Special Psychiatric Hospital where he remained until September 1964, one of the longer periods of confinement of a dissenter whose case is well documented.

The *Chronicle* reports that Samsonov's hospital psychiatrists considered him mentally well (just as Dr Kalinin had considered Pisarev well three years earlier). However, they advised him to concede that he had been of unsound mind when he wrote his heterodox document. Such an admission, they argued, would "testify to his recovery". After two years of internment and a persistent refusal to acknowledge that he had been mentally disturbed when he wrote "Thinking Aloud", Samsonov was threatened with injections of Aminazin (a tranquillizer in wide use for the treatment of certain severe mental illnesses). These threats did not undermine Samsonov's determination. Only in 1964, after he had actually received Aminazin injections and with his general health failing, did Samsonov sign a declaration to the effect that he had been mentally ill. On his release from hospital he received a pension and worked for two months of each year at a geophysics research institute until his death in 1971.

The facts in Samsonov's case speak for themselves: he attempted to exercise his political independence, was subjected to eight years of confinement in a prison mental hospital, was under incessant pressure to concede that his views were those of an insane person rather than a social critic, suffered progressive deterioration of health, and ultimately had his personal integrity undermined by a forced admission that he was mentally ill when he contributed his political ideas to the Central Committee.

In the Leningrad Special Hospital Samsonov became friendly with Fyodor Shults.[10] At the age of nineteen, in 1919, Shults had joined the Communist party. Eighteen years later he was arrested for criticizing Stalin and spent two decades in prison and exile. In 1956 he was legally exculpated and awarded a special pension in recognition of his services to the régime when young.

A few months later, however, Shults again found himself behind bars. In a letter to *Pravda* he had refuted Khrushchev's statement that there were no longer any political prisoners in the Soviet Union. He cited cases known to him, including that of the Socialist Revolutionary Preobrazhenskaya, aged 106, but still held in prison. Shults had thus dissented in a similar way to Samsonov; and their arrests came within a month of each other.

Shults was ruled not responsible on the recommendation of a commission under Professor Lunts. According to a *samizdat* account, the main material studied by the psychiatrists was his letter to *Pravda* and reports on him from various camps that he had been a constant protester when in captivity during the Stalin period.

Shults spent only a little over a year in hospital, and we do not know why he was released—into the guardianship of his wife—so early. He now campaigned for his own exculpation and for the release of his fellow inmates, in particular Samsonov. The guardianship was soon terminated, and in 1960 he was restored to membership of the party. Four years later he achieved full legal and psychiatric rehabilitation when the USSR Supreme Court ruled that charges against him had been unfounded. As of 1971 he was living in Volgograd as an honoured pensioner. In January 1972 Bukovsky petitioned the court which was trying him to call Shults as one of eight witnesses who would confirm the truth of what he had said about the Leningrad special hospital. The court refused the petition on the (false) grounds that Shults was mentally ill.

All four cases we have described thus far—Yarkov, Pisarev, Shults and Samsonov—evoked no public response either within or outside the Soviet Union, whilst they were confined to a mental hospital. In all likelihood they are representative of a sizeable group—one cannot even guess the numbers involved—of Soviet citizens who during the 1950s and early 1960s were charged with a political offence, diagnosed as mentally ill, declared not responsible, and transferred to a mental hospital for indefinite treatment. The only cases which received some slight Western publicity as early as 1961–62 were those of Alexander Volpin, which we examine in this chapter, and the Leningrad artist, Mikhail Naritsa.[11]

The Tarsis Case: First International Awareness of the Issue
Solid public awareness in the West that Soviet psychiatry was possibly being used for political purposes first arose in 1965, with the publication in Britain of a book by Valery Tarsis, entitled *Ward 7*.*[12] The book was serialized in the press and reached a wide audience.[13] *Ward 7* is an autobiography superficially disguised as a novel. It records the plight of a writer, Valentine Almazov (representing Tarsis), who is forcibly interned in a mental hospital for writing and distributing anti-Soviet literature. Tarsis himself was born in Kiev in 1906 and graduated from the University of Rostov-on-Don in 1929. He worked thereafter as an author and translator. As a young man he joined the party but became disillusioned in the 1930s. In 1960 he finally broke with it and, despairing of ever again being published in the Soviet Union, began to send his manuscripts abroad.

His book *The Blue Bottle*,[14] consisting of two short stories, was published in Britain in October 1962 under a pseudonym. Tarsis later protested at the pseudonymous nature of the publication and made it clear that he was opposed to the concealment of the authorship. *The Blue Bottle* describes the predicament experienced by writers and intellectuals under Khrushchev. Tarsis did not conceal that he had sent it abroad; shortly before its publication, in August 1962, he was involuntarily committed to an ordinary psychiatric hospital in Moscow. A few Western protests followed, not sufficient to win

* The title *Ward 7* alludes to Anton Chekhov's short story *Ward No. 6*, first published in 1892. Chekhov describes vividly the experience of the doctor of a small town who has become bored and stultified by provincial life. He becomes interested in an inmate of the hospital's mental ward and begins to spend much of his time exchanging ideas with the patient. Suspicion is soon aroused that the doctor has become insane. The town's authorities conspire to lure him into becoming a patient of Ward 6, where he spends the rest of his life.

his release, and it was only in February 1963 that Tarsis was discharged. Thereafter he struck many obstacles: he was denied employment time and again and generally harassed by the authorities.

Tarsis nevertheless continued to write and, when possible, sent his manuscripts abroad. Shortly before the fall of Khrushchev in 1964 he smuggled out *Ward 7*, intending it for publication under his own name. In early 1966 the authorities unexpectedly allowed him to accept an invitation to lecture in England. While there, he was stripped of his Soviet citizenship and thereby lost any right to return home. Tarsis later settled in Switzerland, pursued his writing career, but soon faded from public view. His *Ward 7* has remained a primary source of knowledge on the practice of interning sane dissenters in mental hospitals. The book probably contains some emotionally-based exaggerations, but the essential facts in it have been confirmed by subsequent accounts.

Ward 7 is a chilling account of sane people in insane places. Tarsis himself was actually a patient in the Kashchenko Psychiatric Hospital, one of Moscow's largest. It is clearly to this hospital that Almazov is committed by order of the chief city psychiatrist after pressure has been applied by party officials. Two policemen come to his home to inform him that the police superintendent urgently requires to see him. Once at the police station, an ambulance whisks him off to the hospital and so begins his ordeal which is to last several months —civil commitment to a mental hospital and forced detention there. The psychiatric intervention is unsolicited by himself or by members of his family—the initiators are political functionaries.

It soon becomes evident to Almazov that this is the case. In an initial interview with a psychiatrist he is confronted with the question "What's the game, eh?—Writing anti-Soviet letters to foreign embassies?" In the following interview he categorically asserts his views to the examining psychiatrist: "This is the position. I don't regard you as a doctor. You call this a hospital, I call it a prison to which in a typically fascist way I have been sent without trial. So now, let's get everything straight. I am your prisoner, you are my jailer, and there isn't going to be any nonsense about my health or my relations, or about examination or treatment. . . ."

Is this evidence of a paranoid reaction or the coherent, firm stance of a man reacting to the injustice committed against him? In fact Almazov is being hospitalized neither because he has a severe mental illness nor because he constitutes a danger to himself or society. He is detained because of the imminent publication of his manuscript in the West, an act construed by the authorities as anti-Soviet. No one in Almazov's immediate personal life has initiated a request that he be medically helped. There is no history of mental illness in his past.

As the novel unfolds, one's suspicion is aroused that something is terribly amiss in Ward 7. Almazov's revelations about the "patients" he meets and the nature of the medical treatment given, generate the scepticism. Almazov estimates that only one patient of the 150 in his section is mentally ill. "No one in it except Karen was the victim of anything except his lot as a Soviet citizen." He identifies three groups of inmates. First, the failed suicides—mainly young people. They have attempted suicide because of their dissatisfaction with society, while the official psychiatric and ideological view is that anyone attempting suicide because of such dissatisfaction must be abnormal— no one could possibly be unhappy living under the Soviet system.* The second group is referred to as the "Americans"— those who have sought information about emigration from a foreign embassy, or actually applied for an exit visa. The third group comprises young people who have rejected the values and standards of Soviet society. They have manifested their dissatisfaction and rejection in diverse ways, often by not adhering to conventional norms.

In a fictionalized autobiography it is difficult to tease out fact from literary expression, but material emerges through the eyes of Almazov that is both consistent and coherent enough to persuade us that in 1962–63 the Kashchenko contained a fair number of people who were there primarily for their political beliefs rather than for medical reasons. Our impression is confirmed by a report submitted by Tarsis to Amnesty

---

* The notion of suicide as a reflection of mental illness is shrouded with controversy and complexity. Indubitably, many suicides and attempted suicides are symptomatic of serious mental illness. Other suicides are committed with rational insight. In such cases, value-laden judgements abound as to whether such a profound act can be interpreted as normal or not.

International* in 1966.[15] In any case, whatever the degree of accuracy of *Ward 7* as a reflection of events in the early 1960s, it alerted Western observers to the recognition that the Chaadayev episode had a counterpart, and a more alarming one, in contemporary Soviet society.

Soon after the publication of *Ward 7* a second case of Soviet psychiatric abuse attracted much Western attention and ultimately led to an extensive public campaign of protest. The discovery of the forcible hospitalization of Evgeny (Zhenya) Belov was fortuitous; the story begins with a visit to the Soviet Union in 1964 by four British university students. Belov, a student interpreter, is attached to the group through an official Soviet tourist organization.[16] They spend much time together discussing political issues. According to the students' report, Belov makes every effort to convince them that Communism is the optimal system of government. They gain the impression that he is recognized by his own student friends as a model Communist. On their return to England the students correspond with him.

The following summer sees the students' return to Moscow and a further meeting with Belov. By this time he has either changed his views radically or decided to express them more frankly. He believes that the party organization has become bureaucratic and serves only the interests of the ruling group; dissenting views are stifled and crushed. Belov seeks greater freedom for the press and radio and more power for the trade unions, all to be gained through constitutional means. After sharing these observations with his party organization, he is immediately suspended from membership and instructed to go before the Moscow city party committee. Belov refuses; he anticipates that he would be denied a fair hearing. He writes letters instead to Kosygin and Brezhnev, but receives no reply from either. Finally he distributes his proposals for change to the Moscow embassies of several Communist countries.

The students after a brief stay proceed to Tokyo for the rest of their vacation. On their return to Moscow on the way home, they are perplexed not to find Belov at the airport as he had promised. They are soon informed by his neighbours that he

* Amnesty International is an independent organization founded in 1961, which works, irrespective of political considerations, for the release of men and women all over the world who are in prison because of their beliefs.

has been diagnosed as insane and confined to a mental hospital. The students subsequently confirm this through another source: the authorities have notified the Moscow Institute of Foreign Languages, where Belov has been a student, about his psychiatric confinement.[17]

In a letter to Soviet leaders containing the above details, the students assert their belief that Belov was not mentally disturbed when they left him some weeks earlier. They conclude that he is being victimized for his political views and they are obliged to follow their conscience and fight for his release. The battle begins in earnest. The students spearhead a campaign under the aegis of Amnesty International.[18] The hope of the protesters is to promote public disquiet by direct appeals to various professional groups in the Soviet Union. A spirited campaign by the British public ensues. An element of doubt still prevails—can the students be certain that Belov is not really mentally deranged? They can only reply that, to them, it is inconceivable that Belov is insane. Amnesty International states publicly that it has agreed to sponsor the appeal since the Soviet authorities have never replied to its persistent inquiries about earlier cases like those of Tarsis and Volpin. Amnesty assumes therefore that these detentions are politically motivated.

Soon after the Belov case became well known through the press, a British newspaper received a letter from Belov's father, insisting that his son was truly ill.[19] He denied that Evgeny had been forcibly taken to the hospital or expelled from the party. He reported that in the hospital Evgeny was constantly drawing diagrams with the object of reorganizing the world. Belov's father asked the press to cease the "unworthy hullabaloo raised around my son's name". This was nothing more than his family's ill luck being used by the British to promote antagonism against the Soviet Union. A complementary article in *Izvestia* spoke of the protest in vitriolic terms as a "filthy soap bubble launched from the British Isles" and as "yet another anti-Soviet forgery".[20] The paper insisted that the "case of Zhenya Belov was fabricated by an anti-Soviet screech let out jointly by the *Guardian* newspaper and by a group of English students acting on behalf of Amnesty International". This was the first of many a counter-attack by the Soviet media against Western critics (see chapters 4 and 10).

After a lull, the British campaign resumed. The letter from Belov's father was viewed with scepticism and doubts were expressed by experts about whether it was written by him freely. The Evgeny Belov appeal committee conceded that there was no conclusive proof that Belov was not suffering from a mental illness. But it pointed out that if he actually were, the Soviet authorities would have acceded by now to the request that he be visited by an independent foreign psychiatrist. The committee also noted that this was not the first case of its kind. They cited Tarsis and Volpin as past examples of the politicization of psychiatry.[21]

The case of Alexander Volpin is perhaps the most illuminating of the practice of curbing dissent through psychiatric means during the 1950s and 1960s. Volpin was interned in psychiatric hospitals on five occasions over a nineteen-year period. He described his experiences in testimony he gave to an investigating subcommittee of the United States Senate Judiciary Committee in 1972.[22] One of the authors (S.B.) spent most of a day with Volpin in Boston (where he is now a professor of mathematics) in September 1975;* the interview covered his involvement with Soviet psychiatry, his life in the Soviet Union, and an informal evaluation of his mental state.

Volpin was born in 1924, the son of the celebrated Russian poet Esenin. He graduated from Moscow University in 1946 and three years later received his doctoral degree in mathematical logic. In the same year he was arrested for the first time after he had written and recited poems regarded by the authorities as anti-Soviet. Volpin was initially interrogated in Lubyanka Prison and then transferred to the Serbsky Institute, where he was declared insane and not responsible. With the court's acceptance of the Serbsky's recommendations, Volpin was compulsorily committed to the Leningrad Special Psychiatric Hospital, in which he spent the next year.

During the Khrushchev period he was forcibly hospitalized on three occasions: in 1957 for three weeks in an ordinary

---

* The author was impressed with Volpin's vitality and spirit; although recalling a series of unpleasant episodes, he showed no bitterness, he had a keen sense of humour, and he was completely open and honest. There was no doubt that Volpin, in the course of our many hours together, was mentally healthy. There was also no reason to think that he might have been mentally ill in the past.

psychiatric hospital in Moscow, for a twelve-month period in 1959–60 in the Leningrad special hospital, and for four months in 1962–63, again in an ordinary hospital. On the two occasions he was confined in special hospitals, the prodecure followed was that of criminal commitment—a criminal charge of a political kind was laid, a psychiatric examination conducted, and a court order issued that he was not responsible and was in need of compulsory treatment in hospital. However, prior to the three confinements based on civil commitment,* political factors also appeared to play an important part. Volpin details the reason for each commitment: "Once for advising a French woman against accepting Soviet citizenship, once for failure to inform on an acquaintance who had allegedly engaged in treasonable activities, and once for my refusal to denounce American publication of my book *A Leaf of Spring*† and my assertion of the right of everyone to leave any country."[23]

Volpin's hospitalization in 1968 typifies the civil commitment procedure as applied to dissenters. Having applied for a visa, needed to take up an invitation to participate in a scientific conference in the US, he was taken forcibly by the police from his home for a psychiatric examination. this was necessary since he had not reported for some time to the clinic where he had been registered since his previous discharge from hospital in 1963. Yet he had not been invited to attend the clinic for over four years. The abrupt manner in which Volpin was brought for examination, with no request from himself or his family, aroused suspicion about the authorities' real motive.

Volpin ascertained that the diagnosis of his condition made during his hospitalizations had repeatedly been a "simple form of schizophrenia". The diagnoses had not always been identical but three features had remained constant in the reports—he was "psychotically disturbed", his condition was regarded as "incurable", and between attacks he was "in a state of temporary remission only". Despite these clinical conclusions, Volpin was never seriously treated for mental illness. During his 1960 detention he received small amounts of Reserpine, a drug then used as a tranquillizer. At another time a psychiatrist, viewed

* Criminal and civil commitment are discussed in detail in chapters 5 and 6.

† Published by Praeger in New York in 1961.

by Volpin as sympathetic, enabled him to avoid treatment with Haloperidol, a potent tranquillizer used for some major psychiatric disorders.

Volpin has described the nature of his internment in the Leningrad hospital: he was stripped of all basic rights, not permitted the use of writing materials, and constantly felt the threat of long years of emptiness and isolation. He was told that his discharge depended upon his willingness to concede that he had "misbehaved", to acknowledge the appropriateness of the medical treatment and to promise a change in his behaviour. Volpin felt that he had been blackmailed by his psychiatrists when they warned him: "you will be here forever unless you behave correctly".

One might think that Volpin, an intelligent, sophisticated man, failed to learn from his experiences and that the most rational way of contending with his situation would have been for him to adapt to the authorities' prescription of desirable behaviour. Volpin himself explains the reason for his non-compliance in most explicit terms:

> In my work I openly and consistently act on the principle "away with the instinct of self-preservation and moderation". Let them do what they want with me because of it, I do not mind if that is considered madness or not . . . for me the concept of non-adaptation must be sacred! Just for the record, let me explain that I am not against the capacity for self-preservation or an understanding of balance, but I prefer these things to be the result of free reason, not of instinct or the emotions, which can always be influenced.[24]

Volpin's 1962 hospitalization is a clear example of his fearlessness in expressing his "non-adaptation". He had earlier arranged for the American publication of his book *A Leaf of Spring*—a series of poems and a philosophical treatise—in the full knowledge that such an act would place him in jeopardy. The powerful party official in charge of ideology and culture at the time, Leonid Ilichev, was probably not the initiator of the plan to commit Volpin to a mental institution for this allegedly anti-Soviet publication, but he was certainly aware of its execution. A year after the book's publication he exploited it to intimidate other potential dissenters by referring to *A Leaf of Spring* as "anti-Soviet, misanthropic doggerel, the delirium of a luna-tic". How could a "normal person" express such "malicious fabrications repellent to any healthy person"?[25] A few days after this speech, and after Volpin had refused to denounce himself for publishing the book, he was hospitalized.

The Beginning of Opposition within the Soviet Union to Psychiatric Abuse

Volpin's last internment in February 1968 lasted only three months; this was undoubtedly due to the large-scale protest that his detention provoked both in the Soviet Union and abroad. A petition by 99 Soviet mathematicians and scientists was especially effective in securing his release. These colleagues of Volpin protested to the Ministry of Health, the Procurator-General and the chief psychiatrist of Moscow, asserting that his forced confinement was a "flagrant violation of medical and legal norms".[26] Some of the signatories were themselves later penalized for their outspokenness and twelve others withdrew their signatures under pressure. Virtually all were denied the right to travel abroad to attend conferences, and some were actually dismissed or demoted from their posts. One mathematician among them, Yury Shikhanovich, was later himself interned in a mental hospital, clearly on political grounds. This large-scale petition within the Soviet Union itself was highly significant, being the first of its kind in a case of the psychiatric internment of a dissenter. It was obvious to Volpin's colleagues that his detention was politically motivated. The abuse was now brought into the open where it was destined to remain, as the human-rights movement became progressively more concerned with the issue.

Two weeks earlier an *ad hoc* group of twelve Soviet human-rights activists had already made the first generalized protest when they submitted an appeal to a conference of Communist parties, then meeting in Budapest, calling on the participants "to consider the peril caused by the trampling on human rights in our country".[27] Dissenters, they claimed, had been victimised in many ways: by unjust dismissal from jobs, summonses from the KGB, threats of arrest, and "finally —the most shocking form of reprisal—forcible confinement in a mental hospital". Ironically one of the signatories,

Major-General Pyotr Grigorenko, who had himself spent a year in the Leningrad special hospital in 1964, would again encounter "the most shocking form of reprisal" in 1969. We shall return to his case in chapter 5.

The appeal to the Budapest conference was published in the first issue of the *Chronicle of Current Events*,[28] in April 1968. The *Chronicle* (as we shall refer to it from now on) was henceforth the main source of information concerning the political use of psychiatry. It quickly became the best-known journal published in *samizdat*. From its inception the *Chronicle* provided accurate, reliable information on violations of human rights in the Soviet Union. Its origin in 1968, designated International Human Rights Year by the United Nations, was no accident. Dissenters by then had become sufficiently well organized to mount a journal whose aim was "seeing that the Soviet public is informed about what goes on in the country" in the field of human rights.[29] The *Chronicle* is a sober record of such events and contains only a minimum of editorial material; it has reported on the arrests, trials and extra-judicial persecution of dissenters, on the conditions prevailing in prisons and labour camps, on the campaigns of national and religious groups, and on other *samizdat* publications. Issues have generally come out every two or three months since the spring of 1968, although publication ceased for more than a year from late 1972 until May 1974, when the authorities made every effort to suppress it. Each issue which has reached the West has been translated into English and, from No. 16 on, published by Amnesty International. It was the *Chronicle*'s accurate and precise reporting that first provided a sizeable quantity of varied information concerning the political use of psychiatry. For instance, in the first eleven issues the *Chronicle* reported the cases of 27 dissenters detained in special psychiatric hospitals. Items also appeared on the nature of these hospitals, particularly the ones in Kazan and Leningrad, and on the treatment given there.

Some of the signatories of the Budapest appeal became foundation members of the first formally constituted group of dissenters—the Action Group for the Defence of Human Rights—established in May 1969. The fifteen foundation members came from several cities in the Soviet Union, were mainly professional men and women, and were mostly aged under 40. They felt the need for at least a minimal structure for their activities.

Their first act was to submit an appeal to the United Nations Commission on Human Rights on 20 May 1969. The group requested that the commission examine violations in the Soviet Union of the citizen's basic right to hold and express independent convictions. The letter argued that Soviet citizens were deprived of this right and certain individuals, whom they listed, had been condemned in political trials for attempting to exercise it. The group also referred to "a particularly inhuman form of persecution: the placing of normal people in psychiatric hospitals for their political convictions".[30] This was the first explicit mention of the practice in an appeal from a Soviet dissenting group to an international organization.

One member of the group, Natalya Gorbanevskaya, had been a victim of this "form of persecution" for a few days in February 1968, but was destined, as we shall see in chapter 5, for a much lengthier internment later. In addition to Gorbanevskaya, three other members of the action group were later subjected to the very practice they had protested about. Vladimir Borisov, a Leningrad electrician, was arrested less than a month after the group's first letter to the United Nations and sent for psychiatric examination. Declared insane, he spent nearly five years in the Leningrad special hospital.[31] Yury Maltsev, a translator, was the next to be forcibly hospitalized, through a civil commitment.[32] He was summoned to a military recruitment centre and told that he had to undergo a medical examination. In fact, the examination was psychiatric, and its conclusions resulted in Maltsev's admission to the Kashchenko hospital, where he spent a month. Leonid Plyushch, a mathematician from Kiev, was arrested in January 1972, for alleged anti-Soviet activities.[33] Eventually he was sent to the Dnepropetrovsk Special Psychiatric Hospital for compulsory treatment in July 1973. We discuss the cases of Maltsev and Plyushch more fully in chapter 7.

And so four of the fifteen founder members of the action group came to experience the "treatment" they had helped to publicize in the West. Other members were generally harassed; some were brought to trial and sentenced.[34] The cost of their efforts was thus extremely high, and the results far from encouraging. The UN Commission on Human Rights, to which the group had appealed, showed no sign of investigating the information contained in its letters. Only a few human-rights organizations and some Western newspapers responded. When, for example, it became clear that the Soviet postal censorship had intercepted the group's first appeal to the UN, Amnesty International formally delivered to the UN a copy which had been brought out of the Soviet Union unofficially.

Three events occurred during 1970 which brought the abuse of Soviet psychiatry dramatically into focus. The first was the publication in the West of General Grigorenko's account of his psychiatric examinations, which we examine in chapter 5. The second was the nineteen-day involuntary hospitalization of Zhores Medvedev, an internationally-respected biologist. There were almost daily reports in leading Western newspapers providing a blow-by-blow description of the affair, which we discuss in detail in chapter 6.

The third event that attracted considerable attention was the television interview by William Cole, an American journalist, with Vladimir Bukovsky, at that time aged 28, who had devoted all his adult years to the struggle for human rights in the USSR. The interview was filmed in Moscow and then broadcast over the CBS network in the United States on 28 July 1970. Broadcasts followed in other Western countries. The same Bukovsky who a few months later would send to the West copies of the psychiatric case reports of several dissenters interned in mental hospitals, related in the interview his own experiences of Soviet mental hospitals and the political use of psychiatry. He recounted how at the age of 21, in 1963, he was arrested and charged with anti-Soviet agitation. After several months in prison, he was transferred to the Serbsky Institute and there declared insane, not responsible and in need of compulsory treatment. He landed up in the special hospital in Leningrad where he spent over a year. On his release he plunged straight back into human-rights work, only to be arrested some months later for helping to organize a demonstration. Again, internment in a mental hospital—this time he spent most of an eight-month period in the Serbsky Institute. His release occurred without explanation and the charges against him were dropped. A visit to the Serbsky during his stay there by a representative of Amnesty International who talked to its director, Dr G. Morozov, may have been a factor.

After a year of freedom Bukovsky was again arrested and charged with slander against the state. On this occasion he actually stood trial, for the first time, and was sentenced to three years of corrective labour. The punishment did not deter him, for shortly following his release in January 1970 he gave interviews to foreign journalists, fully aware of the dangers involved. In one interview Bukovsky described his "fifteen months of hell" in the Leningrad hospital, the "patients" he met there, and the treatment they were given.[35] It is a chilling description of a hospital where the staff are supposedly treating and caring for the mentally ill but, according to Bukovsky, are mainly preoccupied with devising methods of punishment and intimidation of inmates. The CBS interview revealed more details of life in the Leningrad hospital—the punishments meted out, the untherapeutic *milieu*, and the callousness of the staff. But perhaps most significant of all was Bukovsky's explanation of the reasons for admission of many of the inmates he had met there, and of himself:

At first it seemed to me a strange decision. I couldn't understand the reason for it. I could not understand in what way the doctors who examined me found me abnormal. But once I got to know some of the other inmates of that hospital I discovered that it was a usual decision in such cases. The fact is that the inmates, the patients in that hospital, the prisoners, are people who have done things which from the point of view of the authorities are crimes but which are not criminal from the point of view of the law. And in order in some way to isolate them, to punish them somehow, such people are declared insane and are detained as patients in these prison mental hospitals.

Some time passed before I understood this and before I got to know my fellow prisoners. I believe this is the usual fate for a person who wishes to be himself, who wants to say what he thinks, to act in accordance with his convictions and ideas. Events of recent years confirm my supposition. Many people—tens, hundreds of people—have been declared insane and committed to various hospitals, mainly special ones, like those in Kazan, Leningrad, Chernyakhovsk, Sychyovka, etc.[36]

The allegations of psychiatric abuse now widely publicized in the West were exceptionally grave and constituted a major

attack on the psychiatric profession. Yet were they credible?
To the Western media, they were: newspaper editors knew that
the Moscow correspondents who had been reporting the
evidence for the previous two years were, like Cole of CBS, men
of experience and integrity. The accounts, and especially that
of the Medvedev internment, were also accepted by many
Western scientists as evidence of psychiatric abuse. Zhores
Medvedev, and distinguished Soviet academicians like Andrei
Sakharov, P. L. Kapitsa and N. N. Semenov, who leapt to his
defence, were well-known to them as honest men.

Western psychiatrists seemed less convinced by the allegations
of abuse. Hitherto, no response had been forthcoming from
either individual psychiatrists or official psychiatric bodies to
the steadily accumulating evidence. The forcible hospitalization
of Medvedev, the publication of Grigorenko's prison diary, and
the Bukovsky television interview, however, were disturbing at
least to some psychiatrists in the West, and before long one
national psychiatric association felt sufficiently assured to issue
a condemnation of the Soviet practice.

Chapter 4

THE ISSUE BECOMES INTERNATIONAL

THIS FIRST CONDEMNATION came in January 1971 when the Canadian Psychiatric Association endorsed a report from one of its sections "regarding the alleged wrongful detention in mental hospitals in the USSR of seemingly healthy individuals whose views and attitudes are in conflict with those of the régime".[1] The association concluded that the evidence thus far was as "hard" as could be expected short of an on-the-spot investigation. First-hand evidence was not as yet available to the Canadians (or to anyone else in the West), but their suspicion was sufficiently aroused for them to condemn the use of psychiatry "as a means of terrorizing and dehumanizing any human being in the world who is non-violent and who dissents in general". They specifically denounced the abuse of psychiatry "now being perpetrated in the USSR". The Canadians further resolved to continue campaigning until the unethical Soviet practice had ceased and those responsible for it been curbed.

The Bukovsky Papers
They did not have long to wait before the most persuasive body of evidence became available to them, and to Western psychiatrists generally. On 10 March 1971, in Paris, over 150 pages of documentation, including what were claimed to be exact copies of the official forensic psychiatric reports on six Soviet dissenters, were released to the press by a small French group, the International Committee for the Defence of Human Rights. This material shed more light on the political use of psychiatry than all the preceding evidence put together.

Here for the first time were clinical assessments written by psychiatrists and revealing the details of their diagnostic method. The material came from Vladimir Bukovsky, together with a personal appeal addressed to Western psychiatrists. They were asked to examine the documents and to express an opinion on the need for internment in mental hospitals of the six persons concerned.

The question immediately arose of the authenticity of the documents. Might they not have been forged as an anti-Soviet manœuvre?

Since the case reports in the Bukovsky materials constitute such crucial evidence, we will now explain why we are convinced of their authenticity. One of the authors (P.R.) has received and evaluated *samizdat* material coming out of the Soviet Union for ten years and has become familiar with the reliability of various sources. Bukovsky can be accepted as an impeccable source; his integrity in our view is beyond reproach. Confidence in the authenticity is enhanced by the fact that not one of these documents has ever been questioned or denounced by Soviet authorities. Furthermore, Soviet psychiatrists whose names appear on the case reports have never negated their validity. Both groups, as we shall see later, have repeatedly repudiated Western allegations that psychiatric misuse occurs in the Soviet Union, but at no point in their rebuttals have they questioned the genuineness of the Bukovsky material. Indeed, according to the secretary-general of the World Psychiatric Association, Dr Denis Leigh, Soviet psychiatrists attending the WPA's 1971 congress in Mexico, conceded to him that the case reports published in the West were authentic.

Let us now return to Bukovsky's appeal to Western psychiatrists dated 28 January 1971. In it he expresses his views on the internment of sane human-rights activists in psychiatric hospitals in a restrained and sober way:

> In recent years in our country a number of court orders have been made involving the placing in psychiatric hospitals (of special type and otherwise) of people who in the opinion of their relatives and close friends are mentally healthy. These people are: Pyotr Grigorenko, Ilya Rips, Natalya Gorbanev-skaya, Valeria Novodvorskaya, Ivan Yakhimovich, Vladimir Gershuni, Viktor Fainberg, Viktor Kuznetsov, Olga Iofe, Vladimir Borisov and others—people well known for their initiatives in defence of civil rights in the USSR.
>
> This phenomenon arouses justified anxiety, especially in view of the widely publicized placing of the biologist Zhores Medvedev in a psychiatric hospital by extra-judicial means.

The diagnostic reports of forensic psychiatrists which have served as the basis for the court orders provoke many doubts as regards their content. However, only specialists in psychiatry can express authoritative opinions about the degree of legitimacy of these diagnostic reports.

Taking advantage of the fact that I have managed to obtain exact copies of the diagnostic reports of the forensic-psychiatric commissions which examined Grigorenko, Fainberg, Gorbanevskaya, Borisov and Yakhimovich, and extracts from the report on V. Kuznetsov, I am sending you these documents, and also various letters and materials which reveal the personalities of these people. I will be very grateful to you if you can study this matter and express your opinion on it.

I realize that at a distance and without essential clinical information it is very difficult to determine the mental condition of a person and either to diagnose an illness or assert the absence of any illness. Therefore I ask you to express your opinion on only this point: Do the above-mentioned reports contain enough scientifically-based evidence to indicate the mental illnesses described in the reports, and also to indicate the necessity of isolating these people completely from society through internment?

I will be very happy if you can interest your colleagues in this matter and if you consider it possible to place it on the agenda for discussion by the next international congress of psychiatrists.

For a healthy person there is no fate more terrible than indefinite internment in a psychiatric hospital.

I believe that you will not remain indifferent to this problem and will devote a portion of your time to it—just as physicists find time to combat the use of the achievements of their science in ways harmful to mankind.

Thanking you in advance.[2]

Bukovsky requested two actions from Western psychiatrists: to study the psychiatric reports and express an opinion on the diagnosis of mental illness in the six dissenters and the need to intern them in mental hospitals, and, secondly, to place the matter on the agenda of the next international congress. The congress to which he referred was the impending gathering in

Mexico City of the World Psychiatric Association, scheduled for the end of 1971. The first action was accomplished, the second not. To appreciate what happened in Mexico, it is necessary to follow chronologically developments surrounding the Bukovsky documents.

The documents reached the West in February 1971 and in response, on 18 February, a small *ad hoc* Working Group on the Internment of Dissenters in Mental Hospitals (of which we are both members) was established in London composed of psychiatrists, specialists in Soviet affairs, and human-rights experts. The working group translated and edited the Bukovsky materials,* published his appeal in *The Times*[3] and the *British Journal of Psychiatry*,[4] wrote and circulated a booklet on the materials[5] and sought the views of British and European psychiatrists on their content. We called upon them to reply to Bukovsky's questions. On 16 September 1971, 44 psychiatrists, including many distinguished professors and psychiatric-hospital directors, published a report in the form of a letter to *The Times*. They concluded:

> On the basis of evidence contained in these reports, the undersigned psychiatrists feel impelled to express grave doubts about the legitimacy of compulsory treatment for the six people concerned, and indefinite detention in prison-mental-hospital conditions. Four of them do not appear to have any symptoms at all which indicate a need for treatment, let alone treatment of such a punitive kind. . . . It seems to us that the diagnoses on the six people were made purely in consequence of actions in which they were exercising fundamental freedoms—as set out in the Universal Declaration of Human Rights and guaranteed by the Soviet Constitution.[6]

The letter appeared a little more than two months before psychiatrists were to assemble in Mexico City. Here was an opportunity for Bukovsky's second request to be met. The signatories obviously regarded that forum as suitable for discussion of the issue. They ended their letter with an appeal of their own:

* The work was done mainly by Eleanor Aitken of Cambridge, the group's secretary, assisted by one of the authors (P.R.).

We call on our colleagues throughout the world to study the voluminous material now available, to discuss the matter with their Soviet colleagues, some of whom we know to have doubts as grave as our own, and to raise the issue, as Vladimir Bukovsky requested, at international conferences such as that of the World Psychiatric Association in Mexico City from 28 November to 4 December.

In addition to Bukovsky's appeal, one was also submitted to the psychiatrists meeting in Mexico by the Moscow Human Rights Committee.* In this document, published in *The Times* a month before the congress, the committee asked psychiatrists who were due to attend to initiate an enquiry into "the complex of questions concerning the rights of people ruled to be mentally ill".[7] More specifically, they pointed to the practice of incarcerating normal people in mental hospitals and its harmful effects:

It is easy to understand how a person's psyche can be traumatized if he is interned in a hospital without sufficient medical cause, and then subjected to prolonged isolation from society, to unavoidable association with disturbed people, to the influence of drugs which affect the psyche, and to the whole tortuous procedure of treatment.[8]

Sakharov and his colleagues called for the establishment of permanent commissions of psychiatrists to study the issue in various countries, publish their findings, and create international norms for the civil rights of the mentally ill. The appeal was phrased in these general terms but obviously stemmed from the signatories' own experience of their friends and colleagues being confined to mental hospitals for what appeared to be political rather than medical reasons. This was apparent in their statement that "it should not be forgotten that such abuses can be practised as a method of political persecution, that is, of persecuting people for their beliefs".

* The committee, formed in November 1970, consisted of four notable dissenters—Andrei Sakharov, Andrei Tverdokhlebov, Valery Chadidze and (later) Igor Shafarevich. It became an affiliate of the New York-based International League for the Rights of Man and of the Institute for the Rights of Man in Strasbourg.

The Response of Soviet Psychiatry

The Bukovsky appeal, the public response to it by 44 European psychiatrists, and the appeal by the Moscow Human Rights Committee, were the worst dreams coming true for the leaders of Soviet psychiatry. Professor Andrei Snezhnevsky, the country's most influential psychiatrist, who was to lead the Soviet delegation to the Mexico congress, anticipated the danger there of unfavourable publicity and pressure by Western colleagues.

It is Snezhnevksy who is quoted in a reliable source as disapproving of Zhores Medvedev's compulsory commitment in May 1970. "In a year's time," he complains, "there is going to be an international psychiatric conference in Mexico. How do you think this is going to make our delegation look!"[9] With the criticism levelled against Soviet abuse in September 1971 by eminent psychiatrists in *The Times*, Snezhnevsky had to mount a defence of himself and his colleagues. He gave an extensive interview in October to an *Izvestia* correspondent in which he commented on the "lofty humanism" that had always distinguished Soviet psychiatry and expressed his pride in many of his colleagues, who were well known both in the Soviet Union and abroad. He referred to "those absurd reports that healthy persons are put in psychiatric hospitals in the USSR"; his reaction was "a feeling of deep disgust at this outrageous fabrication". In the interview Snezhnevsky explained how Soviet forensic practice was conducted:

> In the Soviet Union the basis for a court ruling to send a sick person for compulsory treatment when he has committed socially dangerous acts is the report of the medical experts. These reports are compiled and signed by not one but several psychiatrists. The system in widespread use in the USSR for the advanced training of doctors and the raising of the level of their knowledge ensures that even rank-and-file psychiatrists in our country are highly qualified. Thus cases of the confinement of healthy persons in a psychiatric hospital are absolutely out of the question in our country. I want to stress that our colleagues abroad who have become acquainted with the organization of Soviet psychiatric care for the population have a very high opinion of it indeed.[10]

The Resolution of the World Federation for Mental Health
A few days before the WPA met in Mexico, the World Federation for Mental Health, an organization consisting of both lay and professional members, met in Hong Kong. During its conference the federation adopted a resolution which specifically criticized the abuse of psychiatry in the USSR. This was the first occasion that an international psychiatric body had taken action of this sort. After a preamble in which the deprivation of the right to express opinions was considered a severe form of mental cruelty in itself, the resolution stated:

> In recent years there have been numerous public allegations concerning the current misuse of psychiatric diagnoses, psychiatric "treatment", and enforced confinement in psychiatric institutions of persons whose only "symptoms" have been the avowal of opinions disapproved by their society. These accusations have been directed in particular —though not exclusively—against the alleged incarceration of political dissenters in prison-mental hospitals in the USSR.
>
> The World Federation for Mental Health resolutely opposes any such abuse of psychiatric procedures and calls on its member associations throughout the world promptly to investigate all such allegations, and to defend the individual's freedom of opinion where it appears to be threatened. The federation also calls on the mental health professionals and the governments of countries where there are no voluntary mental health associations to investigate all charges of the misuse of psychiatric procedures for political ends and to demonstrate convincingly to the world that such practices are not condoned in principle, nor allowed to continue where they are shown to have occurred.[11]

Here was a resolution couched in forthright terms, containing a specific citation of the Soviet Union. It was soon published in full, no doubt gratefully, by the *Chronicle of Current Events*[12] which had also published the "letter of the 44" to *The Times*.[13] Yet like the Canadian Psychiatric Association's resolution earlier in 1971, the WFMH's resolution was not based on proven fact. It referred to "allegations" and "accusations": the WFMH evidently felt there was as yet insufficient evidence on which to base a firm condemnation. The resolution served, however, in alerting member associations to the potential for the use of psychiatry to repress dissent anywhere and in calling on them to investigate all charges of its occurrence.

The Mexico Congress

On 28 November 1971 several thousand psychiatrists from dozens of countries, including a Soviet contingent of fourteen, congregated in Mexico City for the fifth world congress of psychiatry, under the aegis of the WPA. The psychiatrists occupied themselves with the usual scientific and social programmes that characterize such professional gatherings. They were, however, unaccustomed to one feature which mushroomed into a highly controversial issue: the two appeals submitted to them concerning the use of psychiatry for political purposes.

This was an unprecedented event: psychiatrists were being informed, in appeals addressed directly to them, of serious and gross unethical conduct by their Soviet colleagues, and close collaborators of these very colleagues were participating in the congress. The issue was discussed animatedly by many psychiatrists throughout the week. Various groups had disseminated materials presenting the evidence. Copies of the book *A Question of Madness* by Zhores and Roy Medvedev, vividly describing the forcible detention of Zhores in a provincial psychiatric hospital, were prominently available for sale at the meeting.

The stage was set. Bukovsky had initiated the action and was at the time of the congress in detention awaiting trial, the severity of his sentence clearly in the balance. The working group had, in the summer, supplied the WPA with translations of the Bukovsky materials and had been in frequent correspondence with its secretary-general Dr Denis Leigh. The latter had informed one of the group's members, Professor F. A. Jenner, that the issue would be discussed in Mexico.[14] Now the question was what attitude the congress would take on a matter which the 44 psychiatrists viewed as "grave" and as a serious indictment of their profession.

It seemed as if the WPA would indeed respond to the challenge when the president of the congress, Dr Ramon de la

Fuente, in his inaugural speech, referred to documents that had been received about "some places in the world" where political opposition was treated as mental illness. He argued that: "to keep silent about such an ignominious situation would weigh heavily on our conscience".[15] But in the event silence was precisely the congress response. To understand why de la Fuente's speech was ignored, it is useful to summarize some basic facts about the WPA and to examine congress developments chronologically.

The WPA is a young organization, founded in 1961, without strong roots or traditions. At its world congresses, held every five to six years, a new executive committee is elected.[16] However, two of the six members of this committee, the secretary-general and the treasurer, are elected for terms of no less than ten to twelve years. This remarkably long tenure, coupled with the fact that the executive committee normally meets only twice a year, means that the two principal office-holders potentially wield enormous power. They must account to four colleagues only twice a year, and the whole six-man committee must account to its electors only once in five or six years.

Further, the member societies usually feel that their obligations to their own members and to other professional and governmental organizations in their own countries come before those to the WPA. Thus it can be difficult—a fact much bewailed by Dr Leigh—for the secretariat to maintain close liaison with member societies.

All these factors facilitate a situation in which the secretary-general in particular has extensive freedom in the taking of initiatives. He can either be very active, and afterwards persuade his few colleagues on the executive that he has done the right thing. Or he can be very passive, and later explain, if challenged, that no member society asked him to do this or that. In other words, he can usually, if he wants, "play it both ways". In many contexts, in fact, the WPA is virtually a "one-man (or two-man) band"; it is certainly an organization with weak democratic control.

Such a structure doubtless has a number of advantages if its two semi-permanent officers are men of vision and sensitivity as well as administrative skill. Regarding the development of international relations in psychiatry, Leigh, through his tireless travel and organization of regional and world conferences, seems to us to have remarkable achievements to his credit.

However, on the issue of Soviet psychiatric abuse his actions at Mexico strike us as misconceived and devious: he succeeded in suppressing public debate of the Soviet matter by arguing a spurious legalistic case, as we shall see below.

The Soviet abuse was first raised at a meeting of the WPA Committee (composed of 24 members from different nations and, *ex officio*, the six members of the Executive Committee) on 28 November. Dr Leigh reported that the secretariat had received the first letter on the issue in August 1970. Subsequently, correspondence had come from several sources including Dr Norman Hirt (spearhead of the Canadian campaign mentioned earlier), who had called for the WPA's attention to the abuse. The Working Group on the Internment of Dissenters in Mental Hospitals had sent a series of documents, copies of the Bukovsky materials, which had been distributed to the Executive Committee. And Leigh had informed Professor Snezhnevsky, the representative of the Soviet member society, in September 1971 of the allegations being made against his colleagues, and later despatched the Bukovsky documents to him.

The secretary-general proceeded with an explanation of the WPA's legal position, and completed his report by drawing these conclusions:

> Nowhere in the statutes is there any mention of the WPA making itself responsible for the ethical aspects of psychiatry, nor is there any relevant statute or by-law relating to complaints made by one member society against another member society. I think it is legally quite clear that the WPA is under no obligation to accept complaints from one member society directed against another member society. No complaints have in any case been made by any national member society against any other national member society. The executive committee has studied complaints by individuals and referred them to the appropriate quarter, in this case the All-Union Society.[17]

These statements warrant our careful analysis. First, statute 4 of the association, headed "Purposes", reads as follows: "The purpose of the WPA is [1] to advance international co-operation in the field of psychiatry by co-ordinating on a world-wide basis the activities of its Member Associations, and [2] in other ways to *promote activities designed to lead to* increased knowledge in the field of illness and *better care for the mentally ill*." [Our italics and numbers.][18]

These are the WPA's only two purposes and they are broadly defined. But quite clearly the second one covers concern for "the ethical aspects of psychiatry", as such concern would be "designed to lead to . . . better care for the mentally ill". So Leigh's argument on this point was wrong from the legalistic angle. Oddly enough, it was also nonsensical in terms of his own report. For three paragraphs prior to those quoted above he had written:

> The ethical problems of psychiatry have been of concern to the WPA since its formation. . . . In fact, a three-day symposium was held in London in November 1969, the overall topic being "The Uses and Abuses of Psychiatry". The proceedings were published in newspaper form and distributed to a very large public indeed, possibly 500,000 people.

His second point—that the WPA has no relevant statute or by-law relating to complaints made by one member society against another—was also incorrect, even in legalistic terms. If we bear in mind that "The General Assembly is the governing body of the WPA", and most of the votes in it are exercised by the mandated delegates of member societies, the following provisions clearly contradict his assertion:

> Membership of the WPA, both for individual members and societies, may be terminated by resignation, suspension or withdrawal of membership. Such action can be taken by the General Assembly or by the Executive Committee between meetings of the General Assembly.
> . . .
> Members of the General Assembly may request the addition of items to the agenda, these additions being decided upon by the General Assembly.[19]

These provisions cannot in our view be interpreted in any reasonable way to support Leigh's assertion. On the contrary, one of their clear purposes seems to be to ensure that any unworthy behaviour by a member society is discussed and dealt with in accordance with the wishes of other societies.

Leigh's third point—that the Executive Committee had "studied complaints by individuals and referred them to the appropriate quarter, in this case the All-Union Society"— reflected either a remarkable naïveté or a deplorable lack of concern about the second of the WPA's purposes. For if the Executive Committee believed that the complaints would be resolved by referring them to a society which was run by the very psychiatrists who were being complained against, then it was naïve in the extreme. But if it was not naïve, "closing the book" with the referral to Moscow was consciously neglecting the second of the WPA's purposes.

As psychiatrists are no more assiduous than most professional people at studying their associations' rule books, Leigh's report met no resistance in the committee. The ground was thus well prepared for the General Assembly. But Leigh made doubly sure that this body would not cause problems when, at the following meeting of the committee on 1 December, he reported on the desirability of forming an ethical committee. This was clearly a diversionary proposal, as the committee would be concerned with the formulation of universal ethical principles and not with concrete cases of abuse. He had earlier consulted with a number of international bodies concerned with human rights and concluded that the formation of such a committee to consider the ethical aspects of psychiatric practice was reasonable. It was agreed that proposals for this should be considered by the General Assembly at their meeting later that day.

The General Assembly (the governing body of the WPA composed of the delegates of the 75 member societies, the members of the committee and the Executive Committee) had before it the question of whether to form an ethical committee. The Soviet abuse was not placed on the agenda as a result of Leigh's earlier recommendation and its acceptance by the committee. The Soviet delegate to the assembly was absent, as were the delegates of about half the other member societies. Again, the secretary-general reported on the reasonableness of forming an ethical committee within the WPA. It was then suggested that the Executive Committee be empowered to set it up and give it the task of formulating a code of conduct for psychiatrists of member societies. Professor H. Ehrhardt from West Germany supported the idea, highlighting the urgent need for an ethical committee.

But Professor E. Vencovsky of Czechoslovakia in the name of the Czech and East German member societies (and perhaps tacitly also the Soviet society) opposed the committee's formation. He felt consultation of all societies within the WPA was necessary. One delegate (who wishes to remain anonymous) conveyed to us the way in which Vencovsky addressed the assembly. In an intimidating manner, he created the impression that he was determined to have his way even to the point of his delegation and others withdrawing from the meeting and the congress.

The Brazilian delegate regarded the issue as too complex to be decided upon so quickly. The assembly thereupon approved the suggestion by Professor H. Tompkins, a member of the Executive Committee, that the matter be postponed and considered further by this committee.

Ironically, the meeting of the General Assembly elected as an associate secretary and member of the Executive Committee, Professor Marat Vartanyan of the Soviet Union, who quickly became an outspoken apologist for psychiatric practices in his country. The day after his election, speaking to reporters, he denied that sane people were confined to mental hospitals: "The nature of our system is such that this could not possibly happen." He added: "We were willing to discuss the matter with our psychiatric colleagues on a professional level, but we were not approached."[20]

Dr Leigh later explained to the press that there was "no possibility whatsoever" of the General Assembly passing any motion criticizing the Russians, as none of the 75 member societies represented at the meeting had lodged any complaint against the Soviet Union.[21]

We should note here, however, that some individual psychiatrists, mainly Canadian and American, had pushed at the conference for the drafting of a statement condemning the use of psychiatry as a tool of political repression and they expressed concern about Soviet practice of this type.[22]

Other psychiatrists expressed concern but saw it as a political problem and therefore not an appropriate matter for a scientific meeting or an issue within the purview of the WPA. WPA officials were particularly insistent on these points. They felt that an organized effort had been made to convert the congress into a political forum, and thereby to attack the Soviet Union: the distribution of hundreds of pamphlets outlining the alleged Soviet abuse and arguing the dissenters' case, was an "attempt to involve a scientific association in the cold war".[23] This was, according to the officials, one of the factors behind the General Assembly's decision to avoid action on the issue. Paradoxically WPA officials were attacking the president of the congress himself, Dr de la Fuente, since as we have seen earlier, he had called on participating psychiatrists in his inaugural speech to protest against the abuse of their profession, declaring that: "to keep silent about such an ignominious situation would weigh heavily upon our consciences".

The president of the WPA at the time, Professor J. Lopez-Ibor, apparently strove to generalize the problem of abuse, when he claimed that his organization "is fighting for the elimination of these anomalies . . . many charges are coming to us from various countries; the documents forming a bundle almost 1·2 metres high". The WPA had begun an investigation of each case to determine the veracity of the charges.[24] Lopez-Ibor was possibly hoping to defuse the controversy. He must have feared that by an exclusive focus on, and possible condemnation of, one member society, there was a threat that the entire body might fragment. Various sources report that the Soviet delegation, without making a formal threat, clearly hinted that it would walk out of the congress if the General Assembly discussed the allegations against Soviet psychiatry.

Soviet Psychiatry Responds

During the congress Professor Snezhnevsky and his fellow delegates adamantly defended Soviet psychiatry. He himself expressed his views publicly in an interview with the Mexico City newspaper *Excelsior*; he categorically refuted the charge that sane Soviet dissenters were confined to psychiatric hospitals and attributed the allegations to the "cold war":

It is a "cold war" manœuvre carried out by expert hands. It started—and not by chance—during the preparation period of this congress and on the appearance of the English version of Medvedev's book entitled *A Question of Madness* . . . everything is used in the "cold war". Everything is twisted around in this kind of war to the point of absurdity.[25]

Snezhnevsky proceeded, as he had done some weeks earlier in his *Izvestia* interview, with a description of forensic psychiatric practice in the Soviet Union and suggested that in the cases of the six people mentioned in the Bukovsky documents, normal procedures had been applied. They were found to be mentally ill, not responsible, and in need of psychiatric treatment. He reiterated that it was "absolutely false that healthy persons have been confined to psychiatric establishments".

Dr M. Shchirina insisted that she and her colleagues had come to Mexico to share advances of psychiatry in the Soviet Union, to attend the scientific sessions and to exchange ideas with psychiatrists from other countries. She added that the absence of official Russian interpretation (Russian was not one of the official languages of the congress) precluded discussion on the question, raised by some, of Soviet psychiatric misuse.[26] Dr Boris Lebedev, director of a psychiatric hospital in Leningrad, insisted that the charges that dissenters were detained in mental hospitals for no just reason "are arguments intended to create agitation. . . . No one can say it is true. The affair has been used to create agitation. No psychiatrist would take part in it."[27]

And so the most important congress on the psychiatrist's calendar, held only once every five to six years, ended without a response to the appeals addressed to it. Discussion of the political use of Soviet psychiatry was avoided, and action on the question of the WPA's rôle in upholding ethical standards of practice was deferred. The congress was, however, a vehicle for bringing the abuse into the public eye. Through the two appeals, the distribution of pamphlets and considerable discussion in the corridors, many of the 6,000 psychiatrists present had been confronted with a vital issue of which they had previously known little.

The lack of any response by the WPA in Mexico may have influenced the Board of Trustees of the American Psychiatric

Association when it met a few days later on 9 December 1971. In May 1971 the association had received copies of the Bukovsky documents from the International Committee for the Defence of Human Rights with a request to act on them. So the trustees in approving a position statement which declared that the APA "firmly opposes the misuse of psychiatric facilities for the detention of persons solely on the basis of their political dissent, no matter where it occurs",[28] were treading cautiously, and at some distance from the well-documented Soviet example. Although the statement referred to an abuse for which the Russians had been criticized by both the Canadian Psychiatric Association and the WFMH, it studiously included the last phrase to imply that the Americans were not attacking Soviet psychiatry specifically.

The American Psychoanalytic Association adopted a resolution similar to that of its psychiatric colleagues on 18 December 1971, again omitting any mention of the Soviet Union:

> The American Psychoanalytic Association, in keeping with its concern for standards of ethical conduct, deplores the misuse of psychiatric hospitalization as a political device wherever and whenever this occurs. We encourage our members to inform themselves of such activities in order to be able to effectively express their concern.[29]

The Trial of Bukovsky

Thus Bukovsky's appeal had failed to elicit any response from the WPA, and led to only non-specific statements by two American psychiatric bodies. To those people in the USSR and the West who were well-informed on the issue, this passivity seemed like a tragic betrayal of Bukovsky. If Bukovsky himself knew about it, he must have been at the least disheartened.

He had been arrested long before, on 29 March 1971, three weeks after his appeal was published. Ironically he was sent by the investigators to the Serbsky Institute. Probably because of the pressure applied both within the Soviet Union and abroad, he was transferred back to prison after three months, and then brought to trial on 5 January 1972. He was charged with article 70 of the Russian criminal code—"anti-Soviet agitation and propaganda". This is a charge regularly used against dissenters which we discuss in chapter 5. Bukovsky had been held for nine months when his trial commenced, yet it lasted only a day and was closed to journalists and independent observers.

A detailed *samizdat* account of the proceedings, obviously compiled by surreptitious methods, reveals how salient the issue of psychiatric abuse was in Bukovsky's trial.[30] According to the prosecutor the defendant had conducted anti-Soviet propaganda in "maintaining that in the USSR sane people are placed in mental hospitals where they are subjected to inhuman treatment". Bukovsky confirmed he had made such statements and petitioned for the calling of witnesses like Shults, Pisarev, Yakhimovich and the wife of Grigorenko, who would testify to their truthfulness. This petition was rejected by the judge, as were virtually all others submitted by the defence. The witnesses requested by Bukovsky could not be called since they "are insane people and their testimony would be invalid". This statement was definitely false with regard to at least three of them—Shults, Mrs Grigorenko and Pisarev—and probably to others as well.

When given the opportunity to reply to the indictment, Bukovsky focused mainly on the subject of psychiatry and described carefully his own experience and that of other dissenters, including Nikolai Samsonov (see chapter 3), in the Leningrad special hospital.

For the prosecutor, however, Bukovsky's views were based on ignorance: "After all, he is taking it upon himself to instruct and contradict medical specialists, representatives of the Soviet school of psychiatry which has won respect and recognition in the whole world." Indeed, she declared, according to "the famous Soviet scientist . . . Academician A. V. Snezhnevsky . . . 'the absurd reports that in the USSR sane people are put in psychiatric hospitals are just a wild invention which cannot but evoke feelings of deep indignation' ".

Bukovsky's final speech, erudite and legally well informed, pointed to the considerable range of juridical infringements that had typified his trial. All his activities had been perfectly lawful; he had only exercised the right, given to him by the Soviet constitution, to express his convictions. He was probably right when he asserted: "In condemning me, the authorities are pursuing the aim of concealing their own crimes—the psychiatric repression of dissenters."

The guilty verdict was entirely predictable. He received the maximum sentence of twelve years: two in prison, five in a labour camp and five in exile.

Perhaps Bukovsky's appeal came too soon and there had not been sufficient time to assess the import of the case reports he had sent abroad. Although the suspicion of Western psychiatrists was aroused, many of them could not believe the allegations of abuse without confirmatory evidence. Over the next few years a considerable volume of new evidence became available from a variety of sources: consistently reliable *samizdat* reports, mainly in the *Chronicle*, press reports, first-hand accounts by ex-inmates of mental hospitals and Soviet psychiatrists who had emigrated, and, paradoxically, statements by psychiatrists in the Soviet Union, defending their profession against Western criticism. There was even an occasional admission in the Russian press—the work perhaps of critically-minded journalists—that abuse did in fact sometimes occur. Just after Bukovsky's trial an article appeared under the cleverly chosen heading "An Unbelievable Story", recounting how a woman had criticized her boss. Following a heated argument the boss picked up his 'phone, summoned an ambulance, and had the woman interned in a mental hospital for six days. The woman's legitimate claim for reimbursement of lost earnings was, the journalist wrote, still going through the courts.[31]

Chapters 5 to 9 consider this and other material. In chapter 10 we resume the story of Western responses to the Soviet abuse, of which this chapter has told the uneven, some would say inglorious, beginning.

Chapter 5

THE PRACTICE: CRIMINAL COMMITMENT

DISSENTERS FORCIBLY CONFINED in mental hospitals arrive there by way of either a criminal or a civil commitment. In this chapter we examine the process of criminal commitment, then illustrate its application in the cases of two dissenters, Pyotr Grigorenko and Natalya Gorbanevskaya.

The History of Criminal Commitment in the Soviet Union
Article 14 of the "Basic Principles of Criminal Law" of 1919 stated that no one could be subject to criminal trial and punishment for an act which was committed in a condition of mental illness. Medical measures were indicated in such cases.[1] The provision was sufficiently broad to ensure that people accused of criminal acts, who pleaded a mental illness corroborated by psychiatric examination, were to be hospitalized rather than punished. Moreover, the new revolutionary society avowed that crime was basically a socio-medical problem, a result of the injustice and inequity of the tsarist régime.

This view of crime was soon amended. The courts progressively assumed greater responsibility in determining the responsibility or otherwise of a defendant. Revised criminal codes referred to the appropriateness of punishment for those persons who had committed "socially dangerous acts" if they "acted intentionally or negligently and foresaw, or should have foreseen the socially dangerous consequences of their acts".[2]

In the 1930s the emphasis on individual responsibility for crimes grew, as an increasingly paranoid régime developed the need to unmask millions of "saboteurs", "enemies" and "spies". These people could not have their "evil, subversive" activities explained away as insanity. This would undermine the image of an embattled régime heroically overcoming the attacks of counter-revolution and foreign subversion.

Psychiatrists were still called on to prepare medical reports for the court, but these were increasingly unfavourable to the defendant, and in any case the final decision regarding the sanity of the defendant rested firmly with the court itself. The records of the Serbsky Institute demonstrate the increased emphasis on personal responsibility. In 1922 nearly half the "psychopaths" examined there were declared not responsible for their criminal acts. By 1945 the proportion had dropped to only 12 per cent.[3] This new pattern appears to have persisted since, as reflected for example in a standard text-book *Psychiatry*: "Psychopaths, as they are not mentally ill, are in the majority of cases declared to be responsible."[4]

No federal criminal code exists in the Soviet Union. However, a set of federal Basic Principles exists for the guidance of the fifteen constituent Soviet republics in drawing up their own codes of criminal legislation and procedure. The Basic Principles now in force were drawn up in 1958 under Khrushchev, and by 1960 the republics had produced their own codes. These codes eliminated many of the legal provisions which had facilitated police terror and arbitrariness and introduced a number of safeguards for defendants. Each republic's code contains provisions for the mentally-ill offender. Article 11 of the Criminal Code of the Russian Republic (RSFSR) for example states that:

> A person shall not be subjected to criminal responsibility who at the time of committing a socially dangerous act is in a state of non-responsibility,* that is, cannot realize the significance of his actions or control them because of a chronic mental illness, temporary mental derangement, mental deficiency or other condition of illness. Compulsory measures of a medical character may be applied to such a person by order of the court.[5]

The compulsory medical measures are again referred to, in article 403 of the Code of Criminal Procedure:

> Compulsory measures of a medical character provided by article 58 of the RSFSR Criminal Code shall be applied by

* The Russian word *nevmenyaemost*, which can also be translated as non-imputability, has a similar meaning in Soviet law to that of the word non-responsibility in British and American law.

a court to persons who have committed socially dangerous acts provided for by the criminal law while in a state of non-responsibility or who, after committing a crime, having contracted a mental illness which deprives them of the ability to realize the significance of their actions or to control them, if such persons represent a danger to society because of the character of the act committed by them and their state of illness.[6]

Similar articles for the mentally-ill offender are to be found in the codes of the other Soviet republics.

The Rôle of the Forensic Psychiatrist

Forensic psychiatry in the Soviet Union is practised within the framework of the Ministry of Health according to a set of directives co-ordinated by the ministries of Health, Justice and Internal Affairs, and the Procurator's office.* An expert psychiatric examination can be requested at any stage of the criminal procedure.

The right to initiate the examination rests with the investigating organs and the court, but the accused, his family, guardian or defence counsel may appeal for a psychiatric consultation. The court, however, has the right to refuse them.

The examination is conducted by a commission of three or four psychiatrists (in remote areas a smaller commission is permitted) who are employed by the Ministry of Health. The examining experts are regarded as neutral and independent, on the grounds that their employer is neither the Ministry of Justice, nor the Procurator, nor the defendant; their judgement is thus viewed as impartial and objective.† The Soviet model contrasts sharply with British and American law, in which expert medical evidence can be called as of right, by both prosecution and defence, with each side having the right to introduce additional expert evidence in rebuttal.

In the USSR the psychiatric examination may be conducted

---

* The Procuracy has two different and, critics maintain, conflicting rôles. It is responsible for ensuring that all the many departments of state observe the law in their procedures, and also for prosecuting in criminal cases.

† In a system as authoritarian as the Soviet one, this is, we should note, far from always the case.

in a hospital, clinic, court or remand prison. The observation period allowed in a hospital is 30 days, but this can be extended if necessary.

On the basis of the data obtained from the clinical examination, reports from other agencies, and the legal documents of the case, the psychiatric commission prepares a report and presents it to the investigator or to the court (whichever has initiated the examination). The commission expresses its opinions on the presence or absence of mental illness, its severity if present, whether the defendant is responsible or not, his ability to stand trial, the need or not for medical treatment, and, if need exists, the form of treatment. The report also includes a detailed biographical history of the accused, his past medical history and the results of physical and psychological tests.

Each psychiatrist on the commission signs the report unless he dissents from his colleagues. In this case he may submit a separate opinion. All members of the commission share equal responsibility for an agreed report. Should the commission not reach a conclusion because of inadequate data it can indicate this and receive the additional material it requires.

The commission's report forms only part of the evidence. The task of the court is to appraise all the evidence, and only it can decide on how to proceed with the case. The court alone makes a final pronouncement on the sanity of the accused, the question of responsibility, and the need for medical treatment. Although the court generally accepts the recommendations of the psychiatrists and acts accordingly, it is not obliged to do so. Their report may be rejected and another course of action pursued, or a second psychiatric commission established. In the latter case the Ministry of Health arranges for a new examination.

With two psychiatric opinions before it, the court must weigh up all the evidence and select the recommendations it believes are appropriate. A third examination is permissible if the first two reports are in conflict. An opinion from the Serbsky Institute is usually (almost always in cases affecting dissenters) accepted by the court and viewed as more authoritative than that of commissions functioning elsewhere. The defence counsel has the right, at the trial, to request the participation of specific psychiatrists in a second examination. The court decides whether such requests will be acceded to or not.

Other procedural guarantees include mandatory participation of a defence lawyer and the holding of the trial in an open court, except where state secrets or certain sexual offences are involved. By contrast, the presence of the accused during the trial is not mandatory, and the court decides whether he will be permitted to attend or not.

Certain conditions must be satisfied before the court can rule the accused not responsible. It must establish that he has actually committed acts for which the law prescribes criminal responsibility; and that while committing them, he was suffering from a mental illness which prevented him from appreciating their significance and/or from controlling them.

If these conditions are met, the court has several options before it. It can refer the defendant for compulsory treatment to a special or ordinary psychiatric hospital, or place him in the custody of relatives or guardian on condition that he remain under medical supervision. This decision is dependent on the nature of the defendant's mental illness and the degree of danger he poses to society. In referring a person for compulsory treatment, the court does not specify its duration but rather states that treatment is needed until recovery occurs.

There is provision in the law for a systematic check of the patient's clinical course. The patient must be examined at least every six months by a psychiatric commission, which is obliged to submit its report to the court.

If the report recommends transfer to an ordinary psychiatric hospital, under compulsory or voluntary conditions, or release, it is reviewed by a court. The court is not, however, bound by the recommendations, and can reject them. The patient may also be transferred to a psychiatric colony, which usually results in life-long internment.

Relatives or other interested persons can petition (under article 412 of the RSFSR Code of Criminal Procedure) for the discontinuation of compulsory treatment, but cannot insist that the psychiatrists of their choice participate in any examination. The patient himself has no right of appeal; he has automatically been classified as mentally incompetent and therefore unfit to submit legally valid documents.

On release from hospital the patient may, on his psychiatrist's recommendation, be placed by the court under the psychiatric supervision of a district clinic, i.e., "put on the psychiatric register". This involves the legal obligation to obey the orders of the clinic. In some cases the patient may emerge with the legal-psychiatric label "mentally incompetent", i.e., without the rights of a legal person and subject to a relative's guardianship. He may also have been assigned by a Medico-Labour Examining Commission to one of three categories of invalidism. These categories govern whether or not he is legally obliged to work, and whether or not he should receive a disablement pension on the grounds of his mental state, and if so, of what size. Finally, he is secretly categorized in two further ways. His psychiatrist assigns him a degree of social dangerousness on a scale from one to five, and the security organs, after receiving the psychiatrist's report, assign their own danger rating in the light of this and of all their other sources of information. If this rating is high, because, say, he has a propensity to demonstrate, he will henceforth be liable to short internments during big public holidays.

Criminal Commitment in Cases of Dissenters

We shall illustrate criminal commitment as applied to dissenters in our discussion of Grigorenko and Gorbanevskaya. However, some general comments first. The legal process usually involves the arrest of the dissenter by the KGB, and its investigation of the alleged criminal offence. This may last up to nine months according to the law, but can in practice be extended further by a special decree of the Supreme Soviet. During this period the dissenter may be sent by the investigator for psychiatric examination. This is conducted as described earlier. After the examination, a list of detailed charges is drawn up by the procurator. At this stage—often six months after the dissenter's arrest—a defence lawyer is admitted to the case, and he and the accused are allowed to study the case materials.

The charges most often brought against dissenters are articles 70 and 190-1 of the RSFSR Criminal Code.* (Each republic has similar articles in its criminal code, with different identifying numbers.) Article 70 reads:

* The articles most often used against religious dissenters are 142 and 227.

Agitation or propaganda carried out with the purpose of subverting or weakening Soviet authority or in order to commit particular, especially dangerous, crimes against the state, or the oral dissemination for the same purpose of deliberate fabrications which defame the Soviet political and social system, or the dissemination or manufacture or keeping for the same purpose, of literature of such content, shall be punishable by deprivation of freedom for a period of from six months to seven years, with or without additional exile for a term of two to five years, or by exile for a term of two to five years.[7]

Article 190–1 does not cover subversion and therefore provides for less severe punishment:

The systematic dissemination in oral form of deliberate fabrications which discredit the Soviet political and social system, or the manufacture or dissemination in written, printed or other form of works of such content, shall be punished by deprivation of freedom for a period of up to three years, or by corrective tasks for a period of up to one year, or by a fine of up to 100 roubles.[8]

Dissenters are frequently declared insane and not responsible for their alleged criminal act by a psychiatric commission. Almost without exception, the court accepts the recommendation of the commission and the trial becomes a mere formality. The witness list is thoroughly revised and may be dispensed with altogether. The defendant is almost invariably barred from participating in his trial. As he is mentally ill, the court argues, the proceedings are only likely to exacerbate his condition. The dissenter's family and friends are normally forbidden access to the trial through packing of the court with police and other functionaries, or occasionally by an official statement that the trial is a closed one. Sometimes two or three close relatives are admitted, but rarely any friends. Often access is made freer for the reading of the court's verdict.

The dissenter's counsel usually attempts to persuade the court that his client is indeed sane by disputing the findings of the psychiatric commission. His request for a second opinion (or a third if two commissions have previously reached contradictory conclusions) is customarily turned down by the court. Good illustrations of the court's refusal to recognize the request of the defence are provided by the cases of Grigorenko and Gorbanevskaya. Their lawyer, as we shall see, argued in each case for their sanity and pointed out the need for a third examination since the results of the first two were discordant. In both cases the request was denied by the court and the second opinion, that of a Serbsky Institute commission, accepted. In all cases of dissenters the Serbsky report has taken precedence over any other. It is in fact extremely rare that a Serbsky recommendation is not formalized by the court.

Defence counsel may appeal for a new trial to the supreme court of the republic in which the first trial has taken place. Among the reasons presented may be the need for a further psychiatric examination. Such appeals in cases of dissenters have proved futile—the judgment of the lower court has been invariably confirmed. Dissenters declared not responsible usually find themselves faced with compulsory treatment in a special psychiatric hospital for an indeterminate period. The commission normally recommends treatment in a special rather than an ordinary hospital because of the nature of the dissenter's illness and/or the danger he poses to society. Less commonly, he is referred to an ordinary hospital (this occurred, for example, with Ivan Yakhimovich and with Ilya Rips, two cases which have become well known in the West) or is released into the custody of relatives.

While in hospital, the dissenter is examined at six-monthly intervals by a commission, whose report is presented to the regional court. Dissenters are generally transferred to an ordinary psychiatric hospital from a special one, prior to their ultimate release. The six-monthly commissions may continue over a period of years before transfer or discharge is recommended. Dissenters' internment periods have ranged from some months to many years. Once released from the hospital, dissenters are normally obliged to register at their district psychiatric clinic and are then subject to periodic supervision. They are also rated in terms of the degree of "social danger" they represent, this information being needed by both medical and police authorities. If the rating is high, the dissenter concerned is then subject to police control at the time of major holidays or visits by foreign statesmen. He will be interned in a mental hospital for about two weeks or compelled to travel out of town.

THE CASE OF PYOTR GRIGORENKO

Pyotr Grigorenko's case is an excellent example of the process of criminal commitment as applied to dissenters. Abundant material about, and by him, is available. Many of his own writings have been collected in a volume entitled *The Grigorenko Papers*.[9] A background history of the man and a knowledge of his political life are necessary preliminary steps in understanding his involvement with psychiatry and the law.

Grigorenko's political awareness began early when he became the first in his Ukranian village to enrol in the Komsomol or Communist Youth League. In 1927, at the comparatively young age of 20, Grigorenko became a member of the party. Two years later he entered the Kharkov Poly-technic Institute, ushering in an illustrious academic career in military science. Soon recognized as a gifted student, he was transferred to a prestigious engineering academy by party directive, and graduated there in 1934 with distinction. Service followed in various high-ranking Red Army engineering posts. Grigorenko returned to a military academy, however, before the second world war, graduating with distinction. During the war he entered active service and earned the respect of his fellow soldiers as a competent and courageous fighter. His military achievements were recognized by the award of several decorations, among them the Order of Lenin, two Orders of the Red Banner and the Order of the Red Star; and in his progressive rise in rank culminating in 1959 with his promotion to major-general.

After 1945 Grigorenko returned to military academic life, occupying a position in the Frunze Academy, the most notable institution of its kind in the Soviet Union. During the seventeen years he taught there Grigorenko published dozens of academic papers and was repeatedly promoted, ultimately attaining the chairmanship of the Cybernetics Department. His transfer to the Far East as Chief of Army Operations in 1962 was a distinct demotion, the result of his first major entry into the

political arena. His military career rapidly crumbled thereafter, to be replaced by a growing political activism which soon
brought him in conflict with the law and into the hands of
psychiatry. Grigorenko had as early as 1941 drawn a reprimand
from the party for criticizing Stalin's military shortsightedness.
This "stain" certainly delayed his promotion to the rank of
major-general until 1959: it had been repeatedly recommended
by his associates from 1946 onward.

In 1961 Grigorenko criticized the Khrushchev administration at a party conference. He cited the exorbitant salaries
and special privileges granted to officials and called for the
rotation of all party officers. He warned that these practices
were giving rise to a new personality cult, that of Khrushchev.
As a result of this challenge the major-general was removed
from his academic post and strictly reprimanded by the party.
He considered its reactions unjust and arbitrary and was
spurred to even greater activism. It was some months after
this episode that his demotion and dispatch to the remote Far
East took place. Grigorenko continued nevertheless to be outspoken in his criticism of Khrushchev's leadership and also
complained about the neglect of the human rights of Soviet
citizens.

In November 1963 Grigorenko founded a small dissenting
group, the "Group for the Struggle to Revive Leninism". The
group's objective was the re-establishment of Leninist principles
of government. In an effort to spread its beliefs, it began to
distribute leaflets. The leafleting campaign was immediately
interpreted by the KGB as propagation of anti-Soviet material
and the predictable arrest of Grigorenko ensued on 2 February
1964. Charged with anti-Soviet agitation under article 70, he
spent some weeks in Moscow's Lubyanka Prison; then, on the
initiative of the investigator, he was transferred to the Serbsky
Institute for a psychiatric examination.

An understandable ignorance of the use of psychiatry for
political repression is reflected in his initial reaction to entering
the Serbsky (the practice became well known only later in the
decade):

I arrived in the second (political) section of the Serbsky
Institute on 12 March 1964. I had not previously even heard
of such a method of repression in our time as the declaration

of a healthy man to be of unsound mind. I was unaware that this "Chaadayevan" system existed in our country [see chapter 3]. I realized it only when I myself was presented with a committal order for a psychiatric examination.[10]

The Serbsky commission concluded after five weeks that Grigorenko was suffering from a "psychological illness in the form of a paranoid development of the personality involving delusions, combined with the first signs of cerebral arteriosclerosis".[11] He was declared not responsible and in need of compulsory treatment in a special psychiatric hospital. The commission gave these grounds for its diagnostic conclusion:

> His psychological condition was characterized by the presence of *reformist ideas, in particular for the reorganization of the state apparatus* [our italics]; and this was linked with ideas of over-estimation of his own personality that reached messianic proportions. He felt his experiences with emotional intensity and was unshakeably convinced of the rightness of his actions. At the same time elements of a pathological interpretation of his surroundings were observed, together with morbid suspicion and sharply expressed excitability.[12]

The Serbsky's recommendations were accepted by the Military Collegium of the USSR Supreme Court. Thus Grigorenko, on the basis of article 58 of the criminal code, was confined to the Leningrad special hospital where he remained from August 1964 to April 1965.

During the investigation he was not permitted to meet a lawyer nor was he granted the right to participate in either the investigation or the trial. Indeed, the general and his relatives never saw the Court decision. Two weeks after his admission to hospital Grigorenko was demoted to the rank of ordinary soldier, deprived of his pension and expelled from the party by his local committee, under pressure from the Central Committee. These steps were highly irregular. According to the law a military officer declared mentally ill is provided with a pension according to his rank. As regards the party, the membership of a mentally ill person is suspended until his recovery. In Grigorenko's case both the law and the party rules were flouted. In March 1965 Grigorenko was examined by a commission which confirmed the Serbsky's conclusions of a year earlier, but pointed out that he was no longer mentally ill: "He is in remission, does not require in-patient treatment, and shows only features of sclerosis of the brain."[13] The commission recommended Grigorenko's release and periodic visits to his district psychiatric clinic.

From the time of his discharge the following month until his re-arrest in May 1969, Grigorenko became progressively more active as a dissenter. His first campaign was of a personal nature. He embarked immediately on a programme to reverse some of the injustices he considered had been perpetrated against him. He demanded for example restoration of his army pension, but this was given after a prolonged delay, and then only one-third of his due as a major-general. He was reduced to working as a porter to earn his keep until ultimately gaining the correct pension. He also pressed the medical authorities to have him removed entirely from a category of invalidism: on his release from hospital he had been certified as an "invalid of the second category".*

From early 1966 Grigorenko became indefatigably pre-occupied with the promotion of human rights: he wrote letters to government leaders, participated in public protests,† wrote commentaries and delivered speeches.[14] Through all these endeavours he became recognized by the unofficial human-rights movement as one of the champions of its cause. Here was a man who had accomplished much during his career, which had culminated in his appointment as a major-general; he was older than most of his fellow dissenters; and he was fearless in confronting the régime, despite his previous internment in the Leningrad hospital.

---

* An "invalid of the first category" is barred from any employment and given a state pension. A second category invalid may or may not be allowed to work, while in the third category, work is obligatory, as for other Soviet citizens. All three groups must attend their local psychiatric clinics at specified intervals, if their status derives from mental illness.

† When he and some friends planned in February 1966 to demonstrate against re-Stalinization trends within the régime, they were all detained and given a lecture by General Svetlichny of the KGB. The latter's unusually frank words confirmed official policy on two points: "If you go out on the street, even without disturbing the traffic, with banners reading 'Long Live the Central Committee!', we shall *still* put you in lunatic asylums!" *Possev*, Frankfurt, 16 September 1966.

At the same time that his human-rights colleagues viewed him with admiration and esteem, the KGB had its eye on him as well. Grigorenko himself records:

Two or three months after my release . . . the KGB . . . once again took an interest in me . . . I have been subjected to continuous surveillance: constant, round-the-clock trailing of myself, members of my family and my visitors; uninterrupted observation of my apartment by visual and other special means; the tapping of my telephone, inspection of my correspondence, and the confiscation of some of my letters.[15]

Grigorenko was summoned several times to the KGB for "talks", and once to the military-registration office, where he was threatened with the loss of his pension if he did not curtail his dissent. The military also prevented him from joining an organization for retired officers.

In 1966 Grigorenko met the writer Alexei Kosterin, who had waged a struggle for several years, calling on the government to recognize the rights of minority national groups in the Soviet Union. He was especially identified with the cause of the Crimean Tatars. Stalin had had the entire Tatar population of the Crimea deported to central Asia in 1944, alleging that they had collaborated with the Germans. Despite their exoneration in 1967, they had been refused permission to return home as they wished. Grigorenko was immediately attracted to both the significance of the cause and to Kosterin's dedication. Their friendship blossomed as they joined forces to tackle the plight of the Tatars. The Tatars themselves had struggled ever since the mid-1950s for restoration of their rights but now received new inspiration from Kosterin and Grigorenko.

Both urged the Tatars on to new heights of protest. This was particularly so after Grigorenko delivered a passionate speech in Moscow, in which he called on the movement to adopt new, bold methods in its campaign. Rather than address "meekly written pleas" to the leadership, the Tatars "must learn that what is prescribed by law should not be requested; it should be demanded. Start to demand! And demand not bits and pieces but everything that was unlawfully taken from you—demand the re-establishment of the Crimean Autonomous Republic . . . strengthen your demands by all means available to you under the Constitution. . . ."[16] Grigorenko exhorted the Tatars not to confine their activities to their own problems alone, but to forge contacts with other nationalities that were subject to similar indignities.

This was fiery language. Grigorenko himself was aware of the change that had come about in him. At Kosterin's funeral he proudly disclosed that despite their friendship of only three years, the poet had "made me: he turned a rebel into a fighter. I will be grateful to him for this to the end of my days." He also used the occasion to condemn the totalitarian nature of the régime, and those who were converting Lenin's democracy into a "heartless bureaucratic machine".[17]

The authorities, obviously concerned about Grigorenko's stirring encouragement of the Tatars, applied various tactics to discredit them, but were up against a revitalized force. Kosterin's death in November 1968, although a great loss to the Tatars, spurred them to fight even more determinedly. After a spate of protests the authorities reacted by bringing many of them to trial.

Many other dissenters were arrested about this time, including one of Grigorenko's closest colleagues, Ivan Yakhimovich, who was subsequently declared not responsible and committed to a Riga mental hospital. The KGB were obviously intent on arresting Grigorenko too and tried to set various traps for him. Finally, in early May 1969, one of these succeeded. He was telephoned and invited to come to Tashkent to support a group of Tatar leaders who were about to face trial, by appearing in court as a "social defender" (that is, a form of character witness, provided for by Soviet law). In fact he suspected, and discovered on arrival, that the KGB had fabricated the invitation. Despite his plan to return to Moscow immediately, his arrest took place at Tashkent airport. He was charged with distributing politically defamatory literature under article 190–1. While in a KGB detention cell, Grigorenko was brutally beaten and generally maltreated. He was deprived of contact with his lawyer and family, who in turn lost his army pension. The authorities ignored his demands for immediate release, or transfer of the investigation to Moscow, the site of the alleged crimes and where the incriminating documents had been found. They clearly intended to hold his trial in Tashkent, far from his many friends and supporters in Moscow who would otherwise have demonstrated outside the court and in various ways generated publicity.

He now began a hunger strike and was force-fed by his jailers. This was no ordinary prisoner the KGB had on its hands. The KGB resorted some weeks later, on 18 August 1969, to the use of psychiatry. They organized a psychiatric examination of Grigorenko on KGB premises. The three-hour assessment was conducted by a team headed by Professor Detengof.*

On the basis of their clinical observations and an examination of criminal and medical documents, the commission concluded that:

> Grigorenko at the present time shows no symptoms of mental illness, just as he did not show any in the period of the offences incriminating him (from the second half of 1965 to April 1969), when he understood the nature of his activities and was capable of directing them. He was responsible for his actions. Grigorenko's activity had a purposeful character, it concerned concrete events and facts, arose from his personal convictions and in many cases from the same convictions as his fellow thinkers', and it did not contain sick or hysterical symptoms. All his life Grigorenko has developed correctly from the neuropsychological point of view although he has always shown certain original traits of character, such as perseverance in the attainment of a goal, a certain tendency to over-estimate his capabilities, and a desire to affirm his own opinion. At the same time he has revealed good intellectual capabilities, has through steady effort achieved good general development and stature in the spheres of work and social life. He had good relationships in collectives, was a leader and an educator. No appreciable break or change in the development of his personality has been observed. . . .
>
> Grigorenko does not require in-patient investigation, as his personal characteristics and psychological condition are amply described in documents of the case, in data acquired through observation of him in the investigation prison, and

* Fyodor Detengof, who died in 1973, was an eminent figure in Soviet psychiatry, and for many years the chief psychiatrist of the Uzbek Republic.

also in the data acquired through examination of him as an outpatient. *No doubts concerning Grigorenko's mental health have arisen in the course of the out-patient investigation. In-patient investigation at this time would not increase our understanding of his case, but, on the contrary, taking into consideration his age, his sharply negative attitude to residence in psychiatric hospitals, and his heightened sensitivity, it would complicate a diagnosis.*[18] [Our italics.]

Here was a confidently-based conclusion ("no doubts have arisen") and an explicit statement that in-patient investigation would be harmful to Grigorenko. Yet the sequel was precisely that. The KGB flew Grigorenko to Moscow two weeks later and placed him in the Serbsky Institute. We can only speculate why they ordered a second investigation. Perhaps Professor Detengof's team had defied pressure from the KGB during the first one? Or perhaps the authorities had changed their mind later as to what diagnosis suited them best?

The psychiatric examination at the Serbsky was conducted by a commission which included Drs G. Morozov, V. M. Morozov and D. R. Lunts. They found him to be:

Suffering from a mental illness in the form of a pathological, paranoid development of the personality, with the presence of reformist ideas that have appeared in his personality, and with psychopathic features of the character and the first signs of cerebral arteriosclerosis. Confirmation of this can be seen in the psychotic condition present in 1964, which arose during an unfavourable situation and which expressed itself in ideas of reformism and of persecution which had strong emotional colouring. Subsequently, as is evident from the documents of the criminal case and the data of the present clinical examination, the paranoid condition was not completely overcome. The reformist ideas have taken on an obstinate character and determine the conduct of the patient; in addition, the intensity of these ideas is increased in connection with various external circumstances which have no direct relation to him, and is accompanied by an uncritical attitude to his own utterances and acts. The above-mentioned condition of mental illness precludes the possibility of his being responsible for his actions and

controlling them; consequently, the patient must be considered not responsible. The commission cannot agree with
the out-patient forensic psychiatric diagnosis formulated in
Tashkent because of the presence in Grigorenko of pathological changes in his psyche, as recorded in the present
report; these could not be revealed in the conditions of an
out-patient examination because of his outwardly well-
adjusted behaviour, his formally coherent utterances and
his retention of his past knowledge and manners—all of which
is characteristic of a pathological development of the
personality. Because of his mental condition Grigorenko
requires compulsory treatment in a special psychiatric
hospital, as the paranoid reformist ideas described above are
of obstinate character and determine the conduct of the
patient.[19]

The examinations by the Tashkent and Serbsky commissions
were conducted within a three-month period, and yet resulted
in radically discordant conclusions. The Tashkent psychiatrists had "no doubts" concerning Grigorenko's mental health
and firmly recommended that he not be hospitalized for
further examination; the Serbsky psychiatrists concluded that
"the patient must be considered not responsible" and that he
required "compulsory treatment in a special psychiatric
hospital".

Comparison of the Two Psychiatric Case Reports

It is illuminating to compare the two reports further. The
Serbsky's refuted the Tashkent diagnostic formulation by
asserting that Grigorenko's outwardly well-adjusted behaviour,
his formally coherent utterances and his retention of his past
knowledge and manners—all characteristic of a pathological
development of the personality—prevented the out-patient
examination from recognizing his underlying mental illness.
Scrutiny of the two reports, however, shows that both commissions made similar sets of observations. The salient difference
between them, besides the conclusions reached, was in the
interpretation of, and attitude towards, Grigorenko's political
and social activities. Professor Detengof's commission was of the
opinion that "Grigorenko's activity had a purposeful character,

it concerned concrete events and facts, arose from his personal convictions and in many cases from the same convictions as his fellow thinkers', and it did not contain sick or hysterical symptoms". Morozov's commission, by contrast, viewed the same activity in a totally pathological context. It found in Grigorenko "a clear over-estimation of his own activity and of the significance of his personality and his reformist ideas, of the rightness of which he is unshakeably convinced". In reference to the political ideas that Grigorenko exhibited during the 1964 examination, the commission wrote: "He does not, even now, renounce the views he expressed then."

While the Detengof commission interpreted Grigorenko's political struggle within a normal framework and accepted that his ideas were shared by others and were not delusionary in character, the Morozov group concluded just the opposite— that Grigorenko's "reformist" beliefs were indeed false, held with conviction, and emanated from his inflated self-image. This is a crucial difference, central to the entire issue of viewing dissenters as mentally ill, to which we return in chapter 8.

As for the rest of the examination, there was considerable agreement on other features of Grigorenko's behaviour and personality. Both commissions found that Grigorenko had insight into his social situation, made normal emotional contact, though he became angry and excited when questioned about his "illegal" activities. He generally behaved in a courteous and dignified fashion. Importantly, he showed no disorder of intellect, memory or concentration. These faculties, we may note, are usually affected, at least slightly, in the condition of cerebral arteriosclerosis.

Grigorenko's Own Record of the Psychiatric Examinations
Grigorenko kept a sporadic diary of his experiences from the time of his arrival in Tashkent on 3 May 1969 through to the end of his stay at the Serbsky Institute. The diary is entirely coherent and shows that Grigorenko was well aware of what was happening to him throughout this time. His comparison of the two psychiatric commissions is revealing. The Tashkent examination lasted three hours, during which all four psychiatrists participated actively, each conducting aspects of the assessment, and often checking those done by a colleague.

There were long discussions, even arguments, between members of the team. Grigorenko was impressed with the thoroughness and conscientiousness of the process: "I approached the commission with apprehension, feeling certain that my insanity had been predetermined. However, the business-like and friendly atmosphere throughout the examination gradually made me feel at ease, and I even began to believe in a possible objective conclusion."[20]

Grigorenko saw the Serbsky examination session as a mockery in contrast to his experience with Professor Detengof and his colleagues: "No medical examination, a mere interrogation conducted by only one man [G. Morozov]. Maya Mikhailovna [Dr Maltseva] scribbled in a notebook, while the two remaining members of the committee sat by half dozing." He gained the impression that a decision had already been made and the session was merely a rubber stamp. The commission members, according to Grigorenko, spent only 20 minutes with him, and were indifferent to the conversation between him and the chairman.

Criticisms of the conclusions reached by the Serbsky commission have come from several quarters. The group of 44 British and European psychiatrists in their letter (quoted in chapter 4) to *The Times* in 1971, contend that Grigorenko, whose case reports they have examined, "does not appear to have any symptoms at all which indicate a need for treatment, let alone treatment of such a punitive kind". The appraisal of the same documents by one of the authors (S.B.) and two psychiatric colleagues, led them to "believe that the data reveal no cause for compulsory detention in a psychiatric hospital".[21]

Dr Semyon Gluzman, a Kiev psychiatrist (see chapter 8), and two other anonymous Soviet colleagues, studied all the available evidence in the case and concluded that his "actions were rational and purposeful in character"; he was

> not suffering from mental illness and his condition during the period of his activities to which the charges relate cannot be considered a psychotic one of non-responsibility ... the decision of the [Serbsky] commission that Grigorenko is mentally ill is not legitimate because it is not stated explicitly what changes in his personality gave grounds for equating his condition with mental illness.[22]

Professor von Baeyer, one of Germany's most distinguished psychiatrists, and with long experience in forensic psychiatry, criticized the Serbsky report mainly on the basis of its reliance on "reformist ideas" as a manifestation of mental illness. Von Baeyer believed that the

> views held by Grigorenko and like-minded people contain nothing which in themselves can be considered absurd, bizarre, or egocentric as would be the case, for instance, in a paranoid schizophrenic delusion. In the documents that have reached the West, it is striking that the forensic diagnosis of psychiatric disturbances rests overwhelmingly on such "reformist ideas". Yet such ideas cannot be used as a proof of a mental disturbance with however much determination and feeling they may be expressed.[23]

He argued further that the arbitrary association between "reformist ideas" and defective "critical faculties, responsibility and self-control" would be considered inadmissible by German and other schools of psychiatry. Von Baeyer was forced "to suspect that assessments are not made on scientific and clinical grounds but are based on political and opportunist considerations".

Grigorenko's Trial

Grigorenko's trial took place in February 1970 in Tashkent. He was returned there to face charges of disseminating deliberate fabrications which defamed the Soviet system. He was not present at the proceedings, since he was declared "too ill" to defend himself. The recommendations of the Serbsky commission were accepted by the court, those of the Tashkent commission disregarded. As a result, Grigorenko was declared not responsible for the criminal acts with which he had been charged, and dispatched to the Chernyakhovsk Special Psychiatric Hospital for treatment.

The judicial process featured a series of procedural infractions that severely violated Grigorenko's legal rights. Prior to the trial, Mrs S. V. Kallistratova, his defence counsel, had petitioned the court on well-informed grounds for the conduct of a new and thorough investigation of her client's mental state. With compelling logic she pointed out that there were "two diametrically opposed conclusions of the commissions concerning Grigorenko's psychological condition".[24] According to the Uzbek Code of Criminal Procedure the conclusions of both commissions were subject to the appraisal of the court, and neither could take precedence over the other. Defence counsel argued that only a third opinion could resolve the court's predicament. She further contended that the Serbsky report was deficient on several grounds: there was no precise diagnosis of mental illness contained in it; the report contained a number of "inaccuracies, distortions and arbitrary assessments"; the diagnostic conclusion was clinically unsubstantiated. The works of many Soviet authorities were quoted in her arguments, including those of two of the very psychiatrists who had examined Grigorenko at the Serbsky, G. V. Morozov and D. R. Lunts. She used the latter's own published works to prove the fallaciousness of their Serbsky report. Kallistratova considered it essential that the court obtain and include in the file, specified medical documents which were highly pertinent to the question of Grigorenko's sanity. Finally, she requested that the court permit, according to article 144 of the Uzbek Code of Criminal Procedure, her client's choice of psychiatric experts for inclusion in a third commission.*

Kallistratova's petitions fell on deaf ears. None of her recommendations were accepted and Grigorenko's fate remained sealed by the Serbsky report. In April her appeal to the Uzbek Supreme Court was rejected and the decision of the lower court approved. On 26 May 1970 Grigorenko arrived at the special hospital in Chernyakhovsk.

About this time, Academician Andrei Sakharov and three colleagues filed a "supervisory complaint" about Grigorenko's case with the Procurator-General of the USSR. Under Soviet law, procurators are entitled to intervene in judicial procedures to correct irregularities; any citizen can request them to do so. Sakharov's group pointed out several infractions: the illegal use of physical force on Grigorenko in Tashkent, the rejection of defence counsel's insistence on correcting procedural

* Professors N. N. Timofeyev, chief psychiatrist of the Soviet Army, E. A. Shternberg of the Institute of Psychiatry of the Academy of Medical Sciences, and L. L. Rokhlin of the Institute of Psychiatry of the RSFSR Ministry of Health were designated as Grigorenko's choices.

infractions during the trial, the interrogation of only five witnesses in court out of the 30 listed, the examination of only three documents out of the 300 declared to be criminal, "the absence of a well-founded decision by the court on the question of Grigorenko's mental responsibility, and the over-ruling of defence counsel's request for a third examination to clear up the contradictions between the first and second".[25]

Obviously little heed was paid to the supervisory complaint, for Grigorenko remained in Chernyakhovsk and no additional legal proccedings were initiated.

Grigorenko's Hospital Internment

Grigorenko's four-year confinement in mental hospitals (three-and-a-half years in Chernyakhovsk and the remainder at an ordinary psychiatric hospital at Stolbovaya, just outside Moscow) was perhaps more harrowing than an equivalent camp term. The court had referred him to a hospital for medical treatment, but what he experienced bore little resemblance to conventional psychiatric care; the institution was considerably more like a prison in its operations than a hospital.

From the first days at Chernyakhovsk Grigorenko was harassed, and, along with his fellow inmates, legally deprived of all his basic rights. The attitude of the staff towards him was punitive rather than therapeutic. On his wife's first visit to the hospital, she was made to wait eight hours.[26] A warder, who was present throughout their meeting, threatened to stop it should the couple not confine themselves to a discussion of family matters. Mrs Grigorenko was refused access to her husband the following day, supposedly on account of their failure to adhere to the warder's instructions during the first meeting. Ultimately a short 20-minute session was allowed. Later, prior to their son's wedding, Grigorenko's wife, his son Andrei, and Andrei's fiancée, were refused permission to see him without explanation.[27]

These restrictions typified Grigorenko's internment. He also suffered other deprivations. He was regularly refused the opportunity to exercise or work; he was held for lengthy periods in solitary confinement; he was deprived of paper and pen, except for brief periods when he could write letters, duly censored; and at one stage, despite a painful infection of his bladder, he was not permitted a bed-pan in his room and access to a toilet was severely curtailed.

The patient was examined every six months by a commission which recommended repeatedly his continued detention at Chernyakhovsk. Ultimately, in January 1973, after nearly three years there, a commission advised the court that Grigorenko be transferred to an ordinary psychiatric hospital (the commission was composed of a visiting Serbsky psychiatrist, the chief psychiatrist of the Chernyakhovsk hospital and Grigorenko's personal doctor). The Chernyakhovsk city court, however, rejected this recommendation on the grounds that "Grigorenko, after his first discharge in 1965, had resumed his former activities".[28]

Legally, the court had the power to make this judgment, however questionable, as it had the final say over the disposition of a patient sent to hospital through a criminal commitment. Definitely illegal, however, was its failure to summon Grigorenko's wife, his legal representative, to the proceedings, or even inform her about them. She learnt of the court's decision only three months later and was thus deprived of the opportunity to appeal at the appropriate time, a right guaranteed by the procedural code. She now resorted to an appeal to the Kaliningrad regional court, explaining the irregularities of the lower court and arguing that "such a court decision distorts the very essence of the institution of compulsory medical detention, and transforms compulsory treatment into unlawful deprivation of freedom without a definite term".[29]

The Kaliningrad court heard the appeal, revoked the decision of the Chernyakhovsk city court and sent the case back to it for review.[30] In July 1973 a revised decision was issued that Grigorenko be transferred to an ordinary psychiatric hospital near his home. The Procurator, however, contested the decision because it stipulated the location of the hospital. The appeals court again reviewed the case and satisfied the Procurator by ordering Grigorenko's transfer to an ordinary hospital without specifying its location. According to Soviet law the court decides only the type of hospital for compulsory treatment but not the location; this is left to the administrative organs. In Grigorenko's case Ministry of Health officials in his residential district were responsible for the selection of the hospital.

It is chilling to think that had he not been supported by his wife and son and many members of the human-rights movement, all of them well acquainted with the intricacies of Soviet law, he might have languished at Chernyakhovsk indefinitely, despite medical recommendations that special hospital care was no longer required.

Official Manipulation of Foreign Visitors

The final court decision, taken on 31 August, enabled the health officials to avoid transferring Grigorenko to a hospital near his home, where he could have received numerous visitors, including foreign journalists. Instead they chose one 60 kilometres from Moscow, safely beyond the 40-kilometre limit which foreigners cannot cross without special permission. But at least the officials felt unable—in view of the mounting pressures at home and abroad[31]—to delay the transfer any longer. On 1 September a letter in *The Times* called on psychiatrists due to attend a World Psychiatric Association (WPA) conference in the USSR a month later to demand to visit Grigorenko in Chernyakhovsk, and on 8 September Sakharov made a similar appeal at a press conference.[32] So, as foreigners could not be allowed to see the conditions in the special hospitals, and as an outright refusal would look bad, prudence dictated a quick transfer.

On 19 September 1973 Grigorenko was transported to psychiatric hospital No. 5, at Stolbovaya Station. The same day a mysterious "quarantine" was announced in the hospital, applicable to his section only. The result: he could receive no visitors or parcels.[33]

On top of this, Grigorenko also became the object of more intricate official manœuvres. When the secretary-general of the WPA, Dr Leigh, arrived early in the USSR to prepare for the conference, he was immediately summoned, on 5 October 1973, to see the deputy minister of health, Dr Dmitry Venediktov. Among other things, Venediktov announced his readiness to allow Western psychiatrists to visit Grigorenko.[34] Leigh had not requested this, but the Western campaign against Soviet abuses had become intense, and to the Soviet authorities it was crucial to defuse it.

The plan was carefully thought out. By offering a visit to a particular dissenter in specially-prepared circumstances, and by doing so before the conferees arrived, the latter's anticipated requests to visit other dissenters in the highly secret special hospitals could probably be diverted. And so it turned out.

Grigorenko was a good choice. His case had been much publicized in the West, he had been moved to a civilian hospital situated beyond the 40-kilometre limit, and he could be presented—when psychiatrists and journalists reached the hospital, but not before!—as "essentially cured after four years of careful treatment" and "soon due for release".

The last device was especially astute, as it would neatly, and at the last minute, deprive any seriously concerned foreign psychiatrist of what he most wanted: a chance to examine a well-known dissenter who was in a condition claimed by the authorities to require compulsory treatment.

On 15 October, after the WPA conference, Dr Leigh and Dr Carlo Perris of Sweden were taken to Stolbovaya. But here the official plan began to go awry: Grigorenko declined to talk to them until his wife was allowed to join the group with an interpreter in whom he had confidence. As Leigh and Perris failed to insist that this request be met, the worried authorities decided they could afford to play safe. By abandoning the whole enterprise they were bound to lose some face; but they would avoid the unpredictable consequences of Mrs Grigorenko arriving with an interpreter friend, and Leigh and Perris suddenly finding themselves confronted with a more equal situation: too much of the truth might then emerge, and after the visit not only would the hospital doctors and Leigh and Perris be able to give their versions to the press, but also Mrs Grigorenko.

The squandering by Leigh and Perris of the opportunity which Grigorenko had given them to set up a serious discussion caused keen disappointment to his family. His son Andrei wrote later: "The fact that the Western psychiatrists who visited Father in the hospital did not take steps to obtain an impartial interpreter, and were prepared to conduct a conversation through the official Soviet interpreter, can be explained only by an amazing lack of comprehension."[35] The two visiting psychiatrists did, however, ask the general how he felt. In reply, according to his own testimony, he said only this: "By comparison with Chernyakhovsk, here things are better."[36]

As his wife and son bitterly noted later, these words of a man so exhausted that he could not at the time even write, were mysteriously misreported and then constantly repeated, in their distorted form, through various media.[37] Oddly, the most accurate report came from Dr Georgy Morozov, who quoted Grigorenko as stating that he had "recently been feeling better".[38] Leigh, on the other hand, told the press that Grigorenko had said he was now being treated "very well".[39] And according to a widely-published article by a Soviet medical correspondent, Leigh had informed her: "General Grigorenko told me that he was content both with the care and with the treatment, which was having a beneficial effect on his health."[40]

Further mysteries surrounded the question of Grigorenko's ultimate release. Perris told reporters that the hospital director had informed him that a commission would recommend his release in a month's time.[41] Three days later Leigh gave an interview specially to deny this: "It could not be true. . . . No Soviet doctor had made any suggestion that the dissident might soon be released."[42] How Leigh knew what the hospital director had said to Perris better than Perris himself was not explained.

Still more mystery enveloped the matter of the general's sanity. First Perris told *Der Stern*: "Unfortunately he did not want to speak with us, and without our own investigation and conversations with him we cannot judge whether he is being held in the institution justly or unjustly."[43] Leigh took the same position. Three weeks later, however, Tass reported: "Professor Carlo Perris of Sweden testifies that the former General Grigorenko 'is really ill'. . . . 'I consider that my Russian colleagues have carried out a correct diagnosis of Grigorenko. . . .' This statement was carried by the Stockholm evening newspaper *Expressen*."[44] Efforts by Amnesty International members in Sweden to obtain from Perris an explanation of his extraordinary *volte-face* met with no success.[45]

Although these multiple mysteries clearly contained much more that was helpful than unhelpful to the Soviet authorities, and though neither doctor had breathed a word of criticism of Soviet psychiatry, the major propaganda coup the authorities had hoped for had, thanks to Grigorenko's foresight, eluded them. So they quickly turned to see what could be accomplished by allowing a selected Western journalist to visit the hospital.

The journalist chosen was Klaus Lempke of *Der Stern*, one of West Germany's largest weekly magazines. On 17 October 1973 Lempke and his photographer travelled to Stolbovaya, and two weeks later an illustrated article of eight pages appeared, to be syndicated soon after in various other countries.[46] Lempke reported on his two preliminary sessions with Dr Morozov in the Serbsky Institute, his talks with the Stolbovaya doctors, and an interview with Perris. But why had he not interviewed Grigorenko? Or his family? Or his friends? Regarding family and friends Lempke gave no explanation. As for Grigorenko himself, photographs had been permitted by the hospital officials but no interview. Under these distorted circumstances the bias of the article becomes more understandable, if not more excusable: nothing prevented Lempke from hearing the other side of the story from Grigorenko's family and friends.

The Serbsky sessions appear to have been carefully planned. In his long exposition of forensic-psychiatric methods in the Soviet Union, Morozov included numerous half-truths and one or two false statements (possibly caused by mis-translation), such as "The patient has the right to remove a psychiatrist from the examining commission". He then handed Lempke a copy of Grigorenko's case history, the yellowed pages of which gave the German the impression of genuineness.

But the document Lempke then quotes is clearly a falsified summary of the official psychiatric reports and other documents. Equally clearly, the falsification was done carelessly. The summary notes that Grigorenko was arrested in 1969 and ruled not responsible for a second time. Then it blunders: "Detention in a special clinic in Kazan." Grigorenko has of course never set foot in Kazan. The summary (as quoted by Lempke) also lies more subtly, this time about his activity prior to his 1969 arrest: "The patient again writes memoranda and leaflets: he is the only person who can reform the state." Grigorenko had never written anything of the sort, and not even the 1969 Serbsky report, with all its bias against him, had gone as far as to say he had.

Lempke then draws his own conclusions. Prominent people have protested about Grigorenko's internment, "but do they know whether Grigorenko is healthy or ill? When have they last seen him, spoken with him, lived with him?" Moreover,

"Where does the boundary lie in the Soviet Union between normality and madness?" Grigorenko wants to do something regarded as mad in the USSR, to found his own party: "Warnings do not deter him; on the contrary: his conviction that he is the only person who can save his country grows still stronger." (Here Lempke repeats the lie in Morozov's summary, and also the latter's distortion in calling Grigorenko's tiny group of 1963 a party.)

Then comes Lempke's apologia, which, because of the falsified summary and the absence of any corrective from interviews with family or friends, must have seemed quite plausible to the uninformed reader: "What is the result? His act is regarded as one of irrationality, of self-destruction. Is it surprising if the psychiatrists in this country regard his behaviour as sick?"

Here Lempke had presumably been influenced by the summary, one of the major falsifications of which had been the convenient omission of any mention of the Tashkent commission. However, had he done his homework and read that commission's report—published in the German edition of the Bukovsky documents the previous year—he would quickly have seen through Morozov's deceptions. Both the falsification of the summary and the fact that eminent psychiatrists like Professor Detengof saw nothing irrational in Grigorenko's actions would at once have been clear to him. At the last moment he would have been saved from the apologetics towards which Morozov and his own failure to interview Grigorenko's friends and relatives had been influencing him.

Lempke's article was not of course a full-blown apologia. From the Soviet viewpoint this was to the good: *Stern* readers would not have believed such an article. But his conclusions would clearly help to create doubts and to defuse protests. More had been achieved, in fact, through his widely-syndicated article than through the abortive Leigh–Perris visit. As for Grigorenko himself, the article provoked him, when he later read it, to a state of cold fury.[47]

Release and Subsequent Course

In January 1974 a psychiatric commission recommended the continuation of Grigorenko's treatment on the grounds that there was no guarantee that he would not resume his former activities. According to Grigorenko's son, Dr A. A. Kozhemya-kina, the deputy chief doctor of Stolbovaya, revealed her thoughts on Grigorenko when she said that "his death would suit all parties".[48] We surmise, however, that he in fact won his eventual release because the authorities feared the resultant publicity were he to die in a psychiatric hospital.

Grigorenko was by now 67 years old and in poor physical health—his heart condition was particularly serious. In May 1974 Grigorenko's wife and son held a press conference in which they reported that the hospital psychiatrists had informed the Serbsky Institute of the severity of Grigorenko's physical state and the need to discharge him. Ten days later, a commission recommended his release. Only after six weeks, on 24 June, did the court accept this recommendation. Mrs Grigorenko first learned of the court hearing when she received a telephone call on 25 June at 5 pm instructing her to come for her husband the following morning.

As for the "patient" himself, Grigorenko was informed only at 8 am on the morning of his discharge that he would be returning home later in the day. The actual timing may not have been fortuitous: this was the eve of President Nixon's visit to Moscow, and two days before, Andrei Sakharov, in an open letter to both Nixon and Brezhnev, had appealed for the release of 95 prisoners of conscience, among them Pyotr Grigorenko.

In chatting with foreign newsmen the same day, Grigorenko thanked all those who had supported him "for securing his release and prolonging his life". To one journalist he appeared "tired but completely rational after his five years of confinement".[49] At this point he only wanted to rest: ". . . I have become very tired, especially as my health has collapsed, my heart in particular; I want to rest and recover".[50] He would not indicate whether his political views had altered. His wife did say, however, that he had refused to disavow his attitudes on human rights throughout his internment, up to and including the final commission which recommended his discharge.

In the succeeding months little was heard about him. Grigorenko had endured a harrowing odyssey; many a time, as succeeding commissions reconfirmed his "insanity", he despaired of ever regaining his freedom. Now his natural need for rest was, ironically, supported by the KGB. Zinaida Grigorenko was summoned a few days after his discharge and advised to take him off to the country to relax. The KGB's motive was far from altruistic. It simply wanted the family out of reach of enquiring foreign journalists.[51]

Grigorenko soon interrupted his rest, however, with an appeal he initiated to the military authorities, asking for the payment of pension income of which he had been deprived during his hospitalization. Dissatisfied with their negative response, he brought the matter to a court in May 1975, which ruled that it was not competent to judge the issue.[52] Later in the year he addressed a public letter, with eleven others, in support of Sakharov, who had just won the Nobel Peace prize. The group congratulated Sakharov on his achievement and defended him from the vitriolic attacks that had been launched against him in the Soviet press.[53] Two months later, on Constitution Day, Grigorenko and Sakharov led a silent protest in Pushkin Square. With some 50 other Russians, they were demonstrating against what they regarded as the government's pervasive violations of the Soviet Constitution.

Grigorenko also resumed his support of the Crimean Tatars. In November 1975 he appealed to the Procuracy for the release of one of their leaders, Mustafa Dzhemilev, indicating that he was prepared to stand bail for him. After this was refused, Grigorenko participated in a press conference at which Western correspondents were provided with material about Dzhemilev's case; he also appealed to the UN for its intervention.[54] In May 1976 he issued a *samizdat* article on Dzhemilev and included a summary of the latter's major historical work on the Tatars.

The same month nine Soviet dissenters, Grigorenko among them, announced the creation of a citizens' group whose purpose was to monitor the observance by the Soviet government of the 1975 Helsinki agreement.[55]

With this spate of dissenting activity, it was perhaps no surprise that the KGB summoned Grigorenko in early 1976 to warn him to stop taking an interest in Dzhemilev's case.[56] At about the same time a threatening article appeared in the Soviet press attacking Grigorenko, and alleging ominously that his wife had received money from dubious sources abroad.

The intent was clear: hinting at the possibility of a criminal case being brought against his wife, the authorities might deter Grigorenko from his dissent.[57]

THE CASE OF NATALYA GORBANEVSKAYA

Natalya Gorbanevskaya, an accomplished poet, achieved widespread recognition as a leading dissenter with the publication in the West of her book *Red Square at Noon* in 1970.[58] At noon on 25 August 1968 she and six other demonstrators sat peacefully for some minutes in Moscow's Red Square to protest against the Soviet invasion of Czechoslovakia. Her book is a vivid account of that extraordinary event and its sequel. Almost as soon as their banners were unfurled, plainclothed KGB men rushed up to the protesters, tore their banners away, and assaulted them. All were immediately arrested and detained, but Gorbanevskaya was released some hours later, possibly because she had a three-month-old child. Her co-protesters were subsequently punished by prison or exile, or in the case of Viktor Fainberg committed to a special psychiatric hospital.

Three days later, as the only protester still at liberty, she sent a letter to the editors of several foreign newspapers informing them of what had occurred. The final paragraph of her letter reveals the robustness of Gorbanevskaya's spirit:

My comrades and I are happy that we were able to take part in this demonstration, that we were able, if only for a moment, to interrupt the torrent of bare-faced lies and the cowardly silence, to show that not all the citizens of our country are in agreement with the violence which is being used in the name of the Soviet people. We hope that the people of Czechoslovakia have learned, or will learn about this. The belief that the Czechs and the Slovaks, when thinking about the Soviet people, will think not only of the occupiers, but also of us, gives us strength and courage.[59]

The Red Square protest was one of many notable episodes in Gorbanevskaya's career as a human-rights activist. Only in December 1969 did the KGB eventually silence her by resorting to psychiatry. As in the case of Grigorenko, the Serbsky

Institute played a prominent rôle when it declared her mentally ill and not responsible. The result was Gorbanevskaya's confinement in a special hospital in Kazan.

She early became aware of the psychiatric repression of dissent. In 1966 she wrote a biting poem on hearing that her friend Yury Galanskov, a dissenter who became a *cause célèbre* and focal point in *samizdat* circles in the mid-1960s, had been forcibly admitted to the Kashchenko hospital.

> In the madhouse
> wring your hands,
> press your pale forehead against the wall
> like a face into a snow drift.
> Into the hosts of violence
> with cheerful face
> Russia falls
> as if into mirrors.
> For her son
> a dose of Stelazine,*
> For herself—the Potma convoy.†[60]

Gorbanevskaya's sensitivity to human rights and her general political awareness showed themselves for the first time in 1956 when at the age of twenty she began to write poems with a political flavour. She had her first encounter with the KGB the following year in Lubyanka prison. The one-and-a-half day interrogation there is a painful memory for her because of the evidence which she eventually gave against her friends. Undeterred, Gorbanevskaya continued her dissent by contributing poems to two *samizdat* magazines, *Phoenix* and *Syntaksis*, and by composing other poems critical of various injustices she believed were practised by the régime.

In 1959 she voluntarily admitted herself to the Kashchenko hospital with complaints of irritability, extreme fatigue and insomnia. She had been both working and studying by correspondence and felt completely worn out. A prominent symptom then was an unpleasant sensation in her fingertips. She could not touch paper or bear others to touch it. She felt

---

* A tranquillizer widely used in the treatment of certain major mental illnesses.

† Potma is one of the main prison-camp complexes in the USSR.

irritated by its rustle. When she mentioned the KGB interrogation of two years earlier, the attitude of her psychiatrists altered
dramatically. Was this a delusion of persecution, a feature of a
psychotic mind? The doctors could have checked easily
enough with the KGB to confirm the Lubyanka episode, and
according to Gorbanevskaya, probably did. Nevertheless,
schizophrenia was diagnosed.

It was this diagnosis that was to prove so fateful for her in
April 1970 when a Serbsky commission examined her to determine whether she was responsible or not for her alleged slander
of the Soviet system. The commission's report stated of the
Kashchenko episode in 1959: "She did not mind the hospital
surroundings, but suddenly asked the doctor for her discharge,
saying she was afraid she would become mentally ill through
auto-suggestion."[61]

Gorbanevskaya's recall differs: "During these two weeks I
became so ill that when I finally got out I swore never to go
into hospital again. I should add that in spite of the diagnosis,
'schizophrenia', in all the years that have passed since, I have
never had cause to contemplate further hospital treatment, nor
has any doctor suggested it."[62]

We are uncertain about the exact nature of the illness in
1959. Gorbanevskaya displayed various features of neurotic
depression and anxiety. The abnormal sensation in her fingertips was in all probability an example of an hysterical conversion reaction in which, typically, intolerable emotions are
converted into an abnormal bodily change, such as paralysis
of a limb, anaesthesia of an area of skin, blindness or deafness;
the changes are reversible through hypnosis or psychotherapy
and have no organic basis.

During the first year after her discharge, Gorbanevskaya was
classified as a third category invalid and treated at her local
psychiatric clinic. Her insomnia rapidly disappeared (she told
us that the 1970 Serbsky report erred when it stated that she
continued to be troubled by poor sleep). In 1963 she graduated
from Leningrad University and began to work as a translator
and editor. At the same time she became progressively more
active as a dissenting poet and human-rights activist. During
the next five years she was exceedingly productive: several
collections of verse, eager participation in the human-rights
movement; and no further need for psychiatric consultation.

The trial of Galanskov and Alexander Ginzburg in January 1968 provoked Gorbanevskaya in a very personal way. She had become acquainted with them at the time they had been involved with the publication of *Phoenix* and *Syntaksis*. Now she instigated a collective letter to the chairman of the Moscow city court demanding an open trial for the defendants and asking permission for the signatories to attend.[63] Gorbanevskaya was also one of the 30 who sent a letter to *Komsomolskaya Pravda* expressing their protest against its publication of an article dealing with the trial, which they stated was full of distortions.

A month later, probably as a result of her vigorous defence of her friends, she was forcibly transferred from a maternity hospital where she was being treated for a threatened miscarriage to, once again, the Kashchenko hospital. The transfer was arranged under the most bizarre circumstances, without warning to the patient, and without her family's knowledge.

Gorbanevskaya's account of this episode in her essay "Free Medical Aid" reads like a horror story.[64] The maternity hospital, she found, had an "utterly depressing effect" on her and she "came to the conclusion that she would feel better at home". For three days her doctors agreed that she was free to leave but stalled repeatedly, as if their hands were tied. The uncertainty of the situation, the mysterious delaying tactics of the staff and the news that Alexander Volpin (see chapter 3) had been forcibly committed to Kashchenko at about the time of her admission, all served to intensify her sense of distress and insecurity.

Her anxieties mounted on the fourth day, when she suspected more than ever that she might be destined to share Volpin's fate. A duty psychiatrist arrived to interview her and inquired about her mental-hospital admission in 1959 and why she had "refused to eat" the previous day. Gorbanevskaya explained that she had felt upset and had lost her appetite, but that later in the day she had eaten a meal. (Serbsky psychiatrists would later refer to this episode and falsely state that Gorbanevskaya had been transferred to Kashchenko because of her refusal of food.) The next day two friends who had come to the hospital with the hope of taking her home were informed that she had been transferred to Kashchenko the evening before because of her strange behaviour, her repeated requests to be discharged and her refusal to eat.

Paradoxically, after a week in Kashchenko Gorbanevskaya was discharged as not in need of treatment. According to the later Serbsky report, she exhibited no active psychological disorder during this week; yet the Kashchenko's diagnosis had been "sluggish schizophrenia".*

Gorbanevskaya's concluding paragraph in "Free Medical Aid" starts with conjecture but ends on a note of defiance. The harrowing episode evidently fortified her resolve to protest against such injustice:

> If I had not been pregnant, I would not have been taken from the maternity hospital but straight from home in the first place, brutally and openly, as was done with Volpin. . . . I do not know whether my conviction that the KGB was mixed up in this convinces other people. Whether it was or not, the arbitrary nature of it all is obviously a blatant injustice. The final thing I ought to say is that if they wanted to frighten me, unbalance me, traumatize me, they did not succeed. I await the birth of my child quite calmly, and neither my pregnancy nor his birth will prevent me from doing what I wish—which includes participating in every protest against any act of tyranny.

Gorbanevskaya was in fact no mere participant in her next enterprise. As revealed later, she was "the moving force in the founding in spring 1968 of the *Chronicle of Current Events*. She organized the *Chronicle*'s publication, and her activity determined in many ways its style, structure and principles."[65]

In August of the same year Gorbanevskaya took part in the Red Square demonstration. Although released within a few hours, she was taken eleven days later to the Serbsky Institute for an out-patient examination. The explanation for this lay in her past history of psychiatric illness and her two admissions to Kashchenko.

Her own description of the encounter has a touch of the absurd. The commission was chaired by Professor Daniil Lunts. He played the dominant rôle in an interview which bore only slight resemblance to a conventional examination:

* We discuss this peculiarly Soviet concept in chapter 8. The Russian word is *vyalotekushchaya*. The term connotes a mild, continuous form of schizophrenia.

I knew very well what Lunts stood for and how little the outcome of the examination would depend on anything I said. Nevertheless, I behaved properly and answered all the questions—about my past illness, about Czechoslovakia, and whether I liked Wagner. I do not like Wagner. What possible import can such a question have during a psychiatric examination? Who is to be declared sane—the person who likes Wagner or the one who does not? No—that is just me asking myself questions now. At the time I simply told Lunts that, no—I did not like him. "Whom do you like then?" "Mozart, Schubert, Prokofiev."[66]

A week later Gorbanevskaya heard the result of the examination—"deep psychopathy, the possibility of sluggish schizophrenia is not excluded", and the commission's recommendation—"should be declared not responsible and placed in a special psychiatric hospital for compulsory treatment".[67] However, in a rare example of non-compliance with a Serbsky recommendation, the Procurator closed the case against Gorbanevskaya in the light of her insanity and because she had two young children. Instead, she was placed under her mother's guardianship. Gorbanevskaya surmised at the time that "the possibility is not excluded that Professor Lunts's conclusion may yet re-echo in my life".[68] She was justified in anticipating more of the same. Eighteen months later she would once again enter the portals of the Serbsky, and on this occasion the legal authorities would abide by its recommendation.

While free, Gorbanevskaya continued to dissent with unabated vigour. She set about compiling a documentary record of the Red Square demonstration and the trial of her fellow protesters. *Red Square at Noon* appeared in *samizdat* in late 1969 and was read widely. In May of that year she became a founder member of the Action Group for the Defence of Human Rights, which we discussed in chapter 3. On the first anniversary of the invasion of Czechoslovakia a group of dissenters, including Gorbanevskaya, issued a declaration expressing "the pain we feel for our homeland, which we wish to see truly great, free and happy". The group was firmly convinced that "a people which oppresses other peoples cannot be free or happy".[69] Three of the seventeen signatories—

Gorbanevskaya, Grigorenko and Leonid Plyushch—were all destined for criminal commitment to a special hospital.

October 1969 saw another psychiatric examination. Gorbanevskaya received a 'phone call from the office of Dr. I. K. Yanushevsky, Moscow's chief psychiatrist. Would she please attend for examination on 19 November as he considered it desirable to remove her from the psychiatric register. She interpreted this development as KGB inspired—probably her arrest was impending and there was a plan afoot to have her sent to a camp rather than to a psychiatric hospital. A clean bill of mental health was required.

The "patient" met Dr Yanushevsky and about a dozen of his colleagues for half an hour. She recognized some of her examiners as psychiatrists from the clinic she had attended in the past. Among the enquiries, they asked about her stay in the Kashchenko almost two years before, about her alleged refusal of food whilst she was a patient in the maternity hospital, and whether she now regarded herself as mentally ill. After a two-hour conference Yanushevsky disclosed the commission's conclusions to her: no symptoms of schizophrenia were present, but she had a psychopathic personality. Although this was not an illness *per se* but a description of her character, it could give rise to complications in her mental health. It was therefore advisable that she should remain on the register to receive supervision when necessary. The official conclusion of the commission, included among the Bukovsky documents, is an accurate summary of what Yanushevsky explained to her: "On the basis of a study of the history of the illness, of her medical record over more than ten years, and of an examina-tion—there are no grounds for a diagnosis of schizophrenia. Psychopathic personality with symptoms of hysteria and a tendency to decompensation. At the present time she has no need of treatment in a psychiatric hospital."[70]

Gorbanevskaya was baffled by the Yanushevsky episode and by the large number of examiners on the commission. She remained so when we discussed this with her in 1976. She has two slightly different hypotheses. Either the KGB had now definitely destined her for a labour camp, not a hospital, and had therefore hinted to Yanushevsky that it would be con-venient for her psychiatric slate to be wiped clean. Or Yanushev-sky realized that KGB action on her was imminent and *on his own initiative* wanted to stymie the KGB option of psychiatric internment out of a desire to avoid further involvement in the case: at this time Soviet psychiatric abuse was beginning to attract publicity. Gorbanevskaya had not long to wait: the KGB soon showed its hand.

On 24 December 1969 she was charged with slander of the Soviet system under article 190–1. Because of a minor scuffle during a search of her flat, when an investigator attempted to confiscate some highly personal material, she was also charged under article 191 for resisting police in the performance of their duties.

After three months of detention in the Butyrka prison, she was transferred to the Serbsky Institute and examined by a commission which included Dr G. Morozov and Professor Lunts. The psychiatrists concluded:

> Gorbanevskaya is suffering from a chronic mental illness in the form of schizophrenia ... the present psychiatric examination reveals in Gorbanevskaya the presence of changes in the thinking processes and in the emotional and critical faculties, which are characteristic of schizophrenia. Therefore, as a mentally-sick person, and in relation to the actions incriminating her, performed in a state of illness, she must be ruled not responsible. Because of her mental condition and in connection with the persistence of the pathological features which determine her conduct, Gorbanevskaya should be sent for compulsory treatment to a psychiatric hospital of special type.[71]

Comment on the Serbsky Report

Puzzlingly, the conclusion of the Yanushevsky commission is sharply contradicted soon after by the Serbsky diagnosis of *chronic* schizophrenia. The latter is reached on the basis of a change in Gorbanevskaya's thought processes held to be characteristic of schizophrenia; but the only reference to her thinking describes it as "at times paralogical and inconsistent". No illustrations are provided of the alleged thought disorder. The same deficiency appears with regard to the other criteria the Serbsky commission considers typical of schizophrenia— pathological changes in the emotional and critical faculties.

These details would be crucial to a diagnosis of schizophrenia. Indeed, the details that *are* provided in the report point to a person who is aware of the reasons for her examination, converses willingly, remains calm, and admits to the brief episode of mental illness in 1959.

Striking is the psychiatric interpretation of her political views. During the examination, Gorbanevskaya expresses her ideas on why she is being examined and the moral basis on which she conducts her life. Her comments are placed in quotes in such a way as to convey the impression of a paranoid mind. However, they make considerable sense in the light of her rôle as a dissenter. She feels that she has been sent for examination "so that there should be no noise", "because it suits the procurator". Later we will argue that the use of psychiatry for political repression is in part motivated by these very factors.

Gorbanevskaya is also quoted as stating with reference to her dissent "that she acted thus so as not to be ashamed in the future before her children". So, while she explains her moral need to express her political convictions, the psychiatrists deem her comments to reflect a lack of critical faculties. The commission reports that she "does not renounce her actions, thinks she has done nothing illegal" and is "unshakeably convinced of the rightness of her actions". It then implies that she was too disturbed to recognize that writing *Red Square at Noon*, sending a letter to the UN Commission on Human Rights, and other similar acts, were actually criminal in nature.

In a study by one of the authors (S.B.) and two colleagues of the available documents on Gorbanevskaya, as well as of the writings of the poet herself, no significant evidence could be marshalled to warrant a diagnosis of schizophrenia.[72] The group of 44 British and European psychiatrists, in their evaluation of Gorbanevskaya, acknowledge that, according to the official diagnostic reports, she suffered symptoms of mental illness at an earlier period in her life, but "these were minor involving only a two-week voluntary stay in hospital and there was apparently no recurrence of them for seven years preceding the Red Square demonstration". The group infers that Gorbanevskaya was diagnosed and hospitalized on political rather than medical grounds.[73]

A British psychiatrist who carefully examined the documentation arrives at a similar conclusion. Dr Sidney Crown writes in a lengthy report that there seems

> to be little acceptable evidence that she is suffering from a severe mental disorder such as schizophrenia. In particular it seems impossible that in terms of the two psychiatric examinations made upon her a few months apart she could change from having a diagnostic formulation of psychopathic personality with hysterical features, the diagnosis of Dr Yanushevsky, to a diagnosis of "a chronic mental illness in the form of schizophrenia". In addition to this, no unequivocal, and particularly no detailed evidence is given to suggest changes in thinking and emotional response that would be necessary in Gorbanevskaya to make a diagnosis of schizophrenia.[74]

Dr Crown considers that compulsory treatment is not indicated, but rather treatment on an out-patient basis involving tranquillizing drugs, psychotherapy and a return to the family environment.

Gorbanevskaya's Trial

Gorbanevskaya's trial took place on 7 July 1970 in the Moscow city court. A 20-page *samizdat* account of the proceedings is available[75] which clearly owes much to V. Chalidze, an active member of the human-rights movement. Out of some twenty friends who tried to attend only Chalidze was allowed into the court-room.

The trial, like that of Grigorenko, was held without the presence of the defendant, on account of her "illness". Professor Lunts, the psychiatric witness, later indicated that medical opinion generally opposed the participation of a mentally-ill defendant in his own trial, since the patient was not only the object of investigation, but also an invalid whom doctors were obliged to care for.[76] Gorbanevskaya was thus deprived of the chance to participate in her own defence.

Her counsel, Sofia Kallistratova, who also acted for Grigorenko, responded to the judge's call for petitions and requested a postponement, as she had been given only two days to study the several volumes of trial documents. Counsel also requested that the case be referred back for further investigation: the charges against her client failed to specify what acts she was accused of, and when precisely they were committed; instead it was almost a verbatim quotation of article 190–1. Defence counsel could not therefore determine which of her acts were viewed by the investigators as falling under the article.

Kallistratova's third petition was an exact replica of her defence of Grigorenko some months earlier and concerned the crucial need for a new psychiatric examination. In the space of five months, counsel argued, Dr Yanushevsky's commission had declared that there were no grounds for a diagnosis of schizophrenia and no need for institutional treatment, while Dr Morozov's commission had reached an entirely contrary formulation. Kallistratova contended further that the Serbsky report left much to be desired—"no mention is made of the form of schizophrenia, not a single symptom of mental derangement is adduced".

Defence counsel also petitioned for inclusion in the case of Gorbanevskaya's letters to her mother and children, and for the summoning of witnesses who had known the defendant over many years and were qualified to testify to her character.

The prosecutor objected to all these petitions: there was no reason for appointing a new commission; the expert findings could not be declared groundless before their evaluation by the court; and the materials of the case were adequate, precluding the need for additional documentation or testimony. The prosecution concurred with only one petition from the defence, that Gorbanevskaya's mother gain admittance to the trial as her legal representative. The court accepted this last petition but rejected all the others. This judgement resulted in at least two probably critical omissions, the letters written by Gorbanevskaya to her mother and children, and the testimony of two close friends from which we quote below.

Gorbanevskaya's pre-trial letters are not available, but those written in Butyrka prison after sentence are.* They reveal

* Vladimir Bukovsky appended a note to the copies of these letters which he sent to the West. In this, he states that the earlier letters (referred to by Kallistratova) were similar in character and it was "no accident that the psychiatric experts refused to study them". See reference 74 (Weissbort, p. 124).

facets of her personality which contradict a salient feature of the Serbsky report. The letters are tender, warm and completely logical; there is nothing to suggest any abnormality in her thinking or emotional faculties. The following excerpt from a birthday letter to her son, Yasik, is typical:

> In general, I remember everybody all the time, regardless of birthdays, and you too Osenka, and granny, always. How are you helping granny? Have you learned how to use your time well so that there is enough of it for everything: school-work, pleasure, and household work? Here is an assignment for you. Before your next visit (it will be in December), arrange matters so that you won't waste any time pointlessly. When you come back from school, change your clothes quickly, do your homework quickly, and then by all means read, take a walk, or listen to music. And of course help granny particularly in her chores with Osik. And when you come for the visit, you will tell me how you carried out your assignment. Do you agree? I am already waiting impatiently for this visit. I was so happy to see you and very much want to see you again soon. Write me letters every week, find time for this on Saturdays or Sundays. Send me some drawings. I kiss you tenderly, tenderly.[77]

The Serbsky findings of a disturbance in Gorbanevskaya's critical faculties is not borne out by this excerpt from a letter to her mother:

> Mummy, I'm very sorry that my letters haven't been reaching you. I'll try to say the most important things quickly. I consider that everything I've done is morally right and justified. But I suffer because you and the children have to pay for my morally right activities. The weight that has fallen on you—this weight I have only fully appreciated in prison; before that, it seemed to me that suffering and deprivation would affect me alone. For this reason, believe me, no matter when I get out, and from whatever institution that may be, I will do everything I can so that you may live your remaining years in tran-quillity, and I will abstain (sad as that may be) from all this activity.[78]

The Serbsky commission obviously considered the nature of Gorbanevskaya's relationship with her mother and children as germane to its diagnosis: "She reveals no anxiety about her own future or the fate of her children"; she displays "an unfriendly attitude toward her mother".[79] The quoted excerpts from the letters clearly refute this evaluation. In addition, in her testimony in court her mother contradicted the Serbsky report by insisting that Gorbanevskaya was a "conscientious mother who loved her children very much". Although mother and daughter had had their differences, there was "no question of hostility" between them, and Natasha "had always been solicitous towards her".[80]

The testimony of two friends, mentioned above, took the form of an open letter to Soviet psychiatrists. It not only supports her mother's court statement about relationships within the family, but also attests to her sanity:

> We, her close friends, have known Natasha well for a long time, her character, her way of thinking and acting. And we affirm that the diagnostic conclusion is untrue. We have not noticed in Natasha any symptoms at all of mental illness; and if such symptoms had appeared we would have been the first to take the necessary measures for her treatment. We know, contrary to the claims of the diagnosis, that Natasha's relation to her children and mother was and is one of deep affection and care (her letters to them bear witness to this); and that her literary translations from various languages made it financially possible for her to maintain herself and her family.[81]

To return to the trial, Professor Lunts, in his evidence, buttressed the judgements and recommendations in the Serbsky report. Yet to specific questions raised by Kallistratova, he replied in the same general terms which typify that report. He commented for instance that "sluggish schizophrenia is not characterized by explicit, well defined, psychotic phenomena such as delusions, hallucinations, etc. The illness takes its course without affecting the patient's fitness for work or his former intellectual levels and skills."[82]

Defence counsel actually posed eleven specific questions for Lunts, six of which the court permitted. The procedure that ensued was curious, and seriously undermines the argument of Soviet psychiatrists that they serve the court system as wholly independent witnesses. Lunts, on hearing the list of questions submitted to him, expressed a need to consult medical documents kept at the Serbsky. This would necessitate a delay in reply until late the next day. The judge's subsequent announcement of an adjournment until then was reversed almost immediately and thereupon a break of an hour followed. Much of this period, Lunts, the prosecutor, judge and two assessors, spent in a huddle in an adjoining room. On the resumption of the hearing, Lunts replied to the defence's questions.

According to the professor, Gorbanevskaya was suffering from a sluggish form of schizophrenia which "has no clear symptoms" but results in abnormal changes in emotions, will and thought patterns. Memory, former knowledge and habits, by contrast, remain intact. She exhibited mental changes which superficially resembled improvement, but could not be viewed as such "from the theoretical point of view".[83] Gorbanevskaya might appear normal to her fellows, but an underlying illness still existed from the viewpoint of the psychiatrist.

Why was a *special* hospital necessary for the defendant? Lunts argued that in these hospitals a régime prevailed which facilitated the patients' adaptation to the conditions they would encounter on discharge. In addition, Gorbanevskaya's illness, characterized by psychopathological changes including the lack of insight into her own abnormal state but with the preservation of certain personality features, constituted a particular danger to the public. Further probing by Kallistratova produced an equally vague explanation—socially dangerous patients required not only drugs, but also a specific treatment régime, provided solely in psychiatric hospitals of special type. In chapter 8 we examine further these obscure points, also the form of schizophrenia which "has no clear symptoms".

What was this socially dangerous behaviour and how did Gorbanevskaya pose a threat to the public? Lunts at no stage clarified these crucial points. There was certainly no evidence of any propensity to act violently towards others. Was he referring to her beliefs—the convictions which had led her to "slander the state"?

The prosecutor, however, was more than satisfied. Lunts, he said, had explained in detail to the court that the defendant was suffering from a mental illness and required treatment. The authoritative findings should be respected, Gorbanevskaya exempted from criminal punishment and treated in the way recommended by the commission. As for the crimes committed by the defendant under article 190–1, these were several. She had taken part in an action which gravely violated public order when she protested in Red Square. Thereafter, she had written a tendentious letter to editors of foreign newspapers. She had circulated among her friends a book, *Red Square at Noon*, which gave a biased account of the demonstration; she had helped to compile the *Chronicle of Current Events*, a journal that maligned the Soviet Union and created the impression that arrests for anti-social activities made by the authorities were illegal; and she had written an essay, "Free Medical Aid", in which she claimed that the KGB had forcibly placed her in a maternity hospital and subsequently in a psychiatric hospital. Thus, the prosecutor argued, the documents in the case established that Gorbanevskaya had systematically prepared and circulated slanderous fabrications defaming the Soviet system.

Defence counsel requested a postponement of her final speech until the following day as the hour was late and she was utterly fatigued. The judge announced a five-minute recess. Kallistratova's request, like all the others she had made during the proceedings except for one, was denied. She thereupon asked that an entry be made in the record stating that the judge's denial was a violation of the rights of the defence.

Kallistratova now contended that her client, a talented poet and translator (this had been ignored by the Serbsky report), had until her arrest worked usefully in her field, earning adequate funds to support her family. This satisfactory situation would be ended were her client to be hospitalized. Moreover, the evidence of mental illness in Gorbanevskaya was unsubstantiated. The Serbsky report revealed a large number of irregularities and its conclusions contradicted those of the Yanushevsky commission. The rejection by the court of the defence's petitions aimed at studying the Serbsky's conclusions was a violation of the defendant's rights.

Defence counsel then challenged each charge levelled by the

prosecution. The content of Gorbanevskaya's letter to foreign editors after the Red Square protest had been described as tendentious, but not as deliberately false and slanderous; therefore it could not be judged as criminal under article 190–1. Similarly, her book *Red Square at Noon* was not deliberately false and was critical of one criminal trial only; it did not express opinions about the Soviet political and social system as a whole. There was lack of evidence pointing to Gorbanevskaya as an author or distributor of the *Chronicle*. Testimony by one witness concerning a visit to Estonia by the defendant, supposedly to gather information for publication in the *Chronicle*, had been refuted by two other persons interrogated during the pre-trial investigation but denied access to the court as witnesses. The defence's petition to summon them had been unjustifiably denied.

Kallistratova did not regard Gorbanevskaya's essay "Free Medical Aid" as criminal. She had not asserted in it what the prosecution had charged—that the KGB had forced her into a maternity hospital and then transferred her to Kashchenko; rather, she had merely speculated about this possibility. As with other material cited by the prosecutor, "Free Medical Aid" contained no defamatory, anti-Soviet statements.

And so ended defence counsel's speech and, following the verdict, the trial. Gorbanevskaya was found guilty under articles 190–1 and 191. Because of her mental illness, however, she was declared not responsible and committed to a special hospital for an indefinite period, there to receive compulsory treatment.

An appeal against the court's decision heard three months later was rejected.[84] Thus in January 1971 Gorbanevskaya was transferred to the hospital in Kazan.[85] By now she had been detained for over a year. A further thirteen months followed before her final release, nine of them in Kazan and the remainder in the Serbsky. While awaiting transfer to Kazan, she declared a hunger strike. Her declaration conveys well her strength of spirit:

As a symbol of solidarity with the political prisoners in the Mordovian camps, in the Vladimir, Lefortovo and Butyrka prisons, in the Leningrad, Kazan and Chernyakhovsk special psychiatric hospitals, and in other places of imprisonment; as a protest against anti-constitutional political persecution, and in particular against my own arrest, protracted imprisonment and the deliberately false judgement that I am of unsound mind, I declare a hunger strike from 5 December, Constitution Day, to 10 December, Human Rights Day.[86]

In Kazan

Gorbanevskaya has described some aspects of her experience in Kazan. About the drug treatment given to her she reports: "They gave us Haloperidol every day without a break. I soon felt severe side effects; I had symptoms of Parkinsonism, that is, tremor of the hands. I suddenly could no longer read or write coherently. It was hard to sleep."

The attitudes of her doctors were "absolutely cynical". She describes two of them:

> The head of one section was Volkova. She was like a wild animal; she hated all political prisoners. When I told her that I did not tolerate Haloperidol very well, she said that this was only because the dose was too low and she doubled the amount. In the other section the head doctor was Nikiforova. She was more pleasant though not very intelligent. . . . She was sorry for me because of my children. She reduced the dose of Haloperidol and allowed me to receive antidotes from home, i.e. medication to counter the side effects. In Soviet clinics they do not have sufficient amounts of these antidotes.[87]

Gorbanevskaya described Dr Nikiforova to us as a deeply provincial and conformist woman. She revealed her ignorance of Soviet law by commenting: "We have never had such an anti-Soviet person as you." Yet Gorbanevskaya had been charged under the minor article of 190–1 whereas many other Kazan inmates had fallen foul of much more serious political articles such as 70. On another occasion she let slip a view typical of the Stalin period, that it was quite natural for anti-Soviet writers to be executed.

The "patient" discussed recantation several times with her doctors. Gorbanevskaya agreed to recant ultimately but only orally, not in writing. Her motive was simply to get out of the institution and back to her children as quickly as possible. She admitted that she had performed her criminal acts while in a state of mental illness and promised that she would not repeat such acts after her release. She strongly suspects that the psychiatrists appreciated the insincerity of her recantation and realized that it was only a charade. In fact they joked about it: even if the recantation was simulated, they said, she was ready for discharge. After all, competent simulation also signified clinical improvement!

The validity of her recantation was also raised by Professor Lunts in June 1971 when he examined Gorbanevskaya in Kazan as a member of the regular six-monthly commission; but he did so more obliquely, cautioning her: "If you are let out your friends will quickly drag you back into your previous activity even though you promise now that you will not resume it. It would be better to change your circle of friends."[88]

Gorbanevskaya's recantation has never been publicized nor was it ever mentioned when she attended the psychiatric clinic after her release. But it could of course be used against her, or the dissent movement, by the Soviet authorities in the future.

The fact that both Lunts and the Kazan psychiatrists clearly favoured her release was due above all, Gorbanevskaya believes, to the fact that she was well known in the West and her internment was attracting increasing publicity. Her book had been published in Germany and, more important, the Bukovsky documents were reaching a wide audience and arousing concern about the Soviet abuse. As Gorbanevskaya figured prominently in the documents, and as the Mexico WPA congress was approaching, she was becoming uncomfortably "hot to handle". The June commission from the Serbsky recommended the release of an unusually large number of Kazan inmates, including a substantial proportion of politicals. It also decided "in principle" to recommend Gorbanevskaya's release, subject to confirmation by an in-patient examination in the Serbsky itself.

In all these circumstances Gorbanevskaya was transferred to the Serbsky in October 1971. Two months later a commission confirmed the "in principle" decision. Then a two-month delay ensued until a court sanctioned her release. The official hesitancy revealed by this unprecedented stay in the Serbsky probably reflects Soviet nervousness over the WPA congress. When this ended in early December without any condemnation of Soviet psychiatry the KGB may have wavered over releasing her, just as it decided not to release a number of politicals in the Leningrad special hospital who had been prepared for discharge. But her book was now appearing in other languages, and this fact may well have tipped the balance. When she returned to her family in February 1972, two years and two months had passed since her arrest.

Subsequent Course

During the four years between her release and her emigration to France Gorbanevskaya resumed activity in the dissent movement, but in unobtrusive ways. She did not sign appeals, join a human-rights group, or stage demonstrations. Instead she contributed anonymous items to the *Chronicle* and took part in the movement's welfare work. She corresponded with political prisoners, and even managed to visit one of them twice in the Sychyovka special hospital. She also circulated in *samizdat* the poem she wrote on the death of her friend Yury Galanskov. She had protested about his trial in 1968, and now, five years later, he had died in a labour camp at the age of 33.[89]

Although this activity involved her in no direct dealings with the KGB, the latter maintained a careful surveillance through the psychiatrists at her local clinic. In March 1973, for instance, she returned from a holiday in Leningrad, where she had noticed people tailing her. At once she was called to the clinic: "Why have you been to Leningrad? Whom did you meet there? Whom did you stay with?"[90] Not typical psychiatric questions! Similar police-type enquiries were regularly posed during her visits to the clinic, which, though she was summoned monthly, in fact took place every two or three months.

Formally speaking, the psychiatrists dealt with her as an out-patient with a chronic illness, but in practice they never considered prescribing treatment. Their approach was in marked and revealing contrast to that of the Serbsky staff who had administered Haloperidol twice or thrice daily, even during the two months after recommending her release. They had impressed on her that she would have to take drugs indefinitely, as her schizophrenia—though now in remission—would be with her for life.

For two years Gorbanevskaya tolerated the clinic's psychiatrists, pretending not to be annoyed by their patent police rôle. In 1974, however, her patience, in the face of the regular summonses, eventually broke. She complained in a statement to the clinic director that her interviews amounted to nothing more than KGB surveillance: in future she would have no truck with them.

But Dr Ogorodnikova had formidable powers at her command. Gorbanevskaya was, after all, on the clinic's register and thus had no legal right to decline a summons. The doctor's response was to exclaim: "What's all this nonsense! If you refuse to come to the clinic, we'll come to you!"[91] At this point Gorbanevskaya recalled her promise not to cause suffering to her mother, and yielded. She would continue to attend but insisted that her complaint remain on the record.

Despite this retreat, she pursued the possibility of obtaining removal from the register. But this, she was told, would require a wait of at least five years from the moment of her application to the chief city psychiatrist. Even then, Gorbanevskaya reckoned, with her record as a "notorious dissenter", and with the KGB breathing down the doctors' necks, the chances of success would be minimal. Free in one sense—no longer an inmate of Kazan, she was a prisoner in another, trapped in a legally sanctioned vice of the KGB and psychiatry.

Not surprisingly she resorted to the only other viable option—emigration. From the time that she first applied for an exit visa until her eventual departure almost a year later, the clinic never once summoned her. The "treatment" was no longer necessary!

On 18 December 1975 Gorbanevskaya and her two sons arrived in Vienna. Two days later she issued an appeal for Vyacheslav Igrunov, an electrician from Odessa, whose trial was about to begin.[92] Charged with *samizdat* activity, Igrunov had been examined by a Serbsky commission and diagnosed as not responsible. Gorbanevskaya's appeal may have contributed to the result that Igrunov was committed to an ordinary, not a special psychiatric hospital.

She made her home in Paris and there joined the staff of *Kontinent*, a literary political journal founded by Russian émigrés in 1974. She continued to be closely concerned with violations of human rights in the Soviet Union and the plight of her fellow dissenters still languishing in prisons, labour camps and mental hospitals.

This concern, as well as her compassion, commonsense and intelligence, were abundantly clear to us when we had two long meetings with her in July 1976. We found it hard to believe that she had once been labelled a "sluggish schizophrenic".

The Serbsky Institute

In chapter 3 we briefly discussed the Serbsky in the 1940s and 1950s, and now we have seen its rôle in the cases of two well-known dissenters. In view of its key position in the system of criminal commitment and release we round off this chapter with a summary profile of it.

The Central Scientific Research Institute for Forensic Psychiatry—to give it its full title—named after V. P. Serbsky, is the subject so far of only one detailed account by an independent author. This is an as yet unpublished manuscript of 200 pages by a dissenter, Victor Nekipelov. By profession a pharmacist and a poet, Nekipelov was arrested in 1973 for his *samizdat* activity, through which he had become friendly with Leonid Plyushch in Kiev and numerous colleagues of his in Moscow. Charged under article 190–1, he was sent in January 1974 to the Serbsky, where he spent two months. At the end he was ruled responsible—thanks, he believes, to the Western campaign of 1973 against Soviet abuses—then sentenced to two years of forced labour in a camp.[93] After his release, he published in *samizdat* in 1976 his *Institute of Fools: Notes on the Serbsky Institute.*[94] The manuscript is based in part on the diary he kept during his two-month in-patient examination, in part on his accurate memory, and also, to a small extent, on the reports of fellow-dissenters. It is of the greatest value because, although it contains no startling revelations, it confirms what we know from various sources, including official ones, and presents a careful, systematic account, with much detail and numerous examples. Nekipelov also takes pains at each step to indicate the limits of his knowledge, stressing, for example, that in most respects his information does not extend beyond section 4 of the institute, the one to which apparently all dissenters are assigned. The following is, then, in the main, a short résumé of Nekipelov's evidence, which we hope will soon be published in full.

Nekipelov has no doubt that the Serbsky, though ostensibly under the Ministry of Health, is effectively controlled by the Ministry of Internal Affairs, or MVD. He believes that virtually all its personnel have military-style MVD ranks, the doctors being officers, and the nurses and orderlies sergeants and privates. The security guards who patrolled the corridor of section 4 in three shifts wore, under their white coats, the uniforms of ensigns. And Lunts, according to "well-informed people" (clearly Serbsky employees), was, in 1974, a major-general. In chapter 8 we quote corroborative evidence that Lunts is indeed an MVD officer.

The institute is headed by Dr Georgy Morozov, who as we have seen, plays an active part in the work of section 4. The Serbsky has seven sections in all for inmates, of whom there were in 1974 about 300. Overcrowding existed in two of the sections, where some prisoners had to lie on mattresses on the floor. Section 4 specialized in certain types of schizophrenic, section 7 in alcoholics, and number 5 contained women. Sections 1, 2, 3 and 6 apparently specialized in other types of mental illness. Numbers 1 and 2 were the largest, the first containing about 100 inmates. The institute had a big lecture-hall and catered for students of law and medicine by running seminars and other courses.

Section 4 contained 34 beds laid out in six wards, as can be seen from the ground-plan. Three wards, with ten beds in all, held those inmates of the section who had been charged with the most serious offences both of a political and of a criminal, i.e. non-political nature. These wards, known as "the box", were sealed off, specially guarded, and self-contained; in two months Nekipelov learnt virtually nothing about who was in them. As a political charged under article 190–1, he himself could have been placed either in "the box" or, as in fact happened, in one of the three wards where the inmates could move about rather freely. These contained 24 beds, and as the average person stayed for one month, he saw about 50 fellow prisoners, of whom he spoke with over 30. Only two of these, whom he met on arrival, were politicals. Fortunately, the *Chronicle* fills a gap by naming seven politicals who at this time,

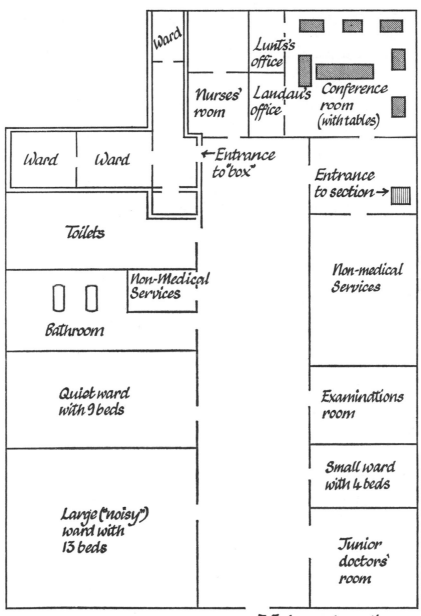

Ward

Lunts's office

Nurses' room

Landau's office

Conference room (with tables)

← Entrance to "box"

Ward

Ward

Entrance to section →

Toilets

Non-Medical Services

Non-medical Services

Bathroom

Quiet ward with 9 beds

Examinations room

Small ward with 4 beds

Large ("noisy") ward with 13 beds

Junior doctors' room

↖ Entrance to section from side facing yard

Ground-plan of section 4 of the Serbsky Institute, 1974, as drawn by Viktor Nekipelov

January 1974, were in "the box",[95] so we can be sure that in section 4 there were then not less, and probably not more, than ten politicals in all. One or two women politicals—an estimated average figure—were probably held in section 5 at the same time.

Nekipelov describes the diagnostic and research tests carried out on him and other prisoners, and reaches the conclusion that the quality of the equipment and the research seemed to be poor. On the other hand, the prisoners' conditions were mostly excellent. The ward was clean, the food tasty and abundant, the beds had sheets, and parcels could be handed in by relatives once a week. Many inmates—but not politicals—were even allowed meetings with relatives. By contrast, a major inadequacy was that, as exercise periods were not provided for in the winter, the prisoners got no taste of fresh air. Nekipelov made repeated protests on this point and was eventually, by way of exception, allowed a short walk in a yard.

More importantly, Nekipelov criticizes in his book certain procedures much used in section 4. Many inmates underwent injections of "truth" drugs,* accompanied by doctors' interrogations and even, as Nekipelov once witnessed, by female doctors' sexual advances. Also extensively practised was the administration of tranquillizing drugs, and their occasional use in large doses as punishment for misdemeanours. This Nekipelov deplores, as the doctors' job was only diagnosis and they had no authority to administer compulsory treatment—a measure which can be ordered only by a court. In addition, he condemns the strong pressure put by psychiatrists on several patients to agree to undergo lumbar and ventricular punctures, and describes the frightening effects on a friend of his of one such puncture which was incorrectly carried out.

Finally, Nekipelov draws psychologically penetrating portraits of almost all the staff in section 4, including each of the eleven doctors. While Lunts apparently headed the section, Dr Yakov L. Landau, whom we mention in chapter 8, ran it when Lunts was absent, and seemed to have a similarly high status. Their deputy was Dr Margarita F. Taltse, and slightly junior to her were four psychiatrists with doctoral degrees,

* He is much less sure than Bukovsky and Gluzman in their "Manual" (see appendix VI) that these are ineffective.

Lyubov I. Tabakova (Nekipelov's psychiatrist), Alfred A. Azamatov, Albert A. Fokin, and a woman with the first name and patronymic of Svetlana Makarovna.* The doctors assiduously concealed their surnames, and of the four most junior ones Nekipelov could find out the full name only of Valentina V. Lavrenteva. The first names and patronymics of the others were Gennady Nikolaevich, Alla Ivanovna, and Maria Sergeyevna.

Nekipelov discusses with imagination and compassion the formative influences on these doctors, pointing to the ironic fact that while part of their time went on proving sane dissenters insane, against their will, most of the rest went on frustrating the will of criminals who were simulating mental illness to try to avoid fifteen-year terms in camps—or the death penalty. Like Morozov,[96] he stresses that only the most tricky, borderline cases (from all over the country) are normally sent to the Serbsky, and he estimates that no more than about 15 per cent of all its inmates are ruled not responsible. He concludes, however, that in their treatment of dissenters the doctors are, in the final analysis, consciously unethical. Their motives are mostly the humdrum ones of careerism and intellectual and political conformism, vices often laced with straightforward cynicism, laziness or stupidity. Fanaticism does not feature in his account, which tends to support the theory of the banality of evil. He believes that one day the doctors will be brought to trial for their actions. But he hopes, as a humane and sensitive man, that such trials will be more educational than vengeful in their purpose. We return to this crucial theme of psychiatrists' motives in chapter 8.

* Probably S. M. Gerasimova. See *Chronicle* 32.

Chapter 6

THE PRACTICE: CIVIL COMMITMENT

THE ALTERNATIVE TO criminal commitment is civil commitment. In this chapter we examine the procedure and its application to dissenters. Two cases are described to illustrate how civil commitment forces the "patient" into hospital—those of Zhores Medvedev and Gennady Shimanov. Shimanov serves also as an excellent example of how psychiatry is used to suppress certain types of religious activity.

The Procedure of Civil Commitment

A set of instructions, entitled "Directives on the Immediate Hospitalization of Mentally-Ill Persons Who Are a Social Danger" was formulated by the Ministry of Health in coordination with the Procurator's office and the Ministry of Internal Affairs in 1961.[1] Although this is an important legal document, it is, oddly enough, virtually unobtainable for both Soviet citizens and foreigners. It was only with much difficulty that we obtained the Russian text; its revised form of 1971, moreover, is to our knowledge still not available in full in the West.

The 1961 directives govern the way in which the medical profession intervenes in a case of a person requiring urgent and compulsory hospitalization; the focus is on the prevention of dangerous acts by the mentally-ill person to those around him or to himself. The directives state: "If there is a clear danger from a mentally-ill person to those around him or to himself, the health organs have the right (by way of immediate psychiatric assistance) to place him in a psychiatric hospital without the consent of the person who is ill or his relatives or guardians."

A single psychiatrist can effect a civil commitment and, in districts lacking psychiatric institutions, a general doctor may do so. The doctor is obliged to provide full details of the medical and social reasons for his judgement. He may be assisted by the police when relatives or guardians or the ill person himself resist the hospitalization. In the psychiatric institution, the committed person must be examined by a three-member panel of psychiatrists within 24 hours. The panel decides on the appropriateness of the commitment and the need for further compulsory treatment. Closest relatives must be informed of its decision.

The mentally-ill person is placed in a section of the hospital appropriate to his condition, to receive treatment. A commission of three psychiatrists is obliged, without exception, to examine the patient at least once a month (in contrast to the minimum of six months in cases of criminal commitment) to determine the need for continuing the compulsory treatment. When the mental condition has improved or the social danger has passed, the commission arranges for the patient's release. His relatives are informed as to where he must attend for follow-up care, should this be made a provision of his release. In the case of a person without family or still in a condition requiring supervision, the hospital arranges for suitable guardianship.*

The above points in the directives are relatively unambiguous, but their catalogue of mental states which justify commitment is, on the contrary, nebulous and ill-defined, and, significantly, does not lay down any boundaries: "The indications for immediate hospitalization enumerated above are not exhaustive but are only a list of the more frequently occurring illnesses which present a social danger." This clause allows the psychiatrist infinite scope in determining who requires involuntary treatment. The vagueness of the list of conditions is compounded by the inclusion of a statement to the effect that any of the listed conditions "may occur with externally correct conduct and dissimulation".

The terms used in the catalogue of indications are psychiatrically obscure and non-specific. For instance, "psychomotor excitement with a tendency towards aggressive actions", refers to nothing more than what it states—both physical and mental agitation—and has no special psychiatric connotation. More psychiatrically-based is "incorrect behaviour caused by

* The discharged patient may, depending on circumstances, be liable to all the categorizations described on p. 102, with the resulting duties and known and unknown restrictions.

a psychiatric disorder"; this indication specifically cites the abnormal states which may be associated with social danger —hallucinations, delirium, psychic automatism, disordered consciousness, and pathological impulsiveness. Delirium is repeated in a separate category, associated with chronic deterioration, but again would be acceptable to most psychiatrists as a potential source of social danger.

The final indication also contains the term "delirium" but in a way that is baffling. This indication is apparently the one most relevant to the civil commitment of dissenters: "Hypochondriacal delirious conditions producing incorrect, aggressive attitudes in the sick person to *particular persons, organizations or official institutions*" [our italics]. Firstly, "hypochondriacal delirium" is an obscure concept, not listed in Western diagnostic systems or included in standard textbooks of psychiatry.* Secondly, though it is of course possible that a person may act in an aggressive manner towards an organization or an institution, e.g. address threatening letters to a government department, the nature of that behaviour, particularly its justification, is much more liable to differing interpretation than aggression directed towards "particular persons". In the latter case, the justification for commitment is likely to be much less ambiguous. Evidence suggests that this particular provision is applied to people who persist in pressing claims against official organizations after these have been rejected.†

---

* The term "Hypochondriacal Neurosis" is listed in the diagnostic manual of the American Psychiatric Association, but it would be most unlikely for a patient with this diagnosis to require urgent, forcible hospitalization. See *Diagnostic and Statistical Manual of Mental Disorders*. 2nd Edition. American Psychiatric Association, Washington, 1968.

† Dr Felix Yaroshevsky, an émigré Soviet psychiatrist now in Canada, told us of the procedure whereby a person persevering stubbornly in having some matter attended to by a government department, e.g. seeking housing, a pension, may find himself trundled off to a mental hospital at the instigation of that department. Academician Sakharov notes in his book *My Country and the World* (Collins, London, 1975, p. 12) that desperate citizens "besiege waiting rooms of important officials, from which many of them (especially the annoying ones) are taken straight to psychiatric hospitals". In 1976 the dissenter Yury Orlov quoted a reliable source who had informed him that of those people who petitioned the Supreme Soviet about twelve per day were forcibly interned in mental hospitals for examination, and about half of these were not then discharged. See AFP dispatch from Moscow, 12 October 1976. See also Chapter 9.

The problems of wide interpretation, ambiguity and vagueness that arise from the 1961 directives were intensified with the promulgation of a special decree in 1969 entitled "On Measures for Preventing Socially Dangerous Behaviour on the Part of Mentally-Ill Persons", by the ministries of Health and Internal Affairs. According to the person who has studied the document most closely, the historian Roy Medvedev, "the decree notes that the 1961 directive . . . is insufficiently widely applied, and makes its application obligatory for the 'prevention of socially dangerous actions of the mentally sick'."[2] There is a shift between the two documents in the direction of *prevention* of aggressive behaviour through identification of "socially dangerous *tendencies*" in mentally-ill persons. This new concept was not further defined in the decree. Pragmatically, a recording system was introduced in which the files on persons with "socially dangerous tendencies" are to be maintained not only in the local psychiatric clinic, but also in other government health agencies, including at the federal level, and in police agencies.* It is the psychiatrist's responsibility to determine the patient's propensity for socially dangerous behaviour.

The timing of the decree of 1969 may be significant, coming as it did a year after the emergence of an organized human-rights movement. Its reference to the under-use of the 1961 directives may have led to a freer use of them, as is suggested by Zhores Medvedev's internment in 1970. However, the uproar over that case and Soviet apprehensions over the congress of the World Psychiatric Association, which was due to start in November 1971, were probably factors in the decision to revise the directives in August 1971. The revised version, of which we so far have only the extracts provided by the *Chronicle of Current Events*, was approved by the Procurator's office and the Ministry of Internal Affairs and thereupon confirmed by the Ministry of Health.[3] It differs from the 1961 version in certain significant, but not radical respects. Perhaps the most notable change is the apparent omission of the original clause that "the indications for immediate hospitalization enumerated . . . are not exhaustive, but are only a list of the more frequently

* This recording may be a component of the "centralized system for collection and analysis of data on patients in the USSR" described by Alexander Kiselev of the Serbsky Institute, in the *American Journal of Psychiatry*, 1972, Vol. 128, 1019–1022.

occurring illnesses which present a social danger". A catalogue of six indications for emergency hospitalization is provided, but unfortunately, these are not included in the extracts given by the *Chronicle*.

The wide latitude originally available to the doctor in ordering a confinement is thus apparently reduced. Also, introduced in the new directives are explicit instructions against the commitment of persons with certain psychiatric conditions or where socially dangerous behaviour is not accompanied by an obvious mental disorder:

> Affective reactions and anti-social forms of behaviour in persons not afflicted with mental illness but manifesting only such psychic deviations as psychopathic character traits or neurotic reactions, cannot serve as evidence for urgent hospitalization. . . . In those cases where the socially dangerous behaviour of the person provokes suspicion of the presence in him of a mental disturbance, but the latter is not obvious, such a person is not subject to urgent hospitalization. . . .

Two other points are revised in the new directives. The police are obliged to co-operate with medical personnel who request their help in the urgent hospitalization of mentally-ill persons. The police can now intervene when a *possibility* exists of resistance or aggression by the patient or his relatives, or his attempt to escape. Previously, the police were authorized to assist in cases of resistance only when resistance had actually occurred.

Also, the nearest relatives must be informed of the patient's hospitalization "no later than one day after examination . . . by the commission"; the original directives omitted any specification of the timing for notification of the family.

Judicial Review and Civil Commitment

Psychiatrists in any country are likely, no matter how precise and explicit their instructions for civil commitment, to err from time to time by placing a person in a mental hospital unjustifiably, or prolonging his stay there unduly. Judicial review normally enables such mistakes to be rectified. Soviet law, however, fails to provide for such a procedure. The patient is not allowed counsel and has no right of judicial appeal at any point during his commitment. Judge Bazelon noted this deficiency on a visit to the Soviet Union as a member of a United States psychiatric delegation. He argued that in the United States the court plays a pivotal rôle in ensuring that professional standards are adhered to. "It does not pretend to know more about the doctor's field of medicine than the doctor himself. All the court is doing is providing a forum where the doctor's practices can be examined and appraised by other experts in his field of medicine."[4] The judge also pointed out that judicial review enables the community to learn how its mental-health system is functioning and thus be better equipped to "oversee government officials and ensure that they respect all substantive and procedural rights".

According to Bazelon, the Russians explain their lack of judicial review in civil-commitment cases in several ways. They argue that the Ministry of Health maintains constant surveillance of the civil-commitment procedure, so ensuring its correct application; that the patient's family, employer, union and party organization would protest against any improper commitment; and that psychiatrists act fairly and impartially since they have no motive to commit a patient for other than medical reasons. He contends that all these explanations are dubious: the bureaucracy is policing itself; the patient's family and others mentioned above often initiate the commitment and cannot be relied upon to protect the patient; should they protest, no guarantee exists that their protest will be attended to; and judicial review rests on the premise that even the well-intending psychiatrist may occasionally fail to adhere to medico-legal standards.

Indeed, Roy Medvedev, after his brother's detention in 1970, wrote a critical review of civil commitment in the USSR and suggested that both the 1961 directives and the decree of 1969 should be abrogated and supplanted by a new set of measures, formulated to eliminate potential abuse. Further, he regarded it as essential to introduce a special article into the criminal code providing for "criminal responsibility on the part of psychiatrists for the committal to mental hospitals of sane people".[5]

Civil Commitment and Dissent

Ample evidence is available that civil commitment has been used for the compulsory hospitalization of dissenters who were not a danger to themselves or to others and who did not match any of the indications specified in the 1961 directives. One indication, however, commented upon earlier, does bear some tenuous relationship to the detention of dissenters— "hypochondriacal delirious conditions producing incorrect, aggressive attitudes in the sick person to particular persons, organizations, or official institutions". The term "hypochon-driacal delirium" is incomprehensible to us as a psychiatric concept; moreover the notion of aggression towards organizations is so broad in scope as to be liable to a variety of interpretations. How exactly is a person seen to be aggressive towards an organization or an institution? In both the cases we shall describe, the answers to this question apparently provide the sole possible rationale for the commitment of the dissenters concerned. Zhores Medvedev, in his social critical writings, and Gennady Shimanov, in the way he acts out his religious beliefs, are categorized as "dangers to society". To the Soviet régime they are regarded as threats to the *status quo*. Psychiatry is conscripted by the régime as an ally in maintaining the prescribed order.

RELIGIOUS DISSENT AND CIVIL COMMITMENT— THE CASE OF GENNADY SHIMANOV

Gennady Shimanov recounts the saga of his commitment to Moscow's Kashchenko psychiatric hospital in a vivid narrative entitled *Notes from the Red House*.[6] The Red House is the two-storey building in which Shimanov was "treated" for three weeks in May 1969. Who is Gennady Shimanov? Not an active political dissenter, not a member of any human-rights movement, not a renowned scientist or writer, but a lift operator and, to his detriment, a religious man, a believer.

Religion and the Law

To understand why Shimanov was forced into the Red House as a social danger, we need to examine briefly official attitudes to religion and religious practice in the Soviet Union.[7] All three Soviet Constitutions to date contain the principles of freedom of conscience and separation of Church and State. In fact, however, the state began to impose, soon after the revolution of October 1917, constraints on religious practice because of Marxist ideology and Lenin's personal intolerance of religion. At various times the leadership attempted to eradicate public religion: Stalin initiated the compulsory closure of churches on a widespread scale in the 1930s but was forced to reopen them to gain popular support against the Nazi invader; under Khrushchev at least half the religious buildings in the Soviet Union were shut down. In 1929 laws were passed which destroyed the principle of separation and enabled the State effectively to control the Church.

Two articles introduced into the criminal code have especially been applied in suppressing religious dissent. Article 142 decrees punishment of one year in a labour camp or a fine for a first offence, and three years for a second. The offence includes any of the following: distribution of documents calling for the non-observance of legislation on religious cults, arousing religious superstition among the population, organization of religious meetings and ceremonies which disrupt the social order, and teaching of religion to minors. Article 227 forbids the organization or directing of a group carried on under the appearance of preaching religious beliefs and performing religious ceremonies, where harm is done to citizens' health, their rights are infringed, or minors are involved. Imprisonment or exile for up to five years is the punishment for offenders. Active participation in such a group, or the practice of systematic propaganda, is illegal and punished by imprisonment or exile for up to three years.

An addendum to Article 227 provides an opportunity for instruments of social control, other than the courts, to combat religious dissent. "If the acts of the persons . . . and the persons themselves, do not represent a great social danger, measures of social pressure may be applied to them." No specification of what constitutes "social pressure" is provided—it is sufficiently vague to permit our supposition that the psychiatrist may sometimes act as one of the agents of "social pressure". It seems likely that in forcibly hospitalizing Gennady Shimanov, the KGB were guided by the addendum to Article 227.

Shimanov's Commitment

Shimanov's story begins in 1968 with a postcard: Would he attend the district psychiatric clinic for a follow-up visit? Suspecting ulterior motives and sure about his own state of health, Shimanov ignored the card. After all, he had not attended the clinic during the previous six years since his discharge from the Gannushkin psychiatric hospital in 1962.

Shimanov was 25 in 1962 and undergoing a religious awakening. His description of it and of his two and a half months in the Gannushkin are to be found in his autobiography published in *samizdat* in 1969.[8] His life was topsy-turvy: he had resigned his job, he had no money, there was a police threat of him being charged with "parasitism". Above all, he was faced with the "revolution that had taken place in me" and felt desperately the need for rest and freedom to comprehend his newborn religious experience. Shimanov chose "the madhouse" as his temporary sanctuary.

Through simulation of mental illness, he hoped to spend a month or two being fed and kept warm, spared of mundane and trivial concerns. After complaining to the local clinic psychiatrist of insomnia and a fear of hallucinations, he added for good measure that he heard voices intermittently. Referral to the Gannushkin followed, with a provisional diagnosis of schizophrenia.

Shimanov soon discovered that the hospital psychiatrists regarded his belief in God as abnormal. After all, he had not had a religious upbringing: "Your religiosity is a disease, we will treat you, and until we have cured you, you won't be leaving here." And so the "patient" received insulin treatment. Despite this, Shimanov remembers his period in hospital as "reasonably tolerable". The therapy was obviously ineffective. Shimanov's religious conviction grew from 1962 onwards and with it came a desire to convert his friends. Ultimately a group of fellow believers developed around him.

However, the card from the clinic in 1968 was a puzzle to Shimanov; he did not at first perceive any association between it and his religious activities.

The clinic persevered. A nurse visited Shimanov's home on three occasions during the next four months, each time trying to persuade him to attend for examination. All to no avail.

1. Dr Dmitry Venediktov, USSR deputy-minister of health responsible for foreign relations in psychiatry.

2. Academician Andrei Snezhnevsky, director of the Institute of Psychiatry, chief proponent of the officially approved psychiatric school, and frequent apologist for Soviet psychiatry.

3. Professor Ruben Nadzharov, Snezhnevsky's deputy.

4. Academician Georgy Morozov, director of the Serbsky Institute and head of the Soviet society of psychiatrists.

5. Marat Vartanyan, professor at Snezhnevsky's institute and associate secretary of the World Psychiatric Association.

6

6. Professor Linford Rees (left) and Dr Denis Leigh (right), treasurer and secretary-general of the World Psychiatric Association, receive diplomas in 1972 as honorary fellows of the Soviet society of psychiatrists from the USSR ambassador in London.

7. Dr Zoya Serebryakova, chief psychiatrist in the USSR ministry of health.

8. Dr Maslyayeva, deputy-chief doctor of the Kashchenko psychiatric hospital No. 1 in Moscow.

7

8

9

10

9. Dr Semyon Gluzman, Kiev psychiatrist imprisoned for exposing abuses.

10. Dr Marina Voikhanskaya, Leningrad psychiatrist, with her son Misha. After she emigrated, Misha was held in the USSR against his will, as official revenge for her denunciation of political internments.

11. Dr Leonard Ternovsky, Moscow doctor who opposed abuses, with Mrs Sofia Kallistratova, lawyer to several victims of abuse.

12. Professor Fyodor Detengof (1898–1973), leading psychiatrist in Soviet Central Asia, who in 1969 ruled General Grigorenko sane.

11

12

13   14

13. Academician Andrei Sakharov and his doctor wife Elena Bonner, two leaders of the USSR-based campaign against psychiatric abuse.

14. Viktor Nekipelov, poet, pharmacist, and author of an analytical memoir about his internment in the Serbsky Institute.

15. The Action Group for the Defence of Human Rights in the USSR, leaders in the same campaign, 1974, l. to r.: Dr Sergei Kovalyov, biologist, Tatyana Khodorovich, linguist, Tatyana Velikanova, mathematician, Grigory Podyapolsky, geophysicist, Anatoly Levitin, school teacher and writer.

15

16

16. The Leningrad special psychiatric hospital, the wing facing on to Arsenal Street.

17. The Kazan special psychiatric hospital.

18. The Oryol special psychiatric hospital: inmates exercising in yards.

17

18

19. Evgeny Nikolayev, linguist, waving from one of the sections of the Kashchenko mental hospital No. 1 in Moscow.

20. The Chernyakhovsk special psychiatric hospital.

19

20

21

22

21. Nina Bukovskaya, campaigner for her son Vladimir.

22. Vladimir Bukovsky, Moscow, 1970.

23. Alexander Volpin, Moscow mathematician interned five times between 1949 and 1968.

24. Ilya Yarkov (1892–1970), author of memoirs about his internment in 1951–54, with a young child.

23

24

25. Ex-Major-General Pyotr Grigorenko and collective-farm chairman
Ivan Yakhimovich, Moscow, 29
July 1968, after delivering to the
Czechoslovak Embassy a warning
about the impending Soviet invasion.
Later interned, they were two of
the six dissenters whose cases were
documented by Bukovsky in 1971.

25

26. Mrs Sofia Kallistratova (l.),
Grigorenko's lawyer, and Mrs.
Zinaida Grigorenko (r.), 1975.

27. Zinaida and Pyotr Grigorenko
with Sergei Zheludkov, Orthodox
priest and human rights activist,
1975, after Grigorenko's release.

26

27

The four other Bukovsky cases:

28. Viktor Kuznetsov, Moscow painter.

28

29. Natalya Gorbanevskaya, poet and dissenter, with her two sons.

30. Viktor Fainberg (l.) and Vladimir Borisov (r.) of Leningrad, with their friend Maria Slonim, 1974.

29

30

31. Tatyana Plyushch with the writer and family friend Viktor Nekrasov, Kiev, 1974.

31

32. Tatyana Plyushch with Tatyana Khodorovich, during the campaign to free Leonid Plyushch, which they fuelled.

33. Leonid Plyushch with his mother, on the Soviet-Hungarian border, on the day of his release and emigration, 9 January 1976, aged 36.

34. Leonid Plyushch in the 1960's.

32

33

34

35

36

35. Yury Galanskov (1939–72), Moscow dissenter interned in early 1960's.

36. Yury Shikhanovich, Moscow mathematician released from internment in response to campaign of protest.

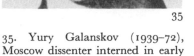

37. Evgeny Belov, Moscow student interned in 1965.

37

38. Mikhail Naritsa, Leningrad sculptor interned in early 1960's for publishing a book abroad.

38

39 40

39. Mykola Plakhotnyuk, Ukrainian doctor interned for *samizdat* activity.

40. Olga Iofe, Moscow mathematics student interned as a "schizophrenic with no visible symptoms".

41. Valeria Novodvorskaya, Moscow student of languages, interned for handing out leaflets.

42. Pyotr Starchik, Moscow guitarist and singer, interned once for distributing leaflets, once for giving informal song recitals in his home.

41 42

43   44

43. Yan Krylsky, Moscow Jew interned on a trumped-up charge after he applied to emigrate to Israel.

44. Ilya Rips, Riga Jew who protested against the Soviet occupation of Czechoslovakia by an attempted self-immolation.

45. MVD order of December 1970 transferring Vladimir Gershuni, Moscow stonemason, from prison to a special psychiatric hospital (in Oryol). Soviet prisoners have their heads permanently shaved.

46. Vaclav Sevruk, Lithuanian philosopher interned for *samizdat* activity.

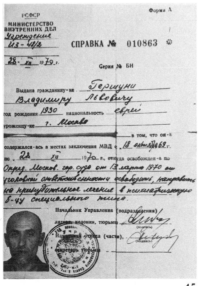

45   46

47   48

Political prisoners sent from Vladimir prison or a forced labour camp to psychiatric institutions, as a means of intimidation:

47. Valentyn Moroz, Ukrainian historian.

48. Lev Lukyanenko, Ukrainian lawyer.

49. Vladimir Balakhonov, official at the World Meteorological Office in Geneva who briefly defected in 1972.

50. Igor Ogurtsov, Leningrad orientalist and leader of underground, anti-Soviet, Christian group.

49   50

51   52

Dissenters interned in ordinary psychiatric hospitals under civil commitment:

51. Oleg Vorobyov, Orthodox Christian from Moscow.

52. Gennady Shimanov, Orthodox layman and writer, with his wife Alla and son, Moscow, 1973.

53. Vytautas Grigas, German mechanic from Lithuania, interned for his role in German emigration movement, photographed in grounds of Moscow's Kashchenko hospital, 1974.

53

54   55   56

Dissenters interned under civil commitment:

54. Yury Ivanov, Leningrad artist, a self-portrait.

55. Yury Maltsev, Moscow translator of Italian literature and member of Action Group.

56. Fyodor Sidenko, Pentecostalist from Soviet Far East, near Pacific coast.

57. Alexander Argentov, member of Orthodox youth seminar, photographed in grounds of Moscow psychiatric hospital No. 14, July 1976.

58. Zhores Medvedev (r.), biologist and *samizdat* author, with his twin brother Roy.

57   58

Shimanov refused, declaring that he felt absolutely well. The explanation provided by the nurse on the third visit differed. This was not just a follow-up visit: there had been enquiries at the clinic from the KGB and Shimanov's employer about his "incorrect behaviour". The clinic doctors were obliged to clarify the situation. They could, if necessary, accomplish this by conducting an examination in his home.

Shimanov relented. At least by permitting the examination he would be rid of the wearisome nuisance. Later in the day, he learned through a friend that an ambulance had called at his apartment, purportedly because of an illness in his child, and not finding anyone at home, had promptly departed. The clinic authorities, presumably under KGB pressure, were obviously determined. Soon his employer, in the presence of a representative from the district party committee, divulged that he had heard reports about Shimanov's misbehaviour. Why not attend the clinic as requested and clear up the matter right away? Again Shimanov relented. He was immediately taken to the clinic by the party representative and there chided by the doctor for having failed to reply to the clinic's multiple requests for his examination. Shimanov asserted his rights: there was no law obliging him to attend the clinic, he felt extremely well. Then why the KGB's enquiries and their request for his psychiatric evaluation, the doctor countered? A reason must exist for the KGB's intervention—participation in a demonstration, distributing leaflets, religious activity?

Religious activity fitted the bill. Yes, Shimanov was an active believer and this was reason enough to warrant a psychiatric examination. The KGB had to be satisfied; Shimanov would require hospitalization. "Just for a few days. We have to tell the KGB something and we can't tell them anything when we have no idea if you are well or not. Please don't think that we as well as the KGB are against you. . . . On the contrary, our duty is to help our patients and to defend them."[9] The clinic's orderlies escorted Shimanov briskly to a waiting ambulance. Their destination was Section 4 of Kashchenko, in the two-storey red building. The civil commitment process was under way.

The next day the "patient" faced the head psychiatrist of the section, German Shafran. As with the clinic doctor, Shafran's salient concern was to establish the reason for Shimanov's commitment, but he simultaneously reassured him that: "I am not an investigator and this conversation of ours is not an interrogation. It is simply that you and I must get clear what the reason is for you having been sent to hospital. I will also phone the KGB to find out what you are accused of."[10]

In actual fact Shimanov had not been accused of anything, and of course had not been either arrested or charged with a criminal act by the KGB. Shafran attempted to identify the activity that had precipitated the KGB's interest in him. Had he had contact with the KGB in the past? Shimanov had actually been summoned in 1967 for interrogation in the cases of Vladimir Bukovsky and Aleksei Dobrovolsky. Shimanov explained that he was a nodding acquaintance of both dissenters and that his telephone number had been found in their diaries. Shortly afterwards, Shimanov had been dismissed from his post as a deputy detachment commander at Moscow's Kuibyshev Academy of Military Engineering. The doctor wished to know whether he had participated in political activity, for in all probability a statement made by him to friends had been misinterpreted and come to the knowledge of the KGB. Dr Shafran assured the "patient" that there was nothing to be concerned about and that he would be discharged within a few days.

Two days later another interview took place. After questions about Shimanov's childhood, his conversion to God, his previous hospitalization at Gannushkin and his recent life, Shafran reached the heart of the matter:

> "It is possible that in the second half of our conversation there may be things that you do not particularly like. . . . You told me just now how you came to religion and joined the Orthodox Church . . . do you talk to everyone about God? —I mean, both with those who believe and those who don't?"
>
> "It depends. I don't have rigid rules."
>
> "Of course you, as a believer, try to convert others to religion?"
>
> "Yes, of course."
>
> "Well, that's it, Gena.* We've come to the heart of the matter. You see, what you do is called religious propaganda. Of course, we have freedom of conscience and freedom to

* Familiar form of Gennady.

conduct religious services, but freedom to make propaganda for religion is something we have not got. Such activity is prohibited by law."[11]

Shimanov explained that he had always acted within the law. Religious propaganda could be interpreted in several ways. Since freedom of conscience was guaranteed by the Constitution, religious propaganda was used in a circumscribed sense to refer to specific activities which he had not practised. "As for conversations about religion over a cup of tea, you won't find a word forbidding them in any code of laws." Shafran agreed. Perhaps the "patient" had not violated the law but the KGB "doesn't give a damn for laws". Shimanov was harming the régime by attracting others to the church. This was not an infringement of the law and although the "patient" would probably win his discharge from hospital without delay on this occasion, the next time he would be compulsorily hospitalized through criminal commitment and receive indefinite treatment until he was "no longer a danger to society". Shafran warned Shimanov that, given that he was a person of integrity, he would, in all likelihood, be unwilling to relinquish his faith and the consequences for both him and his family would be dire.

Was Dr Shafran attempting to help the "patient" escape from a fate that he himself considered unjust and an abuse of his profession, without explicitly revealing his alliance? Was the doctor merely acting pragmatically on the premise that Shimanov was quite well but would not be free of psychiatric pressure until he abided by the KGB's dictates? Did Shafran consider him mentally ill and in need of treatment that would eliminate his "religious delusions"? (We discuss the psychiatrist's rôle in the abuse of psychiatry in chapter 8.) We have only the "patient's" account of Shafran's involvement and so must remain uncertain about his attitudes. Shimanov explained to us that the doctor, while decent and fair, concurrently played out a distinct professional rôle—he had a job to do and senior staff to obey. Interestingly, Shimanov discovered after his release that the same Shafran had served as a medical officer in a prison camp twenty years earlier. According to a friend of Shimanov who had been treated there by him, Shafran was compassionate and kindly.

What we do know is that his "therapy" bore no similarity to conventional psychiatric treatment. The corner-stone of the treatment was practical advice—if you know what is good for you and wish to avoid future suffering for yourself and your family, mute your religious convictions and feelings and keep them entirely private. If not, prolonged, perhaps permanent, internment in a mental hospital will inevitably be your fate.

And so ended Shimanov's first encounter with the psychiatrist. Shafran's promise of an early release melted away when Alla, Shimanov's wife, learned from the doctor that the KGB had instructed the hospital superintendent to delay his release for a further week. Clearly Shafran had limited power to affect decisions of this kind. A few days later he explained that although his opinion was not decisive, he personally would insist on Shimanov's discharge, "as I consider that no drugs will succeed in changing your way of thinking".

Shimanov had obviously paid careful attention to the doctor's original advice for he revealed that he was now prepared, albeit reluctantly, to give up his "religious propaganda". Further advice followed: "Repeat what you have just said, and sufficiently firmly, during the talk which you will have in a few days' time with the deputy medical director. Your wish to change your life may influence the decision of the commission."[12] The "treatment" was working!

Within a day Shimanov faced the four-member commission. (According to civil-commitment procedure, this meeting should have taken place within the first 24 hours of his admission rather than several days later.) Again the preliminary questions regarding Shimanov's work, his relationships with family and friends, and his health since his hospitalization six years earlier. Then came the nub: "Tell us, please, how it was that you came to believe in God?"

Shimanov provides an illuminating description of how he replied. He felt he had to be on guard and give his answers accurately and comprehensibly so that none of them could be construed as a sign of illness.* He explained his conversion to faith in a palpably shrewd manner by referring to the religious

* Five years later Vladimir Bukovsky and Dr Semyon Gluzman were to produce a handbook for dissenters hospitalized in mental institutions, instructing them on how to deal with precisely Shimanov's situation. This is discussed in chapter 8.

faith of Shakespeare, Tolstoy, Dostoyevsky and Pushkin. Were all these great writers crazy too because they believed in God? It was as if a battle were being waged, Shimanov contending that his religious faith was in no way an indication of mental illness whilst the commission was set to "squeeze" him into the established pattern of Soviet orthodoxy. He had a suitable retort for each subsequent psychiatric pursuit of his religious conviction and practices.

A couple of days later, when Shimanov met the hospital's deputy medical director, Dr Maslyayeva, with Dr Shafran present, he was still quite in the dark on how much longer he would remain in Kashchenko. He had already spent two weeks there but as yet received no treatment. The session with Dr Maslyayeva did not resemble a usual psychiatric interview and it warrants our detailed attention. Why had he grown a beard? she asked. Was he a beatnik? Thereupon a discussion about the beard and a curious logic on the part of the examiner. Shimanov admitted that he had not sported a beard on his marriage.

> "So your wife fell in love with you without a beard? Then it's quite incomprehensible. If she liked you without a beard, why did you grow it?"
> "So that she would like me even more."[13]

Then an abrupt switch of topics. Dr Maslyayeva now initiated a more medically-relevant enquiry regarding visual hallucinations:

> "Saints have visions, don't they? What do you call him? Christ?—he appears to them, doesn't he?"
> "It sometimes happens, but very rarely. People more often have hallucinations, that is, not genuine visions. I have not had either visions or hallucinations. I have no talents whatever in that direction."[14]

Shimanov conveys an impression of remarkable poise and wit in the midst of what must have been a tormenting experience. He bounces back assertively and humorously with each psychiatric enquiry. There was nothing thus far to suggest an abnormal mind at work. On the contrary, Shimanov appears alert and insightful. Yet, after the inevitable question about his conversion to God, Dr Maslyayeva declared:

> "You see, Gennady Mikhailovich. . . . Everything that you have just told us confirms us in the view that illness lies at the root of your 'conversion'. Of course, you yourself cannot understand this; but you must have confidence in us; we are specialists. If you had grown up in a religious family or had lived somewhere in the West, well, then we could have looked at your religiousness in another way. . . . But you were educated in a Soviet school, and were brought up in a family of non-believers. . . . You are an educated person; I am ready even to admit that you know more about philosophy and religion than I do. . . . And suddenly . . . wham! . . . you are religious! . . . It's very odd indeed . . . and makes one wonder if some abnormal processes were not already developing in you in your youth, which later on brought you to religion."[15]

Here was the kernel of the psychiatric assessment— Shimanov's conversion to faith as an adult was maladaptive behaviour and thus pathological.* Shimanov characteristically retorted in a reasonable and uncontestable fashion that the Metropolitan Nikodim, a high-ranking dignitary in the Russian Orthodox Church, had also converted to God as an adult, despite having been reared in an atheistic family and having received a Soviet education. Was he too therefore schizophrenic? After all, a long interview with him had recently been published in the Soviet press, indicating in what good standing he was with the party. Dr Maslyayeva side-stepped the issue by asserting that "it is you we are talking about".

The remainder of the session was devoted to an exchange on the compatibility of religion and Marxism which more resembled an intellectual debate than a psychiatric evaluation. The psychiatrist on the one hand argued for the mutual

---

* Shimanov's case appears to illustrate well the current orthodoxy within Soviet psychiatry as regards religion. See, e.g. M. K. Kokin and G. A. Gabinsky, *Religion and Psychic Illnesses* (translated title), Moscow, 1969. This orthodoxy derives in large measure from an earlier trend typified by the book by Ya. V. Mints, *Jesus Christ as a Type of Mentally-Ill Person*, Moscow, 1927. See AS (p. 464), 2765.

exclusiveness of religion and Marxism—it was impossible to reconcile religious belief with the atheistic society that prevailed in the Soviet Union. Shimanov conceded that Marxism denied religious truths but pointed out that the state granted freedom of conscience to its citizens; there was thus no conflict for him in combining his way of life with society's principles:

> "It is quite simple. I work, I earn money. I come home from work, hurry to the shop, buy bread, milk, butter. . . . Nobody there asks me about religion. . . . Then I rest, look after my son's upbringing. . . . I travel by tram, underground. . . . No one there asks me about religion either. . . . And if they did, why should I not answer? . . . What have I to be afraid of? At the moment religion isn't forbidden in this country. . . . So I don't feel any particular conflict with society."[16]

Dr Maslyayeva's rebuttal followed. "All Soviet people are Marxists; everyone acknowledges only a scientific philosophy; but you believe in God, so you are out of harmony with society." She went further, contending that Shimanov, because of his faith, constituted a danger to society—he was an ill man, lacking insight into his condition. The psychiatrist then spelled out her justification for these conclusions.

> [Religion] can be comparatively harmless if it's on the decrease, if it's dying. . . . But if it turns to the attack, if it wins more and more recruits, then it is a socially dangerous phenomenon. . . . We are building communism, we are educating people to be more and more socially aware, and you are corrupting them.[17]
> . . . your symptoms are a one-sided fascination with religion. You have cut yourself off from life. . . . As a result of your illness . . . you have become a person dangerous to society. So we must give you a little treatment . . . in the interests of society . . . and in your own interests, of course.[18]

The picture had changed radically with this disclosure that there was a need for psychiatric treatment. Later Shafran described the nature of the treatment under consideration. His description of its side-effects identifies the drug as one of the major tranquillizer group used conventionally in the treatment of psychotic conditions (we discuss these drugs in chapter 7). Shimanov vehemently protested at this new development. After all, Shafran had assured him of a prompt discharge. Successive assurances had followed and although they had not been kept, Shimanov nevertheless anticipated obtaining his freedom within days. His protest took the form of a hunger strike; he demanded an end to "the experiment of intimidating and oppressing people who think differently from you".[19]

He won his release on the third day of his hunger strike, three weeks after being forced into Kashchenko. The thinking of the psychiatrists was divulged to him by Shafran when he reported that the staff had failed to reach agreement on his case. Shafran himself had insisted on discharge since, as mentioned above, he believed that the "patient" was too resistant to respond to treatment.

Shimanov left the Red House with the notes he had managed to write and conceal from the doctors. He described them as "my only weapon", i.e. as his only defence against a second internment. Soon he was to write them up and publish them in *samizdat*.

Subsequent Developments

Following Shimanov's release in May 1969, he was contacted regularly by the staff of the local psychiatric clinic, usually by a nurse, occasionally by a psychiatrist. This occurred at any time, and invariably before major public holidays. The procedure was still continuing when we met him in Moscow in June 1976. He described to us how in the first eighteen months or so the medical staff acted brusquely and inhumanely. Later, their attitudes appeared to change and they became more cordial and respectful. Shimanov surmised that the improvement reflected the attention he gained at that time in the West through his writings, and the authorities' fear of creating any embarrassing incident around him.

Although, like other dissenters, Shimanov has never been officially informed that he is registered as a social danger, regular visits and enquiries from the clinic make it clear that this is so. Until mid-1976 he had not been threatened with re-admission were he to continue his religious practices and he did not anticipate that the authorities would resort to this tactic. Yet as he succintly pointed out: "Anything is possible."

Shimanov remains a deeply religious man. In recent years he has become a prolific author of *samizdat* essays on religious and social topics. These express his complete loyalty to the Soviet state: he believes that even the state comes from God, and he anticipates the eventual evolution of a benevolently authoritarian Christian order in Russia. Somehow he calculates that his writing activity does not make him vulnerable to another episode of forcible hospitalization. On the other hand he has taken the precaution of not discussing religious matters at work or in other public places, and he and his family have worshipped in a variety of different churches rather than in the one closest to their home.

Over a six-month period prior to his civil commitment, Shimanov entertained a group of friends weekly at his home. Although most were believers and religion was among the topics discussed during their visits, Shimanov carefully explained that these were not formal religious gatherings. But he suspects that the authorities viewed them in this way and resorted to psychiatry to bring the practice to an end. In fact, they were unsuccessful. Shimanov continues to believe that it is his right to invite his friends to the privacy of his home and there discuss whatever they please.

And what of his mental health? Although we were not in a position to conduct a formal psychiatric evaluation, and this was not the purpose of our visit, we spoke at length to him and his wife. We could relate easily to him and were impressed by his warmth and wit. He was completely open and frank in telling his story. He elaborated, for example, on many aspects of his experience in the Red House. There was certainly no evidence during our meeting of any psychiatric disturbance.

Conclusion

Shimanov was hounded into the Kashchenko because of the way he expressed his religious convictions. We conjecture that he succeeded in gaining a relatively prompt release because of two main factors—his own vigorous protest, especially the hunger strike, and the actions of Dr Shafran, who apparently made repeated efforts to secure Shimanov's release but lacked the ultimate power to do so.

Gennady Shimanov exemplifies the use of psychiatry in suppressing religious dissenters. We have more to say about this group of "victims" in chapter 9.

Shimanov would have remained virtually unknown in the West had he not written his notes. At the time of his detention no protest took place either in the Soviet Union or abroad. The following case we describe is radically different in that it achieved instant publicity.

THE CASE OF ZHORES MEDVEDEV

No other dissenter hospitalized through a civil commitment has attracted as much attention as Zhores Medvedev. In 1970 this internationally-known biologist was forcibly held for nineteen days in the regional psychiatric hospital at Kaluga, 70 miles from Moscow. His release followed a spate of protest both in the Soviet Union and abroad. A year later a narrative of the experience by him and his twin brother Roy was published in the West.[20] Not only did *A Question of Madness* provide painstaking detail of Zhores's ordeal, each phase accurately documented; it also revealed to an unprecedented extent the political use of civil commitment.

To appreciate why the authorities declared Medvedev a social danger, it is necessary to know something of his background, particularly of his rôle as a social critic. Unlike Pyotr Grigorenko and Natalya Gorbanevskaya, Medvedev expressed his political and social convictions as an individual. He was not affiliated to any human-rights group. His social activism centred on the rôle of the scientist in the Soviet Union, and his critiques concerned the stringent limitations imposed on the scientist by the Soviet government. He articulated his opinions in his writings rather than through the banner or the leaflet. Later, he was to be informed that his sanity was doubted primarily because of the character of these writings.

Medvedev's status as a biologist of international repute placed him in an excellent position to comment on scientific life in the USSR. His first major critical work was on Lysenkoism, a history of the intense controversy in Soviet biology that took place from the 1940s to the 1960s. (We commented on Lysenkoism in chapter 2.) Medvedev's manuscript was read in *samizdat* in narrow circles on its intitial release in 1962. At that time the Lysenko school of genetics dominated Soviet biology and agriculture. In 1963 Medvedev came under attack from the secretary of the Moscow Party Committee because of his manuscript, and was subjected to hostile criticism in the press. He was also dimissed from his post in an agricultural academy. After 1964, with the fall of Khrushchev, Lysenkoism was officially recognized as pseudoscience and the criticism of Medvedev ceased. However, the manuscript was still not permitted publication. Ultimately it appeared in the West in 1969 under the title *The Rise and Fall of T. D. Lysenko*.[21]

The Medvedev Papers,[22] an account of his many attempts to maintain professional contact with foreign scientists, also circulated in *samizdat* in the Soviet Union prior to its Western publication in 1971. Medvedev describes with care and a spice of humour the difficulties he encountered in attending scientific meetings abroad, corresponding with foreign scientists, and sending and receiving reprints of scientific papers. He demonstrates in detail the firm controls exercised by the Soviet bureaucracy over participation by scientists in conferences abroad, and through shrewd detective work reveals how postal censorship controls correspondence with foreign colleagues. Medvedev argues that these restrictions adversely affect Soviet science, creating a sense of professional isolation. He urges that the restrictions be lifted and communication between Soviet and foreign scientists encouraged.

Undoubtedly as a consequence of *The Medvedev Papers*, he was dismissed as head of the Department of Molecular Radiobiology at the Institute of Medical Radiology in March 1969 after seven years in the post. Medvedev had attained that position at the relatively young age of 37 after a brilliant career in biology which commenced after the second world war. The sacking was initiated by the regional party committee through its application of pressure on the institute's director.

Medvedev's own account of his dismissal in *The Medvedev Papers* sheds considerable light on the factors underlying it. In an interview with the director, he was asked not about his academic work but about his attitude to the Soviet action in Czechoslovakia, the basis of his relationship with Solzhenitsyn, the socio-political journals to which he regularly subscribed, and the reasons for the supposedly inadequate rearing of his son. This "loyalty check" led to Medvedev's loss of a job and continuing unemployment until his hospitalization over a year later. A vindictiveness characterized the entire episode. Medvedev's submission of a grievance to the Academy of Medical Sciences was of no avail. It took him almost a year to acquire from his institute the documents he required to obtain another position.

Medvedev's Commitment

On 29 May 1970 Dr Alexander Lifshits, head of the Kaluga mental hospital, and Dr Y. V. Kiryushin, director of the local psychiatric clinic, accompanied by three policemen, burst into Medvedev's apartment. So began his nineteen-day confinement in a ward at Kaluga. Medvedev was not especially surprised by his commitment. The saga had begun the previous month with an urgent call from the chairman of the town council in Obninsk, where he lived. The chairman informed him of the education department's concern regarding the behaviour of his son. Medvedev's suspicions were immediately aroused on his discovery that the director of the school which his son attended had at no point consulted the education department regarding the boy. He also found it curious that the authorities insisted on him visiting the education department alone, without his wife and son. The authorities impressed on him the need for a psychiatric consultation for his son, despite Medvedev's explanation that he had previously been examined by a psychiatrist and was about to write his final examinations.

Medvedev wondered whether this was a devious way to arrange a psychiatric examination for himself. He was aware of the misuse of psychiatry in cases of persons whom the authorities wished to suppress but who had not actually broken the law. He knew of Grigorenko and Yakhimovich, who were at that moment interned in mental hospitals. Medvedev wondered whether he was destined to share their fate.

He became all the more suspicious on receiving yet another request to consult with the chairman of the town council. On this visit he was faced by her and an official identified only as a representative from the education department. The latter pursued an enquiry about Medvedev's family, in much the same way that a psychiatrist would conduct a family history. He had purportedly come to discuss his son's problems. Medvedev was later to discover the true identity of this official—he was indeed a psychiatrist, Dr Vladimir Leznenko.

In early May Dr Kiryushin invited Medvedev and his son to visit his psychiatric clinic; Medvedev considered this a reasonable request. After all, Kiryushin had served as the original consultant in advising the family on their son's behaviour. What transpired at the clinic, however, was distinctly odd. Medvedev was asked to wait in an adjoining room while Kiryushin interviewed his son. A little later, he observed through the window the boy's departure from the clinic. He tried the door—locked! The room was clearly not a waiting room but a changing room for patients. Medvedev recognized the precariousness of his situation: "I began to bang on the door as hard as I could but very soon stopped, realizing that it might be used against me if my confinement in this little room was not simply a mistake. . . ."[23] Medvedev succeeded in forcing the lock, asked no questions, and promptly departed. Kiryushin, presumably under severe pressure, persevered in his endeavour to lure him back to the clinic. He made several calls on the most dubious of pretexts. Medvedev himself was clearly the target of the psychiatrist's persistence. Kiryushin's appearance at the Medvedev apartment on 29 May, with the police, confirmed finally his true intention. The series of ruses over the previous seven weeks had failed. The authorities were now compelled to resort to the final option, the forcible removal of Medvedev from his home to the Kaluga mental hospital.

In the Kaluga Mental Hospital

A preliminary commission met with Medvedev the following day—Dr Lifshits, Dr Galina Bondareva, the doctor in charge of his section, and the previously unidentified official, supposedly from the education department, Vladimir Leznenko, who was now introduced to Medvedev as director of the Kaluga psychiatric clinic. Their paramount interest revolved around Medvedev's writings. Lifshits obviously had read only parts of *The Medvedev Papers*, while the two other doctors displayed a total ignorance of its content. Nevertheless, the commission wished to ascertain what his objectives had been in writing the work. Why did he now wish to publish the manuscript abroad? How had he come to write his other work on Lysenko and the genetics controversy? By contrast with the enquiry on his written works, a relatively brief period was devoted to issues generally regarded as more pertinent in a psychiatric evaluation: Medvedev's family life, his sleep pattern, and his self-appraisal.

The main commission met a day later. Professor Boris Shostakovich of the Serbsky Institute joined the team as the fourth psychiatrist. Lifshits explained to a querying Medvedev that Shostakovich had come to participate as a general consultant to the hospital and not as a forensic psychiatrist. This issue was to become more acute during a subsequent commission when forensic psychiatrists from the Serbsky again participated in his examination. Shostakovich, the principal interviewer, posed questions very similar to those of the day before. Medvedev came to realize that Shostakovich had read the same portion of his writings as had Lifshits. He hypothesized that Shostakovich could not have read all this material that same morning in Kaluga. He must have been forewarned some days earlier about the likelihood of examining Medvedev. Possibly the staff at Kaluga, recognizing their own inexperience in dealing with "political cases", had arranged for a Serbsky consultant in anticipation of Medvedev's commitment. However, even the presence of Dr Shostakovich, the Serbsky expert, proved in the circumstances to be insufficient for a decisive outcome.

Lifshits later revealed to Medvedev's family that although the Shostakovich commission had not detected any "acute psychological disorder", the examiners felt it necessary to observe the patient clinically over a period of several days. Dr Bondareva meanwhile justified the original commitment to an insistent Roy Medvedev, who was by that time armed with the 1961 directives and well versed in their contents. She indicated that the action had been based on two indications in the directives: "hypochondriacal delirious conditions, producing incorrect, aggressive attitudes in the sick person to particular persons, organizations or official institutions", and "systematized delirious syndromes with chronic deterioration, if they result in socially dangerous behaviour". The diagnosis had been reached by Dr Leznenko after interviewing Medvedev in the guise of an education official, and corroborated by Dr Lifshits on the evening of the commitment.

Six days after his admission the most authoritative commission to date met to conduct yet another examination. The panel included two forensic psychiatrists we have already encountered, G. V. and V. M. Morozov of the Serbsky Institute (both had examined Grigorenko the year before), and R. A. Nadzharov of the Institute of Psychiatry. All three were experienced in the examination of "political patients" and would presumably be well equipped to handle this tricky case.

Like its predecessors, this commission emphasized Medvedev's writings, particularly the segments focused on in the two earlier examinations. The questions followed a similar pattern: What was Medvedev's aim in writing the work? Why had he begun to write works of this sort? Other issues related to his self-evaluation, his opinion on the need for hospitalization, his work record, and his relationships with his family and others. The examination lasted a mere 30 minutes. Lifshits reported the commission's conclusions to the family—discharge from hospital had been recommended and was scheduled for the following day.

Friday 5 June came and passed; Medvedev was still a patient in Kaluga. Saturday saw new investigations performed, including a neurological examination and an electro-encephalogram. A further interview was held with Lifshits and Bondareva. Their central line of enquiry concerned the issue of a history of mental illness in Medvedev's relatives. Struck by Lifshits's microscopic analysis of his records, he surmised that a plan was afoot to search thoroughly for a hint of disturbance in a relative so as to indicate a genetic factor in Medvedev's condition. Further questions, of no psychiatric relevance, were asked regarding his correspondence with foreign colleagues, his work in gerontology and, again, his writings. Such was to remain the character of all subsequent interviews during the next ten days until his release.

Mid-way through his hospitalization, the "patient" received his first "therapy" from Dr Lifshits, and an explanation of his illness. According to Medvedev's summary Lifshits explained that:

To engage in "publicist" writing in addition to one's normal professional work, scientific or other, was a sign of a "split" or "disassociated" personality, an obvious symptom of illness. "In time, of course, the hospital will discharge you," he said, "but you must completely stop all this other activity and concentrate on experimental work. If you continue your publicist activities, then you will inevitably end up back here with us."[24]

Lifshits reiterated this advice several more times during the remainder of Medvedev's hospitalization. At the time of discharge he was to warn him: "If you continue to act along previous lines and don't put an end to your publicist activities, we doctors will be unable to help you."[25] Publicist activities referred primarily to Medvedev's critical writings. Lifshits also explained the psychological disorder that characterized these works. The ideas expressed might be comprehensible and consistent, but they failed to take reality into account and reflected the author's "poor adaptation to the social environment".

The Diagnosis
Although Medvedev was never told in detail about the Morozov commission's diagnosis, a summary of it by Bondareva, submitted to the district psychiatric clinic, was later reluctantly shown to his wife. According to Medvedev's account, the diagnosis included the following points:

> "Sluggish schizophrenia" accompanied by "paranoid delusions of reforming society". The basic symptoms of the illness were also described on the card: "split personality, expressed in the combining of scientific work in his field with publicist activities; an over-estimation of his own personality, a deterioration in recent years of the quality of his scientific work, an exaggerated attention to detail in his publicist writing, lack of a sense of reality, poor adaptation to the social environment". The hospital recommended "out-patient treatment and employment".[26]

As in the case report of Grigorenko, "reformist delusions" are posited as a paramount criterion. Medvedev's critical works on the genetics controversy and on Soviet science constitute the evidence. However, Medvedev's research in these fields has gained him widespread respect. His work on Lysenkoism, for instance, has been published in eight languages, and was initially approved for publication in the USSR in 1967 by the Academy of Sciences. Many eminent Soviet and foreign scientists rallied to Medvedev's support on his detention, affirming the esteem in which he was held.

The notion of a "split personality"—engagement in two unrelated activities—as a criterion of mental illness is ludicrous and has given rise to the ironic term, the "da Vinci syndrome". We would be obliged to certify as insane countless brilliant men and women who have pursued multiple, diverse interests. In Medvedev's case the psychiatrists have also assumed the rôles of literary critic and biochemist. Somehow or another Dr Lifshits in particular acquired sufficient biochemical expertise to detect a deterioration in Medvedev's scientific work, and to assert that his second book, published in 1968, was inferior to his first because it was more theoretical. The fact is that Medvedev's work has been, and remains, valued in international gerontological circles. This is attested to by regular invitations to him to address international congresses, his appointment as a research fellow in the Institute of Medical Research in London, and his scientific publications which number over 100.

The literary criticism concerning the supposedly exaggerated detail in his social writings is an equally dubious criterion for the diagnosis of mental illness. Furthermore, widespread acceptance and acclaim in the West of Medvedev's two socially-oriented works does not support the psychiatric notion of an exaggerated attention to detail. Professor John Ziman in his foreword to *The Medvedev Papers* praises the book when stating that "from the very first page, he speaks to us in his natural voice: spirited, witty, resourceful, and ironical. What he has to tell us is devastatingly simple and clear."[27] Professor G. M. Carstairs in a review of the later work, *A Question of Madness*, refers to the narrative as reading like a "thriller, each stage being carefully documented by notes which the brothers Medvedev kept at the time".[28]

"Poor adaptation to the social environment" is another example of a vague criterion of Medvedev's supposed illness for which no evidence is forthcoming. Since he had never brushed with the law, had achieved stature in his profession, and had lived the quiet life of a provincial family man, the "poor adaptation" could only refer to the critical stance that he had recently adopted in his "publicist writing".

All three commissions somehow ignored important facts: Medvedev had never consulted a psychiatrist prior to this commitment, nor had he suffered from any psychological disturbance. No relative or friend had ever noted odd behaviour in him. There was no family history of psychiatric illness (except for the mild behavioural disturbance in his elder son).

Medvedev's treatment in the hospital consisted mainly of advice. Dr Lifshits also considered drug treatment. He cautiously sought the opinions of both Medvedev and his wife on the possibility of treatment with tranquillizers. The suggestion was swiftly shelved after Medvedev's retort that such treatment would be reminiscent of the medical experiments of Hitler's doctors. If drug therapy were instituted it would undoubtedly require force. Lifshits presumably felt under sufficient pressure by this time, without the added complication of forcing drugs on Medvedev. He was after all receiving a continuous stream of protests in the form of telegrams and letters, as well as having to deal with the tenacity of his "patient's" family.

The Struggle for Medvedev's Release

A major part in the struggle to secure Medvedev's release was played by his brother Roy. He pressed Lifshits from the outset to justify his brother's detention, challenging each point made by the psychiatrist in self-justification. Roy especially pointed to regulations which called for the release of a patient if there were no obvious signs of mental illness. Since the Shostakovich commission had failed to detect any "acute psychological disorder", the hospital was legally bound to release his brother forthwith. Lifshits himself wriggled out of these challenges, flustered by the erudition of Roy's arguments.

Roy solicited aid from a number of influential members of the intellectual community in Moscow, many of them friends and acquaintances of the Medvedev family. Their telegrams of protest cascaded on to the desks of the Minister of Health, the

Procurator-General and Dr Lifshits. Scientists from abroad soon added their own stream of protest, mostly addressed to the Soviet Academy of Sciences. Some friends were particularly assiduous in the campaign for Medvedev's release. Academician Sakharov, for instance, entered the auditorium at the Institute of Genetics, where an international symposium was taking place, to request the delegates' support. A letter from Sakharov to Leonid Brezhnev was widely circulated. Its publication in the Western press generated additional action by the world scientific community. *Inter alia* Sakharov declared:

> This whole action was totally illegal from beginning to end. The health authorities have absolutely no evidence of the kind required by official directives that Zhores Medvedev is mentally abnormal let alone a public danger . . . the health authorities are at this very moment resorting to tactics of subterfuge and delay. . . . I have learned that the relatives have been deliberately deceived and that psychological pressure and intimidation have been brought to bear on Zhores Medvedev himself. Zhores Medvedev must be released immediately. . . . Those who initiated and carried out this illegal action must be severely punished.[29]

An open letter by Alexander Solzhenitsyn was released on 15 June. Solzhenitsyn had first heard of Medvedev in 1964 through his *samizdat* critique of Lysenko. Solzhenitsyn's letter of praise and support at that time had sparked off a friendship between the two men. He was aware of Medvedev's plight but had delayed any comment for two weeks after his detention, uncertain as to the effects of an intervention. Like the Sakharov letter, Solzhenitsyn's protest achieved widespread publicity, both in the Soviet Union and abroad. He condemned the commitment, the criminal actions of the responsible psychiatrists, and more generally, the unjustified application of psychiatry:

> THIS IS HOW WE LIVE:
> Without any arrest warrant or any medical justification, four policemen and two doctors come to a healthy man's house. The doctors declare that he is crazy, the police major shouts: "We are the agency of enforcement. Get up!"

They twist his arms behind his back and drive him off to the madhouse.

This can happen tomorrow to any one of us. It has just happened to Zhores Medvedev, a geneticist and publicist, a man of subtle, precise and brilliant intellect and of warm heart (I know personally of his disinterested help to unknown, ill and dying people). It is precisely for the diversity of his fertile gifts that he is charged with abnormality: "a split personality"! It is precisely his sensitivity to injustice, to stupidity, which is presented as a sick deviation: "poor adaptation to the social environment"! Once you think in other ways than is PRESCRIBED—that means you're abnormal! As for well-adapted people, they must all think alike. And there is no means of redress: even the appeals of our best scientists and writers bounce back like peas off a wall.

If only this were the first case! But this devious suppression of people without searching for any guilt, when the real reason is too shameful to state, is becoming a fashion. Some of the victims are widely known, many more are unknown. Servile psychiatrists, breakers of their Hippocratic oath, define as "mental illness": concern about social problems, superfluous enthusiasm, superfluous coldness, excessively brilliant gifts or the lack of them.

Yet even simple common sense ought to act as a restraint. After all, Chaadayev did not even have a finger laid on him, but we have now been cursing his persecutors for over a century. It is time to think clearly: the incarceration of free-thinking healthy people in madhouses is SPIRITUAL MURDER, it is a variation on the GAS CHAMBER, but is even more cruel: the torture of the people being killed is more malicious and more prolonged. Like the gas chambers these crimes will NEVER be forgotten, and all those involved in them will be condemned for all time, during their life and after their death.

In lawlessness, in the committing of crimes, the point must be remembered at which a man becomes a cannibal!

It is short-sighted to think that one can live by constantly relying on force alone, constantly ignoring the objections of conscience.[30]

Medvedev's Release

Medvedev was finally released on 17 June, nineteen days after his admission. Although Dr Lifshits and his hospital colleagues had the power to release their patients according to their clinical judgement, in Medvedev's case the matter was considerably more complicated. Thanks to Roy's incessant campaign, several high-ranking officials in the Ministry of Health were involved in the case, a vociferous protest both within the Soviet Union and abroad had materialized, and the Western press kept abreast of each development. Clearly the affair had mushroomed into something far bigger than Lifshits could handle; decisions were in the hands of senior politicians in Moscow.

No one could possibly have anticipated the intense furore that occurred. No doubt the original goal of the authorities— probably acting on instructions from the KGB in Moscow—in instigating and persevering with Medvedev's commitment, was his detention for a prolonged period in hospital, followed by long-term supervision in a clinic. All this would have discredited him and his ideas, "trained" him sufficiently to put an end to his social criticism, and made him vulnerable to further episodes of obligatory treatment. Thus his dissenting views could be suppressed, and Medvedev effectively silenced. His relatively brief period in Kaluga reflected the failure of the plan.

Subsequent Developments

The psychiatrists recommended out-patient supervision and employment for Medvedev. He struggled frustratedly to achieve the latter. Despite an offer from an agricultural institute some weeks after his discharge, his path to this post was strewn with a series of hurdles. He encountered minimal co-operation at the Academy of Medical Sciences and the Ministry of Health. Only several weeks later did the institute formally confirm his appointment and then only for an initial trial period. If we bear in mind the psychiatrists' recommendation that Medvedev be employed and that an actual offer of a job had been made, the obstructive tactics practised by various authorities seem vindictive.

One episode is worth recounting to illustrate the type of

treatment meted out to him. Ironically, it is typical of the experiences and observations recorded in *The Medvedev Papers*. In July 1972 he was prevented from participating in the 9th International Congress of Gerontology in Kiev.[31] A year before the congress the council of the International Association of Gerontology had invited Medvedev to deliver a lecture at the Kiev meeting. An invitation by the Soviet organizing committee followed. All the necessary arrangements were made. Shortly before the congress the Soviet committee withdrew the invitation, claiming that there was now a surplus of lectures on the agenda. This action occurred without the knowledge and wishes of the council; its president later expressed his bafflement at this development.

Medvedev's request to participate in the work of the congress was later denied too, on the grounds of a lack of hotel accommodation and inadequate time to settle the formal arrangements. He was informed, however, that admission to congress sessions would be permitted. The KGB concluded otherwise, for immediately prior to the opening session a squad of plainclothes men spirited him off to a neighbouring police station, accused him of disturbing the peace, and ordered him to leave Kiev that night. Nothing was left to chance in the KGB plan, as they escorted him to the Moscow train.

Medvedev experienced other episodes of this kind. A month later, for instance, his request to participate in another international conference in Moscow was granted, but subsequently denied on the grounds of the limited seating accommodation. The restrictions on Soviet scientists, about which Medvedev had written, were once again in evidence.

In January 1973 Medvedev arrived in England to take up an official invitation from the National Institute for Medical Research to spend a year in its laboratories. In August he was summoned to the Soviet Embassy in London and there informed that the Presidium of the USSR Supreme Soviet had stripped him of his citizenship. The presidium had invoked article 7 of the Law on Citizenship and based its decision on Medvedev's alleged "actions discrediting the high title of citizen of the USSR".[32]

Medvedev fought back. He rebutted Soviet press accusations that he had accepted the research position in London following a private invitation, and had continued to spread "slanderous materials discrediting the Soviet state and social system, and the Soviet people".[33] Medvedev had received an official invitation, not a private one, and had accepted it with the backing of the director of his own institute in the Soviet Union. If he had slandered the Soviet state, why had no charge ever been laid against him in the USSR? Why had the procurator not demanded his extradition if he were continuing to commit anti-Soviet criminal acts? He insisted that during his seven months in England he had refrained from making any political statements whatsoever. He denounced the action of the Soviet authorities and called for the restoration of his citizenship. Perhaps realizing the futility of his demands, he sought at least permission to visit the Soviet Union annually in order to see his family and friends. However, neither was his citizenship restored, nor was he allowed to visit the Soviet Union. In 1976 he remained in exile in England.

Irregularities in Medvedev's Commitment

A series of irregularities typified Medvedev's commitment and subsequent "treatment". The patient, according to the 1961 directives, must be a "clear danger . . . to those around him or to himself". This was not the case with Medvedev. He had not exhibited aggressive tendencies or acted violently to others or to himself at the time of his detention, nor was there a previous history of such proclivities. The directives permitted the assistance of the police *in case of resistance* to a civil commitment. A squad of policemen accompanied the doctors on their mission and forcibly entered Medvedev's apartment; the opportunity for resistance was not even provided—the police had participated from the outset and had pre-empted the possibility.

A commission examined Medvedev soon after he entered hospital, as required by law, and by its own admission was unable to find any evidence of mental illness in him. The directives state that the patient gains his release when he is no longer a social danger or when his medical condition has improved, or if there is no evidence of mental illness. As the last condition applied, his release should have followed automatically. Yet the doctors prevaricated, arguing the need for additional clinical observation because of Medvedev's "heightened nervousness".

Even more puzzling was Medvedev's continuing detention for a further two weeks after the second commission had, according to Dr Lifshits's report, recommended his release. Lifshits had revealed that this commission's diagnosis had not provided adequate reason for hospitalization and compulsory treatment.

The participation of forensic psychiatrists in both the commissions, Dr Shostakovich in the first, and the Morozovs in the second, was to say the least anomalous. Medvedev had at no time been charged with, or even investigated for, criminal activity. The medical staff's explanation that the forensic experts were only consulted in their private capacity carried no conviction at all.

Leading Soviet psychiatrists explained the commitment of Medvedev in a meeting at the Serbsky Institute in October 1973 in which several foreign psychiatrists participated. (See chapter 10 for a full account of this meeting.) Professor John Wing[34] documented the account of the case given to the group by its Soviet hosts. The latter included Dr G. Morozov and Professor A. Snezhnevsky, who had both been intimately involved in the Medvedev affair. The account provided differed in crucial respects from that already known through *A Question of Madness*. The Soviet psychiatrists explained for instance that the reason for summoning Medvedev for examination was to determine the suitability of providing him with an invalid pension in the light of his long period of unemployment. His persistent refusal to co-operate with this examination had provoked the decision to arrange compulsory hospitalization. It was conceded that the doctors had erred and should have acted more cautiously. It was Medvedev's wife who had summoned the police at the time the psychiatrists came to interview him. Once examined by an authoritative commission, his discharge had been recommended and acted upon.

These statements are wholly unconvincing when placed alongside the account provided by the Medvedev brothers, the veracity of which there is no reason to doubt and which no Soviet authority has ever publicly questioned. The Soviet psychiatrists at the Serbsky were clearly participating in a cover-up of the original miscalculation in detaining Medvedev, which cast Soviet psychiatry in such a poor light. Why was it necessary to enact a civil commitment of a person merely to assess the issue of an invalid pension? Why had the psychiatrists not released him immediately when it was patently obvious that a commitment for the purpose of arranging an invalid pension was quite inappropriate? Why the need for a commission of visiting forensic psychiatrists from Moscow in a routine case of this sort? All these questions, and others, remained unanswered at the Serbsky meeting.

Both of us have met Medvedev since he left the Soviet Union in 1973. His intellectual and human qualities were obvious to us. They are well reflected in the last lines of *A Question of Madness*:

> Now at the end of this account, I want to stress that it certainly has *not* been written because I feel that there is anything shameful about mental illness. Illness is not a vice, but a misfortune which calls for sympathy and compassion. ... My purpose in writing the present work was certainly not to prove that there is *absolutely* nothing wrong with me. My aim is not so egocentric. It is rather to call attention to the dangerous tendency of using psychiatry for political purposes, the exploitation of medicine in an alien rôle as a means of intimidation and punishment—a new and illegal way of isolating people for their views and convictions.[35]

Chapter 7

THE HOSPITAL AND THE TREATMENT

IN THE PREVIOUS two chapters we illustrated the repression of dissenters through psychiatry by focusing on four cases. Two of them, Grigorenko and Gorbanevskaya, were interned in special psychiatric hospitals (SPHs); the other two, Medvedev and Shimanov, in ordinary psychiatric hospitals (OPHs). Our main objective was to indicate how psychiatry is abused during diagnostic and commitment procedures—we focused less on the hospital conditions and the treatment to which dissenters are subjected.

We now turn to a detailed consideration of these aspects. In the light of the testimony of "ex-patients", we conclude that the treatment of dissenters is a crucial element in the overall picture of abuse. Even if we were to assume, as we do not, that the dissenters were indeed mentally ill and in need of help, the psychiatric treatment they have actually received appears to us wholly inappropriate and often punitive and harmful.

Our conclusion is based on the many accounts of hospital experiences provided by dissenter-patients and their families. We have interviewed eleven "ex-patients" in depth and carefully reviewed diaries and other reports which have appeared in *samizdat*. These accounts of a variety of psychiatric institutions all point to an experience incompatible with what is appropriate for aiding the mentally-ill patient.

Considerable variation exists in what the dissenters have experienced. Much depends on the type of hospital to which they have been confined. Most of the better known dissenters have been dealt with under the provisions of a criminal commitment; by far the majority of these men and women have in turn been treated in an SPH. A small number of criminal-commitment cases, and all those detained under civil commitment, have been hospitalized in an OPH. The hospital experience in the OPH has generally proved less unsatisfactory and punitive.

The Ordinary Psychiatric Hospital (OPH)

As regards OPH conditions, Ilya Rips, who was hospitalized for eighteen months in Riga, was especially fortunate. He was sent there by the city court after it found him not responsible for the "anti-Soviet" offences he committed. The "crime" had been his attempted self-immolation in a Riga public square. He selected this mode of protest after much anguish, to demonstrate his opposition to the 1968 Soviet invasion of Czechoslovakia. Despite the prosecutor's demand for treatment in an SPH, the court, in an uncommon occurrence, ordered Rips to an OPH.

He has described to us his experience there in relatively positive terms. During the first month certain restrictions were imposed, in particular his confinement to his ward. Later, however, he was permitted to walk the grounds in the company of his visiting parents without hindrance. They were allowed to see him twice a week. After some months the authorities permitted others to visit Rips. No observations were made of these visits and free communication was possible.

He experienced no obstacles in obtaining books and had free access to pencil and paper. Indeed he could pursue his studies unmolested, and succeeded in writing several academic papers in his field of mathematics. The "patient" generally enjoyed his doctors, who were mostly kind and benevolent. At no point was Rips actively treated; he received no drugs or psycho-therapy. A regular superficial enquiry from his doctor as to his welfare and progress constituted the entire medical régime.

Doubtless Rips's benign (if long) hospitalization can be attributed to his own co-operative and compliant behaviour. He painstakingly avoided criticism of the hospital authorities on the premise that submissiveness would lead to release. Another likely factor contributing to the reasonableness of his treatment was that it took place in an OPH. This type of hospital is under the aegis of the Ministry of Health and its main function is to serve as a psychiatric facility for the community living around it. Thus for the most part the staff are conducting a conventional psychiatric practice in an institution which is reasonably accessible to the public. Their practices are in some degree exposed to the community and therefore to scrutiny by patients and their families.

But some dissenters have had more unpleasant experiences in OPHs. One of the most detailed and vivid accounts is by Yury Maltsev, whose internment—soon after he joined the Action Group for the Defence of Human Rights—we mentioned in chapter 3.[1] Maltsev is a literary specialist and translator from Italian who was forcibly placed in the Kashchenko OPH in October 1969. The formal procedure involved a military medical commission giving him—as an officer in the reserve—a "routine examination". On the basis that he had applied several times to emigrate to Italy the commission suspected mental illness and transferred him to the Kashchenko.

Here he was placed in a section for disturbed patients. He had no history of mental illness, and his psychiatrist soon concluded: "I personally find nothing abnormal in you. But, you understand, it's not I alone who decide matters." Another psychiatrist asked Maltsev *inter alia*: "Probably you react sharply to injustice?" When Maltsev agreed, he replied: "Unfortunately we can't ease your lot in any way. You'll have to spend at least a month here, because your case is very complex."

Maltsev now managed to get news of his plight to his friends in the Action Group, who in turn succeeded in having it reported in the Western press. This caused some alarm in the hospital. First the head doctor of the hospital and then Professor Viktor Morozov came to assess him. Morozov, whom we encountered in the Grigorenko case, conducted his interview in the presence of all the doctors in the section: "He wearily rubbed his eyes, giving the impression of someone who has long understood everything and to whom everything is terribly boring." How had Maltsev intended to make a living in Italy? How did he now regard his applications to emigrate? Maltsev replied that he now realized they had been useless and he wished he had not made them. Morozov was satisfied with this statement, presumably because it could be interpreted as a recantation. To Maltsev it was more a recognition of the *force majeure* which made emigration impossible. Morozov was interested in Maltsev's assertion that whereas in ordinary situations he was fairly passive, when his basic beliefs came into question he was uncompromising. Later the section's head doctor told him: "The professor explained your actions by the nature of your personality and by a certain tendency to over-valued ideas." The diagnosis, which he learned surreptitiously, was: "Psychopathy: keep under observation of district psychiatrist."

So after a month he was freed, but with a sword of Damocles suspended over his head. He did not know whether the object of the whole exercise had been simply to install the sword in place, or whether he had convinced the doctors of his good health, and this, coupled with the publicity abroad, had frustrated more sinister KGB plans.

Whatever the truth, Maltsev was shocked not only by the perversion of psychiatry in his own case, and in those of unknown dissenters whom he met in Kashchenko, but also by the conditions he had experienced. When he first entered the section: "A nasty smell struck my nose. I had never come across such a stench in any hospital." Also, only six inches separated the beds, while the corridors were jammed with beds down both sides. The windows were barred and the doors constantly locked and re-locked. Most of the patients were heavily drugged and slept or moved about in a daze. The

...smoked without inhibition in the wards, and at night,

...ent, were often drunk. They frequently

...inadequate pretexts, and threatened them

...nful drugs. In the course of a month the

...ut to walk in a small yard only four times.

..., Maltsev never got more than five to six

...it. The food was mostly inedible.

...omplained about conditions to an orderly,

...d how much worse things were in the wards

...: there, not just the corridors were jammed,

...had to be erected in the canteen each night.

...e looked in a mirror and, aged 37, saw "a

...ace . . . the typical look of a prisoner".

...his account immediately after his release

...for publication following his arrival in Italy

...re depressing picture emerges from other

...OPHs. One of these is by a young Moscow

...Dubrov, who had links with the Action Group

...en some *samizdat* articles.[2] In October 1972,

aged 22, he and his mother received permission to emigrate to Israel. At the last minute, however, the permission was revoked on the grounds that he had to do his army service. He refused to comply and—though he had never suffered from mental illness—was dispatched for examination to psychiatric hospital No. 3, known as "The Sailor's Rest" from the name of the street it stands on.

Dubrov was first placed in an observation ward in section 2. In his *samizdat* account written ten days after release he describes the section as being like a prison hospital:

> I looked around. A big ward, or cell, with twenty beds. Bars on the windows. Naked men lie on the beds, tied down, writhing in convulsions, issuing wild cries. From time to time an orderly comes up and gives them a hefty punch in the stomach. From the awful pain they quieten down for a time, just moan, then again they start to shout. From morning to night almost all of them are injected with several doses of Aminazin [a tranquillizer]. . . . The ward is permeated by a sickening smell of rotting: the patients perform their natural functions on the beds they are tied to. . . . It is forbidden to go out into the corridor. Also to walk around the ward. Everyone must lie on his bed. One can go to the toilet . . . only in the presence of an orderly.

After five days, with Dubrov's internment publicized in the West, he was transferred to another ward. The doctor here confessed to his mother that all the staff were terrified lest foreign journalists came to interview him. But the conditions were little better: he was given back his spectacles, without which he was almost blind; yet he still had no exercise period, and only one 60-minute visit per week was allowed. Dubrov describes the daily routine:

> The patients were woken at 7. The grating cry of the nurse rang out: "Come and get your Aminazin!" A long queue of patients would form. At 9 came breakfast. The food was disgusting: usually porridge for breakfast, lunch and supper. . . . From morning till late at night the section was filled with a fearful din—the shouting and the songs which disturbed patients bellowed continuously in the corridor. . . .
>
> The "treatment", at least in this section, was of only two types: injections of Aminazin and tying patients by their wrists, legs, or even chest to their beds. In this position

many were held for five to ten days. They were fed from a spoon. Aminazin is the panacea of Soviet psychiatry. A day before my discharge the following revealing dialogue took place between a patient and his doctor: "Why are you injecting me with Aminazin? You haven't made any diagnosis. . . ." "There are two ways of mending a watch. You can take it to pieces and look at the inside, or you can simply give it a shake. We treat people by the second method."

A commission of five women doctors eventually discharged Dubrov after a two-week internment. The main questions they put to him were curiously non-medical in character: "Do you intend to be politically active in the West?" and "Will you take part in the Zionist movement in Israel?"

In 1973 he eventually emigrated and settled in Vienna.

The Special Psychiatric Hospital (SPH)

Conditions prevailing in the SPHs have, by comparison with those in the OPHs, proved consistently stark and punitive. The SPHs are essentially prison-like institutions and were in fact until recently termed prison-psychiatric hospitals. Their function is to house, compulsorily, persons who have committed serious crimes—murder, rape, arson and an array of other violent offences—and who have been diagnosed as suffering from a mental illness and declared not responsible. Following the procedure of criminal commitment, such mentally-ill offenders are ordered by the court to enter an SPH for an indeterminate period, until their mental condition improves sufficiently to warrant their release. In addition to a supposed therapeutic function, the SPH also serves to protect society from dangerous offenders. Comparable institutions exist in many countries throughout the world: in Britain, for instance, they are the special hospitals of Broadmoor, Rampton and Moss Side.

History of the SPH

The history of the SPHs, and the number of them, are matters still full of uncertainty. Part of the confusion arises out of the simultaneous existence of several slightly different types of institution.

The "purest" sort of SPH is a self-contained institution which contains only inmates who have been sent there under criminal commitment by decision of a court. There are also psychiatric sections in the hospitals of certain prisons.* These are used to hold (apart from temporarily ill inmates from the attached prison) (1) remand prisoners who are either undergoing psychiatric assessment or are awaiting trial after assessment, or (2) prisoners already ruled not responsible by a court and awaiting assignment to an SPH proper. We have seen how the psychiatric section of the hospital of the Butyrka prison in Moscow was used in this last way in Gorbanevskaya's case.

Thirdly, there are institutions designed to deal with prisoners in labour camps who fall mentally ill. These may treat a prisoner and return him to his camp, or they may send him to the Serbsky for diagnosis and possible subsequent dispatch to an SPH.

There are two known examples. One is in Rybinsk on the upper Volga, and appears to be self-contained. The other is block 12 of the hospital in Mordovian camp 3. This hospital serves all the Mordovian camps, but its psychiatric section serves also the political camps in the Perm region, nearly 1,000 miles away. Recent documents describing block 12 suggest that it is an even more inhuman institution than the SPHs proper.[3] Apart from the extraordinary filth of the conditions, the orderlies are reported as exercising a reign of terror. Though common criminals serving their terms, they even have the right to administer injections as punishment.

The first SPH proper was in existence in the 1930s, situated in Kazan. In chapter 3 we included a description of it by a Polish psychiatrist who worked there during the war. After 1945 SPHs were set up in Sychyovka in the Smolensk region, and in Leningrad. The latter is usually referred to as the "Arsenalnaya" because of its location on Arsenalnaya Street. (It has been the place of internment of dissenters such as Alexander Volpin, Pyotr Grigorenko in 1964, Vladimir Bukovsky, Viktor Fainberg and Vladimir Borisov.) The Leningrad SPH was established in a building which served as a

---

* In the early 1950s some of these, at least, contained court-committed inmates: Yarkov, in the psychiatric section of the prison hospital in Gorky, fell into this category.

women's jail up to 1948. The Chistopol SPH may have been opened at about the same time. Certainly it was functioning by 1953–54 when Ilya Yarkov was in it. Whether it still functions is not known: no recent reports have mentioned it.

More than a decade elapsed before the development of other SPHs. The period between 1965 and 1972 saw the establishment of several new hospitals scattered throughout the Soviet Union. An SPH in Chernyakhovsk in the Kaliningrad region opened in 1965 in the building of a former German convict prison (Grigorenko's second hospitalization was here). Another SPH was established in Dnepropetrovsk in the Ukraine in 1968, also occupying a former prison. In the early 1970s SPHs opened in Oryol, south-west of Moscow; in Blagoveshchensk, near the Pacific coast; in Kzyl-Orda in Kazakhstan; and in Smolensk, west of Moscow.[4] Other SPHs exist in Tashkent and Alma-Ata; but we do not know when they began to function.[5] And an ex-inmate of the Arkhangelsk OPH has reported that when he was interned there in 1967–69 he was often threatened with dispatch to a nearby SPH at Zharovikha, which could be seen in the distance. This SPH, and others in Rostov, Ukhta and Perm, are as yet the subject only of individual, unconfirmed reports.[6]

Other SPHs have apparently been established in recent years, but as yet we know little about them. For instance, Natalya Gorbanevskaya has reported the apparent founding, as yet unconfirmed, of a new SPH in Birobidzhan, near the Pacific coast.

We are unclear about the reasons for the increase in the number of SPHs in recent years but speculate that it constitutes a belated effort to catch up with inadequate forensic hospital services. The new SPHs may also be part of the overall expansion of psychiatric hospitals which for many years have been in short supply. Possibly a policy decision was taken that there were too many high-security wards in OPHs, and that dangerous offenders who were mentally ill would be better supervised and controlled in the SPH.

Organization and Staffing of the SPH
The SPH is under the control of the Ministry of Internal Affairs (MVD) rather than the Ministry of Health. This is an

important point as the MVD is also responsible for the administration of the ordinary police (as opposed to the secret police or KGB) and all penal institutions. The MVD's prime interest is law and order.

As in its prisons, so in the SPHs, the maintenance of security is its principal concern; the health and welfare of inmates are secondary issues.

This priority is recognizable in the staff structure and the distribution of responsibility in the SPH. A parallel system of administration prevails comprising the non-medical security staff and the medical personnel. The ultimate responsibility for ensuring that the institution operates satisfactorily lies with the security officers. All personnel are employees of the MVD; the hospital director, senior administrative staff and psychiatrists are MVD officers holding a military-style rank.

The nature of the ranking is exemplified in the titles of the senior staff of the Leningrad SPH—the director of the hospital in 1974 was a colonel and the chief psychiatrist a major. The director of the Oryol SPH in 1971 was a lieutenant-colonel. The director determines policy and runs the hospital, and final authority on all matters rests with him. The chief psychiatrist is his subordinate. It appears that the director is not usually a psychiatrist. The men who in recent years have occupied this position in Chernyakhovsk and Dnepropetrovsk do not seem to have been psychiatrically qualified. According to Vladimir Gershuni, a dissenter confined in the Oryol SPH, its director, Lieutenant-Colonel Baryshnikov, was a surgeon by training and prior to coming to Oryol had headed a sanatorium for tubercular patients.

The day-to-day security is the responsibility of the warder and orderly. The rôle of warder is comparable to that of a prison guard and his activities are supervised by the security administration; he is not subordinate to the psychiatrists. The orderly is subordinate to both medical and non-medical staff, but in practice operates mainly under the direct control of the warder.

Viktor Fainberg, a dissenter who spent four years in the Leningrad SPH, gave us an elaborate account of the parallel systems of maintenance of security and provision of psychiatric care. His description of the orderly is particularly illuminating. As attested in many sources, orderlies are in fact common criminals. After being sentenced for offences like hooliganism, theft, forgery or assault, they are transferred from investigation prisons to an SPH. They are not consulted as to whether they prefer to serve their sentence as an orderly rather than as a conventional prisoner. No proper screening procedure exists; selection appears to be more a function of the authorities' need for staff at any particular time. The basis of the whole policy is not entirely clear but may relate to the difficulty of hiring enough trained nurses for what is a dangerous and unattractive job.

The orderly tends to be easily corrupted; he has little recourse but to adapt to the system. The work is monotonous, the rewards few. The orderly is himself a prisoner, living in prison-like conditions in a hostel which is normally within the SPH.[7] He is fed poorly, sometimes worse than the patients. He may receive one parcel every four months and meet only infrequently with his relatives. The orderly's average sentence is between two and five years and it is in the SPH that he will spend the time unless he is either transferred for good behaviour to a more congenial situation, e.g. working in the construction industry and virtually on parole, or sent to a prison camp for bad behaviour. The latter sanction naturally induces compliance in him. His activities are constantly monitored by the warders and other security personnel. But much of his work remains unsupervised and unchecked. This is crucial, for the orderly has the most frequent contact with the patients, guarding them, holding them down for injections, escorting them to the exercise yard, and the like.

Paradoxically, therefore, a person least fitted to the therapeutic task spends more time with the patient than any other staff. The orderly's frustrations, the circumstances of his own imprisonment, his poor diet, all make for corruption. He tends to take out his frustrations on the patients. He demands food and clothes from them. In return, he allows them an additional visit to the toilet or an extra ration of tobacco.

We have not yet discussed the hospital psychiatrist. Perhaps this is because he tends to play a relatively insignificant part in the system. The need for prison-type security overshadows his rôle entirely. Fainberg, in describing the pattern of power and control in the SPH, highlights this relative impotence of the doctor and the inflated rôle of the orderly:

At the bottom of the two lines of subordination (security and medical personnel) is the orderly, who is subordinate to both of them, but immediate control over him is exercised by the warder, i.e. by a person who has no connection whatsoever with medicine. Such a system not only fails to prevent arbitrariness but, as a result of the process of mutual "covering up" (of one another's misdemeanours) and of well-established hospital traditions, actually encourages it. There are cases of orderlies being instructed by the warder to force their way into a ward and tie up and assault a patient without the knowledge of the nurse. The system at present is such that even people who feel some human sympathy for the patients are in practice unable to help them. Thus a doctor who really wishes to protect a patient from the mockery and blows of the warders and block superintendents is not in a position to do so. A nurse can only ask (not order) a warder to refrain from rudeness and physical violence.[8]

Life in the SPH

Although renamed *special* (not prison) psychiatric hospitals in the mid-1950s, these institutions have retained their prison-like quality in most respects. As mentioned earlier, many of them are housed in buildings previously constructed and used as prisons. A description of the hospital in Dnepropetrovsk depicts the typical character of the buildings.[9] The SPH there is situated within the confines of the city prison. A white brick wall which surrounds it is topped with rows of barbed wire. A second wall is visible behind the outer one, also with barbed wire. Armed guards are perched over these walls in watch-towers, their automatic weapons ready to deal with any attempt at escape. A picture often tells the best tale and the photographs of the SPHs in Oryol and Chernyakhovsk (see nos. 18, 20) highlight the prison-like nature of the buildings.

Within, the features of a prison also prevail. Cells for instance, locked on the outside, house some patients, rather than conventional wards. Patients are confined to a cell or ward for over twenty hours in the day. A daily exercise period of only one hour, or up to two in the summer, is normally permitted, and then usually in a cramped exercise yard. The life of a patient very much resembles that of a prisoner. Vladimir Gershuni, a dissenter who was confined in the Oryol SPH, wrote in his diary on 9 March 1971:

> On the 27 February the latest party of prisoners arrived from Butyrka [a Moscow prison] so the cells are full—before there were seven, now eight people to a 16- or 17-square-metre cell i.e. two square metres per patient. This is all intentional. There is no room to move. One is allowed to go along the corridor, but only if it is absolutely necessary—to the toilet, to obtain items of food from the nurse, or to smoke in the toilet. The toilet here is a cess-pit; four holes in the ground and two taps for 54 people, very reminiscent of railway-station lavatories in the worst sense of the word. . . . There isn't a single locker in the cells, you can only write by squatting beside your bed on the floor. The light is poor.

Gershuni's diary two days later:

> . . . from seven to eight-thirty in the evenings, we are allowed to use the dining room; we can write letters, or play dominoes and chess. The bedlam is indescribable. Your head feels as if it is about to burst. The letters you write in this atmosphere are strange. . . . We only have an hour's exercise (we had two in Butyrka); the exercise yards are so cramped and crowded that it makes your head swim once more.[10]

In Chernyakhovsk conditions in 1970 for Grigorenko were similar to those in Oryol: "His cell is a room of six square metres. There are two people in it: Pyotr Grigorenko and his cell-mate. . . . There are two paces of free space—just enough to get up and dress. The exercise period amounts to about two hours a day—the rest of the time one is locked in."[11]

In addition to these physical restrictions, several dissenters have reported how they have been deprived of the opportunity to occupy themselves creatively. Mrs Zinaida Grigorenko describes in letters to Soviet and international organizations[12] the refusal of the hospital authorities to permit her husband to indulge in any physical activities or to use pen and paper. In one letter she writes:

> Somehow he found a tiny piece of slate pencil. Gripping it with his finger nails he made marks in books. The bit of slate pencil was taken away. He made book marks out of newspaper. These were taken away. He asked for some kind of work to do, as occupational therapy, even if it was just sweeping the yard. Refused.[13]

Writing materials are available, but only at the discretion of the authorities. Gershuni records in one diary entry that he and his fellow inmates were warned that pencils and pens were about to be removed and would only be re-issued if absolutely necessary—to write letters.[14]

Despite this concession, letter writing by inmates entails several restrictions: letters can be sent off only twice a month, outward letters are subject to censorship by the SPH authorities and they may only be sent to relatives. Vladimir Borisov conveys the nature of these restrictions as imposed in the Leningrad SPH: "I have been given permission to use paper and a fountain pen, but I am obliged to give every line into the safekeeping of my doctor (in my own interest of course), lest one of them find its way out of the hospital without having been inspected."[15]

Censorship pervades other aspects of the life of an inmate. Visits for instance are limited to families and take place only in the presence of staff. Discussion must be confined to family matters; revealing facts about conditions in the hospital is forbidden. The guards observe the inmate and his visitors carefully to ensure that no letters or manuscripts are exchanged.[16] Another form of censorship is that of reading materials. Fainberg for example reports that a censorship system exists for all books sent to inmates from outside the hospital and that a total ban operates on books in foreign languages.[17]

Visits are generally permitted only once a month; moreover, the authorities have the power to forbid them. In the case of Grigorenko, for instance, the director refused permission for a visit by his wife, son and future daughter-in-law, despite the couple's wish for parental blessing prior to their marriage, and the length of their trip from Moscow to Chernyakhovsk, a distance of some 700 miles. A month later, son and daughter-in-law were given two hours of visiting time, one hour on the first day and another on the second, but denied a visit on the third day.*[18]

The case of Leonid Plyushch, who was detained in the Dnepropetrovsk SPH from July 1973 until January 1976, and whom we shall discuss later in this chapter, exemplifies the authorities' curious attitude to the visits of patients' relatives. Tatyana Plyushch on occasions experienced considerable difficulty in maintaining contact with her husband. Her first visit to the hospital was not until 22 August 1973, 38 days after Plyushch's admission. At this point, she had not been allowed to see him for over nineteen months, that is, since the time of his arrest. She protested in 1974 to the chief medical officer of the Ukrainian MVD about the hospital's refusal to permit two visits already scheduled.[19]

Other restrictive practices apply to the families of inmates. For instance, they may send only one parcel of food, tobacco and books to their relatives per month.[20]

Brutality and Punishment

The conditions described above might be tolerable were the staff liberal and humane. However, overwhelming evidence points to the contrary being the case. Several accounts of the oppressive, punitive atmosphere have emerged, and they reveal a grim neglect of even the most basic humanitarian considerations normally accorded to the mentally ill. This is not a problem limited to the SPH, or to the Soviet Union for that matter. Individual mental institutions in many countries, particularly those designed for disturbed offenders, have at various times been revealed as inhumane and punitive. But the Soviet SPHs must rank among the most cruel of such institutions in the world.†

* Families are permitted to visit over two or three consecutive days because of the vast distances they have to travel and the long intervals between their trips to the hospital—clearly a policy exists of placing some dissenters in far removed SPHs, so precluding regular contact with their families.

† The SPHs featured in this chapter are in no way exceptional. Conditions in the Smolensk and Sychyovka SPHs in 1972–73, as described by Yan Krylsky (see appendix I) in an as yet unpublished book written by his father Yulius Krylsky, are very similar, and in several respects even more brutal.

A dominant factor in the oppression, mentioned earlier, is the rôle of the orderlies. Their brutality (certainly not confined to this group alone) has been documented vividly by Fainberg in his 1970 appeal to human-rights organizations:

In the summer of 1969 two orderlies from section 8 went into a cell without a nurse or duty officer and beat up a patient called Stanislav Arbuzov. At the end of April 1970 in section 4 a nurse, Anastasia Alekseyevna, gave an injection to a patient called Vladimir Alekseyev . . . and then left the ward to give the orderlies the chance to beat him up while keeping her own hands "clean". Sometimes, for the sake of "convenience", the patient is first tied to his bunk and then beaten up. In August 1970 in section 3 the orderlies beat up a patient called Efimov, first of all pushing him down onto his bunk. Duty officers and block superintendents don't lag behind the orderlies in "feats" of this sort. In June 1969 in section 1 a patient called Vladimir Stepanov was roughly dragged into a different "cabin" from the one he wanted (seriously-ill inmates take their exercise here in cabins, i.e. minute yards more like wooden boxes without lids); the patient, trying to resist, struck Georgy Russky, the block superintendent who, together with the orderly, grabbed hold of him, led him to his section and went on beating him in his cell. Such beatings can be extremely vicious. One patient was taken to the bathroom and brutally beaten up by the orderlies, warders and doctors' assistants. He was thrown onto the tiled floor and kicked, as a result of which his shin-bone was fractured and he had to be sent to Moscow for an operation.[21]

Such incidents of violence by hospital staff have resulted in the death of inmates. The *Chronicle* reports how Popov, a patient in Chernyakhovsk, was beaten to death. In his medical file, it was recorded that he had died of a brain haemorrhage.[22]

Gershuni graphically records his encounter with the brutality of the Oryol staff. While in the midst of a hunger strike, the authorities denied him his period of exercise. Gershuni demanded this right and attempted to join his fellow patients who were being led outside. At this point: "they grabbed me, twisted my arms behind my back, forced me back into the cell, and in the doorway the exercise 'screw' dealt me a blow on the jaw. My gums were rather tender; after all, this was the forty-second day of my hunger strike."[23]

As the above accounts show, the orderly is not the only culprit: the warder and other security personnel also take part in the brutal handling of patients. The nurses and doctors, it would appear, either collude with the beatings or are powerless to intervene. The doctor may act by transferring the injured patient to another section of the hospital. Both Fainberg and Gershuni are critical of the absence of any investigations into the cases of violence inflicted on inmates. The physical injuries are usually explained in various self-serving ways, as described by Vladimir Bukovsky: "There is no supervision of the orderlies by the doctors, so they can beat up the patients with impunity. They can always claim that the patient was not behaving properly, that he was overly agitated because of his illness, so they had no chance to deal with him in any other way. That explanation would be enough: they would receive no punishment."[24]

Several dissenters have recorded the system of punishments that exists in addition to the arbitrary beatings. Presumably the main function of punishment is the maintenance of tight discipline and security.

One mode, described briefly in chapter 3, is the "roll-up" or "wet-pack". Apparently discarded now as a means of restraint and sedation in Soviet psychiatry, the "wet-pack" remains in use as a punitive device. Both Bukovsky and Fainberg[25] provide accounts of its application.

According to Bukovsky's description of its use in Leningrad in the mid-1960s:

This involved the use of wet canvas—long pieces of it—in which the patient was rolled up from head to foot, and so tightly that it was difficult for him to breathe; as the canvas began to dry out it would get tighter and tighter and make the patient feel even worse. But that punishment was applied with some caution—there were medical men present while it was taking place who made sure that the patient did not lose consciousness, and if his pulse began to weaken then the canvas would be eased.[26]

The *Chronicle* reports a form of punishment used at Kazan: "If the patients commit offences—refuse to take medicine, quarrel with the doctors, or fight, they are strapped into their beds for three days, sometimes more. With this form of punishment, the elementary rules of sanitation are ignored: the patients are not allowed to go to the lavatory, and bedpans are not provided."[27]

This "chaining-up" method is also used, according to an eyewitness, in the Sychyovka SPH, sometimes for a period of days.[28]

The Use of Drugs as Treatment and as Punishment

A more common form of punishment has been the administration of drugs. An injection of Sulphazin for instance, a preparation of purified sulphur, leads to a variety of distressing symptoms including high fever, bodily pains and general discomfort. This drug was used for various psychiatric conditions in the 1930s but fell into disfavour when it was shown to have no therapeutic value. Sulphazin has no place in contemporary medicine and certainly does not feature in Western pharmacopoeias. Its application as a punitive measure, however, has been cited by many dissenters. Plyushch reports on its use in Dnepropetrovsk for "misbehaviour" by patients; they suffered excruciating pain lasting up to 24 hours following an injection.[29] Fainberg notes that the drug is "used almost exclusively as a punishment; the patient's temperature rises to 40° Centigrade and for three days it is painful for him even to stir".[30]

Since the early 1950s the class of drugs usually referred to as the major tranquillizers has come to play a vital rôle in psychiatric practice. The tranquillizers have proved of considerable value in treating some of the most severe mental disorders, particularly the schizophrenias, related psychoses, and more generally in dealing with states of extreme excitability. The first drug in this group to be successfully used was Chlorpromazine (common names for this drug in the West are Largactil or Thorazine and in the Soviet Union, Aminazin). Subsequent developments generated other closely-related compounds including Trifluoperazine (in the West known as Stelazine and in the Soviet Union as Triftazin) and Haloperidol (Western names are Serenace and Haldol and the Soviet name Haloperidol). Aminazin and Haloperidol in particular appear to be the commonly-used tranquillizers in Soviet psychiatric practice for the severely mentally ill.

When given to schizophrenic patients, the major tranquillizers initially reduce features of anxiety and excitement; later, major psychotic symptoms such as hallucinations and delusions become less disturbing to the patient; eventually they either disappear or, if they persist, cause less interference to the patient's life. Conventionally, these drugs are administered in high dosage, either orally or by injection, especially in acute attacks of schizophrenia; then the dose is decreased gradually until a low maintenance level is reached.

A range of side-effects and complications can occur with their use such as lowering of the blood pressure, jaundice, allergic skin reactions, abnormal skin pigmentation, weight gain, blurred vision and drowsiness.

One major handicap in prescribing the tranquillizers is the common development of side-effects involving the extrapyramidal system of the brain, responsible for normal movement and co-ordination of the body. Rigidity, slowness and paucity of body movement, tremor, motor restlessness and involuntary purposeless movements of lips, tongue, face and other parts may all occur, and frequently do so in mild forms. These abnormalities are reversible on withdrawal of the drug and indeed can also be prevented in most patients by the concurrent use of other drugs (those normally used in the treatment of Parkinson's disease). There is a danger, however, of the irreversibility of some of these features in a minority of patients.

Most psychiatrists respect both the inestimable value of the tranquillizers in treating psychoses, and also the danger of severe side-effects, particularly those involving the extrapyramidal system. In practice, this results in judicious caution in the setting of the dosage, careful monitoring of side-effects, and the prescribing of an anti-Parkinsonian drug where appropriate. From all accounts, Soviet psychiatrists employ the tranquillizers in a similar fashion to their counterparts in the West. Reports from many dissenters suggest, however, that the drugs are additionally used for non-therapeutic reasons, as for example in the indiscriminate way described by Gershuni:

When our party of prisoners arrived from Butyrka, all 60 of us were prescribed treatment, without undergoing any medical examination. I for instance had my blood pressure measured, but the others did not even have this. Almost all those who arrived were given Aminazin, both orally and by injection. . . . Only two of the group, whose obvious allergies to Aminazin had been established at the Serbsky Institute, were saved from the injections.[31]

More sinisterly, drugs are also used in the SPH as agents of intimidation and, as in the case of Leonid Plyushch, to overcome the resistance of dissenters and force them into what may be the morally self-destructive act of recantation.

The counter-therapeutic application of drugs is reflected in Gershuni's experience at Oryol in 1970:

During a hunger strike in January . . . I felt steadily worse and worse, and after making a complaint, I began to get Aminazin injections in the maximum dose, or very close to it (approximately 6 cc's).* I could not sleep at all, yet the same dose was administered to me for twelve days in a row, until they became convinced that I was still not sleeping, and that the injections had not made me give up my hunger strike. I have been given two tablets of Haloperidol twice daily, that is four tablets in all, and Kozich (the chief psychiatrist) assures me that this will go on for a long time. This medicine makes me feel more awful than anything I have experienced before; you no sooner lie down than you want to get up, you no sooner take a step than you're longing to sit down, and if you sit down you want to walk again—and there is nowhere to walk. By the way, I am not the only one who has had this sort of thing happen to him. Everybody here has their life made miserable by Triftazin, Aminazin and other powerful drugs.[32]

We surmise that Gershuni was indeed administered large doses of Aminazin and Haloperidol in an attempt to end his hunger strike. Hunger strikes appear to be the most potent weapon available to the dissenter confined to an SPH, perhaps his only weapon. In chapter 6 we read of Shimanov's hunger

---

* It is impossible to know how big a dose this actually was since the strength of Aminazin injections varies considerably.

strike and its effectiveness in securing his release. Vladimir Borisov and Viktor Fainberg resorted to prolonged hunger strikes to achieve better treatment for themselves and fellow inmates.

The most blatant misapplication of drugs known to us occurred with Leonid Plyushch. He was born in 1939, graduated from Kiev University in 1962, and until July 1968 worked as a mathematician at the Cybernetics Institute of the Ukraine's Academy of Sciences. He was dismissed from this post after his criticism of a newspaper article about a political trial. A year later he became a founder member of the Action Group for the Defence of Human Rights (see chapter 3). His arrest came in January 1972. After eighteen months of detention the Ukraine Supreme Court, on the recommendation of a psychiatric commission, ordered him to be placed in an SPH. Plyushch was sent to Dnepropetrovsk in July 1973, released two and a half years later, and emigrated immediately thereafter to France. His case illuminates many of the anti-therapeutic practices that characterize the SPH, notably the way in which he was "treated" pharmacologically. Through his wife's ceaseless efforts to attain his release and the support of his friends we have learned much of this aspect of his hospital experience.

Plyushch's letter to his wife written some days after his arrest suggests a warm, well-integrated personality. Excerpts follow:

My darling, dearest Tanchik!
Yesterday I received a parcel from you and it was almost as though I met you. Even your signature delighted me. . . . I feel quite normal, both physically and spiritually . . . I have enough to eat. Books are available. I've got Shevchenko's *Tales*, Kvitko-Osnovyanenko's book, Dubov's *Boy Beside the Sea*, a two-volume edition of Conrad, and Kochetov's *The Zhurbins*. I'm devouring Shevchenko, although of course his tales don't compare at all with his other works. One simply enjoys the inner integrity and refinement of soul that Repnina wrote about. You read and you see the world through his sad, passionate eyes. In his tales he is softer and more sentimental. Maybe, later, I'll really study the Bard [i.e. Shevchenko] and examine different aspects of his psycho-poetics (this term I've invented myself,

and I'm not sure if I'll be able to explain it to you—something along the lines of: what it is in the Bard which reaches the heart, and how).[33]

And to his two children he writes:

> Dima! My son who's almost grown up! You write something to me as well, at least a few lines (providing they're not formal). As regards helping Mama, and your school work, I won't say anything. I think you'll take care of those things by yourself. Describe to me some interesting adventures or books (museums, journeys—you know how much I like all those things).
>
> And now Lesik too! It's a pity I didn't have a chance to say good-bye to you—you were asleep and were seeing something nice in your dream. Well, what should I describe for you? If you like, in each letter I'll send you a bed-time story, so that Dima and Mama can read it to you.

A visit by his wife on 22 October 1973, three months after his admission to Dnepropetrovsk, saw an entirely transformed man:

> ... Leonid Plyushch started to gasp for breath and was seized with convulsions. It was clear from time to time his hearing lapsed and he lost the ability to speak. Plyushch himself asked to have the visit cut short and he was taken back to his ward. ... Shortly thereafter it was learned that he had begun to be forcibly treated with Haloperidol. When his wife visited him again (after a two-week interval) the convulsions had ceased. He may have been given a drug to counteract them. But his general condition is one of great depression, apathy, drowsiness and defeat.[34]

We cannot be dogmatic and insist that the deterioration in Plyushch was in fact due to the administration of Haloperidol, but a causal relationship is most suggestive. Other factors probably operated as well—the influence of deeply-disturbed patients, a sense of hopelessness because of the indefiniteness of his confinement, the separation from his wife and two children and a concern about them. The deterioration is particularly obvious when looking at Plyushch's letter-writing pattern. As the *Chronicle* reported, "Earlier, in August and September,

Plyushch wrote many long and interesting letters. After the beginning of the treatment he ceased writing almost entirely and was even unable to read."[35] These letters later reached the West and confirm the *Chronicle*'s evaluation.[36]

In July 1974 Mrs Plyushch could not recognize her husband: he moved with difficulty and "his eyes had lost their usual liveliness".[37] The Haloperidol treatment had been replaced by Insulin injections* two months earlier. Some weeks prior to the change in drugs, it was learned from Plyushch that all drugs had been withdrawn when he complained of abdominal pain. He himself surmised that the doctors were disconcerted by this development. Without drugs, his condition improved—he began to read again, and to write letters.[38]

In January 1975 we learn that a major tranquillizer was again prescribed. The result by now was predictable—"again: apathy, indifference, tiredness. Now he wrote only one letter of five or ten lines in a month. He could not read, did not work."[39] As the drug was continued, so Plyushch worsened and at a meeting in early March:

> Leonid looked even worse. To his drowsiness and apathy were added serious swelling. He was still in the high-security ward, and still taking the same tablets. In the ward he would try to switch off, retreat into himself. This switching off, already habitual for him, continued even during the meeting. His wife noticed that sometimes his gaze would fade away or would fix itself on something beyond her. At these moments he would neither see nor hear anything. She would have to call out, then he would "return". To questions about his health he answered: "Everything is fine."[40]

Plyushch has given his own account of the use of drugs since his arrival in the West. His testimony demonstrates convincingly their non-medical administration both to himself and to fellow inmates. For instance Anatoly Lupynos, a Ukrainian poet and dissenter, was given medication in large doses after he lodged a protest to the hospital authorities. Until then he had received smaller doses than Plyushch. Another patient, Viktor Rafalsky, a Ukrainian school principal and Marxist writer, was given

* An old-fashioned therapy in psychiatry originally given in a dose to produce a comatose, or sub-comatose, state in schizophrenic patients.

large doses of Sulfazin. A nurse conceded to Plyushch that the treatment was a punishment although the doctors denied it.

In Plyushch's own case, drugs were used for another purpose besides punishment: to destroy him as a dissenter and as a person. As he comments, the drugs had a harmful effect on his whole being:

> I saw in my own case that the first days are meant to break a person morally straight away, break down his will to fight. Then begins the "treatment" with tranquillizers. I was horrified to see how I deteriorated intellectually, morally and emotionally from day to day. My interest in political problems quickly disappeared, then my interest in scientific problems, and then my interest in my wife and children. This was replaced by fear for my wife and children. My speech became jerky and abrupt. My memory also deteriorated.[41]

A third purpose of the drugs was to blackmail his wife. She was informed that his treatment would be made less intensive if she refrained from publicizing his case.[42]

Paradoxically, other dissenters interned in mental hospitals, both ordinary and special, have received no drugs at all despite being given a diagnosis similar to that of Plyushch. Grigorenko and Rips, for example, were spared any medication throughout their lengthy period of confinement; Fainberg was given only two injections over five years. Several explanations are possible. In the case of Grigorenko his age and physical condition would have made him more vulnerable to the dangerous side-effects of the tranquillizing drugs. Since he was well known in the West, and had a particularly well-organized lobby pressing the Soviet authorities for his release, it would have proved embarrassing had he died through the misapplication of drugs.

Fainberg threatened to commit suicide if he were administered drugs; the seriousness of his threats probably deterred the doctors. His abnormal thyroid condition may have been another factor. Rips was treated in an OPH and caused no trouble to the hospital staff; he was an unknown dissenter having made only a single act of protest, and independently of others. He was also a Latvian citizen treated by Latvian doctors and nurses—they could well have sympathized with his ordeal as a reflection of their own antipathy to their Russian "masters".

Plyushch is a complete contrast to Rips. He belonged to a human-rights group and persisted in his dissenting activities, despite repeated pressure on him to cease. The authorities felt they must check him vigorously. His arrest and internment was the result. We speculate that the authorities now decided to use his case for broader, symbolic and sinister purposes.* They may well have opted for maximum brutality against Plyushch as an important element in their suppression of dissenters in general, precisely because he had an unusually well-organized lobby working on his behalf, both in the Soviet Union and abroad. Harsh treatment of the "patient" might ultimately exhaust Western humanitarian concern and generate a sense of futility and despair in both Plyushch himself and fellow members of the human-rights movement. By demonstrating the KGB's readiness to destroy them as human beings, even in defiance of a lobby as powerful as Plyushch's, the régime would intimidate dissenters more than ever before. Eventually, however, the pressure from the lobby became so intense that the authorities found the publicity intolerable and ordered his release.

More generally, we conclude that the indiscriminate use of powerful drugs on dissenters derives from the punitive and intimidatory powers which they provide to the treating psychiatrist. Here is a potent weapon to wear down the dissenter and neutralize his "reformist" thinking, his social dangerousness. The drugs have the potential of inducing a state of apathy, lethargy, depression and physical deterioration. In the face of high doses the dissenter will hopefully "throw in the towel" and make the full-scale recantation which is the KGB's prime goal.

No Legal Redress

Were it possible to mount a malpractice suit against the institution or a particular doctor, the dissenter might be more

---

* Subsequently in 1973–75, when the KGB was crushing dissent in the Ukraine with unusual severity, and when, on the other hand, a powerful campaign was developing in the West, Plyushch's case became a focal one with wide international ramifications.

hopeful of achieving improved medical care. However, a person once committed to a SPH loses all basic rights—he is powerless. No matter how unjust his view of the treatment, no matter that he be beaten or over-medicated or punished unfairly, he has no legal redress whatever. The lot of an inmate is in this respect far worse than a person held in a prison or labour camp.

In a prison or camp an inmate can legally write a letter of protest to the local procurator, who is in theory responsible for ensuring the observance of legal procedures there. Despite the futility of such an act, the penal authorities are obliged to submit the protest to the procurator. A protest letter from a patient is unlikely to get beyond the confines of the hospital ward since it can be immediately categorized as the rantings of a lunatic. In any event the hospital authorities, unlike their MVD colleagues running prisons and camps, are not legally obliged to pass such protests on to the procurator. Grigorenko highlights the complete impotence of the inmate: "An SPH patient lacks even the meagre rights enjoyed by other prisoners. He simply has no rights at all. The doctors can do anything they like with him and no one will interfere or defend him. None of his complaints or those of his fellow patients will ever get outside the hospital. His one and only hope is in the honesty of the doctors."[43]

There is in fact a second path available to the inmate other than the honesty of the doctor. But even to start treading it requires great perseverance and tenacity. We refer to the potential for petitions by the inmate's family, which has the right to ask the local procurator to initiate criminal proceedings against hospital personnel. We know of only one instance of such an action, that of Tatyana Plyushch. In December 1974, when her husband had been a patient in Dnepropetrovsk for eighteen months, and after she had witnessed the progressive deterioration in his physical and mental condition, she requested that the procurator bring charges against the hospital director, Lieutenant-Colonel F. K. Pruss, and Drs L. A. Lyubarskaya* and E. P. Kamenetskaya, Plyushch's two principal psychiatrists. Her action was entirely legitimate, in accordance with the penal code of the Ukrainian Republic. She pointed out that the treatment given to her husband was

* Some *samizdat* documents wrongly identify Dr Lyubarskaya as Dr L. A. Chasovskikh.

tantamount to the "premeditated destruction of Leonid Plyushch's physical and mental health by means of huge doses of drugs administered over a long period and under insanitary conditions".[44]

In reply the procurator informed her that a medical commission would decide on the merit of her complaint, and on whether criminal proceedings should be initiated. Her subsequent enquiries regarding the composition of the commission and other pertinent issues were not answered. Ultimately her request for proceedings against the doctors was denied.

There is no case known to us of a doctor or other staff member of an SPH being convicted for negligence or deliberate misuse of psychiatry. Although the legal machinery exists to initiate a malpractice suit, the likelihood of it getting off the ground is minimal. Perhaps Grigorenko is therefore correct in his conclusion that the honest doctor is the dissenter's only salvation. Only for a very few is there another possible source, namely a powerful Western campaign for their release.

Attitudes to the Patient's Family

Customarily the family of a mentally-ill person plays a crucial rôle in his recovery. Most psychiatrists would exploit the support a family can give, both during the patient's hospital period and later on his release. In the case of dissenters, their families have not only been entirely neglected, but regarded as intruders who may foil the efforts of the psychiatrist. Not surprisingly an adversary relationship is rapidly established between the psychiatrist and the family. After all, the families have not concurred with the process of criminal commitment and the conclusion that their relatives are mentally ill and not responsible. Nor have they seen them as guilty of any crime.

Several accounts illustrate how shabby, sometimes contemptuous, the psychiatrist's dealings with relatives are. Colonel Pruss for instance permits an anxious Mrs Plyushch the chance to see her husband with this terse comment: "As I know you like to make a fuss, you will, despite the quarantine [there was indeed a quarantine in the hospital at the time] be given ten minutes with your husband." Another doctor, in response to her query about the drugs Plyushch is receiving, retorts: "I shall tell you nothing: neither my diagnosis, nor the drugs we are using."[45] We described earlier the authorities' attitude towards the Grigorenko family, reflected in the obstacles placed in the way of their visit to the hospital. Major Belokopytov, the director at Chernyakhovsk, is quoted as replying to the family's request for Grigorenko to bless his son and future daughter-in-law prior to their marriage: "Don't ask, I have no feelings on the job—only instructions."[46]

Indefinite Hospitalization
No matter how severe the conditions of an incarceration, the knowledge of release after a defined period gives the prisoner a sense of hope and anticipation, and the passage of each day reinforces it. Not so in the case of the patient committed involuntarily to a psychiatric hospital. In the Soviet Union a patient can remain confined to an OPH so long as he remains a danger to himself or to others. He has no right of appeal; only doctors can decide the timing of his discharge.

The patient sent to an SPH could remain there all his life. We described earlier the procedure whereby commissions are held at least six-monthly. Only on their recommendation can a patient be released, and even then the final decision resides with a court. As in a civil commitment, the patient has no right of appeal. The patient becomes resigned to the fact that his release depends on the examining psychiatrists. To Grigorenko the indefinite length of his internment was oppressive:

> It is particularly harrowing to realize that one has been put into this position indefinitely. Some scale of minimum periods of detention is applied by the doctors, but I have not seen it. I know that murderers are held for not less than five years. It is said that in this respect political prisoners are equated with murderers, but if they do not recant they may not be released even then.[47]

Elsewhere Grigorenko summarizes the patient's plight like this: "The conditions in a lunatic asylum, the total absence of civil rights and the lack of any real hope of release, represent the most important and most horrifying circumstances encountered by anybody interned in an SPH."[48]

And so dissenters•live from one commission to the next, waiting for a recommendation of release. The wait may last years—Grigorenko himself spent the years 1970-74 in psychiatric hospitals, Viktor Fainberg and Vladimir Borisov were interned for five years, Nikolai Samsonov for eight. There are many other cases, included in appendix I, in which internment has lasted for similar or longer periods.

One factor underlying the indefiniteness of an internment is the vagueness of both the psychiatric report and the court order. The commission, in recommending treatment in an SPH, specifies neither its nature nor its duration. The court normally accepts the recommendation but, again, does not stipulate the type and length of treatment.

The court exercises complete power in accepting or rejecting the subsequent recommendations of half-yearly commissions. The dissenter cannot rely on an automatic confirmation by the court of a commission's recommendation for release or transfer to an OPH. The court often seems to apply a formula whereby the duration of internment should match the sentence which the dissenter would have received for his (alleged) offence, had he been ruled legally responsible. In effect, the period of treatment should apparently correspond to the seriousness of the crime. The case of Grigorenko may illustrate the application of this formula. In January 1973 a commission declared that he no longer required treatment in an SPH and recommended his transfer to an OPH. The court, however, rejected the recommendation, expressing the fear that Grigorenko might resume his former "criminal" activities. Only after an appeal by Mrs Grigorenko was the court's decision reversed; by then he had spent a further six months in the SPH.[49] Similarly, a commission's recommendation for the release of Viktor Kuznetsov from the Kazan SPH in November 1970 was rejected by the court "in view of the gravity of Kuznetsov's guilt".[50] This phrase was in fact used by the procurator, who argued for Kuznetsov's confinement to be continued in Kazan despite the commission's findings. Revealingly the court accepted a procurator's argument rather than a psychiatric opinion on the question of what medical management was then most apt. Kuznetsov was finally released from Kazan in August 1971, nine months after the psychiatric recommendation.

Recantation
A dissenter does have a way of expediting his release from psychiatric confinement—recantation. Renounce your convictions, concede that they are a product of your mental illness, and promise not to re-adopt them following your release. A considerable volume of testimony by dissenters documents these "criteria of recovery". Bukovsky was one of the first to reveal the virtual necessity of recantation for release:

> It is much more difficult to get out of such a place [as the Leningrad SPH] than to get into it. First, in order to get out you must admit openly and officially to the doctors that you were sick—"yes, I was ill, yes"; "I didn't know what I was doing when I did it". The second condition is to admit you were wrong, to disavow what you did. I know of several cases of people who refused to say they had done wrong and spent many long years in that hospital.[51]

Bukovksy goes on to relate the bitter struggle that Nikolai Samsonov (see chapter 3) waged in Leningrad to maintain his integrity, a personal campaign that he endured for eight years. Only following a severe deterioration in his health did he resign himself to the inevitable and sign a declaration that he had indeed been mentally ill.

To achieve these "recovery criteria" might not seem a major hurdle. But for the dissenter—idealistic, dedicated, and a tenacious defender of his rights—the prospect of recanting his beliefs, be they political or religious, is usually viewed with abhorrence. Alexander Volpin conveys the nature of the dilemma well in the case of Grigorenko:

> What would such a requirement [recantation] mean for Grigorenko? No less than this: not only an acknowledgement that he was not responsible when he wrote his letters in defence of the Crimean Tatars, but also an admission of the deliberate falsehood of what was said in them, and of what he had struggled for. Such an acknowledgement is unthinkable for a man of integrity and courage such as we know Grigorenko to be. But that is not all. His recantation would

mean, in practical terms, agreement with the court sentences against which he spoke out. . . . Can one tolerate such forced recantations?[52]

Grigorenko certainly at no time during his prolonged hospitalization renounced his political views. During a commission in 1971 he was asked whether he had changed his convictions. He replied characteristically: "Convictions are not gloves. One does not change them easily."[53] Needless to say, his internment was extended. Fainberg refers to recantation as "moral suicide".[54] To attain his release, a dissenter has to pay the price of disavowing his convictions, but even then, Fainberg maintains, the internment will last another couple of years, until his recantation is complete and full "recovery" achieved. He himself persevered in his refusal to recant throughout his long internment, despite strenuous efforts by the staff. A plan of the chief psychiatrist in March 1971 was doomed at the outset in such a stubborn dissenter: "We'll take away all your writing materials and so forth. We want to give you the opportunity to be alone with yourself, to do some thinking and come to the right conclusion. When a person comes to the right conclusion, he is no longer a danger to society and he is set free."[55]

We speculated earlier that the length of Plyushch's internment may have been related to his dogged refusal to recant. One of the doctors informed his wife that "his views and beliefs" were the symptoms of his mental illness and required continuing treatment. On later visits Plyushch himself revealed that the doctors were insisting on a written recantation of his beliefs, but that he had refused to comply.[56]

Those interned because of their religious beliefs are in an equally trying predicament. They are pressed to relinquish their beliefs and to promise an end to certain religious activities following release. Such was the case with Gennady Shimanov. In chapter 6 we described the dilemma he encountered as an Orthodox Christian.

Vladimir Bukovsky and Dr Semyon Gluzman in their *Manual on Psychiatry for Dissenters** offer explicit advice on recantation. Dissenters are advised to concede to the doctors

---

* We discuss Dr Gluzman and the *Manual* in the next chapter. For the full text see appendix VI.

that they "have reappraised their former unhealthy convictions". They will not necessarily win release but will at least achieve "more or less tolerable living conditions", milder "treatment" and a less oppressive régime. Dissenters must resort to any tactics to demonstrate their "new insight"; "tactical devices" constitute their best method of survival.

However, dissenters like Grigorenko, Fainberg, Plyushch and Borisov adopted a different line. Their refusal to "give in" led to prolonged internments and harsh treatment. Others have opted for recantation, in the belief that this was the best or only solution to their predicament. As we saw in chapter 5, Gorbanevskaya's psychiatrists desired a written statement but were satisfied with an oral "admission" that she had been mentally ill when she committed her anti-Soviet acts.

Yury Shikhanovich, whom we met in 1976 in Moscow, was interned for only six months, and then in an OPH. A mathematician, he was arrested in September 1972 and charged under article 70 with the distribution of the *Chronicle* and other *samizdat* material. A Serbsky commission, including Drs G. Morozov and Lunts, diagnosed him as an "extreme psychopathic personality of the schizoid type; possible presence of a sluggish schizophrenic process", and declared him not responsible. In a rare occurrence Shikhanovich made a partial recantation *before* his trial. In a statement summarized by the *Chronicle* he indicated that "he did not intend to engage in the activities with which he had been charged, and planned on his release to occupy himself only with teaching or editing work".[57]

Probably to reinforce his recantation, the original KGB investigator in his case visited Shikhanovich in the hospital a few weeks prior to his discharge and enquired about his plans. He proceeded to warn him: "Do not make contact with Andrei Sakharov," was one explicit recommendation. The investigator even went as far as securing a job for his "client". This "royal treatment" was probably, at least in part, a *quid pro quo* for his promise to "behave correctly" in the future. But another factor was almost certainly the powerful campaign on Shikhanovich's behalf by Western mathematicians. This is described in chapter 10.

The Effects of Disturbed Patients on the Dissenter

One can easily imagine what it is like for a healthy person to be interned indefinitely with disturbed patients. In the SPH the latter are suffering from severe forms of mental illness and many have committed acts of violence—murder, assault, rape. Grigorenko encountered this frightening aspect of hospital life when first admitted to an SPH in 1964: "The real moment of horror for a healthy person placed in these conditions comes when he begins to realize that he may in time turn into one of those whom he sees around him."[58]

Grigorenko's portrayal of Pyotr Lysak, a fellow inmate in Leningrad interned for a "disloyal" speech, highlights the deleterious effects of a pathological environment on the mental health of a formerly normal person. Lysak had endured seven years of confinement when Grigorenko first met him. Rather than recant, Lysak continued relentlessly to condemn those who had inflicted the injustice of committing him. On one occasion Grigorenko was particularly irritated by Lysak's intransigence: "You talk in such an irrational way that I am beginning to doubt your sanity!" His reply struck Grigorenko forcefully: "He suddenly stopped, gave me a look which I shall not forget until my dying day, and asked quietly, very, very quietly, with a kind of bitter scorn in his voice: 'You surely don't imagine one can spend seven years in here and stay sane'."[59]

Plyushch, recognizing his own deterioration and that of patients around him, mainly because of the drugs they received, reasonably began to fear that he might never recover: "I was afraid that my deterioration was irreversible. I looked at the really serious cases who, they told me, had been quite well a few years ago. . . . Several politicals broke down and gave up before my eyes."[60]

The dissenter is in a minority in the SPH. About him are dozens of patients exhibiting bizarre, frightening behaviour, sometimes grotesque in the extreme. Yury Iofe draws vivid vignettes of patients his twenty-year old daughter Olga had as fellow inmates in Kazan.[61] There was Vera—she had killed her mother with an axe and believed she was the Queen of England. "She crosses herself constantly to keep the demons away. . . . Reptiles are also trying to overpower her. This is

why she keeps asking Olga to take the snake off her back."
Anida, German by nationality, had assaulted and crippled her
father—she believed that Russian patients were being cured
while Germans were being crippled. Lyuba had killed her lover,
deluded that he had robbed her of twenty rubles. Maria was an
imbecile from birth, incontinent, "burrowing round in the
lavatories, carefully collecting the contents and painstakingly
hiding them in the pockets of her dressing gown". These were
the unfortunate mental casualties who constituted Olga's
world in Kazan.

Plyushch describes the atmosphere in section 9 of
Dnepropetrovsk:

> I was put in a so-called "supervised ward" where they put
> the serious violent cases—some fight, others writhe in
> epileptic fits, one cries, another roars with laughter, another
> sings thieves' songs, another describes his case and his
> sexual adventures in a loud voice, another asks to go to the
> lavatory—in short, bedlam.
>
> Then one of the "border-crossers"* asks to go to the
> lavatory. He is incontinent and has the doctor's permission to
> go at any time. But the orderlies do not take this into account,
> so he urinates on the floor in the ward. He is not the only one
> who uses this form of protest. . . .
>
> In the lavatories the picture is even more depressing—it is
> full of people, there's a fight for a place at the hole, people
> search for cigarette stubs among the used lavatory paper.
> Some of the patients also eat their excrement or masturbate.
> I don't want to blacken the picture—this last did not
> happen every day.[62]

How did Plyushch cope with these horrors for two and a half
years? Through deliberate apathy and indifference—what he
described to us as a sort of hibernation. On first entering the
hospital he was acutely sensitive to the suffering of fellow-
patients, but soon he became impervious to it:

> I did not want to hear the cries, the fights, the laughter, the
> crying, the delirium. For whole days on end I lay and tried
> to sleep. The tranquillizers helped me.

* Inmates interned for trying to emigrate by crossing the border illegally.

I did not have a thought in my head. The only thoughts that remained were—the lavatory, smoking and the "bribes" you had to give to the orderlies to get an extra visit to the lavatory. And one other thought—that I must remember everything I saw there, so I could describe it later.[63]

Conclusion

The fate of the dissenter confined to an OPH is mentally and physically bearable by most accounts. The dissenter sent to an SPH however enters an environment so pathological and harsh that there must be few institutions to rival it. Its purpose is to deal with special types of mentally-ill patients—those who have committed criminal acts, often of a violent character. The problem of how to help such people is a severe one and certainly nowhere in the world has it been satisfactorily resolved. The mentally-ill, dangerous offender remains a major challenge for society, and for the psychiatrist in particular.

Society must after all be protected from the mentally-ill offender with a proclivity for violence; the patient in turn must be provided with a milieu from which he may benefit. The SPH may accomplish the former but seems woefully deficient in the latter. The testimony of many witnesses points to the anti-therapeutic atmosphere prevalent in the SPHs or at least in those six on which ample evidence is available; information on the others is still scanty.

We have devoted considerable space to facets of SPH life. The accounts provided by different sources fundamentally agree with each other. We can only draw the conclusion that the SPH is little more than a prison, and perhaps worse, as the inmate lacks the basic rights still retained by prisoners. For the sane dissenter the environment in the SPH is especially horrific. He is stripped of every right and left vulnerable and without hope. As an instrument to oppress him the SPH succeeds.

Chapter 8

THE PSYCHIATRIST AND HIS DIAGNOSIS

WHO IS RESPONSIBLE for the misuse of psychiatry? Is it perpetrated by the entire psychiatric profession or restricted to a minority? What factors underlie the participation of the psychiatrists involved? Is it fear, obedience to the authorities, corruption, ignorance of the ethical issues? Are the diagnoses applied to dissenters clinically reasonable? Would they be acceptable to psychiatrists outside the Soviet Union, or are they shaped to fit the requirements of the régime?

In this chapter we attempt to answer these and related questions.

Who is Involved?

We believe that psychiatrists can be placed along a continuum in terms of their involvement in the misuse of their discipline— a small core group at one end, an even smaller dissenting group at the other, and the vast majority of average psychiatrists between them. These three groups require distinction from one another since they differ markedly in their characteristics. Also in the case of the core and average psychiatrists, they probably differ in their motives when participating in the examination of a dissenter.

The Core Psychiatrist

The core group is well known to Western observers: it includes Professor Andrei Snezhnevsky, director of the Institute of Psychiatry of the Academy of Medical Sciences (AMS); Dr Georgy Morozov, director of the Serbsky Research Institute for Forensic Psychiatry; Professor Ruben Nadzharov, deputy-director of the Institute of Psychiatry; and Professor Daniil Lunts, head of the Serbsky's special diagnostic section.

Dr Snezhnevsky, born in 1904, is without doubt the best known and most influential figure in contemporary Soviet psychiatry. Along with only a handful of other psychiatrists he is a full member of the AMS thus holding the prestigious title of academician. As director of his institute he plays a significant advisory rôle to the federal Ministry of Health on many matters pertinent to psychiatry. His influence is further expanded by his editorship of the Soviet psychiatric journal, the *Korsakov Journal of Neurology and Psychiatry*, by his membership of the presidiums of the AMS and the All-Union Society of Neurologists and Psychiatrists, and by his central rôle in the foreign relations of Soviet psychiatry. He holds honorary membership of the World Psychiatric Association, the American Psychiatric Association and the Royal College of Psychiatrists.

1950 was a critical year in Snezhnevsky's career. During the special joint session of the AMS and the Academy of Sciences held that year to forge Pavlov's ideas into the foundations of Soviet psychiatry (see chapter 2), Snezhnevsky was prominent among the pro-Pavlovian forces. This was a period of intense politico-ideological upheaval which involved a strong element of officially-sponsored anti-Semitism. The Pavlov-oriented psychiatrists triumphed then, and have retained control of Soviet psychiatry since, with Dr Snezhnevsky at the helm. About this time, he took up the chair of psychiatry in the Central Institute for Post-graduate Training of Physicians, and in 1962, became the director of the Institute of Psychiatry, the most eminent academic post in Soviet psychiatry. Earlier, in 1950–51, he was also briefly the director of the Serbsky Institute.

Shortly following the state-directed embrace of Pavlovian doctrine by most psychiatrists in the early 1950s, Snezhnevsky launched his theories on schizophrenia. These evolved into a cogent factor affecting the use of psychiatry to stifle dissent. In essence, Snezhnevsky's ideas broadened the concept of schizophrenia and permitted dissent to be viewed much more readily as a symptom of severe mental illness. We shall return to this theme later in the chapter.

Snezhnevsky's views on schizophrenia led to a protracted battle with other schools of psychiatry, mainly those centred in Leningrad and Kiev, which both adamantly opposed the wider and much more frequent application of the diagnosis. In Leningrad Dr A. S. Chistovich was a central protagonist of the anti-Snezhnevsky school; at a conference in 1954 the battle between these two camps continued. The dissenter Viktor

Rafalsky, for example, was in the 1950s three times ruled sane in Leningrad and three times ruled a schizophrenic in the Serbsky (see appendix I). By the end of the decade the victor had clearly emerged—the Snezhnevsky orientation, with strong official support, had come to dominate the theory and practice of psychiatry, a dominance that has endured to the present day. Vocal opponents had been transferred to less influential positions, often in the provinces.

During the early 1960s the Leningrad Bekhterev Institute still held out, isolated under its director, Dr I. Sluchevsky, but with his death in 1966, it too was soon forced to adopt the Snezhnevsky line. Dr Felix Yaroshevsky, now in Toronto, told us how, as a psychiatrist practising in Leningrad between 1965 and 1972, including a period at the Bekhterev, he noted a major shift in diagnostic practice, particularly the far greater frequency in categorizing patients as schizophrenic.

Along with Snezhnevsky's ambition, shrewd cunning and ability to manipulate people and situations, he also possesses, by all accounts, good clinical skills and considerable personal charm. Colleagues of his whom we have consulted regard him as an unusually complex personality. Since attaining almost complete power in his profession, Snezhnevsky has become the chief defender of Soviet psychiatry against charges that it has been compromised. As we saw in chapter 4, he vehemently denied the allegations of critics at the 1971 congress of the World Psychiatric Association in Mexico City; he has continued to argue that the criticism is nothing more than a "malicious concoction".[1]

Snezhnevsky has participated, either as a member of a commission or as an adviser, in several well-known cases of dissenters who have undergone psychiatric examination. The two most notable instances entail the assessment of Plyushch and his consultative rôle in the Medvedev affair (see chapter 6). He chaired a commission which examined Plyushch in 1972, diagnosed him as a schizophrenic and recommended compulsory hospitalization.[2] After almost two years of treatment and a marked deterioration in Plyushch's health, his wife, in the company of a family friend, managed to visit Snezhnevsky in his home. The friend, Professor Yury Orlov, describes the tense conversation they had with him and their astonishment at hearing him pose the presumably hypocritical question:

"Would it really have been better for him to have got seven years in strict-régime camps?"[3]

Although Snezhnevsky had no part in the detention and diagnosis of Medvedev, quite clearly he played a "behind the scenes" rôle. In their account of the episode (see chapter 6) Zhores and Roy Medvedev graphically describe that rôle. A friend of the Medvedev family gains access to Snezhnevsky, to be told that Zhores is a psychopathic personality with an exaggerated opinion of himself, but that this diagnosis does not warrant compulsory treatment, only his supervision in an out-patient clinic. The following day Academician Andrei Sakharov meets with a group of doctors at the Ministry of Health, including Snezhnevsky. On this occasion, after praising the Soviet psychiatric profession, Snezhnevsky concedes that mistakes are made, particularly in the provinces, where standards are occasionally low. If Medvedev's doctors have erred, he explains, this can be rectified by a directive from the Ministry of Health. Public protest is only liable to damage the reputation that psychiatry enjoys.[4]

Several days earlier, however, Snezhnevsky had participated in a meeting of high-ranking functionaries in the Ministry of Health to discuss the Medvedev affair. By then, international protests were pouring in against his commitment. Snezhnevsky took the opportunity to point out that if internment continued it would be acutely embarrassing for the Soviet delegation to the World Psychiatric Association congress in Mexico a year hence. On this occasion he apparently argued for Medvedev's release; Dr Boris Petrovsky, the Minister of Health, and Dr Zoya Serebryakova, the chief psychiatrist in the ministry, a woman with considerable influence because of her position, opposed his advice and decided that Medvedev should remain in hospital indefinitely. This episode reveals one of Snezhnevsky's prominent qualities, that of political pragmatism. Aware that Medvedev had been committed inappropriately, his concern was rather for the image of his profession than for the welfare of the patient. Presumably he calculated that it was best to release Medvedev in the light of the stormy protests and the forthcoming international congress, but nonetheless he acquiesced to his political superiors at the Ministry of Health.

Georgy Morozov, born in 1920, has since 1957 directed the

Serbsky Institute where many dissenters have undergone psychiatric examination. Since 1974 he has been a full member of the AMS and from 1975 the chairman of the presidium of the All-Union Society (a position comparable to the presidency of the Royal College of Psychiatrists or the American Psychiatric Association). He exerts a marked influence on forensic psychiatry throughout the USSR by virtue of his Serbsky position and his co-editorship of the authoritative Soviet textbook on forensic psychiatry.[5]

Morozov's name has cropped up regularly in the context of the political use of psychiatry. He has served on commissions, often as chairman, in several cases of dissenters (they include Grigorenko, Gorbanevskaya, Medvedev, Fainberg, Shikhanovich and Plyushch), and he is a rebutter of the charges of unethical practice laid against him and his colleagues. In this rôle, he features prominently in chapters 5 and 10.

Dr Ruben Nadzharov occupies the position of deputy-director of the Institute of Psychiatry and like his superior, Snezhnevsky, he wields considerable power and influence. He has been a member of several commissions which have examined dissenters and also a defender of his profession against Western criticism. For instance, Nadzharov participated in the examination of Medvedev which found him to be suffering from sluggish schizophrenia. He also examined Viktor Kuznetsov, a dissenter diagnosed as having sluggish schizophrenia on the basis of his reformist ideas and lack of insight into his illness.[6] Recommended by Nadzharov's commission as in need of treatment, Kuznetsov spent two years in the Kazan SPH.

Nadzharov's defence of his profession is typified by an interview he gave to a Soviet journalist in 1973,[7] in which he berated the critics, asserting that they were motivated only by "unseemly political aims" and actively engaged in anti-Soviet slander. He was also a signatory, like Snezhnevsky and Morozov, of a letter to the Western press, in which critics were castigated.[8]

The psychiatrist viewed by the dissenting movement as most notorious is Professor Daniil Lunts.[9] He was born in 1911 into a well-established family: his father was an esteemed paediatrician, his mother a professor at the Moscow Conservatory. After working in the mid-1930s as a psychiatrist in the hospital section of the main prison in Gorky, he moved to the Serbsky Institute, where in 1940 he became a senior associate and earned the Soviet equivalent of a Ph.D. At the end of the decade he lectured at the college of the Ministry of State Security, the predecessor of the KGB. Lunts, a Jew, survived the anti-Semitic purge which affected the Serbsky and other medical institutions in the early 1950s, and also the special investigation of forensic psychiatry by the party's Central Committee, discussed in chapter 3. However, his position apparently remained tenuous until Georgy Morozov assumed the director-ship in 1957. Lunts has headed the special diagnostic section, concerned with the assessment of political offenders, since at least the early 1960s.

According to Naum Korzhavin, whom we discussed in chapter 3, Lunts first began to work in the special section in early 1948. Korzhavin found him different from all the other doctors: "He was small . . . always guardedly morose, always unfriendly. Once I asked him a simple question, just as I addressed the other doctors who had a kind of respectful attitude to me, and he barked something out in reply. Whether he was at that time a secret police officer . . . I do not know. But the patients all sensed him as an enemy."

Lunts's notoriety rests principally on his clinical approach: the use of the diagnosis of schizophrenia in an extremely loose and broad way. On one occasion Lunts diverged from his usual pattern, and thereby revealed how responsive he was to the needs of the KGB. In 1968 he ruled responsible two dissen-ters whom he had previously ruled not responsible, explaining that his earlier diagnoses had been wrong and his criteria for non-responsibility had become narrower. This ruling was essential to the KGB, as it had pressured one of the two men so that he was ready to give false evidence of the type it needed at the trial. After the trial Lunts reverted at once to his broad definition of schizophrenia and ruled a succession of dissenters not responsible.[10] In a semi-public lecture given in Moscow in 1973,[11] he described examples of people suffering from different stages of one form of schizophrenia—a person who criticized the Soviet socio-political system, a person who hated the police on principle, and a person who tried to assassinate high authorities. The psychiatrist's task was to diagnose this form of schizophrenia as early as possible and, through treatment, prevent its progression. After this lecture the chairman declined to read out any of the written questions addressed to Lunts, on the grounds that, regrettably, they were insulting to him. We noted in chapter 5 the vagueness of Lunts's criteria in the diagnosis of Gorbanevskaya and will see further evidence of his clinical method later in this chapter. He has examined many dissenters including Sinyavsky, Volpin in 1959, Grigorenko in 1969, Gorbanevskaya, Yakhimovich, Fainberg, Bukovsky in 1963 and 1967, and Shikhanovich.

Not surprisingly, Lunts's reputation was well-known to the Medvedev family. Roy Medvedev, on hearing of his selection, categorically insisted on his exclusion from the examining commission for his brother. He was duly dropped.

Lunts became a familiar figure to Grigorenko during his stay in the Serbsky in 1964. He reports that he saw Lunts "on more than one occasion . . . arrive at work in the uniform of a KGB colonel. True he always came into the department in his white coat." [12] No other dissenter has substantiated Grigorenko's observation and one has in fact disputed it, pointing out that if Lunts does hold a military-style rank it would probably be an MVD rank retained since the Serbsky ostensibly ceased to be run by the MVD in 1956 and was formally transferred to the Ministry of Health. [13] This view is strongly endorsed by Victor Nekipelov, who, as we saw in chapter 5, reports Lunts to be an MVD major-general, and also by the fact that he gave his above-mentioned lecture at what was officially described as a "Meeting between Moscow Intellectuals and Representatives of the MVD". In any case this formal puzzle is of little importance as Lunts works closely and apparently smoothly with the KGB, which regularly refers dissenters to his section.

Some personal facets of his character and life may help to shed light on his rôle as "police psychiatrist". A man of small build, he is well-educated and speaks some European languages. By temperament he tends to introversion, suspiciousness and dogmatism. His family life has been marred by tragedy: his wife died in the mid-1960s and at about the same time his only daughter died after a serious illness. In addition he became virtually estranged from his own parents in the 1930s after his marriage to a party member. It was the period of the "great terror": the parents apparently feared being denounced to the police and avoided contact whenever possible.

Less information is available on a number of other psychiatrists who clearly belong to the core group in one way or another. We have mentioned the rôle played by Dr Serebryakova, chief psychiatrist in the Ministry of Health, at the time of the Medvedev confinement, and it seems probable that her part in the misuse of psychiatry is substantial. In the examination of Fainberg, recorded in appendix VII, she lets slip her obvious knowledge that normal people are held in SPHs. Similarly the Minister of Health, Dr Boris Petrovsky, was enmeshed in the Medvedev affair, and later in the Plyushch case; he has also issued blanket denials of Western criticism. According to Mrs Plyushch, Petrovsky intervened in late 1975 to obtain the release of her husband,[14] but this occurred at a time when intense international pressure was being exerted on the authorities for his release.

Professor Marat Vartanyan of the Institute of Psychiatry has had a special function since 1971 as an apologist for Soviet psychiatry. We discussed in chapter 4 his election as an associate secretary of the World Psychiatric Association and we will trace his subsequent manœuvrings in chapter 10. Although he has not examined or treated dissenters, he undoubtedly liaises closely with the core psychiatrists, particularly with Snezhnevsky.

There are in addition some 50 other psychiatrists known to us who have participated in commissions leading to the internment of dissenters. Some, like Drs Viktor Morozov and Yakov Landau, have taken part in several such commissions, and further evidence—such as Landau's high position in the Serbsky, described in chapter 5—also causes us to place them in the core group. Information on most of the others is too sketchy for their assignment with any certainty to the core or the average group.

Motives of the Core Psychiatrist
What motivates the core psychiatrists repeatedly to collude with the state in declaring healthy dissenters mentally ill? The pattern of behaviour in these psychiatrists is too complex to be explained by any one factor. More like a constellation

of motives prevails, which operate in various ways according to the specific situation.

An ideological factor almost certainly applies to some extent —their adherence (sincere or opportunistic) to the view that the party knows best, and that he who questions or criticizes it, and fails to recognize his error, must be mentally disturbed and poorly adapted to his environment. We suspect, however, that the ideology serves as a rationalization, conscious or unconscious, to justify these psychiatrists' misuse of their profession. Whatever the case, the clinical approach of doctors like Morozov and Lunts rests on their consistent contention that those who dissent by propounding ideas on how to change the state are indeed suffering from delusions of reformism.

Even were we to accept that the core psychiatrists genuinely believe dissenters are mentally ill, their recommendations for treatment strongly suggest that—at least in this respect—they knowingly misuse their profession. The recommendation commonly made for treatment in an SPH strikes us as entirely inappropriate for the illness diagnosed and the needs of the patient—a matter we turn to later in this chapter.

Dr Boris Zoubok, a psychiatrist now settled in the United States, formerly worked at the Kashchenko hospital under Snezhnevsky. Zoubok has discussed with us his impression that Snezhnevsky and his colleagues genuinely believe in their method of diagnosis and in the concept of dissent as mental illness. While sharply disagreeing with them, Zoubok grants them the right to their opinion: after all there are many conflicting theories about the diagnosis of mental illness. What is wholly indefensible, in his view, is the customary recommendation by the core psychiatrists for SPH internment, when the latter realize full well what the patient will encounter there.

If we extend Zoubok's arguments, two facts are noteworthy. First, the SPH is primarily designed for mentally-ill offenders who have committed violent crimes and who are a danger to society. Yet no dissenter discussed in this book has ever committed a crime even bordering on violence or manifested intent to do so. Second, in many cases commissions have arrived at a diagnosis of sluggish schizophrenia. For such a relatively mild form of this illness we would expect an OPH to be more suitable and therapeutic.

In the case of Gorbanevskaya for example, Lunts and his

colleagues recommended treatment in an SPH not withstanding the tentativeness of their diagnosis that "the possibility of sluggish schizophrenia is not excluded".[15] At the trial Lunts defended the recommendation of an SPH by claiming, to quote the *Chronicle*'s report, that here, "apart from the actual treatment, a régime existed which met the requirements of patients' subsequent adaptation to the conditions they would encounter on their discharge. A mind that had undergone pathological changes and yet preserved certain of its individual aspects intact was a combination which increased the danger to the public from the patient, as he lacked a critical attitude towards his behaviour and was not conscious of his illness."[16] Thus the possible existence of an illness and, if present, in relatively mild form only, led Lunts to make a medically-inappropriate recommendation. His convoluted language barely concealed, however, his intention that the SPH should induce a recantation and, in consequence, an obedient, conformist citizen.

In addition to a diagnostic method strongly influenced by ideology, we surmise that the core psychiatrists are influenced also by the desire to rise to high professional positions. With such a position come many rewards: the exercise of power, the satisfaction of ambitions, and the more tangible benefits of the "good life".

In chapter 2 we noted the need for political qualifications in a professional person wishing to rise up the administrative ladder, and the high proportion of party members in positions of authority in the health service. Almost certainly, most if not all the core psychiatrists belong to the party, so their subordination to its direction is axiomatic. Clearly psychiatrists like Serebryakova, Snezhnevsky and Morozov have attained top administrative positions in large measure because of their political qualifications. The latter have facilitated their active connivance with the party authorities and permitted the misuse of psychiatry to become a systematic and state-directed policy. In this connivance the core psychiatrist is secure in the knowledge that the party will not allow his victims to call him to account in a court of law or in any other way. In a political system where power is undivided and the expression of protest is strictly controlled, the party can guarantee him this security without difficulty.

The rewards of the good life involve access to a variety of privileges and benefits not available to ordinary Soviet citizens. The core psychiatrist is likely to travel abroad, as a tourist or to attend a conference, to have access to stores selling luxury goods at moderate prices, to have a country cottage, and to holiday at special sanatoria. Their salaries are about three times higher in real terms than those of ordinary psychiatrists.

Rewards are maintained and safeguarded so long as the "contract" between donor and recipient remains undisturbed and respected. The continuation of the reward is the *quid pro quo* for each act of collaboration.

The Rôle of the Average Psychiatrist

Thus far we have discussed the part played by a few powerful psychiatrists. What of attitudes among the rank and file? Interviews with émigré psychiatrists in Britain, Israel and North America lead us to believe that the average psychiatrist has— at least until recently—had very limited knowledge of the political use of his discipline. This is not surprising. Most of the misdiagnoses are concentrated in one institution, the Serbsky, while only a small minority of Soviet psychiatrists work within the SPHs to which most well-known dissenters have been sent for treatment (by far the majority work in psychiatric clinics or OPHs). Access to evidence of the abuse is denied.

Since autumn 1971, however, the average psychiatrist will have read in the Soviet press a number of rebuttals of Western allegations by his "authoritative colleagues". One émigré psychiatrist now in the United States described to us the visit of Georgy Morozov to a conference in Estonia at which he told the participants to disregard Western accusations, as these were nothing but "anti-Soviet propaganda".[17] But how much the average psychiatrist believes such explanations is hard to say: reactions probably vary widely.

One psychiatrist we spoke to in Israel first became aware of something being amiss in his profession only in 1970. He then heard about the Grigorenko case in a broadcast over the Voice of America. Another psychiatrist, now in the United States, learnt of malpractices in 1972, when an article published in France was broadcast on Radio Liberty.[18]

Dr Marina Voikhanskaya, formerly a psychiatrist in a

Leningrad OPH, described to us how her suspicions that psychiatric abuse existed were confirmed in 1974.* On learning that an artist, Yury Ivanov,[19] was a patient in the hospital and seemingly healthy, Voikhanskaya began to visit him regularly and satisfied herself that he was indeed sane and that his internment was unjustified. At first she thought that maybe this was an isolated case of abuse, but soon she found further evidence which convinced her that it was part of something much wider.

We believe then that the average psychiatrist is relatively ignorant of the abuses, and, where better informed, generally passive. What accounts for his passivity? Probably the most cogent factor is the conformism which pervades Soviet society. The psychiatrist, like everyone else, observes those conventions and practices prescribed by the state. He does so largely out of fear and habit. Take a single deviant step and the results will almost certainly be dire. This was the thought behind the advice given to us in Moscow by friends of a psychiatrist who was strongly, but only privately, critical of the abuses. They felt a meeting with us would be too hazardous for her: if it became known to the authorities, her career might well be at risk. We received similar advice in Leningrad concerning another psychiatrist.

Non-compliance with the demands of the state obviously embodies considerable risk and may be tantamount to professional suicide. How then can the average psychiatrist be sure that he will comply with these demands when he encounters a dissenter for examination? Does he have instructions and guidelines to turn to? Yes and no. The Soviet citizen learns from an early age how to "understand". As one émigré psychiatrist put it to us, the Soviet Union is a country of "perfect understanding". Like the core psychiatrist, his "average" colleague, too, usually senses without specific instructions what is expected of him in various situations.

When for example he learns that a prospective examinee is a political offender, he immediately recalls the nature of his unwritten contract: the KGB usually transfers such cases for examination when it wishes the psychiatrists to affix a label of non-responsibility and to recommend compulsory treatment. Similarly, he understands what is expected of him when, as in

* For a detailed report see appendix X.

the case of Medvedev, he is informed that there are good grounds to suspect the sanity of a citizen, the citizen has a record of dissent, and the referral agency is an authority like the local town council.

Yet with his understanding there often comes apprehension and ambivalence. All the émigré psychiatrists we interviewed have emphasized the two tactics that many average psychiatrists resort to: avoidance if possible of the whole task and, if left no choice, as prompt an exit as feasible from the case. Such tactics are characteristic of the Soviet bureaucracy—to which psychiatrists belong. If action is required in an unusual situation where precedent is vague and guidelines nebulous or non-existent, the bureaucrat tends to evade responsibility in whatever way possible. He passes the buck. If evasion is impossible, he avoids taking risks. He performs the task in the manner "understood" to fulfil the wishes of his superiors.

For a Kiev forensic psychiatrist with whom we discussed the question, this generally meant referring "complicated" cases to the Serbsky Institute for a more authoritative opinion, thus sparing the Kiev staff the obligation of making the decision on diagnosis and treatment. According to another psychiatrist, the most useful strategy was to act naïvely, adopt an innocent, apolitical stance and hope to elude responsibility for any unusual matter.

Evasion and retreat are not always feasible. Additional manœuvres must then be undertaken of which moral evasion is among the most helpful. The average psychiatrist cannot afford even to begin pondering whether the action of labelling dissent as illness is unethical. Such a process would entail soul-searching and inevitably pave the way for distressing reactions of guilt and frustration. Further, if the psychiatrist disclosed his uneasiness to colleagues, he could not be sure that one of them might not inform on him and thus render his professional position insecure. According to all the émigré psychiatrists we have interviewed except one, Dr Voikhanskaya, they and their colleagues at no point exchanged their attitudes and feelings on the issue of abuse. Everyone was simply too fearful of the dangers involved in self-exposure. Even when psychiatrists suspected malpractice *vis-à-vis* dissenters, the issue was not broached.

We may have conveyed in our discussion of the average

psychiatrist that all act in similar fashion—as frightened, retreating conformists, attempting at all costs to elude the dissenter as examinee. But exceptions do exist. We have noted how a commission chaired by Professor Detengof in Tashkent apparently failed to "toe the line" when it declared Grigorenko sane and responsible.* Indeed, the commission underlined its conclusion by stating that there were "no doubts concerning Grigorenko's health" and that "in-patient investigation . . . would complicate a diagnosis".[20] As a result, the KGB was compelled to refer the case to more trustworthy psychiatrists at the Serbsky. Predictably they fulfilled their contract and reversed the conclusions of their Tashkent colleagues.

Similarly Dr Yanushevsky, in his assessment of Gorbanevskaya, could find "no grounds for a diagnosis of schizophrenia" and concluded that she had "no need of treatment in a psychiatric hospital".[21] The first commission in the case of Plyushch was composed of psychiatrists from the forensic department of the Kiev regional hospital, who diagnosed him as a psychopathic personality and responsible before the law. Again, the KGB required the services of a Serbsky team to reverse the Kiev findings.

A dissenter, once committed to hospital, may face a variety of attitudes in the psychiatric staff. We noted in the previous chapter the harsh way in which dissenters like Grigorenko, Gershuni, Fainberg and Plyushch were treated, with the collusion and even active collaboration of psychiatrists. By contrast, a few doctors have shown compassion for the dissenter to the extent of assisting him in various ways and even recommending his release after the minimal period they have calculated will satisfy the authorities.

An illustrative case is that of Ilya Rips, who, as mentioned in the previous chapter, spent eighteen relatively comfortable months in an OPH in Riga. He was well cared for by his doctors, who spared him the rigours of drugs or other psychiatric treatment. Even in the SPH there are cases known to us of doctors who have helped their dissenter-patients by, for example, smuggling out for them letters and materials for *samizdat* circulation. We cannot name these doctors, as the publicizing of such acts could even now lead to severe reprisals against them.

* See p. 112 for other possible interpretations of this episode.

But the compassion of a psychiatrist for a dissenter does not normally involve direct collusion of this sort. Usually it is extended within limits set to protect himself. The average psychiatrist dare not articulate his collusion, he cannot afford even to hint to the patient that he considers his commitment unjustified.

The relationship between Gennady Shimanov and Dr Shafran (see chapter 6) exemplifies this cautious approach. In his account of his hospitalization, Shimanov conveys the impression that Shafran made implicit efforts to guide his patient in the way he should behave with the commission that was due to examine him. Shafran also confronted Shimanov with reality when alluding to the power and lawlessness of the KGB in determining the ultimate fate of dissenters: ". . . this régime is pretty strict . . . and will not put up with such religious activity . . . don't you realize that the KGB does not give a damn for laws?"[22]

Another factor that may influence the average psychiatrist involved in the forensic assessment of a dissenter is his rationale that a year or two in a mental hospital under reasonable conditions may be considerably less traumatic and punitive than a long term of imprisonment. This rationale, however, is probably ill-conceived, certainly as regards the SPH, which is in several respects worse than a prison or camp.

The Dissenting Psychiatrist

There are many psychiatrists who act with implicit benevolence towards the dissenter-patient and therefore, in their way, practise passive, veiled dissent against the misuse of their profession. We know of only two Soviet psychiatrists, however, who have publicly displayed their opposition. A few others have expressed criticism too, but anonymously.*

The best known of this minute group is Dr Semyon Gluzman. He was born in 1946, the son of a professor of medicine in the

---

* A good number more have dissented to the extent of declining to rule not responsible people for whom the police clearly wanted such a ruling. Bukovsky has pointed to the young psychiatrists who found him responsible in 1965 in Moscow OPH No. 13 in Lyublino suburb, and to professors Lukomsky and D. E. Melekhov who did likewise in Serbsky in 1971. See *Nature*, 13 January 1977. See also Dr M. Dyakonova's rôle in the case of G. Suprunyuk (appendix I).

Kiev medical school. Following his own graduation as a doctor in 1969, Gluzman commenced psychiatric training, working for two years in regional Ukrainian hospitals. He was then offered a post in the Dnepropetrovsk SPH but declined it because he knew that the hospital was being used to intern dissenters and that he would be compelled to practise unethically. Gluzman embarked on a frustrating job-hunt, ultimately taking a post in a first-aid service in Kiev.

In March 1972 his home was searched and two months later he was arrested and charged under article 62 of the Ukrainian Criminal Code (equivalent to article 70 of the Russian Code) for reading and circulating *samizdat* material. At his trial, from which his parents and friends were barred, the charges revolved chiefly around the fact that he had given someone Solzhenitsyn's novel *Cancer Ward*. The result was a sentence of seven years in a strict-régime labour camp, followed by three years of exile. This was inexplicably savage as the formal charges did not involve Gluzman's composition of any documents, and as it was a first offence of a sort which would normally incur no more than a three-year term.

Almost certainly the real reason for punishing him so harshly was the detailed document he and two colleagues prepared anonymously on the diagnosis of Grigorenko, and his steadfast refusal to inform the KGB about the identity of these colleagues. Entitled "An *in absentia* forensic-psychiatric report on P. G. Grigorenko", the document began circulation in *samizdat* form in 1971.[23] Gluzman and his fellow psychiatrists analyse the reports of the two commissions which examined Grigorenko in 1969, and level detailed criticism at the members of the Serbsky team. The authors also contend that, based on Grigorenko's own writings and the reports of the commissions in both Tashkent and the Serbsky, they are able to conduct their own forensic examination of the case.

The document is thorough and sober and the authors have a solid grasp of the legal aspects of the criminal-commitment process as well as the pertinent psychiatric features in Grigorenko's case. Their analysis of the Tashkent and Serbsky findings is carefully and methodically presented. This is no polemical pamphlet, but through their assessment of Grigorenko they do reach some general conclusions regarding the use of psychiatry for political purposes:

We do not consider our study only as an attempt to restore the truth in the case of P. G. Grigorenko, but also as a professional protest against the system used in such cases in general. Psychiatry is a branch of medicine and not of penal law. The practice of isolating political dissenters without publicity, by confining them to psychiatric hospitals, must be discontinued and the doctors who knowingly commit such inhumane acts should be prosecuted according to the norms of international and Soviet law, as were Professor Dr Hermann Paul Nietzsche [one of the Nazi practitioners of euthanasia] and his collaborators in November 1947.

The three psychiatrists also suggest that the Serbsky experts who diagnosed Grigorenko as not responsible (they name two of them—G. Morozov and Lunts) were either professionally incompetent or deliberately wrote false statements into their report. In the latter case, legal action should be brought against them.

This explicit criticism could not be brooked by the authorities —Gluzman's trial and heavy sentence was their retribution for such potentially contagious opposition. Although the indictment did not state that the defendant was one of the authors of the critical document, Gluzman's severe punishment was undoubtedly intended to deter other psychiatrists who might also feel the impulse to protest publicly against abuse. (The Grigorenko report was at first circulated anonymously and only subsequently, after the trial, was Gluzman's co-authorship made public.) The authorities most likely feared the furore that would ensue in international psychiatric circles were a Soviet colleague to be imprisoned merely for writing a psychiatric report on someone he had not personally examined. After all, there are many accounts by psychiatrists expressing their opinions on public figures whom they have never interviewed, particularly in the United States. Senator Goldwater and President Nixon, for example, were both the subjects of informal but widely publicized assessments. Many may argue that this is unsavoury practice but few would suggest that it constitutes an indictable offence. Gluzman's motives, of course, were different and entirely honourable.

The human-rights movement in the Soviet Union was prompt in its protest against the Gluzman sentence. Academician Sakharov appealed to the international psychiatric community to rally to the support of its colleague who, he argued, was being punished "for his professional integrity".[24] Psychiatrists in the West at first found it difficult to comprehend that a colleague could be penalized so severely for merely criticizing some Serbsky doctors. Later, with more extensive evidence of Gluzman's plight, they initiated a series of protests to their counterparts in the USSR and the Soviet government. By late 1973 all this had led to considerable embarrassment on the part of the authorities. Gluzman records in an open letter of 1974 to his parents how in September 1973 a KGB official had come from Moscow to bargain with him—thereby, we should note, virtually admitting the real reason for his imprisonment.[25] For three days pressure had been exerted on him "to refute the 'lies' of the West about the confinement of healthy people to Soviet psychiatric hospitals". The reward offered in exchange had been "not a small one": the KGB badly needed his help at a time when Western attacks were unusually strong. But Gluzman's integrity precluded his recantation—how could he say that his eminently sane friend Plyushch was insane? He would then become "a colleague of Elsa Koch or Daniil Lunts". So in mid-1976 he was still in a labour camp under extremely severe conditions.

Most of Gluzman's energies during the first four years of his incarceration were devoted to a campaign for the rights of his fellow prisoners and to doing what he could to preserve their health. He took part in several punishing hunger-strikes, and in November 1974 suffered serious heart problems as a result. A statement by him in June 1974 revealed the expertise he had acquired, since entering the camp, on a broad range of legal issues pertinent to prisoners.

A few months later he said in another document that he regretted his imprisonment, because:

If I were free I could be opposing more actively and effectively the criminal certification of healthy people. I am a psychiatrist, and therefore well qualified for this. Yet those who are actively protesting in the USSR against unwarranted certifications are members of the most varied professions but not, unfortunately, psychiatrists. Here I am deprived of the chance to join in. But I also have a personal reason to protest.

My close friend Leonid Plyushch is in a special psychiatric hospital of the MVD. This is my "Klaas's ashes".* In some ways my specialist knowledge is growing even here. In this camp I have observed sadism, as it were, "in vivo", outside the walls of any clinic. One has to console oneself at least with that.[26]

Gluzman also wrote with Vladimir Bukovsky in 1974 *A Manual on Psychiatry for Dissenters*, which we commented on in the previous chapter and to which we again refer below.

Because of these activities, Gluzman was informed in September 1975 that a second case had been initiated against him. He was to be charged as a recidivist with new acts of "anti-Soviet agitation and propaganda". The KGB's official at his Perm camp detailed the charges: sending out information about the collective 1974 hunger strike in which he participated, writing an article on Grigorenko, and preparing the *Manual* with Bukovsky.[27]

In March 1976 Gluzman was transferred to a prison in Perm where the KGB again warned him about the new case it was preparing against him. Its intention to "re-educate" him failed, however, and he was returned to the camp a month later.[28]

Marina Voikhanskaya is the only other Soviet psychiatrist, to our knowledge, who while still in the USSR openly opposed the abuse of her profession (see appendix X). We described earlier how this opposition began. She has given us a vivid and informative account of her colleagues' reactions to the attention she paid to the dissenter-artist Yury Ivanov, whom she tried to support during his internment in her OPH. On hearing that Ivanov was in one of the wards, Voikhanskaya asked his psychiatrist for a report on his clinical state.[29] She was astounded by her colleague's reply that Ivanov was perfectly normal and her warning that she should keep this knowledge completely secret.

Voikhanskaya began to visit Ivanov regularly, bringing him

* A reference to the Till Eulenspiegel legend. Till's father Klaas was burned at the stake by the Spaniards for leading a Flemish revolt. After this Till always carried Klaas's ashes in a bag next to his heart, to symbolize his determination to avenge his father's death.

books and cigarettes. Colleagues started to shun her. After a superior had forbidden her visits for both his and her own good, she saw the artist on Sundays as an ordinary visitor. Consistent pressure by fellow psychiatrists to have her cease the visits failed to deter her. The hospital director finally threatened her with dismissal. During this saga, she was progressively ostracized and ultimately lost the friendship of most of her colleagues; only a few remained loyal to her, and then only in private.

This response to Voikhanskaya's deviant behaviour typifies the attitude of fear of the average psychiatrist discussed above. He retreats quickly from extraordinary situations and from support of a colleague who has broken the rules.

Before long she also actively intervened in the case of Viktor Fainberg, who had been interned in her hospital after issuing a militant statement in support of Bukovsky and other political prisoners. When she learned that Fainberg was being threatened with forcible injections and had stated he would commit suicide in protest, she successfully dissuaded a colleague from proceeding.

In addition to these interventions she became active in the human-rights movement, and soon attracted the attention of the KGB. In April 1975 she emigrated. Our discussions with her lead us to surmise that had she remained in Leningrad the KGB would have stepped up its harassment of her. If this had failed to curb her activities, the outcome would presumably have been a trumped-up charge *à la* Gluzman. In any event, she did not leave the country unscathed; the authorities denied her permission to take her nine-year-old son with her. In mid-1976 they were still holding him as a pawn, in revenge for her public denunciations of Soviet abuse.[30]

Another figure who features in the small group of dissenting Soviet psychiatrists is the anonymous author of some *samizdat* essays on the state of Soviet psychiatry written in Moscow in 1969–70. The one essay which has reached the West is a blistering polemic by a psychiatrist with many years of experience and with extensive knowledge of the practices of his colleagues. Indignation is patent in every paragraph over the way in which "philistinism" has engulfed psychiatry and "encroached upon time-honoured human values". The author conveys the main source of his resentment in the opening lines:

> The story of the compulsory hospitalization of Alexander Volpin, which he has described in his writings, the Chaadayevan verdict of insanity pronounced upon General Grigorenko, and other similar psychiatric "exploits", cannot be a matter of indifference to any person with an informed knowledge of the subject. All the more so because these events are not exceptions: we hear with ever-increasing frequency of the interference of psychiatrists in the thoughts and actions of citizens whose mental health no one had earlier doubted.
>
> The purpose of these essays is to defend psychiatry and to explain to the non-specialist public with a keen interest in the problem that the blame for these outrages lies not with science but with those who have seized power in science.[31]

The author appears to be closely aware of which psychiatrists are culpable for the "exploits". By giving a colourful, detailed history of Soviet psychiatry which highlights its schisms and feuds, he explains how they rose to positions of power.

Figures like Snezhnevsky, Georgy Morozov and Viktor Morozov are discussed and castigated severely. Snezhnevsky is designated as the arch-villain, and the hospitalized dissenters as his victims. He is responsible for the rotten status of Soviet psychiatry, particularly through his overwhelming tendency to "describe almost all syndromes known in psychiatry as schizophrenia. He discerns . . . subtle features of the schizophrenic process which are so subtle as to be quite invisible." Those psychiatrists like Georgy Morozov, who have pleased the "master" and adhered loyally to the doctrine of schizophrenia, have done so for careerist and opportunistic reasons.

How do we assess these forthright accusations? The polemical tone of the essay and its anonymity preclude its automatic acceptance as a reliable document. On the other hand the broad personal knowledge of developments in Soviet psychiatry, of its leading figures, and of its use to suppress dissent, suggest that the author gained a reasonably valid picture over the eighteen years that he worked in Moscow. The psychiatrist's identity and fate remain unknown.

We should also mention three other figures who, while not actually psychiatrists, have worked as professionals in the medical field and have publicly criticized the misuse of psychiatry.

Leonard Ternovsky, a researcher at a Moscow medical institute, circulated the following statement in March 1975 on the occasion of the fourth anniversary of Bukovsky's arrest:

> Bukovsky did what every decent person ought to have done, what only a hero is in fact able to do. . . . I consider myself especially in debt to Bukovsky. The first people to speak up against the shameful and harmful use of medicine should have been doctors. And I belong to this profession. If I had done my duty, then I would now be where Bukovsky is today. But he did it for me.[32]

Dr Elena Bonner, the wife of Andrei Sakharov, was one of the three signatories of an appeal for Yury Shikhanovich (see chapter 7) in July 1973. On receiving the news that Shikhanovich had been ruled not responsible and in need of compulsory treatment, Dr Bonner and her associates in an open letter averred that:

> This treatment will be imposed on a healthy person. Shikhanovich is our close friend. We have consistently and frequently associated with him and consider it our duty to state that we are convinced of his mental health. One of us is a doctor and, guided by professional knowledge and a doctor's sense of duty, hereby testifies that in all aspects of Shikhanovich's personality not the slightest evidence of ill health has ever been noticed. . . .
>
> We live in a society in which no one, including the authors of this letter, can be certain that they will never be struck by the same fate as that of Shikhanovich, Plyushch, Borisov, Fainberg, Grigorenko, Lupynos, Ubozhko and many other inmates of psychiatric hospitals.[33]

Ilya Glezer, formerly a biologist in Professor Snezhnevsky's Institute of Psychiatry, was arrested in February 1972 following

his application to emigrate to Israel and sentenced under article
70 to three years in a labour camp and three in exile. It seems
possible that the heavy sentence was connected, directly or
indirectly, with his condemnation of psychiatric abuse.

As a researcher, Glezer innovated a mathematical approach
to the study of the brain, and wrote two books and numerous
articles. According to an ex-Soviet psychiatrist, Glezer had
initially been victimized in several ways after speaking out
against the abuse. He was under KGB surveillance, was
prevented from submitting his doctoral dissertation, was
demoted from senior to junior status and in 1970 was forced to
leave his post.[34]

Another Classification of Soviet Psychiatrists

We have outlined three broad categories of psychiatrists *vis-à-
vis* the misuse of psychiatry—the core, the average and the
dissenting psychiatrist. In their *Manual* Gluzman and Bukovsky
have also suggested a classification of types focusing almost
exclusively on attitudes to diagnosis: (1) *the novice* views
psychiatry as scientifically sound, and tends in his eagerness and
relative inexperience to over-diagnose mental illness; he may
therefore genuinely view dissent as an expression of mental
illness. (2) *The academic*—psychiatry is a scientific discipline for
him as well. Generally he does not regard dissent as illness and
consequently evades participation in delicate forensic cases;
he understands that there is a potential for psychiatry's misuse
and will endeavour "not to dirty his hands". (3) *The writer of
dissertations* is not as well defined by the authors as the others;
since he tends to broaden the definition of the illness he is
writing about, the dissenter's best chance is to convince him
that his case has no relevance to that illness. (4) *The Voltairean*
is a bright, experienced person, long disillusioned with psychiatry as a science and fully aware of its misuse. Despite his
tendency to cynicism, he will not diagnose a dissenter as
disturbed even under pressure. (5) *The Philistine* is of average
intellect and has highly conventional attitudes and interests.
He considers himself an intelligent and experienced professional
with a life-style that serves as an excellent model for others. His
conformism renders him sceptical of modern poetry and
surrealist art. He cannot understand the dissenter's "lack of

adaptability to Soviet society". "But you had an apartment, a family, a job. Why did you do it?"—he asks in bewilderment. Bukovsky and Gluzman perceive this type as dangerous in that he yields readily to pressure from his superiors and subsequently rationalizes his acts by reference to authoritative psychiatrists. (6) *The professional hangman* deliberately misdiagnoses the mentally healthy as ill. Since he is usually a knowledgeable specialist, the dissenter's only hope is not to provide him with any "symptoms" of illness: the psychiatrist may not want to risk his reputation for competence by resorting to the sheer invention of them.

Soviet Methods of Diagnosis

No matter the type of psychiatrist involved with the dissenter, the Soviet approach to psychiatric diagnosis—particularly the concept of schizophrenia—is a critical help in labelling dissent as mental illness. Our focus will be mainly on schizophrenia, for it is this diagnosis that has usually been applied. Psychopathy, particularly of the paranoid type, is the alternative pigeonhole for dissenters, but is less commonly used.*

What is Schizophrenia?

Although the following discussion of schizophrenia is detailed, we believe it is necessary background for an appreciation of the use of the diagnosis in the Soviet context. Psychiatrists in most

---

* According to the authors of the chapter on "Psychopathy" in the authoritative textbook of Soviet forensic psychiatry, the paranoid psychopath is characterized by a disorder of personality, congenitally determined or acquired early in life. The abnormal features may, however, manifest themselves at any time in life. The patient may show an exaggerated sense of self-importance, believing that others are paying special attention to him. They may have "a passion for scientific invention and reformist work. Their projects and plans usually reveal the narrow range of their interests and knowledge, besides their erroneous nature." In the forensic context the paranoid personality can usually evaluate external reality and govern his actions and is thus declared responsible. Exceptionally, the condition is so deep and the character structure so altered, that it constitutes a mental illness in which the patient is then declared not responsible. ("Psychopathy", chapter 21, by O. V. Kerbikov and N. I. Felinskaya in *Forensic Psychiatry*, edited by G. V. Morozov and I. M. Kalashnik, International Arts and Sciences Press: New York, 1970.)

countries have applied the term schizophrenia since it was first introduced by Eugen Bleuler in 1911, and his concepts have attained a substantial measure of popularity. In recent years, however, schizophrenia has had a checkered career. This is not surprising when one considers the vague and ill-defined features commonly held to constitute the disorder. There is little consensus about it among psychiatrists. The most severe difficulty in diagnosing it stems from a lack of objective criteria. Thus far, no tests have been discovered which permit a definitive diagnosis to be made. Moreover, schizophrenia's cause, notwithstanding an avalanche of research findings, remains obscure.

Given these limitations, schizophrenia is generally defined in terms of its clinical features. Kraepelin, a German psychiatrist, made a pioneering attempt at the turn of the century to classify the major psychotic mental illnesses. The term "psychotic" is a controversial one but is used in this context to indicate the loss of contact with reality by a patient. The symptoms he regarded as characteristic included: hallucinations (perception of stimuli not actually present), most commonly auditory or tactile; unusual and illogical associations of thought resulting in incoherent speech; delusions (false beliefs held with conviction); lack of insight into the illness; withdrawal from the real world; blunting of the emotions; and stereotyped patterns of behaviour.[35]

Bleuler extended Kraepelin's concept by introducing a distinction between primary and secondary symptoms. The former were a direct result of the (undetermined) cause, the latter reflected reactions in the person to the primary symptoms. Bleuler's primary symptoms are: disorder of thought with loosening of associations, blunting of emotions, and withdrawal from reality into a world of fantasy; the secondary symptoms are hallucinations, delusions and diverse behavioural changes.[36]

While the efforts of the German psychiatrist Kurt Schneider[37] and others have aimed at a more disciplined method of diagnosing schizophrenia, other psychiatrists have moved in an opposite direction. Hoch and Polatin for instance introduced the concept of pseudoneurotic schizophrenia, a disorder characterized by multiple neurotic symptoms— anxiety, phobias, obsessions and a tendency to withdraw from reality, but not necessarily involving overt psychotic features such as delusions and hallucinations.[38] The diagnostic manual of the American Psychiatric Association includes these terms under schizophrenia: "latent", "incipient", "pre-psychotic" and "borderline".[39] The comparable manual used in Britain includes a category of "latent schizophrenia"—"to designate those abnormal states in which, in the absence of obvious schizophrenic symptoms, the *suspicion is strong* [our italics] that the condition is in fact a schizophrenia. Eccentric, purposeless behaviour and emotional anomalies could be the basis of the suspicion."[40] All the terms cited above are almost as vague as the Soviet concept of "seeming normality" discussed later in this chapter.

A Danish psychiatrist, Erik Strömgren, comments on the rapidity with which psychiatric terms and concepts change from time to time and from place to place.[41] He points also to the danger of using terms *without concepts*. He argues that confusion may arise in the application of terms through their arbitrary choice, imprecise definition and changing connotation: "borderline psychosis" and "latent psychosis", for example, have both been introduced as diagnostic categories but commonly are applied to patients "where examination and consideration have not given sufficient evidence for making a diagnosis at all".

Some of Strömgren's points were well illustrated by a series of studies undertaken in the 1960s to investigate methods of diagnosis. One group of researchers compared the diagnosis made by American and British psychiatrists and demonstrated major discrepancies between them, particularly the much wider American concept of schizophrenia.[42] The findings showed that despite comparable groups of patients, schizophrenia was diagnosed twice as often in New York as in London and that the New York concept included patients who in London would be labelled as suffering from depression, neurosis and personality disorders.[43]

The World Health Organization, aware of the low level of agreement among psychiatrists in diagnosing schizophrenia, initiated the International Pilot Study of Schizophrenia, a large-scale cross-cultural investigation, involving 1,200 patients in nine countries.[44] The study showed that differences in diagnosis were minimal in cases where a relatively narrow definition of schizophrenia was applied, differences became obvious when the strict limits set were exceeded. Moscow and Washington D.C. diverged from the other seven centres in using the diagnosis more broadly and to cover other psychiatric illnesses. The wider limits occurred in the two centres despite their differing theoretical approaches. Let us now look more closely at the Soviet concept of schizophrenia.

The Soviet Approach to Schizophrenia

The World Health Organization study showed in the Moscow research centre not only a broader concept of schizophrenia but also a unique system of categorizing it. The creator of this system is Professor Snezhnevsky, helped by his associates at the Institute of Psychiatry.[45] They recognize three forms of the condition: continuous, shift-like and periodic, with several subtypes in each form. While clinical features differ in each form, the final criterion for distinguishing between them is the course of the illness. Assignment to a category follows a review of the patient's entire life history: the nature of his personality before the onset of the illness, the age of onset, previous episodes of mental illness, social functioning during periods of apparent health, and the rate of progression of the illness.

In the continuous form, accounting for 25 to 30 per cent of the schizophrenias diagnosed in a series of studies, the patient typically deteriorates in progressive fashion and no remission (i.e. recovery) is possible. Initially, subtle personality changes occur, referred to as "secondary" symptoms—withdrawal, apathy and diminished interests. The development of symptoms may be so gradual that no actual attack of the disease is observable. The "secondary" symptoms are followed by the development of "positive" or psychotic ones like delusions and hallucinations. Sub-types of the continuous form depend on the rate of progression of the disease, hence the descriptions rapid (or malignant), moderate and sluggish (mild). In the malignant course, the symptoms are severe and easily discernible. The moderate course is characterized by slowly evolving paranoid features (ideas of persecution). In the sluggish type, almost full ability to function socially is retained; the symptoms may resemble those of a neurosis and include obsessional, hysterical or hypochondriacal features, or take on a psychopathic or paranoid character. The patient developing paranoid symptoms is usually middle-aged, retains some insight into his condition, but *overvalues his own importance and may exhibit grandiose ideas of reforming the world* or offer new inventions of outstanding significance. Notwithstanding the mild nature of the sluggish type, the clinical course is still progressively downhill and the chance of improvement is minimal.

The sluggish type of continuous-form schizophrenia is frequently diagnosed in the dissenter for reasons indicated by our italicizing of two of its possible features.

A few words on the other two forms. Shift-like schizophrenia, comprising 40 per cent of cases, is, it is held, intermediate between continuous and periodic in that the course is progressive (as in continuous) with attacks of the disorder followed by remissions (as in periodic); the remission is not complete, however, and the patient never returns to his previous level of functioning. As in the continuous form, mild, moderate and severe subtypes occur, depending on the rate of progression.

The periodic form makes up the remaining 30 to 35 per cent of diagnosed schizophrenias. It has the best outlook since the patient's premorbid personality is typically normal and the illness consists only of attacks of delusions and abnormal changes in mood, between which the patient appears and functions normally. A mild abnormal personality change may occur after several years.

The Snezhnevsky school postulates that although the three main forms of schizophrenia are clinically distinguishable and the prognosis is predictable in each, all schizophrenias are biologically interconnected in that they share a common genetic basis. Also, patients tend to belong to one form only, although they may shift from one subtype to another within that form. The emphasis on genetic factors is seen in Soviet studies of schizophrenia, which usually revolve about the search for a genetic cause. By contrast, environmental factors are seen to exert only a minor rôle, as a trigger or precipitant of the illness.

Once a patient is diagnosed as schizophrenic, he is considered thereafter always to be schizophrenic, even if he returns to a normal state, as in the case of the periodic form. A diagnosis of early schizophrenia may be applied to persons who manifest personality changes of the "secondary" kind, despite an absence of any psychotic features. Mild states of the illness are genetically associated with more severe states and therefore are often viewed as a prelude to the latter.

The Soviet view of schizophrenia as an irreversible, deep-seated illness with extremely broad diagnostic criteria leads to serious results for a large number of people who are labelled as suffering from it. They are liable, for example, to be deprived of their driving licences, rejected for jobs, or barred from places in higher education.[46]

Forensic Implications

The forensic implications of this view of schizophrenia are also far-reaching. Dr Edgar Goldstein, a psychiatrist now in the United States who worked in the Leningrad forensic psychiatric service over a six-year period, discussed this issue with us. He summed up the Soviet view in a succint formula—"schizophrenia equals non-responsibility". Dr Morozov authoritatively states that "schizophrenia is a disease in which patients are, with rare exceptions, deemed not responsible".[47] This doctrinaire position matches the absence in Soviet law of any provision for a determination of diminished or partial responsibility in the defendant. The law explicitly calls for a definitive evaluation from the psychiatrist—was the defendant ill or not at the time of committing the offence?*

Consider now the case of a person charged with a criminal offence in which the suspicion of mental illness is raised. Because of the extremely wide limits set in applying the concept of schizophrenia, the diagnosis may be pinned to the defendant on the most tenuous of grounds. And with the diagnosis comes the automatic declaration of non-responsibility. Morozov concedes that "forensic psychiatrists often experience difficulties when psychopathological symptoms are mild and the presence or absence of schizophrenia must be established, or when it is a question of differential diagnosis or an evaluation of remissions".[48] The diagnosis may be made on a history of psychiatric symptoms in the past, i.e. long before the offence was

---

* In recent years, however, a few cases have occurred of defendants being sent to an SPH for treatment, and of the court specifying that they should later be given a full-scale trial on their recovery. See the cases of Kovhar, Plakhotnyuk and Davarashvili in appendix I. There appears to be no basis in Soviet law for this procedure.

committed, and, as we shall now discuss, also in the absence of any symptoms at the time of the offence. The defendant may during the examination appear normal but, according to Soviet concepts, still harbour the illness.

These concepts are well illustrated in the trials of several dissenters. In Gorbanevskaya's trial Professor Lunts defends his diagnosis of sluggish schizophrenia. In this illness, he contends that well-defined psychotic phenomena such as delusions and hallucinations are not characteristically present, indeed this form of schizophrenia "has no clear symptoms". But mental changes which superficially resemble improvement cannot be viewed as such from "the theoretical point of view".[49] Lunts thus calls for the acceptance of a concept that a disease like schizophrenia is "theoretically", but not clinically, present in the patient. This notion also represents the essence of a case argued by a group of prominent psychiatrists, among them Snezhnevsky, Georgy Morozov, Nadzharov and Serebryakova, in a letter of rebuttal sent to their Western critics:

> There is a small number of mental cases whose disease, as a result of a mental derangement, paranoia and other psychopathological symptoms, can lead them to anti-social actions which fall in the category of those that are prohibited by law, such as disturbance of public order, dissemination of slander, manifestation of aggressive intentions, etc. It is noteworthy that they can do this after preliminary preparations, with "a cunningly calculated plan of action", as the founder of Russian forensic psychiatry, V. P. Serbsky, who was widely known for his progressive views, wrote. To the people around them such mental cases do not create the impression of being obviously "insane". Most often these are persons suffering from schizophrenia or a paranoid pathological development of the personality. Such cases are known well both by Soviet and foreign psychiatrists. The seeming normality of such sick persons when they commit socially dangerous actions is used by anti-Soviet propaganda for slanderous contentions that these persons are not suffering from a mental disorder.[50]

The concept of "seeming normality" must thus be added to the lexicon of the psychiatrist—a diagnosis of mental illness in the absence of any signs of mental illness!

Perhaps the most illuminating case of "seeming normality" is that of Olga Iofe. At her trial a member of the psychiatric commission, Dr Martynenko of the Serbsky Institute, has the following conversation with defence counsel Pozdeyev:

Pozdeyev: "Exactly what physiological tests were carried out to establish that she was suffering from an illness?"

Martynenko: "Such physiological tests are carried out on everybody without exception. The absence of symptoms of an illness cannot prove the absence of the illness itself."

Pozdeyev: "On the basis of exactly what remarks did the commission establish that her thought processes were functioning on different levels? Describe even one of the tests administered to Olga, by means of which major disturbances of her thought processes were established, or give even one remark by her which suggested such disturbances."

Martynenko: "I am unable to give a concrete answer, and if the court requires one it will be necessary to send to the Serbsky Institute for the history of the illness. However, her reaction to being taken to the Serbsky Institute may serve as an example of her behaviour. She knew where she had been taken and realized what this meant, but she showed no sign of emotion, the tone of her voice did not even change."*

Pozdeyev: "Do you not ascribe Olga's behaviour to her self-control, strength of will and serenity, of which the witnesses have spoken?"

Martynenko: "It's impossible to control oneself to that extent."

Pozdeyev: "How do you explain the fact that the presence of an illness which, according to the diagnosis, has been developing in Iofe since she was fourteen did not prevent her from successfully graduating from the mathematical school and entering the university?"

Martynenko: "The presence of this form of schizophrenia does not presuppose changes in the personality noticeable to others."[51]

* At this point in the record, as published by the *Chronicle*, the editors refer wryly to another dissenter ruled not responsible not long before: "V. Novodvorskaya showed signs of emotion—too many. The result of the examination was the same!"

Schizophrenia and the Dissenter

In view of psychiatry's lack of sufficiently objective criteria in the diagnosis of schizophrenia, it is irrational to argue that the Soviet concept of schizophrenia, as such, is incorrect. Many differing theories exist and none can yet be regarded with certainty as being more valid than the rest. Nevertheless, we record here our own scepticism of, in particular, three basic features of the Soviet model: the breadth of its diagnostic criteria, the extreme schematism of its classification, and the overwhelming pessimism of its prognosis. We also contend that, even within the context of the model, the application of the diagnosis to dissenters is unwarranted, at least as regards those whose detailed case histories were sent to the West by Bukovsky. We incorporated our own critical remarks and those of other Western psychiatrists into our discussion of the cases of Grigorenko and Gorbanevskaya in chapter 5. We now comment more generally on the clinical criteria usually cited by forensic psychiatrists for the diagnosis of schizophrenia in dissenters.

The most frequently used phrases are: "paranoid reformist delusional ideas" (a variant includes "paranoid delusions of reforming society or re-organization of the state apparatus"), "uncritical attitude towards his abnormal condition" (or "situation"), "moralizes" (or "opinions have moralizing character"), "over-estimation of his own personality" (or "over-inflation of his capabilities"), and "poor adaptation to the social environment". Two or more of these criteria are usually combined in the case reports on dissenters. Three brief examples will suffice to illustrate the pattern:

> He expresses with enthusiasm and great feeling reformist ideas concerning the teaching of the Marxist classics, revealing in the process a clear over-estimation of himself and an unshakeable conviction of his own rightness.[52]

> ... delusional reformist ideas and an absence of criticism towards his own condition and the situation which has developed.[53]

> His political thinking is grossly contradictory. He minimizes his actions and does not comprehend their criminal, treacherous nature. .... He considers himself to be a political

figure of world-wide significance who will be defended by the Commission on Human Rights of the United Nations.[54]

These evaluations are contained in the case reports of Fainberg, Kuznetsov and Yakhimovich respectively. A criterion dominant in all three reports is the dissenter's conviction that society or the state or Marxism-Leninism must be changed. This "reformism" is arbitrarily labelled by the psychiatrists as delusional in character, i.e. the dissenter manifests false beliefs and holds on to them with unshakeable tenacity. Yet it is patently clear that his social and political attitudes, while deemed delusional, in fact involve criticism of specific acts and policies of the Soviet government, such as violations of the Constitution, the lack of rights of minority groups and the 1968 invasion of Czechoslovakia.

The case reports show no evidence of any serious examination by the psychiatrists of the dissenter's criticism to determine whether or not it is delusional. Rather they frequently twist and distort his views to make them appear symptomatic of illness. Thus Yakhimovich's belief that supporters in the West would speak up in his defence is transmogrified into the delusion of grandeur quoted above. Similarly in Grigorenko's case report, his views on human rights are distorted and parodied and made to appear grandiose: "All his energy and activity were 'devoted' to the fight for 'truth' and the creation of conditions which would exclude injustice from the life of the community."[55] As we saw in chapter 5 Gorbanevskaya's interpretation that she was sent for psychiatric examination after her arrest to avoid an awkward trial at which she could make a defiant speech, is reported by the psychiatrists in such a way to suggest that she was paranoid: "Is sure she was sent for diagnosis 'so that there would be no noise'; 'because it suited the public prosecutor'." Her interpretation was soon shown to be correct.[56]

Indeed the clinical reports available to us are full of blatant distortions of many kinds clearly designed, in most cases, to buttress a diagnosis of schizophrenia. The report on Gorbanevskaya deliberately included false testimony to try to show that she had no love for her mother while excluding abundant evidence to the contrary. The report of the Snezhnevsky commission on Plyushch distorts a girl's infatuation with him when they were both students—an episode laughed off as ridiculous and irrelevant by Snezhnevsky during the examination itself—into evidence of his supposedly exaggerated sense of self-importance.[57]

The dissenters whose cases are well documented have not advocated some extraordinary scheme for changing the entire society but have been operating within an internationally recognized movement for the promotion of human rights for Soviet citizens. These are not the bizarre confused thoughts of madmen but rather the political and social views of a group of people closely involved with the realities of their society.

Not only is there no evidence of "reformist delusions" in the thinking of these dissenters, there is also none for concluding that they commonly suffer "an over-estimation of their own personalities". We know of no dissenter, diagnosed as mentally ill, who has believed that he alone could, or would, alter Soviet society, or that the régime would instantly heed his words. On the contrary, many dissenters clearly believe that their campaign to achieve basic human rights for Soviet citizens will necessarily be protracted and frustrating. They understand well that their movement is small and subject to constant erosion through arrest, exile and compulsory hospitalization.

All these points are abundantly documented in the *Chronicle*, one of whose editors even sees the journal's tasks as including the deterrence of any potential revolutionaries from rash anti-Soviet plans or acts. The *Chronicle* achieves this, he believes, by consistently recording the régime's severe repression even of mild criticism.[58]

"Poor adaptation to the social environment" is another commonly cited criterion of the dissenter's schizophrenia. Adjustment to society is widely regarded throughout the world as a criterion of mental health. Although a vague concept, maladjustment is accepted by most psychiatrists as a feature of psychiatric disturbance. Consider a person who devotes his entire energy to the dissemination of his "unique system" for the reorganization of society, and *pari passu* neglects the needs of his family and himself, loses his means of livelihood, and is hostile to those who refuse to support his views. Without question, this person's adaptation to society would be regarded as severely impaired. This is not the case, however, with the Soviet dissenters. Rather than withdraw from reality, they wage a campaign within the boundaries of Soviet law, calling on the régime to respect the fundamental rights of citizens as embodied in the constitution. Their campaign is not an exclusive preoccupation; they continue to work as physicists, electricians, mathematicians, writers, artists, bricklayers (unless arbitrarily dismissed from their posts as a method of punishment). In fact their ranks include men and women who have achieved considerable success in their professional pursuits: Grigorenko as a major-general, Gorbanevskaya as a poet, Medvedev as a biologist, Plyushch as a cybernetician, Yakhimovich as a chairman of a collective farm (he was praised by the Soviet press prior to the onset of his dissenting activities as one of the best collective-farm chairmen in the country),[59] Shikhanovich as a mathematician, and so on. It is striking how these basic facts are almost invariably neglected in the psychiatric examination and omitted from the case report.

It is also interesting to note that many of the dissenters who were interned and later emigrated have adapted quickly and successfully to life in their new homes. Among those we have met, Rips and Volpin were, in 1976, teaching mathematics at universities, Feigin was a trade-union official, Medvedev was a research biologist and writer, Plyushch was preparing to become a mathematics teacher, and Gorbanevskaya was a writer and editor.

Another important factor in the context of adjustment to society is the attitude shown to a patient by his family and friends. In none of the cases of the dissenters we have interviewed have their family and friends regarded them as mentally abnormal or in need of treatment. These people have not submitted complaints to the authorities about the strangeness of the dissenters' behaviour. On the contrary, they have invariably insisted that their relatives are mentally well. It is only the officials and psychiatrists who have maintained otherwise. The same points are true of the great majority of those dissenters listed in appendix I on whom we have the relevant information.*

* We know of only one case when internment has followed the complaint of a relative. Birute Poškiene was hospitalized in an OPH in 1974 after pressure by her husband. Because of her strong religious convictions he and the authorities used psychiatry to deprive her of any influence over their children. See appendix I for more details.

Some psychiatrists have buttressed their argument about the dissenter's poor adaptation by pointing to the tenacity with which he acts out his beliefs despite the odds. In chapter 6 we saw an example of this in Dr Shafran's attempted persuasion of Shimanov to modify his religious activity. The dissenter does indeed operate in dangerous territory; the reaction of the régime is often harsh. But he is fully aware of the risks inherent in his non-conformist behaviour; his moral integrity compels him to take them. Some dissenters have parried the psychiatrists on this point by asking whether Lenin and his colleagues were "poorly adapted" when, in their struggle against the tsarist régime, they were constantly subject to harassment and arrest.

Can the Dissenter Ward Off the Psychiatrist's Diagnosis of Mental Illness?

Bukovsky and Gluzman in their *Manual* have provided systematic advice to the dissenter faced with the possibility of psychiatrists unjustifiably labelling him as mentally ill. The manual illuminates, with unique force, the diagnostic methods of Soviet psychiatry in the context of dissent. The examinee must, above all, be prepared to sacrifice his moral stance and, where necessary, resort to lies. Thus when providing information about his earlier life, he should mention these points: his birth and early development were normal, he enjoyed the company of childhood friends, he experienced no neurotic symptoms as a child, his schooling was satisfactory, he developed an interest in the other sex at the appropriate time, he had no difficulty selecting a career, and he enjoyed a harmonious family life. He should state further that in his current life he engages in social relationships and has a variety of interests in "innocuous areas", but definitely not in philosophy, modern art or religion.

A key recommendation of the manual is the explanation the dissenter should provide concerning his political views. The authors instruct him in these terms:

However disagreeable it may be, the best motivation you can offer for the actions you are charged with is: I wanted to become famous, to be well-known; I did not understand the seriousness of the consequences; I did not stand aside and take a look at myself; I did not realize that I had gone too far, and so on. Unfortunately it is precisely unpleasant reasoning like this which will be interpreted in a positive light by the psychiatrist.[60]

This tactic is aimed at undermining the psychiatrist's argument that the dissenter suffers "an over-estimation of his own personality". The authors also advise against the use of figurative expressions which could strike the psychiatrist as bizarre, for example this explanation by Grigorenko for his dissenting activity—"I could not breathe". Even if the dissenter is convinced that he has been harassed and victimized (and in many cases this is likely to be true), he should not allude to it, as such comments cannot be proved and will be interpreted as a paranoid reaction. Hunger strikes should be resorted to only in extreme circumstances since they will be regarded as examples of "psychopathic negativism". He should show appropriate concern for his family, friends and future, to avoid the label "emotionally dulled or cold".

Conclusion

In the light of our discussion in this chapter it is perhaps no surprise that in recent years hundreds of dissenters have been labelled as mentally ill. First, the authorities can rely on the core psychiatrist to co-operate fully, while the average psychiatrist is too conformist to refuse to participate when called upon. Second, the Soviet approach to the diagnosis of mental illness, and in particular the Snezhnevsky model of schizophrenia, lend themselves more than conveniently to a view of dissent as illness. In the next chapter we look at the victims of this psychiatric system.

We have often been asked how sincere or insincere Soviet psychiatrists are when dealing with dissenters. Do they really believe that dissent is a form of illness? As one cannot see into men's souls the question is a difficult one. Nonetheless, we would like to record our broad conclusion from our research, namely that most of these psychiatrists do not so believe. Bukovsky told us that in his opinion the great majority of those in the Leningrad SPH in the mid-1960s did not in fact regard the political prisoners as ill. Two of the psychiatrists, Drs L. A. Kalinin and

Kelchevskaya, considered Nikolai Samsonov to be mentally healthy, but, in the *Chronicle*'s words, "advised him to admit in writing that he had been ill when he composed his letter to the central committee. Such an admission, they told him, would testify to his 'recovery'."[61] Gorbanevskaya's psychiatrists in Kazan were quite content with her formal and partial recantation, and let her know clearly that they realized it was insincere. Grigorenko's and Fainberg's psychiatrists in Chernyakhovsk and Leningrad likewise hinted that they would be satisfied with formal recantations. Only Plyushch seems to have run up against a psychiatrist, Lydia Lyubarskaya, who genuinely believed he was ill.

By contrast, some psychiatrists have been openly cynical. According to Dr Voikhanskaya, Professor V. M. Morozov likes to say: "It's no secret to anyone that you can have schizophrenia without schizophrenia." And, as noted above, one of Voikhanskaya's colleagues whispered to her about a dissenter in their hospital: "He's perfectly healthy, but don't tell anybody."[62] The doctors in an Ashkhabad OPH told the poet Annasoltan Kekilova that she was "in good health" but that "If you don't give us a signed statement that you wrote to the central committee because you were in a nervous condition, you'll stay in hospital forever."[63] Finally, Dr V. V. Kokorev, head of the psychiatric section of the Mordovian camps' hospital, told a dissenter's parents that "in his opinion their son was mentally healthy, but he refused to guarantee that this would be the diagnosis, and referred to some special instructions he had regarding political prisoners".[64]

Chapter 9

THE VICTIMS

So MUCH FOR the psychiatrists. But what about their victims, that is, for our purposes, mentally healthy dissenters compulsorily confined to psychiatric hospitals? To date we have considered only four of them in detail. In this chapter we estimate their numbers, examine the broad spectrum of activities which led to their internment, discuss which categories of dissenter are *not* represented in their ranks, analyse why some are selected for hospitalization while others are sent to prison camps, and ask why certain victims are interned under criminal commitment and others under civil.

How Many Victims?
At present we have a moderate or substantial amount of information on some 210 people who have been interned in mental hospitals since 1962 for reasons connected with their beliefs. Their cases appear in summary form in appendix I. We choose 1962 as the cut-off date, as prior to that our knowledge is more fragmentary. In the last fourteen years, however, and especially with the emergence of the human-rights movement in the late 1960s, we have received fairly extensive information about the inmates of certain hospitals, usually via the various dissenting groups. This does not mean though that the incidence of political internment was necessarily lower in the period prior to 1962.

The 210 are certainly only a fraction of the total number of victims between 1962 and 1976, as we shall see below. Moreover, this figure does not include a further 50 victims on whom information is not as yet extensive enough. We are confident, in these cases, that they have been interned for their beliefs, but we often do not know the exact nature of the beliefs.[1]

The group of 210 includes a small number of dissenters (about ten), who, we have been told by various reliable sources, have suffered at different times from mental illnesses, usually minor. To give their names here would be invidious. Suffice it to say that in the opinion of their relatives and friends none of them has been in need of compulsory hospitalization, let alone in an SPH. Also, their hospitalization was always a direct consequence of their dissenting activity, and this activity was invariably of a peaceful nature. Appendix I also includes a few people who have become mentally ill as a result of the years they have spent in intolerable SPH conditions.

Numbers in the SPHs

What proportion do the 210 represent of all prisoners interned for their beliefs in the USSR in the period under review? It is impossible as yet to know for sure. Let us look at some of the available evidence.

First, what of those dissenters who have been held in the SPHs? Of the 210 documented cases, about 150 are in this category, the other 60 having been hospitalized in an OPH. What has been the total number of dissenters in particular SPHs at particular times? Fainberg estimates that while the total number of patients in Leningrad oscillated in the period 1969–1973 between about 700 and 1,000, the number of dissenters among them was usually, up to 1972, between 20 and 30. In 1972–73 the numbers dropped sharply, as the dissenters were transferred to other SPHs or to OPHs: this was the administration's way of dealing with the discipline problem caused by the resistance of Fainberg and others. By the end of 1973 only one dissenter, Vladimir Trifonov, remained.

Some of those transferred from Leningrad were sent to swell the numbers in the similarly-sized Dnepropetrovsk SPH. This fact may help to account for there being, according to Plyushch, as many as 60 dissenters held in it at the time of his release in early 1976.[2]

In the women's section of the Kazan SPH, in 1971, Gorbanevskaya reports that there were about fifteen dissenters, half of them political and half religious, out of a total of 150 inmates.[3]

Unfortunately, no more information of this sort is yet available. But given these figures, and the fact that in recent years there have been at least a dozen SPHs operating (see chapter 7), a rough estimate of several hundred dissenters held *at any one time* in the SPHs in recent years would seem plausible.* Our estimate is supported by another method of calculation which focuses on Professor Lunts's special diagnostic section at the Serbsky Institute. The section's function is to examine those persons referred to it by criminal investigators (usually the KGB), who are accused either under articles in the criminal code dealing with serious crimes like those against the state, or under a minor political article such as 190–1. As "crimes against the state" include not only "anti-Soviet agitation" and forming an anti-Soviet organization, but also large-scale embezzlement and murder in certain aggravating circumstances, the dissenters are not, as we saw from Nekipelov's account in chapter 5, the only type of detainee in Lunts's section.

About 80 per cent of the dissenters in Appendix I on whom the relevant information is available have been referred to Lunts and his staff for assessment. The remaining 20 per cent have been assessed exclusively in cities outside Moscow.† However, these figures probably give an inaccurate idea of the overall picture, as the *Chronicle* is less able to gather information about forensic practices outside Moscow. So more realistic figures might, as a tentative estimate, be about 60 per cent for the Serbsky and 40 per cent for the rest of the country.

The three wards in Lunts's section which are collectively called "the box" contain, as noted in chapter 5, those detainees charged with the most serious crimes. Grigorenko reports that in March–April 1964 there were eleven patients in the "box", among whom he expected three to be ruled not responsible.[4] In November 1968 Fainberg tells us that of the four dissenters he himself was the only one to be ruled not responsible. By contrast, during his second spell in February–April 1972 there were nine dissenters, all of whom were ruled not responsible; seven were recommended for SPH and two for OPH treatment.[5] In August–September 1967 Valentin Prussakov lists seven men

* It should be noted that dissenters are often held for some time under SPH-type conditions in ordinary prisons. This is after they have been ruled not responsible and before they are eventually transported, by court order, to an SPH. During this period, which can last up to a year, they are usually held in the psychiatric department of the hospital section of a prison.

† In a few cases like those of Yakhimovich and Igrunov, dissenters are examined first outside Moscow, then in the Serbsky.

accused of political offences,[6] and, as we saw in chapter 5, the *Chronicle* gives the same number for January 1974.[7] To produce the total number of dissenters in the section at any one time, these figures need to be increased by adding in the two or three politicals usually held—if Nekipelov's experience was typical—in wards outside "the box".

As some dissenters in the Serbsky are ruled responsible for their actions, and others are recommended for OPH treatment, it seems that on average only three or four of those under examination at any one time are recommended for an SPH. Since their average stay in the Serbsky is a month, it would appear that Lunts and his team recommend about 35 male dissenters for SPH treatment per year. With women added, the figure rises to perhaps 40* and if this figure is—as suggested above—about 60 per cent of the total for the USSR, then that total would be roughly 70 per year. With the dissenters' average SPH term being approximately five years,† the number of them held in SPHs *at any one time* comes out at about 350.

We should note that the estimate of 350 may not be valid for the whole of the period 1962–75. A forensic psychiatrist from Kiev (who wishes to remain anonymous) told us that the number of dissenters examined there by him and his colleagues rose sharply in 1968 and then remained at a high level, at least until he emigrated in 1973. This rise is not surprising, as 1968 saw the emergence of the human-rights movement and increased activity by many dissenting groups.

We are—as will be clear from the foregoing discussion and what follows—sceptical of the estimate made by one Western psychiatrist that in 1973 there were 7,000 Soviet citizens interned in psychiatric hospitals for political reasons.[8] In any event, however, we do not believe that in the context of psychiatric abuse statistics are the most important consideration.

---

* If, as may be the case, Kazan is the only SPH to which women dissenters are sent, then, as Gorbanevskaya reports, a population of about fifteen in 1971, the total number of them newly interned per year in SPHs would presumably be about three.

† This is the average estimate of the ex-inmates we have interviewed. It should be borne in mind that some of the best-known dissenters have certainly been released "ahead of time", as a result of campaigns in their defence, and that their average stay has therefore been somewhat less than the average for dissenters as a whole.

Numbers in the OPHs
How many dissenters are held in the OPHs? Here our rough
estimating ends and we can only speculate. There are about 200
OPHs scattered throughout the USSR, some mainly for
short-stay, others for chronic patients. Dissenters linked to the
human rights movement have been interned in only a score of
these, and they (through their reports) are almost our only
source of information.

Moreover, although a few dissenters have been held for a
year or more in OPHs, the terms of most of them have been
considerably shorter. As we have seen, Medvedev and
Shimanov spent less than three weeks each in the Kaluga and
Kashchenko hospitals. Yury Maltsev, a member of the Action
Group for the Defence of Human Rights (see chapter 7), was
interned for a month in Kashchenko in 1969. And the Zionist
Grisha Feigin spent three weeks in a Riga OPH in 1970. While
they and a dozen others have described the cases of sane
fellow dissenters interned in their sections, they have not had the
time or opportunity to make estimates of the overall number
of such people in the OPHs.[9]

A relevant factor here is the great size of some OPHs, and the
many categories of inmate scattered in different parts of them.
The Kashchenko for example has 3,000 beds in numerous
buildings covering 40 acres, the available accounts coming
from dissenters who have been confined in sections 3, 4, 5, 15,
27, 32 and 33. Some of these sections are for acutely disturbed
patients, others for mildly disturbed. Some inmates are long-
term, some short-term patients. Some are undergoing obligatory
treatment through civil commitment, others are voluntary
patients.

To make the situation even more complex, the dissenter
population in the OPHs is, beyond doubt, very volatile. At
frequent intervals they are flooded with waves of inmates who
stay only two weeks or so. These are the people mentioned by
Dr Vladimir Dmitrievsky of Kashchenko when he interviewed a dissenter, Evgeny Nikolayev, in 1974 (see appendix
VIII). Pressing Nikolayev to speak frankly "for your own
good", Dmitrievsky warned him that otherwise: "You may
be put in the category of the 'socially dangerous'. Then
you will, as a prophylactic measure, be interned in a mental

hospital before every Soviet holiday, whether you like it or not."[10]

The holidays referred to are the major ones of Labour Day on 1 May and Revolution Day on 7 November. At these times the authorities fear hostile demonstrations, and large-scale preventive detention in OPHs throughout the country is routine.* But not only at these times, as is shown in an account by Fyodor Sidenko, a Pentecostalist, of his internment in an OPH at Ussuriisk near the Pacific coast in 1974.[11] Sidenko was detained only a few weeks, a period which spanned President Ford's meeting with Mr Brezhnev on 23–24 November at Vladivostok, 100 miles away. As he had spent the years 1965–70 in labour camps as a political prisoner and subsequently applied to emigrate, he was clearly on the KGB's list for "preventive detention" in such circumstances. He reports that the OPH was crammed to overflowing because of the influx of dissenters during Ford's visit.

In sum, the number of dissenters held in OPHs at any one time is impossible to estimate. Our impression from reading the available accounts is that probably most hold at least a few, and some, like No. 3 in Leningrad and Kashchenko in Moscow, "specialize" in dissenters and hold considerably more. If this impression is accurate, the OPHs probably contain rather more dissenters at any one time than the 350 we have estimated for the SPHs. And of course their population rises and falls sharply at least twice a year, around 1 May and 7 November.

The Real Reasons for the Internment of Dissenters

Let us now look at the real, underlying reasons for the internment of dissenters, in both SPH and OPH, by taking representative examples from our 210 documented cases. We divide these reasons into five categories, based on the dissenters' aspirations, not on their methods of expressing them. These methods are numerous and include: circulating protests, open letters, bulletins, journals, essays and books in *samizdat*; editing or contributing to a *samizdat* periodical; forming an "anti-Soviet" group; and organizing a protest demonstration.

* For the "socially dangerous" not on psychiatric registers, prisons are sometimes used, also "business trips" out of town which have been ordered by the KGB.

1. *Socio-Political Activity*

The first category, some 55 per cent of our sample, comprises those dissenters who have exercised their civil rights with too much independence, often out of primarily humanitarian motives.* Gorbanevskaya, Grigorenko, Shikhanovich and Plyushch, whose cases we examined in chapters 5 and 7, are good examples. All four were involved, from its inception, in the human-rights movement. This took shape between 1966 and 1968 and reached maturity with the launching of the *Chronicle of Current Events*.

Other dissenters in this category have been more politically oriented. N. I. Yakubenko belonged to a small Marxist group which called on workers to unite and fight for their rights. He drafted a "Programme of the Working Class" and prepared leaflets which were pasted up on walls by a worker friend during a strike in a Ukrainian shipyard. Yakubenko was arrested in 1970, charged under article 70, and interned in a mental hospital. His friend received seven years of imprisonment and exile.

Boris Evdokimov, a Leningrad journalist, was arrested in 1971 for publishing pseudonymous articles strongly critical of government policies in the émigré Russian press. He was charged under article 70 and interned in the Leningrad, then the Dnepropetrovsk SPH. As of mid-1976, he was still a "patient". In the former institution he met Fainberg, in the latter Plyushch. Both regarded him as normal.

Gennady Paramonov, a naval petty officer and a leader in the Komsomol (Young Communist League), belonged to an underground Marxist group, the "Union to Struggle for Political Rights". In 1969 he was arrested and charged with "anti-Soviet agitation and propaganda" and with membership of an "anti-Soviet group". A year later he was interned in Chernyakhovsk. Only in 1975 was he transferred to an OPH, from which he soon emerged.

2. *Nationalist Dissent*

The second category is in many ways a sub-division of the first, yet can usefully be separated out. It comprises 7 per

* Included here are half a dozen dissenters of a kind very different from the rest: those like the Fetisov group (see appendix I) who have advocated totalitarian views.

cent of our sample—those people interned for seeking greater rights for their nation, whether in the sphere of its language, its culture, its education system or its constitutionally guaranteed, but in practice non-existent, political and economic autonomy.

In the Ukraine these issues have existed since the beginning of the Soviet period, and indeed in slightly different forms since much earlier. The contemporary Ukrainian national movement dates back to the early 1960s, when the party alarmed nationally-conscious people in the Ukraine (and elsewhere) by strongly reasserting the doctrine that the peoples of the USSR were growing steadily closer together and would eventually "merge". Unspoken but self-evident was the party's intention that all minorities should be absorbed into the Russian nation, and thus lose their identities. Ukrainian discontent was countered by regular waves of arrests, the best known in 1965–66. However, by 1970 dissenters were sufficiently organized to imitate the *Chronicle* of their Moscow counterparts and produce their own *samizdat* journal, *The Ukrainian Herald*. Like the *Chronicle*, this was written in a critical spirit but from a position of loyalty to the Soviet state.[12]

For helping to produce and circulate this journal a young doctor, Mykola Plakhotnyuk, was arrested with dozens of others in a KGB drive of early 1972. The arrests and lengthy sentences handed down to many of them succeeded in crushing the journal. But Plakhotnyuk was diagnosed by the Serbsky Institute as suffering from "schizophrenia with persecution mania" and ruled "periodically not responsible". He was interned in Dnepropetrovsk and in mid-1976 was still held there. The court also made a ruling, not provided for in Soviet law, that on his recovery Plakhotnyuk should stand trial as a man responsible for the criminal acts he was charged with.

The same legal and psychiatric rulings were made on Boris Kovhar, a Ukrainian journalist and communist, also arrested in early 1972. In 1967 Kovhar became a KGB agent charged with spying on Ukrainian nationalists. Later, however, he changed sides and circulated an open letter in which he revealed his spying activities and described the technology used by the KGB for such work. In mid-1976 he too was still held in Dnepropetrovsk.

Another Ukrainian case is that of the widely-respected

teacher and poet Zinovy Krasivsky, sentenced in 1967 to twelve years of imprisonment and five of exile for his rôle in the underground "Ukrainian National Front". In 1971 he was charged with circulating anti-Soviet poems inside Vladimir prison, then ruled not responsible in the Serbsky, where Fainberg met him. One of his symptoms was reportedly the fact that he was cheerful by day, yet wrote sad poems at night. In 1972 a court dispatched him to the Smolensk SPH. Only in the summer of 1976 was he transferred to an OPH.

The Lithuanian national movement has likewise had psychiatry deployed against it, though to a lesser extent. This may be because the movement has been so strong that there would be no chance of squashing it, even with numerous commitments to SPHs. Since 1972 its main publication, the *Chronicle of the Lithuanian Catholic Church*, has documented in massive detail the persecution not only of the church but also of national traditions and culture, and the resistance which has developed in virtually every Lithuanian village.[13] This dissent movement is the largest in the USSR, larger than the other mass movements, those of the Baptists, the Crimean Tatars, the Meskhetians, the Germans and the Jews.

One Lithuanian victim of psychiatry has been Petras Cidzikas, a 29-year-old student at Vilnius University. In 1973 he was interned in Chernyakhovsk for circulating copies of the Lithuanian *Chronicle*. Another victim was Mindaugas Tamonis, an engineer and poet. In 1974 he circulated a statement calling for democratization, national rights for Lithuania, and a monument to the victims of Stalinism. He was interned in a Vilnius OPH for three months and given "treatment" which induced chronic insomnia, seriously affected his sight, and led to a gain in weight of 36 pounds. In 1975 he went through the same cycle of protest, internment, "treatment" and release. Two months later he was found dead under a train, having committed suicide under the relentless pressure from the KGB.

3. *The Demand to Emigrate*
The third category, comprising twenty per cent of the sample, are those people who have campaigned, or physically tried, to emigrate from the USSR. Their goal has often had a national motivation—Jews wanting to go to Israel, Germans to West Germany—but for others the main desire has been to escape

from what they have regarded as an intolerable existence in their homeland.

In the late nineteenth and the early part of this century, many thousands of Russian Jews emigrated to America, Britain and other Western countries. This period also saw the birth and development of Zionism with a consequent flow of Jews to Palestine. Around 1930 Stalin halted emigration for all Soviet citizens. Only in 1967, inspired by Israel's victory over the Arabs, did large numbers of Soviet Jews suddenly rediscover Zionism. As a result, by early 1971 such a powerful Jewish movement had developed in many parts of the country that the régime felt obliged to start letting them out. Had it not done so, an increasing number of planes would have been subject to hi-jack attempts, the KGB would have found it impossible to keep track of all the underground groups and publications, and Western public opinion would have become dangerously inflamed, especially in the USA, the home of six million Jews. So by 1976 about 120,000 Soviet Jews had been allowed to leave.[14]

One of these was Grisha Feigin, whom we interviewed in Israel. Born in 1926, he enjoyed a successful career in the army, achieving the rank of major in 1955. At about this time he began to protest openly against acts of anti-Semitism. As a result, he was soon demoted to captain and transferred to the reserve. In 1968 he applied to relinquish his citizenship and emigrate. Both requests were refused. Two years later he renounced his rank and handed back his military decorations. In December he was forcibly interned in the main Riga OPH under a civil-commitment procedure. He found himself in a section with about 20 other dissenters, including Grigorenko's friend, Ivan Yakhimovich, one of the six central cases in Bukovsky's appeal of 1971. The psychiatrists' diagnosis on Feigin was chronic schizophrenia. Fortunately his friends at once obtained international publicity for his case. In addition, the critical decision to permit Jewish emigration was taken at about this time. So, after three weeks in the hospital, a new psychiatric commission discharged him. In February 1971 he arrived in Israel.

The KGB has not used psychiatry much against the Jews, as their movement has been too strong to be crushable. The same has been true of the Soviet Union's two million Germans, descendants of the farmers invited to settle on the Volga by Catherine the Great in the eighteenth century. In 1941, when Hitler invaded the USSR, Stalin deported them with great brutality to Siberia and Central Asia. In the 1950s the punitive police régime they had lived under for fifteen years was lifted, and in 1964 they were legally exculpated from Stalin's false charges of treason.

But they were not allowed to return to their homelands on the Volga and in the Ukraine, and a national movement demanding this right rapidly developed. Its insistent lobbying of the authorities met, however, with little or no success. Observing the rise of the Jewish movement, with its militant tactics and goal of emigration, the Germans began in the early 1970s to imitate it. Since they could not regain their Soviet homes, they would seek their ancestral homeland instead. And as their movement grew more militant the authorities began, as with the Jews, to let them out. The numbers climbed from a few hundred a year prior to 1971 to about 6,000 in 1975. To the chagrin of the authorities, the proportion of these people opting to go to East Germany was no more than a few per cent.[15]

One of the movement's leaders in the early 1970s was Vytautas Grigas. In 1971 he was interned in an OPH under criminal commitment. After his release, he applied to leave the Soviet Union but was turned down. With some other leaders he then edited *Re Patria*, a *samizdat* journal on the problems of the Soviet Germans.[16] In January 1974 he took part in a demonstration in Moscow demanding the right to emigrate. He was promptly interned in the Kashchenko OPH for ten weeks and then, soon after his release, allowed with other leaders to emigrate. The KGB hoped to "decapitate" the movement. In West Germany Grigas turned his considerable energy and abilities to organizing a support lobby for the many Germans whom the Soviet authorities would still not let go.

Some other would-be emigrants, apart from a few Jews and Germans, have landed in mental hospitals. Anatoly Chinnov, for example, a Russian biochemist from Leningrad, despaired of ever obtaining permission to leave the country legally. He was arrested when trying to cross the border into Czechoslovakia in 1968. Charged with "betrayal of the motherland", he was interned in the Leningrad and Dnepropetrovsk SPHs.

Here the psychiatrists seized on his religious beliefs and repeatedly told him he would not be released until he renounced them. They subjected him to intensive drug treatment, and his health deteriorated sharply. As the *Chronicle* reports, "he developed chronic gastritis, became extremely thin, and half his teeth fell out". Only after six years did release come.

Another Russian, Nikolai Kryuchkov of Moscow, applied in 1974 to emigrate to the USA. Shortly after, during Nixon's visit to Moscow, he was interned in the Kashchenko OPH. His medical report included this entry: "Reason for hospitalization: wish to emigrate from the USSR."

4. *Religious Activity*

People interned because of their religious faith make up the fourth category, comprising some thirteen per cent of our sample. Gennady Shimanov, whose case we examined in chapter 6, was fortunate by comparison with, for example, Yury Belov. Held in the Sychyovka SPH, Belov was told by his psychiatrists there in 1974 that he suffered from no illness, but nonetheless: "We consider religious convictions to be pathological, so we're treating you." A year later he was still a "patient".

Valery Andreyev, a young Ukrainian worker who turned from a dissolute life to Pentecostalism, was sacked from his job because of his faith. He told a doctor that his religion had saved him becoming depressed about his dismissal. The doctor ruled that in this case he must be ill. Against the protests of his family he was interned in an OPH for two months and forcibly treated with tranquillizing drugs.

The deeply-rooted dissent movement among the Soviet Baptists, which demands a genuine separation of church and state, has also on occasion experienced oppression through psychiatry.[17] Ivan Lazuta, for example, a house painter from Belorussia, was an active member of this movement. In 1970 he was arrested and interned in an OPH in Zhodishki. During an interview with a psychiatrist he asked: "What would happen if I rejected my faith in God and stopped going to prayer meetings? What would you do with me?" The psychiatrist replied: "We'd let you out straight away." Later, after giving Lazuta a course of insulin injections, his doctor asked: "Well, Lazuta, do you still believe in God now?" When his answer was yes, the doctor said: "Okay, now we're going to treat you and rid you of your fanaticism." Then, in the words of Lazuta's fellow-Baptists, "New treatments were prescribed, and as a result the health of our brother became very much worse. From 11 May his arms began to swell, and all his joints began to ache. Since 18 May our brother has been completely confined to bed by illness and he cannot move without assistance."[18]

Buddhists too have suffered similar experiences. In 1972 four intellectuals were charged in Ulan-Ude, near the Mongolian border, with participation in a Buddhist group. By its activity, the group had allegedly infringed the rights of citizens and prompted them to evade their civic obligations. Partly no doubt because these charges were nonsensical, the four men were ruled not responsible (the group's leader, the eminent scholar of Buddhism, Bidya Dandaron, was tried separately). The four were interned in OPHs, from which, thanks probably to international publicity, they were freed within a year of the trial. The local authorities in Ulan-Ude had evidently wanted to launch a major offensive against independent-minded Buddhists, but had later been instructed by Moscow to back off. This followed the unfavourable publicity surrounding the whole case in the West, and in third-world Buddhist countries which the régime was trying to woo.

5. *Being Inconvenient to Petty Tyrants*

The fifth group, some 5 per cent of the sample, comprises those people who, because of their integrity, are simply inconvenient to some petty tyrant. For example a Moscow doctor, L. A. Petrova, was interned in an OPH for five months in 1972 for several times refusing to excuse from work certain malingerers: they happened to be friends of her boss, the chief doctor of a factory polyclinic. Only when 2,000 workers signed a strongly-worded petition was she released and restored to her position. However, to safeguard themselves from prosecution the hospital doctors had ruled Dr Petrova a schizophrenic and an "invalid of the third category".

On learning this the workers again protested and also wrote to Professor Snezhnevsky asking him to examine her. In the words of one of her defenders, Mrs Gusyakova, "Not only has no one ever noticed in her any deviations from the norm, but on the contrary, she is very responsive, calm and kind, and has no history of mental illness in her family. But Snezhnevsky examines people only if he is ordered to from above." Attempts were made to prosecute the doctors: "Five times the workers filed complaints at the Volgograd district court in Moscow, yet no trial ever took place." Gusyakova's final comment is pessimistic: "After all, Petrova is not even one of the dissenters, so how much worse a fate can one expect for them!"

Another example in this category is that of Gusyakova herself, a 61-year-old housewife. In November 1973 she went to the Presidium of the Supreme Soviet of the Russian Republic to complain about illegal acts of the district authorities:

> As the lower officials give no help to us petitioners I asked to be received by one of [chairman] Yasnov's deputies. Mrs Duritsyna agreed to receive me in room 10, but told me to wait in the corridor. An hour later I was called into the room, and three tough men grabbed me and shoved me through a door into the yard (in room 10 there is such a door). They pushed me into a car and drove me off to Psychiatric Hospital No. 13. . . . For the hospital doctors it was a very awkward situation: I did not need treatment, at home I had a seriously-ill husband, yet the authorities demanded that I be kept in a mad-house, as I was complaining about illegal acts by the district authorities.

It took Mrs Gusyakova a week to get out. During this time no one had cared for her husband. "Fortunately", however, "he survived."[19]

This episode is one of the available examples which confirm the accuracy of the following report in the *Chronicle*:

> A number of facts indicate that the reception rooms of the highest official bodies in Moscow either have an ambulance from the psychiatric first-aid service on permanent duty, or are in direct and speedy contact with this service. In many cases people who have come with complaints, usually of a non-political nature, to the reception rooms of the party Central Committee, the Council of Ministers, the Presidium of the Supreme Soviet, the All-Union Central Council of Trade Unions, the KGB and other organizations have not been allowed to put their case, but instead have been forcibly driven off to a Moscow psychiatric hospital, and then, after assessment, to a hospital near their home.[20]

Gusyakova was fortunate, of course: she escaped the last stage. But her summing-up of the situation, in an open letter to *Pravda*, is damning. It indicates, as we saw in chapter 6, how psychiatry is probably abused just as much in suppressing ordinary citizens as well-educated dissenters: "Simple people cannot obtain elementary justice: the most persistent protesters, those who doggedly press for fairness, are dispatched to lunatic asylums from the reception rooms of the Supreme Soviet Presidium and the Central Committee. No, not dissenters, just the persistent—to stop them complaining."

Apart from such petitioners, dissenters in the camps and prisons are also sometimes interned in psychiatric institutions for acting "inconveniently". In 1972, for example, unrest broke out in a Leningrad labour camp when fifteen inmates sewed up their mouths in protest at the severe conditions. Six of them were at once dispatched to the Leningrad SPH without any psychiatric examination or any trial. The apparent aim of the authorities was to halt the unrest by intimidating the inmates with this drastic and arbitrary act.[21] In another instance, Lev Lukyanenko, a Ukrainian lawyer, refused KGB requests to collaborate with it when his fifteen-year term for forming an underground political group was drawing to an end. He was sent in 1974 to the Rybinsk SPH, doubtless in the hope that the experience would make him more compliant. Although regarded as mentally normal by his fellow-prisoners, he was ruled to be ill and returned to the camp as an "invalid of the second category". This would make it easier for the KGB to intern this "unco-operative" man under civil commitment were he to prove troublesome following his release.

Another political prisoner, Igor Ogurtsov, an oriental scholar from Leningrad, served in Vladimir prison the first seven years of a 20-year term for forming an anti-Soviet group.[22] In 1974 he was transferred to a camp in the Perm region. Even though he did not join in acts of protest by other prisoners, the force of his dignity and personality was an inspiration to his fellows and had a marked effect even on the camp personnel. Quite simply, Ogurtsov's qualities threatened the administration. He was interned for five months in a squalid psychiatric institution until, thanks apparently to publicity in the West, he was returned to his camp.

Do Dissenters placed in Mental Hospitals differ from those placed in Camps?

At this point we can conclude that dissenters are, with the partial exception of the fifth category above, placed in mental hospitals for the same range of reasons that their colleagues are confined in labour camps. We should note in passing, though, that a few nationalist movements have, oddly, been more or less immune from psychiatric internment. These include the Crimean Tatars and the Meskhetians, perhaps because their movements are so broadly based and united that it seems futile to the KGB to harass them by the provocative use of psychiatry.[23] The same applies, with some exceptions noted earlier, to the Jews and the Germans. A further factor operates in the case of the Jews. Since the early 1970s their movement has received so much world publicity that the KGB has probably feared to draw massive attention to Soviet police psychiatry by including them among its victims.

We can also say that the psychiatric victims come from the same social groups as the dissenters held in camps, and in roughly similar proportions. A majority have professional and intellectual backgrounds, and only small minorities come from the ruling communist élite, administrative personnel, proletariat and peasantry. It may be, though, that dissenters among the ruling élite are more vulnerable than others to internment: it is more convenient to explain apostasy as a product of mental breakdown than of political revolt or disillusion. Hence, perhaps, the internments of Grigorenko and of Boris Vinokurov, a senior official in the State Committee for All-Union Radio and Television, the equivalent of a ministry. At a party meeting in 1975 he criticized the bad economic situation and the stifling of the media by censorship. The only solution, he declared, was to introduce a two-party system. He announced his resignation from the Communist Party and his intention to form a new party, ending his speech: "After all, someone has to give a lead!" Five days later he was hospitalized, and at the next party meeting it was reported that he, his wife and daughter were all mentally ill, and that his doctor had noted a deterioration in his general health over the preceding months.

The age range of dissenters in mental hospitals does not

appear to differ from that of their fellows in the camps: people of all ages seem to be equally vulnerable to internment, just as they are to imprisonment. The geographical areas they come from are also the same: internment like imprisonment seems to be applied in similar ways throughout the Soviet Union.

Why are Some Dissenters Interned and Others Imprisoned?

By what criteria are certain dissenters selected for one fate, and others for another? Why since 1962 have about one-quarter of all the dissenters whose cases are documented in the *Chronicle* and elsewhere been placed in mental hospitals, i.e. the 210 listed in appendix 1, and three-quarters (about 600) placed in camps? The brief answer is that we do not know. We have no access to the KGB's deliberations.* We can only guess and infer.

The hospital has beyond doubt been the fate of many of the most determined, resilient and respected of the dissenters: Grigorenko, Bukovsky, Plyushch, Borisov, to mention only a few. From the KGB's perspective it is precisely such people whose trials are likely to cause severe problems, as we show below. They are also the most desirable targets for the KGB to intimidate and if possible break: there would then be a chance of destroying the human-rights movement as a whole and thereby winning the gratitude of their political masters in the politbureau.

Both this consideration and the problem of conducting political trials make the "psychiatric gambit" attractive. The trial becomes a brief formality, with the defendant absent and unable to make defiant speeches in his self-defence. Also, the risk of demonstrations by friends outside the court-house— covered by foreign journalists—is virtually eliminated. In an SPH, moreover, isolated from his friends, surrounded by severely-disturbed patients, injected with high doses of drugs, deprived of all rights, and with no limit to his period of intern-ment, the dissenter might eventually be induced to make the

* These incidentally are most unlikely to be committed anywhere to paper: the art of survival in the Soviet bureaucracy—of which the KGB has been a well-integrated part since the execution of Beria—involves careful avoidance of ever being saddled with responsibility for a "tricky decision".

sort of recantation which would break him morally. The whole experience would also intimidate his friends in the human-rights movement by showing that even the morally toughest could be "broken" by psychiatry. And the responsibility, were the operation ever to misfire, would be laid on the psychiatrists, not the KGB!

The gambit is also attractive because, as the resourceful dissenter has carefully avoided breaking the law, there is now no need for the KGB to "cook up" more than a minimum of evidence of any political crime. The brief court hearing will after all be concerned mainly with the psychiatric report.

The gambit is also enticing in those cases where the accused has a psychiatric history, however slight or far in the past. We noted this pattern with Gorbanevskaya in chapter 5. Another example is Fainberg, who had been hospitalized 20 years prior to participating in the Red Square demonstration—on the basis of deliberately false evidence about his behaviour given by his parents! (They hoped to avoid for him—in a period of virulent state-sponsored anti-Semitism—the then much worse fate of many years in a Stalinist concentration camp.) In these cases, as in that of an unstable personality like the engineer Lev Ubozhko, the psychiatrists have something to "work with", some basis for manufacturing a case, part of which may "stick", at least in the minds of uninformed or unsceptical observers.

Finally, as suggested above, dissenters among the party élite appear to be specially vulnerable to internment rather than imprisonment. And the same applies to Marxist dissenters like Plyushch and Medvedev, who did not belong to this élite, but whose ideas might have been attractive to liberal elements within it. All such ideas are particularly dangerous as they might eventually give rise to splits in the party leadership which could prove fatal to it. Thus it is of great importance for the KGB to discredit the ideas as those of madmen—and for this reason not worth consideration. The same aim obtains of course *vis-à-vis* the non-Marxist dissenters, but is perhaps of lesser priority in their case: there is not as yet a political opposition movement in the USSR to challenge the party's monopoly of political power; only small isolated groups have so far attempted this.

Why an SPH for Some Dissenters and an OPH for Others?
Having opted in a particular case for internment, the KGB
then has to choose between an SPH and an OPH. Here again,
we know neither its criteria of selection nor whether these are
applied consistently. Broadly speaking, the following factors
often seem to operate. First, as an OPH internment is usually
short, the KGB can use it when it thinks a relatively brief
punishment will suffice to intimidate the dissenter in question.
Second, the OPH is useful in cases where the dissenter has
carefully avoided breaking any law, and the evidence for laying
a criminal charge is therefore difficult to produce. This was
true of the cases of Medvedev, Shimanov, and (in 1968)
Volpin, which we discussed earlier. Shimanov for example had
not come close enough to running a religious group for the
evidence to convince even a court servile to the authorities.

In some cases of criminal commitment, like that of Shikhanovich discussed in chapter 7, the selection of an OPH probably
represented a compromise. After his arrest, Western protest
began to build up, so an OPH became the best solution: "face"
would be saved for Soviet psychiatry, as the ruling that he was
not responsible would be maintained; yet internment in an
OPH would allow an early release and thus avoid the unfavourable international publicity of a long campaign on his
behalf.

The two-week internments around major Soviet holidays fall
into a special category. As mentioned earlier, these are prophylactic security measures: civil commitment to an OPH is
simply a convenient instrument. It can be used in any case
where a dissenter has been officially classed as socially dangerous and placed on the register at his local psychiatric clinic.
Thus a sword of Damocles hangs permanently over his head:
twice a year, over the major holidays, it may descend, or indeed
at any other time the KGB wishes. Fainberg for example was
released in 1973, and in 1974 launched a hunger strike in
support of Bukovsky. He was soon arrested, just before 1 May,
and committed to a Leningrad OPH on the grounds that
he was suffering a relapse of schizophrenia and had become
a danger to those around him. Eighteen days later he was
released.

Further Types of Victim

Our discussion so far has excluded a considerable number of dissenters who have suffered to a lesser extent than the 210 from the abuse of psychiatry. First, there are those who, though regarded as perfectly sane by their friends and relatives, have been forced after their arrest to undergo a psychiatric examination, at the end of which they have been ruled responsible. These examinations are usually conducted in an in-patient setting and last a month or more. In the period 1962–76 about 100 such cases were recorded in available *samizdat* sources. The investigators' motive in sending these people for examination and later presumably hinting to the psychiatrists that a ruling of "responsible" is required, apparently stems in many cases from their aim of intimidating the accused person into becoming more co-operative in giving evidence: the threat of indefinite internment in an SPH is designed to "soften them up". In other cases, the investigator perhaps hopes that the psychiatrist will unearth some concealed mental "symptoms", and thus present him with a definite option of asking for a ruling of "not responsible".*

Secondly, there are sane dissenters who have only been *threatened* with psychiatric internment. The KGB's threats often reach them indirectly, through third parties or officially-sponsored whispering campaigns. In 1974–75 for example the Odessa police harassed through her party colleagues the teacher and Communist Anna Golumbievskaya, for her persistently sympathetic attitudes to Solzhenitsyn. When she refused to "admit her error", she was threatened with internment. Probably because she vigorously publicized her own case, she suffered only dismissal from her job.[24] Another case is Solzhenitsyn himself. In 1967 official speakers informed closed party meetings that the writer's anti-Soviet views were the product of mental illness.[25] Similar tactics have been used against Andrei Sakharov in recent years.[26]

Where to Draw the Line?

This book is about dissenters, people who are persecuted for

* This argument assumes that the forensic psychiatrists are not infinitely servile, and require at least a few symptoms before making such a ruling.

their beliefs. But where do we draw the line between a political or religious dissenter on the one hand and, on the other, a social deviant who is also a victim of unjustified psychiatric internment? Indeed, can criteria be devised to draw such a line at all? We doubt it. Might not, for instance, all Soviet hippies who are interned because of their deviant life-style be regarded as dissenters? Doubtless some more than others.

An ex-Soviet psychiatrist (who asked to remain anonymous) described to us two cases of this sort. In one, his friend Aleksei Polev was sent in 1972 by the police, as a hippie, for in-patient assessment to a Moscow OPH. Sluggish schizophrenia was diagnosed. The illness had supposedly begun at the age of four, when he began to dream in colour! Polev eventually absconded from the hospital and soon emigrated. The second case involved a radio technician, Viktor Salaty, who was referred by a military draft board for psychiatric examination. Because of his long hair and passion for jazz, he too was diagnosed as a schizophrenic. Later, in 1972, he tried to emigrate by crossing the frontier into Finland. Caught, charged, and ruled not responsible on the basis of his earlier diagnosis, he was interned by court order in an Estonian OPH in Tartu. However, his psychiatrist could detect no psychopathology in him except for sullenness. As a result he was held only six months. Our informant read his case notes and found no evidence in them for a diagnosis of mental illness. The only justification offered was the one word "hippie-ism".

Finally, when Moscow's hippie community gathered on 1 June 1971 for an unauthorized demonstration against the Vietnam war, 150 of them were arrested, many to be subsequently interned for short periods in OPHs.[27] And the same fate can await those whose hairstyle or clothes go too far beyond official norms, or who are too keen on hard rock music or abstract art. This is the observation of Dr Jimmie Holland, an American psychiatrist who worked in Kashchenko with Professors Snezhnevsky and Nadzharov in 1972–73.[28]

We conclude then that the abuse of psychiatry *vis-à-vis* dissenters is probably only the tip of an iceberg. Beneath the surface there seem to be many cases in which psychiatry has been used to suppress individuality, so that the state can maintain a stifling social as well as political control. These "social deviants" are still little known: except for a few groups of *avant-garde* artists, they have not developed the dissenters' sophisticated forms of organization and communication. These artists began in the early 1970s to imitate the dissenters' methods of obtaining publicity for acts of persecution and suppression.[29]

Why has the Psychiatric Gambit not been used more often?
With so many advantages attached to it, the psychiatric gambit might appear to have been under-used by the KGB. It has, however, had one enormous disadvantage. It has touched a nerve in the Western liberal conscience which the orthodox, "traditional" inhumanities of the Soviet forced labour camps have not. Although this conscience spoke but weakly at first, as we saw in chapter 4, from 1972–73 onwards its voice became louder. Thus one of the KGB's basic assignments—to suppress dissent quietly, without protest at home or abroad—could no longer be successfully carried out. From late 1973 therefore the psychiatric gambit was partially curtailed. The story of how this came about is the subject of our next chapter.

Chapter 10

OPPOSITION TO THE ABUSE

"BETRAYAL BY PSYCHIATRY." This was the title chosen by the American journalist I. F. Stone for his article of January 1972 in the *New York Review of Books*.[1] Stone indicted the world's psychiatrists for having swept Soviet abuses under the carpet in Mexico and thus delivered Bukovsky up to his jailers. In particular he castigated the World Psychiatric Association (WPA) and the American Psychiatric Association (APA).

As we saw in chapter 4, the APA had the previous month opposed the use of psychiatry for political purposes. But it had named no names or countries, and its pious, generalized statement had merely said, in effect: "Sin is bad." The WPA had been even weaker, claiming that official action was impossible for reasons of procedure, and not even facilitating unofficial, *ad hoc* responses to Bukovsky's appeal by those of the 6,000 psychiatrists in Mexico City who wished to make them.

In his thorough investigation of what he called "the cop-out in Mexico City" Stone reached these conclusions:

> The bureaucracy of the world organization and of the APA in effect helped the Soviet bureaucracy to shelve and hush protest.... The whole procedure, including just how delegations to the congresses are chosen, is enveloped in a thick bureaucratic fog. The world congress seems to be run by self-perpetuating cliques.... Those at the levers in command of the General Assembly gave in to Soviet wishes.... The most tragic sequel to the congress ... was the savage sentence imposed on Vladimir Bukovsky for having sent abroad the psychiatric reports on which it had failed to act.

In expressing these views, Stone captured the mood of both Soviet dissenters and the informed Western public. At once he was asked to write a similar article for the *New York Times*,[2] which, ten days before the congress, had called on psychiatrists to protest strongly against "Moscow's flagrant abuse". "To the degree that Soviet psychiatry has been perverted into an instrument of political repression," the paper maintained, "it has lost all standing in the outside world."[3] During the congress itself the *Washington Post* had strongly attacked Professor Snezhnevsky and held that neither "incipient political détente" nor a "misguided sense of international or professional delicacy" should inhibit the assembled psychiatrists from condemning "the perversion of medicine which he represents".[4]

Their failure to do this was not only a blow to the informed Western opinion which these and other papers represented; it also dashed the hopes of interned dissenters. As Fainberg later wrote, "Before the congress, chaos reigned in the SPHs and other domains of Soviet psychiatry." Large numbers of political prisoners were prepared for release and "the authorities, with extreme reluctance, improved their living conditions". But when the authorities heard the outcome of the congress, they reacted with "the glee of a cruelty suddenly unleashed. The tortures of which the world's psychiatrists had taken no notice, began again."[5]

Outside the SPHs, the members of the Action Group for the Defence of Human Rights did not express their disappointment publicly. But it must have been keen. In their appeal to the congress to examine the materials sent by Bukovsky and others, they had said: "We are convinced that the opinion of the participants in your international congress will carry great authority and that it could put an end to the practice of interning people in mental hospitals without sufficient grounds." They had also expressed their view that Bukovsky's arrest was a direct result of his appeal to the world's psychiatrists, thereby hinting that his fate was now in their hands.[6]

A month later the Action Group made this hint more explicit. In an open letter issued on 2 January 1972, the eve of his trial, they wrote:

Bukovsky's world fame and the interventions on his behalf (in particular the statement of the 44 British psychiatrists) have already had a positive effect. Of his eight months of pre-trial investigation two-and-a-half were spent under assessment in the Serbsky Institute: the psychiatrists were about to declare him not responsible, when, suddenly, they did an about-turn—no, he's responsible! The nonsense of any other conclusion would have been too blatant, the shame incurred too obvious.

The authors maintained that "Nowadays one can do quite a bit to save a person," and cited as an example the speedy rescue of Medvedev from a mental hospital. They ended by appealing to all those informed about psychiatric abuse to join them in the call, "Freedom for Vladimir Bukovsky!"[7]

In sentencing Bukovsky so severely, the authorities may in fact, from their own viewpoint, have acted unwisely. The weakness of the WPA and APA encouraged them to be, perhaps, overly self-confident. For Bukovsky's twelve years of prison and exile only spurred on those groups of Western psychiatrists and lay people who were less lethargic or indifferent.

Apart from Stone's articles, the International Commission of Jurists denounced as "a travesty of justice" the legal procedures at the trial,[8] the Dutch Labour Party and the Swiss Writers' Association published similar views,[9] French doctors formed a "Committee against the Special Psychiatric Hospitals in the USSR",[10] the Royal Netherlands Medical Association expressed alarm, calling on Soviet colleagues to follow purely medical criteria in their diagnoses,[11] and in Germany and Austria the media paid serious attention both to Bukovsky and to Soviet psychiatric abuse in general.[12] In Britain a letter condemning the trial appeared in *The Times*, signed by 39 prominent cultural figures, politicians and academics and a second one followed from 36 psychiatrists.[13] The latter wrote that "Far from deserving a criminal sentence Vladimir Bukovsky has earned admiration and respect. At great cost to himself he has alerted psychiatrists and doctors the world over to the need for maintaining the highest ethical standards." They concluded with a thinly-veiled rebuke to the WPA and colleagues in other countries: "Those to whom he wrote should have the courage to protest about psychiatric abuse in the Soviet Union, so that his suffering may not be in vain. It is the least they can do."

An additional stimulus to the wave of protest was the appearance of the Bukovsky materials in book form in French, then German, then English.[14] This greatly widened the availability of the evidence. Hitherto the only convenient source had been the booklet "The Internment of Soviet Dissenters in Mental Hospitals", an analysis of Bukovsky's documents published in March 1971 by the Working Group (see chapter 4).[15]

Another stimulus was the steady flow of press reports from Moscow. These concerned not only appeals like that of 52 friends of Bukovsky to UN Secretary-General Dr Waldheim,[16] but also the hunger strikes of Fainberg and Borisov in the Leningrad SPH, their exposés of conditions there, and the urgent appeals of Sakharov and others on their behalf.[17] All this showed beyond doubt that the issue was on the boil in the Soviet Union, and that Bukovsky's six cases were not isolated or exceptional.

A Soviet Policy Develops in Response to Western Protest

In response to these intermittent but growing protests the Soviet authorities gradually evolved a co-ordinated policy. By the end of 1972 it had taken coherent shape. Since then it has remained fairly constant, undergoing only two important changes, both in late 1973. We discuss these further on in the chapter.

In broad terms, the policy of the authorities was to make limited but real concessions to the critics; to camouflage their partial retreat in a smokescreen of righteous self-justification; and to manipulate national and international psychiatric organizations so as to neutralize, as far as possible, future attacks. The concessions were necessary partly because of the strategy of détente with the West, to which the Soviet leaders had committed themselves in early 1971. More generally, they were dictated by the long-standing policy, dating from the mid-1950s, of seeking membership of important international bodies and maintaining it, if necessary, at almost any price. Both policies made intolerable not only the bad publicity about psychiatric abuse which had become steadily more frequent since 1968, but also the associated danger of humiliating boycotts and even expulsion from international psychiatric organizations.

The component of the co-ordinated policy which first came unmistakably into view was the camouflage—the decision to react aggressively, albeit selectively, to Western protests. Prior to October 1971 a tight-lipped silence had been the rule. Subsequently the first responses occurred, but they were sporadic and *ad hoc* in flavour. Apart from Snezhnevsky's interview in *Izvestia*, the Soviet psychiatrists' statements in Mexico City, and two propaganda articles,[18] all occasioned directly or indirectly by Bukovsky's appeal and the WPA congress, the only other high-level reaction was from Mr Kosygin during a visit to Scandinavia. At press conferences in December 1971 he evaded one question on Grigorenko and psychiatric abuse, and replied to another that all the Western allegations were mendacious and his questioner should visit the USSR to see for himself.[19]

For internal consumption there had also been a discreet campaign to boost the image of the Serbsky Institute. Its reputation had been tarnished by the widespread publication of, among other things, Sergei Pisarev's documented attack,[20] summarized in chapter 3, and Grigorenko's prison diary. In July 1971 well-placed critics of the institute had taken advantage of the climate to comment in the Soviet press on its shortcomings, if only from an angle not ostensibly connected with political diagnoses.[21] Under this pressure the Establishment had countered in late 1971, doubtless prompted by the KGB: the Serbsky was solemnly awarded the Order of the Red Banner of Labour. The award decree, signed by President Podgorny, cited the institute's "achievements in the development of public health and medical science and in the training of personnel".[22] In addition, press articles had portrayed Dr Morozov and his institute in the most flattering light.[23] No mention was made of the domestic and foreign attacks.

In July 1972, after six months of silence, the policy of reacting in an orchestrated and deliberate way to Western protests was launched. The most likely explanation of the timing relates to President Nixon's visit to the Soviet Union a few weeks earlier. During this visit détente was officially inaugurated, with the concluding of various agreements. One of these was in the field of health, and among the projects now finalized was joint research into schizophrenia. With the health agreement safely signed, and the danger of protests about psychiatric abuse from the US government and the APA thereby reduced, the Soviet authorities probably felt more confident in embarking on their new policy.

In any case, when a French minister stated in July that in the USSR "those who dare to criticize the régime or its leaders are considered abnormal and asocial and are interned in psychiatric hospitals", the Soviet ambassador lodged an official protest with the French government and also intervened personally with President Pompidou. He did so even though the remark was made only in passing and at a meeting on an unrelated subject.[24]

This was a signal that things had changed. Readers of the Soviet press, who had recently been fed only the assertion that dissenters were psychiatrically interned in Israel,[25] now found an extensive feature in the *Literary Gazette* mocking the very notion that such a thing could happen in the Soviet Union.[26] The feature was a reply to some articles in the West German press which had described the cases of "interned Soviet writers" Valery Tarsis, Gennady Shimanov and others.[27] The author alleged that although Tarsis had been a member of the Writers' Union he was in fact mentally ill, and that the others had never been members and were therefore not writers. They must belong instead, he implied, to that well-known category of mentally-ill people who see themselves as unrecognized geniuses.

The feature, broadcast *in extenso* on the foreign service of Moscow Radio, was supplemented a week later by a long programme about the excellence of Soviet psychiatric services and the Serbsky in particular.[28] The compiler made much use of supposed quotations from respected Western authorities. The British psychiatrist Professor John Wing was quoted as concluding after visits to the Serbsky and other institutions: "I admire the Soviet system because in the USSR everything is done to restore the patient to normal life. . . . I cannot find anything to criticize. I find everything is beautiful." And the Inspector-General of the French Ministry of Justice, Georges Fuly, had studied the work of the Serbsky Institute and then reportedly commented in connection with Western press articles: "I have every reason to believe that everything that has been written is mere anti-Soviet propaganda." Fuly died before he could be asked about this broadcast. But Wing told us that his words had been grossly distorted and that he had made no blanket statement of approval.

The next salvos were fired in articles by a psychologist,

Professor Konstantin Platonov, and Georgy Morozov. The latter confined himself to a straightforward, ostensibly non-polemical account of Soviet forensic psychiatry,[29] but Platonov dismissed Western allegations as "rubbish". "Like a good number of other psychologists and psychiatrists", he frequently gave consultations in the Serbsky Institute, and he could state that "D. R. Lunts and G. V. Morozov are eminent Soviet psychiatrists".[30]

Under the new policy Soviet officials still reacted unpredictably when approached on an individual basis. Although at first Snezhnevsky answered enquiries from abroad about interned dissenters, he apparently did not maintain this practice for long. In September 1972 he replied to Amnesty International in Austria concerning Vladimir Borisov, one of the Bukovsky cases. He had consulted with Borisov's doctors, he wrote in a superficially polite letter, and "once again they have confirmed that he is mentally ill and continues to need treatment as an in-patient".[31]

Health Minister Petrovsky had a harder job in some face-to-face encounters, and not surprisingly gave more away. At a press conference in the USA in August 1972 he hedged when asked if he would grant foreign visitors access to dissenters held in medical institutions, and declined to make any promises.[32] Two months later his interview with a group of American science writers in Moscow was reported like this: "Petrovsky said, 'I don't mind the difficult question,' when asked about committing dissident scientists to mental hospitals. He explained he would 'never think the act of protest itself is considered a symptom of psychiatric disease'. Other factors would contribute to the judgement. He smiled at our scepticism over his follow-on comment that he had observed that 'protest often led' to such disease."[33]

The second component of the co-ordinated policy involved the more active wooing than hitherto of world psychiatric opinion and of two organizations in particular, the WPA and the APA. This effort had been stepped up since Bukovsky's appeal in early 1971. The aim was to head off, or at least neutralize, criticism of Soviet practices by foreign psychiatrists.

The APA was an organization to be reckoned with. The largest national association of psychiatrists in the world outside the USSR, it was also linked to the National Institute of Mental

Health (NIMH), the American body responsible for administering the US–Soviet agreement on schizophrenia.

The WPA's importance derived first from the fact that it was the only well-financed, broadly representative international body concerned exclusively with psychiatry. Second, with Professor Vartanyan as one of its six executive officers, Soviet psychiatry was well entrenched in it.

We examine the Soviet methods of wooing these and other psychiatric organizations later in the chapter.

The third component of the policy was completely new. This was the decision to stop interning well-known dissenters in SPHs (though not in OPHs). From the autumn of 1972 until September 1975 no recommendations for such internment were made.* Even the Serbsky's recommendation of September 1975, for Vyacheslav Igrunov, was changed six months later from an SPH to an OPH. In mid-1976 the third component remained virtually intact.

The fourth component—not recommending well-known dissenters for internment even in OPHs—took effect only in the summer of 1973, and continued for nearly three years until the case of Igrunov.

At this point we should note that by a "well-known dissenter" we mean one whose friends are closely enough linked to the humanitarian groups in Moscow for information on his case to be sure of fairly detailed coverage in the *Chronicle*.

The fifth component was, by contrast, the decision to continue to intern unknown or little-known dissenters, in both SPHs and OPHs. This was safe enough, as publicity would probably not result. Some of the SPH internments have, we should note here, involved dissenters who were initially imprisoned in labour camps, but then prosecuted again for alleged offences committed in captivity. Such prisoners have undergone in-patient assessment in the Serbsky, been ruled not responsible and transferred by court order to SPHs.

The sixth component of the policy worked out in mid-1972 was the decision *not* to release those well-known dissenters who were then imprisoned in mental hospitals. By this the authorities presumably hoped to avoid losing face by not making too many concessions at one time. Only in November 1973, under

* Plyushch was finally sent by a court to an SPH in July 1973, but this was on the basis of a recommendation made nearly a year earlier.

the pressure of their second major crisis, did they start to yield on this. First they released Fainberg, and by October 1974, with the freeing of Gershuni, they had let out all the dissenters well known in the West—except for Plyushch. We later suggest reasons for this exception to the pattern. With the eventual release of Plyushch in January 1976 this sixth component nearly disappeared. In mid-1976 there were *no* dissenters interned who were well known in the West, and relatively few, like Igrunov, who were moderately known. But there were still many who had almost no one to speak up for them, and some of these appear in appendix I; they come within the terms of the still fully-operative fifth component.

A final component has proved to be more of a pious intention than a real fact. According to a *samizdat* document of 1974 whose authenticity has been confirmed by Fainberg,[34] Snezhnevsky felt uneasy at Mexico City about his blanket defence of Soviet psychiatry:

> He decided to study the situation more closely on his return and to have any shortcomings corrected. And he honestly acted on his intention. At his insistence the Minister of Health ordered special commissions to inspect the mental hospitals, especially the famous prison ones. The inspectors were appalled by what they saw. Their general conclusion was: a prison is a prison, and nothing else. Their recommendation: to convert the prisons into hospitals. The result was that on 16 February 1973 the Ministry of Internal Affairs issued Directive No. 022–S, which contained the order "to change the whole appearance of the hospitals from looking like prisons to looking like hospitals"

However, the author asserts, "things have not got better, and according to some reports even worse". Plyushch's testimony on the Dnepropetrovsk SPH seems to confirm this conclusion.

As for Snezhnevsky's original intention, presumably one of his concerns was to make the SPHs more presentable against the day when foreign psychiatrists might mount irresistible pressure to visit them. To date, not one SPH has, to our knowledge, ever been entered by a Westerner, psychiatrist or otherwise.[35] It may have been partially to reduce the risk that foreigners would insist on visiting the dissenters in the Leningrad SPH—

geographically the most accessible to foreigners—that virtually all these inmates were transferred elsewhere in 1972.[36]

Such is the broad outline of Soviet policy as it took shape in 1972, and as it has with certain fluctuations remained. We should perhaps note here that the policy's major concession of halting, with one exception, the criminal commitment of well-known dissenters in the last three years is itself indicative of the political control of the practice. For while well-known dissenters have continued since 1973 to be arrested and charged with political crimes at a rate similar to that of the previous five years, the proportion of them deemed to need psychiatric treatment has abruptly dropped from about a quarter in the previous period to almost nil since 1973. The only factor which has changed, so far as we can see, is the orders transmitted by the régime to the investigators and the psychiatrists. Chance alone could not account for so big a drop. Our view is reinforced by the fact that both criminal and civil commitments of little-known dissenters appear to have continued since 1973 at a rate similar to that of the previous period.

Responses in the USA

To set the scene for the Soviet authorities' second major crisis in the autumn of 1973 we must review the earlier developments in, especially, the USA and Britain, and within the WPA.

American psychiatrists had been able since 1968 to read a steady flow of press reports from Moscow about the internment of dissenters, also the letters of "An Observer" in the *American Journal of Psychiatry* and *A Question of Madness* by the Medvedev brothers. They had been able to see Bukovsky's interview on television, and in May 1971 their APA had been presented with his appeal and documents during its annual convention. But these had been ignored, and six months later in Mexico the American delegate to the WPA General Assembly had not tabled for debate a resolution critical of Soviet psychiatry, which had earlier been approved by the Nassau County Psychiatric Association.[37] Finally, after the congress, the APA had felt impelled to issue its statement that "Sin is bad".

One reason, no doubt, for this sorry response to the mounting evidence was that some of the American psychiatrists most interested in Soviet mental health services had been much involved in the late 1960s in producing a book of a very different nature. This was *The Report of the First US Mission on Mental Health to the USSR*.[38] The mission visited Soviet psychiatric institutions in 1967, and wrote a report which was generally enthusiastic and uncritical. As we saw in chapter 6, Judge Bazelon's contribution stood out because of the questions it posed concerning the absence of judicial review in civil commitment.[39] The book revealed no awareness of psychiatry's use for political purposes. This was partly because the mission had taken place just before solid evidence began to reach the West on a regular basis.

Another reason for the APA's weakness probably concerned the beginning, in mid–1971, of Soviet-American discussions on a health agreement. Shortly before the Mexico congress the director of NIMH, Dr Bertram Brown, was visited by Professor Nadzharov.[40] He proposed that joint schizophrenia research be included in the agreement. Brown and his schizophrenia researchers were receptive, perhaps forgetting, or not knowing, that Nadzharov had played an unsavoury rôle both in the Medvedev affair and in one of the Bukovsky cases. In any event the proposal went ahead, and in March 1972 was incorporated in a draft document worked out by the Soviet-American Joint Committee on Health. In May the agreement was among those signed with much ceremony in Moscow by President Nixon and Mr Brezhnev. It was part of the first formal package in what quickly came to be known as détente.

These official American dealings with Soviet psychiatry may help to explain why, although the APA received the Bukovsky documents in May 1971, it only began to study them almost a year later. I. F. Stone, while writing his article for the *New York Review of Books*, had been so perturbed by the inaction of the WPA and APA, and by Snezhnevsky's repeated references to the US mission's generally favourable report, that he called on the mission's members, and Judge Bazelon in particular, to study the Bukovsky materials and pronounce on them. Stone's request was, however, turned over to the APA on the grounds that, apart from Bazelon, they were not specialists in forensic psychiatry.

As a result, the association appointed an "Ad Hoc Committee on the Use of Psychiatric Institutions for the Commitment of Political Dissenters", consisting of Bazelon and three prominent psychiatrists. It met on 21 April 1972 and soon issued its report.[41] The first paragraph reads:

> The committee was appointed by the Board of Trustees of the APA with the assigned task of studying a set of documents ... which pertain to the alleged use of psychiatric facilities in the Soviet Union for the purpose of suppressing political dissent. The members of the committee have read and examined these documents. While the committee manifestly cannot make a definitive judgement of their authenticity and accuracy, its members were impressed by the scope and quality of the material reviewed. Assuming the reliability of the documents, the committee is of the opinion that they support the above allegations. ... The committee's judgements are sharpened by the fact that there is no provision for judicial review of civil commitments in the Soviet Union.

The committee discussed how abuse could arise not only in the USSR but in any society, although much depended on the prevailing value system. It endorsed the APA's 1971 position statement opposing "the misuse of psychiatric facilities for the detention of persons solely on the basis of their political dissent, no matter where it occurs". And in conclusion it made two recommendations, which were promptly accepted by the APA trustees in early May:

> (a) That the President of the World Psychiatric Association be asked to circulate the APA position statement to all national societies ... requesting their endorsement of the principle expressed in the APA resolution.
>
> (b) That an appropriate international organization (for example the World Psychiatric Association, the World Federation for Mental Health, the World Health Organization, or an appropriate body of the United Nations), be urged to establish a properly staffed agency to formulate internationally acceptable standards and guidelines to safeguard involuntary hospitalization from political influences as far as possible, to receive complaints from any individual or appropriate national body alleging the enforced use of psychiatric facilities for political purposes, and to make investigations of such complaints.

The committee's unanimous report was supplemented by a separate statement from Judge Bazelon, endorsed by committee chairman Raymond Waggoner. Bazelon began by suggesting that the committee had interpreted its brief too narrowly in limiting itself to the USSR and to political dissenters alone:

I think we can learn much from the Russian experience if the materials are authentic. These documents illustrate that the medical model of "sickness" has been substituted for legally relevant criteria of what is socially and politically unacceptable behaviour. Most of the Russian materials we have seen involve persons accused of crimes but who have nevertheless been removed from the criminal process. In place of a trial and a finding of "guilty", these individuals were found "not accountable" for whatever actions they might or might not have committed.

However, the point which should be noted now is that the Soviet psychiatrists involved were not acting on behalf of their individual "patients" but were using psychiatric terminology and techniques on behalf of the state to serve the state's political purposes. Several factors compel me to reach this conclusion. First, although obviously we cannot vouch for the authenticity of these documents, if we admit *arguendo* that the cases reveal clear-cut indications of psychopathology,* the behavioural manifestations of this pathology in no way support the finding of "dangerousness" which is necessary to justify the compulsory commitment of an individual to any kind of mental institution. I cannot accept that the belief in, or advocacy of, ideas could ever constitute such a showing. Second, the majority of these cases were confined in "special" or prison hospitals, in conditions so severe as to belie any suggestion that the patients were receiving "treatment" appropriate for their particular diagnoses.

However, the abuse of psychiatric facilities revealed in

---

* According to 44 British psychiatrists, the cases reveal no such indications of pathology. If the cited traits of "romanticism", "inflated opinions" of self, "rigid thinking" and "uncritical attitude in the appraisal" of one's condition are indications of mental illness, then most of us must suffer. [Bazelon's note]

these materials would still exist were the patients incarcerated in less severe surroundings; left unconfined but given compulsory treatment; or left untreated but labelled "mentally ill". All of these actions would constitute the use of psychiatric "facilities" to suppress political dissent—that is, employment of the medical label of "sick" behaviour to serve political purposes.

This type of abuse of the psychiatric discipline is not confined to the suppression of highly visible political activists. Abuse is imminent whenever psychiatrists abandon their rôle as the patient's ally and use their skills to serve institutional purposes. The Soviet practices are only an extreme example of the dangers for the individual "patient".

The first step in combating these dangers is to identify those practices which contain the seed of abuse and then develop safeguards appropriate to the situation.

At this point Bazelon's statement becomes a short, sophisticated essay which ends with a call for "an in-depth enquiry into the use of psychiatric discipline in the institutions of our own society". In a final paragraph he emphasizes, however, that: "Nothing in this statement should be read to mitigate our condemnation of the practices which the Soviet documents, if authentic, reveal. The trustees should utilize every means within the APA's disposal to protest the hospitalization of these Soviet citizens and to aid in securing their freedom."

For the next four years the APA failed to follow this precept: its potential power was enormous, yet until 1976 its actions were few and generally weak. The trustees accepted with alacrity, within a few days of their composition, both Bazelon's proposal for an enquiry into American practices and the two recommendations of the *ad hoc* committee. The recommendations conveniently exempted the APA from making any deeper examination of Soviet abuses, or any definite judgements, and also enabled it to "pass the buck" to other organizations. Acceptance of Bazelon's proposal would—it was doubtless hoped—somewhat mitigate this abdication of responsibility by showing that the APA was not complacent about problems in its own back yard.

But an abdication it nonetheless was. No preliminary steps were taken to check whether the other organizations would agree to "accept the buck". And when it had been hastily thrown into the void and none of them had in fact decided to catch it, the APA did little to retrieve the situation. Even Bazelon's exhortation that it use every means at its disposal "to protest the hospitalization of these Soviet citizens and to aid in securing their freedom" was virtually ignored.

On the eve of Nixon's departure for Moscow to sign, *inter alia*, the health agreement, the *ad hoc* committee met again and resolved as follows: "They will go no further with the problem in the Soviet institutions, but will turn, instead, to a search for problems that exist on the American scene." No explanation was offered as to why the Soviet problem had to be dropped so completely, or why at least a small part of the committee's efforts could not be directed to continuing the study it had just begun.

It is unclear to what extent, if any, the American buck-passing was caused by direct or indirect pressure from a Nixon administration intent on achieving the coup of détente; or—and this is closely related—by psychiatrists' fears of jeopardizing the embryonic programme for joint Soviet-American research into schizophrenia. But the timing of the various Soviet and American moves at least suggests that these factors taken together may have contributed, and also that the Soviet side played its cards with skill.

In any event, debate in the US on the whole issue now came to a near halt until the autumn of 1973. A group from NIMH toured the USSR in September 1972; the Joint Committee on Health had its second meeting in March 1973; and three months later Brezhnev visited the US to try to give a further impetus to détente. But although press reports of Soviet abuses continued to appear,[42] the APA took no action. It also paid little attention to the testimony given before a US Senate Committee in 1972 by a well-known victim, Alexander Volpin (see chapter 3). Even the publication in December of his revealing evidence, with the Bukovsky materials as appendices, evoked little comment.[43] The same fate befell a letter by five psychiatrists in *Science*[44] and a perceptive paper by Dr Paul Chodoff which analysed the Bukovsky documents and reached conclusions similar to those of the "letter of the 44" in Britain.[45] Chodoff presented his paper at the APA's convention in May 1973 in Honolulu. Here a Czech psychiatrist who had recently emigrated from Czechoslovakia reported that he had left his country in protest against pressures on him to commit people for political reasons, an abuse which he claimed was not rare in Eastern Europe.[46]

Initiatives in Britain

Notwithstanding the "letter of the 44" calling for debate at Mexico City, the Royal College of Psychiatrists in Britain remained even more cautious than its American counterpart about confronting the Soviet establishment. Until the late summer of 1973 most efforts were initiated by members of the Working Group. They published articles on the subject and wrote numerous letters to the medical and general press, stimulating considerable public debate.[47] They called on psychiatrists to alert themselves to the Soviet malpractice and the need for universal safeguards against improper hospitalization. Doctors Shaw, Bloch and Vickers carefully explored in their article the issues involved, and studied the case reports of two dissenters. They concluded that sufficient evidence was then available to confirm the allegations of abuse, and they urged the creation by the WPA of an international commission to "safeguard medical ethics and psychiatric standards and prevent psychiatry from being applied for any purpose other than the welfare of the patient". More particularly, "a commission of this sort would also be in a position to serve as an international 'ombudsman', impartially investigating allegations of psychiatric abuse wherever they should arise".[48]

In addition to writing for publication, the Working Group pursued its efforts on other fronts. Professor Jenner and the authors took part in a BBC radio programme entitled "Protest or Madness?" in which the evidence was comprehensively discussed.[49] Jenner also wrote directly to Snezhnevsky: "Surely with only one side of the argument available, I am right to ask questions and, in the absence of convincing reassurance, to suspect the worst." Snezhnevsky replied that he had covered the Soviet position in detail at the Mexico congress. As there was nothing new in all the subsequent attacks, no rejoinder was called for. He referred to the calumnious nature of the article by Shaw and others: "The organizers of an anti-Soviet campaign are ready to use everything possible," including an "abuse of the facts" and "tendentious interpretation". Proper procedures had been adopted in the cases of the hospitalized dissenters and there was nothing reprehensible in such actions by Soviet psychiatrists.[50]

A powerful stimulus for the group's activity had been news of Dr Gluzman's case, discussed in chapter 8. His trial had been reported in the world press in October 1972.[51] In November Sakharov issued an appeal for him, concluding: "Gluzman has been sentenced for his professional integrity. I call on world psychiatrists to intervene on behalf of their young colleague, and I call on them to demand an immediate international investigation into all the evidence of the use of psychiatry to suppress dissent."[52]

The fact that a Soviet psychiatrist had been harshly sentenced for, *de facto*, defending his profession against the very abuses documented by Bukovsky added a new dimension to the evidence. It confirmed the worst suspicions and cut the ground from under the sceptics' feet.

Thus when Dr Gerard Low-Beer, a Working Group member, organized in early 1973 a series of telegrams to Sakharov, in response to his appeal, he received ready support. The text read:

> To Academician Sakharov. Undersigned psychiatrists and physicians are moved by your appeal dated November 1972. Very disturbed about Gluzman, Grigorenko, and other such cases. World psychiatric opinion now beginning to understand the problem and reaction to it increasing. We will publicize the facts in all responsible ways open to us including this telegram. Best wishes.[53]

Those who signed the first telegram later wrote to President Podgorny quoting its text, after they learned that Sakharov had never received it.[54] Among the 200 eventual signatories were many of Britain's most distinguished psychiatrists. In effect, the original group of 44 who had written to *The Times* eighteen months earlier had swelled greatly in number. This fact reflected the increasing confidence among hitherto cautious and sceptical psychiatrists about accepting the validity of the allegations of abuse.

At about the same time, another Working Group member

Dr David Clark, presented his colleagues in the council of the Royal College with the text of Sakharov's appeal. Their previous reluctance to act on the material Clark had supplied began to melt away. In January 1973 the college broke its silence on the issue with this resolution: "The Royal College of Psychiatrists firmly opposes the use of psychiatric facilities for the detention of persons solely on the basis of their political dissent no matter where it occurs."[55] Other British medical organizations followed suit: "The British Medical Association condemns the practice of using medical men to certify political and religious dissenters as insane and to submit them to unnecessary investigation and treatment."[56] And the Society of Clinical Psychiatrists voted overwhelmingly that: "We believe it is an essential right of all citizens that their doctors be free from any political pressure to give reports that are not a free expression of medical opinion."[57]

All three associations avoided explicit mention of the Soviet Union. Like the APA in its statement of more than a year earlier, the British groups exercised great caution. Yet passage of the resolutions was clearly intended to apply pressure indirectly on the Russians.

One group with both medical and lay membership went further, however. This was the National Association for Mental Health (NAMH), the British affiliate of WFMH. In a statement issued in March 1973 NAMH referred to its parent body's resolution of November 1971 which had called on all member bodies to investigate and oppose the misuse of psychiatry for political ends (see chapter 4). The statement continued:

> We accept that this Resolution would apply to the misuse of psychiatry in our own country, and will maintain the utmost vigilance in this respect. We have, however, watched with increasing concern reports which have been coming from the USSR about the oppressive abuse of psychiatry in that country for political ends. Insofar as such procedures demean the practice of psychiatry and make patients everywhere fearful to present themselves for psychiatric treatment, we condemn what is happening in the Soviet Union.[58]

Developments concerning the WPA

As we saw in chapter 4, the 1971 Mexico congress was the
occasion which produced the Soviet authorities' first major
crisis *vis-à-vis* Western critics. The catalyst for the second one
turned out to be a conference sponsored by the same body which
met in the USSR two years later. But between these crises
came a number of significant developments.

In November 1972, for example, the Soviet authorities
formally expressed their esteem for the WPA's two most
powerful officials, its secretary-general, Dr Leigh, and its
treasurer, Professor Linford Rees. They were invested as
honorary members of the All-Union Society of Neurologists
and Psychiatrists—the only foreigners to be awarded this status
in 1972.[59] The Soviet ambassador performed the ceremony
in his embassy in London, and a photograph was taken to
mark the occasion (see illustration no. 6).

Whatever Leigh and Rees intended, their acceptance of
membership was a considerable coup for Soviet official psychiatry. At a time when public opinion, especially in Britain, was
becoming increasingly concerned about a sinister medical
abuse, their act was bound to be widely interpreted in Britain,
the USSR and elsewhere as an expression of disbelief by the
WPA and them personally in the evidence of abuse, and as a
vote of confidence in Soviet psychiatry.

As regards their own views, this interpretation would seem to
have been broadly correct. Leigh told a number of people at the
time that in his opinion the campaign against Soviet abuse was
a sophisticated and expensively organized operation, with CIA
participation; that he doubted the authenticity of the evidence;
and that Bukovsky was indeed a schizophrenic, or at any rate
had a history of the condition. When challenged in 1972 by
one of the authors (P.R.), Leigh was unable—in responses
which we document elsewhere[60]—to substantiate his points.
Since then, his private and published statements, his minutes of
WPA executive committee meetings, and the WPA's output on
psychiatric ethics, have shown no sign of serious study of the
evidence, despite statements by the president in 1971 (see
chapter 4), and by Rees in 1975,[61] that this was being
conducted. In 1975, Professor Rees still described Soviet
abuses as "alleged", although the Royal College had con-

demned them unequivocally two years earlier. And as of 1976, the WPA had yet to interview any of the ex-victims of abuse, or ex-Soviet psychiatrists, who had emigrated from the USSR since 1971.

In November 1972 the executive committee discussed the APA's position-statement and requested that the WPA circulate it to all member societies; a submission from the West Germans was also considered.[62] According to the minutes, Professor Vartanyan "pointed out that psychiatry was in need of some ethical principles, and that the WPA might well concern itself with the problem". So now, if not earlier, the Soviet authorities, through Vartanyan, supported Leigh, evidently feeling that a committee to formulate universal ethical principles would be an adroit diversion from the real issue. In any event, the executive committee decided merely to forward the American and German statements to member societies for comment.

Why were these documents alone selected for circulation? Why not also the Canadian and WFMH resolutions and the "letter of the 44"? Was it because these items would have provoked debate and concern, whereas the German and American statements would encourage inaction or apathy?

In any case, apathy ensued. After the statements' eventual distribution nine months later, no responses came from member societies, which were, understandably, not moved to action either by the pious generality of the APA, or by the curious ambivalence of the German society. Despite the latter's declaration that the political use of psychiatry was contrary to medical ethics and a violation of human rights, it saw itself as a scientific body with no legal competence to examine actual or alleged cases of malpractice either in West Germany or elsewhere. The Germans also chided the media for inciting public opinion against psychiatry by their publicizing of abuse.[63]

At the time of the executive committee meeting the WPA held a conference on schizophrenia in London. Here Leigh forbade the Working Group to offer literature to the participants either in or near the conference hall. But he arranged an interview for Vartanyan with *The Times*,[64] in the course of which Vartanyan

said the demonstrators referred to a specific group of patients who needed treatment. He said that their delusions were based on political questions. . . . "I can guarantee there are no sane people detained in psychiatric hospitals in the Soviet Union" .... Dr Vartanyan said he believed the regulations concerning certification of patients were not very different in the Soviet Union from those in Britain.*

The Issue Flares Up with New Force

The first half of 1973 was a period of deceptive calm. Only in Britain did protest persist, and then at a low level.[65] In the Soviet Union a determined KGB drive to quell dissent continued, scoring notable successes, especially the suppression of the *Chronicle*, but no new recommendations for the criminal commitment of well-known activists were made. This helped to remove the issue from the news. The American government assisted too, by giving an all-round boost to détente, including the medical exchanges, during Brezhnev's visit to the USA (16–24 June). To the dismay of the liberal press, Nixon and Kissinger apparently noticed neither the intensified Soviet suppression of human rights over the preceding year and a half, nor the use of psychiatry as one of the chosen instruments.[66]

The Soviet psychiatric authorities must have felt pleased. And their gratification undoubtedly increased when, a few days later, the ninth international congress of psychotherapy took the same path in Oslo as the WPA congress in Mexico. The 1,000 participants were presented with a score of petitions from various groups, who pressed them to debate Soviet practices. Amnesty International, which played a prominent rôle in the lobbying, appealed to the Soviet authorities to allow an international commission of psychiatrists to investigate publicized cases of internment.[67]

But the congress neither debated the petitions nor passed a resolution. The organizers hinted clearly that the East European delegations had threatened to walk out if such debate occurred; they did not wish to risk disrupting East–West communication by pressing the issue.[68] The only consolation for Soviet dissenters was the dispatch of a forceful appeal to Brezhnev, signed by 175 of the conferees.[69]

* This was a revealingly incorrect statement. British patients compulsorily detained under civil commitment have an automatic right of appeal (under the 1959 Mental Health Act) to an independent review tribunal, a right which Soviet citizens, as noted in chapter 6, conspicuously lack.

To the KGB the double success of Brezhnev's American trip and the walk-out threat in Oslo allowed an escalated offensive against dissent. It could step up its intimidation of the activists by reverting to the practice it had recently been forced to curtail: that of interning them under criminal commitment.

Thus on 28 June the Serbsky psychiatrists recommended Shikhanovich (see chapters 7 and 8) for internment, and a week later the Ukrainian Supreme Court overturned an earlier ruling and consigned Plyushch to a special hospital. Until then he had spent a year and a half in prison while the authorities wavered over exacting this form of reprisal—one which had been abandoned for people as well known as he in late 1972.

To the dissenters, already under severe pressure, these developments were alarming. In late June and early July four urgent appeals about psychiatric abuse issued from Moscow. One was a direct reaction to what had just occurred in Oslo. Sakharov and his colleagues in the Human Rights Committee wrote:[70]

We have learned that many appeals from individuals and international and national organizations were sent to the world conference of psychotherapists held in Oslo, and that these requested discussion of the practice of psychiatric hospitalization for political purposes in the USSR and the countries of Eastern Europe. The conference refused to pronounce on the matter, so as not to hinder "the currently most progressive process of rapprochement with the countries of Eastern Europe". The Committee has learned of the conference's decision with incomprehension and a sense of bitterness. The confinement of healthy people in psychiatric hospitals will be an eternal stain on our century, just as the "Spanish boot" will always disfigure the Middle Ages.

To close one's eyes to such cruelties means to encourage their perpetration and to betray their victims. Repression through psychiatry not only cripples people's lives, it destroys the moral and legal foundations of human society. One of the expressions of its destructive effect is precisely the decision of the psychotherapists' conference. Where will the forces be found to combat this danger if even doctors desire neither to hear nor speak of it?

We wish eagerly for rapprochement between countries of different political systems, and we see as its purpose that both sides should help each other to develop in the most humane directions. But the decision of the psychotherapists' conference invests the idea of rapprochement with a precisely opposite and frightening meaning.

We appeal to all psychiatrists who feel a responsibility to their patients, their science and humanity to work for a review of this decision.

A similar call appeared in a protest by Sakharov and others about their friend Shikhanovich which we quoted in chapter 8. A third appeal went to the UN's secretary-general, seeking his intervention on behalf of Plyushch and Vladimir Borisov.[71] And the fourth was a 30-page document addressed to the WFMH and the International Commission of Jurists. In this revealing document Tatyana Khodorovich, a linguist and long-standing dissenter, called on these bodies to study her legal and psychiatric analysis of the Plyushch case, make it public, and forward it with their evaluations to the UN.

In her conclusion Khodorovich explained why the authorities had chosen a mental hospital for Plyushch:

His brain has been ruled *socially dangerous.* . . . Imprisonment in a camp . . . would not neutralize the danger from it. After all, there he could associate with *normal* people and have friends. . . . The mad-house, though, is reliable, without term, and sound-proof. Nowadays not even a straitjacket is needed: a few injections of some neuroleptic drug are enough to "straighten out" any rebellious brain, to muffle it in inertia and silence.[72]

These appeals, which were beginning to contain overtones of desperation, evoked some response, especially in Britain.[73] Here the issue had in any case been warming up in recent weeks, following the appearance of two articles by the columnist Bernard Levin in *The Times.*[74] Levin had studied the matter for some time, "and the picture that emerges seems to me so horrifying, its details so little known in Britain, and its history so shot through with appeals from the victims for public pressure on the Soviet authorities to be built up from outside," that he felt he must write about it at length. He discussed the cases of Bukovsky, Gluzman and others, whom he regarded as heroes, and attacked the WPA's refusal to support them. He also denounced Leigh for accepting honorary membership of the Soviet psychiatric society. Finally, he called on the Royal College to criticize Soviet abuses unambiguously at its impending annual general meeting.

This was the first time that the key issues had been expounded so forcefully in the press of any country. Some members of the college responded by criticizing the WPA and suggesting a reduction in the college's support of it.[75] In addition, the International PEN Club intervened for Bukovsky,[76] and the *Observer* published an article quoting from the Human Rights Committee's pained appeal from Moscow and taking the Oslo conference to task for its failure to act. The author also discussed Szasz's view that psychiatry is inherently repressive, and reached this thoughtful conclusion: "If doctors fail to take a stand, and distinguish clearly and publicly between responsible psychiatry and its betrayal in the Soviet Union, Szasz's case will seem to succeed by default. Ultimately, the British psychiatrists are being asked to fight not merely for the Russian victims, but for the integrity of their own science."[77]

But it was only on 29 July 1973 that the issue "took off" at an international level. On this day the *Observer* revealed that the WPA had organized a conference on schizophrenia, to be held in the USSR in October and to be addressed by "compromised" psychiatrists such as Georgy Morozov. The paper also reported: "Dr Leigh ... says that no member-association has ever formally raised the matter [of Soviet abuses] at WPA meetings, and that its rules may, in any case, forbid members to discuss one another's ethical practices." Why Leigh repeated his false surmise of 1971 about the rules, when these contained nothing to support him, was incomprehensible except as a manœuvre to try to stave off criticism of the WPA's inaction on the Soviet issue.

The Soviet authorities were worried by these new attacks both on the WPA and on their own practices, and quickly deputed Professor Nadzharov to rebut them. In a widely-published Tass interview he expressed satisfaction that both the WPA and certain prominent (but unnamed) psychiatrists had "dissociated themselves from the anti-Soviet slanderers," whose lies were "intended to please those circles which are interested in poisoning the international atmosphere".[78]

Over the next few days the temperature rose further, as a separate but related conflict—the struggle between Sakharov and the régime—escalated sharply. In recent months, Sakharov had taken advantage of his partial immunity from arrest, conferred by his fame, to substitute as far as possible for the suppressed *Chronicle* and to issue frequent statements on violations of human rights. But on 12 August the press published something more wide-ranging—a radical critique of the whole Soviet system. In a televised interview he explained in detail why he saw the Soviet Union as "a society of maximal unfreedom".[79] Within days he was solemnly warned by the deputy procurator-general not to make further statements of this kind. Refusing to be intimidated by the clear threat of prosecution, he promptly gave a press conference in which he urged the West not to conduct détente in such a way that the USSR could continue the masked build-up of its military might.[80]

On 24 August a vitriolic and orchestrated press assault was launched against Sakharov. When it became clear that this was probably a prelude to his arrest, Alexander Solzhenitsyn and others mounted a powerful counter campaign, quickly supported by public opinion abroad.[81] In succeeding weeks this campaign interacted with the intensified criticism of psychiatric abuse, the effect being one of mutual reinforcement. While the coincidence in timing was largely fortuitous, a direct and important link was provided by Sakharov's regular statements on the perversion of psychiatry, which he continued to make even when under daily attack.

24 August also saw the publication in *Nature* of Zhores Medvedev's comments on Nadzharov's interview and his discussion of the forthcoming WPA conference. He noted that among the speakers scheduled were Nadzharov, Snezhnevsky, and G. Morozov, who had all played an important part in his own case three years earlier. "With these three 'heroes' of many well-known psychiatric-political cases present," the conference was, he felt, "a unique chance" for scientists to investigate matters at first hand. He urged the Westerners among the 53 psychiatrists due to attend to submit a series of probing questions—which he spelled out—to their Soviet hosts.

Three days later a long correspondence in *The Times* was initiated by an impassioned letter from David Carver, the secretary-general of the International PEN Club. Carver was amazed that Levin's articles in June had evinced no response from psychiatrists, and that now the Royal College was condoning participation by its members in a WPA conference which would be addressed by Morozov and his ilk.[82] In reply to this and other indignant letters the president of the college, Sir Martin Roth, stated that participation was a matter for individual conscience. However, he and his council believed "that the treatment reported to have been meted out to such men as Medvedev, Gluzman and Grigorenko is odious, repugnant and intolerable by any civilized standards". If, moreover, Morozov was to attend the conference, he hoped that Western psychiatrists would "have an opportunity for calling him to account for some of the diagnostic judgements he is reported to have pronounced". The college was concerned to take effective international action on the issue through, for example, the World Health Organization. Hence the generalized nature of its resolution of January 1973. However, "Our statement was not our last word on the subject."[83]

Soviet response to the unprecedentedly severe criticism in the British press began on 31 August, when *Izvestia* reported Snezhnevsky's testimony at the trial of Pyotr Yakir and Victor Krasin, two dissenters who had been broken by the KGB during interrogation and turned state's evidence: "A. V. Snezhnevsky declared that in 50 years of work in the Soviet health service he did not know of any case in which a healthy person had been placed in a mental hospital." Letters from Yakir alleging abuse had, Snezhnevsky maintained, complicated the work of Soviet psychiatrists abroad.[84] Yakir himself then stated that he had invented what he wrote, and a few days later denied at an official press conference that abuse occurred in the USSR.[85]

But Roth's letter provoked a wilder reaction. On 7 September Tass complained that "*The Times* of London has once again dragged out these fables," and published an interview with Snezhnevsky. He "pointed out that he regarded Professor Martin Roth's letter as a regrettable and, of course, hopeless attempt to galvanize an anti-Soviet lie that had long been a propagandist corpse". He had "no wish to enter into any polemics about the motives that prompted the irresponsible statement", but he was "forced to believe that . . . the facts did not interest Roth at all".[86]

Just as the spate of letters in *The Times* began to slacken, the same issues erupted in the correspondence columns of *The Guardian*. Here too Roth published a long letter, this time stressing more forcibly than before that the schizophrenia conference was exclusively a creature of the WPA: "The Royal College played no part in arranging this conference or in choosing Russia as a place in which it should be convened, nor was its council consulted at any stage about the programme."[87] As the college was the WPA's third largest member-society, this statement threw a strange light on Leigh's repeated insistence on the WPA's federal nature, and raised questions as to how exactly the decisions about the conference had been taken. His interview in the *Observer* the next day was not very enlightening on this point. But it was revealing in other ways: "Dr Leigh said last week that critics of the WPA 'can say what they like and we [WPA] can do what we like'." He continued:

> We're not concerned with political matters. We're an association . . . like the United Nations and what our national member-societies do is up to them. . . . Schizophrenia is the most important topic in psychiatry. It's the scourge of the world. The Russians have about 200 people researching on it and they have a good chance of solving it. That's all there is to it. I'm fed up with criticism from public-school socialists.

Leigh would not comment on the evidence of misuse of psychiatry by Soviet doctors: "It is not my place to do so. I am like a trade-union general secretary. I serve my executive."[88]

The *British Medical Journal* discussed what it saw as the WPA's dilemma over whether or not to withdraw from sponsorship of the conference in the light of Medvedev's revelations. Its conclusion was, however, firm on another point: "Whatever its [the WPA's] decision, one course must now be generally expected of it, and that is a declaration that it is aware of the facts and condemns them."[89] The editors must have had a rude shock when they read Leigh's interview.

A British Communist, Dr Leonard Crome, also entered the debate. Writing to *The Times* as a neuropathologist and as the chairman of the Society for Cultural Relations with the USSR, he said he had studied the evidence, "but in my view not even a *prima facie* case has been made out". Moreover, his knowledge and high opinion of Soviet doctors, hospitals, and research institutes made the allegations "inconceivable" to him.[90]

Crome's letter was attacked by many correspondents, including the directors of the Bertrand Russell Peace Foundation.[91] They challenged his society to set up with the foundation a joint commission to examine the charges made by the Medvedev brothers in their book and by Zhores Medvedev in *Nature*. Crome did not reply. Instead, he "smeared" Zhores somewhat deviously when he said in an interview: "I believe he was sincere and honest in his book, but one does tend to shun the printing of things that are unfavourable to the case. It is possible that there was cause in his past medical history to suggest he might be mentally unstable."[92]

While the issues were thrashed out in the British press, with a minority of correspondents favouring a boycott of the conference and the majority urging the invited psychiatrists to attend and pose awkward questions,[93] an American dimension unexpectedly appeared. At first the Soviet authorities must have been elated. On 7 September the US Secretary of Health, Education and Welfare, Caspar Weinberger, in a joint press conference in Moscow with Health Minister Petrovsky, remained silent while his opposite number attacked the US Senate's publication of December 1972 on Soviet psychiatric abuse, mentioned earlier. That it was "based on no serious scientific study" could be seen from the fact that it contradicted the findings of the US mission of 1967. In sum, "This is certainly not a publication which enhances co-operation between our two countries." The two men then inaugurated a direct telex line between their offices in Washington and Moscow.[94] This to the Soviets was détente in action.

Within a week, however, their elation changed to near-panic. First Sakharov urged the psychiatrists invited to the conference to demand to visit dissenters interned in SPHs. If refused, they should boycott the meeting.[95] The next day the US National Academy of Sciences (NAS) cabled its Soviet counterpart, warning that if Sakharov—a foreign associate member—were arrested, and if harassment of him did not cease, scientific co-operation between the two countries would probably come to an end.[96] As the NAS administered the exchanges at the American end, and as the USSR gained more from them than the US, the warning was serious. Indeed, it probably played a more decisive rôle than any other protest in saving Sakharov from arrest.

All these developments, especially the last, now stirred the American Psychiatric Association (APA) out of its détente-induced apathy. Its president, Dr Alfred Freedman, sent this telegram to Snezhnevsky:

> The American Psychiatric Association has for several years been concerned about the alleged involuntary confinement of political dissidents in psychiatric facilities. Several individual members of this Association have made inquiries of Soviet colleagues about this matter and have reported to us that they have received no answers.
>
> Repeated charges that involuntary psychiatric confinement has been used unjustly and without regard to human rights, including the suppression of political dissent, cannot be ignored.
>
> Therefore, the APA calls on Soviet colleagues to meet with a delegation of distinguished United States psychiatrists, in an appropriate professional setting that will assure medical confidentiality, to discuss involuntary psychiatric confinement and specific cases where abuse has been alleged, recognizing that it may be necessary to consider individual patients.
>
> We also recognize that charges about the political uses of psychiatric confinement can be made against any country. Therefore, our delegation would be prepared to discuss alleged misuse of involuntary confinement in the United States and other countries.
>
> The growing suspicion the world over that the profession of psychiatry lends itself to abuses of this genre is cause for alarm by psychiatrists everywhere. If such abuses exist, they should be publicly exposed and corrected with all possible dispatch. We very much hope that Soviet colleagues will join us in this effort, especially in the light of the joint agreements between our nations on scientific co-operation.[97]

To the Soviets the abrupt switch from the friendly Mr Weinberger to the threatening Dr Freedman was a painful lesson in the unpredictability of American pluralism. Two weeks of anxious consultations passed before a counter-strategy was devised. Snezhnevsky then replied: "Apologize for delay with answer. Surprised by your telegram 11 September 1973. However, Soviet specialists have no objection to discussing questions of professional interest after the symposium."[98] Freedman declared that the APA was "much heartened" by this response and was "most hopeful that it will prove an opening wedge to meaningful dialogue with our Soviet colleagues".[99]

However, the relatively polite defensiveness of Snezhnevsky's telegram was soon shown to mask deeper emotions. A long letter from the 21-member presidium of the All-Union Society of Neurologists and Psychiatrists appeared in *The Guardian,* and soon also in other publications.[100] Among the signatories were Snezhnevsky, Nadzharov, G. Morozov, and Serebryakova. The letter was fairly standard apologetics, including for example an exposition of the theory of "seeming normality" discussed in chapter 8. This was presented as a universally accepted fact. But the letter was also an outburst against Western psychiatrists and journalists and Soviet dissenters for their "malicious concoctions ... continuing unseemly attempts to misinform public opinion ... slandering of Soviet psychiatry ... lying concoctions ... concoctions that slander Soviet psychiatry ... propaganda clamour and smear campaigns". The letter concluded that these attacks were "nothing but an attempt to impede the international co-operation of medical men, to damage the developing fruitful contacts between scientists and cultural figures of different countries".

The haranguing tone seemed almost hysterical. But this, as we have seen, was not new. Branding Western critics as malicious slanderers had been resorted to regularly in the past. Another point familiar by now to Western observers was the attribution of praise for Soviet forensic psychiatry to unnamed foreign psychiatrists and jurists who had visited the USSR.

The letter is a classic of its kind, and we include the full text as appendix III. Its immediate effect was to stimulate renewed protest in the British press from Medvedev and others.[101] It also changed the attitude of the British medical journal *The Lancet,* which had previously withheld judgement on Soviet abuses, believing there was insufficient proof. The letter, however, was "by far the most convincing evidence yet that something is seriously amiss with Soviet psychiatry". It was "hard to believe that any scientist . . . could lend his name to such a tirade of emotive rhetoric and unsubstantiated assertion". The exposition of "seeming normality" gave the most away. As for praise by foreign experts, this was well and good, "but who are they, what did they see, and where did they write their findings?"[102]

Official apologetics of this sort also provoked resolute rebuttals from dissenters. The members of the Action Group for the Defence of Human Rights who were still free wrote:

> We continue to assert that in a series of instances psychiatry has been used in our country as a way of locking up people whom the authorities find objectionable. No assertions by Academician A. Snezhnevsky or Professor R. Nadzharov, no repentant statements by P. Yakir and V. Krasin, and no court indictments or decisions can alter the appalling reality of this fact. We direct attention to the fact that while publicly denying the use of psychiatry in the USSR to combat dissent, Snezhnevsky and Nadzharov are themselves *accomplices* in this crime. Their signatures appear on the forensic psychiatric reports of people convicted for ideological reasons. . . . We affirm that Yakir and Krasin, during their investigation, trial, and news conference made false statements. It is tragic that these lies also affect the fate and reputation of all the political prisoners in the camps, prisons and psychiatric hospitals of the USSR.[103]

The Human Rights Committee issued a similar statement on 1 October.[104] It had documentary and other evidence that "precisely people's beliefs and nothing else are regarded by the psychiatrists as proof of illness"; many of the victims were "personally known" to members of the committee, who could vouch for their normality; and the imprisonment of Bukovsky and Gluzman for publicizing the abuse was in itself revealing. The authors also appealed to public opinion, and to national and international psychiatric associations (1) to discuss the issue in depth, (2) to demand that foreign psychiatrists chosen by relatives be allowed to take part in the forensic examination of dissenters, (3) to demand that the WHO, Red Cross, and similar organizations form commissions to investigate serious psychiatric abuses in any country, starting with the practices of five named Soviet SPHs, and (4) to arrange for the transfer of interned dissenters to foreign institutions, where they could be examined and, if necessary, treated. Point 3 had in fact already been demanded by the British Liberal Party in a resolution of a week earlier.[105]

The WPA Schizophrenia Conference in the Soviet Union

In little over a month, from the time of Medvedev's article in *Nature*, the issue of Soviet abuse had become known around the world. As the publicity achieved was greater than in 1971, the spotlight on the WPA conference was intense. Dr Leigh arrived early for it and, as we saw in chapter 5, had a meeting on 5 October 1973 with Dr Venediktov, the deputy minister of health. Apart from offering to arrange a visit to Grigorenko, Venediktov also announced the intention of the All-Union Society to invite the overseas participants to visit the Serbsky after the conference. Leigh welcomed this, and, in his own words, "thanked the minister for his consistently helpful attitude towards the WPA since 1968, when the Executive Committee had first visited the USSR, and for his understanding of the many difficulties facing a non-government organization". Leigh also sought information on Dr Gluzman, about whom he had first enquired in November 1972. According to Venediktov he still could not be traced, but efforts to locate him would continue.[106]

Three days later Snezhnevsky opened the conference in the Armenian capital of Erevan and formally issued the Serbsky invitation. Venediktov was present, but Vartanyan, as a WPA secretary, was the most active Soviet lobbyer. Nadzharov, though billed to speak, was absent on a flimsy pretext, evidently to avoid personal criticism. As one participant recorded, "It was as if the government had placed the responsibility to 'squelch the criticism' on the Ministry of Health, Snezhnevsky, and Vartanyan." Venediktov openly admitted to Freedman: "You gave us a big headache."[107]

Given these preoccupations, it is not surprising that the scientific sessions were of limited value. In the opinion of one psychiatrist, "The Soviets did not much understand the 'foreign' papers, and in general the non-Soviets did not appreciate the Soviet papers. Besides the lower level of scientific discipline, their wordy presentations do not come across well in translation." But the main problem was that "The under-current of a second level of constant meetings—of the WPA Executive Committee, the non-Soviet psychiatrists planning to go to the Serbsky, and the Soviets with themselves and others —drained a large amount of energy from the scientific sessions. These became almost a 'charade' for the *real* agenda—the Serbsky meeting."[108]

Certainly the Soviet device of offering this meeting *after* the Erevan conference succeeded almost completely in preventing discussion of psychiatric abuse during it. Professor Wing did raise the subject discreetly in his paper, but not in a way to cause debate. An American who planned to do so more force-fully was dissuaded by a colleague who feared it might threaten the Soviet-American schizophrenia research programme. The American commented in his diary: "Everyone is hiding behind 'science' as the reason why the issues shouldn't be raised—yet it is the perversion of science for political purposes we're talking about! The other dodge is—well, our system isn't so perfect either. I agree, but all the more reason to question *both*!"[109]

Although the WPA Executive Committee did not meet until the first evening to determine its position on the Serbsky invitation, throughout the day Leigh, according to one conferee, was already "working feverishly to have the Serbsky proposal accepted".[110] The committee promptly welcomed the invitation, after a discussion in which some guests, including Freedman and Snezhnevsky, participated. Freedman found himself isolated in raising practical questions as to what could be achieved in a one-day visit, given the serious problems of language and lack of preparation and legal expertise. If a press conference would follow, he wondered if it would be used to convey a false impression. If serious study were to be under-taken and responsible judgements eventually made, this visit could only be the first of a series.

At this point the minutes of the meeting record:

Professor Vartanyan spoke in reply. Soviet psychiatrists had been greatly offended by the letter of Sir Martin Roth, and, in view of the campaign against them in the press and at international meetings such as the recent psychotherapy conference in Oslo, Soviet psychiatrists could not be silent in front of their colleagues. . . . Professor Snezhnevsky then spoke. He reminded the meeting of the letter published in *The Guardian* from the Presidium of the All-Union Society. He wanted all participants to have the opportunity to visit the Institute, to hear case histories and to participate in a commission of enquiry.

The committee also decided that Leigh should inform everyone of the society's invitation. Why he and not the society assumed this task is unclear. As we saw, he had in fact assumed it even before the meeting. Finally, the committee also endorsed his proposal to set up an ethical committee, subject to the approval of member societies.[111]

One of the informal meetings at which Leigh pressed Western psychiatrists to visit the Serbsky was described by a participant in his diary. On the WPA's rôle, Leigh claimed that his association had no responsibility for the Serbsky meeting,

> yet he had transmitted the invitation and had encouraged people to go. . . . It was as if he wanted it to be both official and unofficial at the same time. . . . The entire discussion was incredibly frustrating, with Leigh obviously obfuscating, evading and diverting attention constantly. He had not made clear to naïve persons that the meeting in the Serbsky was not a WPA thing: he had pressured people subtly . . . Leigh distinguished himself as slippery, evasive, and condescending. He hid behind WPA by-laws when convenient, yet found they could act when it suited *him*.[112]

On the third day at Erevan several of the visitors met to decide how to respond to the invitation. Refusal would enable the authorities to depict them as afraid of learning the truth. So the group agreed to accept, provided that it could issue a press-release in advance. This would say that acceptance did not imply approval of Soviet practices and that no conclusions could be drawn from a single visit. Except for the release of a statement *in advance*, the Soviets accepted the conditions. Eventually twenty psychiatrists signed, including three WPA

Executive Committee members acting in a personal capacity. It read:

A group of scientists taking part in the symposium "Aspects of Schizophrenia" met on several occasions to consider their hosts' offer to arrange a further meeting in Moscow after the conference. This meeting would have the object of discussing the allegations that have recently been made about Soviet forensic psychiatry. The group decided to accept their hosts' offer. The participating scientists would take part in their individual capacity and not as representatives of any organization. The group wished to make two points clear:

1) The fact that members of the group are willing to attend the meeting does not in itself imply any prior acceptance or rejection of the allegations.

2) Such complex and difficult problems cannot be adequately evaluated in one day. It is therefore unlikely that a clear-cut statement of approval or disapproval will be made at the end of the meeting. The intention is to begin what it is hoped will be a series of professional discussions.[113]

On the fifth and last day of the conference, which by now had moved to the Georgian capital of Tbilisi, the Soviets abruptly rejected the statement outright: if it were given to the press in advance the meeting would be cancelled. At this the group complied, and, although the essential points were leaked to a Reuter correspondent,[114] reluctantly decided to release the statement only after the visit.

Apart from the drama involved in this bargaining, a bizarre piece of theatre occurred during a scientific session chaired by Freedman. An intruder rose and demanded to speak, whereupon Vartanyan instantly shouted to Freedman to have the man removed. After some confusion, during which he was heard to say something about dissenters, he was hurried away to a mental institution and there examined, presumably at Soviet prompting, by a panel comprising Leigh, de la Fuente and Rees.[115] According to the WPA minutes, the three psychiatrists "agreed that the man was mentally ill, and had been so for many years; that he was a voluntary patient in the hospital; and that he had no complaint about his treatment".[116] While the circumstances of the episode remain blurred, it seems likely that it was an attempted "provocation" against Freedman, who, as signatory of the APA telegram, had been the target of considerable Soviet hostility throughout. When the provocation failed, credit could still be extracted from the situation: the authorities were liberal and had allowed a panel of foreigners to examine the man freely.

On 15 October thirteen of the Western psychiatrists arrived at the Serbsky.[117] At once the visit to Grigorenko described in chapter 5 was announced, and Leigh and Perris duly departed. The timing was skilful: no one could visit both Grigorenko and the Serbsky simultaneously, and few were likely to sacrifice "a bird in the hand". Later, when the Grigorenko meeting had been abandoned after his request for an independent interpreter, Soviet psychiatrists claimed that his behaviour demonstrated his paranoia, and Vartanyan was still claiming this in 1976.[118] Leigh reported the episode to his executive committee the same evening, which agreed, according to the minutes, on the somewhat misleading formula: "that the press would be informed that no examination had taken place at the general's own wish". The minutes do not record any explanation by Leigh as to why he had not supported Grigorenko's request for an independent interpreter.

In the Serbsky the visitors were greeted by Snezhnevsky, then given a short lecture by G. Morozov on Soviet forensic psychiatry. After a question period, six case histories involving well-known dissenters—among them Grigorenko, Plyushch, and Medvedev—were presented. Each history was accompanied by a short summary in English. Wing managed to transcribe the document on Plyushch,[119] but no participant was apparently allowed to take away copies of the case histories themselves. On Grigorenko, it seems likely that the same material was provided as was shown by Morozov to the German journalist Lempke two days later. As we saw in chapter 5, this contained both subtle and far from subtle falsifications of the clinical history. So did the Medvedev summary described in chapter 6. And the Plyushch document, when measured against the available official evidence, also strikes us as distorted.

We should stress that we are referring here to the second stage of a two-level distortion: as we saw earlier, with rare exceptions like the Detengof report on Grigorenko, the available case histories already contain serious "primary" misrepresentations, designed to justify a diagnosis of schizophrenia.

After questions on the six cases, during which it was disclosed that Gluzman could still not be traced, the foreigners witnessed what was featured as an examination of a dissenter typical of the group just discussed. The anomaly of not presenting an actual member of this group was not explained. So another piece of theatre went ahead. The foreigners were able to question the patient and the examining psychiatrists, and to ascertain that he was indeed a schizophrenic. Perhaps, as the hosts clearly hoped, the more trusting foreigners did believe that he was comparable with Plyushch or Grigorenko.

To Wing, Freedman and Christian Scharfetter, apparently the only three to publish considered accounts of the visit, it fully justified the cautious statement the group had signed in advance.[120] Freedman wrote:

The Serbsky meeting confirmed what I had anticipated. To reach meaningful conclusions, it would be necessary to organize a carefully selected group with experience and expertise in forensic psychiatry, including a lawyer or a judge with special experience and facility in this field. Also, the presence of Russian-speaking psychiatrists would be invaluable. This group would have to prepare itself very carefully by studying the Russian system of justice and Soviet psychiatric practice, as well as forensic psychiatry. There would have to be opportunity for full discussion with appropriate Soviet individuals, private examination of patients and private discussions with various staff personnel. In other words, we would have to organize as we would in this country if we were asked to make a site visit to an institution in which allegations of abuses of one sort of another were made.

I raised this proposal with our Soviet colleagues. While they did not reject it outright, they took a dim view of its feasibility. Finally they said that it was a decision that would have to be made by the Ministry of Health, if I wished to pursue it. However, they looked upon this request as an unwarranted interference in the internal affairs of the Soviet Union. It was often stated that "We don't criticize you for the events which occurred at Tuskegee (where the syphilis experiment took place) and, therefore, it is unwarranted for you to criticize us."[121]

Freedman's desire to act in the spirit of the APA's telegram, and to regard the visit as the first in a series of dialogues, thus received short shrift. The Soviet psychiatrists had not obtained the whitewash they had hoped for, and were angry: they would have to answer for the failure to their political masters. The Westerners had proved less naïve, less easy to "hustle", than expected.

Nonetheless, it was important to salvage as much as possible from the situation, and Vartanyan was first off the mark with a brazen attempt to manipulate the WPA. Within an hour of the Serbsky meeting he drafted a report of it for immediate endorsement by the executive committee. Regarding the five dissenters who had undergone forensic psychiatric examination (i.e. excluding Medvedev), he stated as the committee's opinion: "All five cases had suffered from a mental illness at the time of their respective commissions of enquiry." Whether he hoped that the committee would endorse the report without noticing this sentence, or whether he thought he could cajole any objectors into compliance even though they had not interviewed the patients concerned, remains unclear. In any case, the minutes excluded the false statement, and also recorded Vartanyan's objection to its deletion.[122] Undeterred by this reversal, Vartanyan blithely included the same statement in the leading Soviet psychiatric journal. In March 1974 this reported:

> The members of the Executive Committee expressed their satisfaction with the discussion which had taken place and with the friendly atmosphere in which it had been conducted. *It was agreed that all five of the so-called dissenters who had been discussed at the meeting had been suffering from mental illnesses at the times when they had been examined by psychiatric commissions.* [Our italics][123]

The second Soviet tactic was the traditional one of persuading individual visitors to give press interviews and then publishing and broadcasting them in misleading or distorted form. Tass issued the first such report on the Serbsky visit on 17 October. The author was less blatant than Vartanyan, but nevertheless achieved a similar result. Here are some extracts:

> Howard Rome (USA), president of the WPA, has expressed satisfaction with the activities of the Serbsky Institute. ... Rome said in a Tass interview that the foreign visitors "were able to discuss all questions absolutely freely and were satisfied with the results they were shown, the level of scientific analysis, and the professional actions of the Soviet psychiatrists."
>
> Informing the guests about methods of forensic psychiatric examination, the Soviet scientists showed them the detailed case histories of five persons whose names have been mentioned in the foreign press as allegedly being absolutely sane but as having been placed in hospital on political grounds. The visitors were given a chance to take part in such an examination. ... "We were convinced," said Ramon de la Fuente (Mexico), vice-president of the association, "that medical examination is approached in all seriousness and with due account taken of all aspects of the patient's rights."[124]

Izvestia was bolder, reporting that the visitors had "drawn favourable conclusions about the practice of forensic psychiatric examinations in the USSR and repudiated all the slanderous allegations".[125] *The Literary Gazette* provided an alleged example: "Swedish scientist Professor Carlo Perris stressed that a thorough analysis of the case histories leaves no doubt whatever about the need for special treatment for those patients whose names have appeared in the Western press."[126]

When no objections were raised to these statements and the manner of their presentation, the Soviet propaganda machine became more daring still. A medical correspondent asserted that the foreign psychiatrists: "were in a position to see that all those patients whose 'rights' are defended by the Western press had been under psychiatric treatment long before they committed any anti-social deeds punishable by Soviet law".[127] She proceeded to attack Freedman and to quote approvingly Scharfetter, de la Fuente and Dr J. Angst. The last had supposedly stated: "In saying that dissidents are put in mental hospitals in the USSR, the press distorts the facts. I believe that the persons whose case records we read are mentally deranged." Later, in a private letter, Angst wrote: "The statement attributed to me did not originate, in its present form, from me."[128] But as he apparently made no representations to the Soviet press the statement continued to be published at intervals in later years.[129]

Another "leap forward" into fantasy came in a Moscow Radio broadcast to Britain by Dr Sergei Semyonov, a leading figure in the All-Union Society, and, according to a senior émigré psychiatrist, a close collaborator of the KGB who earlier worked for many years in the Serbsky.[130] He discussed the Serbsky visit and the foreigners' review of "certain cases in which a denial of human rights has been alleged in the West. These specialists met the patients in question, interviewed their doctors, and attended forensic examinations."[131]

The weeks following the Erevan conference saw not only a barrage of these and many similar missiles from the arsenal of Soviet propaganda.[132] Other developments—of mixed desirability from the official viewpoint—also occurred. Dr Malcolm Lader of London resigned as the WPA's symposiums adviser, feeling unable to continue after what he learnt about Soviet abuses while in the USSR.[133] And at the Congress of Peace-Loving Forces in Moscow a Belgian pacifist temporarily spoiled the authorities' design by calling on them to grant an amnesty to all political prisoners: "From Prague and the Soviet Union we ceaselessly receive appeals which we cannot ignore. We cannot in conscience make vanish into thin air the silent minority in camps, prisons and psychiatric asylums."[134] On the other hand, at the same congress the chairman of Amnesty International, Sean MacBride, commented in an interview: "I think there has been a good deal of exaggeration in the foreign press reports in regard to the extent, if any, to which psychiatric hospitals are being used in dealing with political prisoners."[135] These words provoked anger and consternation within Amnesty, which had regularly been publishing the *Chronicle*'s authentic accounts of precisely such hospital use. While MacBride refused to explain himself, it was surmised in Amnesty that a factor in the situation was the "high politics" he was practising in opening talks with Soviet officials about the organization's work. Whatever the case, damage had been done.[136]

Another welcome if double-edged development was a pat-on-the-back from the WFMH. Its executive board said in a statement approving the invitation to visit the Serbsky: "The WFMH salutes the willingness of the Ministry of Health of the USSR to submit its psychiatric procedures to independent examination, and urges that this procedure should be extended to all those cases where wrongful certification has been alleged."[137]

The Royal College of Psychiatrists Condemns the Soviet Abuse

The most serious set-back for the Soviet authorities occurred a month after the Serbsky visit, when the following motion was adopted in London: "The Royal College of Psychiatrists deplores the current use of psychiatry in the Soviet Union for the purpose of political repression and condemns the activities of doctors who lend themselves to this work." The motion's proposer and seconder, Gerard Low-Beer and Harold Merskey, were supported by a number of speakers, including Wing and Lader.

In addition, the college wrote to equivalent bodies in fourteen countries, including the USSR, to propose the creation of an impartial commission of enquiry into the use of psychiatry to suppress dissent anywhere. The college had in mind "a broadly based group of psychiatrists of high repute, drawn from a number of countries". As the WHO and WPA had proved incapable of action, it favoured an *ad hoc* body. Also, "We consider it a matter of urgent necessity that practical steps should be taken in the immediate future."[138]

The Erevan conference and the Serbsky visit had in many ways proved to be stalemates: the Soviet authorities had obtained only a part of what they wanted, and the visiting psychiatrists had failed to take any effective initiatives of the type urged by the dissenters and by sections of Western opinion. But now the authorities could see from the college vote that, at least in one country, the net effect of all the publicity generated was the exact opposite of what they had hoped.

The Cases of Shikhanovich and Plyushch and Developments in France

Against this background the trial of Shikhanovich was an increasing embarrassment. It could no longer be delayed, as his arrest had occurred more than a year before, and support for him was steadily growing. In January 1973 he had been invited to lecture in Britain, and the next month colleagues in Holland, America, Israel, and Britain began to send a steady stream of letters on his behalf to the Soviet authorities.[139] At the same time Sakharov and his associates issued insistent appeals, usually reported at least briefly in the world press.[140] In September a French friend testified to Shikhanovich's eminent sanity in a moving letter in *Le Monde*, and a month later the BBC's Moscow correspondent did likewise in a broadcast.[141]

But the weightiest protest arrived on the eve of his trial in late November. This was a telegram from five members of the 1967 US mental health mission, among them Judge Bazelon, and five other eminent American psychiatrists, including, in their personal capacities, the president of the WPA, Dr Rome, and the president and president-elect of the APA, Drs Freedman and Spiegel. It read in part:

We are deeply concerned that, based on prior psychiatric determination, he might be found mentally incompetent or insane, while the evidence of witnesses suggests that he is fully mentally competent. We are profoundly concerned that this would constitute a violation of basic principles both of psychiatric practice and of criminal justice. We who have known and worked with Soviet authorities in the fields of psychiatry and law urge you to put our concerns at rest by conducting an open trial of Shikhanovich, allowing foreign observers to be present.[142]

Although these requests went unheeded, they were certainly heard. Shikhanovich was dispatched only to an OPH, not an SPH, and within the unprecedentedly short time of six months he regained his freedom.

Meanwhile, his case acted as a catalyst in reviving concern in France about Soviet abuses. This had faded soon after the Committee against the Special Psychiatric Hospitals in the USSR (CSPHU), mentioned earlier in the chapter, had directed a forthright letter of enquiry to Petrovsky in June 1972.[143] Although the letter had eventually been signed by 350 doctors and psychologists, little more took place in France until the

CSPHU came alive again in response to the WPA conference and the Shikhanovich case.

In September 1973 a similar group of signatories appealed to the WPA and the psychiatrists about to confer in Erevan. It pointed out that Petrovsky had not replied to the probing enquiries of the previous year, which now, more urgently than ever, needed to be submitted to senior Soviet psychiatrists at the conference. Therefore, "We ask the WPA president to assume at the conference the responsibilities we expect of him and to intervene in this way. We support those psychiatrists present at the conference who, sharing our anxiety and concerns, are prepared to pose these questions, which seem to us essential."[144] The signatories considered it especially important that a medical commission should make an "on the ground" investigation in the USSR.

These and other initiatives contributed to the formation in the new year of an "International Committee of Mathematicians for the Defence of Yury Shikhanovich and Leonid Plyushch" (ICM).[145] An additional, special factor was that Shikhanovich had translated into Russian works by some of France's most eminent mathematicians. Thus it was not difficult for the ICM to collect the signatures of 550 mathematicians under an appeal for his immediate release. In February 1974 an ICM delegation handed this document to the Soviet embassy in Paris, together with a gift of mathematical volumes inscribed to Shikhanovich. While the books were accepted for transmission to him, officials professed almost total ignorance about him and Plyushch, and denied that psychiatry had ever been abused in the USSR. The only special hospitals were "those reserved, for example, for members of the Academy, where the conditions and medical treatment are even better than in the ordinary hospitals". The visitors expressed their scepticism, and also asked that no obstacles be put in the way of visits to their two colleagues by French mathematicians.[146]

Some weeks later the embassy wrote to the ICM, giving the official version of the two cases. It added that Western psychiatrists including Rome, Freedman and de la Fuente had recently heard the case histories of Plyushch and Shikhanovich and expressed no doubts about their "mental illness and consequent non-responsibility". In reply the two best-known organizers of the ICM, Henri Cartan and Laurent Schwartz, disputed this assertion and enclosed the American telegram in support of Shikhanovich quoted earlier, signed by Rome and Freedman. In addition the ICM secretary, Michel Broué, heard later from Freedman:

> ... I was surprised and saddened to read the letter from the USSR embassy. ... We had been asked by our colleagues to treat the Soviet meeting with high regard for the confidentiality of the material presented. ... The letter you enclose breaches the confidentiality. I must therefore point out that while the case of Plyushch was reported, *that of Shikhanovich was not.* Secondly, the meeting left me particularly unsatisfied and I, in the name of the APA, have renewed our request for further meetings and the opportunity to examine cases in question. ... [Our italics][147]

The ICM grew rapidly, attracting members in thirteen countries, and stimulating many protests: 662 mathematicians in the US signed one petition, 234 in Japan another, and 133 in India a third.[148] After Shikhanovich had been released in July, clearly in response to the pressures from abroad, the committee focused its attention on Plyushch. Information and appeals about him from the USSR had become steadily more alarming since the autumn of 1973, and the ICM and French psychiatrists were active in responding.

When, for example, Sakharov and five colleagues appealed to international humanitarian organizations in February 1974 to save Plyushch's life, seventeen psychiatrists issued an urgent call to all French and foreign doctors to take appropriate action. They were appalled to learn that drug treatment had made Plyushch unable to read or write or take exercise. And they had already sent a telegram to Premier Kosygin making the three demands specifically requested by Sakharov's group: that an international commission inspect the Dnepropetrovsk SPH and similar institutions; that foreign psychiatrists be allowed to examine Plyushch; and that he be transferred to a hospital abroad to recover his health.[149]

In August Sakharov appealed to an international congress of mathematicians in Vancouver "to pass a motion in defence of Plyushch, and to do everything possible to save him". The ICM replied: "We applaud your courage in defending Soviet mathematician Leonid Plyushch. We will work to save Plyushch." It also organized an unofficial meeting at the congress, as a result of which almost 1,000 participants from no less than 31 countries signed a petition calling for his release.[150]

A Second False Start in the USA

The short-lived spurt of concern in the USA about Soviet abuses following the APA's telegram of September 1973 bears a remarkable resemblance to that of February–April 1972. Both episodes turned out to be false starts, and for similar reasons.

As we have seen, the APA's attempt to initiate a serious American-Soviet dialogue on abuses in each other's countries soon collapsed. Freedman's request for further discussion in 1974 evoked no positive response. On the other hand, we may note that the American Psychological Association resolved to consult the APA with a view to "joint action, if such is indicated, to protest Soviet practices";[151] that the American Psycho-analytical Association wrote to Snezhnevsky condemning the USSR's use of psychiatry in its "totalitarian assaults on human rights";[152] that the APA's *Psychiatric News* reported the Sakharov group's urgent appeal for Plyushch of February 1974;[153] and that the journal *Psychiatric Opinion* devoted most of its issue of that month to the involuntary hospitalization of dissenters, especially in the Soviet Union.[154]

But Chodoff, a member of the *ad hoc* APA group discussed early in the chapter, was nonetheless justified in feeling discouraged when he gave an interview to *Psychiatric News* in March: "I think APA ought to be tougher and not so naïve. . . . We ought to seriously consider the course of action of the National Academy of Sciences. We ought to consider whether to continue relations with them on such a friendly basis."[155] He noted that no action had resulted from the APA's resolution of May 1972 urging the establishment of an international agency to guard against hospitalization for political reasons. And he felt that Western psychiatrists had been "kind of conned" at the Serbsky meeting, which the Soviets had exploited for propaganda purposes.

This view of the American scene was in our opinion accurate; yet its publication provoked no upsurge of concern. We suggest several reasons for this. First, the APA was becoming preoccupied with a critical study of the psychiatrist's rôle in American society—a form of self-examination. Second, when the attempt at American-Soviet dialogue broke down, there was no alternative strategy to replace it. True, Freedman initiated discussions on an *ad hoc* international project which would formulate universal standards concerning involuntary commitment; but the project, while potentially of considerable value to Soviet dissenters, seemed over-ambitious, and two years later had not got off the ground.[156] The third, less tangible, reason concerned the effect of détente and the Soviet-American schizophrenia research agreement. A penetrating article in *Science* by Deborah Shapley probed exactly this issue in March 1974. She interviewed most of the Americans involved and concluded that the agreement "may be endangered because of growing doubts on the American side about the Soviet Union's motives".[157] Central to the doubts was the issue of abuse, especially as there was "some evidence that the Soviet authorities use the mental health exchanges for propaganda purposes to whitewash their psychiatric system". Dr Bertram Brown, director of NIMH, the government body in charge of the exchanges, had repeatedly raised the question of abuse: "I received assurances it wasn't so, and remained sceptical." But Brown preferred to continue the exchange, because even if only a little useful research was accomplished, this was better than nothing. Moreover, Sakharov and other dissenters had called for scientific contacts to be maintained; these were "a form of life insurance" to Soviet scientists. However, Brown argued, "If, when they do send people over here, the Russians only send second-rate researchers, or people who are politically safe, that would be a reason to withdraw."

Up to now little real exchange had occurred: while a number of Americans had visited the USSR, no Soviet psychiatrists had reciprocated. A work protocol apparently acceptable to both sides in October 1973 had been signed by Brown in November, but not—four months later—by the Soviets.

The US psychiatrists who had been to Russia were "convinced that the Medvedev and Bukovsky charges are at least in part true". Dr Irwin Kopin, moreover, now believed that the agreement was a "front" for both sides—"for the Soviets to whitewash themselves and for Nixon to pursue his policy of détente". Along with others, Shapley wrote, "he says the group has 'intermittently' considered pulling out". Shapley's own conclusion was: "Of all the science and health accords, this agreement appears to be the one where the professional and political differences between the two sides are most evident. As one of the participants summarized: 'It's a microcosm of détente'."

In June 1974 a clue emerged regarding the Soviet reluctance to develop the schizophrenia exchange. When the Joint Committee on Health met in Moscow, the Russians asked the Americans flatly for a statement by them denying that dissenters were improperly hospitalized. Dr Paul Ehrlich, an American delegate, later told the press: "We indicated such a statement couldn't be issued because we don't have the data. We avoided making any kind of statements that would confirm or deny their use of mental facilities for dissidents."[158] According to Ehrlich, the Americans had suggested that this issue should not "stand in the way of our developing relationship. They [the Russians] don't feel they improperly use their mental health facilities."

The episode confirmed the earlier impression of Americans involved in the exchange: Petrovsky would not allow the joint research to be finalized until he could report to his superiors that he had extracted a suitable whitewash of Soviet psychiatry from the Americans. We might also note that Ehrlich's statement that the US government could not take a position for lack of data sounds odd when we recall that the Royal College felt it had enough evidence the previous year to condemn Soviet abuses unequivocally.

In all these circumstances public debate on the issue virtually ceased in the US for two years.

The Overall Situation in mid-1974

With the release of Shikhanovich, Grigorenko and Gershuni in the summer and autumn of 1974, and with no well-known dissenters now being newly interned, the only such person still in a hospital was Plyushch. At the same time, information on Gluzman became more abundant. Thus, as Bukovsky had been kept steadily in the public eye since 1971, there was— until Plyushch's release in January 1976—a trio of young men for whom Western public opinion interceded with, as we shall see, varying degrees of insistence.

Events in Britain 1974–76
Action by Western psychiatrists on behalf of Gluzman, a colleague with whom they could readily identify, was in general rather weak in 1972–73. His case featured often enough in the intensive press debate in Britain of June–October 1973; but the KGB's foresight in having him sentenced for offences other than the real one, and the pretence by Venediktov, Snezhnevsky and others that they knew nothing about him until November 1973, did not assist the build-up of a strong campaign. Nor did a memorandum about him by Dr Leigh, circulated that month.[159] This stated: "the following facts have been established"; and then purveyed what became for a year the official line—that Gluzman had never been a psychiatrist and his case had no connection with Grigorenko. There was no cautionary note to point out the puzzling contradiction with the careful account of Gluzman's case that Sakharov had written a year earlier.

In 1974, by contrast, the Royal College began to discuss Gluzman's case seriously. In May both the *Chronicle*'s account of his trial and the testimony of an émigré friend became available, and in September another friend, the well-known writer Viktor Nekrasov, settled in Paris and provided further evidence.[160] Two months later an eminent German psychiatrist Professor von Baeyer devoted part of a letter in the *British Medical Journal* to Gluzman.[161] In addition, Sakharov issued a new call, this time to the presidents of nine national psychiatric associations. It ended: "I appeal for your help, relying on your understanding and compassion and on your feelings of professional solidarity. Gluzman is a colleague of whom his profession should be proud. Today he needs your defence and support. Please help him."[162]

Under these circumstances Snezhnevsky was forced to admit, when replying in December to a letter from the college's president, Sir Martin Roth, that Gluzman had indeed had some psychiatric training and clinical experience.[163] This fact was further underlined when the manuscript of the *Manual* by him and Bukovsky reached the West. In translation, the work made a strong impact on those psychiatrists who read it. The *Manual* also impressed journalists and thereby helped to maintain the steady flow of items on Soviet abuse in the British press.[164] This had picked up in October 1974, with the arrival in Britain of Viktor Fainberg, the first ex-victim to devote himself to an unrelenting campaign on the issue. The emigration from Leningrad to London in April 1975 of Dr Marina Voikhanskaya, who joined him in his struggle, further heightened public interest.[165]

A lead also came from Roth when he published a reply to Snezhnevsky in March. After reviewing Sakharov's appeal and other available documents, he concluded: "I believe that psychiatrists in the USSR have a special responsibility to our profession to publish a full account of what is known about the case of Dr Gluzman and to do all they can to mitigate his plight. Everything ought to be done to secure this young man's release from imprisonment. I hope you will feel able to intervene on his behalf."[166]

Not long after, in July 1975, Snezhnevsky received a less polite communication from Roth: "On behalf of the Royal College of Psychiatrists I wish to protest in the strongest terms against the continued incarceration of Gluzman, Bukovsky and Plyushch, which appears a perversion of psychiatric practice and denial of natural justice. Your refusal to take action or to respond constitutes a slur on our profession."[167]

This telegram was followed at once by an animated debate at the college's annual general meeting which resulted in the dispatch of a cable to Gluzman in his camp: "We are sending you this message of support and friendship, and would assure you we will continue our efforts to relieve your present plight."[168]

At this meeting Professor Rees, the WPA treasurer, succeeded Roth as college president. Afterwards, according to a press release, he noted that "national professional bodies could have a big influence on the behaviour of countries abusing psychiatry".[169]

Other developments kept public interest at a high level from then until the time of writing in autumn 1976. In September 1975 an off-shoot from the Working Group was formed—the Campaign against Psychiatric Abuse. Chaired by Dr Henry Dicks, a doyen of British psychiatry and a predecessor of Roth and Rees, it served as a vehicle for Fainberg and other activists, who organized a series of effective public meetings.[170] These passed resolutions and sent telegrams to the Soviet authorities —not only about the trio of Gluzman, Plyushch and Bukovsky, but also about new cases like those of Vyacheslav Igrunov and Valentyn Moroz. In addition, Amnesty International published in November a carefully documented report, *Prisoners of Conscience in the USSR: their Treatment and Conditions*. Part of this analysed the situation of dissenters interned in mental hospitals —a theme specially emphasized in the Amnesty campaign which accompanied publication in several countries.[171] And thirdly, the threat of a new trial of Gluzman in connection with his *Manual* was publicized and caused alarm.[172] Against this background the college passed a new resolution the same month:

> This meeting, noting reports of continuing abuses of psychiatry for political purposes, urges the officers, council and members of our college (1) to sustain their efforts at national level and through our connections with the World Psychiatric Association and other international organizations to secure cessation of such abuses wherever these are discovered to be part of state policy, and in particular (2) to try to bring relief to the prolonged suffering of Soviet citizens Leonid Plyushch, Dr Semyon Gluzman, Vladimir Bukovsky and Zinovy Krasivsky, by our taking the initiative in exploring the possibilities of the formation and despatch of a commission of psychiatrists and jurists to investigate these persons' condition on the spot.[173]

The first draft of this motion, which Snezhnevsky as an honorary fellow of the college received in advance, led him to write to the president with the aim of influencing the meeting. He declared:

> The Royal College has taken a very dubious function of intervening into the inner affairs of national psychiatric associations and using mentally-ill patients for political purposes. I sincerely hope that none of the members . . . seriously believes that in the Soviet Union mentally-healthy people could be forcibly put into mental hospitals.[174]

In fulfilment of the second part of the motion, the college explored how to raise funds for a commission, and also received a favourable response to its approach to the Bar Council concerning the participation of jurists.[175]

The Plyushch Campaign and Developments in France and Switzerland
In October 1974 persistent reports indicated that the Soviet régime was interested in a possible exchange with Chile of high-level political prisoners.[176] Although denied by Moscow, the reports gained credence from the fact that the authorities had by now not only, as we have seen, released all except one of the well-known dissenters in mental hospitals, but had also— unprecedentedly—just released two political prisoners from labour camps only midway through their sentences and allowed them to emigrate.[177]

The possibility of a prisoner exchange apparently evaporated when the Chileans were indiscreet enough to publicize it, and two years were to pass before it re-emerged. Soon Plyushch's chances of release probably vanished too, as Russian-American relations deteriorated sharply. The Soviet government had grudgingly agreed in October to accept the terms of the "Jackson amendment" on freedom of emigration; this was the only way it could gain access to new American technology and large quantities of subsidized credits. At the beginning of January, however, the "Stevenson amendment" snatched most of these credits from under its nose by limiting their volume to a mere fifth of what Dr Kissinger had been promising.[178] To the Soviets this was betrayal, and their im- mediate reaction was an atavistic reversion to type: now Plyushch would *not* be released, he would be "treated" until ready to make a full and humiliating recantation.

Whether or not our interpretation of Plyushch's exceptional case is broadly correct, in December 1974 his condition aroused serious alarm in his wife. A stream of appeals emanated from Moscow;[179] one was addressed directly to the ICM by Tatyana Khodorovich and a friend. They called for urgent intervention, explaining:

> . . . For a year and a half he has been forcibly administered massive doses of neuroleptic drugs. . . . The aim of the

"treatment" is to destroy his personality and force him to accept the official ideology. Plyushch's wife is being terrorized . . . KGB agents hound her in full view of everyone. The aim: to make her keep silent. We draw your attention to the quite special danger which these facts represent: in a very large country which possesses enormous power, it is becoming normal to use modern medicines in a forcible and arbitrary way with the aim of "correcting" free spirits and destroying their consciences.[180]

As we saw in chapter 7, Tatyana Plyushch applied to initiate a criminal action against the SPH staff for deliberately mistreating her husband, and called for the help of "independent international associations of jurists and psychiatrists". In particular, she asked for Dr Low-Beer to participate in the proceedings as a psychiatrist, and for a Western lawyer to take part as well. In February Low-Beer announced his agreement in a letter to *Nature*, and a well-known barrister, Jean-Jacques de Félice, did the same from Paris.[181] Although the legal authorities eventually refused to accept the case for trial, Mrs Plyushch's initiative had helped to throw them onto the defensive. So had the arrival in the West of the Bukovsky-Gluzman *Manual*, carrying the dedication "To Leonid Plyushch, a victim of psychiatric terror". And in Paris Nekrasov began to speak up not only for Gluzman, but also for another of his friends, Plyushch.[182]

To focus the humanitarian efforts in many countries the ICM designated 23 April 1975 as International Plyushch Day. Numerous press articles and readers' letters about Plyushch appeared and telegrams in his support were sent.[183] A letter in Australia, for example, was signed by 88 mathematicians, a telegram from Toronto by 153 scientists, psychiatrists and jurists. Among twelve signatories from Rome was a member of the Italian Communist Party's central committee. And in Paris the ICM and Amnesty International gave a press conference at which two special messages were made public. One was from Tatyana Plyushch, of which we give a few extracts:

The Leonid Plyushch known to me, to his children, relatives and friends, this Leonid Plyushch no longer exists. There exists: an exhausted man, driven to the last brink of suffering, losing his memory, and his ability to read, write and think, and terribly ill. . . .

I am boundlessly grateful to all the mathematicians abroad, to all who are concerned with Leonid's fate. . . . Let me be given back my husband, ill as they have made him, and let us then be allowed to leave this country. [184]

The second message was from an eminent Moscow mathematician and member of the Human Rights Committee, Igor Shafarevich. He wrote: "There are people whose destiny it is to go far beyond the limits of their biography or background. They generalize many people's experiences and become symbols. The name of General Grigorenko has been such a symbol for five years. The same is true of the mathematician Leonid Plyushch." Shafarevich then addressed himself directly to the Western campaigners:

The range and impetus of your endeavour is a ray of hope in our bitter age. But you are defending much more than just one person. You are defending all those who are in the same plight . . . but whose names remain unknown to you.

And I am convinced that ultimately your endeavour will not remain without significance for yourselves. The symbolic fate of Plyushch is a lesson which can help you to comprehend better you own life, and to evaluate your future, the future of your children, the future of your country, and the future of all the human race.[185]

The campaign for Plyushch was also boosted by an Amnesty International symposium on the use of psychiatry for political purposes held in Geneva. Among the speakers were Nekrasov, Fainberg and Voikhanskaya. The last having emigrated only a few days earlier, the symposium could hear the first public testimony ever given by a Soviet psychiatrist with direct knowledge of malpractice. Another speaker was the Belgian, Anthony de Meeûs, who had recently published an illuminating review of the subject.[186]

The participants adopted a "Declaration of Geneva" which called on medical organizations to speak out more militantly than hitherto on Soviet abuses and boycott those involved. It also elected a permanent committee to gather signatures on the declaration and to promote and co-ordinate actions in various countries. The meeting received support from the Swiss Psychiatry Society, which had already made useful interventions with the Soviet authorities in 1973.[187]

The ICM's next and most remarkable initiative proved to be the last that was needed. The Mutualité, one of Paris's largest halls, was packed for a meeting on 23 October 1975 with 5,000 people, who vociferously demanded Plyushch's release. Numerous speakers represented the wide spectrum of mathematical, psychiatric, humanitarian, educational, legal, student and Ukrainian groups which had co-sponsored the meeting. Dr Low-Beer travelled from London to speak for the Working Group.[188]

The next day, the French Communist Party decided that the pressure was now too strong. If it was to retain credibility on the left, it must at last jump on the band-wagon. Its newspaper *L'Humanité* declared: "If it is true—and unfortunately until now the contrary has not been proved—that this mathematician is interned in a psychiatric hospital solely because he took a position against certain aspects of Soviet policy or against the régime itself, we can only confirm with the greatest clarity our total disapproval and our demand that he be freed as soon as possible."[189]

A day later, Tatyana Plyushch was summoned to the MVD in Kiev and told that her request to emigrate with her husband had been granted.

On 10 January 1976 Plyushch and his family arrived in Austria. He had had no chance to meet his friends in Kiev and Moscow who had worked tirelessly to save his life: the authorities had freed him from custody on the Soviet-Hungarian border and put him on a train. A month later he had recovered sufficiently from his profound exhaustion and drug-induced Parkinson's disease to provide a personal account of his experiences to the world's press, and to call for renewed efforts to free Bukovsky, Gluzman and the dissenters still held in the Dnepropetrovsk SPH.[190]

The campaign by the ICM and Amnesty, the publication of a book on the case in French, and Plyushch's press conference and subsequent appeals for the KGB's victims, all generated a powerful commitment by French psychiatrists to oppose Soviet abuses.[191] In 1976 four of their professional organizations joined forces to press the USSR to allow an impartial investigation of the charges, and to ask for the Royal College's collaboration.[192] They received active support from their psychologist colleagues, who had been conducting their own study for two years and who carried out a successful campaign of lobbying at an international psychology congress in Paris in July 1976.[193]

A Soviet Counter-blast

Plyushch's release and press conference triggered off a fresh spate of Soviet propaganda articles and broadcasts—the first for two years—designed to discredit his testimony. The alleged words of Drs Rome, Perris, Angst, de la Fuente and others, whitewashing Soviet psychiatry, were pulled out of the files and pressed into new service, alongside weary denials and apologetics from Nadzharov and Morozov. Vigorous efforts were made to publicize instances of psychiatric abuse in the West.[194]

A dominant theme in the new campaign was the poorly documented claim that most of the dissenters who had been hospitalized and then later allowed to emigrate had subsequently been rehospitalized abroad: this demonstrated the reality and permanence of their illnesses. Among those named was Viktor Fainberg, who, when a British Communist paper incautiously reprinted the charge, sued the paper for damages. On learning the truth, it quickly paid him £750 and published a full apology.[195] Even more fantastic was the statement by a Soviet medical correspondent that Alexander Volpin had, in a state of remission, "returned to the USSR with his peculiar 'views', was here supplied with suitable work and an allowance, and now enjoys the concessions provided in the Soviet Union for all such invalids".[196] In fact, Volpin was busily teaching mathematics at Boston University. . . .

The authorities also resorted to the device of using dissenters' trials as a forum for publicizing denials of abuse. Now, though, there was a new twist. Not Snezhnevsky, but Plyushch's doctor Lydia Lyubarskaya tried to convince a court in Vilnius that Sergei Kovalyov had told deliberate lies in an intercession he made for Plyushch.[197] And Colonel Pruss, just retired from Dnepropetrovsk, carried out the same function *vis-à-vis*

Andrei Tverdokhlebov.[198] But as neither put up a convincing performance, their testimony was little used in Soviet propaganda.

The WPA and the 6th World Congress in Honolulu, August 1977
In 1975 the APA agreed to host the WPA's 6th world congress of psychiatry in 1977 (28 August–3 September) in Honolulu.

Soon after this development, Dr Leigh found himself under pressure to change his line on the Soviet issue. Individuals in the APA felt that this line had facilitated the whitewash of serious abuses and that the WPA's statutes in no way prevented an honest and open debate on the issue—rather the reverse. Moreover, as the APA provided a quarter of the WPA's regular budget and was also putting up $40,000 for the Honolulu congress, it had every right, they believed, to have these points seriously considered.[199]

The pressure was reinforced by the publicized proposal of some British psychiatrists that the Royal College might disaffiliate from the WPA altogether.[200] The discussion of this at the college's meeting in July 1975 helps to explain the following sentence in the subsequent press release: "Dr Denis Leigh, secretary-general of the WPA, associated himself and the WPA with the message to Dr Gluzman, and also with the decision to consider more deeply than hitherto the whole matter of psychiatric abuse and to seek ways of bringing pressure to bear on countries where abuses occur."[201]

The whole episode showed that, when necessary, Leigh could act flexibly and without the inhibition of some non-existent statute: on 6 July, prior to the college meeting, he had been quoted in the press as saying that the statutes did not allow the WPA to take a stand on the Soviet issue.[202] Three days later he did precisely that. The stand taken, moreover, was very different from the WPA's previous and barely concealed policy of trying to protect Soviet psychiatry from criticism.

A specific concern of Leigh's critics prior to this *volte-face* had been a letter from Morozov to the *British Medical Journal* (*BMJ*) in July 1974. Here the Serbsky director had repeated Vartanyan's lie that during the Western psychiatrists' visit to his institute the WPA Executive Committee had "verified that all five of the so-called dissidents were suffering from mental illnesses during the legal examination".[203] When asked by a journalist a year later why he had still published no denial, Leigh said that the matter would probably be discussed at the executive committee's meeting in November 1975. The critics could not understand, however, why such overt manipulation of the WPA was regarded as a matter of negligible importance which could wait for sixteen months.[204]

Here too the college meeting showed that he could act flexibly when necessary. Given its mood, and additional pressure from the lay and medical press, he began to feel that he must publicly rebut Morozov and also explain the WPA's policy as a whole. For example, *The Times* had written in an editorial:

> There is now overwhelmingly convincing evidence that the Soviet authorities quite deliberately use their mental-health service to punish or intimidate political dissidents, a horrible and wicked act of state. Just as it is impossible for a national medical body to ignore irregular behaviour by individual members, it is also impossible for a world body to turn a blind eye to deliberate malpractice; the Soviet psychiatrists who lend themselves to this vile conduct are every bit as guilty as the politicians who order it. . . . What is needed is for Soviet practices to be openly and freely debated without regard to whether or not Soviet representatives walk out. If they wish to sever their links with world bodies they are free to do so.[205]

Leigh's denial of Morozov appeared in the *BMJ* on 30 August 1975. But he side-stepped the challenge posed in *The Times*, as also in the *BMJ*,[206] preferring to describe instead the Mexico congress, his consultations with medical and human-rights bodies, the setting up of a working party on ethics, a seminar on human rights in Strasbourg, and the plan to have a session on ethics in Honolulu. His comment was: "Can it be seriously maintained in view of what has been done, that the WPA has dragged its feet or been ambiguous in its attitude towards the ethical problems of psychiatry?" As for the idea that the WPA might set up a body capable of carrying out impartial enquiries, the association had studied the impressive facilities of the Commission on Human Rights of the Council of Europe, and as a result he concluded: "If justice is to be done, then judicial methods must be used, as at the Commission of Human Rights. The creation of such a commission is quite beyond the financial, professional and organizational scope of international associations such as the WPA. It is either naiveté, ignorance or hypocrisy to suggest otherwise."

With regard to Gluzman, the WPA had supported the college's recent telegram to him, and it was an advantage that WPA officers could meet officials of the USSR and "discuss quite freely and directly the situation of some doctors in that country".

The full implications of some of Leigh's points were clarified in his newsletter two months later:

> I would suggest that we ought to make a declaration at Hawaii of the general principles underlying the ethical practice of psychiatry, very similar to the declarations of the WMA at their meetings. It would be a matter for each national member society whether or not to draw up a detailed code on matters affecting practice in its own country. Thus we avoid problems connected with religion, national policies, forms of political belief and so forth, and can concentrate on the principles.[207]

It now became clear that the ethics committee, whose creation he had advocated since 1971, would be concerned only with principles and not with concrete cases of abuse; the latter could not be investigated anyway, as perfect judicial procedures were unattainable even—as regards Soviet malpractices—by a powerful body like the European Commission of Human Rights, let alone the WPA;* so the only viable path was the quiet diplomacy which the WPA was—supposedly—carrying out already.

Subsequent WPA seminars on ethics in Venezuela and London confirmed that this was indeed Leigh's approach.

More disturbing, though, was the ambiguity of his position on actual Soviet abuses. He had curiously left uncorrected a

---

* The same argument could, we might note, be applied to the investigation of the Nazi concentration camps under Hitler and many other contemporary horrors.

Times leader which stated that he had not supported the Royal College's actions;[208] his *BMJ* letter failed to substantiate the college's statement that he and the WPA intended to consider more deeply than before how to combat abuses; he travelled to Moscow to be a guest at the All-Union Society's congress in December 1975 and was quoted in the press as having nothing but praise for Soviet psychiatry;[209] when Vartanyan came to London for a WPA meeting on ethics in June 1976 he repeatedly and vigorously defended the very man whose lie about the WPA Executive Committee in the *Korsakov Journal* still lay uncorrected two years later;[210] and at this time he could still state regarding conditions in the SPH: "I have no evidence about cruelty. It is hypothetical as far as I am concerned."[211]

In 1976 these episodes helped to provoke a serious challenge to the WPA's position. First the college passed this resolution in May:

> The Royal College of Psychiatrists repeats its support for the steps taken by Council against abuses of psychiatry in the Soviet Union and requests Council to do all in its power at the next world congress of the World Psychiatric Association to secure the passing of the following resolution or one closely similar: "The World Psychiatric Association taking note of extensive evidence of the systematic abuse of psychiatry for political purposes in the USSR joins in the condemnation of those practices which has already been made by the British Royal College of Psychiatrists as well as other bodies."[212]

Then in September, the APA submitted an urgent request to the WPA that a special session on concrete abuses of psychiatry be added to the agenda for Honolulu.[213]

In this way the stage was set by the Americans for a public session, with papers and discussion, and by the college for a debate in the general assembly. Two key member societies had asserted themselves. It remained to be seen, however, whether —in all the circumstances—a Soviet delegation would still come to Honolulu, and also how the ultimate outcome would differ from that in Mexico City six years earlier.

The Release and Emigration of Bukovsky

Certainly the Soviet authorities made things harder for themselves by several actions they took in 1976. First they provoked a powerful and widespread campaign of protest when they threatened to transfer Valentyn Moroz, a Ukrainian historian and long-standing political prisoner, from a prison to an SPH. They eventually backed off under the pressure.[214] Second, they interned under civil commitment a number of dissenters including Vladimir Borisov, Pyotr Starchik and Alexander Argentov, who either were, or quickly became, well known, and thereby provoked new protests. And in December they released Vladimir Bukovsky when he had served only half his sentence, and exchanged him for the Chilean Communist leader Luis Corvalan.[215] Bukovsky was thus free to approach the world's psychiatrists in person, and well in advance of the Honolulu congress.

In the autumn of 1976 a group of dissenters formed a committee to work for the release of Pyotr Starchik. The committee soon evolved into the Working Commission for the Investigation of the Use of Psychiatry for Political Purposes, and was joined by two psychiatrists, who, however, remained anonymous. After succeeding in its campaign for Starchik, it turned its attention to other interned dissenters, including Vladimir Borisov and Yury Belov. In March 1977 documents on some 200 such dissenters were seized from the home of commission member Alexander Podrabinek, a medical assistant, just after the group had announced Borisov's release.* It attributed the release to Western pressure and expressed the belief that the "support of a large section of world public opinion is the most important factor in the struggle against the use of psychiatry for political purposes". "However," the group noted, "there are still hundreds of prisoners of conscience in Soviet psychiatric hospitals and they are in need of defence and support. Their names are little known or not known at all, a fact which makes their situation all the more difficult and enables the police and psychiatrists to act arbitrarily."

---

* See UPI report from Moscow, sent on 15 March; Amnesty International document EUR 46/17/77.

EPILOGUE

WE BELIEVE THAT there is now ample evidence to show that psychiatry in the Soviet Union is being used systematically to suppress dissent.

Sane citizens are interned in mental hospitals for indeterminate periods until they learn to conform. Prior to their internment they have, in most cases, functioned efficiently in society, and their families, friends and colleagues have regarded them as mentally healthy.

We estimate that the scale on which dissenters have been unjustly interned is small in relation to the number of them imprisoned in labour camps. But we also believe that this phenomenon is an integral part of a much wider abuse of psychiatry, which involves the labelling of many forms of social deviance as mental illness. If this is so, then our book has examined only the tip of a large iceberg.

Whatever the scale, however, numbers are not of the essence. The direct victims of the Nazi medical experiments were not especially numerous, and only 350 out of 90,000 German doctors are reckoned to have committed medical crimes.[1] Yet had Hitler's régime survived and expanded its empire, the number of victims and anti-humane doctors would probably have multiplied enormously.

We are further convinced that the treatment of some dissenters in Soviet mental hospitals is not only barbaric and degrading but also sinister. Attempts to extract recantations with the aid of drugs bring Soviet psychiatry to almost the same moral territory as that occupied by the Nazis. The victim is sacrificed to corrupt medicine twice: first his views are ruled to be those of a madman, then he undergoes forcible "treatment" to be purged of them.

If such practices are not resisted, they may become irretrievably entrenched and, at the same time, spread gradually to other countries. For they have an obvious potential appeal not only to repressive régimes of left and right, but also to authoritarian groups in what are still relatively free societies.

It is not surprising, we feel, that medicine should have been worst abused in the two most powerful totalitarian states yet produced by history. The doings of the Nazi doctors are not in our view directly comparable with those of their Soviet counterparts; but certain common features obtain. Both types of practice derive from a total disregard for the rights of the individual; both serve the purpose of the ruling group; both receive justification from that group's ideology; and both, as mentioned above, are potentially open to abuse on a grand scale.

In the political culture generated by Soviet Communism, the suppression of dissent through psychiatry requires close collaboration between politicians and doctors. Yet the process is normally smooth and straightforward: mutual understanding is excellent. It is therefore apt for critics to attack both partners to the practice, but not forgetting that neither acts in isolation. In one sense the politicians are the more important target, as they can do what they did in 1972–73—order the KGB and the psychiatrists to stop the internment of well-known dissenters. But while this development was welcome, it did not and could not ensure that psychiatry ceased to be used as an instrument against lesser-known dissenters and social deviants. The officially promoted near-monopoly of the "Snezhnevsky school" has successfully moulded far too many Soviet psychiatrists for this to be achievable in any short period—even if the party leadership were to desire it.

This leadership is likely to develop such a desire only, we believe, if the political cost—in terms of Soviet loss of international prestige and respectability—becomes too great. By stopping the internment of well-known dissenters, the régime has, for the moment, kept the cost within bounds. As only this category of victim is really newsworthy for the Western press, the amount of unfavourable publicity incurred by the régime has diminished.

Thus the main burden of opposing the abuse now falls, in our view, on Western psychiatrists. They need to be concerned not with newsworthiness but with the inhumane practice of their profession, however obscure the victims. If they succeed in this, Soviet psychiatrists will find themselves under increasing attack within world medicine, subject to boycotts and even expulsion from important bodies. Such a development would once more be newsworthy, and the resulting bad publicity for the USSR could raise the political cost to the point where the régime felt it necessary to deprive the "Snezhnevsky school" of its dominance, or even to outlaw it.

We believe that responsible Western pressure will, if consistently and wisely applied, almost always have an important effect. It has already done so. But there is a long row to hoe. Pressure, boycotts, and threats of boycott should be carefully graduated and differentiated, depending on the individuals involved and other circumstances. Contacts and exchange with able psychiatrists not implicated in abuses should of course be maintained and developed in every possible way. Psychiatric and medical bodies, at national and international level, should study the routine Soviet methods of deception and manipulation, as documented in this book, and develop a consistent policy which will withstand them, based on well-thought-out principles. Perhaps the most important long-term goal is to have the Soviet prison mental hospitals inspected by a well-briefed international commission. At present such a goal may seem unrealistic, but, if pursued relentlessly, it may in the long term become feasible, i.e. after the régime has felt compelled to reform and humanize these institutions. If, at some stage, Soviet psychiatrists should threaten to walk out of particular international forums or organizations, or even carry out their threat, Western bodies should not, in our view, lose their nerve or change their principles. The Soviets will return sooner or later—and probably sooner: their régime's craving and need for acceptance and respectability is, in the post-Stalin era, one of its fundamental features.

If humane psychiatric values should ultimately gain the upper hand in the Soviet Union, one result might indeed be that all imprisoned dissenters would be held in labour camps and none in mental hospitals. If that were to happen, the dissenters would feel elated, their campaign to improve conditions in the camps would be given a boost, and an important victory over the dehumanizing trends in the modern world would have been won.

APPENDICES

APPENDIX I

VICTIMS OF SOVIET PSYCHIATRIC ABUSE: A REGISTER

Note on Abbreviations
Those used in this appendix extend beyond the list on pp. 463–64.
* = case involving civil commitment only (i.e., individuals *without*
an asterisk have been subject to criminal commitment);
Chr = *A Chronicle of Current Events* (see p. 463);
Bourdeaux = Michael Bourdeaux, *Patriarch and Prophets*, London,
Macmillan, 1969;
de Meeûs = see ref. 128 to chapter 10;
Kaznimye = Kaznimye sumasshestviem, Frankfurt, Possev, 1971;
Uncensored Russia = P. B. Reddaway, *Uncensored Russia*, London,
Cape, 1972;
E = Emigration; R = Religion; N = Nationalism; SPA = Social or
political activity; I = Inconvenient. The last five are explained
below.

We have included in the register below people who have, since
1962, been forcibly interned in an SPH or OPH as a result of the
peaceful expression of their beliefs. Half a dozen who have turned
to violence have been excluded, although they too may have been
victims of abuse.* Also excluded are (a) about 100 dissenters who
have been forcibly subjected to psychiatric examination (mostly in
the Serbsky Institute, where the process normally lasts a month),
but have then been ruled responsible and not interned in an SPH
or OPH,† and (b) a further 54 internees about whom the information so far available is not full enough for us to be able to classify
them, e.g. regarding the exact nature of their dissent, with reasonable confidence.‡

* Yury Bondarev (see Chr 39), Nikolai Demyanov, Anatoly Ilin, Pavel
Kuznetsov and Pyotr Trotsyuk-Kozlyuk (all Chr 41), and Vitaly Vodovozov
(document by V. Prussakov).
† Examples can be found in most issues of the *Chronicle*.
‡ (a) Held only or mainly *in Sychyovka SPH*: Boris Davarashvili (Chr 30,
Y. Krylsky); Petukhov and Rotshtein (Krylsky); Mykhaylo Klishch and I.
Uletsky (Chr 39, 41); and Father Chudakov, A. Denisov, M. Maksimov
and I. Makhayev (Chr 39). (b) *In Dnepropetrovsk SPH*: Anatoly Anisimov,

Thus if we add in the 210 dissenters on the register, the total number known to us who have been forced by the authorities to undergo psychiatric procedures or internment is about 365. Virtually none of these, the evidence suggests, would have consulted a psychiatrist had it depended on the wishes of them, their relatives and friends. With rare exceptions, the relatives and friends have regarded them as in no need of psychiatric care, let alone of compulsory treatment.

We should also note that the register includes a few dissenters in these categories: (a) those declared not responsible in Serbsky, their subsequent place of internment not yet being known to us; (b) sentenced prisoners transferred from a camp or prison to a prison psychiatric unit for a month or two as a form of intimidation, even if they have not then been ruled mentally ill and interned permanently in an SPH (Asselbaums, Lukyanenko, Moroz, Ogurtsov); and (c) one dissenter (Makarenko) subjected to so many forcible examinations as an out-patient that the degree of persecution became comparable to that of an internment.

Leonid Efimov and Popov (Chr 39); Viktor Maltsev (Chr 21, 39, L. Plyushch); and Shvedov, Fedosov, Morkovnikov and Palchevsky (Chr 21). (c) *In Chernyakhovsk SPH*: Agafonov, Leonid Kravchenko, Porosenkov and Shaporenko (Chr 41). (d) *In Leningrad SPH*: Lev Fyodorov and Ivan Frolkin (Chr 18); A. V. Kochkin, N. P. Galashov, Panov and Zharov (Chr 27); Panteleyev (Chr 27, CHR 2); and Zabolotny (Chr 27, 39, CHR 2). (e) *In Kazan SPH*: S. M. Stroganov (Chr 27, 39); and Elizaveta Marokhina (Yu. Iofe in *Grani*, 1974, No. 92–93). (f) *In Oryol SPH*: Victor Prikhodko (Chr 19, 39). (g) *In Tashkent SPH*: Lvov (Chr 36). (h) In high security section of *Ussuriisk OPH*: Yury Kryltsov (AS 2007). (i) Psychiatrically interned when serving a camp term: Albert Ugnachev (Chr 34); Ivan Sokulsky (Chr 10–12, 27, 34, where apparently mis-spelled Sakulsky); and V. Berezin (Chr 41). (j) Ruled not responsible, all in Serbsky, but subsequent SPH or OPH not known: Pavel Borovik and Denis Grigorev (Chr 11); Grachev, Nikolai Kopeiko and Ivan Kuzmin (Chr 32); and Alexander Chernogorov (Chr 41). (k) Interned under *civil commitment*: Shtein (in Pavlodar OPH; Chr 22); Nadezhda Gaidar and Alissa Ostrokhova (in Moscow OPHs; Yu. Orlov in AFP dispatch, 12.10.1976); Ivan Titov (in Moscow OPH; his own MS.); Georgy Musatov (OPH in Meshchersky village near Moscow; G. Fedotov letter to Dudko, 11.9.1976;) Viktor Pikhtovnikov (in Ashkhabad OPH, Turkmenia; his own MS.); A. I. Kovalchuk (in Rovno OPH; Baptist documents); Munya Vaisman (?; *Nasha strana*, Tel Aviv, 29.6.1972); and the monks Golovanov, Mirchuk and Shvoruk (Bourdeaux, p. 103). We should also note that the following may have been interned; they were charged as dissenters, then sent for examinations of which the outcome is not yet known: Vasily Trish (in Serbsky; Chr 32); Anatoly Uvarov (Serbsky; Chr 40); Ozhegov (Serbsky; Chr 34); and Anele Paškauskiene (Lukiški prison, Vilnius; Chr 37).

To reduce complex lives and episodes to entries in a chart is inevitably to oversimplify. Our purpose in this register is to provide in condensed form a much broader picture than could be given in our survey of victims in chapter 9, and also extensive data for further research. The entry on "residence" in column 2 normally indicates the town or area where the victim had his most permanent roots prior to his internment. The entry "cause of internment" in the same column is more tricky, and involves judgements based on all the available material about each individual. It denotes what we believe to be not the formal, but the real, underlying reason or reasons why the authorities acted. These reasons usually relate to recent dissenting action by the victim, but can also derive in part from his long-standing behaviour patterns, which may be of a different nature. For example, a long-time religious dissenter may decide, like Sidenko, to seek emigration; as a result he is interned. Thus the entry for him of E–R indicates both the immediate reason for internment and the probable, additional background reason. To put it another way, we believe that by interning Sidenko the authorities wished both to punish him for seeking emigration, and also to deter his fellow Pentecostalists from either doing likewise or committing other acts of dissent.

The category "nationalism" means that the dissent has concerned primarily the cultural, economic or religious rights of a particular nation such as the Ukrainians, Lithuanians, or Russians. "Social or political activity" covers virtually all types of dissent not embraced by the categories already mentioned, but to reduce its scope a little, we have created the small category "inconvenient". This separates— doubtless rather artificially in some cases—dissenters who have pursued a certain line with consistency from people who have "got in the way" of the authorities by resisting particular abuses of power, usually involving themselves, in a more *ad hoc* way.

Name	Birthdate; nationality; residence; cause of internment	Sources of information	Brief summary of case
Sergei Sergeyevich ALEKSEYENKO	1924; Ukrainian?; Kzyl-Orda; E	Chr 18	Army captain. Charged under articles 83 and 15 with trying to cross the border. Declared a schizophrenic and not responsible. In 1970–71 held in Leningrad SPH. Subsequent fate unknown.
A. ANDREYEV	?; Russian; ?; E	Chr 39, 41	In mid-1960s (?) tried to cross the frontier, apparently in the Far East, interned for about 6 years in Blagoveshchensk SPH (or the high-security wing of the OPH, before it was turned into an SPH in 1972). Escaped, caught, interned in Sychyovka SPH c. 1970 (?), released c. 1972–73.
Valery Nikolayevich ANDREYEV*	c. 1950; Russian; Dokuchayevsk, Donetsk Region, Ukraine; R	Pentecostal document	Led a dissolute life, converted to Pentecostalism, transformed, got a job as a labourer, sacked for being a believer. Applied for a new job, at medical exam asked by neurologist Anna Khailo if he was upset at sacking? He said no, because of his faith. She said he must be ill, and against protests of his family he was interned in an OPH (pos. Pobeda, Donetsk City) from December 1974 to February 1975, and given Triftazin and Haloperidol.
Mikhail Fyodorovich ANTONOV	c. 1935?; Russian; Moscow; SPA	Chr 7, 20, 39; Grani, 1971, No. 82, p. 114	Architect. Associate of totalitarian A. Fetisov (see below). Arrested in spring 1968, charged under article 70, ruled not responsible, sent to either Leningrad or Kazan SPH. Released by 1971.
Alexander Aleksandrovich ARGENTOV*	1951; Russian; Moscow; R	Chr 41, 42	Orthodox Christian belonging to an unofficial seminar on religious philosophy broken up by KGB in summer 1976. On 14 July 1976 interned in Moscow OPH No. 14, although had never been on psychiatric register. Dr A. Mazikov said his religion the only reason, and "We'll beat your religion out of you". Examined by commission only on 2 August, ruled mentally ill and in need of compulsory treatment. Released a few weeks later following a powerful campaign of protest in the USSR and abroad.

Name	Details	Source	Description
Boris Timofeyevich ARTYUSHCHENKO	1920; Ukrainian; Kursk; R	Baptist documents	Baptist, arrested in September 1970 for activity in unofficial Baptist Church, sentenced to three years. Interned in May 1973 in an OPH in the Komi republic, but apparently released soon after.
Teodor ASSELBAUMS	1923; Latvian; Latvia; E-N	Chr 39, 40, 42; AS 2229, 2697	Joined the partisans when forced collectivization occurred in Latvia in 1949, captured in 1952, sentenced to 25 years. In 1974 held in Perm camp 35, fought for prisoners' rights, applied to emigrate on release (due in July 1977). November 1974 sent to psychiatric section of Mordovian camps hospital. Doctor said "You've got nothing serious", then ordered intensive treatment with Aminazin, and warned him not to write complaints and not to renounce Soviet citizenship. February 1975 arrived back in Perm camp 35. 1976 wrote letter "with my last bits of strength". Highly regarded by camp friends, including I. Meshener and L. Yagman, now in Israel.
Rolan Teodorovich AVGUSTOV*	1941; Russian?; Uman (nr. Kiev); E	Chr 21	Electrician. In April 1971 detained at the entrance of US Embassy in Moscow after delivering statement renouncing his Soviet citizenship to the Presidium of Supreme Soviet. Forcibly interned in a Moscow OPH, then transferred to the Cherkassy regional OPH in Korsun-Shevchenko. Spent six weeks there. Diagnosed as schizophrenic.
Vladimir AVRAMENKO	1930; Ukrainian?; Moscow; SPA	Chr 39	An engineer, graduate of Moscow Aviation Institute. Read his own poems in company of his friends, in 1972 denounced to KGB and arrested, charged with "anti-Soviet content" of the poems, ruled not responsible, sent to Kazan SPH, still held there in 1976.
Iosif BADUK*	c. 1940?; Ukrainian; Ternopol?; R	Bourdeaux, p. 106	A novice at the Orthodox monastery in Pochaev in the West Ukraine, he went to do his military service. In 1962, while he was away, the authorities launched a brutal campaign to drive out the 140 monks, some of whom were interned in OPHs, and close the monastery. Press articles attacking it appeared over his name. He protested indignantly at this, was arrested, then interned in the Vinnitsa OPH. Unknown when released.

Name	Birthdate; nationality; residence; cause of internment	Sources of information	Brief summary of case
Vladimir Fyodorovich BALAKHONOV	1935; Russian; Moscow; SPA	Chr 33–40; ex-UN colleagues; AS 2229	1969–72 worked in secretariat of World Meteorological Office in Geneva; September 1972 asked for asylum in Switzerland, December 1972 returned to USSR because (a) could not bear separation from daughter, (b) promised by Soviet Embassy there would be no reprisals. January 1973 arrested, tried a year later for treason (article 64), sentence: twelve years. Protested strongly with fellow inmates against conditions in Perm Region Camp 35. January 1975 sent to psychiatric section of Mordovian camps hospital, although his fellows regarded him as perfectly normal. Summer 1975, after publicity on his case in West, returned to Perm camps, but to No. 36. Autumn 1975 transferred to Vladimir Prison as punishment for resistance activity.
Nikolai Ivanovich BARANOV	1936; Russian; Leningrad; SPA?	Chr 18, 27, 39; CHR 2	Worker. Arrested in Moscow prior to 1971, charged under article 70 but diagnosed as psychopathic and ruled not responsible. In 1972 transferred from Leningrad SPH to Alma-Ata SPH, from which he later escaped with a group of inmates. Caught, sent to Kazan SPH, in 1975 receiving large doses of drugs and in bad condition.
Vladimir Semyonovich BATSHEV*	1946; Russian; Moscow; SPA	Grani, 1966, No. 61; P. Litvinov, Trial of the Four; Chr 25	Poet. Took part in a Moscow demonstration for freedom of expression in April 1965, arrested in December 1965 on suspicion of organizing another one, interned for a short time in Moscow OPH No. 3. In 1966 exiled to Siberia for five years.
Ilya BELAU*	1945; Jewish; nr. Moscow; E	Belau; News Bulletin on Soviet Jewry, 1972, No. 216	Journalist. Applied in late 1971 to emigrate to Israel, active in the Jewish movement. In May 1972 permission given, but revoked a few days later because of his "bad behaviour near the Moscow synagogue"; interned in Moscow regional OPH No. 1. Released within a few weeks and allowed to emigrate.

Leonid BELOBORODOV	c. 1950; Russian?; Kiev?; E–I	Chr 25	Artist. In 1969 tried with a friend to sail a boat across the Black Sea to Turkey. First sentenced to two years for illegal crossing of frontier. Released in 1971 but new charges under article 70, apparently designed solely to prevent him revealing the circumstances of his friend's death in a KGB prison. Declared not responsible, sent to Dnepropetrovsk SPH. Subsequent fate unknown.
Evgeny BELOV*	1937; Russian; Moscow; SPA	*Guardian*, 6.10.65, 7.10.65, 9.10.65, 11.10.65; *Economist*, 11.12.65	Student interpreter. In 1965 called on Communist Party to be more democratic. Was immediately suspended from membership. Wrote letters to Kosygin and Brezhnev and finally distributed his proposals for change to the Moscow embassies of several Communist countries. Forcibly confined to a Moscow OPH. Internment provoked British protest. Subsequent fate unknown. See chapter 3.
Yury Sergeyevich BELOV	1941; Russian; Leningrad; SPA–R	Chr 9, 26, 27, 30, 34, 37, 39, 41, 42; N. Gorbanevskaya; Y. Krylsky	Journalist. Three-year sentence for political offence 1964–67, served in Mordovia. Then exiled, wrote book *Report from Darkness*, sentenced in 1968 under article 70 to five years of special-régime camps for trying to send it abroad. Camp 10 in Mordovia, transferred to Vladimir Prison in 1970. Autumn 1971: new charges of "agitation in the prison", December 1971 sent to Serbsky, ruled non-responsible. May 1972: transferred to Sychyovka SPH, where he and Y. Krylsky became friends. Told by two doctors (named) in 1974 that he had no illness, but "We consider religious convictions to be pathological, so we're treating you". Summer 1975: treatment prolonged. January 1976 transferred to Smolensk SPH, September 1976 to an OPH in Krasnoyarsk Region.
Mikhail Semyonovich BERNSHTAM	c. 1940; Jewish convert to Christianity?; Moscow; SPA	Bernshtam; Chr 38, 40, 41	Historian and orientalist, published academic articles up to 1971. In 1973 arrested for writing a book on Soviet history and for supposedly forming an anti-Soviet group among his students. Ruled not responsible, sent to Rostov-on-Don SPH, released after a year there. Became active in human-rights movement, emigrated October 1976.

Name	Birthdate; nationality; residence; cause of internment	Sources of information	Brief summary of case
Vladimir BORISOV	c. 1945?; Russian; Vladimir; SPA	Chr 8–11, 13, 14	A worker, but with a higher education in literature. Founded Union of Independent Youth in Vladimir. Applied to register it with local government. Its aim was the promotion of socialist democracy. Interned in May 1969 in Vladimir OPH "for investigation", but given injections there. Released in July after public pressure. KGB officials said "stop thinking or we'll put you away in prison". A month later arrested, charged under article 190–1 and in October sent for psychiatric examination. Declared not responsible. In May 1970 hanged himself in hospital wing of Moscow's Butyrka Prison, where in March he had met V. Gershuni.
Vladimir Evgenevich BORISOV	1943; Russian; Leningrad; SPA	Chr 10, 11, 18, 19, 24, 28, 30, 32, 42; V. Fainberg	Electrician, interned in Leningrad SPH 1964–68 (article 70), in 1969 joined human-rights group, arrested, article 190–1; 1969–73 interned in Leningrad SPH; 1973–74 in Leningrad OPH. December 1976 re-interned in OPH No. 3. Released two months later.
Vladimir Sergeyevich BORISOV	1937; Russian; Moscow region; SPA?	Chr 18	A worker, arrested, charged under article 190–1, ruled schizophrenic. Sent to Leningrad SPH in summer 1969, still there in early 1971. Subsequent fate unknown.
David Yakovlevich BOSS	?; Volga German; middle Volga; SPA?	Chr 39, 41	Arrested in 1950, sentenced for "anti-Soviet activity", held in camps; in captivity since then. In early or mid-1960s transferred to Kazan SPH, then to Sychyovka SPH. Held there at least as of 1972. Kind and a man of principle, refuses to attend psychiatric commissions.
Nikolai Ivanovich BRESLAVSKY	1905; Russian?; ?; E–R	Chr 18, 30, 39, 41; Senate Hearing; Y. Krylsky	Worker and Christian, served in Soviet army in Iran during war, defected, settled in Turkey. In 1945 forcibly repatriated by USA on basis of Yalta agreement, sentenced to ten years, released in 1956. At once went to Turkish embassy to seek emigration, arrested at entrance, charged with planning to emigrate illegally, ruled schizophrenic, sent to Leningrad SPH. In 1972 transferred to Sychyovka SPH, where Y. Krylsky knew him, still held there, in bad health, in 1976. (Name misspelled Broslavsky and Bzheslavsky in some sources.)

Name	Details	Source	Description
Yury Petrovich BROVKO*	1939; Russian?; Moscow; E	Chr 35, 39	Physicist, research worker; January 1975 entered Swedish Embassy to enquire about renouncing Soviet citizenship. On leaving was seized and taken straight to Kashchenko Hospital. Had no psychiatric history; unknown if released.
Vitaly Kuzmich BUBLYK	1924; Ukrainian; Batumi; SPA	Chr 39, 41	Worked as a manual road worker in German-occupied Ukraine, imprisoned 1944–56 for "collaboration with the Germans". 1956 settled near Batumi. 1959 visited American exhibition in Moscow, recounted his life-story to a US journalist, detained by KGB at exit, charged, interned in Kazan SPH, then in Sychyovka. Held there at least as of 1972.
Vladimir Konstantinovich BUKOVSKY	1942; Russian; Moscow; SPA	Chr 14, 19, 21–24; Senate Hearing; Survey, 1970, No. 77.	Active on human rights from age eighteen. In 1961 a biophysics student at Moscow University. In May 1963 arrested and charged with anti-Soviet agitation because possessed The New Class by Djilas. Examined at Serbsky and declared not responsible. Sent to Leningrad SPH where he spent fifteen months. Arrested again December 1965 for organizing demonstration. Sent first to OPH No. 13 near Moscow, then to OPH No. 5 at Stolbovaya (judged responsible at both) and finally to Serbsky. Here judged not responsible, but released in August 1966 after Western pressure, and case closed. Arrested January 1967 for organizing a demonstration, sentenced to three years. Obtained copies of forensic case reports on six dissenters which he sent to the West in January 1971, together with an appeal to Western psychiatrists. Arrested March 1971. Assessed in Serbsky, found responsible. Tried January 1972 (article 70), sentenced to twelve years of imprisonment and exile. Following strong Western campaigns, released in December 1976 after being flown to West, in unprecedented exchange for Chilean Communist.

Name	Birthdate; nationality; residence; cause of internment	Sources of information	Brief summary of case
Donatas Ju. BUTKUS	c. 1940; Lithuanian; Vilnius; R	Chr 27, 28	Officer of the Historico-Ethnographical Museum in Vilnius, author of article on Tibetan medicine. Charged in 1972 with belonging to a Buddhist group, article 227, interned in a Vilnius OPH, released within a year, but kept on psychiatric register and barred from work in profession.
Gleb Alekseyevich BYCHKOV	c. 1925; Russian; Sochi; SPA	Chr 41	A taxi-driver, arrested under article 190-1 for statements made in conversation, interned in Chernyakhovsk SPH in 1972. Possibly released by 1976.
v. BYKOV	c. 1935?; Russian; Moscow; SPA	Chr 7, 39	Architect. Associate of totalitarian A. Fetisov (see below). Charged under article 70, ruled not responsible, sent to either Leningrad or Kazan SPH. Released by early 1970s.
Anatoly Grigorevich CHEPULA	1950; Russian?; Pacific Coast; SPA?	Chr 18, 39; *Senate Hearing*	A worker, one of a group of seven, all interned in mental hospitals. Charged under article 70, diagnosed as schizophrenic. Held in Leningrad SPH in early 1971, released by 1976.
Vasily Ivanovich CHERNYSHOV	c. 1939; Russian; Leningrad; SPA–N	Chr 18, 27, 39; *Senate Hearing*	Mathematics lecturer at an Institute of Technology. Wrote poetry, short stories and political and philosophical studies "for his own amusement". A Russian nationalist and Orthodox believer. Arrested March 1970, charged with anti-Soviet propaganda. Diagnosed as a chronic paranoid schizophrenic, placed in Leningrad SPH, given drug treatment. In January 1971 wrote an "Appeal to Soviet Society". In 1972 transferred to Dnepropetrovsk SPH. Still there in early 1976.
Anatoly Fyodorovich CHINNOV	1938; Russian; Leningrad; E–R	Chr 26, 27, 30, 34, 39; V. Fainberg	Biochemist, tried to cross border with priest Boris Zalivako in 1968, ruled sane in Lvov, schizophrenic by Serbsky Institute. In Leningrad SPH c. 1971–72; in Dnepropetrovsk SPH c. 1969–71 and 1972–75. Refused to renounce religious beliefs. Released in 1975.

Name	Details	References	Notes
Petras **CIDZIKAS**	1944; Lithuanian; Vilnius; N–R	Chr 34, 36, 39	Student of Vilnius University, charged in 1973 with circulating *samizdat* (article 190–1?), interned in Chernyakhovsk SPH, still there in 1976. When younger, simulated mental illness to avoid military service.
Nikolai Nikolaevich **DANILOV**	c. 1936; Russian; Leningrad; SPA	Chr 5, 8, 9; CHR 5–6	Law graduate from Rostov, worked as a procuracy investigator in Sakhalin 1960–63, then as a worker and a lawyer in Leningrad. Also published poems. Arrested in early August 1968, charged under article 70 for his part in informal human rights group, ruled not responsible, interned in Leningrad SPH. Insulin shock treatment made his health deteriorate. Released in 1970, was working in 1973 as a lawyer in Odessa.
Kim Saifullovich **DAVLETOV**	1932; ?; Moscow; SPA	Chr 24, 25, 34, 39	Much-published scholar on folklore; active Communist; arrested December 1971 for publishing a Stalinist brochure in Albania, article 70, interned. As of early 1976 still in Kazan SPH.
Aleksei Aleksandrovich **DOBROVOLSKY**	1938; Russian; Moscow; SPA	Chr 1; *Kaznimye*	Imprisoned 1958–61 on political charges. Rearrested 1964, ruled not responsible, sent to Leningrad SPH, released 1965 (?). March 1966 re-arrested for planning a demonstration against rehabilitation of Stalin, interned in Moscow OPH No. 3 for a short time. Arrested in January 1967, charged under article 70, ruled responsible, turned state's evidence at trial, given two-year sentence. Lunts gave evidence as for Galanskov (see below).
Andrei Vasilevich **DUBROV***	1950; Russian; Moscow; SPA–E	Chr 25, 27, 29, 30; AS 1294, 1295	Student, expelled from institute for dissenting activity. In October 1972 got permission to emigrate, but this was soon revoked on grounds he had not yet done military service. Refused to do it, was interned in Moscow OPH No. 3 for two weeks. Released after campaign of publicity. Soon emigrated. See chapter 7.

Name	Birthdate; nationality; residence; cause of internment	Sources of information	Brief summary of case
Ivan Grigorevich DVORETSKY*	c. 1920; Russian; Kiev; SPA–E	Chr 40	Train driver, just averted a serious train accident in 1967, made possible by criminally negligent management. Tried to have the relevant manager prosecuted, an old party veteran who was "protected" by the party. Dvoretsky was several times interned in OPHs, beaten up by police, interrogated by KGB. Later he applied to emigrate; refused. In 1975 he appealed for help to US railway workers. Judged normal by numerous psychiatrists, but their judgements repeatedly overruled by those servile to the party veteran.
Vyacheslav Anisimovich DZIBALOV	1915; Russian; Leningrad; SPA	Chr 26, 27, 39	Senior engineer at the Institute of Mechanical Processing, member of group to reform society and revive Leninist policies. Arrested March 1971, article 70, trial in January 1972, interned in Leningrad SPH, transferred later in 1972 to Alma-Ata SPH, then to Kazan SPH, where he still was in 1976.
Pyotr Markovich EGIDES	1917; Jewish? Rostov-on-Don; SPA	Chr 13–14, 17–18; B. Zoubok	Party member, Marxist philosopher and author of several works. After the war spent some years in camps but was rehabilitated. Was charged under article 190–1 in March 1970 for circulating proposals for reform of the party and political writings. Lecturer at Rostov University. Declared not responsible in Serbsky and diagnosed as psychopathic personality ("delusions of grandeur and reforming zeal") with arteriosclerosis and paranoid reaction. Court sat in December 1970. Sent to Kashchenko OPH, apparently released within about two years.

Name	Bio	Sources	Description
Vladimir Vasilevich EIKHVALD	1914; Russian?; Tallinn; SPA	Chr 18, 20; Yu. Luri	Radio engineer. Wrote letters of a critical nature to government bodies, including one of protest against the expulsion of Solzhenitsyn from the Writers' Union. Arrested early 1971, charged under article 190–1, and in June 1971 declared not responsible by a court. Sent to an OPH. Released within a few months thanks to vigorous efforts by his lawyer Luri, who failed to have him examined by independent psychiatrists, but who did obtain opinions from them about case materials.
Alexander Sergeyevich ESENIN-VOLPIN	1924; Russian; Moscow; SPA	*Senate Hearing*; Chr 1, 9, 26; *N.Y. Times*, 12.9.71.	Logician and son of the poet Esenin. Detained in mental hospitals five times between 1949 and 1968. In 1949 charged with anti-Soviet agitation, declared not responsible at Serbsky, interned in Leningrad SPH for twelve months. In August 1957 spent three weeks in Gannushkin OPH No. 4 in Moscow. In September 1959 arrested for "anti-Soviet agitation", diagnosed as paranoid schizophrenic and sent again to Leningrad SPH, where he spent a year. Again interned in OPH No. 4 in Moscow between September 1962 and March 1963 after the publication of a philosophical treatise in the West. Last internment was in February–May 1968 in OPH No. 5 near Moscow. All internments related to his human-rights activity. 1968 internment led to protests from fellow scientists and mathematicians. July 1972 advised to emigrate. Has lived since in Boston, USA, working as a mathematician.
Boris Dmitrievich EVDOKIMOV	1923; Russian; Leningrad; SPA	Chr 26, 27, 37, 39, 42; L. Plyushch	Journalist, arrested 1971 for publishing pseudonymous articles in émigré press, article 70. Ruled non-responsible, tried June 1972, interned in Leningrad SPH, transferred in September 1972 to Dnepropetrovsk SPH, still there. Suffers from asthma, heart trouble, high blood pressure. In 1976 in bad physical and moral state.

Name	Birthdate; nationality; residence; cause of internment	Sources of information	Brief summary of case
Victor Isaakovich FAINBERG	1933; Jewish; Leningrad; SPA	Chr 3–5, 8, 18, 19, 24, 27, 28, 30, 32	Worker, graduated 1968 in English studies as evening student, arrested 1968 for demonstration against occupation of Czechoslovakia, articles 190–1 and 190–3, interned in Leningrad SPH until 1973. Transferred to Leningrad OPH No. 5, released after nine months in November 1973. April–May 1974 interned in Leningrad OPH No. 3 for hunger strike and statement in support of Bukovsky. Emigrated June 1974. See appendix VII.
Georgy (Eduard) Alekseyevich FEDOTOV	1950; Russian; Moscow; R	Chr 15, 27; AS 2747	Legal first name Eduard, he assumed name Georgy after conversion to Orthodoxy. Imprisoned for a common crime c. 1965, in 1968 resentenced in camp for circulating among the prisoners leaflets denouncing the invasion of Czechoslovakia. Took part in prisoner protests in Mordovia in 1970, sent to Serbsky in 1971, ruled mentally ill, sent to Leningrad SPH. Released c. 1973, by now a morally reformed Orthodox believer. Harassed by local psychiatric dispensary. Took part in seminar of young Orthodox intellectuals with Argentov (see above). In October 1976 forcibly interned in Moscow OPH No. 14, released in November after brutal treatment and campaign of protest by friends. Doctors admitted aim was to "cure him of his religion".
Grigory Isaakovich FEIGIN*	1927; Jewish; Riga; E	Chr 17, Feigin	Ex-army major. Tried for many years to emigrate to Israel. In May 1970 publicly renounced his military decorations, then, in July, his Soviet citizenship. In December 1970 forcibly placed in Riga OPH. Released in January 1971 and allowed to emigrate in February.

A. A. FETISOV	?; Russian; Moscow; SPA	Chr 7, 39	Economist, party member. Arrested and charged under article 70 in spring 1968. Critic of Soviet political and economic system from totalitarian point of view, an anti-semite and admirer of Stalin and Hitler. Also a neo-Slavophile. Ruled not responsible and sent to SPH in either Leningrad or Kazan. Released by early 1970s.
Roman T. FIN	1941; Russian?; nr. Moscow; SPA	Chr 18, 22; CHR 7; V. Nekipelov	Biophysicist at the Academy's Institute of Biophysics. Graduated from Gorky University in 1966. Arrested in February 1971 and charged under article 190–1 with circulation of samizdat. Refused to admit any guilt, diagnosed as mild chronic schizophrenic. At trial in October 1971 declared not responsible and sent to Oryol SPH. Later transferred to an OPH in Gorky, released by end of 1973. No previous psychiatric history.
G. FORPOSTOV	?; Polish; Minsk; E	Chr 8, 41	A lecturer. Tried c. 1960 (?) to cross the border into Poland, his homeland; caught and charged with intended treason. Held in a labour camp for eight years, then ruled insane, sent to Chernyakhovsk SPH; held there seven years, then released, apparently in 1975.
Yury Timofeyevich GALANSKOV*	1939–72; Russian; Moscow; SPA	Chr 1, 28; Kaznimye; Uncensored Russia	A samizdat essayist, poet and editor from c. 1960. From 1962 to 1966 interned several times in OPHs as a reprisal, for short terms. Last time in March–April 1966. Arrested in January 1967, sentenced to seven years under article 70. Lunts declared at trial that he was completely healthy, and the previous diagnoses had been incorrect: Lunts's earlier definition of schizophrenia had been too broad and he had now changed it.
Vladimir Lvovich GERSHUNI	1930; Jewish; Moscow; SPA	Chr 10, 11, 13, 17, 19, 30, 32, 34	Stonemason, arrested 1969 for samizdat activity, article 190–1, interned 1970–74 in Oryol SPH; April–October 1974 in Moscow OPH No. 13, released.

Name	Birthdate; nationality; residence; cause of internment	Sources of information	Brief summary of case
Valery Mikhailovich GOLIKOV	1945; Russian; Leningrad; R–I	Golikov	In 1967 refused to do military service on religious and other grounds, told he was mad, interned in Arkhangelsk OPH, only a year later ruled not responsible by a court. Stayed in same OPH. Released 1969. Emigrated 1975.
Natalya Evgenevna GORBANEVSKAYA	1936; Russian; Moscow; SPA	See chapter 5	Poet, writer and editor, mainly in *samizdat*. In 1959 voluntarily spent two weeks in an OPH. In 1968 helped found the *Chronicle*, took part in demonstration against invasion of Czechoslovakia, ruled not responsible, but criminal case closed. December 1969 arrested after appearance of her *Red Square at Noon*, judged not responsible in Serbsky; July 1970 court confirmed judgement. Sent to Kazan SPH in early 1971, spent nine months there, made a formal recantation, sent back to Serbsky, released February 1972, emigrated December 1975. Became an editor in Paris.
Vytautas Ernestovich GRIGAS	1937; German; Moscow; N–E– SPA	Chr 32; Amnesty document; Grigas	Grew up in orphanages in Lithuania, only gradually learned he was German, not Lithuanian, worked as a mechanic and engineer in various places. 1971 flat searched, anti-Soviet letter found, charged with parasitism (article 209), ruled non-responsible in Serbsky (5 pp. psychiatric report available in English), interned in OPH No. 5 at Stolbovaya, released August 1972. August 1973 applied to emigrate to W. Germany, edited a journal on the Soviet Germans with two friends; January 1974 took part in Moscow demonstration demanding right to emigrate. Interned in Kashchenko OPH until March. Emigrated to W. Germany two months later. Has established his real name is Herbert Mickoleit.

Pyotr Grigorevich GRIGORENKO	1907; Ukrainian; Moscow; SPA	Chr: most issues; see chapter 5	Ex-major-general, arrested 1964, article 70, interned in Leningrad SPH 1964–65. Arrested 1969 for human-rights activity, article 190–1, interned 1970–73 in Chernyakhovsk SPH, September 1973–June 1974 in OPH No. 5 at Stolbovaya near Moscow, released.
Vasily GUDILIN	c. 1943; Russian?; ?; SPA	Chr 41	Student of an agricultural college, c. 1968 wrote slogans on some political posters and tore them, interned in Chernyakhovsk SPH. Released in 1975 after seven years there.
Vladimir Nikolaevich GUSAROV*	c. 1930?; Russian; Moscow; SPA	Chr 7, 12, 15, 17, 19, 21–23, 25	Writer of samizdat essays and a book on socio-political themes. Interned in Kashchenko OPH No. 1 in March 1971, during the 24th party congress.
GUSYAKOVA*	1912; Russian; Moscow; I	See ref. 19, chapter 9	A housewife. In November 1973 went to the RSFSR Supreme Soviet to complain about illegal acts of local authorities. Forcibly removed to Moscow OPH No. 13. Released after a week when judged normal. See chapter 9.
Vyacheslav Vladimirovich IGRUNOV	1947; Russian; Odessa; SPA	Chr 34, 35, 37, 38, 40, 42; V. Telnikov; Times, 7.12.76	Economist by training, electrician by profession. March 1975 arrested for samizdat activity, article 190–1. Serbsky ruled him non-responsible, trial due December 1975, postponed. March 1976 court ordered an OPH. Sent to Odessa regional OPH No. 1. In September psychiatrists recommended release, discharged early 1977.
Olga Yurevna IOFE	1950; Jewish; Moscow; SPA	Chr 11, 14–18, 20, 21, 25	Economics student. At age sixteen posted up leaflets warning against the revival of Stalinist tendencies. Arrested December 1969, charged under article 70. Diagnosed at Serbsky as chronic schizophrenia. (Lunts and G. Morozov on her commission.) Trial in August 1970. Declared not responsible and transferred to Kazan SPH. Arrived September. In February 1971 transferred to OPH No. 3 in Moscow and released in July. See chapters 7 and 8.

Name	Birthdate; nationality; residence; cause of internment	Sources of information	Brief summary of case
Mikhail IVANKOV (-NIKOLOV)	1921; Russian; ?; E	Chr 8, 39; *New York Times*, 14 January, 28 and 29 April 1956	Radio operator on Soviet ship who asked for political asylum in the US (when ship berthed in Formosa in early 1956). Soon deceived into returning to USSR by Soviet consul's promise of no punishment. On return, interned in Kazan and Chernyakhovsk SPHs, in July 1968 transferred to Dnepropetrovsk SPH. Still there in 1976. Because he tells others about his fate, in each SPH given big doses of powerful drugs, in Chernyakhovsk given beatings; told by doctors he will never be released.
Yury Evgenevich IVANOV*	1927; Russian; Leningrad; SPA	Chr 10, 11, 22, 25, 29; Dr M. Voikhanskaya; AS 1595	An artist, imprisoned 1955–71 on political charges. 1972 declined to give KGB evidence it wanted. April 1973 invited to Leningrad KGB to receive help in getting residence permit, but arrested in the waiting-room and taken by ambulance to OPH No. 4 in Leningrad. June 1973 transferred to OPH No. 3, given Aminazin injections. Released late 1974. See appendix X.
Raisa IVANOVA	1929; Russian; ?; R–I	Chr 33, 35	Sentenced for belonging to an Orthodox Christian sect (article 70?), refused to work in Mordovian camp 3, in October 1974 ruled mentally ill, though regarded by her fellow-inmates as normal. Interned in the psychiatric block of the Mordovian camps hospital, in camp 3.
Antanas JANKAUSKAS*	1942; Lithuanian; Simnas; N?	Chr 22, 23	Worker. Arrested in Simnas at beginning of 1971 for circulating leaflets and placed in a Kaunas OPH. After his release in August 1971, wrote a letter to the party 1st secretary in Lithuania. In October re-interned in an OPH in Novovilnia near Vilnius. "Treated" with Aminazin. Not known when released.
Heino JÕGESMA	1937; Estonian; Tallinn; E	Chr 32, 41	Electrician. Crossed border into Finland, returned to USSR by Finnish authorities. Article 64? Ruled non-responsible in Serbsky c. January 1974, sent to Chernyakhovsk SPH, still there in 1976.

Name	Details	Source	Description
Vitaly Vasilevich KALINICHENKO	1944; Ukrainian; Kiev region; E	Chr 32–35, 38, 41	Arrested in 1966 for trying to cross the frontier, sentenced by Murmansk court to ten years for "intention to commit treason". In 1974 in Perm camp 36 renounced Soviet citizenship and demanded status of political prisoner. Summer 1975 sent for examination to psychiatric section of Mordovian camps' hospital, for a month, then to Serbsky for a month then held for three months in Sychyovka (or Smolensk, according to one source). In February 1976 sent back to camp, March 1976 released at end of sentence.
Yury KALININ	c. 1950; Russian; ?; E–R	Y. Krylsky	Decided, with sister, to convert to Judaism and try to emigrate to Israel. Framed by KGB, charged with a rape he did not commit, interned, held in Sychyovka SPH in 1973, where Y. Krylsky knew him.
Teet KALLAS	1942; Estonian; Tallinn; SPA-N?	Chr 11, 12	Prose writer and editor. Arrested in October 1969, charged under article 70. Ruled not responsible by a court in January 1970. Which hospital placed in, and when released, not known.
Vladimir KARASEV*	c. 1945?; Russian?; Moscow; SPA	Chr 7	Physics student who had just graduated from Moscow University; immediately after the Soviet invasion of Czechoslovakia in August 1968, collected signatures of protest in the main university hall. Beaten up by KGB officials, then interned in an OPH for three months. On release got a job as a stoker.
Annasoltan KEKILOVA*	c. 1925?; Turkmenian; Ashkhabad; SPA-N-E	Chr 22	Poet who has published three books. Wrote letters to 24th Party Congress and Central Committee, critical of shortcomings in Turkmenia. Deprived of job and publication of books stopped. Renounced her Soviet citizenship. Forcibly confined to an OPH in August 1971, although had no psychiatric history. Was told by doctors that she was normal, but "if you don't give us a signed statement that you wrote to the Central Committee because you were in a nervous condition, you will stay in the hospital forever". Refused to recant. Subsequent fate unknown, but probably released fairly soon.

Name	Birthdate; nationality; residence; cause of internment	Sources of information	Brief summary of case
Vasily Nikiforovich KHARITONOV	1936; Russian; Odessa; SPA–R	Kharitonov; Chr 40	Party member, graduated in philosophy at Leningrad University, then taught in Leningrad and Odessa. In 1968 spent three months in Czechoslovakia, strongly influenced by the freedom there. On return to Odessa participated in *samizdat*, became deeply involved in Christianity, resigned party membership. Arrested when KGB pressure failed to achieve a recantation, endlessly interrogated, released after two months and closely watched. In 1970 re-arrested, underwent psychiatric examinations in an Odessa OPH, then OPH No. 3 in Moscow, then at Serbsky. Severe drug treatment. Declared not responsible, interned in the city OPH in Odessa for a year. Released February 1972, and warned that further dissenting activity would land him in an SPH. Resumed this activity, arrested in January 1973, charged under article 70, ruled not responsible in Odessa OPH. In 1974 released into custody of parents, in May 1975 emigrated to USA.
Lev KINDEYEV	?; Russian?; Sakhalin; E	Chr 41	Arrested (not known when) for trying to cross the border into Turkey. Charged, ruled not responsible. Since 1972 held in Kazan SPH, still there in 1976.
V. P. KOLESNIK*	c. 1920?; Ukrainian?; Dnepropetrovsk region; R	C. R. Hill, ed., *Rights and Wrongs*, p. 118	A member of the Baptist Church not recognized by the state. Went to Moscow in October 1966 to ask the party central committee to restore his pension, which had been unjustly stopped. Forcibly taken from the central committee and interned in Moscow OPH No. 15. Interrogated there about church affairs. Soon released.
Evgeny Evgenevich KOMAROV	1930; Russian; Leningrad; SPA?	Chr 18, 23, 27; *Senate Hearing*; V. Fainberg	A worker. Charged under article 70, unknown when. Diagnosed as paranoid personality, ruled not responsible. Held in Leningrad SPH in 1970–72, then apparently transferred to another SPH. Subsequent fate unknown.

Name	Bio	Sources	Description
Faina Nikiforovna KOMAROVA	?; Russian; Vladimir; R	Chr 41	Hospital orderly, Orthodox Christian, see A. N. Kotov. Prior to 1972 had never been on psychiatric register. Interned in Kazan SPH as of c. 1972.
Viktor KOMAROVSKY*	1934; Russian; Moscow; I	V. Prussakov	Research worker in an institute, a sincere Communist and party member. Lived in one room with wife and two children, eventually started complaining that, because of corruption, he was repeatedly being by-passed in the queue for a bigger home. On fourth occasion, in 1967, removed from Supreme Soviet and interned in Kashchenko OPH No. 1. Here wrote protests, resisted injections, swore at the doctors. Apparently charged with a political offence, sent to Serbsky in August 1967. Here behaved meekly. Subsequent fate unknown.
Pyotr KOPYTIN	1949; Russian; Moscow; SPA	Chr 39	Postman, delivered samizdat along with letters, charged, interned in Kazan SPH. Early 1976 (?) transferred to an OPH.
Nikolai KORABLEV	1933; Russian; Tyumen region; SPA	V. Prussakov	Worker, in 1955 spoke against official candidate for local soviet, sentenced to one year. Moved to Novosibirsk, in November 1956 criticized the government at a meeting, interned in a local OPH for three years (under criminal commitment?). In 1959 new chief doctor found him completely normal, but on release taken to court and given three years. In 1960 sent to Vladimir Prison for a year. 1962 charged with planning to form an anti-Soviet group, given five years. Soon before release, in August 1967, sent to Serbsky, ruled mentally ill, sent to an SPH. Unkown which one, or if later released.
Aleksei Nikiforovich KOTOV (mis-spelled Kitov in early sources)	c. 1905; Russian; Vladimir; R	Chr 30, 39, 41; Y. Krylsky	Orthodox Christian, sentenced for religious activity in early 1930s, kept in captivity continuously until transferred to an SPH in (?) mid-1960s. From Leningrad SPH transferred (c. 1970?) to Vladimir regional OPH, in 1971 released into guardianship of F. N. Komarova, an orderly at the hospital (see above). In c. 1972 both he and she arrested, charged with religious activity, he interned in Sychyovka, held there as of 1975. Y. Krylsky knew him there in 1973, and describes him as unbroken by all his experiences, and as an educated man.

Name	Birthdate; nationality; residence; cause of internment	Sources of information	Brief summary of case
Boris KOVHAR	1926; Ukrainian; Kiev; N–SPA	Chr 28, 30, 39	Journalist, museum official, Communist, arrested March 1972 for writing an open letter which revealed that since 1967 he had been a KGB agent spying on dissenters, and also described KGB techniques. Ruled non responsible, but to be tried again after his "recovery". Interned in Dnepropetrovsk SPH. Still held there in early 1976.
KOZLOV	c. 1935; Russian; ?; SPA–E	Chr 39	Worker, arrested and interned in Kazan SPH for his complaints to official bodies. Released, tried to emigrate to join relatives in South America, arrested for this in 1973, apparently charged under article 83 (illegal crossing of the border), ruled not responsible and sent to Kazan again. Reportedly still there in 1976.
Anatoly Pavlovich KOZLOV	1936; Russian; Tomsk region; SPA	Chr 34, 35	Various jobs, including chief factory engineer, in various places. Arrested 1971 for his writings, article 190–1, ruled responsible, sentenced to two years. In 1972 charged with forming anti-Soviet group in camp, articles 70 and 72; May 1972 recommended in Tomsk for SPH, then in Serbsky in September for OPH. Sent back to Tomsk, further fate unknown.
Andrei KOZLOV	1939; Russian; Leningrad; SPA	Chr 26, 39	Arrested in March 1971 as member of same group as Dzibalov (see above), article 70. Interned in Kazan SPH, released in 1974.
Zinovy Mikhailovich KRASIVSKY	1930; Ukrainian; Morshin, Lvov Region; N	Chr 11, 17, 18, 25, 39, 41, 42; V. Sevruk; V. Fainberg	Writer, poet, teacher. Arrested 1967 for participating in *samizdat* journal of clandestine Ukrainian National Front. Sentence: five years' prison, then seven years' camp, then five years' exile. In December 1971, in Vladimir Prison, charged with circulating his poems, article 70. Ruled non-responsible in Serbsky. A symptom of illness was the fact that he was cheerful by day, but wrote sad poems at night. Sent in 1972 to Smolensk SPH, since then suffers from heart trouble. Transferred to Lvov OPH in 1976.

Name	Reference	Details	Description
Sven KREEK	Chr 37, 39	?; Estonian; Tallinn; SPA-N?	Arrested in January 1975, charged under article 70 with circulating his verse in leaflet form, ruled not responsible, interned by early 1976 in an OPH in Tallinn.
Yan Yuliusovich KRYLSKY	CHR 2; Krylsky's memoirs	1951; Jewish; Moscow region; E	Arrested in October 1971 after provoked into a fight by an anti-semite, who later confessed responsibility. Krylsky released. January 1972 his family applied to emigrate to Israel, case re-opened as a reprisal, in March court ruled him guilty but not responsible. April 1972 sent to Smolensk SPH, where treated brutally and he helped initiate a revolt. January 1973 transferred to Sychyovka SPH, where threatened with charges under article 190–1. "Treated" intensively by sadistic staff and felt near death until March, when father's campaign in West began to gain powerful support. June 1973 commission recommended transfer to OPH. Court ruled favourably in September, just prior to the WPA symposium in Erevan and at time of strong campaign in West (see chapter 10). Transfer to Moscow OPH occurred on 2 November, released January 1974, emigrated to Israel.
Nikolai Nikolayevich KRYUCHKOV*	Chr 35	c. 1950; Russian; Moscow; E	Son of famous film actor Nikolai Kryuchkov; February 1974 applied to emigrate to USA. April re-applied, asking also to give up Soviet citizenship; 17 May summoned for talk with a psychiatrist. 22 June forcibly interned in Kashchenko OPH for the duration of President Nixon's visit to the USSR. In the official papers was written: "Reason for hospitalization: wish to emigrate from the USSR". 5 July released.
KUBYSHKIN	Chr 41	c. 1924; Russian; Moscow; SPA	A worker. In past charged under article 70, ruled not responsible, interned in Leningrad SPH. c. 1975 arrested for anti-Soviet statements made in an argument with a neighbour, article 70, interned in Chernyakhovsk SPH.

Name	Birthdate; nationality; residence; cause of internment	Sources of information	Brief summary of case
Mikhail Ignatevich KUKOBAKA	1936; Russian; Vladimir Region; SPA	Chr 27, 30, 34, 39, 40, 41; *Times* 26.11.76, 7.12.76	Factory loader, arrested in 1970 for over-frank writings and statements, article 190–1. In summer 1970 in Serbsky, then held in Vladimir Prison from September 1970. Only in September 1971, after many protests, did he learn he had been ruled non-responsible and a court had, *in November 1970*, ruled he be interned in an SPH. In November 1971 transferred to Sychyovka SPH, where he met Y. Krylsky. Autumn 1974 transferred to Vladimir OPH, where his reading matter was severely restricted. Released May 1976, but re-interned in an OPH in Mogilev, Belorussia, in early November 1976, as "socially dangerous"; released 28 November.
Viktor Vasilevich KUZNETSOV	1936; Russian; Moscow region; SPA	Chr 7, 9, 18–21, 29; *Senate Hearing*; C. R. Hill, ed., *Rights and Wrongs*	A graphic artist, worked for Novosti Press Agency until 1966. In 1965 summoned to KGB after speaking out in a debate at Moscow University. In October 1966 forcibly interned in Moscow OPH No. 1 for three days, then in the OPH at Meshchersky village near Moscow for two months. After release worked as a painter and decorator. Arrested in March 1969, charged under article 70 because of his *samizdat* activity. Diagnosed as a mild chronic schizophrenic (examiners included Lunts and Landau). Sent to Kazan SPH before hearing of his appeal. Released in August 1971.
Ivan Maksimovich LARIN	1939; Russian; Kaluga; SPA?	Chr 18, 39	A worker, charged under article 70. Diagnosed as schizophrenic, declared not responsible, sent to Leningrad SPH; released by 1976.

Name	Born; nationality; place; denomination	Source	Details
Yury K. LAVROV	c. 1940; Russian; Leningrad; R	Chr 27, 28; personal communication	Graduate student (?) at Ulan-Ude Teachers' Training College, arrested 1972 for activity in Buddhist group, article 227, interned in OPH in Leningrad, released in 1973 but kept on psychiatric register.
Ivan Vasilevich LAZUTA*	c. 1925?; Belorussian; Grodno region; R	Chr 16; Appeal from his congregation	House painter, Baptist. In spring 1970 interned for religious activity in the Grodno regional OPH in Zhodishki. Given insulin injections. Told by doctor that he would be released immediately if he rejected his faith and stopped his religious activities. Soon released without this, apparently as result of a campaign by his fellow Baptists. See chapter 9.
Jak LEIWAND	1949; Estonian; Tallinn; E	Chr 24	Tried to cross the border into Finland in August 1971. Declared not responsible, sent to Leningrad SPH. Held there in early 1972. Subsequent fate unknown.
Yury Leonidovich LEVIN*	c. 1935?; Jewish?; Leningrad; SPA	Chr 8, 9	Senior technician in a scientific research institute. Imprisoned 1957-64 for trying to emigrate. In 1968 wrote to US embassy expressing strong criticism of the invasion of Czechoslovakia. Three weeks later interned in an OPH. After ten days' declared healthy and released. In 1969 arrested.
Mikhail LONCHAKOV*	c. 1890?; Russian; Pochaev; R	Bourdeaux, p. 114	A monk at the Pochaev monastery in W. Ukraine, which the authorities tried to close by force in the early 1960s. In November 1964 interned in an OPH, because he was old, while his fellow monks were imprisoned. Not known when released.
Valery LUKANIN	1946; Russian; Moscow region; SPA	Chr 9-11	Arrested in spring 1969 and sent to an OPH, after displaying a poster in his window criticizing invasion of Czechoslovakia. Charged under article 70, ruled not responsible at trial, June 1969. Diagnosis schizophrenia. Transferred to the Kazan SPH in July. Not told about his trial, while mother threatened that she would not be permitted to visit him unless she withheld information about his trial from him. Unknown if and when released.

Name	Birthdate; nationality; residence; cause of internment	Sources of information	Brief summary of case
Lev Grigorevich LUKYANENKO	1927; Ukrainian; Lvov; N	Chr 11, 28, 30, 33, 36; AS 2301	Lawyer, Communist, sentenced to fifteen years in 1961 for forming embryonic underground party, article 64, served first years in Vladimir Prison, sent back there in July 1973 for part in hunger strikes in Perm camp 36. Became religious believer in camps. In December 1974 sent to SPH in Rybinsk, after refusals to co-operate with KGB. Ruled to be mildly mentally ill (2nd category invalid), returned to prison in February 1975. Believed KGB aim: to make it easier to intern Lukyanenko under civil commitment after his release, which occurred in early 1976. Regarded as normal by friends.
Anatoly Ivanovich LUPYNOS	1937; Ukrainian; Kiev; N–SPA	Chr 22, 23, 30, 39; V. Telnikov; L. Plyushch	Served eleven years in camps 1956–67, article 70, came out in grave condition (paralysis of legs, registered as severest category invalid), worked as administrator of musical society. In 1971 arrested after reading his poems in public, article 70, ruled schizophrenic by Serbsky, interned since early 1972 in Dnepropetrovsk SPH.
Vasyl Stepanovych LUTSKIV	1935; Ukrainian; Lvov region; I–N	M. Browne, *Ferment in the Ukraine*, p. 64	Club manager, party member. Arrested 1960 for belonging to underground nationalist group. Turned state's evidence, but received ten years. In 1965 transferred from camp to psychiatric section of hospital in Mordovian camp No. 3 for writing complaints in which he withdrew his compromising evidence as being false and obtained under duress. Held there for, at least, over a year.
Mykhaylo Petrovych LUTSYK	c. 1915; Ukrainian (but see col. 4); ?; N–E	Chr 11, 24, 28, 33, 35, 39	Born in Austro-Hungarian empire, in W. Ukraine, grew up in Vienna, studied in Berlin, arrested by Gestapo in 1939, released c. 1942 and sent to home in Ukraine, arrested by KGB in 1944, released and exculpated in 1956; rearrested 1960, tried April 1961 for Ukrainian nationalism, released 1972. Refused to accept Soviet papers, asserting he was an Austrian citizen. Sentenced to two years for "vagrancy" in autumn 1973, in 1974 sent from camp to Dnepropetrovsk SPH because still

Pyotr Alekseyevich LYSAK	1916; Ukrainian?; Gruyev; SPA	Chr 11, 39; *Senate Hearing*; A. Volpin	Engineer, colonel in the reserves. Spoke out at a meeting in October 1956 against radio-jamming and the expulsion of students for political reasons. Charged under (?) article 70, ruled mentally ill, sent to Leningrad SPH. Transferred in 1965 to Sychyovka SPH, still held there in early 1976.
Vlades MAIJAUSKAS	1947; Lithuanian; Mažiaikiai District, Lithuania; N	Chr 37, 39	Driver, arrested, charged with putting out a Lithuanian national flag in February 1972, interned in an SPH or OPH. In 1975 held in an OPH.
Mikhail Yanovich MAKARENKO*	1931; Jewish; Leningrad; SPA	Chr 16, 41; *Volnoe Slovo*, 1974, No. 12	Worker, party member, later art-gallery director in Novosibirsk. Forcibly subjected to out-patient psychiatric examinations in Leningrad four times between May 1963 and June 1965, three times in the psychiatric unit of the Pushkin district hospital, once in OPH No. 4. Cause: his letters urging the authorities to conduct research into peace and disarmament in a serious way, and his (fruitless) efforts, as an elected workers' representative, to have grievances investigated. Each time the psychiatrists judged him normal, but told him, "If you don't want to be treated, stop writing letters!" In 1969 arrested, sentenced to seven years under article 70 and others. Spring 1976 threatened in Vladimir Prison with being declared mentally ill, although fellow prisoners found him normal.
Alexander MALKHAZYAN*	c. 1940; Armenian; Erevan; E–SPA	Chr 35; French friend	Schoolteacher of physics and maths. In 1968 began to criticize administration of education, health and justice, many pressures and threats as a result. In 1973 arrested in Moscow and interned in an OPH for a week. A few months later interned in an Erevan OPH for three weeks, charged with his criticisms and with planning to emigrate. Now declared schizophrenic by Russian doctors, but completely healthy by an Armenian authority, Prof. Megrabyan. Applied to emigrate, interned again in an Erevan OPH from December 1974 to April 1975. Released after a hunger strike. Early 1976 still not allowed to emigrate.

Name	Birthdate; nationality; residence; cause of internment	Sources of information	Brief summary of case
Yury Vladimirovich MALTSEV*	1932; Russian; Moscow; SPA	Chr 10, 29; and see chapter 7	Translator from Italian and writer, member of human-rights group formed in May 1969. In October 1969 summoned to a military recruitment centre to undergo medical examination. In fact underwent a psychiatric examination and forcibly interned in Kashchenko OPH No. 1 for a month, although had no psychiatric history. First applied to emigrate in 1965, allowed to do so in 1974. Lives in Italy. See chapter 7.
Konstantin Petrovich MALYSHEV	1929; Russian; Kulebaki, Gorky Region, SPA	Chr 34, 39	Chief engineer, arrested for his protests about misdoings to higher authorities, article 190–1, interned in Sychyovka SPH in 1974 or earlier, still held there 1976.
Viktor Mikhailovich MARESIN	c. 1935?; Russian?; Kiev; SPA	Chr 40	Arrested in summer 1974 on suspicion of involvement in a group of counterfeiters. During investigation expressed "anti-Soviet views", in December 1974 sent for psychiatric diagnosis—"schizophrenia in paranoid form". Case separated from that of counterfeiters, investigation halted. Held in Kiev OPH No. 21, threatened with transfer to Dnepropetrovsk SPH. Doctor said that with his views he could not be freed. Situation in summer 1976. His brother subject to a political prosecution in 1975–76.
Roman MARKEVICH*	1941; Jewish; Leningrad; R–E	New Leader, 1.11.71	Chemical engineer. Applied c. 1970 to emigrate to Israel, dismissed from job, found work as labourer. Asked boss for time off to attend a special Jewish service, refused and told he must be crazy to believe in Judaism. Soon after, in October 1971, forcibly interned in an OPH. Apparently released soon.
Andrei MATKO	1950; Russian; Moscow; SPA	Chr 39, 41	Worker, arrested in spring 1975 as member of a militant anti-Zionist group which believed that Jews had infiltrated all the key posts in the régime. Charged under article 70, ruled not responsible in Serbsky, sent to Sychyovka SPH. Had earlier been on psychiatric register.

Name	Details	References	Description
Zhores Aleksandrovich MEDVEDEV*	1925; Russian; Obninsk; SPA	See chapter 6	Research gerontologist. In May 1970 interned in Kaluga OPH because of his *samizdat* writings. Freed after 2½ weeks following powerful campaign in USSR and abroad. 1973 came to England to research, deprived of citizenship. See chapter 6.
MELESHKO	1935; Ukrainian?; Moscow; I	Chr 39	A driver, sought justice at his car-pool, when failed to achieve it, wrote to local authorities; for this charged under article 190–1 in 1972, interned in Kazan SPH. In January 1976 transferred to the "White Cclumns" OPH near Moscow.
Vyacheslav MERKUSHEV	c. 1947; Russian; ?; SPA–E	Chr 27, 35, 41; AS 2229	Served in frontier troops, sentenced to ten years in 1968 for trying to cross border into Turkey. Punished in camp by being sent for three years to Vladimir Prison, 1971–74. In 1974 sent to Serbsky, ruled not responsible in connection with his strongly anti-Communist statements, in January 1975 in psychiatric section of Mordovian camps' hospital, awaiting transfer to Kazan SPH.
Veniamin Mikhailovich MOISEYEV	c. 1925; Jewish?; central Russia; I–SPA	Chr 41	A school-teacher. In 1966 asked the party committee for a flat, rudely refused, got angry and cursed the party. Charged under article 190–1, ruled non-responsible, interned in Chernyakhovsk SPH. By 1976 held there for nine years, had almost completely lost his sight.
Vladimir M. MONTLEVICH	c. 1940; ?; Leningrad; R	Chr 27, 28; personal communication	Ethnographer, research officer at the Leningrad Museum of Atheism and Religions (ex-Kazan Cathedral), arrested 1972 in Ulan-Ude (Buryatia) for activity in Buddhist group, article 227, interned in Leningrad OPH, released 1973, but kept on psychiatric register and barred from work in profession.
Valentyn Yakovych MOROZ	1936; Ukrainian; Ivano-Frankovsk; N	Chr 17, 40, 41	Historian, sentenced for *samizdat* activity and writings, imprisoned 1965–69, re-sentenced to fourteen years of imprisonment and exile in 1970. In June 1976 due to be transferred from Vladimir Prison to a camp. In May 1976 sent to Serbsky, with clear official intention of having him ruled mentally ill and interned in an SPH, where he would not be able to influence other prisoners. Strong international campaign prevented this outcome. Sent to camp 1 in Mordovia in June.

Name	Birthdate; nationality; residence; cause of internment	Sources of information	Brief summary of case
Roald Gashimovich MUKHAMEDYAROV	1931; ?; Moscow; SPA	Chr 14, 15, 24, 25, 27, 29, 34, 36	Worker, writer of camp memoirs and publicist works, arrested 1972 for *samizdat* activity, article 190–1, interned 1973–75 in OPH No. 5 at Stolbovaya near Moscow.
Sergei MUSATOV	1953; Russian; Moscow; E	Chr 39	In 1973 tried to escape to Austria while serving in the Soviet army in Hungary. Caught, charged with treason, interned in Kazan SPH. In January 1976 transferred to the "White Columns" OPH near Moscow.
Maria Semyonovna MUSIENKO	?; Ukrainian?; Leningrad; SPA	Chr 26, 39	Arrested in March 1971 as member of group of Dzibalov (see above), article 70. Interned, evidently in Kazan SPH. Released by 1976.
Mikhail Aleksandrovich NARITSA	1909; Russian; Leningrad; SPA	Chr 16, 24, 27, 38, 40, 41; *Senate Hearing*	Artist, teacher and writer. Arrested in 1935, spent five years in camps. Arrested again in 1949, exiled to Karaganda for life. Exculpated after Stalin's death. In 1961 arrested after sending his book *An Unsung Song* to the West and applying to emigrate. Ruled not responsible, spent three years in Leningrad SPH. 1965 renewed request to emigrate refused. Wrote account of time in SPH. November 1975 arrested again after renewed applications to emigrate. Psychiatric examinations in a Riga OPH and in Serbsky both found him responsible. Charged under article 190–1, but in May 1976 case dropped and authorities hinted he would now be allowed to emigrate.
Lyubov NASTUSENKO	c. 1934; Ukrainian; Kolomiya; N	Chr 18; *Ukrainian Herald* 1, 3	Nurse, arrested in September 1969 and charged with "nationalist agitation" in Kolomiya, W. Ukraine. Declared not responsible, interned in a special prison section of a mental hospital. In autumn 1970 held in a Kharkov hospital, evidently an OPH (but possibly with a prison-type section). Told her sister the conditions and treatment were indescribably severe, and among genuinely mad people she might become mad herself. Sister told by administration not to visit again, unless she wanted to be interned in a similar institution. Unknown if

Bronius NAUDŽIUNAS*	1938; Lithuanian; Vilnius; E	*ELTA Information Service*, New York, 1976, No. 5	In 1971 started applying to emigrate to join relatives in Canada, and writing appeals. Arrested after coming to Moscow and phoning the US embassy, interned in Moscow OPH No. 15 for a month, where he found himself among dissenters of various types as well as ill patients. Psychiatrists paid no attention to his health, only asked why interned. Soon arrested again in Vilnius, judged sane by a psychiatrist, sentenced in January 1972 to one year in camps. In 1974 re-interned in a Vilnius CPH (Vasara St) for a month. Then managed to get into Canadian embassy, emigrated July 1975.
Vasily Nikolayevich NIKITENKOV	1928; Ukrainian?; Klin, nr. Moscow; E	Chr 19, 20, 24, 35, 38	Doctor, arrested in March 1971 in Moscow on US Embassy ground when entering with wife and children to enquire about emigration. He and wife interned in a Moscow OPH under civil commitment. May 1971 managed to circulate an appeal for help from the OPH. Then charged under article 70 for letters to the UN, etc., recommended by Serbsky for OPH, but in January 1972 court sent him to Kazan SPH. In early 1975 transferred to Taldom OPH in Moscow Region, in May 1975 released.
Evgeny Nikolayevich NIKOLAYEV*	1937; Russian; Moscow; SPA	Chr 16; CHR 12	Biologist, linguist, polyglot, author of many published articles about language. In 1970 lost his research job at an institute when he declared that he did not let the party order him around. Soon after, in October 1970, interned in Moscow OPH No. 16, though he had never before consulted a psychiatrist. Re-interned on two later occasions, once in Moscow OPH No. 15, where he described his socio-political views to a doctor and was at once transferred to OPH No. 5 at Stolbovaya, near Moscow, for eight months. In February 1974 interned for the fourth time, in the Kashchenko OPH No. 1, following the appearance of an article of his in the *samizdat* journal of the Soviet Germans, *Re Patria*, 1974, No. 1. Released by 1976 at latest. See appendix VIII.

Name	Birthdate; nationality; residence; cause of internment	Sources of information	Brief summary of case
V. NIKOLAYEV	?; Russian; ?; E	AS 1595	Tried to cross the frontier. In 1973 held in OPH No. 3 in Leningrad, met by Yury Ivanov, author of AS 1595, who reports watching him reduced to a pitiful state by intensive drug treatment. Subsequent fate unknown.
Valeria NOVODVORSKAYA	1950; Russian; Moscow; SPA	Chr 11–14, 20–21, 23	Student of languages. Arrested in December 1969 for distributing leaflets protesting against the invasion of Czechoslovakia. Charged under article 70. Diagnosed at the Serbsky as a schizophrenic and a paranoid personality. Ruled not responsible at trial in March 1970, sent to Kazan SPH in June. In August 1971 transferred to a Moscow OPH, released in February 1972. See appendix IV.
Olga NOZHAK	c. 1925?; Russian; Moscow; SPA	N. Gorbanevskaya; Yu. Iofe in *Grani*, 1974, Nos. 92–93.	A school teacher. Arrested in 1955 for writing letters to press protesting against the internment of people who in despair bring complaints against local authorities to the Supreme Soviet, etc., in Moscow. Charged under article 70, ruled not responsible, interned in Kazan SPH. Had been there sixteen years when Gorbanevskaya left, because she denounced the psychiatrists as conscious oppressors. She had retained her will and her extrovert personality. No information since 1971.
Igor Vyacheslavovich OGURTSOV	1937; Russian; Leningrad; I-SPA	Chr 1, 2, 4, 9, 11, 17–19, 24, 26, 27, 32, 33; CHR 10	Oriental scholar, sentenced in 1967 to fifteen years' imprisonment and five of exile for leading an underground revolutionary Christian group. Spent seven years in Vladimir Prison, then sent to Perm camp 35, but after only three weeks there transferred in April 1974 to Perm prison for psychiatric exam, then in June, with diagnosis "rheumatism of the brain", to the Mordovian camps' hospital, psychiatric block. In September, after publicity in West, returned to camp 35.

Name	Bio	Source	Description
Efrem OKININ	c. 1910?; Russian; ?; R	Chr 39; Y. Krylsky	Orthodox priest, interned c. 1971 (?) principally for describing Pimen, the new Patriarch, as the KGB's choice, and for attacking certain priests as secret agents of the KGB (article 190-1?). Held in 1973 in Sychyovka SPH, where Y. Krylsky knew and revered him as a true martyr. Constantly tormented with injections, forcible undressing in front of women, and forcible removal of the cross hung on his chest, and people instigated to insult his religious beliefs. *Chronicle* believes he may still have been held in early 1976.
Pyotr ORESHKIN*	c. 1940?; Russian; Moscow; SPA	Chr 32	A professional writer, worked on journal *Technology for the Young*, and in films. 28 June 1974 during Nixon's visit to Moscow, detained, taken to a police station, asked questions there by the district psychiatrist such as "Are you interested in politics? Are you unhappy about any aspects of Soviet policy?" Then interned in Moscow OPH No. 15. Later fate unknown.
Valentin Vladimirovich OVECHKIN*	1904–68; Russian; Moscow; SPA	*Kaznimye*	Well-known writer on rural and agricultural themes, an editor of *Novyi mir* and party member. In 1962 was a candidate for the Supreme Soviet, criticized the new cult of Khrushchev's personality in a speech, was removed as candidate. Autumn 1962 wrote to the party central committee asking for a reform of the farm system on the Yugoslav model. Interned in an OPH, but soon released after news reached West. Not published in press thereafter.
Vladimir PANTIN	c. 1935?; Russian?; ?; I	P. Grigorenko in N. Gorbanevskaya, *Red Square at Noon*	Arrested c. 1958 (?) for a petty theft, pressed by investigator to give false evidence which would convict an innocent man of murder, refused. Investigator: "Ah, so you don't want to help me! Well in that case I'll have you put away in a place which will make you remember me forever!" Ruled not responsible, sent to Leningrad SPH, where spent six years and was friend of Grigorenko in 1964. Lawyer eventually had diagnosis revoked. Re-tried, freed.

Name	Birthdate; nationality; residence; cause of internment	Sources of information	Brief summary of case
Gennady Konstantinovich PARAMONOV	c. 1940; Russian; Paldiski, Estonia; SPA	Chr 10, 11, 15, 17, 33, 37, 38–40	Naval petty officer, Komsomol leader, arrested 1969 for forming "Union to Struggle for Political Rights", 1970 interned in Chernyakhovsk SPH; September 1975 transferred to the Perm regional OPH, in March 1976 released.
Boris Petrovich PAVLOV	?; Russian; Stavropol; SPA	Possev, 1974, No. 1, p. 9	Psychiatrist and senior lecturer at the Stavropol Medical Institute, with a doctoral degree. Arrested late 1972, charged with samizdat activity. His writings containing an original interpretation of Freudianism confiscated. Early 1973 declared not responsible, interned, after trial, in an OPH (?) in Novocherkassk.
L. A. PETROVA*	1939; Russian; Moscow; I	See ref. 19, chapter 9	Doctor in a works polyclinic, in 1972 refused to excuse from work certain malingerers who were friends of her boss. Interned in an OPH for five months, released through pressure of workers. See chapter 9.
PINTAN	c. 1918; Latvian; Australia; E	Survey, 1972, No. 83, p. 129; Senate Hearing, p. 34; V. Bukovsky	Latvian-born, he emigrated to Australia but subsequently returned to Latvia to visit relatives. Told he was, as a Latvian, a Soviet citizen, so return to Australia barred. Charged and committed to Leningrad SPH for persisting and contacting foreign embassies. Held there in 1964, friend of Bukovsky, who saw little chance of his quick release.
Mykola Hryhorevich PLAKHOTNYUK	1936; Ukrainian; Dnepropetrovsk region; N–SPA	Chr 24, 27, 28, 32, 39, 42; L. Plyushch	Doctor who graduated with distinction, worked in a sanatorium. Arrested January 1972, charged with Ukrainian samizdat activity (article 70 or 190–1?), declared hunger-strike in Serbsky in August–September 1972 in protest at conditions, diagnosis "schizophrenia with persecution mania; periodically not responsible". In November 1972 court ordered an SPH, then trial on "recovery" (a procedure not provided for in Soviet law). Held in Dnepropetrovsk SPH, still there in mid-1976, with a disease of the lungs.

Name	Details	References	Notes
Alexander PLENAINEN*	1943; Finn; Lvov; E	*NY Times*, 18.11.74; *Possev*, 1976, No. 8	Soviet Finn, artist, who wanted to emigrate to Finland from age of seven, when forced to learn Russian. First interned, in Moscow OPH No. 7, when he came to visit the Finnish embassy in 1961. Considered that only four out of 25 in his ward were really ill. Escaped after a few weeks, caught, re-interned, transferred to a Lvov OPH, soon released. Interned seventeen more times before eventually succeeding in emigrating in 1976; one of these followed his participation in an unofficial art show in Moscow in September 1974.
Leonid Ivanovich PLYUSHCH	1939; Ukrainian; Kiev; SPA	Chr 1, 5, 8, 11, 14, 24–28, 30, 32–40; Plyushch	Mathematician, sacked from research job in 1968 for *samizdat* activity, 1969 joined Moscow-based human-rights group; January 1972 arrested, charged (article 70), examined by three psychiatric commissions, interned July 1973–January 1976 in Dnepropetrovsk SPH. Released January 1976, emigrated same day. Now in Paris. Foreign pressure important factor. See chapters 7, 8, 10.
Anatoly Dmitrievich PONOMARYOV	1933; Russian; Leningrad; SPA–E	Chr 23, 26, 27, 35, 38, 39; V. Fainberg	Research engineer, arrested 1970 for *samizdat* activity, article 190–1. Ruled non-responsible in Leningrad OPH No. 2, January 1971, interned in Leningrad SPH, late 1972 released. September 1974 applied to emigrate as he could not get work in his profession. Immediately interned in Leningrad OPH No. 3 in ward 8 (for severest cases), but given no drugs. 1975 released, but then re-interned in October 1975 in OPH No. 3.
POPOV	?; Russian; Oktyabrskoe, Bashkiria; SPA	Chr 40	Arrested in early 1976 (?) for some "anti-Soviet" poems, ruled not responsible, and sent to an OPH or SPH. His friend, a law student at Ufa University, asked to be called as a witness at the trial, and at a Komsomol meeting in April 1976 said Popov was mentally normal and a good man; his persecution was unjust. The meeting voted by only a small majority to expel the friend from the Komsomol.
Vladimir Vasilevich POPOV	c. 1945; Russian; Leningrad; SPA	Chr 18, 26, 39	Graduate in architecture. Following his arrest and ruling of non-responsibility, sent to Leningrad SPH in August 1970. Wife told he would not be able to practise as an architect after treatment. In June 1972 court ordered transfer to an OPH; in 1973 released.

Name	Birthdate; nationality; residence; cause of internment	Sources of information	Brief summary of case
Birute POŠKIENE*	?; Lithuanian; Kaunas; R	Chr 36, 39	School janitor, she became a Protestant sectarian and vegetarian. Her husband objected and in September 1974 got a court to deprive her of her maternal rights, having earlier had the children baptized as Catholics. October 1974 Supreme Court of Lithuania heard her appeal, rejected it. October 29 forcibly interned in a Kaunas OPH (75 Kuzmos St). Only her husband had asked for this. Her friends asserted her normality and the two courts did not suggest she was ill. The procurator at the first trial had stressed her good health. Put in ward 3 of OPH (for severe cases), given strong drugs, temporarily lost her sight, could not walk. Doctors and husband insistently demanded she renounce her protestantism, then she would be freed as being well. Situation in January 1975.
POTAPOV	?; Russian; Moscow region; E–R	Y. Krylsky	Baptist, tried to emigrate to USA so as to serve God freely, interned in the late 1950s (?) in Kazan SPH, then Sychyovka SPH, where Y. Krylsky knew him in 1973, and by when he had begun to become mentally unstable.
Sergei POTYLITSYN	1952; Russian?; Transcarpathia; E	Chr 39	Charged with "illegal crossing of the border", held in Dnepropetrovsk SPH since 1971. Still there in 1976.
Nikolai Grigorevich PRISACARU	c. 1918; Rumanian; Moldavia; SPA	Survey, 1972, no. 83, p. 129; Senate Hearing, p. 33; V. Bukovsky	Rumanian by birth; after over ten years in France (Marseilles) migrated to the Soviet Union "to see with his own eyes the construction of Communism". Interned in the Leningrad SPH 1962–65 because of his participation in a strike at the Moldavian footwear factory in which he worked. Friend of Bukovsky there.

Name		References	Description
Sergei **PURTOV**	c. 1940?; Russian; Leningrad; SPA	Chr 23, 24, 26, 27, 39; CHR 2; Yan Krylsky; L. Kvachevsky	Engineer, arrested in March 1971 under article 70. His group had called for a return to true Leninist policies. At trial in January 1972 declared not responsible; sent to the Leningrad SPH. In February supported hunger strike of Fainberg. In July given drug injections although therapist declared them contra-indicated. In August 1972 transferred to Smolensk (*not* Dnepropetrovsk) SPH, where Y. Krylsky knew him in late 1972. In early 1976 the *Chronicle* believed tentatively that he was in Sychyovka SPH. Later in 1976 reportedly held in Kashchenko OPH near Alma-Ata, Kazakhstan, and in poor health.
Viktor Parfentevich **RAFALSKY**	c. 1920; Ukrainian; W. Ukraine; SPA	Chr 40; L. Plyushch	Fought in war, then became school headmaster in W. Ukraine. Also a writer and poet. In 1954 arrested for belonging to clandestine Marxist group, interned in Leningrad SPH. 1954–59 underwent six psychiatric examinations, three in Serbsky (all found him schizophrenic and not responsible), three in Leningrad (all found him responsible). Freed 1959. 1962 re-arrested for links with a Marxist group and for some "anti-Soviet" literary works. Interned in SPH for two years, renounced any concern with politics. 1968 re-arrested because an old "anti-Soviet" novel of his found in his flat, even though no proof he had ever shown it to anyone. Interned in Dnepropetrovsk SPH. Early 1970s told by doctors he was sane, but would not be freed except into someone's guardianship. All efforts to find a guardian then sabotaged by KGB. In 1975 punished with heavy drug treatment, health deteriorated.
Ilya Aronovich **RIPS**	1948; Jewish; Riga; SPA	Chr 8, 14, 20; Rips	Brilliant mathematics student. April 1969 attempted self-immolation on Freedom Square in Riga as protest against the Soviet invasion of Czechoslovakia. Charged under article 70 and found not responsible. Confined to a Riga OPH. Released April 1971, emigrated to Israel in December. See chapter 7.

Name	Birthdate; nationality; residence; cause of internment	Sources of information	Brief summary of case
Vasyl RUBAN	1942; Ukrainian; Kiev; N	Chr 30; Ukrainian Herald, 4, 6, 7–8	Poet, worked for journal Molod Ukrainy for some years, then his work began to be censored for being too nationalistic. Arrested in 1972, ruled not responsible, in 1973 interned in Dnepropetrovsk SPH. Unknown whether or not released. Chronicle 30 apparently confuses him with Nikolai Ruban (Chronicle 17).
Izrail RUSTAN*	c. 1940?; Uzbek; Tashkent?; SPA	Private communication from fellow inmate	A student sent to study in India, informed there about the Tashkent earthquake of 1966. Twenty-three of the Soviet students in India wrote back to the USSR they believed there had been an underground atomic explosion, not an earthquake. Summoned home, interned in Kashchenko OPH No. 1 in Moscow. Given Sulfazin. Subsequent fate unknown.
Alexander RYBAKOV	?; Russian; Novosibirsk; SPA	Chr 24, 25, 27	Technician at Institute of Mineral Processing. Arrested March 1972 in connection with case to suppress Chronicle, after a hectograph and samizdat had been found during a search (article 70?). Diagnosed as schizophrenic at Serbsky in August 1972. Subsequent fate unknown.
Viktor SALATY	1948; Estonian?; Tartu; E	Doctor's personal communication	Radio repair technician. In 1973 attempted to cross the frontier into Finland. Declared not responsible as supposedly being a "hippie" and interned in an OPH in Tartu for six months. See chapter 9.
Eduard Valentinovich SAMOILOV	c. 1953?; Russian?; Kazakhstan-Moscow; SPA	Chr 37, 39	Fourth-year student of journalism (from Kazakhstan) at Moscow University when arrested in May 1975 and charged under article 70. During a search his heterodox work on the history of the USSR and the party had been confiscated. Labelled non-responsible in Serbsky, but as of early 1976 outcome of trial unknown.

Name		Chr refs	
Nikolai Nikolayevich SAMSONOV	1906–71; Russian; Leningrad; SPA	Chr 8, 18; V. Bukovsky	Eminent geophysicist. Wrote essay calling for a return to Leninist principles of government. Charged in 1956 under article 70 (then 58/10). Judged not responsible by commission under Dr Torubarov of Serbsky. Sent to Leningrad SPH, friend of Bukovsky. Released in 1964 after eight years and an eventual insincere recantation. Until death worked for two months per year at a geophysics institute and received a pension. See chapter 3.
Yury Petrovich SAPEZHKO	1936; Ukrainian?; Petrozavodsk; E	Chr 18, 39	Charged under articles 83 and 15 with intention to cross the border illegally. Diagnosed as schizophrenic, ruled not responsible, in early 1971 held in Leningrad SPH. Released by 1976.
Vaclav Leonidovich SEVRUK	c. 1937; Lithuanian; Vilnius; SPA–N	Chr 15, 22, 24–26, 29	Sociologist and philosopher, worked in History Institute. Arrested January 1972, charged with *Chronicle* connections, article 70. In January 1973 Vilnius court ordered an OPH in Vilnius. Released July 1973, emigrated 1974, lives in New York.
Evgeny Viktorovich SHASHENKOV	1932; Russian; Leningrad; SPA	Chr 5, 8, 18, 26; CHR 5–6	Engineer. Arrested in 1950 as a student at Leningrad University for a letter to Stalin, interned in an SPH; re-interned in 1963–64. Arrested in early August 1968 for rôle in human-rights group, charged under article 70, diagnosed as non-typical manic depressive psychosis. Sent to Leningrad SPH, transferred in June 1972 to an OPH, soon released.
SHATRAVKI brothers	c. 1950 and 1952; Ukrainian?; ?; E	Chr 40; L. Plyushch	Crossed the border into Finland, caught, handed back by Finnish authorities. Charged, ruled not responsible, interned in Dnepropetrovsk SPH, where Plyushch met them in 1975.
Yury Aleksandrovich SHIKHANOVICH	1933; Jewish; Moscow; SPA	Chr 2, 5, 9, 24, 25, 27–30, 32	Mathematician, arrested September 1972 for *samizdat* activity, article 70, sent by a Moscow court in November 1973 to OPH No. 9 in Yakhroma, Moscow Region, released July 1974. Foreign pressure important factor. See chapters 7 and 10.

Name	Birthdate; nationality; residence; cause of interment	Sources of information	Brief summary of case
Gennady Mikhailovich SHIMANOV*	1937; Russian; Moscow; R	See chapter 6	In 1962 committed himself voluntarily to Gannushkin OPH No. 4 in Moscow, stayed two months as he went through an inner crisis and became an Orthodox believer. "Treated" for his belief. Later entered the army, but had to leave in 1967 when questioned by KGB about his links with dissenters. May 1969 forcibly interned in Kashchenko OPH No. 1 because of his influence as an Orthodox layman around whom people gathered. Released after three weeks following his hunger strike.
Vladimir SHLEPNYOV	?; Russian; Moscow; E	Chr 26, 39	In 1971 charged with intent to commit treason after he had tried to cross the border. Declared not responsible, sent to Kazan SPH. Released in 1973.
Svetlana SHRAMKO*	c. 1945?; Russian?; Ryazan; SPA	Solzhenitsyn in NY Times, 30.9.74	Sent complaints to various bodies about pollution caused by a fibre plant. June 1974 interned in an OPH in (?) Ryazan. Released five weeks later, went to Moscow, told her story to NY Times correspondent. Subsequent fate unknown.
Lyubov SHTEIN	1949; ?; ?; E	Chr 39	In 1971 escaped from the USSR, but arrested in Czechoslovakia, handed back to USSR, charged with treason (article 64). In early 1976 held in Kazan SPH.
Vladimir SHUNENKOV	1949; Ukrainian?; ?; SPA	Chr 41	An airforce pilot, he lost his job in 1972 following a stay in a mental hospital. Six months later arrested for "anti-Soviet activity", ruled not responsible, interned in Chernyakhovsk SPH. Still there in 1976.

Name	Description	Source	Details
Fyodor Akimovich SIDENKO*	Served sentence 1965–70, article 70. 20 November 1974 forcibly interned in OPH in Ussuriisk in Far Eastern Region (163 Sukhanov Str, evidently because Brezhnev and Ford were due to confer on 23–24 November in Vladivostok (100 miles away). A Pentecostal Christian, he was insistently questioned by psychiatrists about his desire to emigrate, then given drug injections which made him unable to walk or sit and caused terrible pain. Evidently released after a few weeks. The OPH appears to be partly an SPH, as the orderlies (or some of them) were ordinary criminals serving their terms. It was filled to overflowing during Ford's visit to Vladivostok. The politicals were treated sadistically in it, the genuinely ill inmates much better.	AS 564, 2007	1938; Ukrainian; Partizansk (nr. Pacific coast); E–R
Olga Filippovna SKREBETS*	Medical doctor working in tuberculosis research institute. Announced in 1971 that she was resigning from the party on religious grounds and because of the invasion of Czechoslovakia. Hospitalized in the Pavlov OPH in Kiev and diagnosed as an early schizophrenic. Dismissed from job on release from the hospital. Found work in an ambulance service.	Chr 21	1938; Ukrainian?; Kiev; R–SPA
I. N. SLISHEVSKY	Arrested in c. early 1971, charged apparently under article 70 with writing anonymous letters. Declared not responsible and sent to a psychiatric hospital. The chief accused in a case where a second accused received seven years of camps and exile. Unknown if and when released.	Chr 22	?; Russian?; Sevastopol; SPA
Oleg SMIRNOV	Architect. Associate of totalitarian A. Fetisov (see above). Charged in 1968 under article 70, ruled not responsible, sent to Leningrad SPH. Released c. 1972.	Chr 7, 8, 18, 39	1934; Russian; Moscow; SPA
Viktoria S. SMIRNOVA*	In c. 1969 started applying to emigrate, also wrote to the UN to U Thant. In March–April 1971 interned for a month in Leningrad OPH No. 3, during 24th party congress. Told by doctors: "Stop writing letters to the UN and no one will put you in the mad-house." Chief psychiatrist of Leningrad, V. Belyayev, tried to persuade her she was hearing voices. Fate since early 1972 unknown.	AS 1071a, b and c	?; Russian; Leningrad; E

Name	Birthdate; nationality; residence; cause of internment	Sources of information	Brief summary of case
Oleg Georgiyevich SOLOVYOV	c. 1937; Russian; Stavropol; SPA	Chr 27	Chemical engineer. Arrested in March 1969, charged under article 190–1 as the (self-admitted) author of samizdat manuscripts. Declared not responsible by a commission in Stavropol, north Caucasus. Transferred from Stavropol OPH to Chernyakhovsk SPH in November 1970 and then to Oryol SPH in January 1971. In July 1972 transferred to Stavropol OPH and released a month later.
Vasily SPINENKO	1945; Ukrainian; Nizhny Tagil, W. Siberia; SPA	Chr 33, 24; V. Bukovsky	Graduate of Philosophy faculty of Donetsk University, arrested March 1971, charged under articles 70 and 72 with being theorist of an underground political group (seven other members imprisoned for two to five years each), examined for one month in the forensic psychiatric section of the Sverdlovsk regional OPH, judged healthy and responsible, transferred to Serbsky, where after two months diagnosed as schizophrenic with persecution delusions and not responsible. Bukovsky knew him there in October. In November 1971 Sverdlovsk court ruled that he be interned. In 1974, according to a friend, held in Chernyakhovsk SPH. Unknown if and when released.
Pyotr Petrovich STARCHIK	1939; Russian; Moscow; SPA–R	Chr 25, 26, 28, 34, 35, 39, 42	Store administrator in psychology institute, arrested April 1972, charged with circulating anti-Soviet leaflets, article 70; December 1972 court ordered a SPH. Psychiatric diagnosis included his religious beliefs as a symptom of his "sluggish schizophrenia". Held in Kazan SPH, transferred in November 1974 to OPH No. 15 in Moscow, February 1975 released. September 1976 reinterned in OPH No. 5 at Stolbovaya near Moscow for giving recitals of unofficial songs in his flat. Released in November after a strong campaign in his defence and the formation of a committee for his release in Moscow.

Name	Details	Source	Description
Algis STATKEVIČIUS	1937; Lithuanian; Vilnius; SPA	Chr 17–19, 22; private communication	Former official of Sociological Research Bureau in Lithuanian Ministry of Finance. Arrested May 1970 in Vilnius. Charged with authorship of *A Critique of the Communist Manifesto*. In November ruled not responsible by a court and sent first to the hospital section of the Lukiški prison in Vilnius, then, after nearly a year, transferred to a Vilnius OPH. Released by 1973.
Alexander STEPANOV	1936; Russian; middle Volga; SPA	Chr 39	Radio technician, wrote several letters (one to science fiction writer Kazantsev) about his science fictional view of the world, in which the Communists appeared unattractive. Arrested in 1970, article 70, sent to Kazan SPH, still there in 1976, his health bad and receiving contra-indicated drug treatment.
Pavel Nikolayevich STOROZHEVOI*	c. 1920?; Russian; N. Caucasus; SPA–I	Tarsis in *Kaznimye*	An army major. In 1962 he protested against the gross corruption of the commander of his military district, interned in Kashchenko OPH No. 1 in Moscow. Was retired prematurely from the army. Unknown when released.
Elena STROYEVA*	c. 1930–75; Russian; Moscow; SPA–E	Chr 10, 19, 21, 26	Editor, human-rights dissenter, Orthodox. In 1971 applied to emigrate, in March joined a Jewish group lobbying the procurator-general about arrests of Jews. Arrested with husband Titov, interned in Kashchenko OPH No. 1 for two to three weeks. May 1972 emigrated to France.
G. SUPRUNYUK*	c. 1935?; Ukrainian?; Penza; SPA	AS 1407	Policeman, tried to combat corruption of colleagues in Krasnodar. As reprisal, disciplinary case against him begun in 1967, then in 1968 a criminal case fabricated. Arrested, sent for repeated psychiatric examinations, but saved from ruling of non-responsibility by courage of the chief psychiatrist of the Krasnodar regional OPH, Dr M. Dyakonova, who strongly opposed abuses of psychiatry. In early 1971,

Name	Birthdate; nationality; residence; cause of internment	Sources of information	Brief summary of case
			by great efforts, got the case quashed, moved to Penza. In May 1971 went to Moscow to seek retribution for those who had illegally prosecuted him, but forcibly interned in OPH No. 3 "for examination". This consisted of instruction not to meddle in the wrong things, and of a severe beating by orderlies. Fought for release, obtained it within a week. In 1972 appealed to International Red Cross to protect him from future persecution (AS 1407).
Mindaugas TAMONIS*	1940–75; Lithuanian; Vilnius; SPA–N–R	Chr 35, 38, 39; CLCC 10, 12, 20	Engineer, poet, circulated in April 1974 a statement calling for democratization, national rights for Lithuania and a monument to the victims of Stalinism. 17 June forcibly interned in a Vilnius OPH (5, Vasara St), given eighteen insulin injections, which induced (a) chronic insomnia, (b) seriously affected his sight, (c) made him gain 36 pounds in weight. September 1974 released. 25 June 1975, wrote an open letter similar to the first, 27 June re-interned, released a month later. Summoned again, he refused to go, and on 5 November he was found dead under a train, apparently having committed suicide under the pressure of continuing persecution.
Stanislav TAMOSHEVICH*	c. 1945?; Belorussian; Brest; E	Private communication from fellow inmate	A student. He asked permission to emigrate, was interned in Kashchenko OPH No. 1 in Moscow. Held there in 1966. Subsequent fate unknown.
Yury Pavlovich TARAKANOV*	1940; Russian; Leningrad; SPA–E	Chr 39	Teacher of English, imprisoned 1962–64 under article 70. Interned in Leningrad OPH No. 3 during the 24th party congress in 1971. In 1975 refused a visa to emigrate to the USA. In early 1976 again held in OPH No. 3.

Name		Sources	Description
Adrian Aleksandrovich TARASOV*	1945; Russian; Moscow; SPA	Chr 29; V. Prussakov	December 1963 arrested, ruled psychopathic but responsible in Serbsky, sentenced to eight years for treason (article 64, speaking too freely to French friends). In September 1964, a new trial gave him three years under article 70. December 1966 released, 1967 sentenced to six months for violating residence regulations by visiting mother in Moscow. July 1967 arrested in same circumstances, taken to Gannushkin OPH No. 4 in Moscow, ruled schizophrenic. Since then he has been kept in various OPHs under civil commitment, as, having been ruled mentally incompetent, he can be discharged only into the care of his family, yet this can't be done as his mother lives in Moscow and his earlier sentence under article 70 excludes him living in Moscow and other big cities.
Valery Yakovlevich TARSIS*	1906; Russian; Moscow; SPA	See chapter 3	Successful writer of stories, translator, party member until 1960. In 1962 published two stories abroad, in August interned in Kashchenko OPH No. 1. Released February 1963 after Western protests, wrote Ward 7, published it abroad. February 1966 allowed to go to UK to give lectures, then deprived of citizenship. Settled in Switzerland. See chapter 3.
Iosip Mykhaylovich TERELYA	1942; Ukrainian; Vinnitsa; N	Chr 11, 18, 27, 30, 39, 41; A. Radygin; Times, 26.11.76	Serving a term for a common crime, then, in camp, given eight years for nationalist activity in late 1960s. Served term in Mordovia, then from 1969 in Vladimir Prison. Tried again c. 1972 for agitation in prison (article 70), ruled not responsible, sent to Sychyovka SPH. Transferred to Chelyabinsk OPH in 1975, released April 1976. Married fiancée, a doctor, ruled fit for both work and army service, took job as a joiner. November 1976 interned in Vinnitsa regional OPH as being "socially dangerous". An amateur poet and artist. (Name mis-spelled as Vareta, Tereza, Terelli, in early sources.)

Name	Birthdate; nationality; residence; cause of internment	Sources of information	Brief summary of case
Valiakhmed Khaidarovich TIMOKHIN	1947; Tatar?; Vladimir region; N	Chr 41	An artist and restorer, arrested November 1975 in Strunino, charged under article 70 with circulating leaflets. These called for the creation of underground groups to remove the "Brezhnev clique" and re-order society along traditional Russian nationalist and Orthodox lines, as advocated by Solzhenitsyn. Held in Vladimir Prison for investigation, but refused to co-operate. Sent for psychiatric examinations, first locally in Vladimir, then in Serbsky (January–February 1976). Ruled not responsible, interned in Sychyovka SPH.
I. TIMONIN	?; Russian; ?; SPA–R	Chr 18; *Senate Hearing*	A Christian who registered a political protest by pouring ink into a ballot box. In 1971 was held in Leningrad SPH, where his religion was being mocked and the doctors said they would not release him until he renounced his faith.
Vladimir Grigorevich TITOV	1937; Russian; Kaluga region; E–SPA	Chr 27, 30, 37, 39, 41; Y. Krylsky	Graduated from KGB training school, rank of first lieutenant. Native city Kiev. Became disgusted with KGB's methods. Sentenced to five years in 1969 for writing a statement in which he renounced his citizenship, article 70. Served term in Mordovia, then from 1971 in Vladimir Prison. In 1973 charged again under article 70 for a letter written in prison. Ruled non-responsible, sent in 1973 to Sychyovka SPH, became close friend of Y. Krylsky. In 1975 transferred to Kaluga OPH No. 1, evidently because family lives there.
Yury TITOV*	c. 1930; Russian; Moscow; SPA–E	Chr 10, 19, 24, 26	Artist, dissenter, Orthodox. In 1971 applied to emigrate. In March 1971 arrested with wife Stroyeva (see above) and interned in Kash-chenko OPH for two to three weeks. Emigrated May 1972 to France.

Name	Details	References	Description
Gennady Nikolaevich TRIFONOV*	1945; Russian; Leningrad; SPA	Chr 42	Writer. Recruited by KGB as an informer in 1967, while in army; spied on writers to whom he was secretary, but heart not in it, deliberately avoided harming them. August 1973 asked to resign, request refused, September made suicide attempt, then dismissed from KGB. Told friends about previous work, so interned in late 1974 in Leningrad OPH for a month. KGB officials visited him there, tried to recruit him again, he refused. Warned by psychiatrist after release that if he revealed true circumstances of his internment he would be interned again. In 1975 became active in artistic and literary dissent circles, in 1976 applied to emigrate to US to join relatives. In July US embassy informed him he would be given an immigrant visa. In August arrested after KGB had told him he had committed treason and would receive long imprisonment in a camp or SPH.
Vladimir Ilich TRIFONOV	1938; Russian; Kalinin; SPA	Chr 26, 34, 39; V. Fainberg	1965 expelled from teachers' training college on political grounds. March 1968 arrested for making "anti-Soviet statements" (article 190-1), paranoia diagnosed, interned in autumn 1968 in Leningrad SPH, still there in 1976. Considers himself healthy but refuses to attend psychiatric commissions, regarding them "a farce".
Viktor TSELYKH	?; Russian?; Krasnoyarsk; SPA?	Chr 41	A programming engineer, arrested c. 1971 and charged with duplicating samizdat (article 70?). Refused to co-operate with investigators, ruled not responsible. In 1974 held in Smolensk SPH.
Lyubov TSYGANKOVA	c. 1920?; Russian; Wanderer; R	N. Gorbanevskaya	An Orthodox wanderer who, in the Russian tradition, wandered from village to village, for ten years, staying with strangers and preaching God's word. Arrested in 1958, ruled not responsible, sent to Kazan SPH, held there twelve years, but preserved her will and intellect. Autumn 1971 transferred to an OPH. Subsequent fate unknown.

Name	Birthdate; nationality; residence; cause of internment	Sources of information	Brief summary of case
Aleksei Lvovich TUMERMAN*	1942; Jewish; Moscow; SPA–E	Chr 19, 26, 27; *British Journal of Psychiatry*, 1973, p. 237; AS 1237	Had psychotherapy in early twenties, but no more contact with psychiatrists until became a dissenter seven to eight years later. Imprisoned for fifteen days in March–April 1971 during the 24th party congress, after his protest with other Jews, demanding to emigrate. Two days after release interned in OPH No. 8 for two to three weeks. Released under parents' guardianship. May 1972 held for nine days in OPH No. 5 during Nixon's visit to Moscow. February 1973 emigrated to Israel, then USA.
Stanislav Ivanovich TYSTSEVICH	1924; Belorussian?; Moscow; SPA?	Chr 27	Economist. Arrested in April 1967 under article 70 for writing anonymous letters of a political nature (denied authorship). Declared not responsible at Serbsky (Lunts was one examiner) and later sent to the Kazan SPH. In September 1967 transferred to Chernyakhovsk SPH and in January 1971 to Oryol SPH. In September 1971 transferred to an OPH in Moscow and released in June 1972.
Lev Grigorevich UBOZHKO	c. 1935?; Ukrainian?; Moscow; SPA	Chr 13, 15–19, 36, 37, 39	Physicist, arrested January 1970 in Sverdlovsk on trip to take law exams as external student of Sverdlovsk Univ., sentenced for *samizdat* activity to three years, article 190–1 (his lawyer spoke of a certain mental instability). Served term near Omsk, after one-and-a-half years new charges preferred under article 70. Ruled non-responsible, interned in Tashkent SPH 1972–74, transferred to OPH No. 2 in Chelyabinsk region (central Siberia). In early 1975 friends feared a third prosecution in connection with case against his friend Lvov. In mid-1975 he escaped from the OPH, by early 1976 caught and returned to it.

Yury Aleksandrovich VETOKHIN	?; Russian; Leningrad; E	Chr 21, 42	Tried to cross the frontier, charged, ruled not responsible, interned. In 1971 held in Dnepropetrovsk SPH, in early 1976 still there.
Boris Dmitrievich VINOKUROV*	c. 1915; Russian; Moscow; SPA	Chr 35, 39	Head of a personnel department in the State Committee for All-Union Radio and Television (in fact a ministry), he said at a party meeting on 19 February 1975, that the situation in the media and the economy was bad, and that the only solution was to allow a two-party system. He announced his resignation from the Communist Party and his intention to form a new party. He ended: "After all, someone has got to give a lead!" On 24 February he was hospitalized, and at the next party meeting, in early March, it was reported that he, his wife and daughter were all mentally ill, and that a doctor had said that Vinokurov's health had recently deteriorated. His career had been long and honourable. In 1975 held in the Kashchenko OPH. Unknown if released since.
Julia VISHNEVSKAYA*	1949; Russian; Moscow; SPA	Chr 9, 15–17, 19, 22	Poet. Interned in a Moscow OPH in December 1965 for taking part in demonstration in defence of Sinyavsky and Daniel. Soon released, active in human-rights movement. Arrested outside courthouse at the time of Gorbanevskaya's trial in July 1970. Charged under article 191 —resisting the authorities. Transferred to Serbsky on 22 July and diagnosed as sluggish schizophrenia. Held there till 12 October, then released and placed under care of parents. In March 1971 placed in Kashchenko OPH by police during 24th party congress. Given injections by force. In November emigrated to Israel. Later moved to Germany, became a research worker at Radio Liberty.
Nikolai Ivanovich VLADYKIN*	c. 1925?; Russian; Tula; R	de Meeûs, p. 48; AS 1320, 1321	Dissenting Baptist, in December 1972 came to Moscow with wife (see below) to ask for return of their house, confiscated because the Baptists held meetings there. Arrested, interned in an OPH for short time.

Name	Birthdate; nationality; residence; cause of internment	Sources of information	Brief summary of case
P. R. VLADYKINA*	c. 1925?; Russian; Tula; R	As above	Wife of above. Arrested, released, went to visit her son in Glukhov, interned in the Glukhov OPH because of her trip to Moscow. Given forcible injections, released within two weeks.
VOLKOV*	c. 1900; Russian; Volgograd; I	Tarsis in *Kazŭimye*	Chairman of the auditing commission of the Volgograd regional party committee. In 1961 refused to approve accounts which clearly masked massive corruption. Interned in Volgograd, then Kashchenko OPH No. 1 in Moscow. Already in his second year when Tarsis met him, expected to die there.
Oleg Ivanovich VOROBYOV*	1940; Russian; Moscow; SPA	Chr 10, 11, 16	A teacher of literature. While a student at Moscow University, was sent to Serbsky in January 1966 after taking part in demonstration in Pushkin Square. Declared responsible, not prosecuted. In September 1969 forcibly interned in Moscow's OPH No. 15, held for five weeks. Supported Action Group's first appeal to UN in 1969. 1970 received a six-year sentence (article 70).
Ivan Antonovich YAKHIMOVICH	1931; Latvian; Jurmala, near Riga; SPA	*Senate Hearing*; Chr 1, 3-4, 6-7, 9, 13-20	After working as a teacher, became chairman of a collective farm in 1960, began dissenting activities in January 1968. Expelled from party, and as chairman, soon thereafter. In March 1969 arrested under article 190-1. Underwent psychiatric examinations, the last at Serbsky in December 1969. Ruled not responsible, interned in April 1970 in republican OPH in Riga. After recanting, released April 1971 as invalid of second category.

Name	Details	Sources	Description
YAKOVLEV*	1953; Russian; Smolensk region; SPA	Chr 28	Soldier in an army unit near Moscow. Interned in Kashchenko OPH in Moscow in early 1972 for criticizing army procedures and compulsory military service. Held for one-and-a-half months, without treatment, then discharged from the army as mentally ill.
N. I. YAKUBENKO	c. 1940?; Ukrainian; Kerch, Ukraine; SPA	Chr 22, 33	Took part in small workers' rights group, wrote "A Programme for the Working Class", in 1971 arrested, ruled non-responsible, interned in SPH or OPH. Later fate unknown.
Vyacheslav Antonovich YATSENKO	1948; Ukrainian; Nikolayev; SPA	Chr 40; L. Plyushch	Studied at ship-building institute in Nikolayev. Sentenced to one year for attempt to cross the Finnish border, then, c. 1973, charged under article 190-1, judged not responsible in an OPH near Nikolayev; May 1975 arrested again, charged (190-1) with circulation of anti-Soviet letters. Ruled not responsible in Serbsky in autumn 1975, interned in Dnepropetrovsk SPH; became friendly with Plyushch, who describes him as an independent Marxist.
Viktor Aleksandrovich YUDIN*	1938; Jewish?; Luga, nr. Leningrad; E	AS 1968; Neue Zürcher Zeitung, 3.3.75	Driver. In August 1973 handed to the KGB in Luga an appeal to Brezhnev to allow his family to emigrate to W. Germany. Arrested the next day and interned in an OPH, where given drug injections and ECT. Released after four-and-a-half months and kept on the psychiatric register. Doctor wife has relatives in Switzerland.
Gennady ZADKOV	1940; Russian; ?; SPA?	Chr 39	While in a camp, charged under article 70, ruled not responsible, in 1968 sent to Kazan SPH, still there in 1976.
Alexander I. ZHELEZNOV	c. 1945?; Russian; Moscow?; R	Chr. 27, 28; private communication; AS 1240	Student at teachers' college in Ulan-Ude, capital of the Buryat Republic. In 1972 charged with belonging to an illegal Buddhist group, article 227. With three friends, declared not responsible by Ulan-Ude psychiatrists (for extracts from official reports, see AS 1240); court in November 1972 ordered an SPH, but in fact sent to an OPH in (?) Moscow. Released within a year, but kept on psychiatric register.

Name	Birthdate; nationality; residence; cause of interment	Sources of information	Brief summary of case
Algirdas Pranas ŽIPRE	1927; Lithuanian; Lithuania; N–I	Chr 32, 34; AS 2229	Fought with Lithuanian partisans, believed the amnesty declared in 1956, came out of the forests, arrested one-and-a-half years later, in April 1958, sentenced to 25 years, but believed the sentence was only fifteen years, as fifteen had been recently declared the maximum for any prison sentence. In early 1973 told he had ten more years to serve, began writing complaints and protests, believing his sentence had been falsified. October 1973 sent from his camp to psychiatric section of Mordovian camps hospital, in camp 3, then ruled mentally ill, the only symptom being his letters to official bodies. In July 1974 sent to Serbsky, ruled responsible, returned to same section of camp hospital, still there in January 1975, not yet returned to camp.
Mikhail Stefanovich ZVEREV	1925; Russian; Pyatigorsk; SPA	Chr 39, 40	Electrical engineer, arrested February 1975, charged under article 70, considered not responsible by Serbsky ("paranoid development of the personality", "delusions of reformism"), ruling upheld by a court in Pyatigorsk in September 1975. After appeal, sent to Chernyakhovsk SPH, arrived late December. Head wound in the war, but wife considers him normal. Was never on psychiatric register. Charged with circulating twenty articles defaming the Soviet system and with producing and circulating leaflets.

APPENDIX II

OUR RECOMMENDATIONS FOR COMBATING AND PREVENTING ABUSE

What could be done to try to bring the Soviet misuse of psychiatry to an end, and to prevent its spread elsewhere? Drawing upon a variety of sources, and pondering the problem ourselves, we believe that several steps can, and should, be taken. Our proposals relate primarily to desirable, indeed necessary, changes within the Soviet Union, but some are also relevant to potential abuse in other countries. We also present a group of suggestions which are more general in their scope and which would be applicable universally. What we propose here is *in addition to* the pressures (documented in chapters 4 and 10) which can often be effectively exerted through publicity in the world media and through action by national and international bodies in the fields of, in particular, psychiatry, law and human rights.

Proposals for Change in Soviet Law and Procedure

We would be over-ambitious to hope to convince the Soviet government that it should strike out from the criminal code articles such as numbers 70, 190–1, 227, and the like, used widely in the last decade to suppress dissent. Although these articles are incompatible with the Soviet Constitution, and would be untenable in a Western-style democracy, they are clearly regarded by the régime as indispensable. What we can more reasonably propose, however, are changes of specific points of Soviet law and procedure regarding both civil and criminal commitment, which hitherto have facilitated the political use of psychiatry. Our proposals are based, to a large extent, on the excellently prepared sets of recommendations issued by both Amnesty International[1] and the Moscow Human Rights Committee.[2] We are not legal experts ourselves.

A. *Civil Commitment*

1. The criteria for a civil commitment should be stipulated as specifically and unambiguously as possible and revolve around the likelihood of the patient doing serious harm either to himself or to others. There should be clear evidence of dangerousness and an

absolute need to protect the patient or the public. The concept of dangerousness to an institution or organization, and the concept of "socially dangerous tendencies", are both too vague and broad to constitute reasons for compulsory hospitalization.

2. Compulsory hospitalization by civil commitment should be permitted for a limited period only. The patient should then be allowed to gain voluntary status or his release from the hospital. Only if the level of dangerousness in the patient warrants an extension of compulsory treatment, should this be legally permissible. (The current procedure of assessment once monthly permits a civil commitment to continue indefinitely with the onus in effect on the patient to prove that this is no longer necessary.)

3. There should be a provision for judicial review and the patient and his family should be made fully aware of it. The patient should be entitled, by right, to have private access to a lawyer at regular intervals, and to be able to appeal to a court against his compulsory treatment or confinement.

4. The patient should have the right to lay charges against a psychiatrist or other hospital personnel for malpractice. A specific clause should be added to the criminal code, which would recognize the criminal responsibility of medical personnel for an unjustifiable commitment in the first place, and for the continuation of compulsory confinement for non-medical reasons.

B. *Criminal Commitment*
1. In a criminal investigation in which the mental health of the detainee is suspected, private access to a lawyer should be a right once a charge is laid against the detainee. The access should be allowed throughout the legal proceedings, including the period during which an accused person might undergo a forensic-psychiatric examination. Meetings between the accused and his lawyer should be private with no restrictions imposed on their frequency or duration. (At present access to a lawyer before the end of the investigation, which usually last several months, is banned except in unusually complex cases, and then only at the discretion of the investigators.)

2. Bail should be granted (unless there is evidence that the accused might abscond) so that there would be less chance of the investigator sending the accused, without justification, for psychiatric examination in e.g. the Serbsky Institute.

3. The accused should be fully informed of the charges against him and be permitted to submit evidence or petitions he regards as pertinent.

4. The accused, his family, and his lawyer should have the right to submit (if they so wish) their own choice of experts for a psychiatric examination, or at least a choice of two of the three experts. If there is any evidence of possible bias in a psychiatrist nominated for a forensic commission, the accused should have the right to have him excluded from it.

5. The accused should be provided with the result of his psychiatric examination and be allowed to pose questions to the experts, challenge them, or make statements for inclusion in the psychiatric commission's report.

6. The accused should not be subjected to any excessively disturbing or prolonged methods of psychiatric examination while under investigation; he should not be administered any treatment unless absolutely necessary.

7. The defendant should have the right to be present in court during his trial unless there is overwhelming evidence that he would disrupt the proceedings. If unable to be present for this reason, the defendant should be allowed to submit written statements to the court and be represented by his family and/or friends of his choice, in addition to his lawyer.

8. The defendant's family and friends should have the right to be present during the entire trial. The proceedings should be completely open to the public, including the press, both local and foreign.

9. The defendant's lawyer should have the right to submit petitions, to cross-examine witnesses, to draw on extra witnesses, and, of special importance, to call for another psychiatric examination with psychiatrists of the defendant's choice, if the findings of any previous commission are not acceptable to him and his lawyer. In fact, both prosecution and defence counsels should have the right to call for additional medical evidence as well as the right of rebuttal of that evidence.

10. A clear distinction and separation should be made in the proceedings between the determination that the defendant is guilty or not of the charges, and the question of his responsibility. If he is found not guilty, the case should, of course, be dismissed, and any question of his need for medical treatment should become the concern exclusively of the health authorities.

11. The concept of partial responsibility should be incorporated into the legal procedure.

12. The defendant and his family, in appealing to a higher court against a ruling which they dispute, should be able, if desired, to

include the evidence of another psychiatric commission of their own choice as part of the appeal.

13. A defendant found both guilty of the charge and not responsible because of mental illness should be committed for compulsory treatment in an SPH only if he poses a definite danger to himself or to others. If at all possible the patient should be treated in the community or in an OPH.

14. If confined compulsorily to an SPH, a patient should have the following rights:

(a) private access to a lawyer with no restrictions placed on the frequency and duration of meetings.

(b) judicial review—the right to appeal to a court at regular intervals against forcible treatment or forcible hospitalization or for a review of the decision of a psychiatric commission.

(c) as in civil commitment, the right to lay charges against a psychiatrist or other hospital personnel for malpractice.

(d) a guarantee that the court will accept the recommendation of a psychiatric commission for release. The decision for release should be based entirely on medical factors and not on the gravity of the original crime or other legal considerations.

(e) the right to adequate and humane treatment and provision of information regarding the nature of his treatment.

(f) the right to: regular and private visits by his family; regular parcels of food, books, etc.; recreational and occupational activities; reasonable periods of daily exercise; pen and paper; private correspondence without restriction; access to newspapers, books, and journals without censorship; and free association with other patients.

(Points (e) and (f) are, of course, also applicable to the OPH.)

15. The SPH should undergo the following administrative changes:

(a) the SPHs should come under the administration of the Ministry of Health, and their subordination to the Ministry of Internal Affairs should be ended in all respects.

(b) convicted criminals should not serve their term in the SPH as orderlies or in any other capacity.

(c) warders and other staff concerned with security should not have close contact with the patients. Rather, psychiatrists, trained nurses and orderlies should have exclusive responsibility for their care.

Proposals for Universal Application
We believe that three measures could be taken at the international level, both to combat the Soviet misuse and to prevent its occurrence

elsewhere. One measure is the creation of a *Universal Code of Ethics for Psychiatrists*. Codes do exist for the general medical profession (e.g. Hippocratic Oath, the Geneva Convention Code of Medical Ethics), but they fail to cover several ethical questions which are unique to psychiatry. Compulsory hospitalization, criminal responsibility, the right to treatment, provision for judicial review, informed consent for treatment—these are but a few of the taxing issues with which psychiatrists have to deal. Precedents exist for more specialized codes concerning specific medical situations, e.g. the Declaration of Oslo on therapeutic abortion, the Declaration of Tokyo on torture, and the Declaration of Helsinki on clinical experimentation. A code setting high ethical standards for the psychiatrist would, at the least, help to enhance his moral sense.

Who should set the standards? Professor Alfred Freedman of New York has proposed the establishment of a group of psychiatric and legal experts drawn from around the world, and independent of any national government, who would devise "a set of standards for psychiatry in relation to human rights that could have great impact on an international scale". This *ad hoc* group would submit its proposals to member nations of the World Health Organization and World Psychiatric Association for approval and adoption. The proposals would also be submitted to the UN Commission on Human Rights, the International Red Cross and the International Court of Justice "for consideration in cases of abuse of the human rights of the mentally ill brought to their attention".[3]

The World Psychiatric Association embarked on a similar enterprise in 1973 when it appointed a three-man working party to study the principles of psychiatric ethics. The working party, helped by a series of WPA seminars, proceeded to produce a draft code of ethics (as yet unpublished) within the framework suggested by Dr Leigh (see chapter 10). It was planned that the code should be adopted as the Declaration of Hawaii at the 1977 world congress of the WPA.

Another, perhaps equally important, task is the drafting of a *Universal Code of the Rights of the Mentally Ill*. An authoritative, international human-rights body, perhaps the UN Commission on Human Rights, should presumably take on this job; organizations like the World Federation for Mental Health and the WPA, and national psychiatric associations, could serve as consultants. It would involve devising a code spelling out the fundamental rights of mentally-ill patients, applicable in all countries. The existence alone of such a code would expand the citizen's awareness and understanding of his rights should he or a family member become mentally ill. Only an enlightened public can apply pressure effectively on the psychiatric profession to maintain its integrity and honcsty, and mobilize pressure against those psychiatrists who disrespect their own ethics and the rights of their patients.

Finally, we would like to see the establishment of a permanent, international commission of experts, comprising psychiatrists, lawyers and human rights specialists, to "receive complaints from any individuals or appropriate national body alleging the enforced use of psychiatric facilities for political purposes, and to make investigations of such complaints"—as proposed by the American Psychiatric Association in 1972.[4] The commission could either operate in some relation with an existing institution like the World Health Organization or the International Court of Justice, or function as a new, autonomous body under the aegis of the UN, or have consultative status with the UN, like the International Commission of Jurists and Amnesty International. Failing these alternatives, the commission might have to start as a wholly independent body, relying for its authority mainly on the stature of its members.

The commission's representatives would come from several countries and would all be distinguished both for their professional competence and their integrity. (The International Court of Justice seems an appropriate model.) The charter of the commission would ideally permit the full investigation of cases submitted to it, with no restrictions imposed by the government or psychiatric authorities of the country concerned. If required as a part of the investigation, the commission would be permitted free access to relevant institutions, to medical and legal files, and to the patient, his lawyer, his family and friends. Psychiatrists or other professional staff concerned in the case under investigation would be obliged to co-operate. The commission would rely on canons of international law, and, if available, the envisaged *Universal Code of Ethics for Psychiatrists* and *Universal Code of the Rights of the Mentally Ill*, in arriving at their judgement.

The commission's reports of its investigations would be communicated to the relevant governments, in the hope that they would take appropriate action. They would also be made public through an official, regular publication which would, in addition, serve in disseminating information on the broader topic of the ethical practice of psychiatry and the rights of the mentally ill.

As with any international organization, political factors would be likely to complicate the commission's functioning. Governments could well hinder investigations in their own countries, and it would be impossible to guarantee effective sanctions against them. However, the commission could then resort to the only weapon readily available to it—the impartial report, in its official publication, that a particular country had blocked the normal operations of the commission. The implication would be clear that the country had something to conceal and this would be taken as *prima facie* evidence that psychiatric abuse did exist, until proved otherwise. Indeed, the mere existence of the international commission, as an ethical watchdog, would have a restraining influence and would serve as a deterrent to those who are tempted to misuse psychiatry for non-medical purposes. This would be of enormous value.

APPENDIX III

A Letter from the Presidium of the All-Union Society of Neurologists and Psychiatrists (The *Guardian*, 29 September 1973)

Sir,—Malicious concoctions have been expressed lately in some organs of the press, radio and television of Western countries and in statements by individual Western psychiatrists alleging that in the Soviet Union mentally healthy people are being placed in mental hospitals for their "dissenting" political views.

This, allegedly, is done by way of declaring these persons mentally sick by a panel of experts on forensic psychiatry. Going even further than this, it is falsely charged that these persons are given medicines that are damaging to their health.

Prominent Soviet psychiatrists, in their articles in the press and in the process of scientific contacts with their foreign colleagues, in particular, at the International Congress of Psychiatrists in Mexico City in 1972 [actually in 1971], have already pointed out the falsity of such contentions and that they are absolutely untrue.

But the continuing unseemly attempts to misinform public opinion compel the Presidium of the All-Union Society of Neurologists and Psychiatrists, which unites all physicians of these specialities in the Soviet Union, to express its indignation and emphatic protest against the slandering of Soviet psychiatry and thereby of medicine in general.

In our country forensic-psychiatric examinations and the placing of mental patients in psychiatric medical institutions are conducted strictly in accordance with legislation on public health.

Expert examination is in the charge of public-health authorities and is conducted by qualified psychiatrists-clinicists, if necessary in hospital conditions.

In especially complicated cases, the leading psychiatrists of the country are invited to take part in the examination.

Insane persons may inflict damage to themselves and to the people around them and urgent hospitalization is a form of preventing socially-dangerous actions on their part.

Such hospitalization is envisaged by Article 36 of the Fundamentals of Legislation on Public Health of the USSR and is effected by public-health agencies for the period that the patient presents a danger. Such hospitalization, as is known, exists in most countries. In some of them this is entrusted to the police after the appropriate medical conclusion is drawn up, although in recent years the tendency observed there is also to hand over urgent hospitalization to medics as the most competent persons in this field.

A detailed regulation of urgent hospitalization, providing for its substantiation, control over it and the discharge of patients, is contained in a special instruction of the USSR Ministry of Public Health which clearly states the indications and contra-indications for urgent hospitalization.

In accordance with this, during examination by forensic-psychiatry experts and compulsory treatment of mental patients who were declared insane, only such methods of medical investigation and treatment of patients are used that are certified for use in all medical establishments of the country and are generally accepted abroad. Only gross delusion or malicious intent can explain allegations about any harmful influence of these medical preparations on patients.

The leading clinical psychiatric institutions of the country, including the Serbsky Central Research Institute of Forensic Medicine, systematically and extensively familiarize the medical and juristic community of our country with their work as well as many prominent representatives of the psychiatry and jurisprudence of foreign countries, who have repeatedly assessed the activities of these institutions high after visiting them.

On what grounds, considering this state of affairs, do the authors of concoctions that slander Soviet psychiatry permit themselves to judge the correctness of psychiatric conclusions and the administered treatment without seeing and knowing the patients?

But such slanderous concoctions, utilizing the layman's notions that it is possible to confine mentally-healthy people to psychiatric hospitals, are by no means a novelty in the West.

As long ago as 1911, delivering his report "Draft Legislation on Insane Persons" at the First Congress of the Union of Russian Neurologists and Psychiatrists, the prominent psychiatrist, N. N. Bazhenov said: "The press, especially the West European, often takes up the subject of the arbitrary confinement of mentally-healthy people to psychiatric institutions for selfish or even political aims. This prejudice is less widespread in Russian public opinion than in the West."

There is a small number of mental cases whose disease, as a result of a mental derangement, paranoia and other psycho-pathological symptoms, can lead them to anti-social actions which fall in the category of those that are prohibited by law, such as disturbance of public order, dissemination of slander, manifestation of aggressive intentions, etc. It is noteworthy that they can do this after preliminary preparations, with "a cunningly calculated plan of action", as the founder of Russian forensic psychiatry V. P. Serbsky, who was widely known for his progressive views, wrote. To the people around them such mental cases do not create the impression of being obviously "insane". Most often these are persons suffering from schizophrenia or a paranoid pathological development of the personality. Such cases are known well both by Soviet and foreign psychiatrists.

The seeming normality of such sick persons when they commit socially-dangerous actions is used by anti-Soviet propaganda for slanderous contentions that these persons are not suffering from a mental disorder.

The fact that certain foreign circles proceed from unseemly aims was confirmed once again by the open trial of the criminal case of Yakir and Krasin, who were condemned for subversive propaganda and the dissemination of malicious concoctions about the Soviet Union, and by the subsequent press conference by Yakir and Krasin in the presence of foreign correspondents.

The lying concoction that healthy people are placed in mental hospitals, as was admitted by one of the condemned—Yakir—was fabricated by him and accorded with the desires of some correspondents of the bourgeois press and the organizations backing them, and which circulated it using all means of the mass media.

It should be stressed at the same time that of the persons against whom criminal proceedings are instituted and who are subjected to a forensic-psychiatry expert examination in connection with the above-mentioned offences, most are declared sane. But this is stubbornly ignored by those who slander Soviet psychiatry, just as they hush up the fact that most of the patients mentioned by them have had psychiatric treatment long before they were subjected to examination by forensic-psychiatry experts.

The propaganda clamour and smear campaign against Soviet psychiatry rudely contradicts the lofty tasks of psychiatry and the interests of the health of people.

This is nothing but an attempt to impede the international co-operation of medical men, to damage the developing fruitful contacts between scientists and cultural figures of different countries.

Yevgeny Schmidt. President of the Presidium, Academician of the Academy of Medical Sciences of the USSR, Professor, Director of the Research Institute of Neurology of the Academy of Medical Sciences of the USSR.

Georgy Morozov. Vice-President of the Presidium, Corresponding Member of the Academy of Medical Sciences of the USSR,

Professor, Director of the Serbsky Central Research Institute of Forensic Psychiatry of the Ministry of Public Health of the USSR.

Levon Badalyan. Vice-President of the Presidium, Professor, Doctor of Medical Sciences, Head of the Chair of Nervous Diseases of the Department of Pediatrics of the Second Moscow Medical Institute of the Ministry of Public Health of the Russian Federation.

Vadim Mikheyev. Vice-President of the Presidium, Professor, Doctor of Medical Sciences, Consultant of the Chair of Nervous Diseases of the First Moscow Medical Institute of the Ministry of Public Health of the USSR.

Members of the Presidium:

Nikolai Bogolepov. Academician of the Academy of Medical Sciences of the USSR, Professor, Head of the Chair of Nervous Diseases of the Second Moscow Medical Institute of the Ministry of Public Health of the Russian Federation.

Andrei Snezhnevsky. Academician of the Academy of Medical Sciences of the USSR, Professor, Director of the Research Institute of Psychiatry of the Academy of Medical Sciences of the USSR.

Grigory Avrutsky. Professor, Doctor of Medical Sciences, Head of the Department of Psychopharmacology of the Moscow Research Institute of Psychiatry of the Ministry of Public Health of the Russian Federation.

Yuri Aleksandrovsky. Doctor of Medical Sciences, Senior Scientific Staff Member of the Moscow Research Institute of Psychiatry of the Ministry of Public Health of the Russian Federation.

Eduard Babayan. Candidate of Medical Sciences, Head of the Department for the Introduction of New Medical Preparations and Medical Equipment of the Ministry of Public Health of the USSR. Chairman of the Standing Committee on Narcotics of the USSR Ministry of Public Health.

Vasily Banshchikov. Professor, Doctor of Medical Sciences, Consultant at the Chair of Psychiatry of the First Moscow Medical Institute of the Ministry of Public Health of the USSR.

Yevgeny Borisov. Learned Secretary of the Department for the Introduction of New Medical Preparations and Medical Equipment at the Ministry of Public Health of the USSR.

Nikolai Zharikov. Professor, Doctor of Medical Sciences, Head of the Chair of Psychiatry of the First Moscow Medical Institute of the Ministry of Public Health of the USSR.

Grigory Lukacher. Doctor of Medical Sciences, Senior Scientific Staff Member of the Serbsky Central Research Institute of Psychiatry of the Ministry of Public Health of the USSR.

Taisia Morozova. Candidate of Medical Sciences, Senior Scientific

Staff Member of the Serbsky Central Research Institute of Forensic Psychiatry of the Ministry of Public Health of the USSR.

Rostislav Murashkin. Candidate of Medical Sciences, Senior Psychiatrist of Moscow Region.

Ruben Nadzharov. Professor, Doctor of Medical Sciences, Deputy Director for Research Work of the Research Institute of Psychiatry of the Academy of Medical Sciences of the USSR.

Lev Petelin. Professor, Doctor of Medical Sciences, Head of the Chair of Nervous Diseases of the Central Institute for the Advanced Training of Doctors of the Ministry of Public Health of the USSR.

Irina Sapozhnikova. Candidate of Medical Sciences, Head of the Dispensary Department of the Moscow City Psychiatry Hospital No. 8.

Sergei Semyonov. Professor, Doctor of Medical Sciences, Deputy Director for Research Work at the Moscow Research Institute of Psychiatry of the Ministry of Public Health of the Russian Federation.

Zoya Serebryakova. Doctor of Medical Sciences, Chief Specialist on Psycho-Neurology of the Main Department of Treatment and Prophylaxis of the Ministry of Public Health of the USSR.

Gennady Ushakov. Professor, Doctor of Medical Sciences, Head of the Chair of Psychiatry at the Second Moscow Medical Institute of the Ministry of Public Health of the Russian Federation.

APPENDIX IV

FALSE FRIENDS IN A QUAGMIRE OF SLANDER
by K. Bryantsev (*Izvestia*, 25 October 1971)

Again and again she read the address on the parcel which arrived here at the Kazan psychiatric hospital addressed to her. It seemed as if it was all intended for her. But who was the Mrs Juliet Spiegel from Amsterdam who had sent the parcel, and what was the meaning of those strange gifts—the notepaper with Israeli flags, the envelopes and the sugar? At her next meeting with her mother after this incident, Valeria* told her of the unsolicited gift which she had refused. "I am extremely indignant at this outrageous provocative act on the part of foreign 'benefactors'. My daughter and I have never had, and do not have, any relatives or friends living outside our Fatherland," writes Nina Fyodorovna Novodvorskaya. She begs us to protect her sick daughter from presents "serving provocational anti-Soviet aims".

The mother's feelings are easy to understand. How much harder it is to measure the full extent of the moral decline of those who have blasphemously chosen as the object of their dishonourable game people who are defective, suffering from serious illnesses of the psyche, in other words, the mentally ill.

It sounds monstrous, but it is so. In the pages of the Western press, from the anonymous émigré journal *Possev* to the American *International Herald Tribune* which has pretensions to respectability, and in various radio stations (with Munich's Radio Liberty trying to drown them all with its lamentations, as usual), the most wild and far-fetched tales are systematically being spread about "perfectly healthy people" allegedly being confined in psychiatric hospitals in the Soviet Union. In order to lend their evil-minded fabrications a grain of verisimilitude, they drag out a string of surnames of persons who have at one time or another been under investigation or on trial for the commission of criminally-punished acts. It is not given to every film star in the West to receive such "publicity" as some of these people. What do the slanderers care if the doctors have established the presence of mental illness. These malignant slanderers are concerned with one thing alone: to depict the mentally-sick person as a great "fighter for an idea".

* i.e. Valeria Novodvorskaya, see appendix I.

Especially zealous is the notorious Amnesty International, whose unscrupulous methods we have already related to you in the pages of *Izvestia* (no. 64). One of the reports of the British section of this organization states that representatives of the intellegentsia in the Soviet Union are sent off to psychiatric hospitals "without any trial". Tales of "psychiatric isolation cells for healthy persons" are unfailingly accompanied by a hypocritical refrain about "martyrs", condemned, apparently, to spend the rest of their days behind impenetrable walls.

In reality, we are dealing with persons who have committed socially-dangerous actions while of unsound mind, or who have, during the course of the investigation, the trial, or after the sentence has been passed, become mentally ill, thus making it impossible for themselves to take account of their own actions or control them. In accordance with existing laws, such persons, on the basis of a diagnosis made by a competent team of forensic psychiatrists, and at the court's ruling, are subject to be sent for treatment to a psychiatric hospital of the ordinary or special type. Moreover, they may be discharged from the same if psychiatrists testify (at least once every six months)—and it is confirmed—that the implementation of the recommended measures of a medical nature as a protection is no longer necessary.

And this is exactly what happens in practice. For instance, Olga I. [ofe], who was brought to trial last year in Moscow and declared of unsound mind, spent some time in a psychiatric hospital of the special type undergoing compulsory treatment. At the present time, because of the improvement in her state of health, she has been discharged from hospital. Incidentally, compulsory treatment of one of the people about whom a lot of fuss has been made in the West, was also stopped several years ago, on the recommendation of a forensic-psychiatric diagnosis team.

The Western ideological saboteurs who babble all kinds of rubbish about mentally-ill persons, do not even notice what a ridiculous position they are putting themselves in: they are, after all, taking it upon themselves to preach at and refute medical specialists, representatives of the Soviet school of psychiatry, which has earned the respect and recognition of the whole world. Here is what A. V. Snezhnevsky, the well-known Soviet scientist and director of the Academy of Medical Sciences' Institute of Psychiatry, says:

> Yes, I too have read these absurd reports that healthy persons are put in psychiatric hospitals in the USSR. Like all my colleagues, I cannot refrain from expressing my feeling of deep disgust at this outrageous fabrication. Soviet psychiatrists form a detach-

ment of many thousands in the ranks of Soviet medical workers; of course they do not need defending against insulting attacks of this kind. Both in our country and abroad psychiatrists such as Academician A. D. Zurabashvili, corresponding members of the Academy of Medical Sciences, V. M. Morozov, G. V. Morozov, A. A. Megrabyan, professors N. N. Timofeyev, R. A. Nadzharov, B. A. Lebedev, N. M. Zharikov, S. F. Semyonov, G. K. Ushakov, and many others, are well known and enjoy well-deserved authority. A number of Soviet psychiatrists have been elected members of international psychiatric societies and associations.

Russian and Soviet psychiatry has always been distinguished for its lofty humanism, its striving to help the sick man not to feel himself outside society. It is sufficient to remind you that as early as 1919, during the period of famine and civil war, Professor P. B. Gannushkin created a system of district psychiatrists which grew in later years into [a network of] neuro-psychiatric clinics—the basis of the modern organization of psychiatric help throughout the world. It was in our country that the bases of resocialization were formulated—the restoration of the mentally-sick man's capacity to work. This method has now been widely adopted in many countries of the world.

The confinement of sick persons in psychiatric hospitals in our country has always been carried out exclusively on the basis of doctors' findings. The finest traditions of the Russian school of psychiatry have been developed further under the Soviet régime. In the Soviet Union, the basis for a court ruling to send a sick person for compulsory treatment when he has committed socially-dangerous actions, is the findings of medical experts. These findings are compiled and signed by not one but several psychiatrists. The system in widespread use in the USSR for the advanced training of doctors and the raising of the level of their knowledge ensures that even rank-and-file psychiatrists in our country are highly qualified. Thus incidences of the confinement of healthy persons in a psychiatric hospital are absolutely out of the question in our country. I want to stress (says A. V. Snezhnevsky) that our colleagues abroad who have become acquainted with the organization of Soviet psychiatric help for the population have a very high opinion indeed of it.

The professor holds up an attractively produced book bound in blue with gilt lettering. The cover says: "Special Report: The First U.S. Mission on Mental Health to the USSR". The report's authors are leading figures in the world of American psychiatry: Stanley Yolles, director of the National Institute of Mental Health;

Walter Barton, medical director of the American Psychiatric Association; David Bazelon, chief Judge of the Columbia District Federal Appeal Court; journalist Mike Gorman, executive director of the National Committee against Mental Illness; Alan Miller, head of the New York State Department of Mental Hygiene; Philip Sirotkin, programme director at the National Institute of Mental Health and the director of the Illinois State Department of Mental Health, Harold Visotsky.

What conclusion did these seven prominent American specialists reach after becoming acquainted with the Soviet organization of psychiatric aid? Comparing the way these problems have been solved in the USA and the USSR, the authors unanimously conclude: "It all looks as though the Soviets are ahead." The American guests stress the high level of effectiveness of Soviet psychiatric first-aid posts, and their superior staffing by comparison with American ones. Their acquaintance with psychiatric hospitals convinced them that "every effort" is made to "discharge the patient as soon as this becomes possible". "Again and again the delegation was struck by the emotional concern and individual attention shown to psychiatric patients, including deeply disturbed ones suffering from schizophrenia or senile dementia."

The American specialists also gave serious attention to questions of forensic psychiatry. After visiting the Serbsky Institute, they stated that the findings of Soviet psychiatric experts were "far more detailed and contained more useful information about the personality and the environment of the accused than findings presented in American courts". As for compulsory treatment, the opinion of the report's authors was that the Russian standard was essentially identical with the American. The approach of Soviet doctors "in many respects is not so different from the views of some American doctors. . . . Perhaps these doctors, both Russian and American, are right. Perhaps people who need treatment ought to be compulsorily hospitalized for their own good."

Finally, A. V. Snezhnevsky showed me a lengthy article on Soviet psychiatry printed in the French journal, "Information on Psychiatry" vol. 46, No. 9, for 1970. In it French scientists are full of praise for the activities of psychiatric institutions in Moscow and Leningrad. A. V. Snezhnevsky adds that such views are not isolated instances. The notable American specialists J. Wortis, N. Kline, I. Ziferstein, and a number of others have expressed their high opinion of Soviet psychiatry.

The organizers of anti-Soviet scandal-mongering will very likely include the above-named American and French psychiatric workers among the ranks of "communist agitators". They are, of course, no such thing. They have simply spoken the truth. But for these loud-mouthed characters, suffering from a pathological hatred of the Soviet system, the truth is quite contra-indicated. We can vouch for the accuracy of this diagnosis but we shall not attempt treatment. These people are hopeless cases.

APPENDIX V

A Samizdat Reply to Bryantsev's Article

This article was written in late 1971 and circulated in *samizdat*;
it appeared in summary form in *Chronicle* 22

On 25 October 1971, the newspaper *Izvestia* published an article by
K. Bryantsev, "False Friends in a Quagmire of Slander". The
article concerns the question of the detention in Soviet psychiatric
hospitals of mentally-healthy people. Bryantsev describes as nonsensical rumours the reports on this subject "broadcast by various
radio stations", and asserts that all the "foreign friends" are
incompetent to judge on questions which can be fully understood
only by specialists. He devotes a good half of the article to an
interview with the director of the Institute of Psychiatry of the
USSR Academy of Medical Sciences, Professor A. V. Snezhnevsky.

The main assertion in Snezhnevsky's long statement is that "In
the USSR cases of deliberately incorrect placing of healthy people
in mental hospitals are quite inconceivable". As confirmatory
evidence Snezhnevsky quotes the high opinions about the achievements of Soviet psychiatry held by a number of foreign psychiatrists,
mostly American.

Director of the Institute of Psychiatry and a full member of the
USSR Academy of Medical Sciences, Andrei Snezhnevsky is now
in effect the monopolistic ruler of the whole science of psychiatry in
the USSR. His rise began in 1950, after the so-called "Pavlov
session" of the Academy of Sciences and the Academy of Medical
Sciences. For a time he was director of the Serbsky Institute of
Forensic Psychiatry, and in that capacity he was—with V. M.
Banshchikov, I. S. Strelchuk, and O. V. Kerbikov—one of the
co-authors of the report "On the General Position in Psychiatry in
the Light of Pavlov's Teachings", which was presented at a joint
meeting of the Presidium of the Academy of Sciences and the
Academy of Medical Sciences in 1951. The consequence of this
report, and of decisions taken in the light of it by the meeting, was
the arbitrary dismissal from their posts in many tertiary institutions
and research institutes of very eminent scientists (M. O. Gurevich,
R. Ya. Golant, A. S. Shmaryan, A. L. Epshtein, and many others),
on charges of "anti-Pavlovian activity".

Soon after this, Snezhnevsky got the chair of psychiatry at the

Central Institute for the Advanced Training of Doctors, a chair from which his teacher M. Ya. Sereisky had just been dismissed for "anti-Pavlovian errors". Snezhnevsky held this post for some years, organizing instruction—in the ideas he had "developed"—for the doctors who came for higher-training courses. These ideas can be succinctly described as a limitless widening of the diagnostic criteria for an illness which is extremely controversial as regards its symptoms, and which has come to be called schizophrenia.

As Snezhnevsky and his collaborators entrenched themselves (among them were V. M. Morozov and R. A. Nadzharov, whom he describes in the article as eminent scientists, as well as others he does not mention), a fairly broad movement developed in Soviet psychiatry, opposed to the subjective diagnosis of schizophrenia and even denying its very existence. But gradually Snezhnevsky succeeded in completely monopolizing the situation, in some cases through arbitrary dismissals, in others by waiting for death or illness to remove his opponents. Using the *Journal of Neurology and Psychiatry*, of which he became an editor in 1952, he also succeeded in spreading his ideas throughout the USSR, ideas which many eminent (but now mostly dead) Soviet psychiatrists regarded as completely unscientific and fantastic.

The result of this uncontrolled hegemony of Snezhnevsky over Soviet psychiatry has been his creation of a "school"—a multitude of practising doctors, including forensic psychiatrists, who, against common sense and centuries of psychiatric experience, diagnose "schizophrenia" when there are no grounds for doing so. This has had serious consequences in society: people so diagnosed are deprived of their driving licences, are often rejected for jobs or for entry to tertiary educational institutions, while for people who have "committed socially-dangerous acts" the result is compulsory treatment in a mental hospital.

The actions on 5 December 1969 of Valeria Novodvorskaya, who is mentioned in Bryantsev's article, were carefully thought out and purposeful, and were not the product of any illness. "Schizophrenia" was diagnosed in her by a psychiatric commission, because . . . after a personal crisis typical of her young age she had made a suicide attempt.

The grounds for a similar diagnosis made in the Kaluga mental hospital on Zhores Medvedev (among those who "examined" the "patient" were V. M. Morozov and R. A. Nadzharov) were even more laughable: "a strange split in the personality" expressing itself in the fact that an able biologist is, at the same time, an able publicist.

All the other reports of forensic-psychiatric examinations which, despite the secrecy surrounding such documents, specialists have managed to study—likewise contain no serious scientific arguments, while their descriptive sections contain facts which have often been extremely crudely manipulated.

While, on the one hand, these exceedingly important documents represent the carrying-out of directives from the police to rule insane as many enemies of the régime as possible, on the other they express "the triumph of Snezhnevsky's ideas".

So there is nothing surprising in the fact that he saw in the exposure of the illegal and inhuman acts of our psychiatrists a threat to his own prosperity, and, no less emphatically than Bryantsev, "rebuffed the slanderers".

It is characteristic that until very recently Snezhnevsky's name has not been mentioned in connection with the internment of mentally-healthy people in mental hospitals. The only time his name has appeared in the press was in a brief report on the psychiatric examination of Ilin (the episode of January 1969 in the Kremlin).* Ilin was ruled to be suffering from schizophrenia by a commission consisting of A. V. Snezhnevsky, G. V. Morozov (Director of the Serbsky Institute) and V. M. Morozov. But Snezhnevsky declined to participate in the commission to examine Zhores A. Medvedev, just as he has declined to take part in commissions in many other such cases: he has handed over this work wholly to G. V. Morozov and D. R. Lunts.

But the extent to which the criminal actions of the psychiatric services have been exposed is now apparently sufficient for Snezhnevsky to be unable to remain any longer in the shadows; he has now had to admit, obliquely, his involvement in the use of psychiatry for purposes of repression.

---

* Ilin apparently intended to assassinate some of the Soviet leaders but fired at cosmonauts by mistake. For the press report referred to, see *Izvestia*, 21 March 1970.

APPENDIX VI

A Manual on Psychiatry for Dissenters*
by Vladimir Bukovsky and Dr Semyon Gluzman, 1974

(dedicated to Lenya Plyushch, a victim of psychiatric terror)

> Pushkin: You're a madman yourself!
> Chaadayev: Why am I a madman?
> Pushkin: You understand equality, but you live in
> servitude.
> Chaadayev (pondering): Then it follows that you
> are right: I am a madman.
> (A. Platonov, "Pupil of the Lycée")

Introduction

It is well known that in the Soviet Union today large numbers of dissenters are being declared insane, and there is reason to fear that this method will be used on an even greater scale in the future. It is not difficult to find an explanation for this phenomenon. From the point of view of the authorities, it is an extremely convenient method: it enables them to deprive a man of his freedom for an unlimited length of time, keep him in strict isolation, and use psycho-pharmacological means of "re-educating" him; it hinders the campaign for open legal proceedings and for the release of such people, since even the most impartial man will, if he is not personally acquainted with a patient of this sort, always feel a twinge of uncertainty about his mental health; it deprives its victim of what few rights he would enjoy as a prisoner, and it provides an opportunity to discredit the ideas and actions of dissenters, and so on.

There is, however, another, no less important side. Dissenters, as a rule, have enough legal grounding so as not to make mistakes during their investigation and trial, but when confronted by a qualified psychiatrist with a directive from above to have them declared non-responsible, they have found themselves absolutely powerless. All this has, inevitably, engendered renewed fear and dismay in dissenting circles and is a reason for cases of unexpected "repentance" and recantation which have occurred in recent months.

---

* For Russian text see CHR, 1975, No. 13. This text was typed out in Moscow from the original hand-written text smuggled out of forced labour camp no. 35 in Perm region.

Forensic psychiatry has thus renewed the fear of persecution, which a knowledge of the law and skill in applying it had previously dispelled. A mood of resignation to one's fate, a sense of one's powerlessness to resist this method of persecution, has become widespread.

All this demonstrates the need for a handbook generalizing the experience gained from many psychiatric examinations and setting out the basic tenets of psychiatric theory, having the format of a guide to the kind of behaviour which will give the experts as little basis as possible for pronouncing the examinee insane. The present authors, one a former "mental patient", the other a former psychiatrist, hope that by combining experience with professional knowledge of the subject they will succeed in producing a work that fulfils as far as possible the aim outlined above.

This manual lays no claim to be an exhaustive analysis of the problems of psychiatry; some aspects have been deliberately simplified, as the handbook is designed for as wide a readership as possible.

Legal part (schematic)

You can be seen by a psychiatrist, even without your consent, in the following three cases:

I. Compulsory examination or compulsory hospitalization within the framework of normal medical regulations. Your convictions, openly expressed public stance, actions or acquaintances have made you an object of the close attention of a KGB squad. Because of certain unalterable circumstances, it is undesirable to institute criminal proceedings against you. In this case, the KGB (often not directly, but through the police, the procuracy, the local council, informers, etc., etc.) will tell medical establishments that they believe you are suffering from mental illness, and will indicate the reason for their interest in you.

A psychiatrist in a clinic, health centre, hospital or city first aid post is, in these circumstances, obliged to examine you and, if he considers it necessary, to have you admitted to a psychiatric hospital of the ordinary type.

A psychiatric examination of this kind may be carried out at home, at your place of work, at the scene of the "incident", in a preliminary detention cell, in an appropriate institution or in some other place.

If the psychiatrist finds that you show symptoms of an illness to a degree which does not require in-patient observation and treatment in a psychiatric hospital, you will be registed at a psychiatric clinic or in the psychiatric department of a polyclinic. You may be placed in a psychiatric hospital of the ordinary type if you show evidence of the following:

(1) mental derangement constituting a danger to yourself
(2) mental derangement constituting a danger to other people
(3) mental derangement verifiable only by in-patient examination
(4) pronounced mental derangement which cannot be successfully treated in out-patient conditions
(5) state of "acute psychosis" (i.e. what the ordinary person would call "going berserk").

Your removal from an out-patient psychiatric register, or discharge from an in-patient institution depends, formally, solely upon medical evidence (i.e. upon a psychiatrist).

If your condition is diagnosed by a doctor as abnormal, the forwarding (in psychiatric in-patient conditions) and investigation of your complaints, statements, petitions and letters depends wholly on the professional competence and conscience of your doctor, since the law makes this his responsibility. Relatives, friends and other interested persons may make requests and lodge claims regarding your case with the medical authorities (to the chief psychiatrist of the USSR, republic, region, area, town or district).

Mistakes can occur in psychiatric practice, as in any other form of human activity; the law does not define a doctor's liability for a professional error.

This state of affairs may be used by the authorities to explain a compulsory hospitalization which later turns out to have been unwarranted. For the same reason, an incompetent or morally irresponsible psychiatrist can give an incorrect assessment of your mental state without any damage to his own future reputation.

II. *Forensic-psychiatric examination following the institution of criminal proceedings.* After selecting the preventive measure to be taken in your case (usually arrest), the investigative organs or the procuracy may send you for forensic-psychiatric examination. For this purpose, a document is drawn up listing statements made or actions performed by you which cast doubts upon your mental health.

Normally the investigator (or procurator) does not make his doubts known to you, nor does he show you the relevant documents. He does not inform you, either, of the very fact that you are to undergo a psychiatric examination, or of how long it will take or where it will be carried out.

Forensic-psychiatric examinations are performed by commissions of not less than three psychiatrists. You may be subjected to either of the following forms of forensic-psychiatric examination: (1) out-patient; (2) in-patient.

An out-patient examination is normally carried out in a medical establishment or in a remand prison; it may last from a few minutes to several hours.

An in-patient examination is carried out in a psychiatric in-patient establishment (the Serbsky Institute of Forensic Psychiatry in Moscow, or investigation or ordinary "acute" admission wards in ordinary-type psychiatric hospitals; psychiatric sections of prison hospitals).

The length of an in-patient examination is not specified by law; usually it lasts from a few weeks to several months.

You will most likely not be informed of the experts' decision, if you are declared not responsible. From that moment, a defence counsel is permitted access to your case but you yourself will probably be barred from participating in the investigation.

The law provides for an unlimited number of repeat and supplementary examinations to be performed. The investigator (or procurator) has the responsibility of deciding which finding is correct, if the opinions of the commissions of experts differ.

Normally a non-responsible person is not called to attend the court hearing and is not informed of the court's ruling on his case.

Sometimes the psychiatric examination is performed in court. Essentially, it is no different from the ordinary out-patient examination. On the court's decision, legal proceedings may be suspended while the accused is sent for in-patient examination. The type of hospital to which the non-responsible person is to be sent (an ordinary hospital, or a special psychiatric hospital under Ministry of Internal Affairs jurisdiction) is determined by the court. It is, unfortunately, most unlikely that the court will order observation by a psychiatrist at your home, without depriving you of your freedom.

III. If you are a witness in a case, it is also possible that you may have to undergo compulsory out-patient examination. In this case, the formal pretext is that doubt has arisen in the mind of the investigator (procurator, court) as to your ability to grasp correctly circumstances which have an important bearing on the case and to give the correct evidence about them. In this case, in-patient examination can take place only with your express consent (which we hope you will not give).

Notarial law gives you the opportunity to safeguard your evidence by arming yourself in advance with an objective psychiatric report on the state of your mental health. At your written request, a notary will issue a decree ordering an examination, with indications as to the form it will take and the place where it is to be held. All you then have to do is pay for this formal notarial assistance and do everything necessary to ensure that if you are arrested and attempts are made to have you declared mentally ill, this psychiatric report on you becomes generally known (see *Statute on RSFSR State Notarial System*, articles 66, 67, and "Instructions regarding the procedure for carrying out notarial transactions in state notarial offices of the RSFSR," pp. 139–146).

General information on psychiatry

"Where we lack concepts, words promptly step in to take their place" (Goethe's *Faust*). The principles governing the activity of the human brain are still unclear to us. Neurophysiology and the other concrete brain sciences are still unable to comprehend the "psychic" phenomenon of psycho-pathology. Equally mysterious and difficult to place within the strict framework of a systematic science are the concepts of health and sickness; the conceptual vagueness character-istic of medicine in general is especially marked in psychiatry. Madness is regarded both as a biological and a social (historical, philosophical, legal) problem.

In contemporary psychiatry as a whole, there is no firm basis for the system of categories in use or even for the system of classifying diseases of the psyche. Thus, for example, at a diagnostic symposium in Leningrad, 20 leading psychiatrists pronounced twelve different diagnoses on one and the same patient.

All mental illnesses can be divided into two groups: (1) those which have supposedly been defined, i.e. provisionally separated out from a chaotic mass of data accumulated over centuries and given individual identities, and (2) true mental illnesses with a cause known to science and characteristic dynamics. If the model for the first is purely "rhetorical", the second type is based on concrete scientific discoveries and its models are "demonstrable".

The basic method of clinical psychiatric investigation is still the subjective observation of the behaviour, speech, memory, etc., of the patient. Used in conjunction with this is information—again subjective—about the patient obtained from his associates, friends, relatives, from official documents and such-like. Other methods (laboratory analyses, ECG investigations) are of secondary importance.

The vagueness with which mental illness is defined does not unduly concern working doctors, since treatment is more often than not determined not by diagnosis, but by particular symptoms of illness.

In psychiatric theory, there are no generally-recognized standards of "sickness" and "health". A mass of abstract concepts exists from the philosophical to the cybernetic, all of them absolutely useless in psychiatric practice. Nevertheless, the day-to-day activity of the doctor would be impossible without the use of some standard of health, even if it is only an arbitrary one. So practical psychiatry uses an arbitrary standard of mental health which is convenient, simple and easy to understand: that of the so-called *"rentier* living off the income from his shares". A *rentier* is a person of mediocre intellect and bourgeois tastes, civilized rather than cultured, who is unwilling to take chances. He is content with his low but stable social position ("the higher you fly, the harder you fall"), and never lets himself get carried away; he has no creative aptitude whatsoever, and is the mainstay of any authority; the guiding light in his life is his instinct for self-preservation. His life is monotonous but tranquil: he regards his life-style as the only correct one and indeed the wisest and safest one in our existence fraught with adversity.

The concept of the *rentier* is not a scientific one and is not mentioned at all in Soviet psychiatric literature. But applied psychiatrists use it every day in their work, though not always consciously, and of course, not as a hard and fast rule. (You will see below why the concept of the *rentier* is so dear to the so-called "average psychiatrist".)

Dissent as a psychiatric problem

The freedom of each of us as an individual is restricted by society's interests. The law and morality are expressions of such restrictions. The behaviour of a mentally-ill person who is not breaking the law is "foolish", "odd" and so on, and society regards it as undesirable.

It is with the protection of citizens from behaviour of this kind that psychiatry is concerned. Forcible incarceration in a mental hospital is justified from the social as well as the medical point of view. And if "health" is "desirable behaviour" and "sickness" is "undesirable behaviour", then the social aim of psychiatry is the transformation of undesirable behaviour into desirable. Thus, force used against a mentally-ill person is justified by the resulting benefit to society. This use of "evil in a good cause" was the reason for the breakaway of an "anti-psychiatry" school of thought from classical Western psychiatry. The "anti-psychiatrists" declare that "the substance of psychiatric science is the repression of the revolutionary sub-conscious in the name of the state; the history of psychiatry is the history of the methods by which society has striven to break down psychological resistance to the prevailing conditions of life."

You will agree that, in view of the vagueness of the categories it uses and the existence of a multitude of "scientific schools of psychiatry", it is quite possible for psychiatry to extend its competence beyond legitimate limits.

And under the conditions of the "social command" as practised by various totalitarian régimes, psychiatric norms are defined by the needs of the particular moment, rather than by scientific and historical reasoning (compare this with the "anti-psychiatrists' " assertion that psychiatry, in fulfilling the demands of a class society, has always turned revolutionaries into psychopaths).

The Soviet use of psychiatry as a punitive means is based upon the deliberate interpretation of dissent (in the well-known sense of the word) as a psychiatric problem. In his monograph *The Theory and Practice of Forensic-Psychiatric Diagnosis*, Professor D. R. Lunts asserts that any illegal act, by virtue of its illegality alone, merits psychiatric analysis (in so far as it does not fit in with the *rentier* concept), and substantiates his remarks by claiming that under socialist conditions there are no social causes for criminal acts. Lunts attributes to *capitalism* the phenomenon of crime resulting from social disharmony.

Exculpation, i.e. declaring non-responsible dissenters who, in one way or another, express their disagreement with particular aspects of the Soviet government's domestic and foreign policy, is now being practised with single-minded determination. Basically, two psychiatric diagnoses are being used for this purpose: sluggish schizophrenia, and paranoid development of the personality. Other diagnoses are hardly ever mentioned, that is, dissent does not, even in theory, enter into them (fortunately for you, otherwise you would have to familiarize yourself with psychiatry in much more detail).

Sluggish Schizophrenia. To quote an expert of some experience, Professor Timofeyev: "The more one studies mild and attenuated (*stertye*) forms of schizophrenia (i.e. sluggish schizophrenia—the authors), the more difficulties one encounters in diagnostics. The question still remains problematical, since some psychiatrists do not recognize these particular forms of the disease, while others regard them as having a relatively independent existence." In another work Timofeyev asserts that "dissent may be caused by a disease of the brain in which the pathological process develops very slowly and mildly (sluggish schizophrenia—Gluzman), while its other symptoms remain for the time being (sometimes until a criminal act is committed) imperceptible." Thus Professor Timofeyev recognizes the existence of sluggish schizophrenia: "It is typical of persons of precisely this age-group (20–29—the authors) to exhibit a heightened propensity for conflict, the desire for self-assertion, the rejection of traditions, opinions, standards, etc.: this has contributed to the creation of the myth that some young people (who are actually suffering from schizophrenia) are being wrongfully placed in psychiatric hospitals and are being held there allegedly because they think differently from every one else."

By sluggish schizophrenia is understood a form of the disease in which all its symptoms are "barely" or "only slightly" manifest, while symptoms as explicit as the presence of hallucinations are absent altogether. Its normal symptoms are (according to a text-book for students at medical institutes): unsociability, sluggishness, loss of interest in life, mild attacks of pessimism and melancholia; concentration on inner experiences, inadequate thoughts and actions, stubbornness and inflexibility of convictions, suspiciousness, etc. So if you are reserved, inclined to be introspective and uncommunicative, if you do not wish to alter your convictions since you do not regard them as "unsound", and if your allegations that you are being shadowed and that your telephone is tapped are viewed as "suspiciousness" and sometimes even as "persecution mania", when these things really are happening to you—the conclusion is obvious . . . The fact that you are coping successfully with your official responsibilities or your creative work, that you show an interest in them and are even making progress in your career, will not save you. Although formally the presence of pathological psychiatric symptoms does not rule out the possibility that you are still legally responsible, the outcome of your examination is predetermined.

According to the data of the Serbsky Institute of Forensic Psychiatry, approximately one half of all cases of sluggish schizophrenia are declared mentally competent. But we know of no case where a schizophrenic has been declared legally responsible. That most experienced diagnostician Professor Lunts favours introducing into civil legislation the concept of "limited" or "partial" competence, yet deliberately pronounces criminal diagnoses of insanity on healthy people, for "every class, every profession has its own ethical code". (*N.B.* limited competence and responsibility are indeed necessary, and exist as legal terms in the jurisprudence of all civilized countries.)

Paranoid development of the personality. A diagnosis which is, similarly, dubious and unspecific. To understand what lies behind this terminological label, one must be aware of the following:

(1) psychiatry distinguishes three kinds of ideas (apart from normal ideas):
   (a) The obsessive idea: observed in healthy people who are preoccupied by some aspiration and are wholly engrossed in a developing thought.
   (b) The over-valued idea (pathological): a notion, usually rational in content, but the importance of which has been over-estimated beyond all reason. Objectively the importance of an over-valued idea is negligible in comparison with the individual's subjective evaluation of it.

(c) The delusional idea (pathological): an erroneous notion, having no real basis and incapable of alteration. A concentration of such ideas is known as a delusional state.

(2) Two types of the several types of delusional state are of interest to us:

   (a) Reformist delusions: an improvement in social conditions can be achieved only through the revision of people's attitudes, in accordance with the individual's own ideas for the transformation of reality.

   (b) Litigation mania: a conviction, which does not have any basis in fact, that the individual's own rights as a human being are being violated and flouted; the reasons become "clear" to him, and he begins to send in complaints and demands to have "justice" restored.

(3) A pathological development of the personality is known as psychopathy. Alongside this there exist extreme variants of the normal personality—the borderline between these and psychopathy is indistinct and vague. The dynamics of psychopathy involve what are known as periods of compensation (in the social respect) and periods of decompensation.

Only one of the types of psychopathy is of interest to us: paranoid psychopathy. It is characterized by suspiciousness, mistrustfulness and a greatly increased propensity to over-valued and delusional ideas; by rigid, one-track, sluggish thought-processes; and by a tendency to dwell at length on experiences connected with insignificant events. In conflict situations, paranoid psychopaths have paranoid reactions. In time, these turn into a paranoid development of the personality, that is, an orderly delusional system, in our case, litigation mania or reformist delusions.

Its development takes the following pattern: an obsessive idea arises, which then gives way to an over-valued idea, and finally to a delusional idea; the formation of an orderly (that is, outwardly convincing and not absurd) delusional system is followed by a systematized delusional state, then a systematized persecution mania, with a tendency towards over-estimation of one's own personality (all interpretations are those given in the psychiatry course for students at medical institutes in the USSR). As you can see, the demonstrability of this type of psychopathology is highly relative. And vice versa: try proving that your opinions on the occupation of Czechoslovakia or on the absence of democratic freedoms in the USSR are not erroneous, with no real basis in fact. . . . Or that the surveillance of yourself and your close friends is not "persecution mania". Or that your own subjective appraisal of internal political life in the USSR is not at all insignificant in comparison with the real facts. . . . Or that your being "relieved" of your job after you had been one of the signatories to a "declaration of protest" is a violation of your rights. . . . Doctors of Medical Sciences Pechernikova and Kosachev, experts at the Institute of Forensic Psychiatry, openly state: "Ideas of fighting for truth and justice most frequently arise in personalities with a paranoid structure," or: "The litigious-paranoid state develops following psychotraumatizing circumstances which affect the interests of the person concerned, and is typified by accusations of encroachment upon the legal status of the individual," or: "A characteristic feature of these (over-valued—the authors) formations is the conviction of the individual's own rightness, an obsession with asserting his 'trampled rights', the importance the sick person attaches to his own feelings as an individual," or: "They use the court hearing as a platform for making speeches and appeals."

But how are the psychiatrists to assess the mental state of a Georgy Dmitrov who makes a speech at his trial! . . . Or of many other public activists with their all-consuming belief in an ideal and their renunciation of their personal life? . . . For our psychiatrists, to be healthy means to be cautious, not very clever, "to keep one's wits about one". For wit leads to trouble.* It only remains for a new type of mental pathology to be officially introduced into psychiatry, called the Chatsky complex.

Finally, a diagnosis of paranoid psychopathy and paranoid development of the personality does not automatically mean certain exculpation. According to official statistics from the Institute of Forensic Psychiatry, 95·5 per cent of cases are declared responsible. But this figure exists only on paper. There is a different set of statistics for dissenters, and they are not published. Pechernikova and Kosachev have given a very detailed account of the development of paranoidal litigation mania, but they have "forgotten" to tell us the percentage of "paranoid litigants" exculpated.

The psychology of the psychiatrist
The twentieth century has confronted us with the problem of communication. Nowadays, people in different professions who speak the same language have difficulty in understanding each other. In the psychiatrist's consulting-room, too much will depend on your ability to communicate. Try to ensure that the expert

* In Russian, a pun based on the title of Griboyedov's comedy *Woe from Wit* (*Gorye ot uma*), in which the hero Chatsky is a socio-political non-conformist.

understands you in precisely the way you intend: do everything you can to prevent the expert's "goal" of having you declared non-responsible, if such is his aim, from becoming a documentable diagnosis. Remember that the psychiatrist is an ordinary man possessing no supernatural powers. The view which exists in certain circles that the psychiatrist can "fathom your soul with his gaze, read your thoughts, or force you to tell the truth" is absurd. There are no therapeutic, hypnotic or pharmacological pressures that can reveal your secret thoughts and make you talk if you do not wish to. Neither is the idea of the psychiatrist as a person of extremely high intellect and with a profound knowledge of human psychology (in the everyday sense of the word) always valid.

The psychiatrist is a doctor who spends the greater part of his time within the walls of a psychiatric institution, amongst people who are mentally ill. He is accustomed to seeing suffering, violence, the most incredible perversions and grief. His patients are madmen —mad children and mad adults, women and men. Hence the very desire of a person to choose this profession, and his successful completion of a "probationary period" in psychiatry (for many people, the critical time), presuppose certain initial specific features in his character. Years of daily contact with this "graveyard of lost reason" leave their imprint on the personality of the doctor and work irreversible changes.

Here are the most characteristic types of working psychiatrist.

The Novice Psychiatrist: sincerely loves psychiatry and regards it as a fully-fledged scientific discipline. Because of his insufficient worldly and professional experience and the paucity of his knowledge, he discerns mental pathology where it undoubtedly does not exist. He does not understand the artificiality of psychiatric concepts. Thus he is very susceptible to suggestion and may sincerely "detect" that you have a pathological mental condition. He does not participate in forensic-psychiatric diagnostic commissions, and he is not dangerous, since it is not he who will decide your fate. The types of mature psychiatrist merit more detailed examination, for it is they who will determine your future.

The Academic: has retained his "youthful" passion for psychiatry and regards it as his vocation. For him, psychiatry is a scientific discipline (though with reservations). As a rule he sees (or "does not see": original unclear—Russian copyist) dissent as falling within the competence of psychiatry. He does not like participating in diagnoses concerning non-responsibility: "I am a doctor, not an investigator. . . ." He is sober enough to understand the state of affairs, but tries "not to dirty his hands": help him by using the right tactics.

The Writer of a Dissertation: chief characteristic: he is unconsciously extending the boundaries of the disease which he is describing in his dissertation. . . . Persuade him by your behaviour that you are not suitable "material."

The Voltairian: a clever and experienced person and psychiatrist. He has become long since disillusioned with psychiatry as a science. He is highly intelligent, loves art and literature, and can talk at great length about them. He is socially inactive, since he does not believe in the success of any social transformations (the wisdom of Ecclesiastes); but a conformist stance in public is not excluded. He is something of a coward, and a cynic. He understands the state of affairs perfectly well, but even under "pressure" he will find you mentally healthy, moreover, by virtue of his cowardice he will do it convincingly and demonstratively, to remove any suspicion of "sympathy" towards you: "so that nobody can pin a thing on to him".

The Philistine: intellect and specialist knowledge no higher than average. Considers himself an intelligent and experienced doctor and his life-style a desirable standard for others. Within the framework of political conformism he is socially active, and he has a well-developed adaptability to external conditions ("social mimicry"). He does not understand phenomena such as surrealist art ("do horses really fly?"), modern poetry ("but where are the rhymes?") and suchlike. He sincerely regards your social position as abnormal; his basic argument is: "But you had an apartment, a family, a job. Why did you do it?" We do not advise you to talk to this contemporary *rentier* about abstract subjects, philosophy, theoretical physics, etc., or about modern art; try to keep to his level. He is dangerous and may detect a psycho-pathological condition. He yields easily to pressure from above, and always justifies himself (in his own eyes) by citing authorities and psychiatric "schools".

The Professional Hangman: deliberately practises the exculpation of mentally-healthy persons. He is usually a competent specialist. Therefore your only possible course is not to allow him to detect a single "symptom". In that case, he may, out of a certain sort of professional self-esteem, decide he does not want to "dirty his hands" by "blatant forgery".

Practical recommendations on tactics

The punitive organs have one important advantage over dissenters: they are actively amoral. The principle of "the end justifies the means" is used by the state against citizens who behave like the boy in Andersen's famous fairy-tale about the emperor with no clothes. Pseudo-scientific theses on the class character of morals permit the state to take openly immoral measures against "enemies of the

Soviet people and the socialist system". But what is morality? Truth is moral, but falsehood is not, sincerity is moral, sympathy is moral, and so on. As a rule, dissenters adhere to precisely this kind of "classless" morality. In the context of the preliminary investigation, trial and psychiatric examination, this kind of morality implies the following:

(1) that you give truthful testimony on all matters which interest the KGB or the court, knowing that this will be your ruin as a person under diagnostic observation

(2) that you report to the KGB or to the court on circumstances and motives about which they had no knowledge, thus giving the psychiatric expert the necessary "material" to build up a picture of your "symptoms"

(3) that you show impermissible weakness towards the investigator for whom it is "imperative to carry out the investigation successfully", or to the witness who turns coward "for fear of losing his job", and so on.

Unfortunately these are the facts. Lying is a vile thing to do: but bear in mind that your fate hangs on your decision and ability to act immorally towards persons and organizations which profess the morality of savages. On the basis of our own experience and that of hundreds of our comrades, we can tell you that the abstract morality which governs the behaviour of the person undergoing investigation, trial, or psychiatric examination, works against his vital interests. The correct behaviour to display during a period of psychiatric examination (as during criminal investigation or trial) entails not only a necessary minimum elementary knowledge of psychiatric theory and practice, but also a "worldly" morality.

All our recommendations are aimed at the "average dissident". Naturally we cannot take account of the multitude of individual circumstances, interests and fortunes. You are not obliged to follow a specific recommendation if it is objectively at variance with reality in your case. Indeed, to do so would be harmful. It is senseless, for example, to deny a brain injury in the past, if your documents refer to one; or to deny that you stammer, if such is the case, and so on. It is desirable that your potential witnesses should be able to give equally correct and "clean" evidence about your mental character. The information you give a doctor may not coincide with that contained in the materials of the criminal investigation. In the first place, the law does not prohibit a suspect or an accused from giving deliberately false testimony; and in the second place, the information at the disposal of the psychiatrists, although not kept secret from the KGB (in Soviet law, medical confidentiality exists as a purely formal category), may not be used during the investigation or court hearing. Always remember, however, to exercise caution when giving the psychiatrist any information about circumstances which specifically interest the KGB, since this information may in time be "strategically exploited".

General information about your life. Your mother's pregnancy and your birth were normal. You were born a healthy child and you learned to sit up, walk and talk at the proper times. In your childhood you showed an interest in your peers and derived pleasure from contact with them. You showed no preference for playing games alone, all by yourself, nor any propensity to daydreaming, lying or obstinacy; all your habits, actions and opinions were those normal for your age and sex. You showed a moderate or somewhat heightened interest in books, and you preferred books suitable for your age. You did not suffer from nocturnal fears, sleepwalking, disturbed sleep, stammering, exaggerated fear of the dark, herds of animals or heights, etc. You displayed no fitfulness of moods, weakness of will, over-sensitivity, no sudden aggressive reactions; you did not play truant from school or home; you made good progress in your studies and never stayed down to repeat a year, you showed interest in classroom, school and playground life and did not try to avoid joining in it; you were liked by your school-mates (but you were not too "exemplary" or lacking in initiative), your friends were always of your own age. During your teenage years there were no peculiarities or difficulties with your behaviour. You took failures calmly, but not without some concern; you felt no attraction for quiet and solitary pursuits, nor any aversion to sport, large crowds or mass entertainment. You were absorbed in the interests of your age-group and milieu: you loved the cinema, you loved books (but not just science fiction), you loved games; you felt love for the members of your family; you were absorbed in the interests and concerns of your family; you felt for your near and dear ones, you shared their illnesses, their troubles and their joys; you were not secretive, you shared your interests and your news with your family. Your interest in the opposite sex arose at the right time; you were not apathetic about choosing a career; you always displayed lively, vivid and adequate emotions; you sincerely sympathized with those close to you in their troubles and failures. You are not irascible by nature, your contacts with people are not superficial; you do not restrict yourself to the interests of your home and work environments. If you *are* a secretive and withdrawn person, the reason is that you are shy and not that you lack the need for social intercourse; you are not indifferent towards your professional obligations and feel no aversion towards them; unless your studies or your profession require it, you show no interest (and never have) in philosophical problems (for there is a term "metaphysical intoxication"), in psychiatry, parapsychology or mathematics. Bearing in mind what you already know about the psychology of the psychiatrist, do not display any interest in modern art, and, especially, any understanding of it. You do not devote your spare time only to individualistic pursuits such as reading, gardening, or the contemplation of nature and works of art. You have hobbies, you are interested in sport (if only as a fan or a spectator). If you are unmarried, do not explain the fact by saying that you feel no attraction for the opposite sex or that you are repelled by the idea of family life; find some other reason (you have no apartment, your salary is too low, you were about to get married but were prevented by your arrest . . .). In respect of sexual behaviour, you have never overstepped the bounds of "decency". You have never been inclined to make "peremptory judgements", you understand—you have always understood—that "in life the crooked line is often shorter than the straight"; you have never performed any actions that were not justified by circumstances. If there is objective knowledge of any special peculiarities in your character, for example, that you have had "breakdowns", show an ability for critical self-analysis. You have never suffered brain injuries or had convulsions, fainting fits, hallucinations, memory disorders or diseases of the nervous system (the brain); you do not indulge in alcohol to excess; if you do drink, you have always preferred dry wines. Your social views have altered with age and have been corrected by the people round about you, by events and by reading books, etc., etc. Your reactions to injustices against you have never been excessively sharp, impetuous, effusive or long-lasting. Your dissenting views arose under the influence of books, tales of eye-witnesses and victims of repressions, your home upbringing and school education (if the circumstances allow you to offer this information painlessly), and as a result of a sober, objective appraisal of reality. However disagreeable it may be, the best motivation you can offer for the actions being imputed to you is: "I wanted to become famous, to be well-known; I did not understand the seriousness of the consequences, I did not stand aside and take a look at myself; I did not realise that I had gone too far", and so on. Unfortunately it is precisely unpleasant reasoning like this which will be interpreted in a positive light by the psychiatrist. We do not insist that everyone takes this advice on every occasion; but remember that circumstances may sometimes call for this kind of defence measure, especially as your moral stand (refusal to "ruin" your friends, "blacken" your past, etc.) will not suffer from this enforced tactical device.

During the period of investigation, dissenters are, as a rule, deprived of their freedom as a preventive measure. Denied the opportunity to see your family and friends, torn from your primary environment and your "life-stereotype," you become a participant in a fight with the KGB which you have already lost. It is in the investigation period that your behaviour and the circumstances of the case will predetermine whether or not you are to be declared non-responsible. The simplest way of safeguarding against exculpation is to give the KGB all the information it wants about all the persons in whom it is interested; not to spare family, friends, or anyone else and to disavow your "criminal past", etc., etc. As a rule, this guarantees that you will not end up in a mental hospital, even if you are a psychopath or a chronic alcoholic. There have indeed been instances of this. Happily, very few people resort to such an objectively and subjectively amoral way of protecting their interests. We hope that this simple, elementary method is unacceptable to you too.

During the period of the investigation, your behaviour will be influenced by the following factors:

(1) total isolation from the outside world
(2) anxiety about the future
(3) psychological pressure from the investigator
(4) the virtual certainty that you will have to share your cell with a prisoner who acts as an informer and directly or obliquely exerts psychological pressure upon you.

The informer will have been specially planted in your cell and his purpose is to bring influence to bear upon you, by any means, to the KGB's advantage. His methods include persuading you to give evidence, to show sincere repentance and thereby win a pardon; in the process, he cites himself or his friends as examples. Sometimes he "accidentally" finds that you and he had mutual friends in the past, and, referring to what they have told him, he informs you that he knows the "truth" about your wife's or fiancée's "infidelities". He squeezes the information out of you which the investigators need, creates an utterly intolerable psychopathic atmosphere in your cell, and prevents you from sleeping, eating, reading, etc. The investigator is, as you will quickly realize, organically incapable of keeping to the law in his actions; he will use persuasion, intimidation and blackmail, will infringe procedural norms for compiling investigative documentation, and so forth.

Alexander Volpin's *Instructions on behaviour while under investigation,* which are widely known to readers of *samizdat,* have, it is now clear, one important defect: the "legal stand" he advocates for persons under investigation (insistence that the investigator adhere to the letter of the law, precise knowledge and assertion of one's legal rights) hampers the investigator from making a "clean sweep" of your case, from intimidating your witnesses during confrontations, from juggling with testimonies in interrogation records, and so forth. This exhausts the investigator and forces him to resort to seeking mental flaws in your character and to apply to have you sent for psychiatric investigation. You run a special risk of having the "experts" brought in, if you refuse outright to testify (although this is not prohibited by law). We therefore recommend that you only resort to such means of conducting your case in extreme situations.

If circumstances permit, do not carry on conversations with the investigator about subjects which have "emotional" significance to you; often the investigator deliberately conducts talks of this kind on subjects to which you are not indifferent, and in a tenor calculated to provoke you to an emotional reaction. This is how Leonid Plyushch, for example, was "prepared" for his examination, so that a documentary record of his "fantasies" could be compiled.

Be prepared in advance for the investigator to make false claims that he has "evidence" against you and "depositions which expose you". Remember that you will not be able to prove to the investigator (nor to the court) that you have been shadowed, that provocations have been staged against you, and so forth, for obvious reasons. If you do, the experts will add "persecution mania" to your "diagnosis". For the same reason, do not insist on these aspects if the circumstances of the case allow. Try to argue your opinions, not on the basis of personal experience nor by analyzing reality, but by referring to literary sources, statements by authorities, etc. (Otherwise the experts' findings will include "over-estimation of your capabilities".) Do not be shy of expressing anxiety about your family, relatives and friends. This is essential evidence in favour of your "emotional integrity".

Protest hunger-strikes are desirable only in extreme necessity: if you want to strike, your refusal to take food may be interpreted as a pathological symptom of mental illness (which happened in the case of Pyotr Grigorenko).

In no case should you make any mention of disillusionment with life, lack of the desire to go on living, or of plans to put an end to your life. This will immediately incur the suspicion that you are mentally sick and may be a weighty argument in favour of exculpation. You must not utter a single word about any thoughts or plans to do away with yourself.

Do not be afraid that pharmacological substances may be put into your water or food; do not refuse treatment if you are ill—the evidence about such methods has not, as a rule, been confirmed.

We do not believe that these methods of exerting pressure are practised, since they involve certain purely technical difficulties and would not, in fact, be very effective.

There are no "scientific" methods which can force you to act against your will and your conscience. The same applies to hypnotic suggestion, which is quite ineffective in such situations.

The period of psychiatric investigation and actual diagnostic examination. We shall take in-patient examination as being the most complex situation.

You have been taken under escort to the reception room at a psychiatric institution, where, from the moment of your arrival, you find yourself under observation by medical personnel. In the reception room you undergo a health and hygiene check and have your first talk with a doctor. Don't refuse to submit to the health and hygiene routine, to talk or to undergo the medical examination, since this may be interpreted as "mental negativism." In the ward (or cell) you will meet other patients under examination. They may include people who are mentally sick, and you will have to get used to their presence. Don't be frightened of them; even aggressive mental patients are not as dangerous as rumour would have it, especially in the hospital environment of a psychiatric institution where methods of "deterrence" are practised. Remember that even here the possibility of the presence of an informer cannot be entirely ruled out. Usually each ward has an orderly or medical assistant who is there at all times and whose duties include continuous surveillance and, when necessary, the controlling of aggressive behaviour, over-excitement, etc., by means of injections with drugs and various forms of tying down.

The medium-ranking medical personnel in psychiatric establishments keep a diary of their observations, to maintain a detailed record of all the peculiarities in the behaviour of patients and persons under examination, their statements, their requests, etc. Therefore you must keep a check on your every action and word: all will be reported to the doctor in charge of you (the so-called "reporting doctor" who will submit your case to the commission of experts). Your conversations with the "reporting doctor" will largely determine the commission's diagnosis. Be reasonably polite to him (whatever your feelings about him), answer all his questions, as far as is possible; some questions may seem "stupid" ("What is the date today? What day of the week is it? What year? What is a hundred minus thirty? What is the meaning of the proverb: 'You are sitting in the wrong sleigh'?" and so on). You will have a chance to determine the psychiatrist's intellectual level and his way of conducting a conversation; your aim should be to talk with him "in the same language, on the same conceptual level".

We have already given a great deal of advice on the tactics to use when talking to a psychiatrist and the content of your conversation in other sections of our manual. Try not to make use of expressions which may be regarded as "symbolic associations" (for example, Grigorenko was asked to give the "reasons" for his "anti-social activity". He replied: "I couldn't breathe.")

Do not categorically state that you have been shadowed, victimized, eavesdropped upon, provoked, etc. (Pechernikova and Kosachev: "As paranoid reactions develop and escalate into a pathological development of the personality, the basic psycho-pathological formations gradually begin to acquire ramifications of delusional ideas about persecution, other people's attitudes, 'grand interpretations.' ")

Hunger strikes should only be declared in extreme circumstances, since they, too, will be interpreted as a manifestation of "psycho-pathic negativism". You will be unable to convince the psychiatrist of the objectivity and the social causes of your convictions (precisely because he too is well aware of the facts); consequently, we do not advise you to become involved in discussions on socio-political themes, otherwise you may be discovered to be "over-estimating your capabilities". (Pechernikova and Kosachev: "over-valued notions give place to interpretative delusions, which acquire the characteristics of incorrigibility, conviction, para-logicality; then there arises over-estimation of the individual's capabilities".) "Circumstantiality of thought" may also be noted (as happened with Grigorenko).

Naturally, if the psychiatrist has made up his mind to discern in you a pathological condition, any answer or action by you may be interpreted accordingly. Zhores Medvedev, for instance, was found to have a "split personality" on the grounds that he was a biologist by profession but also wrote poetry.

Your behaviour must be as natural as possible; do not hide your fears about the future, about your family, close friends and acquaintances, lest you be diagnosed as "emotionally dulled" or "cold".

Deny all knowledge of our manual, do not tell the doctor that you have ever been interested in psychiatry, parapsychology, philosophy or religion (if possible, base yourself on objective facts and circumstances).

Remember that a Soviet doctor cannot give you any assurance that he will observe his code of professional secrecy. Do not give him any "strategic" information which might be used against you or your friends.

After a certain time, the "reporting" doctor will present you to the commission, inform its members of his observations, and of the nature and content of his conversations with you, offer a preliminary analysis and announce his findings of responsibility (or non-responsibility).

Finally, rumours of "pharmacological" interrogations in psychiatric institutions are not without some foundation. A method exists called the "amytal interview", in which you may be given an intravenous injection of sodium amytal. Shortly after the injection (within seconds), the victim goes into a brief period of intoxication similar to an alcoholic state; he then passes into a deep sleep. The principle is the rather banal one of "drinking loosens the tongue". The "disinhibition" method, for so it is officially called, is used in cases when it is desired to bring to light the patient's concealed delusions, hallucinations and so forth. We can competently state that the method is ineffective; do not be afraid of it, stay in control of your condition (this *is* possible), and the effect of "loosening your tongue" will not be achieved.

Behaviour in the psychiatric hospital

The worst may happen: in spite of the fact that you have followed our advice in every respect, you are declared non-responsible and the court has ruled that you be sent for compulsory psychiatric treatment. The mental patient is totally deprived of his rights, and his situation is an unenviable one. But do not despair! Scores of your comrades have been undergoing compulsory treatment for long years without any serious injury to their health. Despite the whole arsenal of psycho-pharmacological methods and shock therapy, contemporary science has—fortunately—not yet reached the point where it can work irreversible changes in the human individual or destroy a man's personality.

Every six months, you are required by law to be presented to a regular psychiatric commission. Who knows, perhaps one of these commissions will find you "cured". There are no grounds for relying on the conscience of doctors; and unfortunately, the pressure of world opinion has had little effect either as regards the criminal use of psychiatry in the USSR.

Practice has shown that in order to create more or less tolerable living conditions for yourself in a psychiatric hospital (a less marked "regimen of oppression", permission to read books, milder "treatment", with longer intervals between courses), it is essential that you tell the doctors that you have "re-appraised your former unhealthy convictions". With all due respect for the courage of Leonid Plyushch, who is deliberately refusing to resort to any "tactical devices" in the Dnepropetrovsk Special Psychiatric Hospital, we strongly advise you to make use of them all the same. For they, and they alone, are your only hope of salvation.

Conclusion

Professor Ushakov, who diagnosed one of the authors of this manual, writes the following in his textbook for medical students: "Scientific ideas, which are dominant in the consciousness of the scholar, and the fanatical ideas of the religious believer are variants of the over-estimation of ideas (that is, of over-valued, pathological ideas)."

After that, can one wonder at the widespread use of the practice of exculpating dissenters?

Today, a knowledge of the elementary tenets of psychiatric practice and an ability to behave consciously and competently in the presence of a psychiatrist are essential requirements for many people. Certain circumstances in our life have prevented us until now from generalizing our experience in written form and offering it to readers.

Our manual is also designed to help in a situation in which you might have to appear as a witness during an investigation. Upon your evidence will depend the fate of other people.

Our concise format has prevented us from going into some questions of psychiatric theory and the interrelationship between psychiatry and the law as deeply and as seriously as we would have liked. For those of you who wish to acquaint yourselves in more detail with the problems we have touched upon in our work, we recommend the following reading.

Together with this work, we earnestly ask you to publish "An *in absentia* forensic-psychiatric report on P. G. Grigorenko" with Gluzman's authorship acknowledged.

If necessary, supply a glossary of terms at the end of the work.

V. BUKOVSKY, S. GLUZMAN,
Vladimir Prison—Perm Political Camp.

Recommended reading

1. Criminal Code (commentaries).
2. Criminal-Procedural Code (commentaries).
3. Fundamentals of Public Health Legislation of USSR and Union Republics (article 36).
4. RSFSR Law on Public Health (articles 54–56).
5. Directives on the immediate hospitalization of mentally ill persons. RSFSR Ministry of Health.
6. ...... [illegible]
7. ......

8. Medvedev, Zh. *A Question of Madness* (*samizdat*).

9. Grigorenko, P. *Memoirs* (*samizdat*).

10. ......

11. Gilyarovsky, V. A. *Psychiatry* (Moscow, 1938).

12. Gannushkin, P. B. *Selected Works* (Moscow, 1964).

13. Timofeyev, N. N., Timofeyev, L. N. Problems of medical deontology in clinical forensic-psychiatry, in *Korsakov Journal of Neurology and Psychiatry* (1973), No. 5.

14. Pechernikova, T. P., Kosachev, A. A. "Some peculiarities in the development and diagnosis of paranoid syndromes in psychopathic conditions," *Forensic-medical Examination* (1973), No. 4.

15. Timofeyev, N. N., "The deontological aspect of the identification of schizophrenics," *Korsakov Journal of Neurology and Psychiatry* (1974), No. 7.

16. Shmanova, L. M., *Clinical aspects of sluggish schizophrenia based on data from long-term follow-up observation* (doctoral dissertation) (Moscow, 1968).

APPENDIX VII

A Psychiatric Examination of Viktor Fainberg

This appendix consists of extracts of a *samizdat* record of the psychiatric interview of Viktor Fainberg by a commission on 17 March 1971 in the Leningrad SPH. The members of the commission were Professor R. Nadzharov, deputy-director of the Institute of Psychiatry of the Academy of Medical Sciences; Dr Z. Serebrya-kova, chief psychiatrist in the federal Ministry of Health; Dr V. Belyayev, chief city psychiatrist of Leningrad; Colonel P. Blinov, director of the Leningrad SPH; Dr L. Zemskov, head psychiatrist of the Leningrad SPH; and General N. N. Timofeyev, head of the Department of Psychiatry of the Military Medical Academy.

The record was summarized in *Chronicle* 19, and published in part in French in *Esprit*, 1971, No. 7–8, pp. 54–58. It is document AS 1276. The record, compiled by Fainberg, was kindly translated by Lowry Wyman.

Nadzharov: "We are psychiatrists from various civilian hospitals. Tell us what is troubling you."

Fainberg: "For the last two years I have been accustomed to seeing only doctors in military uniform."

Nadzharov: "No, we are civilian psychiatrists."

Fainberg: "But can't I find out what institutions you represent, or is that a secret like everything else here? (A vague silence.) So it's a secret. But please tell me then what sort of thing you have in mind. There is a great deal that interests me."

Nadzharov: "We are not going to get into a discussion of politics. Each of us has his own views."

Fainberg: "So I imagine. Well, since you are psychiatrists and you apparently want me to express my views on a broad range of topics, I should like particularly to touch on those issues which should also be of interest to you as specialists."

Nadzharov: "Please do."

Fainberg: "I have been here for two years now. During this time I have seen and heard many fantastic things. And I am aware that similar things go on at other special psychiatric hospitals like Chernyakhovsk and Kazan as conditions are identical every-where."

Nadzharov: "What do you mean?"

Fainberg: "The worst things are of course the beating of the patients, the rudeness and arbitrariness."

Nadzharov: "Who beats the patients?"

Fainberg: "The orderlies, the duty warders, even the block warders."

Nadzharov: "Unfortunately such things occur in civilian hospitals too. We are of course trying to fight this evil, but believe us, it's very difficult. The newspapers write about the nurse problem, but no one writes about the problem of orderlies—no one wants to work for such low wages."

Fainberg: "Yes, but you must agree that a criminal is not the best sort of orderly."

Nadzharov: "You mean to tell us that criminals work as orderlies here? But that is not at all true."

Fainberg: "If you are going to deny the obvious from the outset, it is going to be difficult to talk to you."

Blinov to *Nadzharov:* "Indeed, prisoners do work as orderlies here."

[Fainberg proceeds to comment on juridical, clinical and treatment aspects of the SPH—he describes in detail episodes of brutality, similar to accounts we included in chapter 7.]

Fainberg: "I should like now to turn to a personal issue: the predicament of political prisoners in special hospitals. I do not regard this issue as simplistically as the KGB, which simply orders the psychiatrists to declare certain political prisoners as mentally ill."

Nadzharov: "Of course not. We're not going to get into politics. Everyone has his own views on the subject."

Fainberg: "But it's impossible to avoid, doctor. In order to understand this problem you have to examine it in all its complexity. All the more so, since in this instance the political ingredient is the dominant element. Let's begin with the commission. It's the politicals who most frequently undergo psychiatric examination. Moreover, it's common knowledge how vague and diffuse psychiatry's diagnostic criteria are. And so the doctor . . . often pronounces a completely sane person as mentally ill. And the patient is sent away to undergo compulsory treatment. Thus, a person who has committed acts for which his colleagues will be sentenced to a term in a labour camp, and which are committed with the same motives, is declared insane and sent to a special hospital to have his head fixed. Although his colleague's term of imprisonment is fixed in a court judgement it is internment for him until he renounces his convictions. The doctors even say as much: 'Your release depends on your behaviour. And by your behaviour we mean your opinions precisely on political questions. Your behaviour is completely normal in every other respect. Your illness is heterodox thinking. As soon as you renounce your views and get back on the right track, we'll release you.' Thus, completely sane people are condemned to imprisonment forever if they refuse to alter their convictions."

Nadzharov: "But that can't be."

Belyayev: "Which doctors told you that?"

Fainberg: "Why list them? All the doctors that I've had to deal with. But this can't be through their own initiative. They're carrying out specific instructions from the top. According to this line of reasoning, you'd have to put the greater part of humanity in special hospitals. Hundreds of millions of people consider the invasion of Czechoslovakia to be what it was in fact—undisguised aggression. Thousands demonstrated in front of our embassies, hundreds of organizations deplored it in one form or another, including the leading circles of several of the biggest Communist parties: the Italian, French and British. So if our government were to gain control of just the European continent, many prison hospitals would have to be built! And you'd have to find a place for the parties' leaders—Luigi Longo for instance."

Belyayev: "You don't understand anything about psychiatry; your thoughts are extremely superficial."

Fainberg: "You don't have to be an expert in psychiatry to see that dozens of completely healthy people are confined under guard for many years without any hope of being released, only because they hold the convictions of the greater part of humanity. Some are 'treated' with walls, others with drugs which have a strong effect on the brain. Is it possible to deny that this is the most despicable torture? You speak about a commission of examiners! Every one of them pours forth a nauseating stream of official clichés. One is told that the invasion of Czechoslovakia was not an act of aggression, and other such nonsense. They demand that one says black is white and white is black. One answers these people sharply, but they are impervious: they've been wallowing in their clichés for so long that the same things are repeated over and over again at every meeting of the commission."

Serebryakova: "Isn't it true that you've never been able to give up your views even for a time?"

Fainberg: "If all these people had given up their views, doctor, we'd still be living in the Stone Age."

Serebryakova: "But it's the 20th century; for just this reason you ought to be more flexible!"

Fainberg: "But not at the expense of one's conscience, doctor."

Nadzharov: "Viktor Isakovich, people are declared mentally ill not because they hold one or another set of views and not because they have committed a crime with the same motives as healthy people. They are sent away for treatment because they were ill prior to that, and they undergo compulsory treatment until they're no longer a threat to society. And we psychiatrists can judge whether they are ill or not." (All three look at Fainberg triumphantly. Serebryakova impatiently looks at her watch.)

Serebryakova: "That's it. The 'circle' is closed."

Fainberg: "But really, this is casuistry. Dozens of completely healthy people are rotting here, in Chernyakhovsk, in Kazan! People whom nobody, except you, consider to be ill. They are rotting only because of their political convictions! Are you going to assert that General Grigorenko is ill? Or Natalya Gorbanevskaya?"

Belyayev: "You're repeating yourself. You've already been given proof."

Nadzharov: "And the point that you're being pressed into renouncing your views—that can't be."

Fainberg: "Now you're no longer indulging in casuistry, but calling black white. So it's useless to argue on such a level. But you yourselves are getting into this vicious circle; you think that you've got me into it. That's just the point—the only symptom of illness, please note, the only symptom, is considered here to be precisely one's political views. Where then is your circle? You're using casuistry and you want me to discuss calmly in an academic way the fate of decent people who are undergoing torture only because they had the courage to fight against arbitrariness and crime."

(To General Timofeyev who has arrived shortly before this interchange):

"You, Nikolai Nikolaevich, call General Grigorenko your friend: 'My friend, Grigorenko, also a general.'* You are generals from different armies! Here you sit with the commission and decide people's fate, but Grigorenko's fate depends on an illiterate orderly who can decide, excuse me, whether or not to let him go to the lavatory. And now he is suffering from an inflammation of the bladder. That's how a man is dispensed with, a man who has shed so much blood for his country!"

Nadzharov: "We're not going to talk about politics, everyone here has his own views."

Fainberg: "I'm not asking you for your views, that's dangerous in our country. But——"

Belyayev: (interrupting) "That's an insulting and vulgar remark."

* Timofeyev was responsible for Grigorenko's release from the Leningrad SPH in 1965. He also earned the gratitude of Leningrad Christian oppositionist Igor Ogurtsov when declining to diagnose him as mentally ill in 1967. (On Ogurtsov see Appendix I.)

Fainberg: "No need to get all worked up, doctor. My joke shocked you perhaps because it's so close to the truth, because it's impossible not to say that it almost coincides with it. You can leave out the word 'almost'. But Dr Nadzharov has emphasized that everyone has his own views so many times that I felt obliged to exhibit my trust in him in precisely this way."

Belyayev: "You take the rôle of a hero and unjustly extol some people and show contempt for others."

Fainberg: "It's incomprehensible to me on what grounds you attribute to me the rôle of a hero. To be sure, there are heroes in the human-rights movement and I take my hat off to them. But I do not consider my colleagues, let alone myself to be heroes. Our movement is not heroism; it's the ordinary human conscience. I also don't understand whom you have in mind when you accuse me of showing contempt for people. The hooligan-like orderlies and their patrons? And if you're alluding to the fact that I'm making a differentiation, then I would like to be perfectly frank in my response. Great social movements are always started by a minority. This is an established rule of history. Of the majority, each individual must decide for himself to which faction he belongs: the sympathizers, the liberals, the conservatives, the opportunists, or simply the crooks."

Belyayev: "I understand you mean that every man decides for himself?"

Fainberg: "It's very nice that you have finally understood me correctly."

Serebryakova: "Why have you stopped eating?"

Fainberg: "My colleague Borisov [Vladimir Borisov] and I have made a written declaration to the administration on this point. You of course know of him. We have stipulated that all discussions concerning our hunger strike be held with us together."

Timofeyev: "You've become involved with an anti-Semite."

Fainberg: "Nikolai Nikolaevich, you're getting confused again. Chernyshov is the anti-Semite, and it is Borisov and I who have begun a hunger strike. With regard to Chernyshov, we demand that the injections be stopped, since he was given them as punishment for his perfectly justifiable hunger strike."

Nadzharov: "What's all this about your not being allowed to see a lawyer?"

Fainberg: "Right, we're considered not responsible. Borisov, for instance, is a completely healthy man who was declared insane only for having written a letter with others to the UN Commission on Human Rights about the unlawful arrest of Grigorenko and Gabai. He was refused permission to see his lawyer. The lawyer was told that Borisov's health didn't permit it."

Serebryakova: "What restrictions apply to the literature that you can read?"

Fainberg: "Many books in the hospital library aren't lent out to us because we're mentally ill."

Serebryakova: "What for instance?"

Fainberg: "Dostoyevsky is banned."

Serebryakova: "Well, we read Dostoyevsky during our childhood."

Fainberg: "And it wouldn't be a bad idea now for many to re-read him. In this day and age everything is perceived differently, particularly Dostoyevsky."

Serebryakova: "What else?"

Fainberg: "A whole ream of books. We can't have Mager's four-volume *Universal History*; I personally received a copy from the doctors in wards 4 and 5. But this is exceptional. The doctors had taken it out on their own library card."

Serebryakova: (smiling) "Then you should be grateful to the doctors."

Fainberg: "Of course I'm grateful. But really it's a matter of luck; everything depends on the doctor's character. In principle, such literature is forbidden for us."

Serebryakova: "What other books?"

Fainberg: "Quite a long list: Pokrovsky's *History of Russia in the 19th Century*, Ovsyaniko-Kulikovsky's *History of Literature in the 19th Century* and La Rochefoucauld's *Maxims*. Practically speaking, anything of interest. In addition it's very difficult to obtain permission to receive books from the outside. I'm a philologist and a specialist in Germanic studies. My field is actually English language and literature. Language is like a sport; you simply disqualify yourself through lack of practice.... I haven't received any books from the outside for six months. I was told to send a statement in writing to the hospital director. There was no reply for a long time. Finally I was given an oral response from the colonel, who said that because of my health I wasn't allowed to receive books from the outside; and that I couldn't read books at all, only periodicals."

(an uneasy silence)

Serebryakova: "You've stopped eating?"

Fainberg: "I'm being force-fed through my nose. Here you're allowed to fast for only four days."

Serebryakova: "What do you do now?"

Fainberg: "Gymnastics and shower, three times a day. The rest of the time I spend reading—English, German and history."

Belyayev: "You've said that some people have been here for thirteen to fifteen years. Can you recall their names?"

Fainberg: "Certainly. Lysak was here thirteen years—he refused to renounce his convictions. Kogan is in his seventeenth year."

Serebryakova: "Lysak! That one is really mentally ill." [*sic*]

Fainberg: "For all practical purposes, he is a perfectly sane man."

Nadzharov: "Viktor Isakovich, we've heard you out. We shall consider what you have told us."

Fainberg: "I'd like to be able to believe that."

APPENDIX VIII

A Talk with a Psychiatrist

The following is the text of a talk between Evgeny Nikolayev, a scientist, and the psychiatrist Vladimir Nikolayevich Dmitrievsky, head of section 15 at the Kashchenko Psychiatric Hospital in Moscow. It took place in March 1974. On Nikolayev see appendix I.

D [*Dmitrievsky*]: "Why were you hospitalized?"

N [*Nikolayev*]: "I don't know. I never did anything bad to anyone. The psychiatrists arranged the hospitalization in such a way that it came like a bolt out of the blue. I don't know why, or for what."

D: "Couldn't it have had some connection with your remarks?"

N: "What remarks?"

D: "Well, remarks about our society, for example."

N: "I don't know. In official organizations I never made any remarks."

D: "And in unofficial ones?"

N: "I am quite simply unfamiliar with unofficial organizations."

D: "Why were you hospitalized in 1970?"

N: "I don't know. That hospitalization, too, was arranged in the same manner. So you have more information on it than I have."

D: "But after all, your wrong-headed views were first manifested a long time ago, when you were nineteen."

N: "My views have nothing to do with psychiatry. And mistaken views are not always a symptom of illness. For example, a mistaken view can be due to a lack of information."

D: "I gather that you were expelled from the Komsomol*."

N: "I was not expelled from the Komsomol. I withdrew from it."

D: "Why did you withdraw from it? Was it because of your views?"

N: "That has nothing to do with psychiatry."

D: "No, but the fact is that this is the fourth time you have been put in a psychiatric hospital. After all, not everybody who drops out of the Komsomol is sent to a psychiatric hospital."

N: "I left the Komsomol eighteen years ago. That's an outworn topic."

D: "Of course. I'm not giving it special emphasis. What is your profession?"

* Communist Youth League.

N: "I'm a biologist."

D: "Do you know foreign languages?"

N: "Yes."

D: "Many?"

N: "Quite a few."

D: "Where have you worked?"

N: "Four years at the All-Union Institute of Scientific and Technical Information and one year at the disinfection institute."

D: "Why did you have conflicts with your colleagues?"

N: "I didn't have any conflicts with my colleagues."

D: "What else did you study besides biology and languages?"

N: "Whatever I felt a need for."

D: "Have you been interested in philosophy? In problems of the state and law?"

N: "No. Of course I studied all those subjects at the university, but I've never gone back to them since."

D: "And you have taken no special interest in philosophy?"

N: "No."

D: "What can you say about our society?"

N: "If you're interested in our society, you'd do better to ask people more competent than I am. I've already said that after passing my exams on political subjects I never looked at the textbooks. So my remarks wouldn't be worth more than a 'D'."

D: "I'm not interested in your knowledge of university courses. I'm interested in your own opinions. The clinic that sent you to the hospital had received a phone call about your mistaken views of our society."

N: "Whatever my views are, they have nothing to do with psychiatry."

D: "If that were so you wouldn't be here. If your views of society didn't represent a social danger, you wouldn't have been hospitalized. Isn't it true that three times before you were in psychiatric hospitals for long periods of time?"

N: "Yes."

D: "And you are familiar with our governmental machinery. We are all subordinated to the appropriate organs; and if we get instructions from those organs, we are obliged to carry them out."

N: "And that is why you are so interested in my views of society?"

D: "Yes. But you have been putting up a kind of wall between us. And believe me, it's not to your advantage. The more stubbornly you refuse to answer questions, the longer you'll stay in the hospital. I'm asking you these questions for your own good. Surely you've noticed I'm not taking notes."

N: "I'm not taking any notes, either."

D: "Moreover, you can be classified as socially dangerous. In that case, before every Soviet holiday, by way of a preventive measure you'll be put in a psychiatric hospital, whether you like it or not."

N: "I'm aware that there is such a practice in our country."

D: "Just remember, you're not an important figure like Solzhenitsyn. He was expelled from the country for his views and remarks. But for your views and remarks, you'll just be put in a psychiatric hospital."

N: "And to no purpose, because my views do not represent a social danger. As for those who disagree with my views and make calls to the clinic about them, they are simply exaggerating them—probably because they're full of phobias. It's perfectly true that I enjoy no such popularity as Solzhenitsyn. But I'm rather well known among people interested in foreign languages. And any time I'm hospitalized, it can only have an adverse effect, since I can't contribute my knowledge and skill to that society about whose security you worry so much."

D: "Still and all, where did you voice your incorrect attitude towards our society?"

N: "I think you'd do better to put that question to the employees of those organs that telephoned the clinic."

D: "That may be. But I'd like to hear it from the primary source."

N: "In this case your primary source is the person who denounced me. I don't know who did it, and I can't even guess, since I didn't make any disloyal remarks."

D: "But you're here. *Ergo*, you made such remarks about our society, and those remarks represent a social danger."

N: "You're mistaken. Tell me: Have there been any complaints about me in your section?"

D: "No, there have been no complaints from the personnel about you. Your behaviour has been irreproachable."

N: "But if I were really socially dangerous, my behaviour could not have been irreproachable."

D: "It's not your behaviour that is socially dangerous but your views."

N: "I think not. Whatever my attitude towards our society, that society won't change. If I damn it, it won't become worse; and if I praise it, it won't become better. What I say can't make it either better or worse. Therefore my views can't be dangerous to society."

D: "And which do you prefer: to praise society or damn it?"

N: "I prefer to stick to the principle that it's not my concern."

D: "That attitude towards society also represents a social danger. If you continue to follow that principle, you'll be continually confined in psychiatric hospitals."

N: "I'm aware of that. I've been through it. How long do you intend to keep me in the hospital?"

D: "I can't tell you that. Everything depends on you. You won't get off with one month."

N: "I've already been here three weeks."

D: "You'll be released by a medical commission convened for that purpose. If you continue to evade all the critical questions when the commission meets, it won't be to your advantage."

N: "From past experience I've become convinced of the contrary. When I told a doctor at Psychiatric Hospital No. 15 about my attitude towards society, he sent me to the Stolbovaya suburban hospital where I spent eight months. As you can see, it's dangerous to express one's views. And I've learned from you that it's also dangerous to say nothing. Apparently I have to choose the lesser of two evils."

D: "Get me right. There are good reasons for my questions."

N: "I'm a healthy man, and my views have nothing to do with psychiatry."

D: "But all the doctors at various hospitals who treated you and, more than anything else, were disquieted by your views—surely they cannot have been wrong?"

N: "Quite possibly the doctors weren't wrong. After all, you yourself said that people in official positions are subordinated to the appropriate organs and are obliged to carry out ·their instructions."

D: "How were your relationships with your family?"

N: "That's not a matter ot immediate concern."

D: "At various times in the past, you have published a great many articles."

N: "Yes. In the *Moskovsky komsomolets*, and in a few newspapers in the Moscow region—in Kaluga and Obninsk. Also, my most recent articles were published in Kamchatka."

D: "Did you write about your views of society in those articles?"

N: "No, those articles dealt with an intensive method for learning foreign languages. They were addressed to those interested in that problem."

D: "Where, and under what circumstances, did you propagandize your disloyal views?"

N: "Nowhere. And in the final analysis, to put a person in a psychiatric hospital for his views is quite simply a cheap trick and unworthy of the title of physician."

D: "I have to make my rounds now, but we'll continue this talk later. I have to ascertain your attitude towards society. I'll probably prescribe other medication for you shortly."

7 March 1974

APPENDIX IX

A Letter from Dr Semyon Gluzman, 1974

Gluzman wrote this open letter to his parents in August 1974, from camp 35 in Perm region, after he had been deprived of the right to see them. It was typed out in Moscow from a barely legible original.

My Dear Ones: On August 9th I learned of your trip here an d your unsuccessful attempts to visit me. I learned this from your letter, since until that time no one had told me of your coming here. They were afraid to talk—afraid of my comrades' reactions. This time it is not easy for me to write. But I shall try to avoid too much emotion since paper catches on fire so easily!

I don't know how the camp superintendent described my transgressions to you. I was deprived of my right to see visitors because of my refusal to help build the camp prison. I had been put in a punishment cell twice, but it was not until July 26th that I was deprived of the visit, on orders from the KGB operations office. The KGB learned of your impending arrival, and the provocation succeeded beautifully. During the month-long hunger strike, Commandant Pimenov said, "From now on we're going to do our job more thoroughly," and his promise was fulfilled. Legally, everything was well-grounded. . . . There is only one "trifle" you don't know: during all that time there were several opportunities for me to be assigned work, and I requested it repeatedly. . . But the "interests of state security" demanded a different approach.

You will remember that last year I was allowed a visit, at the cost of a compromise with myself. Not long before receiving your letter, I was sent to spade up the ground in the security zone that runs around the camp. To put it simply, I participated in guarding myself.

From a prisoner's viewpoint, that was immoral. I did it for your sake—for the sake of the visit. That was my only compromise, and my last one. Captain Utyro, the KGB operations chief, once said that I had one weak spot—my parents. He was mistaken: I have no weak spots. I cannot allow myself such a luxury. Just as I am virtually deprived of the right to correspondence, to proper medical care, to visits by my parents, to human dignity, so I am deprived of the right to emotion. Such is my day-to-day life in camp: always cold, always hungry, always realistic.

You write that I should reconsider my values. Daily and hourly, my physical being and personality are being killed. The watchdog outside the fence gets better food, with more calories, than I do. It is not fed rotten cabbage and stinking fish. Right now I am wearing a thin cotton tunic of the same infamous cut that Stalin wore, with a name tag on my chest. My head is shaved. I am always hungry, and I freeze on the cement floor of the punishment cells. I must march in formation, and at any moment I may be stripped naked or forced to squat countless times. I am a slave. Any sadist has the authority and right to force me to do any humiliating labour. I am the convict Gluzman, S. F.—an especially dangerous state criminal. But I'm not Yakir and I'm not Dzyuba.* They are probably the ones you call "ringleaders". As if talking about a gang. I don't have the ability to see roses blooming on a barbed-wire fence, and I am not a chronic alcoholic who can see hallucinations. During my investigation they told me of the "recantations" of Franko, Seleznenko, and Kholodny.† They used "persuasion" on me: Seleznenko was across the street in the Kiev Restaurant, drinking cognac and eating shashlik, "while you're in prison". I'm not accustomed to eating shashlik washed down with cognac; my gastronomical tastes provided no reason for "recanting".

I would have to deny myself—to deny the moral principles I learned in your family, from Uncle Lev—and, Father, from your friend Misha Yavorsky, who perished "somewhere". Investigator Gunikhin (?) [illegible—copyist] tried to convince me that in the years of the "cult of personality" there were no "substantial" abuses; that only five million persons were arrested, the majority of them under ordinary articles of criminal law, and that "not really very many" perished . . . Should I go on? You were eyewitnesses in '37.

I was accused of circulating "libellous fabrications" to the effect that Komsomolsk-na-Amur was built by Zeks [prisoners]. Just remember the late writer Abram Kogan (?) [illegible—copyist], your acquaintance. He worked on that great "Komsomol" construction project. Some of my fellow-prisoners in this camp worked on similar construction projects. But that kind of thing never happened, right? Remember the "Doctors' Plot". And that never happened either? And there were never any atrocities committed by Garanin,

* Pyotr Yakir, a Moscow dissenter who in 1972–73 broke under pre-trial investigation and betrayed his friends; and Ivan Dzyuba, a Ukrainian dissenter who recanted after his arrest in 1972.

† Zinoviya Franko, Leonid Seleznenko and Mykola Kholodny, Ukrainian dissenters who recanted in various degrees in 1972.

never any revolts in the camps, never any night arrests? Come now! Those things happened in your day, not mine! Recently, in our camp, they pulled down a shaky building put up in 1949. On one of the roof beams we saw a graffito: "25 years of forced labour, 12 yet to go. Maksimov, A. G." That graffito on the roof-beam was all that remained of a human being. Of the former zeks in the Urals, only very few survived. They used the example of the Urals camps to frighten the prisoners of Norilsk and Vorkuta. Now they are used to frighten the zeks of Mordovia.

But even if it comes to the worst I am not threatened by oblivion—thanks to my comrades, known and unknown, and to the Chronicle of Current Events. In court one young witness, still really a girl, responded to a question as follows: "The Chronicle of Current Events exists so that people can learn the truth about closed trials like this one." That girl was not a "ringleader." She was not even a regular *samizdat* enthusiast. But would not any "reconsideration of my views" be a betrayal of her? And what should I revise? My negative attitude toward the cult of personality—instilled in me by teachers in school and college, and by books, films, and even official Party documents? Should I forget the dozens of personal acquaintances who have experienced all the horror of our modern-day Oprichnina?* I'm a doctor—I have seen death, and to some extent am accustomed to it. But the kind of death I have seen was always that of a single person, alone, when science was powerless and the end was inevitable. And it is hard for me to imagine the death of millions—healthy people, young people, old people. Death from starvation, bullets, torture. The death of millions is not one death but millions of deaths. Nothing can justify the death of innocent people.

The procurator once asked me: "Why do you put so much emphasis on the period of the cult of personality? Was anyone in your family imprisoned?"

Yet in your letters you lecture me. You believe the words of a professional policeman—a man without convictions—thus making it easier for them to put pressure on me. Pimenov once told my friend Meshener: "I can stand you on your head if I want to." The humanism of the socialist penitentiary system consists in just such acrobatics. I have experienced it on my own skin. Yesterday, for example, a sixty-two-year-old man named Prishlyak, who has endured the torture of camp life for more than twenty-two years (and I am only twenty-seven), was sent to a punishment cell. And the reason for that "humanitarian" act was Prishlyak's refusal to paint the fence around the security zone. Apart from any moral considerations, the zone had been spaded up before that, and who

* Ivan the Terrible's secret police.

could guarantee that a man wouldn't be shot there "while attempting to escape"? Such things have happened before. . . . In Mordovia, for example, on May 3, 1970, while dozens of zeks were looking on, twelve shots were fired at a man in the garb of a hospital patient. They shot at him despite the shouts from the zeks. "Don't shoot! He's crazy!" And despite the fact that Baranov (such was his name) put up his hands after being hit the first time. That's only one example, and not the most horrible. The history of the "Gulag Archipelago" offers even more bitter examples.

Do you realize that when we are marched from one place to another, stopping or taking one step to the side is considered an attempt to escape? (I know this from personal experience.) Or that when the temperature was $-58°$ F. I was forced to lie down in the snow at night, guarded by an Alsatian dog straining at the leash, "just in case"? This is the basis of my values; I can have no others. Therefore, there will be no compromise. Can I forget the conditions in the punishment cells at the Kharkov Transfer Prison? The bestial cruelty of the guards in the railroad cars taking prisoners from one camp to another? Or how the officer commanding those guards "educated" a convicted prostitute by taking her into his compartment for the night?

So is everything fine in "the far kingdom"? You are Communists. Then why is it that you, worthy citizens of "the state of socialism and democracy", are not allowed to familiarize yourselves, even superficially, with the materials in my case? Why weren't you allowed to attend the trial of your own son? Why weren't you given a copy of the sentence?

Why did the "interests of national security" require an attempt to conceal from everyone the charges against me—having a copy of Albert Camus' Nobel Prize speech, a parody of Kochetov's novel, *What Do You Want?*, an article by Böll (?) in the Reporter, Arkady Belinkov's open letter to the Union of Soviet Writers? Why did they conceal the testimony of witnesses who all said there was no "anti-Soviet agitation and propaganda" in my utterances or actions? I knew the length of my sentence even before the preliminary investigation was completed. I was told by Lt. Col. N. P. Borovin, chief of the investigative section.

I had the following dialogue at that time with Borovin about my convictions.

B: "You still have time. Take back what you've said, and tell us what we want to know, and you won't get ten years."

I: "Do you really think I'd change my convictions just because I've been arrested and am under investigation?"

B (interrupting): "Who's interested in your convictions? That's not what the case is all about."

Need I comment on this variation of the dialogue between the Devil and Faust?

It's hard on you—unspeakably hard. Your expectations have been blasted . . . [illegible—copyist] instead of a scientific and medical career, and finally my family—none of this has come to pass. But is this the whole truth? I have written my dissertation: "An In-Absentia Forensic Psychiatric Examination in the Grigorenko Case." And I thank God I'm a bachelor. The KGB agents who eavesdrop in the camp visitors' building cannot be witnesses to my adultery. I have been spared at least that one humiliation.

Again, both as a psychiatrist and a close friend of Leonid Plyushch, I cannot "revise" my belief that he is absolutely mentally healthy. You know that in September 1973 Georgy Trifonovich Dyagas, an agent from the central KGB, came to see me. Secretly, and without any authorization from the procurator, I was taken to the visitors' building of Camp 36, where for three days, with no witnesses present, I was subjected . . . [illegible—copyist] processing. No deal was made, because I refused. But it was obvious that someone badly wanted my help. "Suppose Gluzman agrees to refute those 'fabrications' in the West about confining healthy people in Soviet psychiatric hospitals?" And the price offered me was no small one.

Would you really have approved such a recantation? You—conscientious and honest people, and doctors? No, you would not have. Because then I would really have become a criminal—a colleague of Elsa Koch (?) [illegible—copyist] and Daniil Lunts. I am not strong enough to violate my own conscience. And not weak enough. Here in this concentration camp I am leading an authentic spiritual life. I am happy, despite everything I have to endure. I say this even though declaring a hunger-strike is the only means available to me and my comrades in happiness (this is no slip of the pen: I am really happy) for demonstrating our human dignity to all the thugs around us; even though refusing to help build the camp prison is one of the few ways I can affirm the morality of my convictions and my civic creed.

I am a Jew, and my Jewishness is not merely a matter of remembering the victims of genocide and of persecutions resulting from prejudice elevated to moral dogma: it is not just a matter of these memories. My Jewishness lies in the knowledge that today there exists a people possessing their own state—a people with a history, a future, and (fortunately) weapons. My Grandfather Abraham, who was shot at Babi Yar, would never have allowed me to "reconsider my values." Because every September his spirit grows restless—and you know why.*

* i.e. During the anniversary of the mass liquidation of Soviet citizens, mostly Jews, at Babi Yar in Kiev in 1941.

My dear ones! It's very hard for you. I realize you are afraid to wait. But please believe in the sincerity of this letter, which will by-pass the censor. Everything is all right with me. Whatever may happen in the future, I am complaining of nothing and am really satisfied with my fate. I know it's hard for you to understand that. Your generation was shell-shocked by '37 and the years that followed. Fear, fear, fear. It's unbearable to fear your own desires. During the investigation and the trial I felt sorry for the witnesses testifying against me. They were pale, they stammered, they couldn't look anyone in the eye. What they said about me—my views, my words, my deeds—was said out of fright alone, with no malice toward me. They were afraid. Their fear was somehow transcendental, Kafkian. Then am I not fortunate that I have no such fear—that my conscience is clear? Is that a mere trifle?

It's hard on you, yes. But would you really want me to betray the mother of Jan Palach? (After all, I was incriminated for what I said about the occupation of Czechoslovakia in '68.) She has lost her son—forever. So what could my "reconsideration of values" be called except betrayal?

One does not have to become a paid "source" for the KGB, to testify against those who share one's views. Suffice it to mention what Dzyuba did.

I must close this letter—time is pressing. It will strike you as confused, but that can't be helped. I lead a restricted life, and I don't know when I'll have another chance to send you a line by-passing the many censors—to tell you the truth about myself once again. Don't be surprised by the glibness of my [other] letters to you. The fact is that I can't answer your questions. I can't write about my comrades (or even mention their names); about punishments, my own illnesses, our diet, and many other things. All those things are a carefully-guarded state secret.

So goodbye, my dear ones. I kiss you.

Slava.
[Gluzman's nickname]

APPENDIX X

Life in an Ordinary Mental Hospital: the View of a Soviet Psychiatrist

by Dr Marina Voikhanskaya

Dr Voikhanskaya worked for five years in Leningrad's Psychiatric Hospital No. 2, then moved in 1967 to No. 3. Here she was a staff psychiatrist until she emigrated in 1975. Soon after her arrival in England she wrote this article, translated by Hilary Sternberg, which first appeared in *New Psychiatry* [31 July 1975] in slightly different form.

An enormous, poorly lit, old-fashioned hall with columns and a high ceiling, and the ghostly pale figures of mental patients creeping along the walls. My heart thumped with fear and curiosity; at any moment now they would bring him in, this artist who had done fifteen years in prisons and camps and was now in the terrible ward for violent patients; and I would have to make a diagnosis of sick or healthy. He came in, an embittered, despairing man who at once began shouting that I was a KGB agent; but after we had talked for a little while he began to believe in me and trust me. He was healthy, yes, but he was a very tired, broken man. I believe that this meeting was probably the turning point in my fate—my fate as a doctor and my fate as a human being.

In the past 25 years Russian psychiatry and all its past glories have been debased, reduced to a semi-amateur level by Academician Snezhnevsky and his "school". What was once a flourishing science has now been replaced by a single doctrine about schizophrenia. This "unanimity of thought" is very convenient for the powers-that-be: alcoholism (which is on the increase) and alcoholic psychoses can be labelled schizophrenia; congenital idiocy in the children of alcoholics, premature schizophrenia; and dissent—eureka!—dissent too is not the flower of the nation or its pride and joy, but schizophrenia with delusions of reform.

Psychiatry has therefore become a very easy and very lucrative profession; any philistine with a doctor's diploma can make a diagnosis of schizophrenia if he has a smattering of gentlemanly jargon at his command. "Everything that is not like ordinary people—i.e. like myself—is schizophrenia." A favourite dictum of

Professor V. M. Morozov, one of Snezhnevsky's closest confederates, is: "It's no secret to anyone that you can have schizophrenia without schizophrenia."

Translate this into ordinary language and you find you can have disease without disease, happiness without the symptoms of happiness. This is the kind of absurdity that is taught in the departments of the Moscow Institute for the Advanced Training of Physicians, which every year turns out hundreds of trained psychiatrists ready to see a schizophrenic in Leonid Plyushch because he knows and thinks too much; or in Viktor Fainberg because he dares to have an opinion of his own and, what is more, to express it openly; or in Tolya Chinnov because he believes in God; or in Pyotr Starchik because he recited the poems of Tsvetayeva and Pasternak from memory while he was in prison; or in General Grigorenko because, in spite of his high post and the material benefits he enjoyed as a consequence, he refused to keep silent. . . .

Without fear of being made to answer for it you can have a hapless young metallurgist bound hand and foot and sent to a psychiatric ward simply because he was unhappy at work and had come to a psychiatrist for advice and sleeping pills. A student who was cheated in a restaurant and all but arrested for hooliganism when he tried to protest very soon found himself in hospital. Back in his hostel, in a burst of anger, he began criticizing the Soviet régime, and all someone had to do was telephone a psychiatrist for the boy to end up in our section with a diagnosis of schizophrenia.

Ch—, a practising Orthodox Christian, was hospitalized because his behaviour seemed strange first to his neighbour (a drunkard) and then to a psychiatrist at a district clinic—for what did he mean by going to church, feeding the birds, never using foul language, always praying and observing fasts, and being kind and gentle to everyone? A quiet, mild-mannered youth with a heart condition also ended up in our section—the therapist had grown tired of hearing his complaints. I could continue with the list *ad infinitum*.

The hospital where I worked is in the outskirts of Leningrad and consists of several old and rather beautiful buildings erected at the turn of the century through the generosity of private benefactors, and three new wings built in the last eight years to replace the crumbling old buildings which were quite unfit for use. The hospital is designed to accommodate 1,500 patients, but it normally houses 2,500. It is directed by the chief physician who has absolute medical and administrative authority.

For the last few years the chief physician has been M. P. Isakov, a man of about 50 with extremely limited intellectual powers and a poor medical and general education, and whose spoken Russian is slightly ungrammatical. He has four deputies:

a medical affairs deputy, who was once a good doctor and a decent human being but is now over 70 and afraid of losing his job;

a scientific deputy—a lady who has no connection whatsoever with science and was given the job (which does not figure in the hospital staff list) as a reward for personal services rendered. Her name is L. A. Zhivotovskaya and it was she who directed that V. Borisov and V. Fainberg be tortured;

there is also a deputy for military training, usually a retired colonel; and lastly, a deputy for finance and administration.

The hospital consists of 31 sections, each in the charge of a section head with no more power than a puppet, and a number of house-doctors and surgeons with between 35 and 40 patients each under their care. All doors in all sections are kept locked. Patients wear standard, badly-laundered pyjamas. In summer they can take three- to four-hour walks in a small locked garden; in winter walks are not allowed because there are no warm clothes.

There is one bath-house for the entire hospital, and patients visit it in queues under staff supervision once every ten days. There are baths in the sections, but only for patients who are weak. All examinations and physiological treatment are carried out under supervision. Visits to the lavatory, access to personal belongings, and smoking are permitted only at certain times. In each section there are three hours daily of work therapy. The patients dislike it because it is primitive and monotonous, and they do it under duress.

A patient is assigned to a particular doctor for the whole of his stay in the hospital. Visits from relatives are allowed once a week, on Sundays; parcels are accepted on Wednesdays, but the quantity and range of products permitted is strictly limited. For some reason meat is prohibited; the hospital food is very bad, which means that patients may have to live for years on meagre rations. Only a very limited number of patients are released for holidays—it is less worry to keep them under lock and key.

In the wards beds stand only 20 to 30 centimetres apart, sometimes right up against each other (like double beds). Patients have no place for their personal belongings—indeed, these are not allowed. The sections have no libraries; there are a few old books with their beginnings and ends missing. The hospital takes the national newspapers but the patients hide them and use them as toilet paper. For the really sick patients these conditions are almost unbearable. . . .

Most of the nurses have had only one or two years' training, sometimes no more than six months. They are frequently casual workers whose level of culture is low; they treat patients condescendingly and address elderly patients familiarly and without due respect. They make patients run errands for them and reward them with extra cups of tea or cigarettes. . . . For Jewish patients here conditions are even worse because of the anti-Semitism which exists.

A hundred doctors work in the hospital; 80 of these are psychiatrists. There are blatant scoundrels and careerists, typical examples of *homo sovieticus*, but the majority are decent and humane people.

But then in May 1973 on the orders of the chief city psychiatrist, Belyayev, the artist Ivanov was sent to section 8, for the most disturbed patients in our hospital. The woman head of the section, a young, witty and crafty philistine, and two other section doctors, also women, all realized that Ivanov was a healthy man; but they kept him in the section without telling this to anybody. I learned of him from Viktor Fainberg in January 1974. When I asked the head of the section (until then a friend of mine) about the state of Ivanov's health she hissed at me through her teeth: "He's perfectly healthy but don't tell anybody."

She gave me permission to visit him, and I began going every day because I realized that he felt a need to speak his mind, and he was very tired.

I brought him books and cigarettes. The doctors in the section stopped saying good-morning to me. In March a new section head was appointed, a cynical man, fond of the good life and prepared to do anything to please the authorities. He called me to his office and said "Can I give you a piece of friendly advice? Stop visiting Ivanov, for your own good and his." When I refused he shouted at me and forbade me to visit Ivanov. So I decided to go and see the artist on Sundays, like a visiting relative.

On the very first Sunday I was searched by the doctor on duty in the ward, whom I had previously regarded as a very nice woman. During my meeting with Ivanov nurses were posted at either side of the bed; a detective stood in the corner of the room and afterwards accompanied me back to my own section. From that day I sensed I was being shadowed but, inexperienced as I was, I brushed the thought aside. In the middle of the following week deputy chief physician Zhivotovskaya summoned me to see her and tried at great length to "dissuade" me from paying any further visits to Ivanov; when next Sunday it was discovered that I had again visited him, the offensive against me was launched in earnest.

The next morning, as I was on my way to work, a car, painstakingly washed and sparkling, with a uniformed chauffeur, drove out of an alley, coasted very slowly along in front of me and accompanied me for some way, the driver all the while staring fixedly at me; then the vehicle abruptly gathered speed and vanished. When I came home from work the whole procedure was repeated exactly. And so it continued for the rest of the week; they weren't following me, just trying to frighten me.

At the end of the week I was told that the chief physician had forbidden me to visit Ivanov and that I was to be interviewed by him on Monday. On Monday morning as I was leaving my house and going down the front steps I noticed an estate car waiting nearby (I live in a quiet street). Catching sight of me the driver accelerated and as I stepped down I was almost knocked over and had to jump aside on to the grass. The driver was the same man but this time in plain clothes. Slowly he turned the car round and drove off; and I went to my interview with M. P. Isakov.

For two solid hours the hospital director shouted at me, threatened me with dismissal, and demanded that I cease my visits to Ivanov, whom, incidentally, he called a schizophrenic and an anti-Sovietist. Vile rumours about me began to spread through the hospital; they had been concocted by the secretary of the hospital's party organization, the secretary of the local party committee and the head of section 8.

I was isolated in a vacuum. Several psychiatrists who had been my closest friends broke off relations with me. None of the psychiatrists in the hospital would agree to take parcels to Ivanov while I was away on holiday.

In May 1974 a commission headed by Professor Sluchevsky examined Ivanov and declared that he could be discharged, but instead he was transferred to another Leningrad psychiatric hospital. There were to be many more commissions and hospitals after that. Not until March 1975 was he discharged.

REFERENCES

The following abbreviations are used in these references:

1. *Senate Hearing*
   This refers to a volume published under the title *Abuse of Psychiatry for Political Repression in the Soviet Union,* which contains the record of a "Hearing before the Subcommittee to Investigate the Administration of the Internal Security Act and Other Internal Security Laws of the Committee on the Judiciary, United States Senate, September 26, 1972". It also contains, as appendices, the "Bukovsky documents" and other materials. It was published first by the US Government Printing Office, Washington, D.C., 1972, then by Arno Press, New York, 1973. The latter edition is distributed in Britain by Aris and Phillips, Warminster, Wiltshire.

2. *Senate Hearing, 27 October 1972*
   A record of the testimony given to the same sub-committee mentioned above by Dr Norman Hirt, plus related appendices. Published as vol. II of the above title in 1975 by the US Government Printing Office, stock number 052–070–02750.

3. *CHR*
   Short for *A Chronicle of Human Rights in the USSR.* This bi-monthly journal has been published by Khronika Press (505 Eighth Avenue, New York, N.Y. 10018) since 1973, and edited by V. Chalidze, P. Litvinov, E. Kline, and P. Reddaway. It appears in separate Russian and English editions.

4. *Chronicle* designates *A Chronicle of Current Events,* a journal produced in typescript every two to four months in Moscow by an anonymous and changing group of human rights activists. The first eleven issues appeared in English in Reddaway, P., *Uncensored Russia,* London, Cape, and New York, McGraw-Hill, 1972; issues 12–15 were circulated by Amnesty International (53 Theobald's Road, London, W.C.1.) in duplicated form, and issues 16–33 have been published by Amnesty in eleven separate volumes. Further volumes will appear. The original Russian texts (title: *Khronika tekushchikh sobytii*) of issues 1–27 were published by Possev Verlag, Frankfurt, and issues 28–41 have appeared from Khronika Press (see above). Issues 1–5 are dated in 1968, 6–11 in 1969, 12–17 in 1970, 18–22 in 1971, 23–28 in 1972, 29–31 in 1973, 32–34 in 1974, 35–38 in 1975, and 39–41 in 1976.

5. Minutes of WPA Executive Committee (or WPA Committee). WPA is short for World Psychiatric Association. These minutes are circulated to all the WPA's 75 member societies, in whose offices they are (presumably in most cases) filed.

6. *AS*

   Arkhiv samizdata, i.e. the Samizdat Archive of Radio Liberty in Munich, which assigns numbers to all the documents it receives. These are regularly published in limited editions in the original language (usually Russian), copies of all volumes being deposited in the Library of Congress, the British Museum, the Bodleian Library (Oxford), Die Bayerische Staatsbibliothek (Munich), the East Europe Institute of Amsterdam University, the Hoover Institute (Stanford), M.I.T., and Ohio State University.

7. *SWB* designates *Summary of World Broadcasts*, daily publication of the BBC Monitoring Service, Caversham Park, Reading.

Chapter 1: The Vulnerability of Psychiatry

1. Busse, E. W., "APA's Role in Influencing the Evolution of a Health Care Delivery System", *American Journal of Psychiatry*, 1969, vol. 126, pp. 739–744.

2. Waggoner, R., "Cultural Dissonance and Psychiatry", *American Journal of Psychiatry*, 1970, vol. 127, pp. 1–8 (read at the 123rd Annual Meeting of the American Psychiatric Association in May 1970).

3. For an appreciation of the views of the radical psychiatry movement, see Talbot, J. A., "Radical Psychiatry: An Examination of the Issues", *American Journal of Psychiatry*, 1974, vol. 131, pp. 121–128.

4. Liefer, R., "The Medical Model as Ideology", *International Journal of Psychiatry*, 1970, vol. 9, pp. 13–21.

5. Szasz, T. S., *The Myth of Mental Illness*, New York, Delta, 1961.

6. *Diagnostic and Statistical Manual of Mental Disorders*, 2nd edition, Washington, American Psychiatric Association, 1968.

7. *A Glossary of Mental Disorders*, Her Majesty's Stationery Office, London, 1968.

8. Socarides, C. W., "Homosexuality: Findings Derived from 15 Years of Clinical Research", *American Journal of Psychiatry*, 1973, vol. 130, pp. 1212–1213.

9. Gold, R., "Stop it, You're Making Me Sick", *American Journal of Psychiatry*, 1973, vol. 130, pp. 1211–1212.

10. Liefer, *op. cit.*

11. Szasz, T. S., *Ideology and Insanity*, New York, Doubleday, 1970, p. 213.

12. McGarry, A. L., "The Question of Dangerousness", *Psychiatric Spectator*, 1974, vol. 9, pp. 14–15.

13. *Ibid.*
14. For a full account of this subject, see Kittrie, N. N., *The Right to be Different: Deviance and Enforced Therapy*, Baltimore, Johns Hopkins Press, 1971, pp. 54–101.
15. *Sunday Times*, 21 May 1972.
16. Miller, K. S., Simons, R. L. and Fein, S. B., "Compulsory Mental Hospitalization in England and Wales", *Journal of Health and Social Behaviour*, 1974, vol. 15, pp. 151–156.
17. For an overview of some of the issues relating to dangerousness and civil commitment, see Shah, S. A., "Dangerousness and Civil Commitment of the Mentally Ill: Some Public Policy Considerations," *American Journal of Psychiatry*, 1975, vol. 132, pp. 501–505.
18. *Psychiatric News*, 16 July 1975.
19. For an overview of the concept of the "right to treatment", see Stone, A. A., "Overview: The Right to Treatment— Comments on the Law and its Impact", *American Journal of Psychiatry*, 1975, vol. 132, pp. 1125–1134.
20. In 1972 for instance, a celebrated Hungarian stage actor, Zoltan Latinovits, was pronounced "mentally not responsible" and confined to a mental hospital following a political demonstration he initiated on the stage of the National Theatre. (*Baltimore News American*, 16 May 1972. See also *Valosag*, Budapest, October 1975, and *Sunday Times*, 31 November 1975, for accounts of inhumane conditions in Hungarian mental institutions, and hints of political implications in psychiatric practice.) A report emerged from Poland two years later that a Roman Catholic priest had been detained in a mental hospital to await trial after his complaints about police persecution. Father Zabielski had used his home to celebrate mass at a time when the church hierarchy in Poland was publicly protesting against harassment by the authorities. (*The Times*, 3 January 1974.) In 1976 Wilhelm Lange had been held for five years in a psychiatric hospital in East Germany, following his request to emigrate. Born in 1908, he protested against the building of the Berlin wall in 1961 and, as a result, spent much of the next ten years either in prison or under restricted residence. (Amnesty International, British Section *Bulletin*, May–June 1976, No. 15.) Professor Robert Havemann, a prominent East German physicist, issued a statement in 1976 protesting against such abuses of psychiatry in his country. (*Le Monde*, 20 June 1976.)

Yet it would seem that none of the East European régimes employ psychiatry to suppress dissent on a scale that resembles the Soviet practice. The reasons for this are not clear, but the following points may be relevant. Communism is a more recent phenomenon in Eastern Europe so there has been less time for the traditional German school of psychiatry to be remoulded to suit Marxist–Leninist ideology. Second, the régimes mostly avoid courting unnecessary unpopularity from their peoples, subtly suggesting to them, indeed, that they would be more liberal if it were not for the military *force majeure* of the USSR—a real threat in view of the invasions of Hungary and Czechoslovakia. Third, because of the overwhelming reality of the *force majeure* there is usually less overt political dissent for the régimes to deal with than is the case in the Soviet Union: dissenters are realistic about their chances.

As for China, no reliable evidence of psychiatric abuse is available to us. But the apparently widespread practice of trying to cure mental illness by inculcating Maoism into patients so that they should think "correctly" arouses the suspicion that psychiatrists may also be involved in the "thought reform" practised on dissenters in labour camps. (See: Bao Ruo-Wang (Jean Pasqualini), *Prisoner of Mao: An Eye Witness Account of China's Forced Labour Camp System by One of its Few Survivors*, London, Deutsch, 1975, and Walls, P. D., Walls, L. H. and Langsley, D. G., "Psychiatric Training and Practice in the People's Republic of China," *American Journal of Psychiatry*, 1975, vol. 132, pp. 121–128.)

Dissent has been stifled by the use of psychiatry in Western countries too. In 1971 a prominent academic and political activist in Barcelona, Professor Carbonell, was confined in the city's prison psychiatric ward after he had defiantly answered police interrogators in his native language of Catalan. (*Sunday Telegraph*, 24 January 1971.) A clear-cut case occurred in the United States in 1932. A teacher at the New York City College was an early campaigner against fascism and encouraged his students to join him. Dr Kraus began a hunger strike when the college attempted to curb his political activities. The resultant publicity embarrassed the college, which persuaded Dr Kraus to undergo a medical examination on the pretext of his physical condition. He found himself, however, under examination by psychiatrists and following their pronouncement of him as mentally unsound, was discharged from his post. Although several eminent psychiatrists later vouched for his sanity, Dr Kraus was unable to reverse the college's decision. Finally, after nearly four decades, Kraus triumphed in his battle to regain his rights, when the college acknowledged its mistake of the imputation of mental illness in him. (Lord Chorley, "The Case of Dr A. J. Kraus",

Association of University Teachers Bulletin, April 1970.) Perhaps Ezra Pound is the most notable American case in which the action of psychiatrists had profound political implications. His case is, however, too complex and the issues too blurred to be discussed here.

Chapter 2: Soviet Psychiatry: Evolution and Character
 1. Raskin, N., "Development of Russian Psychiatry Before the First World War", *American Journal of Psychiatry*, 1964, vol. 120, pp. 851–855.
 2. *Ibid.*
 3. Sigerist, H. E., *Socialized Medicine in the Soviet Union*, London, Gollancz, 1937.
 4. Holland, J., " 'State' Hospitals in the USSR: A Model of Governmental Psychiatric Care", in Suzman, J. and Bertsch, E. F. (eds.), *The Future Role of the State Hospital*, Lexington, Massachusetts, Lexington Books, 1975, pp. 373–385.
 5. Field, M. G., *Soviet Socialized Medicine: An Introduction*, New York, Free Press, 1967, p. 73.
 6. Medvedev, Z., *The Rise and Fall of T. D. Lysenko*, New York, Columbia University Press, 1969.
 7. Ziferstein, I., "The Soviet Psychiatrist: His Relationship to his Patients and to his Society", *American Journal of Psychiatry*, 1966, vol. 123, pp. 440–446.
 8. Visotsky, H. M., "The Treatment System", *American Journal of Psychiatry*, 1968, vol. 125, pp. 650–655.
 9. *Survey*, 1971, No. 81, p. 114. Translation of Physician's Oath originally published in *Meditsinskaya gazeta*, 20 April 1971.
 10. Ziferstein, *op. cit.*
 11. *Survey*, *op. cit.*, p. 114.
 12. Field, M. G., *Doctor and Patient in Russia*, Cambridge, Massachusetts, Harvard University Press, 1957, p. 73.
 13. *Ibid.*, p. 74.
 14. *Soviet Socialized Medicine*, *op. cit.*, p. 33.
 15. *Doctor and Patient in Soviet Russia*, *op. cit.*, p. 74.
 16. Sakharov, A., *My Country and the World*, London, Collins/Harvill, 1975, pp. 21–23.
 17. *Literaturnaya gazeta*, 22 September 1976. Article by Anatoly Rubinov.
 18. *Izvestia*, 31 August 1976, article "Istoriya bolezni". The author states that what he describes is typical only of a hospital in Odessa; but the Soviet press would not publish such an article unless officials wanted to draw attention to a widespread problem. Recent emigrants have told us that such bribery is indeed widespread.

19. *Narodnoe khozyaistvo SSSR v 1974 g.*, Moscow, 1975, p. 734; and article by A. G. Safonov on government policy towards psychiatry in *Zhurnal nevrop. i psikhiatrii*, Moscow, 1976, No. 6.

Chapter 3: Psychiatric Abuse: Its History and How it Became an Issue in the Soviet Union

1. Quoted in Medvedev, Z. and Medvedev, R., *A Question of Madness*, London, Macmillan, 1971, pp. 196–197.
2. Steinberg, I. Z., *Spiridonova: Revolutionary Terrorist*, London, Methuen, 1935, p. 241.
3. *Ibid.*, pp. 241–242.
4. Balabanoff, A., *My Life as a Rebel*, New York, Harper, 1938, pp. 237–238.
5. Letters in *American Journal of Psychiatry*, 1970, vol. 126, pp. 1327–1328; 1970, vol. 127, pp. 842–843; 1971, vol. 127, pp. 1575–1576; and 1974, vol. 131, p. 474.
6. Reddaway, P., *Uncensored Russia*, London, Cape, 1972, p. 237.
7. Yarkov, I. P., "Reconvicted: 1951–1954", chapter 7 of autobiography, *samizdat* manuscript dated 27 May 1967; *AS* 2455.
8. Pisarev, S. P., "Soviet Mental Prisons", *Survey*, 1970, No. 77, pp. 175–180.
9. *Chronicle* 18. Reprinted in *The New York Review of Books*, 10 February 1972. Another case from this period is that of the Georgian doctor Nikolai Samkharadze, interned in 1959; see *Chronicle* 42.
10. Undated *samizdat* document, compiled in 1971; *AS* 589.
11. *Senate Hearing*, pp. 178–190.
12. Tarsis, V. Y., *Ward 7*, London, Collins/Harvill, 1965.
13. In Britain the book was serialized in the *Observer* on 2, 9 and 16 May 1965.
14. Valeriy, I., *The Blue Bottle*, London, Collins/Harvill, 1962.
15. Tarsis, V. Y., unpublished report for Amnesty International, 1966.
16. *Guardian*, 6 October 1965.
17. *Ibid.*, 7 October 1965.
18. *Ibid.*, 9 October 1965.
19. *Ibid.*, 11 October 1965.
20. *Ibid.*, 8 November 1965.
21. *Economist*, 11 December 1965.
22. *Senate Hearing*, pp. 2–16.
23. *The New York Times*, 12 September 1972.
24. Esenin-Volpin, A. S., *Let Pyotr Grigorenko Have a Fountain Pen. Samizdat* manuscript dated 20 July 1970; *AS* 406. Published in Russian in *Kaznimye Sumasshestviem*, Frankfurt, Possev, 1971, pp. 346–365. English translation in our possession.

25. *Guardian*, 13 May 1965.
26. *Senate Hearing*, p. 4.
27. Reddaway, *op. cit.*, pp. 86–87.
28. See introductory note to these references.
29. *Chronicle* 5.
30. Reddaway, *op. cit.*, pp. 150–151.
31. On Vladimir Borisov, see appendix 1.
32. On Yury Maltsev, see chapter 7.
33. On Leonid Plyushch, see chapters 7, 8 and 10.
34. Reddaway, *op. cit.*, pp. 154–168.
35. *The Washington Post*, 17 May 1970. The journalist was Holger Jensen.
36. The interview was printed in *Survey*, 1970, No. 77.

Chapter 4: The Issue Becomes International

1. *Survey*, 1971, No. 81, p. 113.
2. *Ibid.*, pp. 112–113.
3. *The Times*, 12 March 1971.
4. *British Journal of Psychiatry*, 1971, vol. 119, pp. 225–226, letter by Dr Derek Richter.
5. Mee, C., *The Internment of Soviet Dissenters in Mental Hospitals*, London, Working Group on the Internment of Dissenters in Mental Hospitals, 1971.
6. *The Times*, 16 September 1971.
7. *The Times*, 23 October 1971.
8. *Ibid.*
9. Quoted in Medvedev, Z. and Medvedev, R., *A Question of Madness*, London, Macmillan, 1971, p. 63.
10. *Izvestia*, 24 October 1971.
11. Resolution of the World Federation for Mental Health, Hong Kong, 25 November 1971. Published in *Chronicle* 24 and *Senate Hearing*, 27 October 1972, pp. 63–64.
12. *Chronicle* 24.
13. *Chronicle* 22.
14. *World Medicine*, 3 October 1973.
15. *Mexico City News*, 30 November 1971.
16. Here and infra see *World Psychiatric Association: Organization and Statutes*, London, WPA, 1974, pp. 47–59.
17. Minutes of WPA Committee meeting on 28 November 1971.
18. *World Psychiatric Association, op. cit.*, p. 47.
19. *Ibid.*, pp. 48 and 54.
20. Reuter dispatch from Mexico City dated 2 December 1971.
21. *Ibid.*
22. *The New York Times*, 3 December 1971.
23. Reuter dispatch, 2 December 1971.

24. *Excelsior*, Mexico City, 30 November 1971.
25. *Ibid.*, 1 December 1971.
26. *Ibid.*, 30 November 1971.
27. *Ibid.*
28. *Psychiatric News*, 5 July 1972. On the APA's failure to take any action between May and December 1971, despite a promise to do so, see *Senate Hearing*, pp. 17, 20.
29. Quoted in a letter from Dr B. E. Moore, president of the American Psychoanalytic Association to Professor A. V. Snezhnevsky dated 21 January 1974. Published in *Senate Hearing*, 27 October 1972, pp. 66–67.
30. *Survey*, 1972, No. 83, pp. 123–160.
31. *Leningradskaya pravda*, 23 January 1972. A similar type of article appeared in 1967 in *Krododil*; see V. Zorza's summary of it in the *Guardian*, 24 October 1967.

Chapter 5: The Practice: Criminal Commitment

1. Berman, H. J., *Justice in the USSR*, Cambridge, Massachusetts, Harvard University Press, 1963, p. 315.
2. *Special Report: The First US Mission on Mental Health to the USSR*, Chevy Chase, Maryland, NIMH. 1969. Public Health Service Publication No. 1893, p. 74.
3. *Ibid.*, p. 74.
4. Banshchikov, V. M. and Nevzorova, T. A., *Psikhiatriya*, Moscow, 1969, p. 292. Cited in *Survey*, 1971, No. 81.
5. *Vedomosti Verkhovnogo Soveta RSFSR*, 1960, No. 40. A slightly different translation can be found for this article and the two to which references 6 and 7 apply in Berman, H. J., *Soviet Criminal Law and Procedure. The RSFSR Codes*, Cambridge, Massachusetts, Harvard University Press, 1966.
6. *Vedomosti Verkhovnogo Soveta RSFSR*, 1960, No. 40.
7. *Ibid.*
8. *Ibid.*, 22 September 1966.
9. Grigorenko, P. G., *The Grigorenko Papers*, London, C. Hurst, 1976.
10. Reddaway, P., *Uncensored Russia*, London, Cape, 1972, p. 228.
11. *Senate Hearing*, p. 66.
12. *Ibid.*, p. 66.
13. *Ibid.*, p. 60.
14. Grigorenko, *op. cit.*
15. Statement of 4 December 1968 in Brumberg, A., *In Quest of Justice*, New York and London, Praeger, 1970, p. 364.
16. Speech of 17 March 1968 in *ibid.*, p. 212.
17. Reddaway, *op. cit.*, p. 130.
18. *Senate Hearing*, p. 64.

19. *Ibid.*, p. 70.
20. *Ibid.*, p. 87.
21. Shaw, D., Bloch, S. and Vickers, A., "Psychiatry and the State", *New Scientist*, 2 November 1972, pp. 258–261.
22. "An In Absentia Forensic-Psychiatric Report on P. G. Grigorenko", circulated in *samizdat* in 1971. Published in Russian in *Russkaya mysl*, Paris, 12 April 1973 (also *AS* 1243); French translation in *Cahiers du Samizdat*, Brussels (105, drève du Duc), 1973, No. 9; English translation in our possession.
23. Letter in the *British Medical Journal*, 9 November 1974, pp. 341–342.
24. *Survey*, 1971, No. 81, p. 150.
25. *CHR* 9, 1974.
26. *Chronicle* 14.
27. *Chronicle* 15.
28. *CHR* 2, 1973.
29. *Ibid.*
30. *CHR* 3, 1973.
31. Grigorenko's wife had spearheaded the campaign for him from the start, issuing numerous appeals. See, e.g. *Chronicles* 12, 18, 24, 32. A film about him, made by Granada TV in Britain in 1970, especially spurred foreign concern.
32. *The Times*, 1 September 1973, letter from K. Coates and C. Farley; and (Sakharov interview) *Daily Telegraph*, 10 September 1973.
33. Grigorenko, A. P., introduction to Grigorenko, P. G., *op. cit.*, p. 10.
34. WPA Excutive Committee minutes of meeting on 8 October 1973, p. 10.
35. Grigorenko, P. G., *op. cit.*, p. 8.
36. See document *AS* 1683b, dated 2 May 1974 and signed by Grigorenko's wife.
37. *Ibid.*
38. *Der Stern*, Hamburg, 31 October 1973, p. 26.
39. *The New York Times*, 16 October 1973.
40. *Sowjetunion Heute*, Köln, February 1976, article by Eleonora Gorbunova.
41. Reuter dispatch from Moscow dated 19 October 1973.
42. *Guardian*, 23 October 1973.
43. *Der Stern*, loc. cit.
44. Tass dispatch from Stockholm dated 10 December 1973, published in English translation in *Summary of World Broadcasts*, SU/4473/A1/5.
45. Personal communication from Karin Gawell of Lidingö, Sweden.

46. *Der Stern,* 31 October 1973, pp. 18–26; *Paris Match,* 10 November 1973; the *Daily Express,* London, 9 November 1973.
47. Personal communication from a close friend of his who witnessed the scene.
48. *Chronicle* 32 and document *AS* 1683, dated 2 May 1974 and signed by Grigorenko's wife and son.
49. *The New York Times,* 27 June 1974.
50. *Chronicle* 32.
51. *Ibid.*
52. *Chronicle* 37.
53. *Chronicle* 38.
54. *Ibid.*
55. *Guardian,* 15 May 1976; *Chronicle* 40.
56. Personal communication from Andrei Grigorenko.
57. *Komsomolskaya Pravda,* 21 February 1976.
58. Gorbanevskaya, N., *Red Square at Noon,* London, Deutsch, 1972.
59. Reddaway, *op. cit.,* p. 100.
60. *Senate Hearing,* p. 133.
61. *Ibid.,* p. 111.
62. *Ibid.,* p. 118.
63. Brumberg, *op. cit.,* p. 102.
64. *Senate Hearing,* pp. 118–134.
65. *Chronicle* 38.
66. Gorbanevskaya, *op. cit.,* p. 68.
67. *Ibid.,* pp. 68–69.
68. *Ibid.,* p. 69.
69. Reddaway, *op. cit.,* pp. 107–108.
70. *Senate Hearing,* p. 110.
71. *Ibid.,* p. 113.
72. Shaw, Bloch and Vickers, *op. cit.*
73. *The Times,* 16 September 1971.
74. Weissbort, D. (ed.), *Selected Poems by Natalya Gorbanevskaya with a Transcript of her Trial and Papers Relating to her Detention in a Prison Psychiatric Hospital,* Oxford, Carcanet Press, 1972, pp. 127–131.
75. *Ibid.,* pp. 135–154.
76. *Ibid.,* p. 137.
77. *Senate Hearing,* p. 116.
78. *Ibid.,* p. 117.
79. *Ibid.,* p. 112.
80. *Chronicle* 15.
81. *Senate Hearing,* p. 113. The authors of the letter were T. Velikanova and V. Lashkova.
82. *Chronicle* 15.

83. *Ibid.*
84. *Chronicle* 16.
85. *Chronicle* 18.
86. *Ibid.*
87. *Die Welt*, 6 February 1976.
88. Gorbanevskaya, N., personal communication, 4 July 1976.
89. *Vestnik RSKHD*, Paris, 1972, No. 106, p. 354.
90. Gorbanevskaya, N., personal communication, 4 July 1976.
91. *Ibid.*
92. *Observer*, 4 January 1976.
93. See *Chronicles* 29, 30, 32.
94. See brief summary in *Chronicle* 42.
95. See *Chronicle* 32, sections on S. Pirogov and on H. Jogesma and others.
96. See, e.g. his interview in *Der Stern*, 31 October 1973.

Chapter 6: The Practice: Civil Commitment

1. "Directives on the Immediate Hospitalization of Mentally Ill Persons Who Are a Social Danger", published in Russian in Saarma, J., *Kohtupsühhiaatria*, Tallin, Valgus, 1970, pp. 286–287.
2. *Senate Hearing*, p. 25. The decree is No. 345–209 of 15 May 1969.
3. *Chronicle* 28. The directives are summarized in general terms in article 56 of the Health Law of the RSFSR of 29 July 1971. For an English translation of the article see Dr T. M. Ryan's letter in *The Times*, 10 September 1973.
4. *Special Report: The First US Mission on Mental Health to the USSR*, Chevy Chase, Maryland, NIMH, 1969. Public Health Service Publication No. 1893.
5. *Senate Hearing*, p. 27.
6. *Ibid.*, pp. 191–224 (this translation has been amended by us in some of the quotations we give).
7. For more on this see Bourdeaux, M., *Religious Ferment in Russia: Protestant Opposition to Soviet Religious Policy*, London, Macmillan, 1968; and Berman, H. J. (ed.), *Soviet Criminal Law and Procedure. The RSFSR Codes*, Cambridge, Massachusetts, Harvard University Press, 1966.
8. Shimanov, G., *Before Death (Pered Smertyu)*. This work, briefly summarized in *Chronicle* 13, appeared in a second edition in *samizdat* in 1974. See pp. 31–35 of this edition, a copy of which we possess.
9. *Senate Hearing*, p. 195.
10. *Ibid.*, p. 199.
11. *Ibid.*, pp. 201–202.

12. *Ibid.*, p. 207.
13. *Ibid.*, p. 212.
14. *Ibid.*, pp. 212–213.
15. *Ibid.*, p. 213.
16. *Ibid.*, p. 214.
17. *Ibid.*, p. 216.
18. *Ibid.*, p. 214.
19. *Ibid.*, p. 219.
20. Medvedev, Z. and Medvedev, R., *A Question of Madness*, translated by Ellen de Kadt, London, Macmillan, & New York, Random House, 1971. (Translation slightly amended.)
21. Medvedev, Z., *The Rise and Fall of T. D. Lysenko*, New York, Columbia University Press, 1969.
22. Medvedev, Z., *The Medvedev Papers*, London, Macmillan, 1971.
23. Medvedev, Z. and Medvedev, R., *op. cit.*, p. 20.
24. *Ibid.*, p. 146.
25. *Ibid.*, p. 155.
26. *Ibid.*, p. 175.
27. *The Medvedev Papers*, *op. cit.*, p. vii.
28. *Nature*, 1972, vol. 235, pp. 399–400.
29. Medvedev, Z. and Medvedev, R., *op. cit.*, pp. 115–117.
30. *Chronicle* 14. See also reference 20, pp. 135–137.
31. *Chronicle* 26.
32. *CHR* 3, 1973.
33. *Ibid.*
34. Personal communication, Professor John Wing of the Institute of Psychiatry, University of London.
35. Medvedev, Z. and Medvedev, R., *op. cit.*, pp. 201–202.

Chapter 7: The Hospital and the Treatment

1. *Novyi zhurnal*, New York, 1974, No. 116, pp. 30–71.
2. *AS* 1294, dated 18 November 1972. For more details on Dubrov see *Chronicle* 27, Amnesty International edition.
3. See *CHR* 10, 1974, document on I. Ogurtsov; and *Chronicle* 34, p. 36 of Russian edition.
4. *Chronicle* 8 describes the development up to 1969; *Chronicle* 19 the opening of Oryol (see Gershuni's diary); *Chronicle* 24 of Blagoveshchensk and Kzyl-Orda; and that of Smolensk, an unpublished book by Julius Krylsky about his son Yan's internment in Smolensk, then Sychyovka. A copy of Krylsky's book, which contains vivid and alarming descriptions of these SPHs, is in our possession.
5. See *Chronicle* 36, item on L. Ubozhko; *Chronicle* 39, items on Baranov and Dzibalov.
6. Personal communication of May 1975 from V. M. Golikov

(see appendix I); regarding Rostov, personal communication from M. S. Bernshtam (appendix I); regarding Ukhta and Perm, see so far unpublished letter of G. Fedotov to D. Dudko, 11 September 1976.

7. Personal communication from Viktor Fainberg.
8. *Senate Hearing*, p. 142.
9. Khodorovich, T. (ed.) *The Case of Leonid Plyushch*, London, C. Hurst, 1976, p. 89.
10. *Chronicle* 19. On Vladimir Gershuni, see appendix I.
11. *Chronicle* 14.
12. *Chronicle* 18.
13. *Possev*, 1971, No. 5, pp. 5–6; also *AS* 603. English translation published in *International Socialist Review*, New York, 1972, No. 6, pp. 42–44.
14. *Chronicle* 19.
15. *Senate Hearing*, p. 152.
16. *Ibid.*, p. 7.
17. Unpublished *samizdat* document, Moscow, Spring 1974.
18. *Chronicle* 15.
19. *The New York Times*, 19 December 1974.
20. *Survey*, 1970, No. 77.
21. *Senate Hearing*, p. 140.
22. *Chronicle* 8.
23. *Chronicle* 19.
24. *Kaznimye sumasshestviem*, Frankfurt, Possev Verlag, 1971, p. 367.
25. *Senate Hearing*, p. 141.
26. *Survey*, 1970, No. 77.
27. *Chronicle* 10.
28. Khodorovich, *op. cit.*, p. 91.
29. *The Times*, 4 February 1976.
30. *Senate Hearing*, p. 141.
31. *Chronicle* 19.
32. *Ibid.*
33. Khodorovich, *op. cit.*, pp. 7–9.
34. *Chronicle* 30.
35. *Ibid.*
36. Khodorovich, *op. cit.*, pp. 7–79.
37. *Chronicle* 32.
38. *Ibid.*
39. *Chronicle* 34.
40. *Ibid.*
41. Khodorovich, *op. cit.*, p. 151.
42. Unpublished account of meeting with Leonid Plyushch by H. Fireside, at the New York Academy of Sciences, 29 March 1976.

43. Gorbanevskaya, N., *Red Square at Noon*, London, Deutsch, 1972, pp. 277–278.
44. *Chronicle* 36.
45. Khodorovich, *op. cit.*, p. 100.
46. *Chronicle* 15.
47. Gorbanevskaya, *op. cit.*, p. 278.
48. *Ibid.*, p. 279.
49. *Chronicle* 30.
50. *Chronicle* 18.
51. *Survey*, 1970, No. 77.
52. See reference 24 to chapter 3.
53. *Chronicle* 18.
54. *Senate Hearing*, p. 139.
55. See appendix VII.
56. *Chronicle* 32.
57. *Chronicle* 30.
58. Gorbanevskaya, *op. cit.*, p. 276.
59. *Ibid.*, p. 274.
60. Khodorovich, *op. cit.*, pp. 151–152.
61. *Ibid.*, pp. 92–95. On Olga Iofe see appendix 1.
62. *Ibid.*, p. 148.
63. *Ibid.*, p. 151.

Chapter 8: The Psychiatrist and his Diagnosis

1. *Guardian*, 29 September 1973.
2. *Chronicle* 29.
3. Appeal by Yury Orlov dated 22 April 1975, *AS* 2165. Published in French translation in *Cahiers du Samizdat*, 1975, No. 28.
4. Medvedev, Z. and Medvedev, R., *A Question of Madness*, London, Macmillan, 1971, pp. 129–130.
5. Morozov, G. V. and Kalashnik, I. M. (eds), *Forensic Psychiatry*, New York, International Arts and Science Press, 1970.
6. *Senate Hearing*, p. 160.
7. *Izvestia*, 10 August 1973.
8. *Guardian*, 29 September 1973.
9. We have received information on Professor Lunts from dissenters who have been his patients: Viktor Fainberg, Alexander Volpin, Natalya Gorbanevskaya and Yury Shikhanovich; Alexander Lunts, a distant relative now living in Israel; and a Moscow dissenter who has asked to remain anonymous.
10. See entries on Galanskov and Dobrovolsky in *Kaznimye sumasshestviem*, Frankfurt, Possev, 1971.
11. *CHR* 3, 1973. The source, who attended Lunts's lecture, is known to us personally, but wishes to remain anonymous.

12. Reddaway, P., *Uncensored Russia*, London, Cape, 1972, p. 228.
13. Personal communication from a Moscow dissenter who desires anonymity.
14. *The Times*, 29 November 1975.
15. Gorbanevskaya, N., *Red Square at Noon*, London, Deutsch, 1972, p. 68.
16. *Chronicle* 15.
17. Personal communication, 18 December 1974.
18. Personal communication, 27 September 1975. Both psychiatrists wish to remain anonymous.
19. On Yury Ivanov see appendix I.
20. *Senate Hearing*, p. 64.
21. *Ibid.*, p. 110.
22. *Ibid.*, p. 202.
23. See reference 22 to chapter 5.
24. *The Times*, 9 December 1972.
25. See appendix VIII.
26. *AS* 2090, October 1974.
27. *Chronicle* 38.
28. *Ibid.* 40.
29. See appendix X.
30. *The Times*, 30 August 1976.
31. *Survey*, 1973, No. 89.
32. *Chronicle* 35.
33. *CHR* 3, 1973.
34. *News Bulletin on Soviet Jewry*, 1972, vol. 2, No. 217, and personal communication (the psychiatrist wishes to remain anonymous).
35. Kraepelin, E., *Dementia Praecox and Paraphrenia*, Edinburgh, Livingstone, 1919.
36. Bleuler, E., *Dementia Praecox or the Group of Schizophrenias*, New York, International Universities Press, 1950.
37. Schneider, K., *Clinical Psychopathology*, New York, Grune and Stratton, 1959.
38. Hoch, P. and Polatin, P., "Pseudoneurotic Schizophrenia", *Psychiatric Quarterly*, 1949, vol. 23, pp. 248–276.
39. *Diagnostic and Statistical Manual of Mental Disorders*, 2nd edition, Washington, American Psychiatric Association, 1968.
40. *A Glossary of Mental Disorders*, Her Majesty's Stationery Office, London, 1968.
41. Strömgen, E., "Uses and Abuses of Concepts in Psychiatry", 1969, vol. 126, pp. 777–788.
42. Kendell, R. E., "Diagnostic Criteria of American and British Psychiatrists", *Archives of General Psychiatry*, 1971, vol. 25, pp. 123–130.
43. See Cooper, J. E., Kendell, R. E., Gurland, B. J. *et al.*,

Psychiatric Diagnosis in New York and London, Maudsley Monograph No. 20, London, Oxford University Press, 1972, for more details of US–UK differences in diagnosis.

44. *The International Pilot Study of Schizophrenia*, vol. 1, Geneva, World Health Organization, 1973.

45. We are indebted to Dr J. Holland of the Albert Einstein College of Medicine, New York, for her invaluable help in clarifying the Soviet model of schizophrenia. She worked in Professor Snezhnevsky's Institute of Psychiatry on an exchange programme in 1972–73 for eight months with Professor R. Nadzharov and others, and has made a significant contribution to the understanding of Soviet concepts. See "Concept and Classification of Schizophrenia in the Soviet Union", in press, *Schizophrenia Bulletin*, Washington D.C., and "Schizophrenia in the Soviet Union", in press, *Annual Review of Research in Schizophrenia*, vol. VI, (ed.) Cancro, R.

46. See appendix V.

47. Morozov and Kalashnik, *op. cit.*, p. 221.

48. *Ibid.*, p. 222.

49. *Chronicle* 15.

50. *Guardian*, 29 September 1973.

51. *Chronicle* 15.

52. Report No. 35/S., *AS* 574. English translation in our possession; extracts published in Russian in *Kaznimye sumasshestviem*, Frankfurt, Possev Verlag, 1971, pp. 200–203.

53. *Senate Hearing*, p. 163.

54. *Ibid.*, p. 167. Professor N. Timofeyev argues that dissent *per se* is a symptom of schizophrenia and that it constitutes a sufficient basis for this diagnosis in the absence of any other symptoms:

> ... dissent is a different way of thinking ... a way of thinking which is in disagreement with that of other people. It can be of various origins ... it may also be determined by a disease of the brain in which the morbid process develops very slowly (sluggish form of schizophrenia) so that its other manifestations remain imperceptible ... diagnostic difficulties increase if the subject relates in a formally correct way to the environment. ...

See Timofeyev in "Deontological Aspects of Diagnosing Schizophrenia", *Zhurnal Nevropat. i Psikhiatrii*, 1974, vol. 74, pp. 1065–1069.

55. *Ibid.*, p. 69.

56. *Senate Hearing*, p. 69.

57. See reference 42 to chapter 7.

58. *Chronicle* 32.
59. *Senate Hearing*, p. 165.
60. The *Manual*'s authors then state that they do not insist that all dissenters should take this advice on every occasion; but they urge the dissenter to remember that the "enforced tactical device" may be necessary in certain circumstances.
61. *Chronicle* 18.
62. See appendix IX.
63. *Chronicle* 21.
64. The dissenter was Igor Ogurtsov. See *CHR*, 1974, No. 10.

Chapter 9: The Victims
1. The 210 figure does not include, either, the quite numerous dissenters who have been interned in the Serbsky Institute for examination for some weeks, then declared responsible and tried. See discussion at the end of this chapter.
2. Khodorovich, T., *The Case of Leonid Plyushch*, London, C. Hurst, 1976, p. 146.
3. *Die Welt*, Hamburg, 6 February 1976, and personal communication.
4. Reddaway, P., *Uncensored Russia*, London, Cape, 1972, pp. 228–229; *Chronicle* 11.
5. Personal communication.
6. Unpublished memoir "Meetings in the Serbsky Institute", sent to us by the author (see *Chronicles* 1, 12, 14, 25, 26) in 1973.
7. *Chronicle* 32.
8. Dr Norman Hirt in *The Vancouver Sun*, 18 April 1973; see also his testimony in *Senate Hearing*, 27 October 1972, p. 28.
9. Among the additional witnesses are Ilya Rips, Valery Tarsis, Alexander Volpin, Valery Golikov, Evgeny Nikolayev, Andrei Dubrov, Pyotr Patrushev, Yury Ivanov, Fyodor Sidenko and Victoria Smirnova. See appendix I.
10. *CHR* 12, 1974.
11. *AS* 2007, dated 19 December 1974; French translation in *Cahiers du Samizdat*, Brussels (105, dréve du Duc), April 1976, No. 35, pp. 19–22. Concerning Sidenko, who was imprisoned on political charges from 1965 to 1970, see also *AS* 564 and 2575.
12. This journal has not yet appeared in English. In Ukrainian, Nos. 1–4 and 6 (produced in 1970–72, *AS* 994–999) have been published in four separate books under the joint imprint of Smoloskyp (PO Box 6066, Patterson Station, Baltimore, Maryland 21231, USA) and P.I.U.F. (3 rue du Sabot, 75006 Paris). Nos. 7–8 (1974), produced by new and militantly anti-Soviet editors, have been published in English by Smoloskyp as *Ethnocide of Ukrainians in the USSR*, 1976.

13. 23 issues had been published between March 1972 and mid-1976. Their contents has been summarized in almost every issue of the *Chronicle* since No. 27. No. 4 and succeeding issues of the *Chronicle of the Lithuanian Catholic Church* have been published in English translation as booklets by the Lithuanian Roman Catholic Priests' League of America, 64–14 56th Road, Maspeth, New York 11378. Extracts and commentaries have appeared in many issues of *Religion in Communist Lands*, Keston College, Heathfield Road, Keston, Kent, U.K.

14 Since No. 6 the *Chronicle* has regularly carried material on the Jewish movement. See also Leonard Schroeter, *The Last Exodus*, New York, Universe Books, 1974; and the weekly *Jews in the USSR*, 31 Percy Street, London, W.1.

15. Since No. 32 the *Chronicle* has reported often on the Soviet Germans. See also *CHR* 7, 10, and 12, and Sheehy, Ann, *The Crimean Tatars, Volga Germans and Meskhetians*, Minority Rights Group, 36 Craven Street, London W.C.2., 1973.

16. *AS* 1776, published in full in *Volnoe slovo*, Frankfurt, Possev Verlag, 1974, No. 16. A second issue appeared in 1975, but has yet to be published.

17. On the Baptists' movement see Bourdeaux, M., *Religious Ferment in Russia*, London, Macmillan, 1968; Bourdeaux, M., *Faith on Trial in Russia*, London, Hodder, 1971; Vins, G., *Three Generations of Suffering*, London, Hodder, 1976; and numerous materials in *Religions in Communist Lands* (see ref. 13).

18. *AS* 855, English translation in *East–West Digest*, Petersham, Surrey, UK, July 1971, pp. 202–203. See also *AS* 856–858.

19. *Zhit ne po lzhi: sbornik materialov, avgust 1973-fevral 1974*, Paris, YMCA, 1975, pp. 62–63.

20. *Chronicle* 20; see Reddaway, *op. cit.*, p. 247.

21. *Chronicles* 24, 25.

22. See *Chronicle* 1; *CHR* 10, 1974; and Dunlop, John B., *The New Russian Revolutionaries*, Belmont, Massachusetts, Nordland Press, 1976.

23. On their movements see Reddaway, *op. cit.*, chapters 12 and 13, and numerous issues of the *Chronicle*; also Sheehy, *op. cit.*, and *Tashkentskii protsess*, Amsterdam, A. Herzen Foundation, 1976.

24. *Chronicles* 34, 35, 36; *AS* 2098.

25. Labedz, L., *Solzhenitsyn: A Documentary Record*, Harmondsworth, Penguin, 1972, p. 152, speech by M. V. Zimyanin, editor of *Pravda*.

26. See *Sakharov Speaks*, London, Collins/Harvill, 1974, p. 50; also *Chronicle* 40.

27. *Chronicle* 20, pp. 252–253 of Amnesty edition; *Newsweek*, New York, 15 December 1975, p. 17.

28. *Psychiatric News*, Washington, D.C., 6 and 20 March 1974; and a paper by Dr J. Holland, "Schizophrenia in the Soviet Union" (see chapter 8, reference 45).

29. See, for example, the account in *Chronicle* 34 of an unofficial Moscow exhibition in September 1974.

Chapter 10: Opposition to the Abuse

1. Dated 10 February 1972, the issue in fact appeared (as per usual) about two weeks earlier.

2. Published 15 February 1972.

3. *New York Times*, 19 November 1971, reprinted in the *International Herald Tribune*, Paris, 20 November 1971.

4. *Washington Post*, 1 December 1971, reprinted in the *International Herald Tribune*, Paris, 2 December 1971.

5. Fainberg's appeal of 15 April 1974 (*AS* 1677) appeared in extracts in *The Times*, London, 7 May 1974, and in the *Observer*, London, 19 May 1974.

6. Appeal (*AS* 1280), dated 26 November 1971, published in extracts in Reuter and AP dispatches from Moscow, 28 November 1971, and in *Chronicle* 23.

7. Extracts from the appeal (*AS* 1146) appear in *Chronicle* 23, where it is dated 29 December 1971.

8. See extracts in the *Guardian*, London, 12 January 1972.

9. See text in *Der Bund* and *Berner Tagblatt*, both Bern, 20 January 1972. The former lists the 75 signatories. We have the text of the Dutch protest, dated January 1972.

10. Formed on 10 May 1972. See founding statement with 85 signatories in the Trotskyist paper *Rouge*, Paris, 27 May 1972.

11. Letter of 15 February 1972 addressed to the Soviet Medical Workers Union. Text in our possession.

12. For Austria see the documents in *Wiener Tagebuch*, Vienna, 1971, May, No. 5, also big articles in *Die Volksstimme*, Vienna, 20 January 1972, and *Die Presse*, Vienna, 29 January 1972. For Germany see big articles in *Der Spiegel*, Hamburg, 1 November 1971, and *Der Stern*, Hamburg, 23 January 1972. German TV carried serious interviews on the subject with the eminent psychiatrist Professor W. von Baeyer (10 December 1971, channel 2) and with the well-known writer Heinrich Böll (10 January 1972, channel 1).

13. *The Times*, 31 January and 30 March 1972. See also the letter by Dame Peggy Ashcroft in support of the first letter, *ibid.*, 2 February 1972.

14. V. Boukovsky, *Une Nouvelle Maladie Mentale en URSS: L'Opposition*, Seuil, Paris, 1971 (introduced and edited by Jean-Jacques Marie); W. Bukowskij, *Opposition: eine neue*

Geisteskrankheit in der Sowjetunion?, Hanser, Munich, 1972 (translated from the French edition). Some of the documents appeared in English in *Survey*, London, Autumn, 1971, No. 4 (81), pp. 111–164, but fuller publication was in *Senate Hearing* (December 1972).

15. Available from Hon. Sec., Working Group on the Internment of Dissenters in Mental Hospitals, 13 Armitage Road, London NW11, England. Summarized in the *Guardian*, London, 30 March 1971.

16. This appeal (*AS* 1079) was summarized in an AP dispatch from Moscow of 23 January 1972. See also: agency reports of 22 February 1972 on the rejection of Bukovsky's appeal against sentence; *The Times*, London, 7 February 1972, for the text (*AS* 1069) of Bukovsky's final speech at his trial; and the *Daily Telegraph*, London, 4 May 1972, for an appeal by 20 of his friends to Amnesty International concerning the blocking of his letters (*AS* 1284).

17. On all these see: the *New York Times*, 19 March 1971; *Le Monde*, Paris, 4 April 1971; *Esprit*, Paris, 1971, No. 7–8; *The Times*, London, 3 January, 29 February and 7 March 1972; *L'Express*, Paris, 31 January 1972; agency reports from Moscow sent on 2 August 1972; a Reuter report from Moscow, 6 October 1972; and a UPI report, 6 December 1972.

18. For the interviews see chapter 4. The articles appeared in *Moscow News* (by Yevgeny Makarov), Moscow, 11 December 1971, and in *Die Volksstimme*, Vienna, 20 January 1972.

19. The press conferences took place in Oslo on 7 December and in Aalborg, Denmark, on 5 December 1971. See *Morgenbladet*, Oslo, 8 December 1971, and various Danish papers, 6 December 1971.

20. Its publication as a feature article in the *New York Times* on 6 July 1971 may have been of special relevance here.

21. See the article by forensic psychiatrist B. Frankshtein in the monthly journal *Sotsialisticheskaya Zakonnost* (*Socialist Legality*), Moscow, July 1971, No. 7. The author proposed setting up a centralized forensic-psychiatric institution in Moscow which would relieve the over-worked Serbsky of all but a few unusually complex cases. His suggestion was supported by the editors, who asked the Ministry of Health to consider it. The journal is an organ of the Supreme Court and the Procuracy. The article may have been an indirect attempt by legal authorities to undermine the Serbsky and thereby reduce the KGB's influence over forensic psychiatry.

22. Decree dated 22 October 1971 and published in *Vedomosti Verkhovnogo Soveta SSSR*, 1971, No. 43, p. 581.

23. These appeared in the weekly *Knizhnoe Obozrenie*, Moscow, 1971, No. 40, and in the trade unions' paper *Trud*, 26 January 1972.

24. See an AP dispatch from Paris dated 14 July 1972 and *Le Canard Enchainé*, Paris, 19 July 1972.

25. *Pravda*, Moscow, 18 May 1972.

26. *Literaturnaya gazeta*, Moscow, 9 August 1972, feature by Alexander Krivitsky; broadcast by Moscow Radio in German on 15 August 1972. See *SWB*, SU/4069/A1/5, 17 August 1972; also *Chronicle* 27.

27. Two articles by Wolfgang Kraus in *Der Tagesspiegel*, West Berlin, 6 April and 27 June 1972.

28. Moscow Radio in Romanian, 24 August 1972. See *SWB*, SU/4078/B/1, 29 August 1972. The programme was almost certainly broadcast in other languages also.

29. *Anglo–Soviet Journal*, London, Summer 1972, pp. 40–42, 64–65.

30. *Golos Rodiny*, Moscow, 1975, No. 75, p. 4.

31. Letter of 11 September 1972. Copy in our possession.

32. Dispatch of the Jewish Telegraph Agency from Washington in *The Jewish Press*, New York, 18 August 1972.

33. Article by Robert Cowen in *The Christian Science Monitor*, Boston, 18 October 1972.

34. This document, written in 1974, is *AS* 1684.

35. A marginal exception to this statement is the Polish psychiatrist, "An Observer", who worked in the Kazan SPH during the second world war. See chapter 3.

36. See *Chronicle* 27.

37. See I. F. Stone, "Betrayal by Psychiatry", *New York Review of Books*, 10 February 1972.

38. Published by the National Institute of Mental Health, Chevy Chase, Maryland, 1969; Public Health Service Publication No. 1893.

39. Judge Bazelon also contributed an introduction to the American edition of the Soviet text-book *Forensic Psychiatry*, edited by Georgy Morozov and Ia. Kalashnik, International Arts and Sciences Press, New York, 1970.

40. This paragraph is based mostly on the article by Deborah Shapley, "US–USSR Exchange: Americans Split on Schizophrenia Program", in *Science*, New York, 8 March 1974, vol. 183, pp. 932–935.

41. The report has not to our knowledge been published, but it is summarized, with commentary, in the APA's publication *Psychiatric News*, Washington, D.C., 5 July 1972. We have worked from complete texts of this and related documents.

42. See, e.g. *Time*, New York, 7 February 1972, *Christian Science*

Monitor, Boston, 17 March 1972, and *The National Review*, New York, 9 June 1972.

43. I.e. the volume *Senate Hearing*. Its publication was reported in a UPI dispatch from Washington, D.C., published in some papers on 4 December 1972.

44. *Science*, New York, 23 March 1973, letter from Drs P. L. Watson, L. Hartmann, J. P. Nahum, C. Nadelson, and M. A. Leibovich of the Harvard Department of Psychiatry.

45. "Involuntary Hospitalization of Political Dissenters in the Soviet Union", eventually published in *Psychiatric Opinion*, Framingham, Massachusetts, vol. 11, No. 1, February 1974, pp. 5–19.

46. See brief report in *East–West Digest*, Petersham, U.K., 1973, July, No. 14.

47. See the following letters by: David Markham in the *British Journal of Psychiatry*, vol. 119, October 1971, p. 471; Julius Telesin in the *Guardian*, 28 October 1971; Dr Suzanne Shafar in the *Lancet*, 1 January 1972 (replying to an editorial of 18 December 1971); large groups in *The Times*, 31 January, 2 February and 30 March 1972 (see note 13); Professor John Ferguson and 35 other academics, politicians and Bishops in *The Times*, 11 September 1972 (an appeal for Fainberg and Borisov and a Greek prisoner); Dr Steven Rose in *New Scientist*, 9 November 1972; Dr Gery Low-Beer and Gwynneth Hemmings (separate letters) in *ibid.*, 16 November 1972; Drs Sidney Bloch and David Shaw in the *Lancet*, 11 November 1972; Dr Harold Merskey in *ibid.*, 9 December 1972 (where an editorial comments on the letter); Dr Gery Low-Beer in *The Guardian*, 30 November 1972; and Dr Harold Merskey in the *British Journal of Psychiatry*, February 1973.

See the following articles by: Drs Shaw, Bloch, and Vickers in *New Scientist*, 2 November 1972; Drs Shaw and Bloch in the *Lancet*, 24 February 1973; Peter Reddaway in *The Times*, 9 December 1972 and 11 July 1973; Bernard Levin in *ibid.*, 12 and 14 June 1973; and Professor F. A. Jenner in the *British Journal of Psychiatry*'s supplement *News and Notes*, July 1973.

48. "Psychiatry and the State", *New Scientist*, 2 November 1972, pp. 258–261.

49. BBC Radio 3, 17 January 1973. The programme provoked letters in the *Listener*, London, from Jacqueline West, 8 February 1973; and from Godfrey Stadlen and F. A. Jenner, 15 February 1973. It was favourably reviewed in the *Sunday Times*, 21 January, and *The Times*, 27 January; more critically in the *Guardian*, 20 January.

50. Unpublished letter from Professor F. A. Jenner to Professor

A. V. Snezhnevsky, 5 February 1973, and the reply, 4 April 1973.

51. See agency reports sent from Moscow on 20 October 1972.

52. See full text in *The Times*, 9 December 1972, also in *CHR*, 1973, No. 1.

53. First telegram sent on 28 February 1973.

54. Letter dated 7 May 1973 from Professor Sir Aubrey Lewis, Professors D. R. Davis, R. Doll, G. M. Carstairs, F. A. Jenner, E. Stengel, G. Russell, D. Pond, W. H. Trethowan, and Dr P. Sainsbury.

55. See editorial in the *British Medical Journal*, London, 8 September 1973.

56. *Ibid.*

57. See letter from the Society's chairman Dr A. C. Woodmansey in *The Times*, 1 September 1973.

58. Statement of 1 March 1973 by NAMH, 39 Queen Anne Street, London, W.1. See also a report in *The Times*, 2 March 1973.

59. *Zhurnal nevropatologii i psikhiatrii imeni S.S. Korsakova*, Moscow, 1973, No. 3, p. 473; TASS release, broadcast in English by Moscow Radio on 16 November 1972, see *SWB*, 20 November 1972. See also Bernard Levin's article in *The Times*, 14 June 1973.

60. The circumstances of this episode are as follows. On 21 January 1972 a British writer and journalist, John Chandos, interviewed Leigh about interrogation methods for an article he was writing on torture: Leigh was a consultant psychiatrist to the Ministry of Defence and the British Army had recently been charged with using a form of torture—sensory deprivation—during interrogation of IRA prisoners in Ulster.

At one point the conversation diverged to take in the Mexico congress and related issues. Leigh expressed concern for the damaging effects on East–West relations in psychiatry of the allegations of Soviet abuse made in Mexico, and said he doubted their validity. Chandos said he was surprised, because the evidence from many independent sources seemed to him irresistible. Leigh replied that he was not convinced about the independence and authenticity of the evidence, and suspected that there had been an elaborate operation by Russia's enemies to defame her, perhaps with CIA involvement. He added that he would welcome new evidence on the matter from any quarter.

Three days later Chandos mentioned this fact when interviewing Reddaway, also Leigh's suspicions about the authenticity of the evidence. On February 3 Reddaway wrote to Leigh, described his conversation with Chandos, and asked

Leigh if he would kindly supply copies of any inauthentic documents so that he could examine them and offer his opinion. The next day Leigh telephoned Reddaway. Chandos was wrong, Leigh said, to have implied that he suspected the forgery of documents. He was concerned only with the official psychiatric reports on dissenters, not with any others (he declined to say why not). The authenticity of these had been confirmed to him in Mexico by Soviet psychiatrists. What evidence did he have, then, of inauthentic evidence or CIA involvement? Here Leigh became uneasy, but eventually said that a "Radio Free America of Miami" had pestered the congress secretariat, asking for a condemnation of the Soviet Union, and that he thought this station might have CIA connections. Was there any other evidence? Well, actually, no.

Leigh then volunteered that in his opinion Bukovsky was a schizophrenic, or at any rate had been in the past. He had spoken in Mexico to one of the psychiatrists who had examined him in the mid-1960s and who had described Bukovsky's symptoms to him. He dismissed the evidence of Bukovsky's sanity provided by Reddaway's friends, who had met Bukovsky in 1970 and 1971. Leigh thought that the new sentence on Bukovsky was cruel, but was partly to be accounted for by protests like the "letter of the 44" in *The Times*, which did more harm than good. He was pleased that he had got the "very nice" Professor Vartanyan onto the WPA's executive committee. Also, Snezhnevsky had offered to let him inspect the Serbsky Institute from top to bottom whenever he wished.

Finally, Leigh said that the situation in the Soviet Union was now improving, as could be seen by the recent transfer of the prison psychiatric hospitals from the jurisdiction of the Ministry of Internal Affairs to that of the Ministry of Health. When Reddaway replied that he had not heard about this himself, Leigh insisted that his information was correct. Reddaway agreed that if this were true it would be a welcome change. It turned out not to be true.

This episode illustrates well the fact that while Leigh has consistently claimed that he is neutral, just a servant of the WPA's executive committee and member societies, in fact he has repeatedly taken the initiative in ways that have assisted the Soviet psychiatric establishment and frustrated the growing body of opinion within member societies which condemns Soviet abuses. When pressed, he has justified his line by suggesting that it is more effective to combat the abuse—as he sometimes claims to be doing—by maintaining a dialogue with the Russians than by risking the severance of contacts.

The trouble here is that, as we have seen and will see again, he has several times let slip that he does not believe that any abuse exists. So his claim to be combating it fails to carry conviction.

It is hard to know men's motives; but many observers have discerned in Leigh the perhaps understandable pride of the empire-builder, and they have felt that this influences unduly his attitude to the USSR. For it was he who brought the All-Union Society of Neurologists and Psychiatrists into the WPA in 1967, thereby recruiting one of the two largest national bodies of psychiatrists in the world, with over 20,000 members. If this society were to be forced out of the WPA— so observers have argued—the blow would be severe, not only to Soviet prestige, but also to the empire-building pride of Dr Leigh.

Finally, Leigh's claim that the campaign against Soviet abuse was sophisticated and expensive deserves a brief comment. As the main organizer was in fact the Working Group, whose bank balance had never exceeded £150, whose honorary secretary had been writing her letters to Leigh in longhand because she had no typewriter or secretary, and whose literature had been distributed at the congress by Mexican friends out of sympathy for the group's aims and because no group member could afford to attend, the claim was decidedly eccentric!

61. See his interview in *New Psychiatrist*, London, 17 July 1975.
62. Minutes of WPA Executive Committee meeting of 12 November 1972.
63. Resolution of the Deutsche Gesellschaft für Psychatrie und Nervenheilkunde, adopted 21 January 1972, drafted by Dr H. E. Erhardt. See Erhardt's account of the circumstances of its composition in *Der Nervenarzt*, 1972, No. 43, pp. 223–224.
64. *The Times*, 17 November 1972. The report appeared only in early editions.
65. See reference 47.
66. See, for example, the leading articles in the *Washington Post* and the *New York Times*, printed in the *International Herald Tribune*, Paris, 21 June and 25 June 1973 respectively.
67. This call echoed a similar one made by Sakharov in his appeal for Dr Gluzman of November 1972, quoted earlier in the chapter. The appeals of the various groups were reported in, e.g. *Aftenposten*, Oslo, 25 and 27 June 1973, and *Verdens Gang*, Oslo, 22 June 1973.
68. See the *Observer*, London, 1 July 1973; a Reuter dispatch from Oslo of the same date; and *Verdens Gang*, 29 June 1973.

69. This petition, organized by Bishop M. Norderval, was reported in *Morgenbladet*, Oslo, 27 June and 29 September 1973.

70. Statement dated 9 July 1973, signed by Sakharov, G. Podyapolsky and I. Shafarevich. Russian text in *CHR*, 1973, No. 3. A slightly different draft of the same statement appears in *Chronicle* 30.

71. "Open appeal" of 25 June 1973 to Dr Waldheim, signed by Sakharov and Podyapolsky. Text in *CHR*, 1973, No. 3.

72. Full text, dated June 1973, published in Russian as *AS* 1550 and in T. Khodorovich, *Istoriya bolezni Leonida Plyushcha*, Amsterdam, A. Herzen Foundation, 1974; condensed text in French translation in T. Mathon and J-J. Marie, *L'Affaire Pliouchtch*, Paris, Seuil, 1976.

73. See, for example, articles in *The Times* and the *Daily Telegraph*, 11 July 1973.

74. *The Times*, 12 and 14 June 1973.

75. Private information from participants in the college's meeting.

76. Letter in *The Times*, 13 July 1973, from the PEN Club's president and secretary, Heinrich Böll and David Carver.

77. The *Observer*, 22 July 1973. Article by Laurence Marks.

78. *Izvestia*, 10 August 1973. See also *CHR*, 1973, No. 3; *Soviet News*, London, 14 August 1973.

79. See, e.g. the *Washington Post*, 12 August 1973.

80. For Sakharov's interview with Deputy Procurator-General Malyarov (16 August) see *CHR*, 1973, No. 3, and a full transcript in the *New York Times*, 29 August 1973. His press-conference of 21 August was widely reported in the world press the next day.

81. This counter-campaign is extensively reported in *CHR*, 1973, No. 4, and in *Chronicle* 30.

82. *The Times*, 27 August 1973. The Royal College had already been sharply prodded on 19 August by the *Observer*, in a note appended to a letter from the college's Registrar. The college was charged with complacency and failure to realize the seriousness of Soviet psychiatrists' "systematic cruelty".

83. *The Times*, 4 September 1973. The earlier letters had been from Dr M. Markowe (29 August), D. Markham (31 August), and K. Coates and C. Farley, M. Owen, and Dr A. C. Woodmansey (all 1 September).

84. *Izvestia*, 31 August 1973, and a Reuter dispatch from Moscow, 7 September 1973.

85. *Pravda*, 6 September 1973.

86. *SWB*, SU/4394/C/1, 10 September 1973. Extracts published in *The Times*, 8 September 1973.

87. *Guardian*, 8 September 1973, in response to a leader of the

previous day. Other letters appeared from Dr G. Low-Beer (11 September), A. Haddow, E. H. Hutten (13 September), K. Coates and C. Farley (15 September), Dr A. Clare (21 September).

88. *Observer*, 9 September 1973. Leigh also refused to comment on Soviet abuses to the *Guardian* (10 September).
89. *British Medical Journal*, 8 September 1973.
90. *The Times*, 5 September 1973.
91. *Ibid.*, 8 September 1973.
92. *World Medicine*, London, 3 October 1973, p. 20.
93. Letters not previously listed are those in *The Times* from Dr R. Lawson, Dr P. Bowden (both 8 September), Dr T. Ryan (10 September), Dr H. Merskey (12 September), H. Innes (13 September), and J. Pringle (20 September).
94. *The Times*, 8 September 1973 (Reuter report).
95. *Daily Telegraph*, 10 September; *Washington Post*, 11 September 1973.
96. Published in the world press on 10 September 1973.
97. APA press-release dated 11 September, summarized in the *New York Times*, 12 September, printed in full in *Psychiatric News*, 3 October 1973.
98. Cable dated 24 September, published in *ibid.*
99. *Ibid.*
100. *Guardian*, 29 September 1973; also published in *Soviet News*, 9 October 1973 (a different translation, made from the Russian text published in *Meditsinskaya gazeta*).
101. Letters in the *Guardian* from G. Panayi, M. Jones, D. Markham (2 October), and Zh. Medvedev (3 October).
102. *Lancet*, 13 October 1973.
103. *Chronicle* 30. Signed by T. Velikanova, S. Kovalyov, A. Levitin, G. Podyapolsky and T. Khodorovich.
104. *Ibid.*, also *CHR*, 1973, No. 4.
105. *The Times*, 24 September 1973.
106. Minutes of WPA Executive Committee meeting of 8 October 1973.
107. Diary of an American participant whom we know personally.
108. *Ibid.*
109. Diary of another American participant whom we know.
110. *Ibid.*
111. See ref. 106.
112. See ref. 109.
113. Press-release of Dr A. Freedman, 2 November 1973, published in full in French translation in *Bulletin* No. 3, March 1974, pp. 13–15 (see ref. 143), and summarized in the *New York Times* and *Washington Post*, 5 November 1973.

114. Reuter dispatch from Tbilisi dated 12 October, printed in *The Times*, 13 October 1973.
115. See ref. 109.
116. Minutes of WPA Excutive Committee meeting of 14 October 1973.
117. See ref. 113.
118. Private information from a psychiatrist in whose presence he said it, in Oxford, at the end of June 1976.
119. To be published in J. K. Wing, *Reasoning about Madness*, Oxford, O.U.P., 1977.
120. For Wing's account see *ibid.*, for Scharfetter's see *IBRO News: a Quarterly Newsletter of the International Brain Research Organization*, 41 Queen's Gate, London S.W.7, 1974, No. 3.
121. See ref. 113.
122. Minutes of WPA Executive Committee meeting of 15 October 1973.
123. *Zhurnal nevropatologii i psikhiatrii imeni S.S. Korsakova*, 1974, No. 3, p. 472.
124. *SWB*, SU/4428/C1/1, 19 October 1973.
125. *Izvestia*, 30 October 1973.
126. *Literaturnaya gazeta*, 7 November 1973, p. 9, article by A. Kurov.
127. *Soviet Weekly*, 5–12 January 1974, article by E. Gorbunova. An earlier version of the article was issued on 14 November 1973 by the Soviet Embassy in Washington.
128. Anthony de Meeûs, *White Book on the Internment of Dissenters in Soviet Mental Hospitals*, International Committee for the Defence of Human Rights in the USSR (28 place Flagey, Brussels), 1974, p. 58.
129. E.g. in *Sowjetunion Heute*, Köln, 1 February 1976, and *Sotsialisticheskaya industriya*, Moscow, 15 February 1976.
130. Private information from this psychiatrist, who now lives in the USA.
131. Broadcast of 5 January 1974, *SWB*, SU/4494/C/3, 8 January 1974.
132. E.g. Moscow Radio commentaries on 10 and 23 October, *SWB*, SU/4433/C/1, 12 and 25 October; and interviews with Drs A. Portnov, S. Semyonov and E. Babayan in *Soviet News*, 16 October 1973.
133. See his interview in the *Daily Mail*, London, 8 November 1973; also the minutes of the WPA Executive Committee meeting of 21 May 1974.
134. Reuter dispatch from Moscow dated 28 October; *The Times*, 29 October 1973.

135. Interview with C. S. Wren, *New York Times*, 2 November 1973.

136. On these talks see *ibid.* and the introduction by Martin Ennals to *Prisoners of Conscience in the USSR: their Treatment and Conditions*, Amnesty International Report, London, 1975.

137. Dated 13 October 1973, the statement appears in full in the minutes of the WPA Executive Committee meeting of 21 May 1974.

138. Press release of the college dated 14 November 1973. Summarized in the *Guardian*, 17 November; the *Observer*, 18 November.

139. Appeal by eighteen of his friends, *Daily Telegraph*, 27 November 1972; lecture invitation from Professor H. L. Price of Leeds University, *Yorkshire Post*, 9 July 1973; appeals by foreign colleagues, *CHR*, 1973, Nos. 1–3 and 5; Zh. Medvedev's open letter in *Nature*, 24 August 1973; articles by B. Levin (12 June) and P. Reddaway (11 July) in *The Times*.

140. Reuter dispatch from Moscow dated 11 February 1973, printed in the *Guardian*, 12 February; *Daily Telegraph*, 11 July 1973; Reuter dispatch dated 8 October 1973, printed in *The Times*, 9 October. For full texts see *CHR*, 1973, Nos. 1–4.

141. Letter by the psychologist Tania Mathon, *Le Monde*, 4 September 1973; broadcast by Erik de Mauny, published in the *Listener*, London, 18 October 1973.

142. Telegram dated 25 November 1973, summarized in *Washington Post*, 27 November, in *CHR*, 1973, No. 5–6, and in *Chronicle* 32. The other signatories were Drs W. Barton, A. Miller, H. Visotsky, S. Yolles, A. Stone, and J. Visher.

143. *Rouge*, Paris, 27 May 1972; and *Bulletin* No. 1 of the CSPHU (205 boulevard de la Gare, 75013 Paris), June 1972.

144. *Bulletin* No. 3 of the CSPHU, March 1974, pp. 11–12.

145. *CHR*, 1974, No. 7; *Chronicle* 32; and *Bulletin* No. 1 of the ICM (18 rue du Général Pajol, 77130 Montereau, France), 19 February 1974.

146. *Chronicle* 32; *Bulletin* No. 2 of the ICM, 2 June 1974; also *L'Affaire Pliouchtch*, *op. cit.*, a book which contains documents and commentary on the whole campaign for Plyushch's release.

147. *Bulletin* No. 3 of the ICM, 31 July 1974.

148. *Ibid.* Another protest at this time was a letter in the *Guardian*, 26 February 1974, from nineteen friends of Shikhanovich, mostly mathematicians, who had recently emigrated to Israel and elsewhere, and who testified to his sanity.

149. *Bulletin* No. 3 of the CSPHU, March 1974, pp. 22–23. For the appeal of Sakharov's group (*AS* 1714) see *ibid.*, also *CHR*, 1974, No. 7. A member of this group was Andrei

Tverdokhlebov, who had earlier published two letters in defence of Plyushch in the *New Scientist*, London, 11 October 1973, and (*AS* 1678) in *CHR*, 1974, No. 7.

150. *Bulletin* No. 4 of the ICM, September 1974; *CHR*, 1974, No. 10; article by P. Reddaway in *The Times*, 23 August 1974. The ICM's actions in Vancouver were co-ordinated by Professor Lipman Bers of Columbia University.

151. *American Psychologist*, June 1974, p. 394.

152. Letter of 21 January 1974; copy in our possession.

153. *Psychiatric News*, 20 March 1974.

154. Issue contains articles by Drs P. Chodoff, R. R. Rogers, P. Ottenberg, and J. Lopez Ibor.

155. *Psychiatric News*, 20 March 1974.

156. Described in an interview, *New York Times*, 31 March 1974; also in the *Observer*, 5 May 1974.

157. *Science*, 8 March 1974, vol. 183, pp. 932–935.

158. UPI dispatch of 11 July 1974 from Washington, printed in the *Washington Post*, 12 July.

159. Dated 8 November 1973, copy in our possession. Summarized by B. Levin in *The Times*, 7 May 1974.

160. *Chronicle*'s account is in No. 28; friend's account is in an article by L. Marks in the *Observer*, 5 May 1974; Nekrasov's statement of November 1974 was circulated by the Working Group, and in French in *Bulletin* No. 4 of the CSPHU, March 1975. See also Dr H. Merskey's letter in *World Medicine*, London, 8 May 1974.

161. *British Medical Journal*, 9 November 1974.

162. *AS* 1947; published in *CHR*, 1974, No. 12; circulated in English by the Working Group, and in French in *Bulletin* No. 4 of the CSPHU, March 1975.

163. Roth's letter dated 18 October 1974, Snezhnevsky's 8 December 1974, texts in *News and Notes* (monthly supplement to the *British Journal of Psychiatry*), July 1975. In November 1974 the college debated Gluzman's case, but passed only a generalized resolution on psychiatric abuse. See *ibid.*, May 1975.

164. Prior to the autumn, the most notable items in the British press in 1974 not yet mentioned had been a review by Dr H. Rollin of Amnesty International's *Report on Torture* in the *British Medical Journal*, 5 January; an article "Psychiatry in the Soviet Union" by Professor J. K. Wing in *ibid.*, 9 March; related letters in *ibid.* by Dr G. V. Morozov (6 July), A. King (27 July), J. Wing (10 August), and I. Atkin (7 September); an attack on Wing's article of 9 March by Dr Louis Goldman in *World Medicine*, 24 April; questions in parliament by P. Whitehead, P. Cormack and C. Mayhew, *Hansard*, 1 May,

columns 1139–40; Bernard Levin's article in *The Times*, 7 May; and Dr W. L. Tonge's article "Psychiatry and Political Dissent" in *The Lancet*, 20 July.

165. See Fainberg's interview in the *Observer*, 20 October 1974, and his article "People Listen but do not Hear" in *ibid.*, 5 January 1975; Vera Rich's article in *Nature*, 22 November 1974; UPI dispatch dated 18 December 1974 from Moscow about the Manual; appeal for Bukovsky by five eminent doctors, the *Guardian*, 3 March 1975; V. Nekrasov's open letter to Snezhnevsky in the *Sunday Times*, 16 March 1975; the full publication in June of the Manual, *Survey*, London, 1975, No. 94–95; Valerie Kaye's and Bernard Levin's articles in *The Times*, 27 June and 3 July 1975; an editorial in *ibid.*, 4 July 1975; a report of a press conference given by the Working Group and Amnesty International in *ibid.*; articles by William Shawcross and Viktor Fainberg in the *Sunday Times*, 6 July and 3 August 1975 respectively; letter from Dr S. Shafar and others in the *British Medical Journal*, 28 June 1975; editorial in *ibid.*, 9 August 1975; letters in *The Times* from Dr A. Storr (18 July 1975) and Dr H. Dicks (22 July 1975); a leader in *ibid.*, 22 July 1975; Dr Voikhanskaya's article "Psychiatry Betrayed" in *New Psychiatry*, 31 July 1975; a letter by Dr H. Dicks and P. Reddaway criticizing the WPA and Drs Leigh and Rees in *ibid.*, 28 August 1975; letter by Dr S. Shafar in *ibid.*, 11 September 1975; article by Dr H. Merskey in *Soviet Jewish Affairs*, London, 1976, No. 1.

166. Full text dated 24 March 1975 in *News and Notes*, June 1975.

167. Press release of the college, undated but *c.* 15 July 1975.

168. *Ibid.* The meeting was reported in the *Guardian*, 10 July, *The Times*, 17 July, the *Observer*, 20 July, and *Nature*, 17 July 1975.

169. See ref. 167.

170. See reports of meetings in the *Sunday Times*, 29 February 1976, and *New Scientist*, 1 July 1976; and of a letter by Dr Dicks to Snezhnevsky in the *Observer*, 16 November 1975.

171. See ref. 136.

172. E.g. by P. Reddaway in *The Times*, 23 October 1975.

173. *News and Notes*, February 1976. Motion passed by 51 votes to 3.

174. Full text in *ibid.*, April 1976.

175. *Ibid.*

176. Reuter dispatches of 16 October from Chile and 17 October from Moscow; AP dispatch of 20 October from Chile; and *The Times*, 21 October 1974.

177. Silva Zalmanson emigrated to Israel and Simas Kudirka to the USA. Both had ten-year sentences. See *CHR*, 1974, No. 10, and *Chronicles* 33 and 34.

178. See P. Reddaway's chapter in Archie Brown and Michael Kaser, eds., *The Soviet Union since the Fall of Khrushchev*, London, Macmillan, 1975.

179. See *Chronicle* 34; *CHR*, 1975, No. 13; No. 6 of the *Bulletin* of the ICM, March 1975; No. 4 of the *Bulletin* of the CSPHU, March 1975; *AS* 2006.a to 2006.e and 2057–2059.

180. Appeal of T. Khodorovich and Yury Orlov dated 28 December 1974. *AS* 2006.d, published in French in *Bulletin* 6 of the ICM, March 1975.

181. Appeal signed by T. Plyushch, T. Khodorovich and Yu. Orlov, dated 20 December, published in *ibid.*; in *CHR* 1975, No. 13; and *Le Monde*, 2–3 February 1975. For Low-Beer's letter see *Nature*, 27 February 1975. On de Félice see *Bulletin* 7 of the ICM, June 1975.

182. See his open letter to Snezhnevsky in *ibid.* and in the *Sunday Times*, 16 March 1975; and his article in the Colour Magazine of the *Observer*, 20 July 1975.

183. See details in *Bulletin* 7 of the ICM, June 1975; *CHR*, 1975, No. 14; *Chronicle* 36.

184. *AS* 2127; published in *Chronicle* 36 and in T. Khodorovich, ed., *The Case of Leonid Plyushch*, London, C. Hurst, 1976, pp. 128–129. This book contains the items on Plyushch in *Chronicles* 32–37.

185. *AS* 2126; summarized by P. Reddaway in *The Times*, 24 April 1975; full text in *Bulletin* 7 of the ICM, June 1975.

186. See ref. 128. This book appeared also in a French edition. The symposium proceedings (and a useful collection of statements by psychiatric bodies on Soviet abuse) were published as an illustrated booklet, *Les Abus de la Psychiatrie à des Fins Politiques*, Amnesty International, B.P. 276, CH-1211 Geneva, November 1975. Agency reports dated 20 April 1975 appeared in many countries the next day; other reports appeared in the *Guardian* and *The Times*, 21 April, and *Le Monde*, 22 April. Tass denounced the symposium and quoted again alleged statements by Western psychiatrists of 1973. See *SWB*, 26 April 1975.

187. Statement published in *Bulletin des Médecins Suisses*, 10 October 1973, and *Journal de Genève*, 13–14 October 1973. Twenty-eight Geneva psychiatrists also wrote an open letter to Health Minister Petrovsky in early 1973. See extracts from both documents in *Les Abus de la Psychiatrie . . .*, *op. cit.*

188. See details and numerous documents in *Bulletin* 8 of the ICM, November 1975; *L'Affaire Pliouchtch*, *op. cit.*; *Chronicle* 38; *CHR*, 1975, No. 17; *The Times*, 23 October 1975.

189. *L'Humanité*, 25 October 1975.

190. For Plyushch's press statement of 3 February 1976 see Khodorovich, *op. cit.*, pp. 143–152; extracts in the world press on 4 February. On the last months of his captivity see *Chronicles* 38 and 39, and *L'Affaire Pliouchtch, op. cit.*

191. The book refereed to is *ibid.* It reprints the strong appeal for Plyushch in *Le Monde* of 22 October 1975 by nine prominent psychiatrists, which reinvigorated the CSPHU. See also the record of a meeting of the Société-Médico-Psychologique addressed by Dr G. Ferdière in *Annales Médico-Psychologiques*, 1976, No. 4.

192. They formed a "Working Commission on Internment Procedures and Involuntary Treatment in Special Psychiatric Hospitals", closely tied to the CSPHU. The academic secretary was Dr J.-P. Descombey and the administrative secretary Martine le Guay (205 boulevard de la Gare, 75013 Paris). The four organizations were Syndicat des Psychiatres Français, Syndicat des Psychiatres des Hôpitaux, Syndicat National des Psychiatres Privés, and Evolution Psychiatrique. In April 1976 the Commission wrote to the Soviet ambassador in Paris asking for copies of the official documents in the Plyushch case.

193. See *Le Monde* 24 and 25 July 1976; *Le Quotidien de Paris*, 18, 23 and 26 July 1976; *L'Humanité*, 27 July 1976.

194. See Tass report of 8 January 1976, *SWB*, SU/5104/B/1, 10 January; Dr G. V. Morozov's interview on Moscow Radio, 21 and 23 January 1976, *SWB*, SU/5117/A1/7, 26 January; *Literaturnaya gazeta*, 4 and 11 February 1976; article by N. Efimov in *Sotsialisticheskaya industriya*, 15 February 1976; a similar broadcast by him, see *SWB*, SU/5179/C1/1, 7 April 1976; Moscow Radio commentary, *SWB*, SU/5130/A1/1, 10 February 1976; *Soviet Weekly*, 28 February 1976; Nadzharov interviews in *Moscow News*, 21 February 1976, and, reported by Tass, 24 April, *SWB*, SU/5193/A1/7, 27 April. Attacks exclusively on alleged foreign abuses appeared in *Pravda* and *Krasnaya Zvezda*, 27 March, and in *Literaturnaya gazeta*, 28 April and 29 September 1976. See also an interview by Dr A. B. Smulevich in *La Libre Belgique*, Brussels, 23 June 1976; and a Tass dispatch in which Archer Tong, director of the International Council for Prevention of Alcoholism and Narcoticism, fulsomely praised the Serbsky Institute, *SWB*, SU/5268/A1/5, 24 July 1976.

195. *Morning Star*, 5 and 23 February 1976; *Daily Telegraph*, 23 March 1976; see also the letter from Drs H. Dicks and G. Low-Beer in *The Guardian*, 1 March 1976. Dr Boris Tsukerman later obtained a similar apology in the *Morning Star*, 30 November 1976.

196. Article by Novosti medical correspondent E. Gorbunova in *Sowjetunion heute*, Köln, 1 February 1976.
197. *Chronicle* 38.
198. *Chronicle* 40.
199. Minutes of a meeting of the Organizing Committee for the Sixth World Congress, held in Anaheim, California, on 7 May 1975.
200. *Sunday Times*, 6 July 1975.
201. See refs. 167 and 168.
202. See ref. 200.
203. *British Medical Journal*, 6 July 1974.
204. See ref. 200.
205. *The Times*, 22 July 1975.
206. Editorial of 9 August 1975.
207. WPA *Newsletter* No. 31, October 1975.
208. See ref. 205.
209. *Soviet News*, 13 January 1976. This praise was described by Dr H. Merskey in a letter in the *Lancet*, 6 March 1976, but Leigh made no reply to either publication.
210. E.g. in the *Guardian* and the *Daily Mail*, 30 June 1976. Earlier he had said, equally remarkably: "The Soviet All-Union Society of Psychiatrists behaves perfectly properly as a member of the WPA", *Sunday Times*, 6 July 1975. For other reports on Vartanyan's visit see *Daily Telegraph*, 29 and 30 June 1976, *The Times*, 30 June and 1 July.
211. *Daily Mail*, 30 June 1976.
212. *News and Notes*, November 1976. Motion passed by 60 votes to 3 on 4 May 1976.
213. *Psychiatric News*, 1 October 1976. The ground had been partially prepared in the U.S. by letters in *ibid.* from Dr H. Dicks (6 February 1976) and Drs D. Charry and M. G. Brook (both 19 March), and by speeches made at a New York public meeting in March 1976 by Dr P. Chodoff and L. Plyushch, *ibid.*, 4 June and 7 May respectively. Earlier, Representative P. M. Crane had raised the matter forcefully in Congress, *Congressional Record*, 10 November 1975, p. E5972; on the other hand, Dr M. Sabshin, the APA's medical director, had attended a conference in Moscow, been quoted in Soviet media as having only praise for Soviet psychiatry (*Soviet Weekly*, 3 January 1976, *Soviet News*, 6 January 1976), and apparently let the reports stand without comment.
214. *Chronicles* 40 and 41; *CHR*, 1976, No. 20–21.
215. See reports of his arrival in the world press of 19 December 1976.

Epilogue
1. See A. Mitscherlich and F. Mielke, *The Death Doctors*, London, Elek, 1962.

Appendix II: Our Recommendations for Combating and Preventing Abuse
1. *Prisoners of Conscience in the USSR: Their Treatment and Conditions*, London, Amnesty International, 1975, pp. 141–144.
2. Chalidze, V., *To Defend These Rights. Human Rights and The Soviet Union*, London, Collins/Harvill, 1975, pp. 247–290.
3. *Psychiatric News*, 15 May 1974.
4. *Ibid.*, 5 July 1972.

INDEX

This is an index of proper names, medical institutions and other organizations. For further assistance on the book's subject matter see the detailed Table of Contents.

The appendices are covered in this index, but not, with two exceptions, the references.

The titles Professor and Doctor are given only for medical doctors, not for others.

Abbreviations used: SPH = Special Psychiatric Hospital; OPH = Ordinary Psychiatric Hospital; Acad. = Member of the Academy of Sciences.